MEDIA, REVOLUTION AND POLITICS IN EGYPT

The Reuters Institute for the Study of Journalism at the University of Oxford aims to serve as the leading international forum for a productive engagement between scholars from a wide range of disciplines and practitioners of journalism. As part of this mission, we publish work by academics, journalists, and media industry professionals focusing on some of the most important issues facing journalism around the world today.

All our books are reviewed by both our Editorial Committee and expert readers. Our books, however, remain the work of authors writing in their individual capacities, not a collective expression of views from the Institute.

The Reuters Institute would like to acknowledge the assistance of Naomi Sakr and Jean Seaton as editorial advisers on behalf of the Institute.

MEDIA, REVOLUTION AND POLITICS IN EGYPT

THE STORY OF AN UPRISING

ABDALLA F. HASSAN

Published by I.B.Tauris & Co. Ltd in association with
the Reuters Institute for the Study of Journalism, University of Oxford

Published in 2015 by
I.B.Tauris & Co. Ltd
London • New York
www.ibtauris.com

ISBN: 978 1 78453 217 8 (HB)
978 1 78453 218 5 (PB)
eISBN: 978 0 85773 981 0

A full CIP record for this book is available from the British Library
A full CIP record is available from the Library of Congress

Library of Congress Catalog Card Number: available

Typeset by Riverside Publishing Solutions, Salisbury, SP4 6NQ
Printed and bound in Great Britain by T.J. International, Padstow, Cornwall

For my parents and sisters with love

Rebellion! I do not know when that Rebellion will come,
it might be in a week or in a hundred years,
but I know . . . that sooner or later justice will be done.
(George Orwell, *Animal Farm*)

Contents

Foreword ix
John Lloyd

1. Prologue to Revolution 1

2. Eighteen Days 37

3. Politics and the Press under Military Rule 75

4. Revolutionaries versus the Generals 115

5. Fall of Military Rule and the Islamists 143

6. An Overthrow, a Revitalised Police State, and the Military Presidency 175

Epilogue: Media Matters 215

Timeline 223

Notes 233

Index 265

Foreword

This is at once a careful account of journalism's roller-coaster ride during the course of a decade in Egypt, and the testament of a liberally minded writer, fully engaged with the country's politics and culture and its struggle for a civil society in the Middle East's most populous state. It is rigorously detailed and sourced, and breathes the air of liberation – from the stifling rule evident from the early 2000s, reaching its flood from the uprising of 2011 through 2013, when an inept and unyielding Muslim Brotherhood government was toppled, then closed down once more by a more favoured military-backed order.

Abdalla Hassan is no romantic. He sees that the regime of Field Marshal Abd al-Fattah al-Sisi, elected president in 2014, is a popular one because of its strongly patriotic stance and its appearance of strength in combating the (quite real) jihadist terrorism at work in Egypt. The news media, raucously free for a few years, have – with a few exceptions – come to heel, apparently of their own volition.

Still, something happened – and is still, in a subterranean way, happening. The authorities, as in other repressive states, have lost the ability to completely control the news media they could claim in the early years of military rule, in which Gamal Abd al-Nasser, one of the group of officers who overthrew the monarchy in 1952, was pre-eminent. The internet and social media do not make or sustain a revolution, but they provide networks of revolt and dissidence much harder to rub out than in the pre-digital age.

State propaganda, however, has also become stronger, in part by using the same digital tools, in larger part by controlling the messages that television, by far the strongest medium, puts out. Propaganda can be ignored or mocked, as it was in the closing years of President Hosni Mubarak's 30-year term, but it is potent when there is a real fear of external machinations and internal subversion, and when the theme of patriotic unity is hammered home day after day. In Egypt, the distance between the intelligentsia (including the media) and the people is usually much greater than that between the people and the army.

The media take on an extra importance in Egypt, as in all authoritarian states, when they are suppressed, and are mixed in with the arts. Where politics is quelled, everything becomes at least potentially political, especially the novel, theatre, and cinema. Hassan makes this wonderfully clear, by giving the plots and the reception of so much that was published and shown.

Like many who were relieved at an end to the Muslim Brotherhood government, he is appalled by the harshness of military-dominated rule. He sees, clearly, that a refashioned authoritarianism presently sustains itself by the support of an approving public, who have made plain they prefer the hard smack of control by army officers to the soft jihadism of the Brotherhood.

Yet though the Arab Spring went straight to winter, it threw up a challenge, which for a while saw the press, and above all television channels, open up to the many voices loosed by the protesters and the would-be democrats. Although such manifestations as China's Tiananmen Square protests of 1989, or the large-scale protests in Russia in 2011–12, have been put down, it is hard to believe that the causes for which they were mounted have ceased to exert a pull, especially on the younger generations.

One of these causes is that journalism be allowed to seek something closer to the truth about the society in which it operates, and to provide a forum for wide debate and the deployment of new ideas. Abdalla Hassan has shown, uniquely well, the forces at play in Egyptian society that attempted to break through to such a space, as well as the presently greater force that stops it doing so. The result is a most valuable testament.

John Lloyd
Contributing Editor at the *Financial Times*
and Senior Research Fellow, RISJ

1

Prologue to Revolution

> *The newspapers' sting at first seemed slight and was conveniently disregarded, but its cumulative effect proved dangerous. By aggressively projecting political messages to its readers and generating active political debate among an expanding reading public . . . the press helped create a climate for political action that would eventually undermine the British hold on the country.*
>
> (Ami Ayalon, *The Press in the Arab Middle East*[1])

Early in the morning of 20 March 2003 bombs began falling on Iraq. The allied invasion had started. Hours later, demonstrations erupted on university campuses around Cairo. At noon, protesters converged on downtown Cairo's bustling Tahrir Square in a demonstration that continued for 12 hours, dubbing the area the 'liberated territories' of Tahrir, which itself means 'liberation'. The demonstration was largely peaceful until riot police turned water cannons on protesters, some hurling stones, as they attempted to march to the United States Embassy nearby. As night fell, demonstrators continued chanting, lighting candles, and singing.

The next day, a Friday, observant Muslims gathered at the Sayeda Zeinab Mosque, one of Cairo's largest and oldest. Set among crowded tenement blocks and street markets in an impoverished neighbourhood, it has been home to impromptu protests against US Middle East policy in the past. The day after the bombardment began, the imam recounted Islam's early military victories but made no direct mention of the war in Iraq. Following congregational prayers, worshippers stood in prayer for the souls of deceased Muslims in 'America's war'.

In sidewalk cafés across Egypt television sets were tuned to Al Jazeera, the Qatari satellite news channel, as Iraq faced a showdown with the world's greatest military powers. Al Jazeera regularly showed images of dead and wounded Iraqi civilians, many of them children – the fallout of what had been billed as a surgical, hi-tech war. Not shying away from controversial political issues, Al Jazeera broke barriers with its revolutionary style and approach. The network gained enemies everywhere. Arab states disliked its examination of internal politics and its habit of offering dissidents from across the political spectrum, from secular pro-democracy advocates to die-hard Islamists, airtime to defend their political views. Censorship was more elusive in the world of satellite broadcast and live news coverage.

A nearby café was broadcasting Al Jazeera, reporting that an estimated 50,000–55,000 protesters were rallying at al-Azhar Mosque. Al Jazeera's cameras showed images of security forces turning water cannons on the demonstrators. Organisers had planned the protest to begin at al-Azhar and make its way to Tahrir Square in the afternoon. The interior minister had warned that no demonstrations or rallies were to take place in public squares or major thoroughfares. Security forces cordoned off Tahrir Square early on, but demonstrators began gathering in the surrounding streets. Riot police with sticks, dogs, and water cannons charged at protesters. As demonstrators fled into nearby buildings and alleys, security forces chased them, often beating and striking protesters as they retreated.

In a nationally televised address the day before the start of war, President Hosni Mubarak had blamed Iraqi leader Saddam Hussein for making war inevitable. 'My hope is that the Iraqi government will realise the seriousness of the situation in which it put itself – and us – in,' Mubarak told his audience. Many viewers were apparently not convinced. '*Irhal, irhal, ya Mubarak* – Leave, Mubarak, leave,' many shouted at the 21 March demonstrations. Outrage was not just about a war in Iraq, but dissatisfaction with how things were at home.

Protesters increasingly criticised the Egyptian government for its handling of the ruined economy, widespread corruption, and the perpetual renewal of Egypt's draconian emergency laws. The state of emergency gave the government broad powers to arrest and detain individuals indefinitely without charge or try them in extraordinary State Security courts where verdicts cannot be appealed. 'That's the danger of using brute force [to suppress demonstrations],' said one protester questioned about the new willingness to risk criticising Mubarak in public. 'It brings the enemy close to home.' A wave of arrests quickly followed. While daily demonstrations continued to attract thousands of students on university campuses, the security forces' iron-fisted policy managed to stop unsanctioned street protests.[2]

Until the end of his days

In his first speech as president in 1981, Mubarak said he would not serve more than two terms and his name would not grace buildings or his likeness feature on monuments. Both promises were broken. In 1993, with Mubarak's second term in its final year, parliament approved a constitutional amendment, voted on in a public referendum, which allowed him to run unchallenged for an indefinite number of terms. 'Here in Egypt, we don't have previous or future presidents,' wrote best-selling Egyptian novelist Alaa Al Aswany in a *New York Times* op-ed, 'only the present head of state who seized power through sham elections and keeps it by force, and who will probably remain in power until the end of his days.'[3]

Much to the chagrin of human rights defenders, the regime maintained emergency laws in effect, imprisoned and detained political dissidents, and narrowly restricted access to the political process. Power was firmly concentrated in the hands of the executive branch. The legislature, dominated by the ruling National Democratic Party, merely served to rubber-stamp presidential directives. By the 1980s the Muslim Brotherhood had become the main organised opposition group in the People's Assembly.

On public university campuses, corruption was endemic, ruling party loyalists controlled university appointments, political freedoms were stifled, the quality of education suffered, the Islamist trend commanded a strong presence, and the security apparatus kept tabs on students and professors. When the novelist Miral al-Tahawy entered college in the late 1980s the Brotherhood dominated campus activities, everything from sports and excursions to theatre and publishing. This Islamic alternative to what many saw as a nation's corrupt and failing institutions persuaded many Egyptian students to cling to hopes of change through religion. Without other channels for political action on the campus of Zagazig University, al-Tahawy joined the then-underground religious organisation. She was selected to write for the magazine of the Muslim Brotherhood, *Liwa' al-Islam* (Banner of Islam, formerly *al-Da'wa* or 'The Call'), focusing on themes of morality and virtue within a literary narrative.

It is a phase she has described as her 'political adolescence'. The first and essential lesson for recruits of the Muslim Brotherhood is to listen and obey, recalled al-Tahawy. 'Soldier, obedience; obedience, soldier; command, inhibition', the words rolling off her tongue in a staccato marching order. 'It makes you feel as if you are in the army of salvation,' she said. 'You are not engaged in political action, you are engaged in military action.' Instead of finding greater freedom, she found herself in a setting that was more dictatorial. 'The world of the Brotherhood is not democratic,' she said. 'It is very oppressive to any member who thinks, or discusses, or objects.'[4]

Novelist Sonallah Ibrahim publicly refused a state literary prize in 2003. 'I have no doubt that every Egyptian here realises the size of the disaster besetting our country,' he declared at the award ceremony.

> *We no longer have theatre, cinema, scientific research, or education. We only have festivals and a fund of lies. We no longer have industry, agriculture, health, or justice. Corruption and pillage spreads. And whoever objects faces abuse, beatings, and torture. The exploitative few have wrested our spirit from us. The reality is frightening, and in light of this reality, a writer cannot close his eyes or be silent.*

For this reason Ibrahim chose to reject an award 'from a government that in my opinion does not possess the credibility to grant it'. He stepped away from the podium to wild cheers and applause, leaving a stunned minister of culture holding the award cheque of 100,000 Egyptian pounds ($17,000).[5]

Mubarak tended not to jail the literati, yet his regime had other tools at its disposal, from blacklisting artists from state cultural institutions to buying the loyalty of the cultural elite. 'He allowed a margin for the arts and culture limited by boundaries he wanted to place,' said the colloquial poet Gamal Bekheet. 'We were on opposing sides with the regime. Between us was a game of tug of war. He reached a conviction at one time that the best thing for him to do is to dissipate the emotions of people: Let them say what they want and we will do what we want.'[6]

A message in comedy

Catering to an elite audience, theatre offered a unique space for expression, portraying the realities of despotic regimes through parody. The 1989 comedic play *Takharif* (Delusions), directed and starring Muhammad Sobhi, has a dictator reigning over the fictional land of Antika. Having attained power, the ruler of the island nation announces plans to govern democratically by declaring a dictatorship and jailing everyone who helped him stage a coup. Attired in boots and a trench coat, the dictator, who bears a striking resemblance to Adolf Hitler and slips into the cadences of former President Anwar Sadat, issues one unintelligible decree after another: 'If you find a citizen who understands me,' he orders, 'arrest him!'

A messenger comes to the ruler, who now has been in power for 20 years, and informs him that the population is rebelling because they cannot find bread. The dictator issues decree number 48,933 ordering the arrest of the bakers, declaring them enemies of the people.

'The bakers say they can't find flour,' says the messenger.

'Then arrest the flour traders!' barks the dictator.

'The traders did not receive flour from the farmers.'

'Arrest the farmers!'

'Then we will not find anything to eat.'

'Arrest those who won't eat!' quips the dictator.

When the dictator discovers a bomb in his desk, foiling an assassination attempt, he is determined to find out what the people truly want. He requests to speak with a citizen. Clothed in rags, citizen number 1,591 is brought before him.

'You are the representative of the people,' the dictator tells him. 'Talk without fear. Talk. Release what is in your head. Let out what is in your heart. *Without fear!* Do not be afraid of anything. You are free, and the son of the free. This is your historic hour. You are at the pinnacle of justice and democracy, so you should speak. Talk with your soul for today you will be asked before the people. *Without fear!* Do not be afraid of anything at all. Today you are envied. Why? Because you are standing before your servants, not your rulers. *Without fear!* I have a question and I want an honest answer. Are you an absolute supporter of me, my rule, and my government or do you belong to the opposition? *Without fear!* You do not need to be afraid of anything at all. Talk. Talk freely and democratically. Talk for today you are before your father. I am your father – better than the ones who gave birth to you. You are in my heart. If you took a knife and opened my chest, you'll find my heart. Do not be shocked, for it is one of the organs of my body. If you severed my heart in two – left chambers, right chambers, and an aorta – and you found yourself situated there, know that you are in my heart of hearts. You are forever in my heart, my blood, my tears, and my smile. Talk. Answer my question. Ah, you might have forgotten the question. Look at me as I ask the question. Fellow citizen, are you an absolute supporter of me, my rule, and my government *(nods his head)* – do you understand? – or are you, God forbid, from the opposition *(gestures throat being slit)*? And do not forget that you are in my heart.'

'The dictator who demands the support of people . . .' begins citizen 1,591.

'Thank you, fellow citizen,' says the dictator. 'By the constitution, I allowed him to speak. Now go home to your mother.'

The dictator's wife cajoles him to allow the citizen to finish what he was saying.

'But that is against the constitution,' he informs her.

'Give me the microphone and I will tell you that the world supports me,' says the poverty-stricken citizen.

'Give you the microphone?' admonishes the dictator. 'Do you know how much it costs? Give you the microphone so you can take it apart and sell it? Give you the microphone so that you can walk among the people, who you know are mostly illiterate?'

'You have been in power for 20 years. No one but you benefits from keeping the people illiterate,' the citizen challenges the dictator.

'I gave the people their freedom. I was not greedy,' the dictator says. 'And when they have their freedom, they use it against me. We are your masters, not your rulers!'

The citizen describes how low wages and high taxes have forced people to work less and accept bribes. 'Believe me, no one can fool the people, either in Antika or anywhere else in the world.'

In his 1991 satire *Mama Amrika* (Mother America), Muhammad Sobhi portrays Arab states as bickering siblings, made obvious by his open character impersonation of Hosni Mubarak, who views it in his interests to court America. The play's message is a strong condemnation of the US and its ally Israel, who exploit the weak and powerless for self-interest. Sobhi's character Ayish Shahat (literally: living as a beggar) is tricked into marrying the wealthy Amira Kamel (symbolising America), who claims to stand for human rights as she conspires with her cousin Shuman al-Shaffat (symbolising Israel) to drug and swindle Ayish. When he discovers the plot and demands a divorce, he finds himself accused of being a terrorist. 'A call from an impoverished Egyptian citizen to all the capitals of the world: Watch out for the new world order that aims to destroy our nation by those who kill for profit,' warns Sobhi's character.

Films have used humour to broach the topic of the Arab world's long-reigning rulers, such as the 2006 comedy *Zaza*, starring actor Hany Ramzy. Censorship authorities did not want comparisons with Egypt's regime to be obvious and so a made-up flag was represented in the film and there was no mention of the name of the country. The nation's autocratic ruler aims to achieve a veneer of democracy by announcing contested presidential elections, but the state assassinates opposition candidates because they pose a threat to the regime.

When the interior minister is invited on a talk show, Zaza's job at a television station is to mimic various callers asking whimsical questions. In one call, he interjects by saying, why do we even need presidential elections in the first place, since the one we know is better than the one we don't. Zaza sticks to the script as the minister's agents menacingly stand watch over him. Interior minister Gaber Mansour quietly dismisses the notion that the government was behind the accidental death of two presidential candidates. Yet the incidents have scared away potential opponents, and with two days left until the close of nominations, no one has come forward. To convince at least one candidate to run, Mansour announces that the state will insure the life of a political contender to the tune of five million Egyptian pounds.

Television presenter Rasha Basbous also works in league with the Interior Ministry and decides to help Mansour find a candidate for the ruse elections. She drugs Zaza and accuses him of rape. To avoid charges, Zaza reluctantly agrees to be the presidential candidate. The chief of staff informs President Metwally al-Hennawy that a citizen has been found who will run against him in the elections. 'All this is because of external pressures,' the chief of staff explains.

In television appearances Zaza vows to address the needs of the masses. 'I am a citizen just like you. I feel your hunger and poverty. I dream your dreams. And what's more important is that I love you. I love you all – the poor above the rich, the weak before the strong,' he tells viewers. 'I wish to do a lot of things and above all to restore our dignity: I want to prevent citizens from being subject to insult and humiliation.'

The political newcomer skyrockets in popularity. 'Zaza made us dream in an age when dreaming was forbidden,' remarks one citizen. 'If he dies, our dreams die.' President al-Hennawy has Zaza and Rasha Basbous arrested and referred to military trial, an act that receives global condemnation. Ambassador John Marsh and the Secretary of State Old Spice meet al-Hennawy and demand their release.

Zaza meets the president for the first time in a presidential debate. When the sitting president is asked about his platform, he promises pay raises, housing for those in need, land to peasants, and jobs for graduates.

Zaza's platform centres on love, freedom, and justice. Oppression and inequality have increased, he tells al-Hennawy.

'I was never an oppressor and oppression is not something I like,' the president says in his defence. 'You are trying to distort my image. My door is always open.'

'Yes, to the clique that you put between yourself and us – not to the people. Those around you tell you that our country is heaven and that all the people kiss your feet,' says Zaza.

'Your words are not true. They are lies. What you say has not been mentioned in the reports I receive,' says al-Hennawy.

'You receive information from reports that benefit whom? The person who raises his voice is a terrorist and the person who minds his business is a villain. What have they told you about the high bills and long queues?'

'How will you rule the country?' asks the president.

'No barriers or doors will be placed between myself and the people. No clique or relatives or friends. The people will have my mobile number. Whoever needs me will find me.'

'You will rule the country with your mobile?' al-Hennawy says disdainfully.

'No, I will rule it with my heart. The people need a heart to rule them, not a mind to control them,' replies Zaza as the audience cheers. 'We are with you with our hearts,' the crowd roars back.

Zaza wins 90% of the vote on election day. When introduced to the ministers, the president-elect says, 'I know them all. Since I was born they haven't changed.' He takes the ministers undercover to a police station where a detainee is being whipped as he hangs by his feet. Zaza strips the lapels off the officers committing the violations and sends them off to jail.

Ambassador Marsh goes to see President Zaza. His country has decided on a military strike against a leader in the region and requests that Zaza approve the use of his nation's airports and facilities for the attack. Zaza's willingness to go along will be in exchange for economic assistance.

To protect his nation's sovereignty and transform it into a regional power, Zaza cleverly negotiates a deal to purchase advanced weaponry from a European country. In his first speech to the people, Zaza announces a programme for development that includes punishment for those who have robbed the nation's wealth and an end to the system of graft that benefits those with money and connections. He issues his first decision as president: accept the Cabinet's resignation and investigate the violations government ministers have committed against the people. Zaza receives word during his speech that the arms shipment he brokered has arrived. His second decision is to refuse all foreign aid, which has always come with strings attached. The crowds enthusiastically exclaim, 'Keep the aid and leave us alone!'

Ambassador Marsh now orders the president's assassination. A sniper is in position. Zaza issues his third decision: a review of all international agreements that have been signed during previous eras. A shot rings out, striking the young visionary president. 'We will speak, even if we die,' cries the song at the end of the film, delivering a powerful message against dictatorship and foreign control. While packaged as a comedy, the allusions to Mubarak and his rule were all too plain.

The 2009 comedic film *al-Diktatur* (The Dictator) takes place in the strategically placed nation of Bambouzia. The story begins when an army general, Shanan al-Geyushi, assumes power by assassinating the ruler in a palace coup. When Shanan has a nightmare that free and fair presidential elections have unseated him from power, he rounds up the opposition and has them shot. The dictator's twin sons, Hakim and Aziz, are groomed to assume positions of power. An extravagant playboy, Aziz is sent off to Egypt where his antics are concealed from public scrutiny, while Hakim embarks on a privatisation drive where everything in Bambouzia is up for sale to foreign investors. When rebellion breaks out across the land, military officers turn against the ruler. Shanan and Hakim are arrested, tried in a military tribunal, and sentenced to death, but miraculously escape. Not exactly a warning to despots, the film ends with Shanan and his sons returning to power.

Hany Ramzy played the role of citizen 1,591 in the play *Delusions* while studying acting by day at Cairo's Higher Institute for Performance Art. As a film star his run-ins with the censors started with the 2001 *Gawaz bi-qarar gumhuri* (Marriage by Presidential Decree), the first and last film where Mubarak made a cameo appearance with the aid of computer graphics. Ramzy's character, Amr Bayoumy, is a low-level employee at the Foreign Ministry's archives and the son of a struggling actor. Engaged to his childhood sweetheart Reham, he sends a wedding invitation to the president on a whim. Seeking to appear closer to common Egyptians, the president surprisingly accepts. Crooked politicians and apathetic officials become attentive, vigilantly beautifying the impoverished quarter where the street wedding will be held. Residents find through Amr the only way to reach the president. The prospective groom receives thousands of letters containing their simple requests. Yet the glare of the spotlight splits the young couple apart. What ensues next is comic drama as the chief of staff, determined not to disappoint the president, goes to great lengths to get them back together. At the film's conclusion, the president appears at the wedding where Amr and Reham, reunited, hand him thousands of citizens' demands.

'Among the red lines were personalities that have halos around them, eliciting panic, fear, and concern. They could not be touched, like the president of the Arab Republic of Egypt,' said Ramzy. An appeal to the president's sons, Alaa and Gamal Mubarak, finally got *Marriage by Presidential Decree* to clear the censors, the actor disclosed. The problem was not just with Mubarak's presence but with allusions to a corrupt regime unaware of the problems of citizens or negligent in solving them. 'The people that he has as governors, members of the People's Assembly, ministers – each one of them is a guise, the "clique of beneficiaries", as they say,' remarked Ramzy.

The screenplay of another film where Ramzy played the lead role, the 2003 *'Ayiz haqi* (I Want My Rights), remained in the censor's drawers for six years, denied filming approval. And when it was finally made, it faced a host of problems from the censoring body, which demanded revisions to eliminate similarities with known political leaders. Ramzy plays Saber al-Tayib, a taxi driver who comes across articles in the constitution that declare public property to be owned by the people and each citizen is entitled to a portion of national production. Engaged for six years yet lacking sufficient savings for marriage, Saber decides to sell his allotment of the nation's assets. He wages a campaign to gather proxies from 51% of the population, allowing all of them to sell their national stake. He is arrested for being a gang leader, jailed, battered, charged with inciting the public, placed on trial, and finally acquitted. But when it comes time to sell a majority of the nation's assets at a public auction to a group of anonymous multinational investors, Saber decides to abort the deal.

Zaza was originally scripted as a fantasia set 50 years in the future. 'Why a fantasia? Why not make it a reality?' thought Ramzy, who played the part of Zaza. 'When we came to make it a reality, the censors opposed. So we decided to say that in some country at a certain time. But the important thing was that people understood that we were talking about Egypt.' *Zaza* faced quandaries with film censors not the least because the film expressed the audacious notion of actually voting out a sitting president. One of the parts of the film snipped out by the censors was of the former ministers being placed on trial.

Another scene the censors objected to was when Zaza, touring with ministers as they inspect police stations and government agencies, abandons his retinue and drives off. He notices a prostitute. She initially thinks the president is propositioning her but he wants to understand what motivates her to sell her body. The dialogue between Zaza and the woman could have been one the film's most moving. She pulls out a strip of drugs. Zaza asks her if she is an addict. She says no, but that if she were ever arrested by the police she would swallow the pills and take her own life to save her family from shame. 'There were moments where the woman was crying and I was crying for her,' recalled Ramzy. The censors were unwavering in their disapproval. Prostitution could not be acknowledged and a fictional leader could not be seen fraternising or sympathising with a working girl. In negotiations with the censors, Ramzy and the producers reluctantly agreed to the cut in order to have the film approved.[7]

A louder protest movement

Demanding political reform, the Egyptian Movement for Change, or Kifaya (Enough) as it was commonly called, emerged in the summer of 2004 to oppose the uncontested election referendum that would hand Mubarak another six years in power. The activist coalition comprised of sundry political trends also rejected the inheritance of political power from father, elder Mubarak, to son, Gamal, already a prominent figure in the National Democratic Party, known for its opaque, backroom policymaking. Kifaya sought the right to protest in the streets and took risks in directly criticising the president.[8] Their rallies were virtually ignored by Egyptian state television.

Under growing international pressure to create a façade of greater political participation, Mubarak in a televised speech on 26 February 2005 announced that article 76 of the Egyptian constitution would be amended to allow for the nation's first contested presidential elections. But when the amendment was drafted, it outlined such stringent standards that it would have meant the ruling party choosing its opposition in presidential elections. According to a confidential US Embassy cable, Mubarak told a visiting congressional delegation that he was 'begging' candidates to run in the presidential election. The constitutional amendment was for 'the future, not for me', he said. 'But all must be done at the right speed, Mubarak cautioned, saying he could not make the people do "a high jump" yet,' the diplomatic cable reported. Mubarak laughed off the notion of having presidential debates, 'suggesting that such activities were inappropriate for Egypt's political process'.[9]

In an interview with the Kuwait newspaper *al-Siyasa* (Politics), reprinted in the state-owned *al-Ahram* (The Pyramids) and *al-Akhbar* (The News) on 14 May 2005, Mubarak alleged that Kifaya protesters were paid and that their demonstrations were chasing away foreign direct investment and worsening unemployment. Denouncing the sham constitutional changes, Kifaya activists held street rallies, including one on 25 May, the day of the national referendum, in two locations in central Cairo – in front of the Journalists' Syndicate and at the mausoleum of nationalist leader Sa'd Zaghlul. Women protesters were harassed, beaten, and sexually molested by plain-clothes policemen and thugs allied with the regime as riot police looked on, an incident recorded in images that generated widespread outrage. The movement earned international media attention, focusing criticism on the government's heavy-handed tactics.

State television on the other hand reported a record turnout for the referendum that would bring Egypt one step closer to democracy, showed voters casting their ballots and heaping praise on the president. Kifaya, which has spawned other grass-roots movements calling for greater freedoms, organised a silent candle-lit vigil expressing anger at the indecent assault of women activists. Creative in their use of signs and slogans, activists again took to the streets a month later when Mubarak nominated himself for the presidency.

When the Islamist movement Hamas emerged victorious in the January 2006 Palestinian Legislative Council elections, any external pressures on Mubarak to implement gradual democratic reform dissipated. Security agencies restricted the spaces for human rights campaigning, the media, and activism, particularity the right to protest, which had opened up in 2004 and 2005, yet a greater public awareness and a demand for rights had already become rooted. Judges and activists staged sit-ins and protests lobbying for the independence of the judiciary, which were met with massive police presence, arrests, and violence against protesters and journalists.

The independent newspaper *Sawt al-umma* (The Nation's Voice) published the initials of judges believed to have been accomplices to electoral fraud. Counsellors and vice presidents of the Court of Cassation Hesham al-Bastawissy and Mahmoud Mekki[10] were charged by a disciplinary council with defaming a judge in *Sawt al-umma* by accusing him of vote rigging. Rallying for the independence of the judiciary, judges and activists took to the streets on 25 May 2006 in a demonstration in front of Cairo's High Court of Justice, one year after the flawed constitutional referendum.

Activist blogger Wael Abbas got involved in online chat forums in the late 1990s, which evolved into a Yahoo! Group he formed called 'Former Internet Junkies', so named because it focused on political, religious, and social discussions rather than frivolous internet obsessions. At the time Arabic publishing online was still new and few software tools were available for Arabic enabled sites. Abbas began publishing his work in online journals and electronic forums to reach the widest possible audience. Subscribers to Former Internet Junkies brought up topics, including the president's family dealings and rumoured plans for his son's succession, which were then taboo subjects to be examined openly. The group's members reached 10,000 before being hacked.

In 2004 Abbas started blogging, a task that did away with the chore of designing web pages and made his work immune from revision or censorship by moderators of digital publications, plus it had the element of interactivity. He also had the freedom to upload videos and as many photos as he liked. Abbas followed the burgeoning protest movement in his blog, a subject that the new independent print media was cautious about covering consistently or in-depth. Abbas soon found the images he posted being reproduced in newspapers. He doggedly pursued police torture allegations and sexual harassment incidents, posting videos on his YouTube channel that broke the story open, eventually gathering a flurry of media attention. His actions have not come without security harassment. Nonetheless, Abbas was joined by other devoted political bloggers.[11]

The April 6 Youth Movement leapt into prominence as a Facebook group in spring 2008 supporting a factory workers' strike in the Nile Delta city of al-Mahalla al-Kubra. Channelling the organising power of social media, the organisers called for a nationwide general strike in solidarity with strikers and as an act of civil disobedience against corruption, political stagnation, and economic hardships. The passive protest, which encouraged people to wear black, not to attend work or school, and abstain from shopping, was largely successful, although violent clashes between police and protesters erupted in al-Mahalla al-Kubra with several deaths reported.[12] The Facebook group became an active political discussion forum for a wide range of grievances against Mubarak's regime, becoming

Egypt's largest with more than 70,000 subscribers and articulating public opinion in a way that far surpassed what could be written in newspapers or discussed on television talk shows. The regime cracked down hard, arresting the group's creators, strike organisers, and online activists. Another general strike was organised a month later, on 4 May, to coincide with the president's 80th birthday. Employers threatened termination or docked pay for workers who did not show up to work, and this form of civil disobedience died down. Yet the April 6 Youth Movement did not.

Recognised by its clenched fist logo, the group continued its action online and on the streets. Activities of the group were closely monitored and organisers were routinely arrested and tortured by State Security. The mobilising efforts of the group – inspired by the non-violent political philosophy of Gene Sharp and the youth movement Otpor! that overthrew Serbian nationalist Slobodan Miloševic – would be a fulcrum of popular revolution two and a half years later, paving the way for a legion of online and offline activists, thereby reducing the risk threshold of political participation.

At 10 am on 6 April 2010, two years after the start of the movement, the first text message was sent, calling on members of the April 6 Movement to take to the streets and loudly recite the national anthem. A second text message at noon instructed the crowds to move quickly and in groups to make their way towards the parliament buildings. They carried signs demanding democratic reforms. Once there, the protest rally lasted only minutes. 'We won't leave!' and 'Long live Egypt!' they bawled. Security forces and plain-clothes officers faced off against protesters in downtown Cairo and Alexandria, walling them in, breaking or confiscating mobile phones and cameras, assaulting journalists, and beating and detaining dozens.

New forms of resistance emerged, with several waves of sit-in protests. On a hot afternoon in late April 2010 wheelchair-bound Mahrusa Salem Hassan and her five-year-old daughter Noor camped outside the People's Assembly; it was the 46th day of their sit-in. For months she had lobbied officials for a kiosk, which would provide her and her family with a means of living, only to be met with shut doors. She sought a law to gain rights for people with disabilities and was joined by tens of other disabled men and women calling on the government to give them a helping hand. 'Why do you marginalise me?' she asked, addressing government bureaucrats unconcerned with her plight. 'Why don't you help me to be a person who is productive and useful, and not someone who feels alienated?'

She has had to wait. 'All these people have left me out of their calculations,' she said, adding that she does not feel this country is hers and does not know how to teach her daughter to love her country when deep inside she despises it. Sit-in protests in front of the People's Assembly became a common occurrence in the last year of Mubarak's presidency. The picketers, whether laid-off textile workers or real estate tax collectors demanding a payrise, often came in supplication; in the end they wanted to walk away with something. 'There is no one but our father, our father who is Hosni, the honourable president. There is no one better than him who can stand up for these people,' said Mahrusa.[13]

From student activism on public university campuses to rural inhabitants blocking a road demanding that clean water reaches their village, protest action has bravely taken place in defiance of five or six laws and risking varying prison terms. 'People are engaging in sit-ins without being too afraid that the penal code, or the emergency law, or the law of assembly, or the law of associations will be applied to them,' expressed Hossam Bahgat, a human rights advocate and executive director of the Egyptian Initiative for Personal Rights. 'It is not that the regime is allowing more rights that it did not offer before. There are differing levels of civil disobedience – sometimes bordering on suicidal – which challenge the current laws. If it succeeds, it motivates others to try it.'

The same experience held true for the private print and broadcast media, which gambled in crossing red lines until a new norm was established. And for protesters, the press was an important catalyst. Bahgat outlined:

> *One, they know that the media is concerned with their movement and will transmit their voice. Two, they have seen on these same media outlets other people doing the same thing and that is why they are struggling to get their rights. Three, they have a desire to reach the media in order to achieve what they want. But what is most important is that they have greater confidence in themselves after the regime for years routinely destroyed the confidence people had in themselves and their ability to effect any change.*[14]

Activism and political expression against Mubarak's regime expanded to a greater extent on social media. Songs lampooning the social climate proliferated on Facebook and YouTube. Harnessing the social space, Egypt's underground rock and hip-hop groups delivered a politically and socially aware message that got the young more involved. Social media have become a free space for ideas and political debate in Egypt, but the security-minded state intervened when it became a means to organise politically.

Press restrictions

While portrayed as Egypt's larger than life father figure, Mubarak was no longer quite as untouchable as he once was by 2005, when the first contested presidential elections took place. The president was subject to more direct and unprecedented criticism in the press, where prior to 2003 denunciation of him was virtually unheard of. The independent *al-Dustur* (The Constitution), known for its adversarial and nonconformist approach, took the lead. The paper returned to news-stands on 23 March 2005 following a seven-year court battle to reinstate its publishing licence, revoked by the Ministry of Information. 'An American Magazine: Gamal Mubarak Owns a Company Worth 600 Million (Egyptian) Pounds', announced a headline above the masthead of the 7 July 2005 edition. The Mubaraks' family wealth was not a subject previously discussed in the press.

Taking advantage of the freer boundaries, a 2006 edition of *al-Dustur* had a headline asking the rhetorical question, 'Is Hosni Mubarak a Dictator?': 'The size of powers granted by the constitution to President Mubarak – may God extend his life – and his successor makes us affirm, without sarcasm, that if a white angel with wings of silk ruled Egypt based on this constitution, he would immediately be transformed into a tyrant.'[15] A front-page article asked whether it was even possible to have free presidential elections when student union elections in universities were rigged. 'Who was the government afraid of?' asked *al-Dustur*. Alongside the question were three multiple choices: (a) the people; (b) the Brotherhood; (c) the Americans.[16] The press stood clear of directly associating the president with corruption.

In February 2004, Mubarak announced that the penal code would be amended to abolish prison sentences for journalists charged with defamation. It was not until June 2006 that Mubarak interceded with the speaker of the People's Assembly to strike a controversial article from the penal code amendments that would impose prison sentences on journalists who falsely accused public officials of corruption. Journalists still faced stiff fines and could be jailed for defaming the president.

The chief editors of four independent and opposition papers – Wael Elebrashy of *Sawt al-umma* (The Nation's Voice), Ibrahim Eissa of *al-Dustur* (The Constitution), Adel Hammouda of *al-Fajr* (The Dawn), and Abd al-Halim Kandil of *al-Karama* (Dignity) – in a case filed in 2006 by members of the ruling National Democratic Party all faced charges of slandering the president, his son, and key political leaders in the NDP, spreading rumours, and damaging Egypt's image abroad. In September 2007, a civil court ruled that the editors must pay 20,000 Egyptian pounds ($3,540) each in fines, the maximum allowed by law, and were sentenced to prison for a year. On 7 October, a national holiday marking the start of the 1973 War, 22 independent and opposition newspapers did not go to press in protest at the government's action against press freedom. A Cairo appeals court on 31 January 2009 upheld the fines against the four newspaper editors but cancelled the one-year prison sentences.

In another case, Eissa was taken to court for spreading false rumours and harming Egypt's economic interests when he speculated about the president's ill health in a front-page column titled 'Gods Don't Get Sick'. 'The president in Egypt is a god and gods don't get sick,' wrote Eissa. 'For this reason President Mubarak and his associates and hypocrites hide the fact of his illness, leaving the country to feed on rumours and hearsay.'[17] Contemplating presidential succession and the power forces in play, Eissa goes on to say that the president's wife Suzanne is encouraging him to retire and transfer power to their son Gamal within his lifetime but the president clings to authority and wishes to remain in charge for as long as he can. Following an appeal, the court handed down a sentence of a two-month prison term on 28 September 2008, and when it was met with public outcry Mubarak commuted the punishment eight days later. In 1999 the rotund, moustachioed Eissa penned a self-published mystery novel staged in the corridors of presidential power called *Maqtal al-rajul al-kabir* (The Murder of the Big Man). He contracted with a state-owned publishing company to distribute 3,000 copies, which were quickly confiscated by State Security. The audacious whodunit circulated as underground literature before being republished in 2008.

But the firebrand journalist, whose columns were lauded for telling it as it is, would face what seemed like an orchestrated dismissal. In a battle of egos, Eissa was fired from *al-Dustur*, of which he was the founding editor, in October 2010 in a row with the paper's new owners, who objected to the publication of an opinion piece by democracy advocate Mohamed ElBaradei. In the article, ElBaradei noted that 37 years after the October

1973 War with Israel to liberate the Sinai, Egypt had not advanced politically or economically 'on the path to victory'; instead the nation had regressed. 'The October victory was a triumph of discipline and planning in work, which certainly represents the reverse of a culture of chaos and randomness known by Egyptian society after that,' wrote ElBaradei.[18] Eissa's hard-hitting nightly talk show *Baladna bil-masry* (Our Country . . . in Egyptian) on the satellite network ONtv, owned by billionaire telecom mogul Naguib Sawiris, was abruptly cancelled a month earlier, evidently due to pressures from above and ahead of parliamentary elections. Ibrahim Eissa has said that it was not enough for the government to fix elections; they did not want anyone to *talk* about fixed elections.[19]

Wider freedom within boundaries

Ra'is al-tahrir (Editor-in-Chief), a current affairs and talk show by the outspoken veteran journalist Hamdy Kandil, was the boldest show to appear on Egyptian state television, running from 1998 to 2003, but the prerecorded show often featured jarring cuts. Kandil freely criticised American designs in the Middle East with war looming in Iraq, and pushed the boundaries of expression on state television. The programme featured his review and commentary of the Arabic and foreign press. He numbered each press clip so viewers would know when television censors had deleted items. Kandil left Egyptian television when he felt the heavy-handed censorship violated his principles. His show moved to private Egyptian satellite channel Dream before it went off the air when the presenter refused to tone down his outspoken commentary.[20]

A popular interview programme broadcast on state-owned television with a mildly critical perspective of businessmen and government officials was *Min qalb Masr* (From the Heart of Egypt) hosted by Lamis al-Hadidi,[21] who worked as a public relations adviser in Mubarak's presidential campaign. She is the wife of Amr Adeeb, scion of a family media and entertainment conglomerate who has his own talk show on Saudi-owned Orbit satellite television, *al-Qahira al-youm* (Cairo Today), and is known for his self-styled populism that is often loud and aggressive. Amr Adeeb's brother, Emad Eddin Adeeb, the oversized chairman and CEO of the Good News Media Group and the presenter of *'Ala al-hawa* (On the Air), was given an exclusive interview with President Hosni Mubarak in the run-up to the 2005 presidential elections. The rare one-on-one interview with the president, broadcast in three episodes on state-owned Channel One, was meant to portray the ageing ruler as a man of the people.[22]

With such vested interests at stake, it seemed apparent that uncomplimentary programming was only allowed to go so far. In October 2010, Amr Adeeb found his popular talk show off the air for broaching the delicate subject of a safe exit strategy for the president. The official reason given was unpaid bills to majority state-owned Media Production City, where *Cairo Today* had its studios. As a general ally of the regime who took a few jabs at government officials every now and then, his departure had a chilling effect for other broadcasters.[23]

Dream TV, owned by Egyptian businessman Ahmed Bahgat and launched in November 2001, became the first private Egyptian satellite channel. Enjoying cosy relations with the regime, Bahgat was able to secure huge loans from public sector banks to establish manufacturing ventures, a theme park, and Dream TV. When he fell out of favour because of programming on his channel that was considered disparaging to the presidency, public sector banks recalled his loans, forced him to sign away his holdings, and seized a controlling stake in his business enterprises. He was prevented from leaving the country and only allowed to travel to Atlanta in 2007 for a heart transplant by special permission of the president. While recovering in intensive care Bahgat was forced to sign an amended agreement with the banks or risk having all his assets held in escrow.

Bahgat's Dream TV caused a stir in the closed political system, especially through its popular night-time programme with presenter Mona al-Shazly called *al-'Ashira misa'an* (Ten at Night), which broadcast interviews with policy-makers and politicians that included challenging questions about Egypt's social and political realities. Talk shows like *Ten at Night* gained loyal audiences of Egyptian viewers in a sea of free-to-air satellite channels. While private Egyptian satellite channels have played a significant role in connecting with the man on the street, the government and its security agencies have had ways of pressuring producers and presenters, or more pointedly, the channel's owners, who are businessmen with interlocking interests with the government.

An expanding press landscape has broken the cast of conformity characterising regimented, authoritarian societies, where any form of dissent is decidedly not encouraged. The multi-layered complexity of political discourse has emerged. Arabic satellite television introduced topics for discussion that would never have made it onto state-run television, breaking rules, flaunting conventions, and taking audiences along for the ride. But that freedom was never unfettered. 'It can give the impression of freedom without boundaries, which is not true. We all know this. During times of crisis we discover red lines linked with the politics either of the station's financing or the hosting country,' said Naglaa El Emary, programmes editor at BBC Arabic. 'From time to time, it becomes apparent.'[24]

Within the larger media world made possible by satellite communication and the internet, the state's role in shaping what Egyptians see has shrunk considerably. Add to that the fact that Egypt's role politically, culturally, and economically has eroded in recent decades. 'In reality, Egypt will not achieve the role it had played in the world and regionally,' remarked Hussein Abdul Ghani, Al Jazeera's Cairo bureau chief. 'The cultural influence was one of the sources of power for Egypt – the soft power of Egypt was its journalism, its intellectuals, its books, and its cinema industry.'[25]

Al Jazeera charted new ground in covering political news and opened the floodgates for free and open political discussion. Al Jazeera commanded audiences not only with news but with investigative documentaries and popular interview and debate programmes. State media around the Arab world, by comparison, could no longer hold on to their once dominant position. By losing hegemony of the broadcast image, they no longer had the same tools to mould public opinion.[26]

The Arab public holds a high degree of distrust of the government press, said Abdul Ghani at his office in downtown Cairo, where on the wall panel behind his desk hung the calligraphic teardrop emblem of the Qatari news station. 'The independent press has won ground so you can expect that there would be a resistance, then a regression and suppression.' Abdul Ghani and his staff have been arrested and detained on dozens of occasions. They have had video equipment broken and footage confiscated. 'The harassment increases during times of crisis,' said the Cairo bureau chief, 'when the government feels that the critical spirit of independent press coverage is pressing on its nerves.'

And there was much to hide from the scrutiny of the press. 'Each time a journalist is pushed away it is an attempt to avoid exposing new corruption. Each time the press is pushed away it is a way of hiding an illicit association between a businessman and a minister,' said Abdul Ghani. 'Each time the press is pushed away the more it reduces the chance of there being free choice to elect representatives who will hold the government accountable.' The government has used heavy-handed attempts to control the imagery that comes out of Egypt and restrict the actual practice of journalism on the streets.

Power and the press

The primary function of censorship has always been political, asserted novelist Alaa Al Aswany. Religion and social morality, he said, are used as convenient covers by authoritarian regimes, serving to preserve their power and shield them from criticism. The authorities did not consider an author's connection with his readers to represent a significant threat, added Al Aswany. 'They fear and place restrictions on television. The viewership of some programmes reaches 40 million.' This, he argued, is a shortsighted and erroneous measurement since effecting change does not necessarily correlate with the numbers of people being influenced. 'If I galvanise 30,000 readers among the intellectuals, I can change the whole country. It is not necessary that I reach a large number.'[27] That was a lesson lost on Egypt's British occupiers. In the late nineteenth century, agent and consul-general Evelyn Baring (Lord Cromer) gave the press generally free rein not out of a sense of benevolence but because he felt it was essentially harmless since only a small minority of Egyptians were literate. With a burgeoning nationalist press clamouring for an end to foreign rule, the British administrators of Egypt would eventually come to regret that decision.

While official state media served the useful function of shaping public information in the past, its credibility has eroded in a more open media space. In an odd language of contradiction, Egyptians believed the opposite message of what was being reported in the state press. 'When the government says there are no summer diseases, it means that there is an outbreak of cholera,' Al Aswany explained. With public denials by Gamal Mubarak, including a prime-time interview on state television's Channel One on 28 March 2006 stating that he was not interested in the presidency, Egyptians knew the stage was being set for the former investment banker to succeed his father. While the elder Mubarak also dismissed the notion that his youngest son was being groomed to be the head of state, he kept the vice-presidential post vacant.

Facing competition from a vibrant and expanding independent and private press, the state media's flagship daily *al-Ahram* saw its circulation and reputation diminish. The president and an ever-youthful first lady were for a long time front-page fixtures of the main state-owned dailies and the government perspective was given the benefit of the doubt. News items seemed oddly sanguine. Each day lauded the initiation of a new factory and the job opportunities it would create, even in the face of high unemployment. The common retort was that it was the newspaper of another country.

The blogosphere expanded the arena of expression for traditional media in addition to serving the complementary role of being a media watchdog. *Al-Ahram* famously and embarrassingly doctored a photo taken at the September 2010 Middle East peace talks in the resort city of Sharm al-Sheikh to have Mubarak leading the troop of world leaders; behind him were US President Barack Obama, President Mahmoud Abbas of the Palestinian Authority, King Abdullah II of Jordan, and Israeli Prime Minister Binyamin Netanyahu. In the original photo, Mubarak was trailing the pack.[28] The gaffe was discovered by an Egyptian activist and blogger, dispersed on social media, and quickly made headlines around the world.

'*Al-Ahram* as it stands now under editor-in-chief Osama Saraya can be studied in media schools as an example of failure. The Ministry of Interior dominates *al-Ahram* from A to Z. Maybe the only section that it does not control are the obituaries. That is an area where the Ministry of Interior cannot lie,' Al Aswany said before the 25 January revolution, citing the running joke on what can be trusted in the state-owned print media.[29]

The newspaper's headline on 4 May 2010 – Mubarak's 82nd birthday – was, 'A Day Egypt Was Born . . . Anew'. Saraya penned a sycophantic and laughable front-page column titled 'The Maker of the Future', lauding the achievements of the president in 'building a modern Egypt'. 'Today, political life is organised and freedom flourishes throughout the country, and every Egyptian man and woman experiences the freedom to participate and write and say what he or she wants in all issues of the homeland without fear or hesitation,' wrote *al-Ahram*'s chief editor, who goes on to mention other glowing accomplishments. The global economic crisis 'has not affected a single Egyptian', 'a strong country has stood by its citizens and children amid the escalating crises', and implemented programmes 'to root out poverty'. 'Each day, Mubarak handles the large battles for change in the lives of Egyptians,' enthused Saraya.

> *Do not forget to wish him happy birthday on this grand, beloved day. We tell him with our hearts filled with joy at his recovery following treatment,*

when he returned to work tirelessly, internally and externally, to maintain Egypt's prestige, its central role in the interest of all brotherly Arab states of preventing war, restoring peace, and building the nation.[30]

Let them bark

A confluence of factors accelerated the creation of a wider space for an independent press, particularly from 2004 onwards, giving room for dissidents and critics of the regime to express their opinion. What Egypt used to have before then was a government press and a loud, noisy, and scurrilous opposition press that often lacked true credibility. New print arrivals presenting a strong challenge to the state-owned media came on the scene. With the existence of a private press, a much larger middle ground opened up where Egyptians sought to know what the truth was – not by just demagoguery but by actually looking for sounder facts. Movements on the street like Kifaya took on a deeper role, openly railing against the décor of political reform and voicing trepidation in the run-up to the first contested presidential elections on 7 September 2005, where Hosni Mubarak faced off against nine other challengers and won 88.6% of the vote, according to the official count. Combine that with increased pressure from the administration of George W. Bush for Egypt to at least make the appearance of moving towards reform, even as the US was aiding violations in human rights through its notorious renditions programme and proxy CIA prisons, which made Mubarak's cooperation particularly useful.

Mubarak's reluctance to implement political reform was well known to his American ally, which delivered billions in aid to an 'ossifying and increasingly out of touch' regime. 'In all likelihood, it will not be possible to make great progress on democratic reform as long as President Mubarak remains in office,' asserted US ambassador to Egypt Francis J. Ricciardone Jr in a 2006 embassy cable. 'We do not have a silver bullet, but we can press reforms that will lead, inexorably, to the "death by 1000 cuts" of Egypt's authoritarian system. There will be no "Orange Revolution on the Nile" on Mubarak's watch, but we must aim to consolidate each modest democratic advance.'[31]

Evening talk shows and news magazine programmes were where most Egyptians got their news and information. They had replaced the basic function of the local evening newscast on state-owned terrestrial channels, which led with a story about the president (even if something as mundane as his telephone conversation with another world leader), prime minster, or top-ranking government official, reported a factory opening or other ceremonial occasion, and quickly moved on to cover news outside Egypt.

Mubarak's government had the means to pressure the private press. There are ways to teach outspoken journalists a lesson, too. They include arrests, beatings, prosecution, travel restrictions, being monitored and having phone calls tapped by the security agencies, or by having allies of the regime tie up journalists in expensive and time-consuming court cases. Journalist Abd al-Halim Kandil, known for his caustic editorials against Mubarak and the regime, was abducted in November 2004 in front of his home, beaten, stripped naked, robbed of his wallet and thick spectacles, and left on a desert road. 'So you'll stop talking about the big guys,' he was told. Yet the treatment did not deter him; his 2009 polemic was titled *Kart ahmar li-l-ra'is* (A Red Card for the President).[32] Some media professionals were up for the challenge of battling against forces of entrenched power, others were not. Journalist Andrew Hammond expressed it this way: 'For journalists, it's a game of daring an official mindset that rules by instilling fear of its ability to strike at any time. Many decide that cohabiting with and being co-opted by the authorities is the better part of valor.'[33]

Security agencies often got involved in the affairs of the press through hidden means, becoming what Abd al-Moneim Aboul Futouh, who was a prominent figure in the opposition Muslim Brotherhood, called the 'security press':

> *The security press is a number of journalists in different places, some of them are editors-in-chief of state-owned publications. Their role is to be an instrument of the security agencies. The security agencies use them to harm a political opponent, to defame his reputation, or to injure an organisation like the Muslim Brotherhood. I call this group the security press, the press that gets its instructions from the security agencies, that does not practise the function of media and journalism as professionals – neutral, honest, clean.*[34]

The state-owned press routinely referred to the Muslim Brotherhood as the 'banned group'. Egyptian television blacklisted opposition figures. Even as the secretary-general of the Arab Medical Union, Aboul Futouh was prevented from appearing on Egyptian television to talk about purely medical matters. The barrier of allowing Brotherhood members airtime to defend their views was broken first by Al Jazeera and occasionally by private Egyptian satellite channels.

The Egyptian regime exerted a firm level of control on forms of political expression, particularly through the state's one-million-man-strong security apparatus. 'EGIS [Egyptian General Intelligence Service] Chief Omar Soliman and Interior Minister [Habib] al-Adly keep the domestic beasts at bay, and Mubarak is not one to lose sleep over their tactics,' described a US Embassy cable.[35] A freer press has been called 'the right to scream' or 'the right to bark', but when Egyptians attempted to organise politically, the security state cracked down. While 'freedom to talk' expanded, 'freedom of action' had its limits. 'So you can criticise, give the opposite opinion, accuse the authorities, and question their legitimacy,' described Gamal Ellatif, strand editor at BBC Arabic. 'But when it comes to action on the ground then it is met with negative consequences. They call it the freedom to vent *(tanfis),* not the right to implement *(tanfiz)*. So say what you like but do not implement what you say.'[36]

While the press in the last years of the Mubarak presidency was allowed a wider space for criticism, that did not end rigged elections or promote true political reforms. 'What is worst is the lack of responsiveness,' contended Awatef Abdel Rahman, professor of journalism and mass communications at Cairo University. 'The private and opposition press uncovers corruption and the government does nothing.'[37] That sentiment was echoed by Aboul Futouh. 'Criticism of the executive branch has no value if it is not followed by action. We don't have free expression in Egypt; we have the right to yell.'[38] Take any number of issues that have been heated topics of discussion, he continued. Ultimately nothing has happened to change the realities on the ground. 'There is no response or solution to most chronic problems. So what's the value of expression? Is it a form of venting? Psychological help? Is that going to be the goal? If its role is psychological, it should be played out at the doctors' offices and not in the press.' To have a noticeable impact, the right to free expression needs to diffuse all levels of society, including the street, posited Aboul Futouh. 'What will lead to change is popular action.'

Alaa Al Aswany entertained no illusions about literature's ability to bring about change. 'The function of literature is not to change the political realities in Egypt or anywhere else,' said the novelist. 'Literature is not a political strategy. If you want to change the political reality, be involved in activism.'[39] Al Aswany's literary and political salons used to take place in downtown Cairo cafés, but when the owners were pressured by the security agencies not to host the gatherings, they eventually moved to a crumbling building, home to the opposition Karama (Dignity) Party, in the Cairo district of Munira. A dentist by profession, Al Aswany has penned regular political articles, where he advocated democracy, human rights, and the rule of law to replace an authoritarian system that favours those with power, wealth, and connections. He ended his columns with the words, 'Democracy is the solution.'

In one opinion piece in the independent daily *al-Shuruk* (Sunrise) published in April 2010, Al Aswany recounted the history of the Iranian revolution and how its ruler had become completely oblivious to how his people were living. 'The dictator lives in complete isolation from the life of his citizens and does not truly know what happens in his country . . . but only its image, transmitted to him through reports raised to him by the different intelligence agencies.' It is in the interests of these agencies to shroud the truth so as not to receive the dictator's wrath, Al Aswany continued. He linked the example of the shah of Iran's detachment with the ruler of his country.

> *What do you think President Mubarak knows about what happens in Egypt? Does he know that more than half of Egyptians live below the poverty line? Is the president bothered that millions of Egyptians live in slums without access to water, electricity, or sewage? Is he distraught by the spread of unemployment, poverty, disease, and hopelessness? Does the president know that Egypt has sunk to the bottom in all fields? Did he hear about the poor who die waiting in queues in search for loaves of bread or propane gas canisters? Has he heard about the boats of death through which thousands of youth try to escape despair and are found drowned at sea? Has anyone told the president that thousands of wage earners and their children lie in protest for months on the sidewalks before the People's Assembly because their lives have become unbearable? Has President Mubarak thought of the employee who earns 100 Egyptian pounds a month to spend on his whole family when a kilo of meat has reached 60 pounds? I really do not know how the president thinks. And were I to guess, according to the phenomenon of the isolation of the dictator, President Mubarak is completely detached from the reality of what is happening in Egypt.*[40]

Al Aswany concluded his column by calling on the president to end his years of rule with true democratic reform, and amend the constitution to allow for honest competition between candidates and transparent elections that allow citizens to choose representatives who will end Egypt's ordeal.

It was these sorts of hard-hitting and widely read columns that forced the authorities to take action, closing a paper factory belonging to newspaper publisher Ibrahim al-Mu'alim because of alleged safety violations. The message was clear: stop publishing Al Aswany's columns. State Security officers routinely called al-Mu'alim after the articles appeared in the paper and warned him there would be consequences. Al Aswany refused to tone down his criticism of the president and the ruling clique, and submitted his resignation to *al-Shuruk* in October 2010 after al-Mu'alim's factory was shut down a second time. Al Aswany was willing to pay the price for his words, but he was not prepared to have factory workers or the owner suffer in his place.[41]

Even as the state cracked down on the media, an Egyptian public became more informed, public debate was heightened, and there was an expectation of hearing different perspectives and viewpoints. 'It is one area where there really has been quite deep reform with profound impact. It is not a matter of having a few more-or-less independent newspapers with pretty good circulation,' added Max Rodenbeck, the Middle East bureau chief for *The Economist*. 'There is a sense of airing grievances. This is presumably a part of government policy to let things open a little bit. Cynics would say that the policy is to let people shout just to let off steam but I think there had been a very marked widening of the circle of freedom of speech.'[42]

A political challenger arrives on the scene

Coming together via the power of networking, thousands of Egyptians crowded the terminal at Cairo International Airport awaiting the arrival of the former director general of the International Atomic Energy Agency and 2005 Nobel Peace Prize winner Mohamed ElBaradei in Egypt on 19 February 2010. Supporters waved banners and posters declaring ElBaradei 'The Hope of Egypt', cheering with nationalistic slogans, and singing the national anthem. They came to express their support for ElBaradei's vision for greater democratic representation, a respect for human rights and the rule of law, and an end to the corrupt authoritarianism that has long defined Egyptian-style politics. His arrival from Vienna – and the Egyptian people's reaction – was reported around the world. The regime was caught off guard, unaware exactly how to handle this public relations nightmare.

'Mr ElBaradei is also fortunate that one of the few chinks in the armour of Mr Mubarak's state is a relatively free press,' *The Economist* opined shortly after his arrival in Egypt. 'Despite a flood of innuendo and calumny from regime mouthpieces, independent newspapers and television channels have given the newcomer a fair hearing.'[43] Egyptian presenter Mona al-Shazly conducted a live three-hour-long interview with ElBaradei on 21 February 2010. 'My party is the people,' proclaimed the democracy advocate. 'I don't have a government or an army. I have a thought.' Egyptians, he said, were alienated from political life, feeling that elections were nothing more than a staged performance. Since 1952 a vanguard rooted in the military had held sway over Egypt's political destiny. 'It is time we talked about democratic validity,' he said, adding his common refrain that 'poverty is the biggest weapon of mass destruction.'[44]

The control the state had over the media was seen with coverage of the regime's latest liability. As an emerging political contender, ElBaradei's access to the media would be severely restricted. ElBaradei's campaign, called the National Coalition for Change, began on 4 December 2009 when the recently retired chief of the UN's atomic energy watchdog announced that he would consider running for the presidency in his native Egypt if political reforms were made to open the political process to greater participation and transparency.

Through the coalition's website and in door-to-door canvassing by volunteers, Egyptians were invited to sign a seven-point petition that demanded an end to wide-ranging powers granted to the state by emergency law, complete judicial supervision of elections, monitoring of elections by civil society and international non-governmental organisations, providing equal opportunities in the media for candidates, enabling Egyptians abroad to exercise their right to vote at Egypt's embassies and consulates, ensuring the right to stand in presidential elections without arbitrary restrictions, and constitutional reform. ElBaradei's petition drive resulted in more than one million signatures. His courage in criticising the lack of democratic representation earned him a following, one he nurtured through regular postings on Facebook, Twitter, and YouTube.[45]

Mubarak's Egypt was careful about who shared the political limelight and government office holders who seemed to be gaining admirers were promoted out of influential posts and eventually their stars faded. That served to entrench the idea that there was no one, save

Hosni Mubarak and his son and heir apparent, who had the experience to lead a country as large and complex as Egypt. Loyalists in the state-owned media and the business elite around the president's son doggedly promoted the notion of dynastic succession as the safest course for Egypt.[46]

The regime had always made the case abroad that democracy has to progress at a snail's pace since no ally wants the Islamists ushered into power. The time is not quite right, they maintained, for true representative democracy with free and fair elections. That was an argument that British agent and consul-general Lord Cromer had advanced during the era of monarchy a century earlier: 'It is absurd to suppose that Europe will look on as a passive spectator whilst a retrograde government, based on purely Mohammedan principles and obsolete Oriental ideas, is established in Egypt,' he wrote in 1908 in a two-volume history titled *Modern Egypt*. 'The material interests at stake are too important, and the degree of civilisation to which Egypt has attained is too advanced, to admit of such a line of conduct being adopted.'[47]

Aside from a series of interviews about the need for democracy and signatures gathered on a petition, ElBaradei did not succeed in generating a movement for change that Egyptians could latch on to and the initial euphoria that met his arrival largely dissipated. Taking frequent trips abroad, he had been reluctant to go beyond rhetoric and do the real work of grass-roots mobilisation that was needed to bring about change.

Political challengers were also up against insurmountable obstacles. 'The security agencies are what rule Egypt. The criminality and the intervention of the security corrupt any act of reform,' said Muhammad Mahdi Akef, the former supreme guide of Egypt's most organised political opposition, the Muslim Brotherhood. 'We are not able to resist neither the military nor the security.' Sentenced to death during the reign of Gamal Abd al-Nasser, Akef spent the next two decades in prison. In 1996, under Mubarak's rule, he received a three-year sentence handed down by a military tribunal. Before the revolution, he said:

> *ElBaradei is someone with integrity, who has an international reputation. The likes of ElBaradei are many; hundreds are like him. But they do not succeed in accomplishing anything. And ElBaradei won't succeed in doing anything because the political will of the military and security does not want this to happen. If the regime has the political will, then everyone will cooperate for change, and the best methods of*

> *change. Change can work if the nation is united behind a core concept and one set of demands.*[48]

It looked unlikely that ElBaradei or any other challenger would be able to replace an entrenched authoritarian system with one that was more democratic, but it meant the regime would have to work overtime to weather the electoral cycle in 2010 and 2011. In street demonstrations and online campaigns, activism expanded as much as the security state would allow. These organised efforts calling for genuine political change lacked the infrastructure of a party and embraced a rejection of an increasingly unpopular system. Even the security agencies were hard pressed to handle formations that were essentially leaderless and represented more or less a collective will for something different.

The 2010 parliamentary elections, a harbinger of what could be expected in the 2011 presidential race, laid to rest the hope that gradual democratic reform was in the offing. With the security apparatus as accomplices, Mubarak and the ruling party intended to secure a tighter grip on power. Full supervision of elections by Egypt's judiciary, the only hope for a semblance of fair elections since international observers were not permitted, came to an end with amendments to the constitution in 2007. In June 2010, the National Democratic Party won 80 of 88 contested seats in the Shura Council, the upper house of parliament, amid claims of vote buying, voter intimidation, and election rigging. Another 44 seats were allocated by presidential decree.

The outcome was no different in elections for the People's Assembly five months later, which guaranteed the ruling party a landslide win. Candidates of the Muslim Brotherhood running as independents, the largest opposition bloc in the outgoing People's Assembly with 20%, received no seats in the first round of voting on 28 November 2010 and boycotted the runoff elections on 5 December. Maintaining its political dominance, the National Democratic Party won 420 of 508 seats in the People's Assembly amid allegations of fraud. With calls for reform gaining momentum, the state began tightening systems of control over the media in a run-up to elections. State Security determined who was allowed to appear as a talk show guest and who was not. In a 12-minute message posted on YouTube following the parliamentary elections, ElBaradei warned, 'If we must, we will resort to civil disobedience', adding that violence may be the inevitable result of a system unwilling to change. 'There are limits to oppression. And if repression persists, we must know that there will come a day of reckoning.'[49]

Social media breaks walls

An often-used word of advice to avoid trouble with the authorities was to 'walk close to the wall' – which meant to have nothing to do with anything political. Many Egyptians have internalised that message, choosing to play it safe if they did not want to find themselves in the stranglehold of the security agencies. That psychological barrier began to fall as more Egyptians, particularly internet-savvy youth, sought a political voice. Yet change required a critical mass willing to act and to shed their fears. Social media opened up an arena for political engagement and activism that was having a slow yet transformative effect. Protesters were using mobile phones to stream live footage of political action on the street to the web and to document police abuses. More than being a forum for expression, the internet was being used to monitor and coordinate protests and grass-roots organising. That was evident in a police brutality case that roused outrage against the long-standing emergency law in an unruly police state.

Khaled Muhammad Said was a 28-year-old man beaten to death by plain-clothes police in a cybercafé in Alexandria on 6 June 2010. Graphic photos of Said after his death surfaced on social media, bloodied, disfigured, with a broken jaw and teeth. His death marked a tipping point, and in a matter of days his image was the symbol of national anger against the all too common practice of police torture – a bleak reminder of how the state treats its citizens. The official narrative given by the authorities for Said's death was that he died of asphyxiation when he swallowed a bag of drugs after being apprehended by police.[50]

Facebook expanded the community of online advocates. Postings and shared links were read or watched by an audience that far surpassed many print publications in numbers and influence. Protests and demonstrations followed, including silent vigils on Fridays staged on the corniche in Alexandria. Many Egyptians changed their profile picture on Facebook to an image of Khaled Said with a banner that read, 'Martyr of Egypt'.

The dynamic of the conversation generated online could not be ignored by broadcasters, who had previously been cautious about broaching topics like police corruption and abuse. On 13 June 2010, as the outrage over the beating to death was picking up steam, presenter Tamer Amin gave the Interior Ministry's version of events on the popular evening current affairs show *Masr al-naharda* (Egypt Today) broadcast on state television's Channel Two. 'Everyone tells the story he wants. I am not against any narrative, but I am against a judgement before investigation,' he said. 'From actual records of the Interior Ministry, this youth, Khaled Sobhi Said,[51] 28 years old, is a criminal and has a police record. He has four convictions, four court cases,' explained Amin as he kept count by motioning with his fingers. 'First, evading compulsory military service. Second, carrying a switchblade. Third, sexually harassing a female. Fourth, attempted robbery using force.'

Amin continued with the official line: when Khaled Said saw the police he ran, swallowing the drugs. 'The forensic pathologist verified that the cause of death was asphyxiation. The bag of marijuana was lodged in his trachea, resulting in him choking. No oxygen was passing through his air passage, so he died.' Amin advised that there should not be a rush to judgement before the public prosecutor had completed a review of the case, but called the police's version of events 'more logical'.[52] Because of the force of social media, the murder remained in the headlines for weeks, even attracting international media coverage, finally pressuring prosecutors to bring charges against the two policemen responsible for Said's death.[53]

The programme *Egypt Today*, in a segment in October 2010, sounded the alarm bells on Facebook, a harbinger that the regime had intentions of reining in the social networking site in the name of national security. Tens of thousands of members massed on the pages of the April 6 Youth Movement and 'We are all Khaled Said' – forums not only for debate but activism – have made Facebook a threat to the security state.

'We have to take a stand and talk about the defects of Facebook,' said presenter Mona al-Sharqawy, who acknowledged that she did not have a Facebook account. 'They can use your personal information for other purposes – the information they know from what you write, the groups you join,' she added. 'They can take it and use it to other ends.'

The presenter took the discussion into more treacherous ground. 'I am also talking about the political danger. As I said in the introduction, intelligence agencies are financing Facebook. Many of you don't know this,' alleged al-Sharqawy. 'We are scandalising our country. And if you allow me, some groups are inviting protest and sabotage,' she continued. 'How do we know that the ones telling them to do this are not Egyptians? It could be someone foreign. We have seen it more than once. We have seen it with April 6. We cannot deny that it was a sabotage operation – they were instructed to go out and vandalise Tahrir Square.'

Foreign intelligence outfits were not the only rogue elements behind social networking, according to the presenter. Democracy promotion was another danger. 'It was said about two months ago that Facebook will start funding democracy in countries and especially in countries entering elections, and of course we are entering elections,' announced al-Sharqawy.

'I hope you have absorbed every word we have said today,' the presenter told her audience at the programme's conclusion. 'I speak to all with an open heart,' she said of the information revealed about Facebook. 'On the social level, the results have shown that it is detrimental. They know personal details about us, and they play with it, abuse it, and threaten us with it. On the political level, it is enough for us to say that behind the funding are intelligence agencies. I urge each mother and father and youth who are mature and alert to be extremely careful when they deal with this system and that they do not coordinate with people who incite them in matters that can endanger their country.'[54] In an age of digital communication, the technology gains of immediacy, decentralisation, and magnitude are the censorship authority's Achilles' heel.

The Jasmine revolution

With ever-rising prices, limited employment opportunities, political dissatisfaction, and a strong will to act, more and more Egyptians were becoming politically engaged. In the dusty and crowded streets of Cairo, there was an unsettling feeling of suffocation, malaise, and frustration. So much needed to change: corruption was not only common, it was encouraged; a huge polarisation of wealth existed, with most Egyptians living on the margins of existence. Add to that the shadow of fear – that anyone could be picked up by the authorities, randomly (for being in wrong place at the wrong time) or on purpose (to silence dissent), and subjected to all manner of abuse. Despite all that, people were speaking up in ways they had not done before, armed with social networking tools that made it unacceptable to sit on the sidelines.

The world watched and waited as demonstrations in neighbouring Tunisia reached a crescendo, bringing down the autocratic regime of Zine el-Abidine Ben Ali. The protests erupted after 26-year-old vegetable seller Mohamed Bouazizi doused himself with a flammable liquid and set himself ablaze outside a local government building on 17 December 2010 in the provincial town of Sidi Bouzid after authorities publicly humiliated him and confiscated his vegetable stall, his only means of livelihood. Dying of his burns 18 days later, Bouazizi emerged as a martyr to Tunisians who took to the streets protesting against high unemployment, the lack of political freedom, nepotism, and rampant corruption, notably among members of Ben Ali's family, a quasi-mafia known to live wildly extravagant lifestyles. Strong press censorship kept stories of familial profiteering from being publicised or acknowledged.

News of unrest in Tunisia originated not from the local press or traditional media organisations, which were barred access in a country that heavily restricted press freedoms, but were disseminated on social media despite attempts by the state censorship apparatus to restrict online activity. These testimonies of the ongoing clashes on the streets between security forces and protesters were curated by the media, particularly Al Jazeera. One desperate act by a young man would become the event that set off a month-long uprising in Tunisia that toppled the country's 23-year reigning president, whose promises of comprehensive reforms came too late. 'I heard you. I heard you all, the unemployed, the needy, the politicals, and those who demand greater freedoms,' a tense and shaken Ben Ali intoned in a final televised address on 13 January, one day before he and his wife fled Tunisia. 'I have decided on complete freedom for all forms of media, an end to closure of internet sites, and a refusal of any form of censorship on it, mindful of our morals and the principles of the journalistic profession.'[55]

The events of Tunisia's Jasmine revolution emboldened activists and reformers in Egypt as 2011 turned out to be a watershed year for Arab states. Some pundits were predicting that Egypt would be next. 'Egypt, in particular, seems to bear at least a passing resemblance to Tunisia – a heavy-handed security state with diminishing popular support and growing demands from an educated, yet frustrated, population,' observed Anthony Shadid in the *New York Times* on the day the Tunisian president fled the country.[56]

In a 2008 meeting with assistant secretary of state and former US ambassador to Egypt David Welch, Ben Ali shared his insights on where the region was heading: 'He opined that the situation in Egypt is "explosive," adding that sooner or later the Muslim Brotherhood would take over.'[57] Totalitarianism across the Arab world, long known for its monarchs and presidents for life and their ironfisted rule, did in fact make the region explosive, and the spark of what would be called the Arab Spring was set off by Tunisia's popular revolt. 'What happened in Tunisia over the past three weeks is little short of a revolution whose domino effect many in Egypt hope will not only touch the banks of the Nile, but the capital cities of the entire Arab world,' Rania Al Malky began her editorial in the English-language *Daily News Egypt*, where she was chief editor.

> *Ironically, all the events that led to the Tunisian uprising are daily occurrences in Egypt. . . . Why then do we not sustain the momentum of our protests – which have sadly become like withered embroidery bordering the patchwork of Egypt's so-called democracy? And when Egyptians do come together in modest numbers, why then does the regime not feel obliged to make fundamental reform, satisfied that protestors will welcome the bread crumbs it offers as major victories? . . . [T]he Tunisian upheaval . . . has shown us that it is no longer a choice between civil wars or military coups.*
>
> *There is a third option and the Tunisians are leading the way.*[58]

That editorial got the attention of the state's censorship authority, which has offices right next door to State Security. 'For the first time in six months, I got a call from our friends at the censors,' said Al Malky. He told her they had not had coffee in a while, then got to the point. 'He said what you wrote was incitement,' she recalled. 'We had this short and brief five-minute conversation where his message came across very clearly.'[59]

Anything that made direct links between Tunisia and Egypt was seen as risky in the eyes of the minders. Since the developments in Tunisia, the platoon of state media publications bent over backwards to portray the government as being truly concerned with the plight of the people. Lip service aside, the government was not offering up a modicum of genuine reforms that would indicate that they were at all concerned.

Mubarak was the only president that every Egyptian under 30 years of age – two-thirds of Egypt's population – had ever known. But, as Egypt had so often seen in those three decades, political change was only choreographed by the president himself. He was a man who operated with unbelievable caution. Yet the status quo, which neglected too much of Egypt's population, was unsustainable. Social networks and a renewed sense of activism awakened a force for change that on 25 January 2011 reached breaking point.

2

Eighteen Days

By placing confidence in violent means, one has chosen the very type of struggle with which the oppressors nearly always have superiority.

(Gene Sharp, advocate of non-violent action[1])

A silent protest was organised on 7 January 2011 – Coptic Christmas – against the terror bombing outside the Two Saints Church in Sidi Bishr, Alexandria, on New Year's Eve that killed 23 people and injured scores. Dressed in black, protesters massed on Qasr al-Nil Bridge and at other locations, holding up signs simply proclaiming 'Muslim + Christian = Egyptian'. Security officials displayed only so much tolerance. 'We played around, we fooled around, *now go home!*' howled a security official. The political system would remain monopolised by an elite who would use it for their benefit, equipped with an immense and ruthless security apparatus. It was difficult to hold out much hope – until a week later when Tunisia's dictator was toppled by intense and sustained protests. It was an important lesson for the masses in the Arab world: collectively you have unbridled power to change your societies – even against oppressive and autocratic regimes. In Egypt, the deadly beating by the police of Khaled Said in June 2010 would become that pivot for change. It was on the Facebook page 'We are all Khaled Said' that the silent protest of 7 January and the 'Freedom Revolution' of 25 January were publicised. The April 6 Youth Movement along with youth activists worked on the logistics of organising protests throughout Egypt.

The date 25 January 2011 was chosen to coincide with Police Day, a national holiday declared by President Hosni Mubarak just two years earlier to commemorate a heroic 1952 battle in Ismailia between the police and the British occupation forces where 50 officers lost their lives. 'After more than fifty years, we suffer from the practices of the police, which have become a tool for the torture and humiliation of Egyptians. We have chosen this particular day because it symbolises the fusion of the police with the people and we hope that on this day of demonstration the esteemed officers will join with us because our cause is one,' the organisers wrote on the Facebook page. '25 January is not a revolution by means of a coup but a revolution against the government, to tell them that we've begun to be concerned with our own affairs and we will get back all our rights and not remain silent after this day.'[2]

The page listed four main demands: addressing the problem of poverty by having a minimum wage and improving services for the poor, ending emergency law and the dominance of the security apparatus, dismissing interior minister Habib al-Adly because of crimes and abuses by security officials and security lapses that have led to terrorism, and implementing presidential term limits. Had any genuine attempt been made by the government to address those demands before 25 January, an uprising might never have materialised.

Protests would be held throughout Egypt in locations listed on the page and also start in poor and working-class neighbourhoods. Guidelines were laid down: the protests will be peaceful and refuse provocation by the security forces ('One of the primary goals of the security is to portray protesters as a bunch of thugs who want to ruin the country'); the protest will start exactly on time; when leaving home do not carry anything you won't need; have your ID card, enough money for emergencies, and a bottle of water; bring only an Egyptian flag, not the banner or sign of a party or other affiliation because on this day we are all Egyptian; do not use obscene language or engage in battles with security; avoid deliberately blocking traffic; do not go by yourself, bring a friend. The unified slogans suggested for the event focused on political freedoms, unemployment, and poverty since they were issues of concern to all Egyptians.

Young and courageous, Asmaa Mahfouz announced a protest in Tahrir Square on 18 January to commemorate the death of a jobless 25-year-old man in Alexandria who set himself on fire, perhaps believing his immolation would somehow set off revolt. Three other Egyptians had done the same since Ben Ali's fall. While Mubarak and the regime made no mention of the neighbouring dictator's demise, the state media's coverage in the following days went out of its way to reassure the public that the president was mindful of Egypt's poor and his economic reforms had their concerns at heart.

Mahfouz publicised her protest action online but was disappointed when she was joined by only three other youth. They were met by three trucks of security personnel with others on the way. 'Enough! Enough of what's happening,' Mahfouz recounted in a video she posted on YouTube that night. 'Anyone who dies from the mess and filth that we live in, the newspapers and everything that belongs to the government say he dies because he is disturbed or mentally ill.' She entreated everyone to come out on 25 January to say no to the regime and no to corruption. 'Anyone who says that the numbers will be small and nothing will change, I tell him, "You're the reason for this. You're guilty, like the president, like anyone who's corrupt, like any officer who hits and beats us. . . . If you sit at home then you deserve what happens to you."'[3] Mahfouz uploaded another YouTube video on the night of 24 January, making another appeal for Egyptians to take to the streets. 'Tomorrow if we succeed and stand firm, whatever the security does to us, and we are truly unified – we all come on time and demand our rights peacefully – it will be the first true step for change.'[4]

Day 1: 25 January 2011

On 25 January, Egyptians crossed the fear barrier. What began as a day of protest would evolve into a mass uprising with its own intrinsic dynamic. Tens of thousands of protesters took to the streets, shouted slogans in call and response fashion that not only demanded basic freedoms but the downfall of Mubarak's regime: 'Down with Mubarak!' – 'Revolution in Tunisia. Revolution in Egypt. Revolution in all the streets of Egypt!' – 'Ben Ali, tell Mubarak, "An airplane is awaiting you!"' Crossing into the political arena, hardcore football fans known as Ultras, accustomed to confrontations with Central Security during matches, joined protest rallies.

In the Giza neighbourhood of Dokki just before 4 pm, a group of over a hundred protesters, waving Egyptian flags, called for an end to Hosni Mubarak's rule. The crowd grew larger as protesters marched. In past demonstrations, protesters were penned in by a wall of security forces in riot gear. But on this day the numbers were too many and the protests too scattered.

One middle-aged woman's passionate sentiment summed up what these protests were all about: 'We want to live as human beings,' exclaimed Laila Muhammad. 'The queues for subsidised bread are a wait of two and three hours. . . . The women are the worst off in Egypt. Have the president feel for us. We don't ask for anything other than to have him come down and see the people for himself.'

'I want the whole government to leave. That's all I want,' expressed a young woman. 'I want democracy. I want a country I could be proud of.'[5]

Among protesters was a remarkable sense of solidarity, and expressions of popular discontent – we won't take this anymore: the corruption, political stagnation, spiralling prices, and an octogenarian president who clings to power. If the president was listening to Laila and others like her, he chose neither to acknowledge the anger nor respond to their demands.

Demonstrations numbered in the tens of thousands in governorates across Egypt. The protest originating across the Nile in Dokki was not allowed to coalesce with the burgeoning protest in downtown Cairo's Tahrir Square, blocked at bridges by rows of riot police. Earning a paltry salary, these Central Security conscripts were foot soldiers obeying the orders of officers with gold eagles and stars decorating their lapels. Yet those cadres had more in common with the masses of Egyptians than with a regime that aimed at keeping things the way they are. And it was for this reason that protesters cried out: 'O security, protect us. Tomorrow they will step on both you and us.' Their demand for basic freedoms included everyone, especially those drafted from poverty to be cogs in the machine of state oppression.

Minister of information Anas al-Fiqqi instructed state television presenters to say that the Muslim Brotherhood and other subversive elements had infiltrated protests with the goal of destabilising the country and bringing about chaos. Presenters Tamer Amin and Khairy Ramadan of the popular night-time talk show *Masr al-naharda* (Egypt Today) on state television framed a narrative of peaceful, well-intentioned youth who went out to express legitimate demands only to have rogue forces of the Brotherhood hijack the protests. (Their explanation of events mirrored the statement by the Interior Ministry, which Amin read during the news segment.) According to Amin's colourful description, the behaviour of the crowds smacked of zealotry and sorcery: 'Congressional prayers started to be held, and supplications and calls for relief and rainfall and salvation, and for nightfall to settle and dawn to rise – in addition to religious homilies urging jihad.'

Al Jazeera's coverage of the events in Egypt became another subject of ire for the hosts. 'I am a media personality and a media personality is not innocent. He resorts to sneakiness in order to understand what's happening,' said Ramadan, who despised the Qatari network's live coverage and its messages of 'constant incitement'.

'I am talking here about professionalism – professionalism in transmitting the news,' added Amin. 'It is up to the news channel to report the news and leave viewers to analyse and understand it as they wish.' He discussed a previous story reported by Al Jazeera on the leaked documents outlining negotiations between the Israeli government and the Palestinian leadership. 'Who wants to set Palestine alight? Hamas,' Amin said, answering his own question. He implicated the news channel as serving the same goal with its coverage of the sensitive communications – and being on the 'same line of thinking' – as the militant Palestinian resistance group, which he wildly claimed was responsible for the New Year's Eve church bombing in Alexandria and a bombing at a Cairo bazaar in 2009. Employing far-fetched logic and rhetorical sleight of hand, Amin managed to link Al Jazeera with terror attacks in Egypt.

Ramadan asserted that 'fingers' were trying to exploit the protests that had begun innocently. 'There were citizens who were truly like us, but people slipped in who had objectives, and they were being directed and told how to move,' he said.

'It is external fingers that tried to steal the purity of this demonstration,' charged Amin. 'I get a message from Manila and from Afghanistan saying, move and rise up Egyptians. Who are you? Perhaps – this is an assumption because I do not have a source – it could be the international organisation for the Brotherhood.'

When clips of the day's protests were shown on *Egypt Today*, the footage appeared without audio, and none of the slogans calling for Mubarak's downfall were heard. The programme did not broadcast any footage to back up Amin and Ramadan's most outlandish claims of religious sermonising, a nefarious Brotherhood plot, or text messages from far-flung corners of the earth goading Egyptians to revolt.

'No one can deny or disagree with 90% of the demands. . . . All this is healthy and natural. We call for this in the media and on our programmes – and the newspapers, whether the national, opposition, or private press,' said Amin. 'When you have the Interior Ministry exercising restraint, it means that there was a government decision; the government said that it's the right of people to express their anger.'

Amin and Ramadan struck a tone that validated calls for change but warned of subversives who sought to 'pollute' the protests' noble goals. The days when Egyptians were mute are long over, said Amin. 'That was in an era when whoever uttered a word in a newspaper or even in a café with his friends did not return home,' he said. 'It is people's right to talk and complain and say, "I am a citizen who has all the decent rights of any citizen in a developed country."'[6]

Rassd News Network (RNN) began as a Facebook group, Twitter feed, and YouTube channel in November 2010 to collate reports of citizen journalists during the parliamentary elections. Meaning 'observation', the name Rassd is composed of three Arabic letters, the first letters of the words *raqib* (monitor), *sawar* (photograph), and *dawin* (blog). Plugged into the low-cost, real-time news delivery offered by social media tools, Rassd shot to prominence on 25 January, gaining 150,000 fans on that day alone, and being a source for news and information to rival newspaper websites and television broadcasts. To keep up with rapidly unfolding events across Egypt, the nascent news group with ties to the Muslim Brotherhood posted two mobile numbers where citizens could report on events on the ground and send images and videos. To avoid harassment by the security agencies they set up shop in the Nile Delta town of Mansoura. Rassd also had a team of volunteer correspondents, three of whom were arrested in Tahrir Square on the first day of the uprising.[7]

According to media reports, by midnight 13,000–20,000 protesters were occupying downtown Cairo's Tahrir Square. The last time Tahrir Square had been occupied was at the start of the 2003 Iraq war. Deep and substantive reforms had to come now if Mubarak was to avoid an escalation of the protests. Impatient and fed-up youth networked on social media were not going to wait until the ageing ruler met his natural demise. Ill-fated attempts to block Twitter, Facebook, and live video streaming were ineffectual, with tech-savvy youth one step ahead of the security establishment's obstructions. The events were beyond the regime's power to suppress or control, and the momentum only heightened.

Day 2: 26 January 2011

There was a heavy security presence in downtown Cairo's Tahrir Square on the afternoon of Wednesday, 26 January. At around 12:30 am the night before, security forces charged the square with water cannons, tear gas, rubber-coated bullets, and batons, and succeeded in sweeping out the crowds. The Interior Ministry had prohibited protests and security forces were ready to use force.

'We will live for Egypt! We will die for Egypt! Egypt, Egypt! Long live Egypt!' A demonstration was beginning in Tahrir. 'Let us through! Let us through!' roared the crowd, penned in by helmeted riot police with shields and batons, who were not letting them march. 'The people want the downfall of the regime!'

The encirclement tightened as protesters chorused, 'Peaceful, peaceful,' hoping the security forces would show mercy. An elderly man yelled at cadres, 'Are you with them or are you with us?' Then riot police and plain-clothes officers began striking demonstrators. 'Get lost, you sons of bitches,' an officer shrieked.[8]

Tahrir was closed off. Security personnel cordoned off entire streets around the square and adjacent parliament buildings. The Metro was not stopping at the Tahrir Square station. Hundreds were detained. Shouting 'The people want the downfall of the regime', protesters jumped on train tracks at the Gamal Abd al-Nasser Metro station, one stop away, halting service.[9] While Tahrir would become the symbol of revolution, calls for an end to Mubarak's rule were taking place in all parts of the country in a popular revolt that overwhelmed the logistics of the security authorities. Videos shot on mobile phones and uploaded on YouTube would be part of sustaining the spirit of revolt. They included videos of protesters bravely confronting police, such as one of a young man facing off against an armoured water tank in a street leading to Tahrir Square as onlookers cheered.[10]

Egyptians were taking to the streets, willing to take risks in confronting police, fearless in demanding an immediate end to Mubarak's reign. The youth-driven movement was led *not* by political parties or opposition factions. Their demands were real. The regime was silent. 'We will continue until we hear the words, "I have understood you,"' vowed Nawara Negm, writer, blogger, activist, and the daughter of the poet Ahmed Fouad Negm.[11]

The president did not appear on television. There were no announcements from the government or the ruling party to indicate that they had got the message. In a statement, the ruling National Democratic Party fingered the Muslim Brotherhood for the unrest, the regime's favourite scapegoat, thus seeming to undermine the popular demands expressed by protesters.

Mona al-Shazly, the host of the evening current affairs show *al-'Ashira misa'an* (Ten at Night), began her show by talking about the accusation levelled at her as a media presenter: wanting to 'set Egypt on fire'. Journalists become either the 'devil who speaks or the devil who stays silent', she said, adding that she had a responsibility to journalistic truth and would uphold the values of the profession until her last day on the air. 'Withdrawal is better and easier. It is better than the pressure of responding every day to a thousand questions and a thousand accusations. Withdrawal is better. We want to withdraw. We want to be in a position that the public knows about the media. Media is supposed to be a ray of light, a ray of understanding, a ray of warning,' said al-Shazly.

'Egypt is passing though an exceptional scene. If someone says it is not an exceptional scene then he has a problem with his vision. We have tens of thousands of people who went out in the streets with different demands: some political, some economic, some for individual demands. Those tens of thousands are an exceptional scene, which we cannot ignore or pretend not to see,' noted the presenter, adding that until this moment we had not seen a political step being taken to remedy the issue. 'Those with political remedies are not held to account. Those who have contributed to this scene are not held to account. Who is being held to account? The media. You ask me why and I will tell you that only God knows.'[12]

She discussed a phone conversation with talk show presenter Mahmoud Saad of the programme *Egypt Today* on state-owned television, who chose not to go on the air, giving himself an open-ended vacation because of a difference of opinion with television executives. She said that she and other presenters would be willing to do the same, hinting at the heavy-handed security pressures placed on talk show hosts, often dictating what they can discuss on their programmes. Mona al-Shazly's first report showed footage of protesters being arrested in Tahrir Square that day,[13] followed by reports on demonstrations taking place around Cairo; the security forces clearing Tahrir Square of protesters occupying the square the night before; the sharp 6% drop in the stock exchange's benchmark index; and the quarantining of reporters inside the Journalists' Syndicate by security forces. The internet again witnessed intermittent blockages of sites like Facebook and Twitter. The invited guests on *Ten at Night* included Hossam Badrawi, member of the general secretariat of the ruling National Democratic Party;[14] Magdy al-Gallad, editor-in-chief of the daily *al-Masry al-youm* (The Egyptian Today); and Osama al-Ghazali Harb, chairman of the opposition Democratic Front Party.

'We hope the government and the regime have the responsibility and address the problem with the efforts it deserves. As you said in the introduction, why is it that no official is available to talk about this issue? Why is the Interior Ministry assigned to deal with a political issue?' said Harb. 'It is being dealt with in the same uninformed way and which does not acknowledge facts as in other places in the world.'

'If there are demands, why can't they be discussed politically?' asked al-Gallad. 'Why is it not being discussed until now, 48 hours after these demands were presented? That is a mistake.'

Protests spread across the country, bringing in a cross-section of Egyptian society to demand basic rights of social equality and human dignity. The industrial city of Suez emerged as an epicentre of the uprising. News from the seaport city was sketchy at first, originating from social media, with reports of numerous casualties in confrontations between security forces and protesters – claiming the revolution's first martyrs.

Actor Amr Waked was one of the protesters who came out on 25 January, joining crowds of demonstrators in the densely populated working-class district of Shubra. He was with his brother, who was detained. 'We should not live being afraid to say our opinion or be arrested,' Waked said in a phone call to the programme. He did not know where his brother was.

The NDP's Badrawi, a lone reformer in the ruling party, said he sympathised with Waked. 'Freedom of expression is one of the rights of people we must safeguard and any respectable party must protect it. That is number one. Number two, anyone who does not engage in violence or transgress the law should have the right to know the charge being levelled against him,' he said. 'We cannot demand from protesters that they define a political strategy. In the end, it is an expression of a viewpoint. . . . It is not the role of the security to respond to the people; it is the role of the government to respond.'

Mona al-Shazly asked Harb whether it was in fact young people on Facebook and in the April 6 Movement that organised and took part in the protests and opposition parties 'rode the wave'.

Harb replied that her assertion was an overstatement, that it was not a party or any known movement that moved these demonstrations, but associations of youth that motivated Egyptians to take to the streets. 'The state always plays this game, saying it is the Brotherhood in order to scare the outside world that the Muslim Brotherhood is leading these protests and seeks to be the alternative [to Mubarak].' It is not a choice between authoritarianism and Islamism, he argued.

'Let me say this when Dr Hossam is here,' added al-Gallad. 'One of the main reasons for these protests are the past People's Assembly elections. Why? The National Democratic Party erred in conducting historic sham elections that wiped out the opposition and secured the party 95% of the seats. What has this achieved? Egyptian citizens have lost faith in the executive branch for years. Their hope was in a People's Assembly or parliament to defend their rights and talk about the concerns of the street. With a People's Assembly that was all comprised of NDP members, Egyptian citizens found no one to voice their opinion so they had to go out and express their opinion on their own.'

In response to the interruptions in internet access over the past couple of days, the Ministry of Communication's website had been hacked. On the phone was internet expert Wael Ghonim, who described the blockages of internet traffic, particularly on social networking sites. 'Blockages have never been a solution. We are living in the twenty-first century – this year is 2011 – you cannot prevent people from accessing information,' he said. 'The people don't need a government to tell them what can and cannot be done.'

'Cutting off internet communications is never a wise decision especially during such a time. In the morning, when a group of youth called me and told me that Facebook was blocked, I called to ask and was told, "No, there is no block. The traffic is high so the speed is low, and so on,"' said Badrawi, when asked about breaks in internet traffic. 'The benefit that we have is that we are open to the world and the internet is working, and people are communicating via Facebook and Twitter. This advantage, I believe that any intelligent politician would not forfeit at a time when he is saying, "I am giving you greater freedoms."'

'The rationale is that you are breaking the cycle that caused this headache. Isn't it the internet that caused all these people to organise?' said al-Shazly.

'Just as it organised all these people, it showed you what they are doing and what they are deciding on,' said Badrawi. 'We have to use the benefit we have in Egypt, that we have freedoms. We have people like Osama [al-Ghazali Harb] who says we are not a democratic country on your programme. We have people on the street stating their demands. That is Egypt, that we listen to all. I am against cutting off information and the party is against it.'

Ghonim rejoined the conversation. 'I am personally one of the ordinary users of Facebook, and I could not access Facebook for two hours but I could access the site through a proxy – entering a network outside Egypt and through that network access Facebook,' he said. Four million Egyptians have Facebook accounts and more than 1.8 million Egyptians access the site daily, added Ghonim. 'The solution is not blockage. The solution is that you talk to people and listen to them. We have a big problem in Egypt, Mona, and that is that our government does not listen to us. We want the government to listen to us, to listen to the demands of youth, to listen to the demands of rational people because if you do not listen to the demands of rational people, you will see another set of saboteurs.'[15]

Protest strategies were quickly adapting to security measures. Mass protests were being planned after Friday noon prayers across Egypt, which made them difficult for the security apparatus to contain or control. Thousands of Egyptians continued to pour into the streets demanding justice, democracy, and an end to Mubarak's rule.

Day 3: 27 January 2011

The anger of Egyptians had been ignited and the question was whether the uprising could be sustained or whether it would eventually be crushed. One tactic was to out-strategise intelligence and security personnel, who had been working around the clock since 25 January. Titled 'How to Intelligently Revolt', a PDF circulated by e-mail outlined tactics for confronting security forces on the fourth day of protest, dubbed the Friday of Rage. The demands also increased substantively, calling for the downfall of Mubarak and his ministers, an end to emergency law, freedom, justice, the formation of a new government not comprised of military men, and the sound administration of Egypt's resources. Three tactical goals for civil disobedience were seizing important government buildings, attempting to gather the police and army into the ranks of the people, and protecting fellow revolutionaries.

The locations where protesters would head to included downtown Cairo's television and radio building ('Surround the building from all sides, then enter the building and take over live transmission, announcing a declaration from the people of control of Egyptian television and its liberation from oppressive dictatorship'), the presidential palace, police stations, and the governors' offices in provinces throughout Egypt ('When the governors' offices are seized, the governorate is no longer following the corrupt administration, but is beholden to the free people of Egypt'). Saving injured colleagues was paramount. Vandalising public and private property was not permitted. 'If security forces start striking, the first rows of protesters would recede, to allow for fresh protesters to battle security in a coordinated attack,' instructed the e-mail. Recipients were enjoined to forward the instructions and distribute paper copies, making sure not to 'betray the people of your country' by having the information fall into the hands of the police or army. So even with heavy-handed attempts by the security state to disrupt Facebook and Twitter, organised action found ways to adapt to the control of structures of entrenched power.

Safwat al-Sherif, the secretary-general of the ruling National Democratic Party and at one time the information minister, held a press conference where he said, 'We hold the demands of the people above our heads.' But he mentioned no proposals for any kind of government reforms. With those patronising words, the administration would effectively write its own death warrant. Sherif also denied that Gamal Mubarak was in London, stating that the president's son had attended a party meeting that day. Rumours had been circulating for days that Gamal and Alaa Mubarak and their families had fled the country.

Among activists an air of optimism was building. Images on Al Jazeera – whose broadcasts have a penchant for the emotional, such as stories from the morgue – or uploaded on YouTube were igniting popular fury. Mass protests were having other effects. The benchmark Egyptian Stock Exchange index tumbled the maximum 10% on the last day of trading for the week before trading was halted. The Muslim Brotherhood, which had not endorsed the 25 January protests, stepped into the fray and instructed its membership to join the Friday of Rage. Thirty-four members of the Brotherhood's leadership were arrested on 27 January, including seven prominent figures of the group's governing Guidance Council. Mohamed ElBaradei returned to Egypt to participate in protests on Friday. 'I have been out of Egypt because that is the only way I can be heard. I have been totally cut off from the local media when I am there,' he wrote. 'But I am going back to Cairo, and back onto the streets.'[16] Suez continued to witness the fiercest street battles despite a curfew and blocked mobile phone, landline, and internet communications. When security reinforcements were moved to Suez from the neighbouring Canal city of Ismailia, protests there intensified.

If the regime thought they had the situation under control, they were taking noticeably drastic and desperate measures. Severely restricting Egypt's information exchange with the rest of the world, a systematic shutdown of the internet began that evening and all text messaging was blocked. Social media revolutionised the way people act, organise, and struggle against power. But more than becoming just the struggle of Egyptians for basic freedoms against a dictatorship, the media made this a revolution that the world watched. In a YouTube video by the hacktivist collective Anonymous, an automated voice declared:

The Egyptian people are living under inhumane conditions; being denied their basic rights to freedom of speech, freedom of religion, freedom of association, and the free access to information. By imposing censorship on its own people and condemning these freedoms, the Egyptian government has revealed itself to be criminal, and has made itself an enemy of Anonymous.[17]

The internet and social media have become communication equalisers in a battle against despotism in the Arab world. Facts can no longer be concealed or ignored despite the best efforts of the state, its media, and the labyrinth of security agencies. With those truths emerged the will to organise and involve others through blogs, Facebook, videos on YouTube, and the instantaneous micro-news and commentary of Twitter. Anyone with access to the internet was a potential information provider, chronicling history's first draft. A journalist no longer had to be the designated witness and bearer of news.

The defining moment for revolution in Egypt came when citizens realised they were not as powerless and controllable as previously imagined. Egyptians were for a long time cowed by a fear that convinced them they were no match against a despotic state. Egypt's revolt has been called the Facebook or Twitter revolution. But it was not social media acting in isolation that set in motion a history-making event. It was social media combined with the willingness of people to act – and sacrifice – when reform had stopped being an option and regime change was the only answer.

The 'We are all Khaled Said' Facebook page by this point had reached 418,000 subscribers, becoming a hub for activism, coordination, and information sharing. The 'Friday of Rage' event announced, 'We will go out in rallies from all Egypt's large mosques and churches heading towards the public squares and staging sit-ins until we receive our rights that have been usurped. Egypt's Muslims and Christians alike will come out to fight corruption, unemployment, injustice, and the absence of freedom.' A posting on the wall of 'We are all Khaled Said' stated:

A message to all the youth of Egypt who are going out tomorrow: We don't want another Suez. Please commit to peaceful protest and sit-ins. No one should break or destroy anything. Don't squander the rights of the youth who went out and protested and died by resorting to frustration, brutality, and chaos. We are advocating a right and we are going out to demand our rights. We should all make that pledge before God before we go out.

Wael Ghonim wrote the following on Twitter, hours before his arrest: 'Pray for #Egypt. Very worried as it seems that government is planning a war crime tomorrow against people. We are all ready to die #Jan25.'[18]

On the evening of 27 January, Alaa Al Aswany held his weekly salon in the building of the opposition Karama Party, where the enthused topic of discussion was the revolt that had started two days earlier. 'If we consider the strongest party the one that can move the masses, then I will say in Egypt that it is the party of Facebook,' he said to applause. 'That is a real party, which has allowed a group of youth to get 400,000 people on the streets. No other party, including the Muslim Brotherhood, has succeeded in doing that.'

The regime wildly miscalculated the explosion of anger on the street, believing in its ability to instil fear in the population. 'The message of the people to the regime is that we are no longer afraid,' Al Aswany remarked on the unfolding drama. 'And we are ready to sacrifice. People are dying, whether from poverty, on ferries, trains, or by bullets, people are dying. The regime's message is that I do what I want by force.' When the security apparatus of the state shoots demonstrators, another problem arises, what Al Aswany described as 'the problem of blood'. Protesters will not quietly return home, but will return to the streets and confront security forces with a vengeance.[19]

Day 4: 28 January 2011

The internet remained switched off and all mobile phone communication was cut off around 11 am. These restrictions of basic freedom of expression only added fuel to the fire. Government-allied sheikhs and religious figures were brought on television to exhort the population not to demonstrate. The lead headline in that morning's *al-Ahram* was, 'Mubarak Follows the Events and Calls the Suez Governor for Reassurance on Citizens'. The independent weekly *Sawt al-umma* carried the banner headline, 'The Regime Is on the Verge of Toppling and the Coming Protest Is the Final Blow'.[20]

On this 'Friday of Rage' protests were planned after noon prayers and instead of tens of thousands, as on the first day of revolt, the numbers were in the hundreds of thousands – throughout Egypt millions took to the streets calling for the downfall of Mubarak's regime. The crowds reached fever pitch in the largest mass protests Egypt had ever seen. Mohamed ElBaradei, who had arrived in Egypt a day earlier, attended Friday prayers at a mosque in Giza Square. Following prayers, security forces quarantined ElBaradei and his supporters inside the mosque.

Al Jazeera had become the default news channel in times of crisis. Seen by officials to be urging the uprising, information minister Anas al-Fiqqi ordered the news network's live broadcast signal be taken off NileSat. But even with Al Jazeera's live transmission off the air, Egyptian audiences had other sources of news via a plethora of round-the-clock news channels. The BBC had an Arabic transmission, as did France 24, Deutsche Welle, Russia Today, and the US government's Al Hurra. Al Jazeera English, the BBC, CNN, EuroNews, and other news channels – all with transmissions on NileSat – were closely following developments in Egypt. Meanwhile, state television was reporting its version of the facts on the ground. According to them, on this intense day of uprising, everything was normal and under control, with most Egyptians choosing not to take part in riot-prone demonstrations. In telephone interviews with governors of the various provinces on state television, newscasters emphasised that mass protests as seen on 'some of the satellite channels' were 'exaggerated'. When the swirl of events became inescapable, state news reports stated that 'thousands' of protesters had taken to the streets, turning violent and leading to confrontations with security forces.

For structures of oppression, the millions on the streets amounted to a perfect storm of popular revolt. Security forces using every arsenal at their disposal, including snipers, were no match for the determined masses. Images of the tense stand-off between protesters and security personnel at Qasr al-Nil Bridge, which leads to Tahrir Square, would be memorialised in images surfacing on social media and broadcast on satellite news stations. The footage showed security vans running over protesters, riot police firing tear gas canisters and rubber bullets into the crowds, and water cannons dousing protesters kneeling in prayer.[21] Determined to make it to Tahrir Square past contingents of security forces, unarmed protesters finally won the battle at Qasr al-Nil Bridge.

Soon the headquarters of the National Democratic Party, adjacent to the Egyptian Museum, was in flames, with billowing black smoke signalling the ruling party's demise. Police stations and the ruling party's offices in other cities suffered a similar fate. The day brought the largest death toll of the revolution. Police snipers stationed on the rooftop and balconies of the Ramses Hilton Hotel gunned down protesters approaching the television and radio building. Snipers were also positioned on the roof of the

Ministry of Interior off Tahrir Square, where Habib al-Adly was bunkered. Protesters approaching both locations were shot in the head or chest.

By evening, interior minister Habib al-Adly ordered the complete withdrawal of all security personnel, a move widely believed to be the contingency plan that would reduce the country to looting and lawlessness – a punishment to Egyptians for rising up. The danger on the streets, they calculated, would work to keep revolting citizens in their homes. A contributing factor was the escape of thousands of criminals from the nation's prisons – a strategy allegedly orchestrated by security officials – which unleashed a crime wave, with released inmates looting weapons from jails and police stations. Although the reality of the day's events was hard to ignore, state media reported a different story – the theft and vandalism that gripped the country by nightfall, a story they charged satellite news channels with ignoring. In an attempt to disperse crowds, state television broadcast a siren warning to protesters in Tahrir Square to clear the area immediately because thugs armed with firebombs were making their way to the downtown Cairo landmark.

No truly reliable account of the death toll existed. Media reports cited figures hovering around 300, which were provided by human rights groups from quick tallies at hospital morgues.[22] Additionally, there was the politics of determining the size of protests and the numbers inside Tahrir Square. Was it thousands, tens of thousands, hundreds of thousands, a million, or more? Even if a crowd shot can determine with reasonable accuracy the numbers at any given time, how many had come and gone to be replaced by new protesters throughout the day? Any estimate does not take into account rallies and strikes taking place throughout the country. But numbers and figures seemed to be beside the point when protests embodied such a concerted popular will.

A curfew was in place from 6 pm to 7 am and army troops, tanks, armoured personnel carriers, and military vehicles rolled into Egypt's cities. Egyptians cheered the arrival of the army on the streets, exclaiming, 'The people and the army are one hand.' The trust people had in the army was because conscripts made up its ranks – brothers, nephews, and neighbours' sons completing their required military service. They served to maintain order when security forces made a hasty retreat. A military's role was to defend the homeland against invaders. It would be the height of betrayal for army personnel to shoot down protesters. The security forces with their cache of tear gas, rubber bullets, and live ammunition were no match for the Egyptian masses. How could an army of half a million men fare differently?

Even Tunisia's military refused to turn their weapons against protesters to defend strongman and ex-military man Zine el-Abidine Ben Ali.

In telephone interviews on satellite broadcasts, opposition figures called for the president to step down and for his failed policies to come to an end. Mubarak did not take to the airwaves until past midnight, his first pre-recorded address to the nation since the beginning of the uprising.

Day 5: 29 January 2011

In a 12-minute speech that might have been effective if delivered days before, Mubarak said that he had followed the protests and the calls of demonstrators. 'These protests and what we have seen previously in sit-ins during the past few years could not be possible if not for the wide space for freedoms of opinion, expression, and the press, and other freedoms that were steps in reform for the children of the nation.' Mubarak said he upheld the right to expression as long as it was done legally and within the confines of the law. He referenced the violence that threatened order and social peace: 'Neither democracy is realised nor stability preserved.'

He acknowledged that protests expressed legitimate demands for greater democracy, and addressing poverty and unemployment, improving living standards, and combating corruption – goals he said he strove for each day. 'The youth of Egypt are its most valuable possession and they will determine its future,' he said, adding that they should not allow among them those who seek to plant chaos, looting public and private property, setting fires, and destroying what we have built. 'My unwavering commitment is to political, economic, and social reform for a free and democratic society that embraces the principles of the age and is open to the world,' said Mubarak. 'We will implement new steps to affirm our respect for independence of the judiciary and its rulings, new steps for greater democracy and freedoms for citizens, new steps to confront unemployment, raise living standards, expand services, and new steps to stand by the poor and those with limited income.'

Mubarak added that he bore responsibility for the security of the nation. 'I will not permit fear to grip our citizens.' In the last minute of his speech, Mubarak said that he had called for the resignation of his Cabinet and would assign clear mandates to his new government. 'I will not hesitate in taking any decision to preserve for every Egyptian their safety and security and I will defend the security and stability of Egypt. That is the responsibility for which I swore an oath before God and the people.'[23]

Mubarak's first public address since the start of mass protests fell short of expectations. It contained no concrete proposals for far-reaching reform that would open up the political process. Mubarak did not say he would not run for re-election. He did not propose redrafting the constitution to create an equitable distribution of power between the branches of government. He did not vow to dissolve a parliament elected through fraudulent elections and hold free and fair elections. He did not give up his position as the head of the National Democratic Party or distance himself from businessmen who had profited from influential posts in the party hierarchy. He did not offer to free political detainees, including those arrested during the protests, or rein in the massive reach of State Security. Scrapping three decades of emergency law was not in the offing either.

Throughout the night and early morning, volleys of gunfire were heard on the streets, assumed to be an attempt by the army to scare away bands of looters. On the morning of 29 January, mobile communications were restored but text messaging remained blocked. Private Egyptian satellite channel Dream TV broadcast nationalistic songs to images of fires set ablaze, a fluttering flag becoming a fixture at the top left corner of the screen, an emblem found on Egyptian public and private stations accompanied with slogans like 'Preserve Egypt'. Citizen watch committees and makeshift roadblocks were set up to guard neighbourhoods, especially during curfew hours. Foreign minister Ahmed Aboul Gheit stoutly defended the Mubarak regime, repeatedly proclaiming to diplomats and the media that Egypt would not tolerate meddling in its internal affairs.

Mubarak appointed his old air force colleague and civil aviation minister Ahmed Shafik as the new prime minister charged with forming a Cabinet. He also appointed his long-serving intelligence chief and confidant, General Omar Soliman, as his first ever vice president so he could be the face of the regime in leading a 'dialogue' with the opposition. The top officials were sworn in before Mubarak in a ceremony broadcast on state television. The choice of Soliman and Shafik hinted that the policies of the regime in responding to the crisis were going to be more business as usual. The calls on the street for regime change did not subside, instead they were joined by a chorus of Egyptian luminaries, including Nobel Prize-winning chemist Ahmed Zewail and religious activist and social reformer Amr Khaled, supporting the youth and calling for justice and comprehensive change in the face of a corrupt and oppressive regime. Offers of vague and overdue reforms would do little to quell the uprising.

Egypt's airspace was closed for several hours, a move that alarmed embassies evacuating nationals. In the mid-afternoon thundering fighter jets flew low in the Cairo sky as defence minister and field marshal Muhammad Hussein Tantawi paid a visit to troops in Tahrir Square. 'Your country needs you,' he told the young conscripts stationed outside the Egyptian Museum and the state television and radio building. Protesters had spray-painted tanks and army vehicles in the zone of Tahrir Square with 'Down with Mubarak'.

State television throughout the day broadcast eyewitness reports of roving armed gangs in pickup trucks, motorcycles, and mopeds robbing homes and businesses, alongside images of weapons confiscated by the army. Callers to state television from affluent districts hysterically described their fear of being attacked, calling on the military to secure their suburbs, mouthing apologies to Mubarak, and condemning satellite broadcasters for bringing Egypt to ruin. The state media's fostering a sense of panic helped the regime blame protesters for causing the chaos and paint them as foreign-backed provocateurs. Curfew hours were extended from 4 pm to 8 am. State television broadcast images of empty bridges to show that Cairo was quiet and citizens had abided by the curfew. At the top of the newscasts, state media repeated the refrain, 'Calm has returned to the streets of Cairo.' Using archival footage of the leader's accomplishments, announcers praised Mubarak, who has 'fought for the sake of the nation': 'He has been there and will remain in the coming months and days, exercising the tasks of his authority.'

Day 6: 30 January 2011

'Good morning to the flowers that are blooming in the gardens of Egypt,' said the iconoclastic poet Ahmed Fouad Negm in a telephone interview on Al Jazeera, borrowing lines from his poem dedicated to student protesters in 1972. 'My beloved children of Egypt, you have lit up the world! Don't let anyone tell you, "That's enough." You are beautiful.' While Negm was glowing with praise for the young people who were the force for change, he had derisive words for Mubarak: 'Why are you still here?' he scolded.[24] Al Jazeera's Arabic transmission continued round-the-clock coverage of the developments in Egypt despite having its offices closed and equipment confiscated by order of the minister of information that morning. Al Jazeera's broadcast signal on NileSat went dead before 1 pm but a new broadcast frequency for the Qatari news station was posted on Al Jazeera English and spread by word of mouth.

'The Egyptian people have said one word: President Hosni Mubarak needs to leave. We need to transition to a democratic country by way of a national unity government to produce a democratic constitution and free and clean elections,' Mohamed ElBaradei said in a telephone interview on Al Jazeera. 'Any attempts to ignore popular demands will lead to a degradation of the security situation for which I hold President Mubarak personally responsible.'[25]

Satellite news channels showed a clip of a military general announcing in Tahrir Square that Habib al-Adly, the long-serving interior minister, and Ahmed Ezz, ruling party powerbroker and iron and steel magnate, had been detained by the military. State television asserted that those reports were not true and censured the satellite outlets that reported the news as 'unprofessional'.

On Al Jazeera, a young woman activist from the April 6 Movement had harsh words for the autocrat, demanding that all the money he had stolen be returned. 'Not only will we kick him out, we will put him on trial! What are you waiting for Hosni Mubarak?' She charged the interior minister with opening the prisons and letting more than 23,000 convicts escape in a wicked plot to frighten Egyptians into submission.[26] Mubarak appeared on television meeting with top generals in images meant to show that he was very much in control.

The state media's anchors continued to receive on-air calls from Egyptians who supported Mubarak and wanted a return to normalcy. The state media maintained that the protesters were being manipulated by foreign elements to follow a 'red agenda' to undermine Egypt. Guests on state television pointed accusing fingers at Israel's Mossad, Hezbollah, Hamas, the CIA, Iran, the Qataris (with their menacing Al Jazeera), and any number of dangerous external elements. Protesters were lured to Tahrir Square with promises of money in hard currency and a KFC meal, according to pundits invited on state television. Men and woman alleging to be the youth of 25 January were brought on to fuel suspicion about who was manipulating the protests, and oblige Egyptians to return to their homes and allow the political leadership to take action in rectifying the crisis. That same narrative was echoed in the state-owned press.

Some private Egyptian satellite channels lined up to support the absurd fabrications in the regime's public relations battle. Television host and media mogul Emad Eddin Adeeb made the rounds of talk shows to faithfully defend the president and allege that history would demonstrate that it was the US that was dictating that Mubarak had to go. He claimed to have evidence that bands of non-Egyptians were apprehended with communication equipment and documents that proved they were dispatched from abroad, including Arab states and 'friendly' nations.[27]

Day 7: 31 January 2011

Ahmed Shafik's Cabinet, sworn in before Mubarak on 31 January, comprised 18 ministers who remained in their posts, including information minister Anas al-Fiqqi, who had ordered Al Jazeera's broadcast signal blocked, the licences of the network and the press credentials of its reporters be revoked, their office closed, and their equipment confiscated. Protesters called for a 'march of millions' on 1 February, where Egyptians would descend on Tahrir Square demanding Mubarak step down.

In prepared remarks on Egyptian state television, the newly appointed vice president called for a dialogue with the opposition on 'constitutional and legal reform'. 'As it concerns political and democratic reform,' Omar Soliman said, 'the president emphasised that the decisions of the appeals court in the electoral petitions must be implemented faithfully.' Judicial decisions not in the favour of the regime had been routinely ignored. Soliman only promised new elections in contested districts 'within the coming weeks', which suggested that the National Democratic Party would maintain its control of the legislature.

The demands of the street were dramatically out of sync with the grudging reforms of the regime and its vague promises to deal with unemployment, poverty, and corruption. Protesters continued to occupy Tahrir Square. Journalists continued to be detained by military forces. In an attempt to limit the sustained protests and sit-ins against Mubarak and now Soliman, the curfew was extended from 3 pm to 8 am. To stop Egyptians living in the provinces from flooding into Cairo for a march of millions in Tahrir Square the following day, all train services ground to a halt.

Day 8: 1 February 2011

Al Jazeera, which had been broadcasting on NileSat at a different frequency, was again knocked off the air before noon. Despite curfews and the suspended train service, hundreds of thousands of Egyptians descended on Tahrir Square to call on Mubarak to stand down. 'Under no circumstances will we listen to anyone who was a partner with Mubarak during his lifetime,' former supreme guide of the Muslim Brotherhood Muhammad Mahdi Akef told BBC Arabic. 'Any person who deals with Mubarak today will be held responsible for this crime that is occurring in Egypt.'[28]

In a programme called *48 Sa'a* (48 Hours) on the Mehwar satellite channel, presenters Sayed Ali and Hanaa al-Simary received a caller on the air who claimed she was an activist in one of the youth groups. 'Discussion with a woman trained at the hands of Jews in America to overthrow the government in Egypt' flashed at the bottom of the screen. She was later invited on the programme with her face pixilated and went on to make outrageous claims that she was flown to a host of countries – the United States, Qatar, Serbia, Poland, South Africa – by the 'Zionist American' group Freedom House, taught methods in challenging the regime, and trained in carrying weapons.

'They taught us to overthrow the system according to peaceful means and burning the parliament and institutions of power,' said the anonymous woman, whom the presenters named Shaymaa. Shaymaa said that she was shocked when she arrived in the US to 'find out they were Jews and there were people from Qatar'. The words at the bottom of the screen were: 'A woman active in one of the political movements received training by the Israeli Mossad.' She went on to claim that the Muslim Brotherhood and Hamas were engineering the protests to overthrow the regime after the Brotherhood received no seats in the last parliamentary elections. She started sobbing as she stated that Mubarak was our father and it was unthinkable to kick him out, adding that Egyptians have been brainwashed. Sayed Ali remarked, 'Egypt is not Tunisia and Mubarak is not Ben Ali. We all need to understand that.'[29]

The presenters when later challenged about the veracity of the woman's account produced evidence they say backed her claim – visa stamps, travel records, documents – all of which the presenter Sayed Ali flipped through on his desk but none of it was shown for the camera. The programme and its hosts were accused of violating journalistic ethics by not allowing protest organisers to respond to the allegations of a plot masterminded by foreign agents. This whole spectacle, it turned out, was a performance by Nagat Abd al-Rahman, a journalist with the state-owned magazine *24 Sa'a* (24 Hours), in league with the security agencies. She was found out after work colleagues recognised her voice on the programme.

At 11 pm, Mubarak again took to the airwaves to address the nation in a prepared 11-minute speech delivered from behind a podium. 'Fellow citizens, I speak to you in difficult times that test Egypt and its people and may drift it to the unknown,' he began.

> *The country is experiencing critical events and harsh tribulations begun by honourable youth and citizens. They have the right of peaceful demonstrations to express their concerns and aspiration but they were exploited by those who want to cause chaos, violence, confrontation, and bypass and assault the legitimacy of the constitution. These demonstrations moved from a civilised expression of practising freedom of speech to unfortunate confrontations manipulated and dominated by political groups that sought to throw oil on the fire by targeting the stability and security of the country through provocation and incitement, destruction, looting, arson, blocking roads, attacking national possessions and public and private property, and raiding diplomatic missions on the land of Egypt.*

His message was consistent with the theme of the state media's presentation of events after they had reached a crescendo on 28 January: the protests were started by noble young people and their cause was hijacked by nefarious elements and foreign forces beyond their control.

Mubarak outlined the struggle as one between chaos and stability, and between radicalism and moderation. He noted that he had formed a government that would respond to the demands of the young and assigned his vice president the task of coming to an understanding with political factions on reforms. 'There are political forces that have rejected this invitation for dialogue, holding on to their private agendas,' he continued. 'I never wanted power or prestige and people know the difficult circumstances in which I shouldered the responsibility and what I have given the homeland in war and peace.'

Mubarak said his main responsibility was to restore security and ensure the peaceful transfer of power. 'I say with all honesty and despite the current situation, it was never my intention to stand for the next presidential elections,' he said, the first time he had publicly mentioned that he would not be running for another term. The expectation was that he would run and win, serving as president until death, or choreograph his son's takeover of power. He proposed redrafting articles 76 and 77 of the constitution, which outlined who could run for the presidency and the length of his term. Setting term limits was the only change he suggested in his speech. He gave no specifics about political, economic, and social reforms, creating employment opportunities, combating poverty, and realising social equality – issues he said his government would address.

> *Hosni Mubarak who speaks to you today is proud of his many years spent in the service of Egypt and its people. This dear country is my homeland, just as it is for every Egyptian man and woman. In this country I have lived. I have fought for it. I have defended its territory, sovereignty, and interests. On this land I will die and history will judge me and others, either for us or against us.*[30]

It would be known as the address that split the country in two – between those who felt sympathy for Mubarak and wanted to give him the chance to complete the remaining months of his term, and those who wanted him to leave immediately, believing that the time for talk of reform was long gone.

US President Barack Obama telephoned Mubarak within an hour of his televised remarks, warning him in their final conversation that protests would continue if the reform process dragged on.[31] Mubarak assured Obama that the demonstrations would come to an end within days. The events of the next couple of days would be crucial in turning the tide against Mubarak, as the regime resorted to its favourite weapon of violence to intimidate protesters and rally support for the embattled president.

Day 9: 2 February 2011

A deep sense of solidarity, comradeship, and a near-festive atmosphere enveloped crowds gathered in Tahrir Square the day before. By morning, groups holding pro-Mubarak signs were heading in the direction of the square, the first rallies for Mubarak since the uprising began. One of the men had a wooden sign that read, 'Yes to change. Yes to Mubarak.' People trickled into the square, including more pro-Mubarak groups with signs, banners, and Egyptian flags. The scene in downtown Cairo was of charred vehicles, vandalised police pickup trucks, army tanks, and the heart of a city in pieces. It would only look worse as the day wore on.

Judging from the anger expressed by the pro-Mubarak contingent, there was a sense early on that events were bound to turn confrontational. Mubarak's Egypt had been known to use hired thugs in league with the security apparatus to harass protesters, intimidate opposition candidates and their supporters, and rig elections. As crowds of pro-Mubarak demonstrators flooded into the square, a face-off began with democracy protesters who demanded an end to Mubarak's reign. The scenes unfolding were followed in real time by 24-hour news channels. Men on camels and horseback, who gave rides to tourists at the Pyramids, descended on Tahrir Square and charged at anti-Mubarak protesters in a gambit to drive them out. State television showed only peaceful pro-Mubarak rallies across town in Mustafa Mahmoud Square, while the world watched the harrowing clashes taking place in Tahrir Square that were clearly fuelled by regime and ruling party elements.[32]

The absurd soon turned violent. As riots ensued, journalists evacuated the square and followed the scenes from cameras set up in hotel windows. North of Tahrir Square the pro-Mubarak gang congregated and fortified its position. On the south side were crowds of protesters calling for Mubarak's downfall. The clashes turned into a long-drawn-out street battle. Makeshift barriers were created, rocks and Molotov cocktails were hurled, and fires were lit. The fighting continued throughout the night with the army standing idly by and occasionally firing volleys of shots in the air. The bloody stand-off in Tahrir became known as the Battle of the Camel. Deliverance from repressive rule came from within. 'No one was waiting for a savior,' wrote *New York Times* journalist Anthony Shadid. 'Before nearly three decades of accumulated authority – the power of a state that can mobilize thousands to heed its whims – people had themselves.'[33]

NDP operatives had access to telecommunications links, commandeering mobile phone infrastructure to send text messages to party loyalists.[34] Text messaging remained blocked, but internet connectivity was restored on 2 February. With Egyptians back online, YouTube through its news and politics channel, CitizenTube, and in collaboration with the news aggregator Storyful, highlighted playlists of the latest protest videos being uploaded from Egypt. These videos pieced together the mass actions of an uprising, exposing such callous deeds as an armoured police vehicle running over protesters,[35] and shared them, unfiltered, with an audience around the world.

Day 10: 3 February 2011

At dawn the tense stand-off in a divided Tahrir Square persisted. The battle for Tahrir was eventually won by the revolutionaries, aided by the organisational discipline of Muslim Brotherhood youth and the determined spirit of the Ultras, who collaborated with a legion of protesters to wage an offensive. Vice president and former intelligence chief Omar Soliman in an interview on state television that evening blamed 'foreign elements', channels belonging to 'brotherly countries' that have misinformed the young and ignited their emotions, the Muslim Brotherhood, and some businessmen. Ahmed Ezz, iron and steel industrialist, leading figure in the ruling party, and a confidant of Gamal Mubarak, was being investigated on corruption charges in a move to mollify the masses and save the old guard ruling elite.

Soliman renewed his invitation for dialogue with opposition groups and seemed puzzled about the reasons for the dangerous clashes instigated against protesters by pro-Mubarak forces in Tahrir Square, promising a probe that would get to the bottom of the matter. In the interview with a sympathetic journalist, Soliman labelled the calls for Mubarak to step down as 'a strange demand for the Egyptian people'. When asked to make a closing statement, the newly anointed VP thanked the youth for what they had done, describing them as the flame of reform, and asked them to give the government a chance to fulfil their legitimate demands.

International solidarity with the popular struggle in Egypt had identified Mubarak as the latest face of tyranny, with protesters massing outside Egyptian embassies around the world. Having forfeited legitimacy domestically and internationally, Mubarak's minutes in power were ticking away. 'Obama is a very good man. But I told Obama – quote – "you don't understand the Egyptian culture and what would happen if I stepped down right now"', ABC's Christiane Amanpour said in a broadcast on 3 February, recounting her conversation with Mubarak. 'He said again that there would be chaos and he said that the banned Islamist party, the Muslim Brotherhood, would take over.'[36]

Amanpour followed her report with an interview with the stiff Omar Soliman. 'You don't think it is young people who want their rights, who want their freedom?' she asked the vice president.

'I don't think it's only from the young people. Others are pushing them to do that,' he answered, suggesting that foreign elements were in league with protesters to undermine Egypt's sovereignty.

'Do you believe in democracy?' continued Amanpour.

'For sure, everybody believes in the democracy. But when you will do that?' asked Soliman, then he answered his own question. 'When the people here will have the culture of democracy.'

If the government was more conciliatory in its rhetoric, its actions proved otherwise. The downtown Cairo offices of a human rights group, the Hesham Mubarak Law Center, which had offered respite for protesters and collected medical supplies for the injured, was raided by police and army forces on 3 February, hard disks were confiscated, and 27 lawyers, activists, and organisers arrested.

The Brotherhood was a convenient and over-used excuse why Egypt had not progressed towards democracy under Mubarak. It was an excuse the regime presented time and time again to explain away the closed political system, the human rights violations, three continuous decades of emergency law, political detainees, rigged elections, restrictions on the press, and the massive security apparatus that keeps it all together. The ruling National Democratic Party, a well-oiled patronage machine, commanded an automatic majority in parliament. The constitution delivered to the president far-reaching powers and forbade his questioning or assessment before parliament. No healthy system of checks and balances existed. Mubarak's policy of stifling reforms left only one option open: revolution.

The demands of the revolution crystallised: the resignation of Mubarak, the lifting of emergency law, release of all political detainees, the dissolution of a parliament elected through forged elections, the formation of a national coalition government to manage the affairs of the state during the transition to democracy, investigation of the abuses of the security forces during the revolution, and the protection of protesters by the military.

Day 11: 4 February 2011

Seen as a pharaoh's day of reckoning, 4 February was called the Friday of Departure, where nationwide protests began following noon prayers. Al Jazeera's transmission on NileSat was again knocked off the air.[37] Blocking the Qatari news station only served to give it an increasingly loyal viewership: it was the station the government did not want Egyptians to see, so it must be telling the truth. Colluding against the censorship authorities, ten satellite channels halted their broadcasts to simulcast Al Jazeera's coverage.

'The whole world and not only Egypt now calls on President Mubarak to step down. He has lost his legitimacy. He has lost his credibility,' Mohamed ElBaradei told Al Jazeera in a phone call from Tahrir Square. 'As a military man, he should take the final step.' The uprising is not provoked by foreign elements, as the regime likes to explain, added ElBaradei. 'They have not listened to these demands until the people took to the street by the millions. These are not external demands; they come from the consciousness of the Egyptian people. The Egyptian people want their freedom, want a system that is based on social justice and do not want to be treated as slaves as we have been treated for 30 years.'

Nine of the political activists who were meeting with ElBaradei at his home the evening before were later abducted and detained by security forces – this at a time Mubarak's government was promising greater democracy and a dialogue with the opposition. ElBaradei likened the regime's position to 'a war of attrition'. 'There is a unified vision: we transition to a democratic system, a system based on social justice and equality among all, a modern civil state. That is all agreed on. There is an agreement that there should be a transition period for a year when presidential and parliamentary elections will be held.'[38]

Mubarak seemed bent on defying the odds, perhaps calculating that the protests would inevitably run out of steam. The conduct of pro-Mubarak hooligans in Tahrir Square solidified opposition to the regime. Meanwhile, the ruling echelon pointed an accusing finger at external forces, the Brotherhood, and Al Jazeera to explain away its failures. 'All night the state media had been spewing disinformation about who was behind the attacks and the gunfire that was still heard the next morning,' wrote Rania Al Malky in an editorial in the *Daily News Egypt*. 'The scenarios were not only pernicious lies, but were tantamount to incitement of hatred, even murder.'[39]

The pressures on Al Malky were now from the paper's owners. 'This could get us in trouble. You are aggravating the situation,' were among their unhappy comments. But in those first days of February the situation had escalated beyond reversal. 'I personally, as an editor and a commentator felt, you know what? I am going to say it as it is and I don't care. Come what may.'[40] So it was during those days of revolution that Egypt's independent media evolved and the state-owned media huddled for the regime, exposing wildly gaping disparities.

Ibrahim Kamel, a prominent businessman close to Mubarak, told BBC Arabic radio's Akram Shaban that Mubarak would not leave power before the end of his term, and would not cave in to external pressure from Barack Obama or anyone else. 'Once the president himself announced that he was not going to be running again,' the US president said at a news conference, referring to Egypt's ageing ruler, 'the key question he should be asking himself is: how do I leave a legacy behind in which Egypt is able to make it through this transformative period?'[41]

Day 12: 5 February 2011

A light afternoon rain fell from the sky as crowds waited in line at the entrance of Qasr al-Nil Bridge, which was blocked by two tanks, as soldiers checked IDs and bags, with separate queues for men and women. They confiscated lighters and a small pile formed atop one of the tanks. Across the bridge was another checkpoint that led into the now famous Cairo landmark. Barbed wire was set up. IDs were checked again by a row of soldiers. Friendly volunteer protesters manned the last checkpoint. Entering the square, a row of protesters on either side greeted the new arrivals: 'Welcome to the newcomers. Join the revolutionaries!'

A cross-section of Egyptian society was present in the square: families, including babies and toddlers, and men and women of all ages and social backgrounds. Quite a few protesters were bandaged from fierce confrontations with pro-Mubarak ruffians days earlier. Vendors did brisk business selling Egyptian flags. One man stuck a flag in the dressing around his head. A stuffed effigy, a crude representation of Mubarak, was hanged by its neck from a lamp post in the square. A few of the protesters were giving away flowers. At a corner shop that used to be a Hardee's restaurant, bottles of tap water were being distributed and the mobile phones of protesters were left for recharging – at no cost.

The protesters had a creative sense of humour too, in art and expression and poetry. A man held up a sign for Mubarak that read, 'Leave already! I'm tired of holding up this sign.' Another said, 'Hurry up and leave! The lady is about to give birth and the child doesn't want to see you.' Videos by the online cartoon network Kharabeesh humorously lampooned Egypt's embattled president. In one animated video, Mubarak sat on a rocking chair, plucking flower petals and cursing Ben Ali. He decides to make a speech to the people, hoping they would return to their senses. 'Why can't we be friends? We'll fix things. We'll bring in the plumber and the carpenter and polish up the government,' promises Mubarak. 'I will always be in your lives. And if you don't want me, I want you!'[42] In another skit, Mubarak, glued to a chair that is nailed to the floor, receives calls from Arab dignitaries. 'Don't let a bunch of kids on Twitter and Facebook scare you,' he advises Yemeni strongman Ali Abdullah Saleh. The extravagant and ambitious

Leila Trabelsi, wife of Tunisia's ousted leader, calls to suggest meeting over a cup of coffee to discuss a business partnership. 'I would like to, babe, but I can't,' replies Mubarak. 'I am stuck to the chair and can't move.'[43]

Among the voices to emerge from the uprising was that of Ramy Essam, a 24-year-old architecture student from the Nile Delta city of Mansoura. Strumming a guitar, his tunes strung together protest chants. '*We're all one hand and we demand one thing: Leave! Leave!*' he sang to cheering crowds. Embroiled in the violent confrontation of the Battle of the Camel, he vowed not to stop singing for Mubarak's departure until the despised president left.[44] In art and song, this defiant and creative energy lifted spirits and sustained the resistance to Mubarak's rule.

Platforms were situated around the square. One of the speakers was describing reports in the foreign press assessing the Mubarak family's multibillion-dollar fortune. Estimates of the value of the Mubarak family estate in the international press ranged from \$2–3 billon to a staggering \$70 billion. 'We want our money back!' the crowd boomed. The number of people waiting to enter Tahrir Square swelled by evening.

It was easy to blame protesters for the upheaval. A taxi driver was not particularly sympathetic. He felt the president had done enough; the protesters should go home so things could go back to normal. Some Egyptians believed rumours of lackeys being paid 50 euros a day to demonstrate. At Makani, a restaurant and café in the upmarket neighbourhood of Zamalek, one of the few places open, everyone had an opinion: Mubarak should be given the chance to leave with dignity; the protesters would not achieve any more of their demands; Mohamed ElBaradei could not be trusted; the Muslim Brotherhood would take over and things would be worse; foreign forces were seeking to hijack the protest movement; the protesters' demand for an interim government and the drafting of a new constitution would not work.

The long fight for democracy and freedom came at a price not everyone was willing to pay – harassment, arrest, detention, torture, even death. For those with money and connections, life was good in Egypt – as long as one did not worry too much about a monopolised political system, pervasive corruption, or millions of impoverished Egyptians denied the right to change a system that had robbed them of their dignity. Corruption works for those with ready cash; it is within this system that they feel privileged. Democracy would give the masses too much power.

Text messaging, which had been blocked since 27 January, returned at around 7 pm. The day's curfew also began at 7 pm.

Day 13: 6 February 2011

Media stories detailed an investigation of long-serving interior minister Habib al-Adly, charging him with masterminding the diabolical plot of bombing Alexandria's Two Saints Church on New Year's Eve, a terrorist attack that at the time was pinned on al-Qaeda operatives. The Interior Ministry's motive, according to reports, was to secure Western backing, precipitate a crackdown on Islamists, and keep the Coptic Christian minority in line in their support for the regime, since doing so was presumably in their best interests.[45]

Now a regime in tatters was forced to acknowledge that the massive security apparatus that had buttressed an unpopular political order had fallen to pieces and protest rallies showed no sign of ebbing. Vice President Omar Soliman met with a group of political figures, which included leaders of the Muslim Brotherhood, in a conference room in the presidential palace in which a framed photograph of Mubarak was prominently displayed. A coalition of revolutionary youth groups was among the opposition forces that rejected negotiation unless Mubarak stepped down. The encounter proved to be a photo op. Soliman issued a statement after the meeting that said a 'consensus' was reached on the path to political reform, yet outlined nothing that the regime had not stated earlier, simply reiterating the narrow concessions Mubarak had already made. Criticised by revolutionaries for legitimising a defunct regime by participating in the talks, the Brotherhood along with other opposition politicians denounced the meeting for dialogue as a ploy and refused further involvement.

US Secretary of State Hillary Rodham Clinton argued that removing Mubarak quickly could undermine the country's democratic transition, remarks that angered protesters in Tahrir. Fearing turmoil in Egypt, Western powers seemed content to have Mubarak manage a transition to a more open representative system, one he had stubbornly avoided. Mubarak was betting protests would wane as he engineered divide-and-rule strategies against opponents. He believed he could cling to power a while longer, surrendering little political power – just enough to weather the storm.

Day 14: 7 February 2011

How long would the protests and uprising continue and how many of its goals could it achieve? Sectors of the population were satisfied for the time being with the few concessions Mubarak's regime had made: a reshuffled Cabinet that contained no true reformers; promises to redraft a handful of articles in the constitution (not the entire constitution); scheduling parliamentary elections for seats contested by court challenges (not dissolving a parliament voted in through fraudulent elections and holding new elections); a shakeup of the National Democratic Party (with Gamal Mubarak, the president's son and groomed successor, tendering his resignation); and promising government workers a 15% pay rise (which just about offset inflation).

Could protesters keep the pressure on so that true political reform would become a reality? Egypt's popular revolt could not be called a revolution unless it created a seismic shift in Egypt's political map, sweeping away a despised autocrat, his patronage party, and his security apparatus, and building new democratic foundations. Hundreds of thousands if not upwards of a million visitors passed through Tahrir Square each day, with many camped out for days on end. 'It is enough to have freed ourselves and our country,' said an elderly man settled at the foot of a tank. 'Perhaps our children will enjoy that freedom.'

An emotional hour-long television interview with internet activist Wael Ghonim, who was detained in State Security custody from 28 January to 7 February, was a factor in nurturing the revolution. He was released only a few hours before his appearance on Mona al-Shazly's programme *Ten at Night*. Ghonim, a marketing executive at Google, had spoken with Mona al-Shazly in a telephone interview on her popular programme on private Egyptian satellite channel Dream 2 on the second day of protests. It was a programme the show's presenter and producers thought would be their last.

On Monday, 31 January, Ghonim's friend, Najeeb, a Jordanian colleague at Google, called Mona al-Shazly to tell her that Wael had been missing since Friday. The talk show host contacted everyone she knew who could help. The response was: 'We haven't arrested anyone' or 'We don't have that name on record'. When Ghonim's disappearance was made public, there were persistent calls for his release along with others being detained.

At around 7 pm on 7 February, al-Shazly's mobile rang. 'Wael Google', the number she had saved for Google's marketing executive, appeared on her phone. He spoke quickly, and al-Shazly arranged for him to come on the programme that night, hours after his release.

In an emotional interview, Ghonim started by giving his condolences to the martyrs of the protests, including the police. 'We did this because we love Egypt,' he said. 'We wanted people to say, "We want our rights and we'll get them."'

He took a six-day vacation from his job in the Emirates to participate in protests he helped organise on the 'We are all Khaled Said' Facebook page, which he administered anonymously. He said he did not want anyone to know he was the administrator because he wasn't looking to be made a hero. 'In Egypt, we like to make heroes. I sat sleeping for 12 days [in detention]. The heroes were the ones who went to the streets and protested. The heroes were the ones who were beaten and detained and exposed to danger.'

His involvement, he said, was to type on a keyboard and post on Facebook. 'This is the revolution of the youth on the internet that became the revolution of the youth of Egypt. Then it became the revolution of all of Egypt.' Underestimating the force of the internet generation, the security agencies first derided young activists as just a bunch of kids on Facebook. When he first spoke to State Security interrogators, they were convinced that he was being motivated and financed by foreign powers.

'We are not traitors. We are not traitors, Mona. We love Egypt. We are not working on behalf of anyone's agenda. Among us are people who are rich, living in nice homes, and driving the finest cars. I didn't need anything from anyone and I didn't want anything from anyone.' If he were a traitor, he said, he would have relaxed by the pool of his villa in the Emirates and enjoyed life. 'Like people say, "Let this country go up in flames. This is not *our* country. It's *their* country." That's what I would have said if I were a traitor.'

He chose otherwise. Ghonim's personal life suffered from his devotion to the cause. His wife was going to divorce him because he was ignoring her. His father had lost the sight in one eye and could lose sight in the other. He did not deserve the torment of not knowing where his son was for 12 days. Heading home after visiting a friend, Ghonim was abducted at 1 am on 28 January. He found himself surrounded by four men who shoved him in a car. He was kept blindfolded during his detention. He did not know what was going on in the street.

'The coordination of protests on 25 January did not include anyone from the Brotherhood,' said Ghonim, setting the record straight. 'They were not a party [in organising]. They did not know how the protests would progress. They were just like everyone else who accessed the [Facebook] page. On Friday [28 January], they said they were going to join. If they want to join as a political organisation, it is their prerogative – but in the end, they will not hijack this action. . . . This action belongs to Egyptian youth who fear for and love their country.'

Foreign news channels had been fingered in fuelling the protests by the regime and state television. 'Why are Egyptians looking to these channels?' asked Ghonim. 'It's because their [Egyptian] channels are telling them that everything is great; there is just some mayhem and vandals.'

'On Wednesday [2 February], we were told to say there were "tens" of protesters,' noted al-Shazly, 'and for this reason we said we are not going on the air. Tens of protesters, when we see with our eyes hundreds of thousands.'

Mona al-Shazly ended the programme with photos of 'youth like flowers, like the flowers of a garden' who had lost their lives in the protests. 'These are people who did not want to head a political party, nor were they stricken by poverty,' she said. 'They said, "What past generations could not do, we will accomplish."'

As those images were being shown on the screen, Ghonim broke down in tears. 'I want to tell every mother and father that lost a child that it's not our mistake. I swear to God it is not our mistake. It's the mistake of everyone who held on to power in Egypt and dug in his heels.'[46]

Day 15: 8 February 2011

Within hours, the interview with Wael Ghonim made it around the world, electrifying Tahrir Square the next day, with queues at checkpoints into the square stretching for hours. Protesters devised stratagems to keep the pressure on. Tens of thousands of protesters marched to the parliament buildings, which they included as part of the liberated territory. First, they hatched a ruse to fool the army and secret police, spreading the word that the television and radio building was where they were planning protests and sit-ins, when in fact their target was the legislature.

Day 16: 9 February 2011

The viability of Mubarak clinging to power was in doubt and the institutions of state power knew it. At the flagship state-owned *al-Ahram*, journalists and editors demanded the dismissal of editor-in-chief

Osama Saraya over the paper's unethical and unprofessional coverage. The state-owned print media – facing their own revolt by employees against editors-in-chief and their loyal pro-regime editorial line, a public that had lost all trust in their content, bundles of their papers unsold on news-stands, and free-falling advertising revenue – were compelled to start reporting and publishing more of the basic facts instead of flagrant lies of foreign plotting, or be ignored.

The main headline of the 9 February edition of *al-Ahram* read, 'A Fourth March of Millions Affirms the Rigidness of the Base of the 25 January Revolution'. A new supplement called *Shabab al-Tahrir* (The Youth of Tahrir) carried the headline, '25 January 2011: The Day Egypt Was Born Anew' – eerily similar to the paper's front-page headline on Mubarak's 82nd birthday months earlier. The paper even mentioned the obvious: protesters were calling for Mubarak's downfall. State-owned print media had days earlier described the protests as the work of 'tens' of agitators looking to create chaos. In a 9 February interview on state television, Omar Soliman warned that Egypt was in danger of a military coup – a threat that fell on death ears.

Day 17: 10 February 2011

'There is no single revolution that failed to achieve a change. It could take time,' said Alaa Al Aswany at his dental clinic on 10 February, adding that Egypt was in a 'revolutionary moment'. Out on the streets during the Friday of Rage protests on 28 January, he witnessed two young men close to him shot dead by sniper fire. 'Politically and morally, the regime is over. Mubarak can no longer claim that he is the president of Egypt by killing his own citizens because they dared express their own opinion.'[47]

An army spokesman declared the following on state television, in what was described as Communiqué no. 1 of the army command:

> *In affirmation and support for the legitimate demands of the people, the Supreme Council of the Armed Forces convened today, 10 February 2011, to consider developments to date, and decided to remain in continuous session to consider what procedures and measures that may be taken to protect the nation, and the achievements and aspirations of the great people of Egypt.*

Before Mubarak took to the airwaves in a speech on 10 February, optimistic rumours suggested he would announce his resignation, citing health reasons. That was the talk on satellite channels in those hours of anticipation – a planned trip for the president to the Sinai resort town of Sharm al-Sheikh, followed by a visit to his doctors in Germany.

He finally appeared on state television at 10:45 pm. After 17 days of protests, he again offered a trite apology to the families of the victims – he did not call them martyrs. Protesters saw him as being directly responsible not only for the deaths of the hundreds of Egyptians killed since the start of protests on 25 January but for everyone ensnarled in the security state's death grip since he assumed power in 1981.

The buildup to the speech proved to be another anticlimax. In 17 minutes, Mubarak began by directing his words to the 'youth of Egypt in Tahrir Square'. In prepared remarks he said he was 'speaking from the heart, as a father would to his sons and daughters'. Mubarak's hackneyed words of grief did not come across as being genuine or sincere: 'I tell the families of the innocent victims that I am suffering, as you are. My heart is hurt by what happened to them, as your hearts hurt.'

In the next breath, Mubarak said he would not listen to any directives from abroad and again affirmed he would not run in the upcoming presidential elections. Recycling words from his last speech, he reminded his audience of his military accomplishments and his defence of Egypt and its sovereignty over his 60-plus-year career, adding that his proudest moment was when he raised the Egyptian flag over liberated Sinai. As if to redeem his tattered reputation at home and abroad, he said he had preserved the peace and protected the safety and security of Egypt. 'I trust that the vast majority of the children of the nation know who is Hosni Mubarak.' Still, he was deaf to the seething calls of the street. 'The current events are not linked with my personality; they are not linked with Hosni Mubarak,' he said, suggesting that young people were the most affected by the mounting losses Egypt was facing.

He went on to say that the constitutional committee formed by presidential decree would amend five articles (having to do with electing the president, the People's Assembly, election monitoring, and the passage of constitutional amendments) and do away with a sixth (an article that dealt with combating terrorism). Mubarak mentioned that he would be delegating powers to his vice president, although he did not specify the scope of those powers. Emergency law remained in effect, but might be abolished when Egypt returned to a state of normality, stated Mubarak.[48]

Following Mubarak's comments, vice president and ex-intelligence chief Omar Soliman gave a six-minute speech on state television claiming that change had begun. 'The president has placed the higher interests of the country above all else,' declared Soliman. He added that the president was committed to the reforms he promised, and it was time for a return to 'normal life'. 'We have opened the door to dialogue. We have reached understandings. We have agreed to most of the demands according to the allowed time frame. The door is open for more dialogue.' Not someone with a reputation for championing democracy, Soliman blamed people with 'agendas for destruction' for the crisis in Egypt. He had a message for the 'youth and heroes of Egypt': 'return to your home and work'. Another piece of advice: do not pay attention to satellite channels, which have no other objective than to foment discord, weaken Egypt, and distort its image.[49]

'A halt to resistance rarely brings reduced repression,' writes Gene Sharp. 'Once the restraining force of internal and international opposition has been removed, dictators may even make their oppression and violence more brutal than before.'[50] Waving their shoes in the air, protesters in Tahrir Square, jubilant before the speech, reacted with anger and frustration to Mubarak's remarks, vowing to march to the television and radio building and the presidential palace. And the numbers of protesters the following day would only grow as Egyptians responded to Mubarak's speech.

Day 18: 11 February 2011

At 6 pm Cairo local time, vice president of two weeks Omar Soliman read a 30-second statement that said Mubarak was resigning the presidency and handing powers over to the Supreme Council of the Armed Forces.[51] With those words, the street erupted in euphoric celebration, complete with drumming, dancing, flag waving, and flares lit from aerosol canisters. It was an emotional moment for everyone following 18 eventful days. Two days later the military council suspended the constitution and dissolved parliament, pledging a peaceful transfer of authority to an elected legislature and president within six months.

For 18 days, Egypt was *the* story the world was watching. Started by politically engaged young people on social media and spreading to every corner of Egypt, the 25 January revolution brought Mubarak's reign crashing down. In the space of less than a month, the world witnessed the demise of two Arab dictators. No longer would the ruler have the population's silent obedient consent, surmised activists across the Arab world. 'For the first time, the population went out to oust the divine ruler from his throne,' opined the colloquial poet Gamal Bekheet, 'defeating the notion that he who rules Egypt is a god.'[52]

3

Politics and the Press under Military Rule

> *The illusion of freedom will continue as long as it's profitable to continue the illusion. At the point where the illusion becomes too expensive to maintain, they will just take down the scenery, they will pull back the curtains, they will move the tables and chairs out of the way and you will see the brick wall at the back of the theatre.*
>
> (Frank Zappa, composer and musician[1])

State media and public figures solidly behind the regime until 11 February 2011 had to quickly rebrand themselves as supporters of the revolution and tribunes of the people. A day after Mubarak stepped down, the headline in large red lettering above the masthead of the flagship state-owned daily *al-Ahram* was 'The People Toppled the Regime'. 'We Won' was the banner of the four-page supplement, *Shabab al-Tahrir* (The Youth of Tahrir) and the image a young man clutching an Egyptian flag, his face painted with its colours.

'I invite you to go to the newsroom of *al-Ahram* and meet journalists,' editor-in-chief Osama Saraya told a BBC Arabic correspondent during an on-camera interview when asked about the staff's demands for reform. 'I promise you that I will go to the newsroom right now and talk to people. Isn't that what you requested?' said the journalist, Khaled Ezz al-Arab. 'Now you are fooling around within the organisation and I can refuse what you say,' responded Saraya aggressively, flashing an artificial smile. 'In heated moments, media organisations play this game, I call it the dirty tricks of some of the foreign organisations.' He ended the interview, ripped off his lapel microphone, and disdainfully threw it on the floor.[2]

State television also shifted its editorial line, congratulating Egyptians on their revolution and vowing to be truthful in its coverage. Tendering his resignation a day after the announcement that Mubarak was stepping down, former information minister Anas al-Fiqqi was arrested on 24 February and incarcerated at Tora Prison, along with other apparatchiks, pending investigations into money laundering and corruption. On 28 February, the lead story on state-owned Channel One's newscast was the general prosecutor's order to confiscate the fortune of Mubarak and his family and prohibit them from travelling abroad. Earlier that day the president's wife and younger son had attempted to leave the country aboard a private jet in the Red Sea resort town of Sharm al-Sheikh. Still, changes in the state media were more cosmetic than substantive. The decades-old institutional culture of a state media in thrall to the powers-that-be remained in place, as well as self-imposed censorship, nepotism, and favouritism.

As Egypt's revolution raised the ceiling of press freedoms, the dominance of the security state over the media temporarily receded. Information sources were multiplying in an increasingly fragmented media space, pushing news consumers to access outlets that affirmed their worldview. In the aftermath of Mubarak's downfall 16 new satellite channels took to the air, which did not need State Security clearance to be licensed.[3] Muhammad al-Amin Ragab, an ally of the Mubarak business clique, launched a bouquet of channels called CBC, short for Capital Broadcasting Center. The Muslim Brotherhood opened an affiliated channel called Masr 25.

Mubarak's downfall triggered a wave of popular activism. Students and faculty of Cairo University's School of Journalism and Mass Communications staged a sit-in demanding the dismissal of the dean and regime loyalist Sami Abd al-Aziz. The unsuccessful campaign was broken up on 23 March using military force. In Mubarak's final days, the chairman of the Journalists' Syndicate and former presidential speechwriter, Makram Muhammad Ahmed, was ousted by members of the union because of his cosy ties with the regime.

Friday of Victory: 18 February 2011

A sea of people and Egyptian flags packed Tahrir Square at noon on the Friday of Victory. It was exactly one week since Hosni Mubarak stepped down as president and Egyptians were rejoicing with revolutionary ardour, imbued with a renewed sense of hope and belonging that was absent under Mubarak's authoritarianism. A day earlier, three former ministers (including the hated interior minister Habib al-Adly) and iron and steel monopolist, NDP clubhouse politician, and rabble-rouser Ahmed Ezz were arrested pending a corruption investigation. But those allegations were only the tip of the iceberg. Egyptians were demanding a public accounting of government officials who had profited handsomely from graft and abuse of power, including the former president himself.

Tahrir Square was a soapbox for anyone who could gather a crowd. A woman railed against unscrupulous politicians who siphoned millions at the public's expense. One man stood out with his reprimand in street poetry rhymes. Red, white, and black face paint decorated children's faces. A gigantic flag was lifted above the heads of the crowd. 'Lift your head up high. You're Egyptian!' The promise of freedom unleashed creative talent and roused independent initiative in a way autocracy, with its forced conformity, never can.

Across town, in the square in front of Mustafa Mahmoud Mosque in the upscale neighbourhood of Mohandiseen, a pro-Mubarak rally took place. A few thousand people gathered around a makeshift stage waving flags and listening to one speaker after another honour the conspicuously absent ex-president. Why sympathise with an undemocratic ruler who has been in power for 30 years? A common and often repeated explanation of loyalty to a dictator is the Stockholm Syndrome, where victims empathise with their captors, viewing them as a source of protection and security.

But that is not the whole story. In any order that thrives on insider connections, there are winners and losers. The winners are the ones who know how to manoeuvre around the system and use it to their advantage. Why would they want to change a status quo that has worked to their benefit? In addition to NDP loyalists who benefited from party affiliation, there was the security apparatus, which was fused with the executive branch and the ruling party. Those massive agencies of the state could always be counted on to rig elections, keep tabs on the opposition, and silence dissent. Still, it was refreshing to see a vibrant arena for free speech in Egypt – with the military rulers in charge that was not a sentiment that would last.

A showdown with the prime minister

Novelist and political writer Alaa Al Aswany appeared in the 2 March broadcast of the night-time programme *Baladna bil-masry* (Our Country . . . in Egyptian), a programme on Egyptian satellite channel

ONtv with Prime Minister Ahmed Shafik, appointed by Hosni Mubarak on 29 January, along with veteran journalist Hamdy Kandil and billionaire businessman and the station's owner Naguib Sawiris.[4]

In a tense exchange, Al Aswany pointedly told the sitting prime minister that he should resign and said he would be among the hundreds of thousands of protesters in Tahrir Square that Friday calling for him to step down. Al Aswany challenged Shafik in a grilling of a high-ranking public official that Egyptian satellite television has seldom witnessed.

Al Aswany interrogated Shafik on the systematic use of torture by State Security, reminding him of his phone interview with CNN's Candy Crowley during the revolution, where the prime minister pretended he could not hear the question, repeated several times, on why human rights activists and journalists were still being arrested.[5] 'When you were a minister in Hosni Mubarak's Cabinet, didn't you hear that there was torture in State Security,' Al Aswany asked him forthrightly. 'The prime minister should be more concerned with trying the people who killed the [revolution's] martyrs than presenting candy and chocolates.' Shafik, either as a gesture of goodwill or irony, had made the remark that he would pass out candies to protesters massed outside the parliament buildings.

'Perhaps in your former post or in your military career you have not dealt with State Security. People like the doctor [Alaa Al Aswany] and myself have dealt with them,' said Sawiris, describing the agency as a 'parallel government' that prevents young people from speaking about politics in university campuses, tortures political dissidents, gets involved in businesses and the stock market, and even dictates whom private satellite stations can invite on as guests and who they cannot. 'For example, if they find out that this station has invited someone from the Brotherhood, I find all the telephones ringing off the hook. You have an officer who doesn't have one-millionth the culture or education I have calling me to tell me he is not to appear. There is no better time than now to be honest,' Sawiris, who is Coptic Christian, said to the prime minister. 'I am a liberal channel. I have to bring someone I disagree with, not someone who will beat my drum.'

'The interior minister said that the police performed their role admirably. He said that the protesters had snipers who spoke in [foreign] languages, that those protesters are agents. He also said that the role of State Security will not be touched and it would continue to perform its nationalistic role. Is there a contradiction here or not?' asked Al Aswany.

'The minister should resign immediately, Mr Prime Minister,' Kandil chimed in, later adding, 'I thought you would present your resignation because you know that public opinion does not want this government.'

Shafik suggested that State Security be reformed, not abolished. 'Let's see what State Security looks like after its reorganisation. It's either pass or no pass. It's either go or no go. Either black or white,' Shafik managed to reply, giving no specifics on the purpose of the agency responsible for state repression.

'We want your opinion, since you are with us, to tell us what that role should be,' asked Sawiris.

'Its role is state security, and we will itemise it,' answered Shafik.

'Its role was state security before, too. We mean state security and he means another form of state security,' Al Aswany shot back. He brought the point home with the security vacuum the state had maintained. 'Why leave Egypt, from Alexandria to Aswan, without a traffic officer?' It is a strategy to undermine the gains of the revolution and maintain old regime elements, Al Aswany charged.

> *Something happened yesterday that makes it apparent that it's a plot. Thugs began to attack elementary schools. And those thugs are from the criminals that were released [on 28 January] in order to frighten Egyptians as a penalty for the revolution. All this is documented. I understand that a thug would go to a bank, a company, or to rob me in my house. But if thugs go to a primary school, what are they going to get from schoolchildren? Will they get their sandwiches? The idea here is that your point of weakness is your children, and they make you feel that your kids are not safe. When I say that the demands of the revolution have not been met, people say, 'I don't care. Let the revolution go up in flames.'*

Shafik was not only questioned on the security apparatus, but also about emergency law, the imprisonment of political detainees, and the open powers granted by the constitution to the president. He was challenged about certain ministers in his Cabinet: the justice minister, who in Mubarak's regime was useful in smothering an independent-minded judiciary; and the foreign minister, who loyally defended Mubarak's regime during the revolution.

Then there was the question on why no one was put on trial for the deaths of the revolution's martyrs. 'Have you seen the video of the armoured vehicle that ran over people? What do you think, as the prime minister of

Egypt?' asked Al Aswany. 'What do you think of the people who died and what do you think of the 1,200 people who lost sight in their eyes?'

'Don't wear the role of nationalism more than me. I have a history of patriotism,' howled Shafik, referring to his air force service. An angry exchange ensued.

'Yes, I will tell you what you are supposed to do as prime minister. I am an Egyptian citizen and I have the right to tell you,' bawled Al Aswany. 'Your history is your business. Don't tell me I am wearing the role of nationalism, I am telling you that people died. What have you done for the people who died?'

'You sleep in your house,' snapped Shafik.

'No, it is *you* that sleeps in your house!' responded Al Aswany. 'If your son was run over by a car, would you have said that?'[6]

The following morning Shafik submitted his resignation. The military council appointed Essam Sharaf, a former transportation minister who led protests during the revolution, as prime minister and he was tasked with forming a new Cabinet. Amid crowds following Friday noon prayers on 4 March, Sharaf took the oath of office in Tahrir Square.

For the first time in Egypt's living memory the media had a role profound enough to compel the resignation of a top government official. State Security, an organisation notorious for torture and surveillance of dissidents, was 'disbanded' and replaced by a new agency called Homeland Security, raising concerns that, besides creative rebranding and reshuffling officers, the same agency existed within the Interior Ministry. The security apparatus remained largely intact, maintaining a strategic security vacuum so that Egyptians would pine for the stability of the former regime, as these enforcers – now joined by the military police – kept an eye on objectors through a network of domestic spying and intimidation schemes.

Competing truth narratives

Called the Friday of Cleansing, 8 April 2011 witnessed one of the largest rallies in Tahrir Square since the president's ouster. The main demand of the protesters was the immediate trial of Hosni Mubarak. The army's top generals were also under attack for not moving fast enough in apprehending the powerbrokers and profiteers behind Mubarak's regime. Communiqué no. 1 of the 'Honorable Army Officers' read by an officer in Tahrir Square listed their demands: dissolving the Supreme Council of the

Armed Forces and holding them accountable; the resignation of defence minister Muhammad Hussein Tantawi; the formation of a civilian presidential council consisting of only one military officer; speedy trials of those responsible for corruption, and for the deaths and injuries during the 25 January revolution, above all the ex-president and his family.[7]

In a Facebook note, Omar Kamel, a musician, video producer, and one of the protesters in Tahrir Square, gave this account: 'When the dissenting army officers came to Tahrir, their fates were pretty much sealed,' he wrote. 'The officers had basically thrust their neck out and unless we were there with them, we might as well have hung them dead ourselves.' The officers were in makeshift tents in the centre of the square. In the pre-dawn hours of 9 April 2011, army commandos and security forces charged Tahrir Square, shooting volleys of gunfire and detaining dissenting army officers who had joined protesters. 'They broke through to the tent in the middle, they broke it down, pulled it apart, beat up the protectors, as well as the officers inside, they stormed the tent, and took the officers by force,' described Kamel. 'Some escaped. One died. Some they captured. . . . The rate of gunfire is something I've never, ever, ever, heard in my life before.'[8] Videos surfaced on social media that contradicted the official army account that no shots were fired.[9]

Communiqué no. 34 issued right after the incident and posted on the official Facebook page of the Supreme Council of the Armed Forces, announced the detention of Ibrahim Kamel, a wealthy businessman and National Democratic Party cohort, blaming him and his associates for causing trouble in Tahrir Square the day before. The communiqué concluded with the words:

> *The Supreme Council of the Armed Forces confirms that it will persist with determination and strength after the remnants of the former regime and the National Democratic Party. We also confirm that the armed forces will always and forever be a strong arm committed to protecting and providing for the nation, and guaranteeing security, stability, peace, and the desires of the great people of Egypt.*[10]

The pre-dawn incident stirred distrust against a military high command that ruled the country with presidential and legislative authority and lacked transparency in its decision-making. Setting up barricades, protesters reoccupied the square for days. Other activists felt that it was not wise to engage in a confrontation with the military.

On 10 April, Al Arabiya broadcast a five-minute audio speech made by Mubarak where he responded to critics who said he had plundered the nation and amassed a huge fortune. 'Brothers and sisters, the children of Egypt, I was very much hurt, and I am still hurting – my family and I – from the unjust campaigns against us and false allegations of abuse that aim to smear my reputation, slander my integrity, my positions, and my military and political history for which I struggled for the sake of Egypt and its children, in war and peace,' began Mubarak in his first public statement since he was ousted from power. 'I have stepped down from the position of the presidency, placing the interests of the nation and its children above all else' – words that angered his detractors since it made it seem as if his decision to relinquish authority was entirely voluntary.

'I have spent a lifetime serving the country honourably and honestly. I do not have to be silent in the face of campaigns of falsehood, presumptions, and vilification, and the continued attempts to undermine my reputation and integrity, and to challenge the reputation and integrity of my family,' Mubarak continued. He claimed to own no property or bank accounts abroad and vowed to cooperate with the general prosecutor in the investigations 'so that all will know of the lies reported in the media, in local and foreign newspapers, on the alleged and massive real estate assets that I and my family own abroad'. He also threatened legal action against those who defamed his reputation.[11]

If Mubarak thought his prepared statement would placate Egyptians, he could not have been more mistaken. Shortly after Mubarak's words were broadcast, the general prosecutor on state television announced that he had summoned the former president and his sons for questioning on corruption allegations and the death of citizens during the revolution. On 12 April, Mubarak was hospitalised after reportedly suffering a minor heart attack. The following day, he and his sons, Gamal and Alaa, were under arrest. The former ruling party was dissolved on 16 April and its assets sequestered by the state.

Mubarak's arrest took public scrutiny away from the Tahrir Square raid. Yet a strained relationship between the public, the media, and the military council lingered, especially when it came to the army's practice of torture and other human rights violations against protesters, and its endorsement of a plan to outlaw demonstrations and sit-ins. The divide would only widen in the months ahead as the ruling council referred civilians to military trials, maintained emergency law in effect, and unilaterally managed a long-drawn-out transition period.

Bassem Youssef and political satire

As Egypt's revolution unfolded, bizarre coverage by the local media became the stimulus for a show that drew its inspiration from Comedy Central's *The Daily Show* and *The Colbert Report*. Shot in a spare room in Bassem Youssef's apartment overlooking the Nile in the Cairo neighbourhood of Maadi, *The Bassem Youssef Show* started as an internet production created on a shoestring budget with the aspiration of making it to television. When Youssef made his internet debut in March 2011 in an episode that humorously exposed the absurdities of Egyptian television's coverage of events of the revolution, he was counting on 10,000 hits to his channel within a couple of weeks. Instead, he got a million.

Youssef's satire presented a witty yet serious take on the issues Egyptians were talking about. The then 37-year-old cardiothoracic surgeon went on to strike a television deal that made him one of the top-paid talents on Egyptian television. His television show, called *al-Bernameg?* (The Programme?), debuted on ONtv in the ratings-driven month of Ramadan. The show's second season moved to the CBC satellite network in November 2012 and was filmed before a live audience in downtown Cairo's historic Radio Cinema.[12]

'The revolution exposed a lot of creative talents among Egyptians,' Youssef begins one YouTube episode. Wild imagination, anger, hysteria, and drama were some of the aptitudes on display, he goes on to say, but Tamer from Ghamra was a unique case. 'Tamer was not only emotionally affected, he had a theory that was so different from those who preceded him.' Between sobs, Tamer in a phone-in tells the presenter on state television, 'They are foreigners who speak the English language very well. No one speaks other than English inside [Tahrir Square].' With a mountain of tissues on his desk, Youssef is brought to tears only to learn that Tamer from Ghamra is a performance concocted by the state media. Youssef ends the clip by awarding the caller a faux Oscar.[13]

'I have no problem if you want to take the side of Mubarak. I have no problem if you want to be against the revolution,' Youssef said in an interview. 'But if you want to do this you should not propagate ridiculous rumours and make people think that these people are worthy of being killed or they are traitors or they have been trained abroad.'[14]

In another episode, Youssef tackles the divisive debate on the referendum for constitutional reforms held on 19 March, Egypt's first democratic vote since Hosni Mubarak's ousting.

> *In sum, if you voted 'yes', then you are a member of the Muslim Brotherhood, a Salafi, or the two of them played a joke on you, you're dumb, or you've betrayed the revolution and the blood of the martyrs. And if you voted 'no', then you don't understand anything, want the country to go up in flames, want the army to stay in control, and you are an infidel. That is democracy – to present the other side as a traitor, always placing them in a position where they are defending themselves.*

In a serious tone, he says that a boot had been on the necks of Egyptians for decades and it is natural to hear things we don't like when it is finally lifted. 'Call me what you want, but I remember all these people stood together a few weeks ago in something called . . . *the revolution*. Those were great days,' Youssef says fondly as images of unity in Tahrir Square flash across the screen.[15]

'We were trying to make people think first and laugh later,' said Youssef. 'When we are talking about the tensions between the different sects of the community, Muslims and liberals and Christians, if you would come and preach to people from the first second, they will not actually watch. I had to make people laugh a little bit and then talk straight to the camera and tell them, you know, everybody is mistaken.'[16] Youssef sees the failure to communicate as being the major barrier to bridging divides.

> *The thing I like about Tahrir Square is that this is the only place that people talk to each other. We do not talk to each other. The extreme Muslims and the frightened Christians and the uppity liberals, they don't talk to each other. Everybody thinks that he is right. If you think that it is only the Salafis or Ikhwanis [the Muslim Brotherhood] or extreme Muslims' fault, no, it is the liberals' fault as well. We are as mistaken as everybody else.*

In another YouTube clip, Youssef goes to Tahrir Square and talks with protesters demanding that the ex-president be put on trial. The day is Friday, 8 April. 'The ceiling of your demands increases every day!' he tells one protester with mock astonishment. At the end of the segment, Youssef turns to the camera and says, 'Laughing and sarcasm aside, Tahrir Square is what we have left. What are our demands? Our demands are the same as they were from the first day: The people demand the downfall of the regime. I don't see that the regime has fallen,' he says. 'As long as the regime is in place, merely a change of faces and a change in seats, people will continue coming to the square.'

He held no illusions about the limitations on freedoms of expression. 'Before you are free, you have to be smart. You have to choose your battles. It takes nothing away from your courage that you are not able to speak about a topic,' he said. 'Until there is a president and a People's Assembly, you are under military rule. In any place in the world, military rule has restrictions.'[17]

Prosecuted for blogging

On 11 April 2011, 25-year-old Egyptian blogger Maikel Nabil Sanad was sentenced to three years in prison by a military tribunal on charges of insulting the military establishment and publishing false information. His blog posts spoke of the army's torture of protesters and arraigned the ruling military council. 'I will present all the evidences and documents which prove that the army did not stand by the people's side, not even once during this revolution and that the army's conduct was deceptive all the time and that it was protecting its own interests,' he wrote in a post on 8 March titled 'The army and the people wasn't ever one hand.'[18]

Other bloggers have criticised the actions of the Supreme Council of the Armed Forces, but Sanad's views on military conscription and support for Israel made him a vulnerable target under military rule. Sanad wrote that he would avoid compulsory service in the Egyptian army and persuaded Egyptians to evade conscription. In a YouTube video to Israeli audiences during the revolution, he urged them to support Egypt's uprising as being for the best interests of the Jewish state.[19] After the revolution, he exhorted Israelis not to support Egypt's military leadership. Sanad's case delineated the boundaries of where expression was not allowed to go. A pacifist, Nabil waged a liquids-only hunger strike in prison and boycotted the military trial.

On 14 August 2011, the military prosecutor began investigating 26-year-old activist Asmaa Mahfouz for allegedly inciting confrontations with the military rulers and the judiciary in Facebook and Twitter posts and questioned her for three hours. Facing military trial and years in jail, she was released on bail of 20,000 Egyptian pounds ($3,350/£2,040). Mahfouz had shot to fame in bold YouTube videos urging Egyptians to come out in the streets on 25 January. 'If the judiciary doesn't give us our rights, nobody should be surprised if militant groups appear and conduct a series of assassinations because there is no law and there is no judiciary,' she wrote in a post on Facebook.[20]

Since Mubarak's downfall, more than 12,000 civilians have faced military trial, mainly on charges of 'thuggery' or libelling and slandering the military. Both charges were easily levelled at protesters and dissidents, even when their criticism of the Supreme Council centred on its political role of running the country. Mubarak, as commander-in-chief of the armed forces, was not as unforgiving of his critics as to refer libel and slander cases to military courts.

In Communiqué no. 72, issued on 18 August, the Supreme Council of the Armed Forces announced that it was dropping charges against Asmaa Mahfouz and blogger and activist Loai Nagati, who was arrested in protests in June, charged with thuggery, and referred to military trial. The communiqué followed a meeting between army chief of staff Sami Anan and intellectuals and journalists who objected to the practice of trying young activists in military tribunals. 'The Supreme Council of the Armed Forces', read the communiqué, 'calls on the children of the Egyptian people from media figures, thinkers, intellectuals, and youth to consider expressing their position and ideas in a way that is mindful, responsible, and does not represent an offense or injury, preserving the shining image of the 25 January revolution, which was protected by the armed forces.'[21]

On 14 December, an election day, prisoner of conscience Maikel Nabil Sanad was sentenced in a retrial to two years in prison, fined 200 Egyptian pounds ($33/£22), and ordered to pay an additional 300 Egyptian pounds ($50/£32) for a court-appointed lawyer. Four days before the first anniversary of the start of the revolution, the military ruler ordered the release of 1,955 detainees, including Sanad, held in military prisons. Incarcerated for 302 days, he was set free on 24 January 2012.

The media and the military

On 25 May 2005, in a nearly empty polling station, Bothaina Kamel cast her vote on the referendum to amend the Egyptian constitution to allow for the nation's first contested presidential elections. That evening she faced a studio camera, reading a newscast on state television that declared that the referendum witnessed a record turnout. The vote was marred by violence perpetrated by State Security against protesters denouncing the façade of greater political participation – something that was not mentioned in the broadcast. That got Kamel thinking: was she telling viewers the news or was she conveying government newspeak?

That summer, Kamel along with two other women formed Shayfeen.com – the name means 'we are watching you' in colloquial Arabic – a group to monitor parliamentary elections that have witnessed widespread subterfuge, outdated voter rolls, and low voter turnout. She became a recognised face at pro-democracy rallies. In 2006, Kamel chose not to read newscasts she did not believe to be true on state television, opting for a leave of absence.

Six years and a revolution later, Kamel, a television presenter and activist, had the distinction of being the first woman to announce her candidacy for president in Egypt. She revealed her intention to run for the presidency in April 2011 on Twitter, using social media as her main publicity and advocacy tool.[22] Her campaign motto was simply 'My agenda is Egypt' – an answer back to the state media establishment, which during the revolution derided protesters as having nefarious 'foreign agendas'.

On 8 May, Kamel stood in front of the Church of the Virgin Mary, set ablaze a day earlier, in the working-class district of Imbaba. Sectarian confrontations engulfed this community, where it was rumoured that a Coptic woman was being held in a church because she wed a Muslim man and converted to his faith. The clashes left a dozen people dead and two churches up in flames. Explanations abounded on the reasons for the surge in violence: sectarian conflicts were being engineered by counter-revolutionary forces to halt the gains of revolution; the military rulers were slow to react because they wanted to remain in charge of the country; the wider margin for expression laid bare animosities cultivated by extremists, who thrive on the hopelessness and anger that poverty breeds.

Kamel blamed the military rulers managing Egypt's transition. 'I entered Imbaba saying the police and the army were slow to react,' she said. 'I left Imbaba saying the police and army were complicit.' Those were strong words for a ruling body known for its intolerance to censure. 'I accuse the Supreme Council of dereliction and with helping to aggravate sectarian violence, of failing our revolution,' charged Kamel. 'I am saying you should return to your barracks. You have failed miserably in protecting Egypt. Your place is not security, it is war. We want a civilian presidential council.'[23]

For six years, Kamel hosted a popular weekly radio programme called *I'tirafat layliya* (Night-Time Confessions). Broadcast after midnight, listeners called in to talk about personal dilemmas and seek advice, discussing such sensitive topics as sexual abuse, and premarital and extramarital sex. After six years on the airwaves, the programme was abruptly taken off in 1998, accused by a state committee on religion of damaging the reputation of Egypt and its youth.

She later made the move to satellite television and the Saudi-owned Orbit network. There, she was a presenter for a decade, hosting an interview and talk show called *Arguk ifhamni* (Please Understand Me). But when she chose to do an episode following the revolution on Mubarak's hidden billions, station executives, expecting Saudi Arabia's alleged role in transferring the fortune would come up, informed her that the show was not going on a half hour before airtime. She returned to state television and after reading two newscasts, she found out she had been removed from the newscast schedule without being notified of a reason. One newscast she ended with the words 'Greetings to the revolution and the square.' In another she concluded with 'Our Egyptian Arab revolution continues.'

On 10 May 2011, Kamel appeared on the programme *Shari' al-kalam* (The Street of Words), which hosted a presidential candidate each week. (Kamel was the fourth candidate to appear.) In front of the television and radio building demonstrations raged. 'Copts are protesting the thuggery of the Salafis and the failure of the security,' said presenter Mahmoud Sharaf, explaining the programme's delay. 'A group of Salafis have congregated outside the building yelling, "Islamic, Islamic."'

But before the one-hour programme on state-owned Nile Culture channel ended, the host was instructed to close it in a directive from Sami al-Sherif, the head of the Egyptian Radio and Television Union, to the channel's manager. 'I don't know if I will present this programme again or remain with the station,' Sharaf said on the air.

'I want to ask you, what are you going to do, Mahmoud?' Kamel asked gently.

'If Dr Sami al-Sherif wants to present the programme, he's welcome to do so,' said a dispirited Sharaf, addressing his bosses and the audience. 'Ms Bothaina is stating her opinion freely. There were no transgressions, in my opinion, in what she said. In any case, this is your media and this is the direction you want it to go in.'

'It is worse than the media of Mubarak,' Kamel said, as she and the studio staff started clapping as the programme rolled off the air.[24]

The incident became the talk of the media. Prime Minister Essam Sharaf accepted on 30 May the resignation of Sami al-Sherif, who left the landmark television building amid tight security. On the night-time current affairs show *Akhir kalam* (Last Words) hosted by Yosri Fouda, al-Sherif explained pulling the plug on the programme, as it was the policy for state television not to allow presidential candidates to discuss their electoral programme on the air. In a telephone call to the programme Mahmoud Sharaf said that if there was such a policy he was not aware of it, arguing that his interview with Kamel hardly focused on her electoral platform. Moreover, he had invited other presidential candidates on the programme: Why wasn't anything said then?[25]

For five hours on 14 May, the military prosecutor questioned Bothaina Kamel centring on tweets she wrote following a conversation she had with General Ismail Etman, head of the Morale Affairs Directorate of the Supreme Council of the Armed Forces, where she challenged him on the arrest and abuse of demonstrators by the military police and forced virginity tests for female detainees.

Interrogations by the military prosecutor of journalists and activists continued. ONtv presenter Reem Magued and blogger Hossam el-Hamalawy were called to appear before the military prosecutor on 31 May. The reason was the allegation el-Hamalawy made on Magued's programme *Our Country . . . in Egyptian* on 26 May where he said that there needed to be an examination of the violations by the military police:

> *I hold General Hamdy Badeen responsible. In interviews, Badeen has dismissed reports of torture by the army as being 'fabricated'. Just as Hosni Mubarak did not go down in the street and kill the revolutionaries with his own hands but we are trying him for the charge of killing revolutionaries, General Hamdy Badeen is responsible for the military police, which is involved in violations, and that is something we need to talk about.*[26]

'Are these violations documented?' asked Magued. 'It is documented and on video and in testimonies,' replied el-Hamalawy, mentioning the names of human rights lawyers working on those cases. Several months after abuse of demonstrators made headlines, the military prosecutor wanted to know what kind of evidence el-Hamalawy held. Journalist Shahira Amin was also asked to appear to give testimony before the military prosecutor regarding an article on CNN's website where she cited an unnamed 'senior Egyptian general' admitting that virginity tests were performed on women who were arrested in demonstrations, an allegation previously denied by the military.[27]

Dream TV presenter Dina Abd al-Rahman was let go from the morning show *Sabah Dream* (Dream Morning) on 24 July 2011 when she discussed an opinion article by journalist Naglaa Bedair in the independent daily *al-Tahrir* (Liberation), which was critical of General Hassan al-Roweiny, a member of the Supreme Council of the Armed Forces.

In television appearances, al-Roweiny had provoked the ire of Egyptians. He admitted spreading rumours in Tahrir Square during the revolution, telling protesters that regime figures had been arrested and that all their demands would be met, in order to appease the masses and control the situation. The general also had harsh words for the April 6 Youth Movement, Kifaya, and a number of presidential hopefuls, alleging that they were receiving foreign funding and driving a wedge between the army and the people. The use of the media by military officers to make unfounded accusations against activist groups served the purpose of drumming up public opposition to protest action on the streets.

Major General Abd al-Moniem Kato, adviser to the armed forces on Morale Affairs, in that day's *al-Shuruk* penned an opinion piece where he plainly alleged that two presidential candidates were agents for America and that the April 6 Movement comprised a collection of saboteurs. On the programme *Dream Morning*, Abd al-Rahman had the military adviser on the phone to talk about the indictments he levelled. Kato, incensed at the public criticism of the army in Bedair's article, engaged Abd al-Rahman in a heated discussion.

'This journalist named Naglaa, why are you are sitting there and reading her whole article? She is a saboteur,' began Kato.

'Just a second, you are accusing the journalist Naglaa Bedair of being a saboteur?'

'Yes, a saboteur. Is *that* an article to be said or written? Then you, as a broadcaster, read it to the public?'

'What is it you want, General Kato? Yesterday we received a telephone call from General Hassan al-Roweiny and we had a discussion and we listened to him for nearly an hour.[28] Is it not the right for any journalist to express her opinion and for us to present that opinion?'

'See, the armed forces are trying to teach people the kindergarten of democracy and it is giving everyone the chance to express his or her opinion. But an opinion must be objective. It should be transparent and true. She cannot do such things as write an article that curses the man,' proclaimed Kato.

'She did not curse, and I urge you to read the article again,' asserted Abd al-Rahman. 'It does not contain abuse or curses but it is a reaction to what the general said in statements yesterday. You said that the armed forces are teaching people democracy. Isn't it part of democracy to criticise? Many Egyptians know what is democracy and how to practise it, General.'

Abd al-Rahman turned to the specific allegations he presented in his opinion piece. 'At any rate, our reason for calling you is your statements that two of the presidential candidates are chief agents for the United States of America,' she said.

Kato refused to disclose the names of the candidates. 'We are in a period where we must all unite and stand as one,' he claimed.

'Is uniting and standing as one achieved by throwing around accusations without proof, General?' asked Abd al-Rahman.

'Who says without proof? If Hassan al-Roweiny said so-and-so about the April 6 Movement, undeniably . . .'

'I do not talk about General Roweiny and what he said, I am talking about the atmosphere generally. You have made the accusation about the respected journalist Naglaa Bedair and you have also accused two of the presidential candidates.'

'To Naglaa Bedair I tell her that when you write you should write objectively.'

'Let us go to the subject of the two presidential candidates. In these difficult times that we're passing through, General, and you are an adviser to the Morale Affairs Directorate, could you have evidence against two candidates in the presidential elections, and know that they are spies and agents and are directing movements on behalf of America, and simply leave them?'

'Do not enlarge the subject,' replied Kato. 'All the viewings and readings say that there are truly people who destroy.'

'Are these speculations, General, or do you have information and evidence?'

'These are speculations, of course.'

'Speculations?'

'These are speculations from the readings. There are people who attack and in their attacks they destroy.'

'And how about April 6 Movement, is it speculation or [do you have] information and evidence?'

'No, there is information.'

'Why are they left alone if you in fact have this evidence with you?'

'This becomes a warning,' said Kato.

'Should we have warnings for spies and agents, General?'

'Let's not consider them spies, but people who are paid.'

'People who are paid are spies, sir. Someone receiving financing from abroad and fulfilling foreign agendas is a spy,' said Abd al-Rahman. 'If we have evidence then why don't we begin investigations and apprehend suspects? A suspect is innocent until proven guilty. Calling people traitors and throwing around accusations is what divides people when you want people to be one.'

'We should not throw accusations and all that. We should unite during this period,' said Kato in evident contradiction.

'How can I unite with a traitor, sir? We have a group of nationalists and a group of traitors and spies that are paid to fulfil foreign agendas. How could you call for unity?' said Abd al-Rahman with an obvious hint of sarcasm.

'We invite every honourable Egyptian, if he is wrong, to return to his senses and fall into line,' answered Kato.

'The accusation of being a traitor is unforgiveable for every Egyptian in these circumstances,' said Abd al-Rahman. 'When a group is accused of being agents, it is important that these accusations be said clearly and seriously and that all legal measures be taken to determine if they are truly agents.'[29]

After the programme, Dream TV owner Ahmed Bahgat asked to see Abd al-Rahman in his office and fired her on the spot.[30]

8 July 2011: Friday of Justice and Purification

Under the banner of 'Revolution First', a protest rally was called for 8 July, the Friday of Justice and Purification. Crowds of protesters massed in major squares across Egypt to send a strong and clear message to the military rulers demanding public trials and justice for those who killed the revolution's martyrs, among them Hosni Mubarak and Interior Ministry officials, and a revamping of the police and security force; corruption investigations against government officials and former ruling party bosses; removing ineffective ministers from the Cabinet; combating poverty and having a livable minimum wage; and the end to military tribunals for civilians. With Mubarak quietly secluded in a hospital in Sharm al-Sheikh, the gains of the revolution were in doubt as reports surfaced of police officers intimidating the families of those who were murdered in the uprising.

Platforms were set up around Tahrir Square in a rally and sit-in to last until the revolution's demands were met.[31] Reminiscent of the 18 days of the uprising, the renewed protests in the searing summer heat sent a poignant message that Egyptians were impatient with the slow pace of change. There was a lot to be angry about. More than 840 protesters died during the revolution, yet only one police officer had been convicted – in absentia – of murder.[32] The trials of other officers (and the former interior minister) had witnessed postponements or acquittals, with defendants set free on bail.[33] A march of millions and a general strike were announced for 12 July and other street action mobilising workers and the poor were being organised.

Prime Minister Essam Sharaf on 10 July set out a series of promises after meeting with revolutionary youth: at least 1,400 Interior Ministry officers, including high-ranking officials linked with shooting protesters, would be laid off by 15 July; at least a third of the Cabinet ministers would be replaced; new governors would be appointed; and significant changes would be made to the colossal state media establishment. Despite the promise of reforms, the sit-ins continued. In a defensive and somewhat threatening posture, General Mohsen al-Fangary, assistant defence minister and a member of the Supreme Council of the Armed Forces, took to the airwaves, attacking those who spread rumours and false news that led to 'divisions and rebellion, the ruin of the nation, and plant doubt in [government] decisions, contributing to conflict and instability'. He called for 'the honourable citizens to stand against all the appearances that restrict the return of normal life to our great people and against the blinding rumours'.[34]

The statement by the military council indicated that they were concerned about the support the sustained protests had attained. 'The Supreme Council of the Armed Forces will not relinquish its role in managing the affairs of the state during this milestone period in Egypt's history,' underscored al-Fangary, adding that parliamentary elections would be held first, followed by the creation of a new constitution and the election of a new president.

The rally announced for Tuesday saw tens of thousands flood into Tahrir Square and major squares in Alexandria, Suez, and cities throughout the country. Speakers' platforms and tents were set up around Tahrir. An electricity pole was rigged to supply power. A satellite dish was stationed outside one of the tents. A loudspeaker blared the music and poetic rhymes of the counter-culture duo Ahmed Fouad Negm and the blind Sheikh Imam Eissa, including a 1968 song called 'Guevara maat' (Che Guevara Died), an ode to the Latin American revolutionary and a wake-up call against '*justice that is mute or a coward*'. Mosireen (which means 'we are determined'), an activist media collective, organised nightly video screenings of documentary footage of the revolution and resistance since 25 January. In videos and short films, Mosireen has chronicled the revolution, protest rallies, and citizen action, becoming an online source to counter the state media's narrative.[35]

Yet protesters had to engage in a public relations offensive, particularly with rumours and smear campaigns alleging that drugs and prostitution were rampant in the square. In marches and rallies, tens of thousands again took to the streets in the Friday of Last Warning on 15 July. A march that gathered a much smaller crowd was held in the district of Roxy in the upscale neighbourhood of Heliopolis to support the military and the Supreme Council of the Armed Forces.

In reaction to assertions by military council member Hassan al-Roweiny that activist youth groups were financed by foreigners and were dividing the people and the army, on the evening of 23 July protesters decided to march to the headquarters of the Supreme Council of the Armed Forces in the Cairo district of Abbasiya with a list of demands. Abbasiya Square descended into street fighting with area residents and vigilantes hurling rocks at protesters. The military and security forces unleashed tear gas and blocked off streets and escape routes.

The Tahrir Square sit-in lasted until 1 August, the first day of Ramadan, when the army ripped up tents, prevented photography, and forcibly ejected the remaining protesters after the political forces decided to call an end to the protest during the fasting month but pledged to return if the government and the military council stalled in fulfilling their promises. In response to protesters' demands, state television would broadcast the trial of Mubarak and his cohorts.

A script for arresting the revolution

Alaa Al Aswany's widely read 2 August column in *al-Masry al-youm* was titled 'How to End the Revolution in Six Steps.' 'Dear General, If you were surprised by the revolution, do not panic. Don't be afraid at the scene of millions of angry citizens,' he begins. 'Be calm, take a breath, and keep your temper. Know that the revolution is an exceptional state, a rare moment in humanity where people act with courage and are pushed to death in defence of their freedom and dignity.' People under the weight of oppression will accept injustices and the rule of a cabal, as witnessed by the infrequent number of revolutions in the course of human history, Al Aswany goes on to assure the military ruler. There is no need to fear the roar of the crowds, he asserts, since the masses are but animals gone wild, and can safely be returned to their cages if the following steps are followed:

'*First, celebrate the revolution and curse the ousted dictator*,' writes Al Aswany.

> *You should announce your complete condemnation of a bygone era. You are naturally sympathetic to the former dictator who was your partner and friend for decades but you should curse him in public and chant in favour of the revolution. People will believe you immediately. . . . People will believe you because they want you to be a supporter of the revolution, and they are likely to believe what they want to see happen.*

With song and praise lavished on the revolution, citizens will presume it has truly succeeded, Al Aswany argues, and therefore all events that occur will be inextricably linked in their minds to the revolution.

'*Second, preserve the old regime in totality*. Don't give in to the demands of the revolutionaries or change anything in the old regime,' is Al Aswany's second piece of advice to the General. 'In the beginning they will put intense pressure on you for change. Wait until it reaches a zenith then implement small, symbolic changes that do not touch the rubric of the old regime.' A few hated politicians will be chosen, arrested, and tried. The cases will drag on and be complicated by many procedural matters until they are nearly forgotten. The inmates will be secretly assured that they have nothing to worry about and their incarceration is merely to assuage public anger.

'Never abandon the members of the old regime. They are your loyal soldiers,' writes Al Aswany.

> *The corrupt judge whose sentences are dictated to him over the telephone, the prosecutor who plants evidence of the charge with his own hands upon your request, the famous announcer who receives daily instructions from the security before appearing on-camera, and the tormenting police officer who tortures and kills tens of people in defence of the regime – these models are rare. Never release them from your grasp.*

'*Third, let the conditions of the country deteriorate until they've reached rock bottom*' is Al Aswany's next piece of advice to the General. Here is where he describes the division of society into three: the beneficiaries of the regime, the revolutionaries who are under constant repression, and the passive majority of the population who are harmed by the regime but do not possess the courage to resist. 'Revolution occurred when revolutionaries triumphed in convincing ordinary people to join them. This is the weak point of the revolution where you should strike. Place pressure on ordinary people so they return to their spectator seats.' Factories will close. Irrigation water and fertiliser will be in short supply and crops will perish. Police will be absent and theft, assaults, and thuggery will proliferate. Security informers will infiltrate protests.

> *At the same time, your agents in the media must lead an organised campaign to terrorise the people. They should exaggerate the effects of the crisis and attribute all the problems to the revolution until the notion is rooted in people's minds that the country is closer to famine and chaos because of the revolution – the revolution alone.*

'*Fourth, strike at the unity of the revolutionaries and divide them*,' says Al Aswany. 'Know that the revolutionaries are your true enemies. They do not trust you and understand the dimensions of your plot from the start.' Split their ranks aided by security reports, he continues, and then invent a reason to have a referendum that will isolate the revolutionaries. Secretly ally with one party, he tells the General, advising him to take the side of the religious fascists against democratic forces: 'Fascists are excellent allies because they do not believe in democracy, but only use it to attain power. They feel that they alone possess the whole truth and despise those who disagree with them and do not recognise their rights. Fascists are like an organised army placed entirely at your disposal.' Meanwhile, the hostile rhetoric of this group will lead some to wonder whether removing the dictator was the right thing to do after all. The security services and old regime cohorts will hold rallies exalting the fallen leader. 'The number of revolutionaries will decrease and they will return to how they were before the revolution, a passionate few that people do not sympathise a whole lot with,' remarks Al Aswany.

'*Fifth, besiege the revolutionaries and tarnish their image*,' expresses Al Aswany in his column.

> *You must begin an extensive and organised campaign to discredit the revolutionaries. It is quite simple. You have your followers in the media, police, and the judiciary. It is easy to fabricate records, photographs, and documents confirming that these revolutionaries are traitors and agents of foreign powers, which led them to support the revolution.*

At the appropriate time, announce an investigation into the role of foreign financing in the revolution, suggests Al Aswany.

> *Ordinary people will be troubled and many of them will believe that these revolutionaries are just traitorous agents. You will have a long laugh as you see the revolutionary youth, who were seen a few weeks ago as national heroes, now pursued everywhere with jeers and accusations of being operatives.*

'*Sixth, strike your decisive blow*' is Al Aswany's final advice for the General. Economic and security conditions by this time would have completely deteriorated.

> *Tell the people that the crisis is severe and the situation will only worsen. Ask people to cease the demonstrations and sit-ins until the situation calms down and the wheels of production begin turning. Of course the revolutionaries will not stop demonstrating. They now know that you have deceived them and hijacked the revolution. They realise that you pretended to safeguard the revolution but in reality you contained and stalled it from achieving its objectives.*

The revolutionaries will take to the streets demanding the downfall of the General only to be attacked by the fascists, who desire power and have allied themselves with the General. They will be joined by ordinary people cursing the revolution, when at one time they were willing to die for it. No one will listen to the explanations of the revolutionaries. 'Only then will you have completed the task successfully,' concludes the novelist and political commentator, who saw it necessary to add this caveat: 'I got the idea for this article by reading the history of revolutions in the Republic of Comoros and therefore it is not at all related to what is happening now in Egypt.'[36]

Mubarak on trial

The third day of Ramadan, 3 August, marked the start of the former president's criminal court proceedings, presided over by Judge Ahmed Refaat. In white prison overalls, Hosni Mubarak was wheeled on a hospital stretcher into the iron cage of a police academy that had borne his name and where he had honoured the security forces in a speech two days before the start of revolution. It was Mubarak's first public appearance since his televised address a day before his downfall. Without mass protests that pressured the military council to succumb to the demands of the street, the former commander-in-chief might never have faced such open humiliation.

The only words Mubarak uttered were to acknowledge his presence to the judge – 'Sir, I am here' – and to state his plea – 'I categorically deny all the charges.' Mubarak along with his interior minister, Habib al-Adly, were charged with conspiring to kill protesters. Egypt's autocrat was also charged with selling natural gas to Israel at below market prices and profiteering from an influence-peddling land deal in the resort town of Sharm al-Sheikh. Beamed on state television from nine courtroom cameras, the trial became the passionate topic of conversation among Egyptians on the street, on television talk shows, and social media.

Media reports that had Mubarak in a coma, refusing to eat, and wallowing in depression proved false or pathetically exaggerated as he reclined in the courthouse cage, his hair dyed black, and hovered over by his two sons, who coyly obstructed the camera's view of their father. The front-page headline on the next day's *al-Ahram* declared: 'Present, Mubarak and His Regime in the Grips of Justice'. Above the masthead of the independent daily *al-Tahrir* read the Qur'anic verse: 'Say: "O God Master of the Kingdom, Thou givest the Kingdom to whom Thou wilt, and seizest the Kingdom from whom Thou wilt, Thou exaltest whom Thou wilt, and Thou abasest whom Thou wilt."'[37] The independent *al-Shuruk* carried a headline that was taken from another Qur'anic verse referring to pharaoh: 'That you may be a sign to those who come after you.'[38]

Commotion marked the courtroom drama as lawyers yelled to get the judge's attention. Outside, rock-throwing street battles raged between supporters and opponents of the beleaguered former ruler. The dictator chose as his representative the top lawyer Farid al-Deeb, who had defended the infamous Israeli spy Azzam Azzam as well as Egyptian property developer, parliamentarian, and ruling party heavyweight Hesham Talaat Mustafa, who arranged for an assassin to murder his former mistress, Lebanese pop singer Suzanne Tamim, in her Dubai apartment. Israeli Knesset member and former defence minister Benjamin Ben-Eliezer revealed to Army Radio that he had met with the deposed president in Sharm al-Sheikh months before and offered him asylum in Israel, an overture that was turned down.[39] As minister of national infrastructure, Ben-Eliezer facilitated the controversial gas export deal with Egypt in 2005.

The judge ordered Mubarak to be moved to a military hospital outside Cairo. The trial resumed on 15 August, giving Egyptians another look at their former ruler, transported on a stretcher, and his sons in an iron cage. At the end of the session, Judge Refaat ruled that the live broadcast of the trial would end 'to protect the public interest'. The military ruler Field Marshal Tantawi testified on 24 September in an hour-long closed court session, and did not directly implicate Mubarak in ordering the death of demonstrators. Tantawi's anti-climactic testimony led to suspicions that the military's top ranks would like to see their former commander-in-chief acquitted of the most damaging charges against him.

A transcript of Tantawi's testimony surfaced a day later when Mohamed ElGarhey, the news editor at the daily *al-Tahrir*, leaked the text via his Twitter account in violation of the court's gagging order.[40] Tantawi's laconic responses to 30 questions were immediately retweeted and posted on blogs, generating a flurry of commentary on the field marshal's curt and ambiguous answers.

> *Q: Did the former president of the republic, the accused Muhammad Hosni Mubarak, give orders to the interior minister, Habib al-Adly, for the police to use force against the demonstrators, including shotguns and firearms from 25 January to 28 January?*
>
> *Tantawi: I have no information about this and I do not believe this occurred.*

Tantawi also said he had no explanation for those protesters who were killed or injured. 'The possibilities are many but I do not have information with me.'

> *Q: Is the former president, the accused Muhammad Hosni Mubarak, directly or individually responsible along with whoever carried out the orders to deal with demonstrations, which were issued by him personally?*

Tantawi: If he issued this order – the use of firepower – I believe the responsibility is shared. I do not know if he gave this order or not.

Tantawi was asked if the interior minister could make decisions outside normal protocol without consulting the president. 'I don't know what happened but I think that the interior minister told him or maybe not. I don't know,' responded Tantawi when asked if Mubarak was kept in the dark about the tactics of security forces.

Q: Some generals say that they were asked to forcefully break up the protests. Were the armed forces requested to do that?
Tantawi: I have said in the Police Academy graduation and I say this for history: No one from the armed forces will fire on the people.

State television on 26 September showed Tantawi forgoing his military attire and strolling in the streets of downtown Cairo in a suit, shaking hands and exchanging greetings with shop owners and pedestrians. The move may have been intended to shore up his support by connecting him with the people on the street. *Al-Ahram* journalist Gamal Zayda, speaking on the state television programme *Mubashir min Masr* (Live from Egypt), where the footage was broadcast, articulated that the field marshal would be a suitable candidate for president. 'He has removed his military attire and presented himself to Egyptian citizens and we see on the television screen how people have surrounded him,' he enthused. 'This man is a leader and has proved an ability and striking calmness in managing the transition period.' The host of the programme went on to say that this 'scoop' shows everyone that state television has the ability to surpass private satellite channels.[41] Others saw this treatment by state media as just another indication that it remains enthralled by and subservient to the men in power.

The military council and the Cabinet decided to halt the issuing of new permits to satellite channels on 9 September 2011 and information minister Osama Heikal vowed to clamp down on stations that endanger the safety and security of the nation.[42] On 11 September, authorities raided the offices of Al Jazeera Live Egypt, which began transmission after Mubarak's downfall, confiscated equipment, arrested an employee, and closed the channel because it was broadcasting without a licence. The channel's live programming from Egypt included in-depth interviews, extensive coverage and commentary of Mubarak's trial, and live broadcasts of protests, such as the fervid demonstrations outside the Israeli Embassy.

It was also on 9 September that protesters marched with picks and hammers to demolish a concrete wall erected by the military as a protective barrier for the embassy, which occupied the top floors of a high-rise by the Nile. A group of demonstrators scaled the building to tear down the Israeli flag and ransack an office, hurling documents onto the street. The confrontation by military and security forces with protesters was transmitted on Al Jazeera Live Egypt. The network also broadcast rallies outside the Israeli Embassy when in the early hours of 21 August protester-cum-hero Ahmed al-Shahat took down the Israeli flag and raised the Egyptian flag in its place as an ecstatic crowd cheered. Three days earlier, Israeli troops had crossed the border into Egypt, shooting and killing half a dozen border guards following a terrorist attack in southern Israel that left eight Israelis dead. The offices of Al Jazeera Live Egypt were again raided on 29 September. The crackdown was an attempt to avoid the scrutiny of live, round-the-clock coverage, particularly during upcoming parliamentary elections – conducted under the ongoing state of emergency law and without international supervision.[43]

In arguments to the court, Mubarak's defence team led by the cigar-smoking Farid al-Deeb alleged that it was in fact commandos from Iran, Hamas, and Hezbollah that were behind the killing of protesters during the revolution. To back up his claims, he cited articles in the state-owned *al-Akhbar* and the testimony of Omar Soliman. He added that the defendant he called 'President Mubarak' had not given orders to kill 'honourable citizens' and had every intention of meeting their demands within the framework of the constitution. As for the death of protesters, it was the armed forces that should be held accountable, posited al-Deeb, since they had been in charge on the ground since 28 January 2011. Al-Deeb told the court that his client was still the president of Egypt and had only transferred powers of managing the affairs of state to the Supreme Council of the Armed Forces, but had not submitted a written resignation to the People's Assembly abdicating the presidency. Mubarak, al-Deeb argued, remained the president even after his term expired in September since no head of state had been elected.

Incitement and state media

On 30 September 2011, St George Coptic Orthodox Church in the village of al-Marinab, near the town of Edfu in the southern governorate of Aswan, was set on fire and destroyed. Obtaining the required permits, church officials had begun renovating and expanding the church built in 1940. Local hardline Salafi adherents objected to the presence of the high steeple, domes, and crosses and attacked the church following a mosque imam's incendiary sermon that Friday. Three homes belonging to Coptic families were destroyed in the rampage. In the hours when the church in al-Marinab was being pillaged, no military or police forces intervened. In television interviews by telephone, the governor of Aswan, Mustafa al-Sayid, played down the destruction of the Christian house of worship, stated there was no church in the village to begin with, but a guesthouse and it was demolished by Muslim villagers because it was being built in violation of the permit requirements.[44]

On 9 October 2011, after more than a week in which the grievances of the Coptic community were not addressed, protest marches and rallies were organised in cities across Egypt. The demands included rebuilding the church in al-Marinab and compensation for the damage to property belonging to Christian families, the resignation of Aswan's governor, and a unified law for the construction of mosques and churches. Meeting in front of the state television and radio building, otherwise known as Maspero, the protest gathered men, women, and children.

Live coverage of the events showed armoured military vehicles speeding along Corniche al-Nil Street in front of the television and radio building in an attempt to clear the crowds, running over protesters and crushing some of them to death.[45] An eyewitness account by journalist and blogger Sarah Carr, who marched with protesters from the working-class district of Shubra, described the scene:

> *Two armored personnel carriers (APCs) began driving at frightening speed through protesters, who threw themselves out of its path. A soldier on top of each vehicle manned a gun, and spun it wildly, apparently shooting at random although the screams made it difficult to discern exactly where the sound of gunfire was coming from. . . .*
>
> *And then it happened: an APC mounted the island in the middle of the road, like a maddened animal on a rampage. I saw a group of people disappear, sucked underneath it. . . .*

> *The Coptic Hospital tried its best to deal with the sudden influx of casualties. Its floors were sticky with blood and there was barely room to move among the wounded, the worried and the inconsolable. . . .*
>
> *Even while the wounded were still being brought in, state TV was reporting that Christian protesters stole weapons from the army and killed soldiers, and that the busy foreign hands are back again, still trying to destabilize Egypt.*[46]

Unconcerned with reporting the whole story, state television was accused of fuelling the violence. Newscaster Rasha Magdy narrated events for television audiences in a condemnatory tone:

> *Until now there are three martyrs and more than 20 injured and they are all army soldiers. And by who's hand? Not the hand of Israel or an enemy, but from a group of countrymen. The army that is being attacked now is the one that stood by the revolution. The army is the one that protected the revolution, and refused to fire one shot on any of its citizens. Today we find those who fire bullets at the sons of the army. Any group in Egyptian society, whatever its demands – legal, lawful, the construction of a building – does this deserve completely burning a nation?*[47]

Magdy stated that Coptic protesters, throwing rocks and Molotov cocktails, fired on army personnel assigned to guard the television and radio building. The state media's disinformation campaign could have been an attempt at damage control, spin in favour of the military authority, or defensiveness at a crisis situation that could have been better managed from the start. But like the days of revolution it painted a picture of an imagined reality palatable to those who wanted to believe it. Flashing at the bottom of the screen was the declaration: 'Breaking: Three martyrs and a hundred injured from the army and security forces after they were fired on by Coptic protesters in front of the Maspero building.' The military did not report or acknowledge whether soldiers were in fact killed.

Protesters, including the injured, sought refuge in surrounding buildings. Army personnel forced their way into the eleventh-floor offices of the US government-funded Al Hurra news channel in an apparent search for fleeing protesters. Amr Khalil, the Egyptian presenter of *Birnamig al-youm* (The Today Show) was live on air, the images beamed on the screen were taken from state television as he conducted telephone interviews. Behind the presenter was the avenue where the confrontation raged, the televised images punctuated with the sound of gunfire and ambulance sirens. 'I am on the air. Take your time, take your time,' said Khalil addressing army personnel. 'A soldier from the armed forces is inside the building with his handgun. He entered the studio as I was on the air,' the news presenter explained to viewers.

'Search all you want. Take your time,' he told a howling soldier situated off-camera. 'We are with you.' Soldiers searching the offices of the station ordered live transmission to end just after 8 pm.[48] The broadcast signal of the channel 25 was also taken off the air shortly after 8 pm when soldiers and security officers stormed the station's studios, broke broadcast equipment, and demanded to see the identification cards of employees to identify if any of them were Christian.

'Once again state media, which is owned by the people, has failed in meeting their aspirations to know the truth – simply to know the truth,' said Yosri Fouda on his late-night current affairs show *Akhir kalam* (Last Words) on ONtv the day after the horrific deaths at Maspero. 'Still, Egyptian television tries to convince us that what we see in reality isn't exactly what we see.' The breaking news bar announcing the death of three army and security officers appeared for hours as viewers watched the unfolding events, he added. 'How did state television know with such speed that they were martyred by gunfire? And how did they know who fired the shots – Coptic protesters?' An armed forces source told *Last Words* in a statement Fouda read on the air, 'The military institution by its nature operates in secrecy and does not announce the number of causalities during crises so as not to affect the morale of conscripts and officers and it will announce the correct number at an appropriate time.'

The tragic events of 9 October were not only marred by state television's deceitful coverage, but also in its call for 'noble' Egyptians to come to the streets and *defend the army*. Deepening sectarian fissures, that call was answered by citizens wielding pipes, machetes, and weapons from the impoverished neighbourhood of Bulaq adjacent to Maspero, described Hossam Bahgat, founder and director of the human rights advocacy group Egyptian Initiative for Personal Rights and a witness to the events, on the programme *Last Words*. Bahgat labelled 'criminal' the actions of state television.

> *The first question that should be answered is what is the name and rank of the officers or soldiers that were driving the personnel carriers*

> *that we saw with our own eyes running over protesters and whose crushed bodies we saw in the morgue. I want the name and rank of the officers that were responsible for the group of military police in front of Maspero. I want the name and rank of the officer who issued the order to use violence to clear these gatherings. And I want the name and job titles of everyone who was in the newsroom in Egyptian television at the time they took the decision, which was not spontaneous, that there be one message told to people in their homes, and that is: Save Egypt's patriotic army, which is being attacked by Copts, who are of course funded by America.*[49]

Twenty-seven deaths were attributed to the events at Maspero, among them revolutionary activist Mina Danial. Pictures of other victims, shot, bludgeoned, or crushed beneath the wheels of an army vehicle would appear on social media and broadcast on Coptic satellite channels.[50] A widely circulated photo was of Vivian Magdy crying as she clutched the hand of her fiancé Michael Masaad on the floor of the morgue of the Coptic Hospital. Other bodies, victims of the Maspero massacre, surround them. On the ONtv programme *Manshet* (Headlines) two days later, Vivian emotionally described how a personnel carrier zigzagging through the streets pulled Michael beneath its wheels, crushed his leg, and flung him onto the pavement, smashing his skull. 'Then a soldier with a red beret came to me, yelling and hitting me. When he starting hitting him [Michael], I said, "He is not breathing" and threw my body over his. He [the soldier] hit me on the back with a baton. I said, "Someone call an ambulance!" He hurled curses at me, curses I cannot say, and said "You infidel, what brought you here?"'[51]

It seemed obvious the military had broken a sacred vow never to aim fire on its own citizens. Yet at a press conference on 12 October, a whole two days after the deaths at Maspero, the military stuck to its line that it did not fire live ammunition, no protesters were run over by military vehicles, and no force was used. To substantiate their claims they showed video footage of personnel carriers swerving to avoid protesters and unidentified persons vandalising army property. 'This cannot be blamed on the Egyptian Armed Forces. It can be blamed on anyone else. It cannot be written in history that we crushed someone, even in confrontations with the enemy,' said assistant defence minister General Adel Emara.[52] The generals repeated the mantra that army personnel have never and would never open fire on protesters. Instead the crowd was armed and shot at soldiers, and army vehicles were stolen and commandeered to strike protesters, they insinuated.

Facing off against thousands of unruly protesters, terrified young conscripts acted in self-defence, explained Emara. Notwithstanding, General Mahmoud Hegazy added, the soldiers exercised restraint: 'The weapons of the armed forces are used for killing and not security. If the weapons were used, or we allowed their use, the results would have been catastrophic. But that did not happen.' Showing footage of a Coptic priest declaring that the march would end inside the Maspero building, Emara remarked that it was a clear example of incitement.

Hegazy, a member of the council that has ruled since Mubarak was deposed, said that soldiers were martyred with live ammunition. The names and exact number were not disclosed citing military protocol. (The names of border guards killed by Israeli fire weeks earlier were reported.) The military's whitewashing of the deaths at Maspero aided those who wanted to believe that their military, a sanctified institution akin to Mubarak and his predecessors in their heyday, could do no wrong, and that protesters or rogue elements were mainly at fault. For everyone else, including the Coptic community, it was an embellished fabrication at best and an utter betrayal at worst.

Generals meet the press

In homes, shops, and cafés, Egyptians tuned to *Ten at Night* during the late hours on 19 October, staying up until the show ended at 1:25 am. In a widely watched, nearly three-hour-long interview broadcast simultaneously on Dream 2 and al-Tahrir, two members of the ruling Supreme Council of the Armed Forces, Generals Mahmoud Hegazy and Muhammad al-Assar, were questioned by stalwart veteran journalists Mona al-Shazly and Ibrahim Eissa.[53]

Eissa, ever the firebrand, began the programme by introducing his guests seated around a rectangular table and joking, 'Do you intend to stay long? I don't mean on the programme but generally, in the military council and in managing the country.' A more serious al-Assar replied, 'We're staying for a while.'

Eissa's first line of inquiry centred on the contentious events at Maspero. 'Those who carried out this incident seek evil for the nation, knowing well that two things would harm Egypt: subversion dividing the military and the people, and sectarian strife. Whoever masterminded this incident struck with both stones,' said al-Assar, avoiding allegations directed against Egypt's Coptic Christians.

Eissa brought up the army assault on protesters and the infamous images of armoured personnel carriers crushing demonstrators. Al-Assar referred to the press conference given days earlier where videos were shown to prove the military's narrative on the course of events, adding, 'The goal was not to toss responsibility on the Copts but to confirm that the armed forces were targeted in this incident, like the Copts.'

Hegazy underscored that an independent committee was investigating the events of Maspero. 'What is meant by "independent"?' asked al-Shazly. 'Is there a committee that will find the army at fault?'

'Doesn't the presence of victims, regardless of the reasons, mean that the army is at fault?' added Eissa.

'We, as a people and a nation, awaited and still await the military council to deal with the situation as a main political player. Everything that you said in the press conference and now, no one can question because neither Mr Ibrahim Eissa nor I are members of the investigative committee. We saw and heard, but we do not have the truth,' said al-Shazly, echoing the sentiment that the military rulers have not been particularly transparent in their relations with the public. 'The military council is not using political tools at all. From the events of Maspero until now, no political steps were taken, such as a resignation or an apology,' she said.

'You want decisions before the results of the investigations are known,' replied al-Assar defensively. 'After the results of an investigation are out, there will definitely be decisions taken.'[54]

'We don't know the results of the investigation of events at the Israeli Embassy until now,' interjected Eissa. 'I understood from Mona's question, it is not the legal handling, but the political handling.'

Dressed in olive green military apparel, their lapels decorated with a gold eagle and crossed swords, the generals stuck to their script: Egyptians needed to get back to work and rebuild the country instead of engaging in strikes and sit-ins; the security situation and the economic grievances would take time to correct and would not be solved during the transition period; and the military council was committed to handing over power to an elected civilian government. The generals defended the interim Cabinet of Prime Minister Essam Sharaf, which had all too often been seen as acting under the directions of the military council. Eissa described the government as being 'in a state of permanent failure'.

'We don't understand, is the military council attached to a weak Cabinet, or defending it?' asked al-Shazly.

'Or do they desire a weak Cabinet?' added Eissa.

The protests and sit-ins are negatively affecting the country, maintained the generals, displacing the blame for a weakened economy and an unstable security situation. The budget of the country does not allow the state to fulfil their demands. The solution, they said, was for people to remain calm and allow the wheels of production to turn. Al-Shazly commented:

> *General, I feel as if we are reinventing the wheel. It's as if the messages are direct, from the Supreme Council to citizens. And they are truth. We as the media and citizens, everyone should go to work, everyone should protect the public interest. In the end, countries are not run by consciousness or individual initiatives. There is a government that says, this is the plan and this is what we will do. Firstly, to be explicit, and that has not happened. And second, to implement, and that has not happened. Thirdly, if you erred, to apologise, and that has not happened. I, as a citizen, do not understand. Either the military council in taking on more than it can handle or it is separated from the people and sees that the government's treatment is good and it's the people that are wrong.*

Ten at Night, hosted by Mona al-Shazly and Ibrahim Eissa, delivered the kind of grilling by the media of members of the ruling military council that the unelected decision-makers of Egypt's transition phase had seldom experienced.

The presenters read questions and criticisms submitted on Facebook from viewers that reflected public perceptions of an aloof and unresponsive ruling council: 'Why is it that the army and army commanders are not able to arrest a few thugs in the streets for eight months, or does the presence of thugs in the streets meet their whims?' 'Why haven't the demands of the revolution been met until now? Is it slowness or complicity [with the former regime]?' 'Security, security, and security. If you want production, then the government has to establish security.'

'People are saying this on shows, they say it on Facebook, Twitter, and among themselves. They want to make sure that their sentiments have reached you,' al-Shazly told the generals. The generals insisted that, while they have their critics, they enjoy the support of a majority of Egyptians.

During the course of the programme, the generals glanced at their papers and jotted down notes in a challenging interview for two of the military council's decision-makers. Field Marshal Muhammad Hussein Tantawi has made no similar broadcast interviews. When in power, Mubarak, too, rarely gave media interviews.

'We will not repeat the mistakes of the previous regime and ignore those who oppose,' said al-Assar.

Eissa interrupted with, 'They've increased'.

'We have a connection with all the political powers, evidenced by the fact that we chose your programme. We chose the people who object the most and said we will come on with them,' said al-Assar. 'We are going in the right direction and most of the people are satisfied with us. We want the people who are not satisfied to be satisfied because it is their right to have an explanation.'

Eissa asked how he knew that the people were satisfied. 'From the opinion polls that come out, which are conducted by respectable foreign and Egyptian organisations,' replied al-Assar, citing no specific polling data to confirm the assertion. 'We do not have any desire to remain in power,' he continued. 'But we see this as a nationalist duty we must fulfil. There is no alternative to the council. Those who call for the downfall of the council are calling for the downfall of the country. I believe that most Egyptians are against these people.'

The generals outlined the timetable for the transfer to civilian rule. Following the end of parliamentary elections in March 2012, it would take up to six months to select members of a committee to draft a constitution and another six months to devise a new constitution that would be voted on in a national referendum. Presidential elections would not come before the summer of 2013, keeping the military council in power and holding off transfer to civilian rule at least two and a half years after revolution.

'We made a revolution and overthrew everything we wanted to overthrow,' said Hegazy, a way of stating that the problem was really with those clamorous voices stirring up trouble. 'I believe that a section of the people need a revolution within themselves.' He went on to say that the army and the military council had taken decisions that saved Egypt from peril.

'We created a revolution and you said you will fulfil my demands,' Eissa told Hegazy, who was urging that decision-makers be left to make the ultimate choices for the benefit of the nation. 'General, do you know that famous phrase, "There are three ways to remedy a situation: the right way, the wrong way, and the army way." In a revolution, there are right ways and wrong ways. The way of the army is something else.'

'This is a revolution of the people, of different spectra and categories, including the armed forces,' responded Hegazy.

'Are you saying that the armed forces participated in the revolution with us?' asked Eissa.

'It was part of the revolution and whoever denies this is denying a big reality,' answered Hegazy.

'I am asking how it participated in the revolution,' said Eissa.

'When the army realised that these are the demands of the people, it sided with the people, who own the armed forces, and not with any other side,' said Hegazy. 'An error in estimating the situation could have resulted in consequences that could have cost the country a lot.'

Eissa argued that Field Marshal Tantawi testified at Mubarak's trial that the army was not asked to fire on protesters, so how could the military's role have been so pivotal in the revolution? Hegazy claimed that the army had announced that citizens had the right to protest, they had legitimate demands, and it would not fire on demonstrators.

'Has the Supreme Council of the Armed Forces asked the former president to step down?' asked Eissa.

'We always say that the policy of the armed forces – and this is part of its advancement – is that it respects legality and will not overthrow the regime, or whenever the minister of defence does not like a president, he would overthrow him,' said Hegazy.

'When there are suggestions, voices, or even opposition, it most often means that these are efforts and attempts at collective thinking,' al-Shazly advised the generals shortly before the close of the programme. 'We request the armed forces to stay in the same pattern, to stand at a level ground with all, recognising that criticism is also an effort to present the best for Egypt and it is not a position taken or a quarrel against a great army or the Supreme Council of the Armed Forces, which everyone tries to participate in decisions with.'

'We have collected statistics on the talk shows. There are 25 talk shows. In one particular day this month, there were 12 programmes criticising the Supreme Council of the Armed Forces,' said al-Assar.

'There were 13 that were not criticising,' Eissa noted.

'We welcome the criticism as long as the criticism is within the boundaries of what is permitted,' said al-Assar.

'There are newspapers in which all they do is praise the military council,' said al-Shazly.

'What bothers us is one thing: overreaching, accusations, injury. These are not themes the military institution can accept,' said al-Assar. 'We welcome the criticism. We have a connection to all the political powers. We are on a level ground with all. Our interest is to realise the goal that we promised the people.'

Eissa ended the episode of *Ten at Night* by telling viewers that the revolution would have truly succeeded when a civilian government was elected in free and fair elections.

Military prosecution of civilians

On 30 October 2011, activist, blogger, and software developer Alaa Abd El Fattah was ordered held by military prosecutors in detention for 15 days in connection with the investigation into the deaths at Maspero three weeks earlier. A factor that led to him being summoned for questioning was an opinion piece he wrote in the daily *al-Shuruk*. In the article Abd El Fattah described how he lobbied to make sure that the state coroner's office performed proper autopsies that would aid future legal cases and ensure that victims at Maspero were recognised as martyrs. 'Two days we spent in the morgue. Two days with bodies struggling to hold on to the title of "martyr." Struggling against the entire Mubarak regime – not just the Mubarak military that crushed them, or the Mubarak media that withdrew the title of martyr and labelled them thugs, or the Mubarak prosecution that skirted the search for their rights,' he wrote.

> *The bodies struggled to hold on to the glory of martyrdom in the morgue of an impoverished public hospital lacking facilities. They struggled against the Mubarak-era myth that an autopsy violates the sanctity of the deceased and is not a victory for their rights. They struggled against the sway of the sultan's religious scholars and priests who say that that the seeker of justice in life relinquishes it in the afterlife. They struggled against the sectarianism of Mubarak that made the poor see enemies in others who are poor like them instead of those who rob their piece of bread.*[55]

Abd El Fattah was accused of inciting violence, attacking military personnel, stealing army weapons, vandalising army property, and unlawful assembly. Believing that the army was implicated in the crimes at Maspero, Abd El Fattah refused to answer questions from military prosecutors, who issued a list of 'suspects' in the Maspero massacre that included the deceased 20-year-old activist Mina Danial.

In the evening broadcast of *Fi-l-midan* (In the Square) on al-Tahrir TV, Ibrahim Eissa highlighted the genuine contradiction between the ruling military council announcing that civilians would not be referred to military prosecution or stand trial before military courts, and the jailing of Alaa Abd El Fattah. 'The military council is bleeding out the relations it has with the revolution generation and revolutionary youth, when those youth sharply criticise military trials and the actions of the military police. This is a generation that rejects patriarchal power and does not want to deal with the military council as if commandments from a father,' said Eissa.[56]

In a letter from a six-by-twelve-foot cell shared with eight other men, Abd El Fatah wrote about the return to Mubarak's jails, where he had been incarcerated five years earlier for activism in support of an independent judiciary. Fellow inmates were unimpressed with the accomplishments of the nine-month-old uprising. 'As soon as they learned I was one of the "young people of the revolution" they started to curse out the revolution and how it had failed to clean up the ministry of the interior. I spend my first two days listening to stories of torture at the hands of a police force that insists on not being reformed; that takes out its defeat on the bodies of the poor and the helpless.' Then there is the martyr Mina Danial, who along with Abd El Fattah is 'accused of instigation' by the military rulers. 'They must be the first who murder a man and not only walk in his funeral but spit on his body and accuse it of a crime.'[57]

It was not until fierce street battles in November that claimed the lives of more than 50 protesters, a sequel to the events of Maspero, that the military ruler saw fit to transfer the case of Alaa Abd El Fattah to civilian courts, albeit under State Security prosecution, a separate track of justice created by emergency law. The case later went to an independent investigation judge and charges of unlawful assembly and inciting violence were dropped.

Released on 25 December after nearly two months in prison, Abd El Fattah was greeted with excitement by family, supporters, and his 19-day-old newborn son Khaled, named after the martyr Khaled Said. Abd El Fattah still faced trial in connection with the Maspero massacre and was barred from travelling abroad. Abd El Fattah's case embodied the eroding trust in the military council, particularly in its resort to military justice when it was obvious that the military and not Abd El Fattah were responsible for the murders at Maspero.

A statement for a free media

Articulate and mild-mannered, Yosri Fouda has been one of the Egyptian media's most credible voices. This was most evident during the revolution when his late-night current affairs programme *Last Words* on ONtv gave a trustworthy representation of developments on the street, as other satellite broadcasters were propping the regime. On 20 October 2011, Fouda tweeted that the programme for that day's show would be on reaction to the death of Libya's Muammar al-Qaddafi and an analysis of statements by military council generals given during press conferences and on the previous day's *Ten at Night*. Alaa Al Aswany, Ibrahim Eissa, and Yasser Rizk, a journalist with close ties to the military council, were scheduled to be on *Last Words* with Fouda. His following tweet stated that he would not be appearing on that night's show and would be issuing an announcement the following day.

'There are three things I always try to keep in mind: my conscience before God, my duty towards the nation, and my concern for the values of the profession,' Fouda began his statement, posted on his Facebook page, in which he disclosed that he had decided to suspend his programme. 'It is no secret that much of the pre-revolution mentality is still clearly imposed on us as it had been before, if not worse.' The freedom of the journalism profession in Egypt was gradually deteriorating, maintained Fouda, noting how the media denied existing realities and invented parallel truths.

Concluding that he did not want to be part of a crumbling media establishment, Fouda argued that it had become apparent that 'there are intense efforts to maintain the essence of the regime'. Since Mubarak's overthrow by popular protests, pressures have been placed on those who stand by the goals of the revolution, 'convincing them to voluntarily censor what cannot be silenced or embellished'. While committed to protecting press freedom, 'this is my way of self-censorship: to say what is good or to be silent', stated Fouda.[58]

When General Ismail Etman, called Reem Magued's programme *Our Country . . . in Egyptian* and cajoled, 'Come back, Yosri. We need you,'

Fouda could not help but smile, feeling as if he were some lost child, he later wrote. 'The experience of freedom is, in a sense, like death. Yes, you can visit death, but you cannot go back,' he explained. 'There are limits to self-censorship if one is to respect himself, his audience, his profession, and his nation.'[59]

Fouda's stance was put in sharper focus in Alaa Al Aswany's column in the daily *al-Masry al-youm*. Al Aswany was preparing to go to the studio for the broadcast of *Last Words* when Fouda called him to tell him that the episode had been cancelled and invited him for a chat. 'There were pressures that led to the cancellation of the programme,' Fouda told the author. 'As for me, I have decided to end the programme. I respect only my conscience in my work and I refuse to work according to the instructions of any side, whatever it is.' Al Aswany's column berated the ruling body for 'narrowing serious and sincere criticism'.[60] The writer said he was ready to engage in an on-air discussion with members of the military council, an offer that was not accepted. Yosri Fouda returned to the airwaves after a three-week hiatus and two weeks before parliamentary elections, with in-studio guests Alaa Al Aswany and Ibrahim Eissa. 'This is not a reason for pessimism,' he began his introduction of *Last Words*, 'because the destiny of Egypt is in the hands of the people for the first time in a long time.'[61]

4

Revolutionaries versus the Generals

> *The dictum that truth always triumphs over persecution is one of those pleasant falsehoods which men repeat after one another till they pass into commonplaces, but which all experience refutes. . . . Men are not more zealous for truth than they often are for error, and a sufficient application of legal or even of social penalties will generally succeed in stopping the propagation of either.*
>
> (John Stuart Mill, *On Liberty*[1])

Under decades of authoritarian rule, Egyptians lacked a sense of ownership. 'All of a sudden we are talking about Egypt as if it is ours and that it is our right to think of our future,' described novelist Miral al-Tahawy. 'What happened after 25 January was not a huge change in the regime but a huge change in people's speech.'[2] Ten months since Mubarak's downfall, sentiments among Egyptians went from optimism to sheer frustration as the military council ruling the country made one purposeful misstep after another: jailing activists and prosecuting them in military tribunals; clamping down on the press; stalling in handing power to a civilian government; allowing deteriorating security to erode the confidence of Egyptians in the goals of the revolution; failing to reorganise the security apparatus; carving out special dispensation for the military within a state polity; and watching as Egyptians died and were maimed by security forces and military police. On 19 November 2011 Egyptians drew the line.

Early that Saturday morning security forces violently broke up a sit-in of 150 to 200 protesters; among them were families of the revolution's martyrs and those injured during the uprising. On previous occasions security and military police cleared Tahrir Square with crude force. But on this morning things were different. Demonstrators returned, escalating into a confrontation that only ceased in Tahrir five days later. Armed with shotguns, chemical gas, rubber bullets, and live ammunition, security forces and the army waged an assault to claim and reclaim the square as determined protesters rallied to hold on to ground that was the symbol of revolution. It came at a heavy price: 51 dead and thousands injured, many losing their sight. The assault ignited protests and open-ended sit-ins across Egypt. Among revolutionaries, one demand crystallised: Tantawi's downfall and immediate handover of power to a civilian government.

Tahrir Square changed hands a few times between protesters and military and security officers. By nightfall on the first day, five protesters were reported dead in Cairo, Alexandria, and Suez, with demonstrations raging in Upper Egypt and the Nile Delta towns of al-Mahalla and Mansoura. As the casualties mounted, state news reports repeated the Interior Ministry line that security officers were using the utmost restraint.

Police and military charged Tahrir on the afternoon of 20 November, burning tents, blankets, and a motorcycle – used to ferry the wounded to field hospitals. Several men were piled in the street, either unconscious or dead. An officer dragged a body to a heap of garbage, a gruesome scene captured on video.[3] Other images and videos caught the public's attention: protesters beaten with sticks by soldiers and security forces,[4] a security officer being congratulated by colleagues for firing his shotgun to strike the eyes of a protester,[5] and heartbreaking images of those who had fallen.[6]

Then there was the authorities' incessant and absurd lying: live ammunition, shotguns, and toxic tear gas were not used; the army and security forces do not have shotguns or even sticks and protesters are armed with handguns and shotguns; all the security forces were trying to do was protect the Interior Ministry building; some 'third party' or 'invisible hand' was responsible; we commend the security forces on their 'restraint'; the people in Tahrir Square do not represent all Egyptians.

For days, round-the-clock battles continued between rock-throwing protesters and army and security forces. On the night of 21 November, the military council accepted the resignation of the government of Essam Sharaf. A rally was organised in Tahrir Square on 22 November. Tens of thousands packed the square as the fighting in side streets was in full swing. Field hospitals were receiving more injured patients carried from the conflict zone. An odd normality imbued the square amid the roar of motorcycles transporting the injured and the wailing of ambulance sirens. A huge banner was unfurled on a building around the square as crowds cheered. It read: 'The people have decided the handover of power is now!'

Protesters spent nights on the cold pavement of Tahrir Square, where the air was thick with poisonous gases. Vinegar proved to be an effective antidote to the tear gas used back in January, but the security forces' new stock was a more lethal variety that led to numerous deaths by asphyxiation. Security forces launched a canister at the field hospital closest to the heaviest fighting on Muhammad Mahmoud Street, claiming the life of a young woman doctor. Nothing has changed except, as protesters described with wry humour, the type of chemical agents used against civilians.

On 22 November, Tantawi, in a cap and military attire, made his first speech to Egyptians, standing behind a podium, hands folded, reading from a teleprompter. He underscored that the military has 'not fired a shot at the chest of an Egyptian citizen', did not covet the seat of power, and blamed the unrest on elements that seek the 'downfall of the Egyptian state'. Tantawi ended his address with cautious yet foreboding words: 'We are completely ready to hand over responsibility right away and return to our original purpose in defending the nation, if the people so desire, through a popular referendum if deemed necessary.'[7] The military council would allow the violence to continue days away from People's Assembly elections beginning on 28 November.[8]

In a telephone interview on al-Hayat satellite channel, General Mansour al-Essawy, the interior minister, denied that the sit-in was broken up with force or that journalists were targeted. Only tear gas was used when protesters approached the Interior Ministry building, he claimed, despite ample evidence to the contrary.[9] 'We did not fire one bullet and no one was injured in the area around the ministry, not with ammunition, or buckshot, or rubber bullets.' At the time the interview was conducted 33 protesters had lost their lives. When asked who was killing and injuring them, al-Essawy asserted that it was 'people on the rooftops of buildings'. When asked who they were, the interior minister replied, 'Thugs and drug dealers – lots of people. And these buildings are not currently under our control because it is in the area that is under the control of revolutionary youth.'[10] It was official policy to admit to no wrongdoing, deny basic facts, and make unsubstantiated counter-accusations.

A concession made by the military council was to expedite the handover to civilian rule, projected to be in mid-2013, to take place on 30 June 2012. Two days before the start of parliamentary elections, a young protester at a sit-in outside the Cabinet against newly appointed Prime Minister Kamal al-Ganzoury – a 78-year-old who served as prime minister under Mubarak from 1996 to 1999 – was reportedly crushed to death by a police vehicle.

In an interview on the programme *Masr taqarar* (Egypt Decides), General Mamdouh Shaheen of the Supreme Council of the Armed Forces claimed that there was overwhelming support for the council's handling of the transition phase. If the military council left it would be 'a betrayal to the country,' he added.

'Do you feel trust in the Supreme Council is receding a bit?' presenter Mahmoud Muslim asked.

'That could be the opinion of some but I can tell you that 90%, and I confirm this, 90% are with the Supreme Council.'

'Ninety per cent?' asked Muslim.

'At least,' said Shaheen.

'Don't you think that is a high percentage?'

'No, it's not a high percentage or anything.'

'Ninety per cent are in favour of stability, not with . . .' ventured Muslim sceptically.

'They're with the Supreme Council because the Supreme Council is what will realise stability.'

'Don't you feel your prestige was shaken a bit?' suggested Muslim.

'No, no, no, the prestige of the armed forces can never be shaken,' Shaheen affirmed.[11]

The editor and the *Independent*

Magdy al-Gallad, editor-in-chief of *al-Masry al-youm*, put an end to the publishing and distribution of the second print edition of the English-language weekly *Egypt Independent*, due out on 1 December 2011, because of an opinion column he disapproved of. Titled 'Is Tantawi reading the public's pulse correctly?' military historian Robert Springborg, who taught at the Department of National Security Affairs at the Naval Postgraduate School in California, discussed Tantawi's apparent willingness to hold a referendum on the military's immediate transfer of power. 'This was intended to be a threat to his civilian challengers,' Springborg wrote. 'Reported to be a keen follower of public opinion polls, the Field Marshal and his advisers no doubt calculated that in any such referendum, the majority of voters would support military over civilian rule.'

Springborg outlined two problems with a potential referendum. The first is that voters may distinguish between the Supreme Council, whose performance they might not find commendable, and the institution of military. 'They may see no contradiction in continuing to hold the military in high esteem while blaming the SCAF for the failures of the revolution,' he argued, using the acronym for the infamous council of generals.

> *The second problem is more profound and threatening to the SCAF, namely that many in the military resent the reputation of their institution being abused by the Field Marshal and his 19 colleagues on the SCAF. . . . The present rumblings of discontent among junior officers, Chief of Staff General Sami Anan's greater popularity than the Field Marshal in the military and among Egyptians as a whole, and intensified pressures from the US could all result in the Field Marshal sharing President Mubarak's fate. The military institution could remove him to save itself. If matters became truly desperate, discontented officers not in the SCAF might decide that a coup within the coup would be the best way to save the honor of the country and their institution.*[12]

The entire edition of *Egypt Independent* never made the news-stands. The story was first reported by Alastair Beach of Britain's *Independent*, who described how the article was cleared for printing when the editor-in-chief of the newsweekly's sister publication decided to censor the opinion piece.[13] *Al-Masry al-youm* berated the *Independent* for lacking professionalism:

> *The article that a foreign writer tried to publish in the supplement is an explicit and clear incitement to Egyptian army officers to carry out a coup d'état to seize power. That is what is rejected by the newspaper and the Egyptian people, in order to protect the gains of the revolution for which the blood of youth was sacrificed for the sake of a modern civil state.*[14]

The article does not mention Robert Springborg by name, a historian and academic who has written extensively on Egypt's military and the Mubarak regime. During Mubarak's reign, Springborg's book *Mubarak's Egypt: Fragmentation of the Political Order* was banned. Springborg gave his take on the censorship row in *Foreign Policy*:

> *General Tantawi must be aware that his perch atop both the SCAF and the military (indeed, for the moment, the entire state), is precarious. For years he was Mubarak's instrument to control the military. The measures he employed – including promoting the incompetent over the competent, minimizing training and general preparedness, redirecting the institution's*

primary efforts to economic rather than military pursuits, and ladling out dollops of patronage to retain loyalty – resulted in an indulged officer corps, but also one that harbors profound resentments. Those resentments have been greatly exacerbated by the SCAF's mishandling of the transition, especially the deployment of military units for crowd control, outright intimidation and even killing of demonstrators, and converting military bases into detention facilities.[15]

The staff of *Egypt Independent* in a note to readers posted on their website affirmed that the 1 December issue was internally censored by Magdy al-Gallad after the edition had gone to press. The publication's editorial team wrote:

Because our paper lacks its own printing license right now and is therefore legally considered a 'supplement' of the Arabic paper, we complied and agreed to change what the editor considered the objectionable parts of the article. We did this in collaboration with Professor Springborg, who, with his long experience in Egypt and knowledge of the country's politics and military, understood the restrictions placed on the media, even in the wake of an historic revolution.

After making the requested changes, the censored version was still never reprinted. We never received any calls from authorities outside of the institution to halt the printing process and, to our knowledge, the decision was internal.[16]

The staff went on to criticise the prevalent ultra-nationalist discourse. While Springborg's original column advanced the notion of internal dissent within the military, the editorial team argued, 'This is not advocating mutiny and it does not make him a conspirator against Egypt. It is a descriptive reading by a respected expert on the Egyptian military. Even if this analysis is uncomfortable for some, it deserves to be heard.' The staff refused to work on a weekly print edition in the absence of their own publication licence and guaranteed editorial independence, stating, 'if self-censorship becomes internalized and goes unquestioned, it becomes an irreversible practice'.[17]

Magdy al-Gallad got the last word in a column entitled 'Drink from the Sea!' He talked of 'pressures' to publish the Springborg's column in the 'experimental' English-language supplement, where the writer 'invites army officers and Lieutenant General Sami Anan to seize power in a military coup, particularly after the results of the first round of parliamentary elections, on the basis that Field Marshal Tantawi is allied with the Islamist trend in Egypt!' Springborg made no reference to legislative elections or the political power of Islamists.

Al-Gallad charged the writers and editors working at *Egypt Independent* of not having adequate knowledge of Springborg's background and ties with the Pentagon and the US Department of Defense. 'But I know him well. I stood against the article before it was published. I read it once, twice, and ten times. Then I clearly decided not to publish it,' wrote the editor-in-chief. 'I will not work on behalf of the writer, his superpower, or its brutal and bloody practices around the whole world. I am not afraid of his screams in the British *Independent* or the American *Foreign Policy*, and not from the broken record of "freedom of opinion", which is exploited by the West to achieve its malicious objectives against us, and which it uses inversely to protect its interests and national security.'

Striking a decidedly nationalist tone, al-Gallad accused Springborg of arrogantly seeking to sow chaos and back coups that would 'return Egypt to the point of zero'. 'Yes, I have not and will not publish the article,' he declared defiantly. 'And those who do not like it in America and its servant Britain can drink from the sea, any sea whose waters are turbid, not bound on the north, south, east, or west by the precious land of Egypt!'[18] Al-Gallad left *al-Masry al-youm* in March 2012 to become editor-in-chief of a new daily newspaper, *al-Watan* (The Nation),[19] and a weekly print edition of *Egypt Independent* returned to news-stands on 7 June 2012. But on 16 April 2013, after 49 issues of the newsweekly, the management of al-Masry Media Corporation pulled the plug on *Egypt Independent*. After reviewing the contents of the final issue, the paper's management halted its publication before it went to press.[20]

Clashes at the Cabinet

In an image striking in its cruelty, a young woman lying limp and exposed on the ground was being beaten and stomped on by soldiers with truncheons, who tore the abaya and clothing off her body to reveal a blue bra and a bare torso. Distressing images of the army's violence against women and protesters were displayed in a YouTube clip beneath a soundtrack of a moving song by Egyptian singer Reham Abd al-Hakim titled 'Bil-waraqa wa-l-qalam' (With Paper and Pen). '*Tell me how you will carry on*,' went a line of the song, '*when all this has happened to you?*'[21]

Bloody clashes began on the night of 15 December when protester and Ultras member Aboudy was pummelled by soldiers for an hour inside the parliament grounds.[22] He had approached a vehicle suspected of kidnapping protesters, tapped on the glass, and asked to see the driver's identification. The man behind the wheel responded by saying he was an officer and got out of the car. He picked up his phone and two army divisions arrived, recounted a badly bruised Aboudy from the hospital, his eyes swollen shut. 'He took out his pistol and said, "Yes, I am the one who abducts" and struck me on the head.'[23]

Clashes erupted by dawn. Soldiers positioned atop the Cabinet building pelted protesters in the street with rocks, concrete slabs, broken tiles, and pieces of furniture.[24] On Friday evening, 16 December, al-Azhar scholar Sheikh Emad Effat was shot in the chest and fourth-year medical student and field hospital volunteer Alaa Abd al-Hady was shot in the face supposedly by army bullets.[25] Sheikh Emad Effat had issued a fatwa, or religious judgment, that forbade voting for the remnants of the National Democratic Party in elections. Protests erupted at al-Azhar Mosque, where worshippers prayed for his soul. 'The people want the downfall of the field marshal,' erupted scholars, students, and mourners as soon as prayers ended.[26] 'We don't want the field marshal or any of these animals,' said one of the al-Azhar's scholars. 'The blood of Sheikh Emad, God willing, will not be lost in vain.'[27]

In a press conference, Prime Minister Kamal al-Ganzoury said, 'A ball entered the Cabinet grounds, so one of the individuals went in. He was treated in a way that may not have been correct and was beaten.' To the allegations that protesters were shot, al-Ganzoury said, 'The army did not use any firepower.' He said he consulted all the sources and they denied that bullets were ever used. 'I said and I still say, we will not confront any peaceful demonstrations with any type of violence.'[28]

Shorty after al-Ganzoury's statement on 17 December, the army began a siege of Tahrir and downtown Cairo, burning tents and field hospitals and assailing and arresting bystanders.[29] Soldiers entered buildings and private apartments overlooking the square and confiscated journalists' cameras or flung them from balconies. Despite claims that the army did not carry firearms, photos and videos on social media showed these to be patently false.[30]

All the while, the military and its apologists were advancing the 'hidden hand' theory. State television did its part to defend the official line. In characteristic style, they interviewed detainees arrested by the army and police. Usually mention of the April 6 Youth Movement, the Revolutionary Socialists, or the Ultras was woven into incriminating testimonials. Despite the gunshot deaths of Sheikh Effat and Abd al-Hady and the despicable assault on women, it was repeated by state media and the military council that protesters at the Cabinet were not the 'pure youth of the revolution'. The army, of course, remained blameless and its handling of the events was not given too much scrutiny on the public airwaves. During the 18 days that toppled Mubarak, official media also claimed the honourable youth of 25 January had withdrawn, leaving rogue foreign elements, infiltrators plotting the ruin of Egypt, and the Brotherhood to seize the crisis.

The Supreme Council of the Armed Forces issued Communiqué no. 90 in the form of a YouTube video. 'It is our right to defend the property of the great Egyptian people for which we swore an oath to protect. These are images of the scheme being carried out against Egypt and recordings of it.' The five and a half minutes of footage showed vandals breaking the windows of a government building and throwing rocks; protesters shouting, 'The army and the police are the same dirty hand'; people trying to tear down a fence around parliament, and a clear image of man in a hard hat setting fire to a building.[31] It emerged on social media that the man looked suspiciously like one of the soldiers.

In an episode of *Qalam rusas* (Pencil), Hamdy Kandil advised, 'Don't believe any official announcements – not the announcement of military council yesterday or the announcement of the prime minister today, or any statement from official sources.' The only government information that could be trusted was that of the Ministry of Health on the number of deaths, he added, listing the cascade of events that led to the clashes, beginning with Aboudy's kidnapping. 'Aboudy was not the first of the sit-in protesters to be kidnapped and he won't be the last,' described Kandil. Despite all the official statements that peaceful protest was allowed, 'protesters were threatened, terrorised, and pressured to break up the sit-in'. The army, constructing walls and barbed wire fortifications, was facing off against its own people, he said. With mounting casualties in one outbreak of violence after another, all that were promised were investigations that went nowhere. 'The third party, internal spying elements, unknown powers. We have nothing but ghosts moving the situation,' Kandil sarcastically concluded. 'They are not moved by a council, the government, the army, or the police.'[32]

The general's press conference

In a green beret and uniform, General Adel Emara, one of the commanders on the Supreme Council of the Armed Forces, gave a press conference on 19 December where he steadfastly defended the actions of military personnel over the past few days. 'Events since the beginning of the revolution until now have proven the method of planning to destroy the country, continue the security deficiency, and destabilise the security situation, then to plant doubt in Egypt's honourable judges, and lastly to confront the armed forces and present it in ways that are not appropriate,' he began. The nation is at risk, and soldiers and officers are carrying a heavy burden, Emara intoned. 'Some media outlets are working against the interests of the nation.'

In presenting the case of the armed forces, using 'information that cannot be doubted or fabricated', Emara began the telling of events at dawn on Friday, 16 December by claiming that protesters in the sit-in assaulted an officer.[33] 'The protesters are holding the officer. Then one of the protesters entered the building of the People's Assembly. As a result of the confrontation, the person that entered the People's Assembly sustained some injuries,' said Emara. 'Then he was let go.'

Emara reiterated that the armed forces did not use force against protesters. 'The soldier who protects the facilities, all his weapons have blanks. The weapons used by the other side, like the protesters or anyone else, as you will see in the tapes, are Molotovs and butane canisters and knives. You will see the leg of a soldier nearly torn off by a knife,' he stated dramatically.

Soldiers within the grounds of the legislature and Cabinet faced 1,500 protesters massed outside, throwing rocks and Molotovs, Emara said, painting a scene of motorcycles shuttling to gas stations to fill bottles with petrol, vehicles and buildings set ablaze, plots to storm the People's Assembly, and street children given hard hats to engage in battles with soldiers. 'The other side has a goal to fulfil: to burn the People's Assembly,' he said. At the same time, a group of protesters were making their way to the nearby Ministry of Interior, Emara continued.

On Saturday, 17 December, the military decided to erect a separation barrier, explained Emara. At 2 pm, the Institut d'Égypte, built by Napoleon Bonaparte during the French expedition to Egypt in the late nineteenth century, caught fire. The blaze engulfed the building's collection of rare books and manuscripts as volunteers attempted to salvage what they could from the flames and ashes. 'It is a catastrophe history will judge us on,' admonished Emara, who charged that the library was left to burn because fire fighters were prevented from putting out the fire.

'Regarding what was published in some media of a picture of an Egyptian girl,' he said, pausing to instruct a journalist in the front rows to put away the graphic image, 'who has fallen on the ground – I say yes, this scene happened and we are investigating it, but what I ask – before you open the newspaper and say, what is this, and the army, and violence, and so on – ask about the circumstances in which she fell. What happened, not only in that shot?' He then barked at a journalist who objected: 'I did not allow you to speak. If you talk, I will have you taken out,' he scolded. 'There needs to be order!'

Emara took his first question from a journalist from the weekly newspaper *al-Usbu'* (The Week), who denounced the violence used by soldiers. 'Are you convinced that soldiers used force?' asked Emara and rebuked him for rushing to conclusions. He talked about the need for the media to abide by journalistic ethics, alleging that some media outlets did not wish the best for Egypt.

A women who introduced herself as a military correspondent requested an apology from the military council – not a general apology but a personal apology to the women of Egypt. Emara interrupted her as he read a note passed to him by a soldier. 'I have information that there is a plan today to burn the People's Assembly again. There are large crowds in Tahrir Square now to begin implementation of the plan. This is only information I am passing along to you just to confirm my words of a methodology of planning.'

Emara allowed the woman to continue. 'I ask the military council to issue an announcement apologising to all the women in Egypt,' she said in a tone that was clearly upset.

'All the demands that you have stated will be studied,' tersely responded Emara before moving on to a screening of what he considered was video evidence to back up his claims. Viewers saw black-and-white surveillance footage of small fires and people throwing rocks at a burning building. This was followed by footage of three soldiers who had been injured, one with a bloodied nose, a second with unidentified injuries being carried by stretcher into an ambulance, and the third with a gash across his thigh. And that was when Emara requested the recording be rewound so that his audience could get a better look at the injury. 'He was struck with a sharp instrument by one of the protesters. He cut a vein in his leg and he is in critical condition.' The suggestion was far-fetched; the injury was not blood-soaked or deep enough to have severed a major blood vessel. Moreover, Emara supplied no evidence, not even the testimony of the soldier, to support his claim that the injury was caused by a knife-wielding protester.

Emara devoted much attention to the burning of the Institut d'Égypte. Videos circulated on social media showing soldiers atop the building throwing rocks on protesters below, a detail Emara failed to mention.[34] This was followed by footage of teenagers, who appeared bruised and battered, confessing to taking money to deliver food and blankets, and cook up Molotov cocktails. One teenage boy who resided off Tahrir Square, at 6 Qasr al-Nil Street, which also houses the offices of the Merit Publishing House, told how the publisher Mohamed Hashem would hand out gas masks and hard hats to protesters, and offer them food and a place to rest. A young woman told the interviewer that she ran away from an abusive stepfather and said she had been kidnapped and raped. She mentioned something about getting in contact with a State Security officer when Emara asked the recording to be fast-forwarded (evidently because it had not been carefully vetted) to another remorseful young man, a minor who also looked like he had been beaten, admitting that he was paid to make Molotov cocktails in exchange for food and 100 Egyptian pounds a day.

The next question Emara took was from a woman journalist who was on the verge of tears, arguing that something could have been done to prevent the burning of the Institut d'Égypte. The army was already using water hoses on protesters. 'Couldn't the armed forces save it like it protects the People's Assembly and the Shura Council?' she asked.

'I want you to picture the situation. It is more dangerous than what you can imagine,' replied Emara, theatrically remarking how a soldier sacrificed his life in an apparent attempt to extinguish the blaze.

The final question was from an Agence France-Presse journalist, who said that journalists' camera equipment was either confiscated or hurled from balconies by the army and asked the top general what were the procedures for evacuating a protest? 'First, there were no commands to break up the sit-in – I tell you this in a definitive manner – not by the armed forces or the forces of the Interior Ministry. From what you said about breaking cameras and assaulting journalists, I don't have information but we will investigate this matter.'

Emara read a few more prepared remarks and crowds in the back of the auditorium had their cue to applaud. The press event had come to an end and the general departed the hall.[35]

The response

General Adel Emara used the same line of defence that he did in the aftermath of the Maspero massacre: disavowing basic truths and absolving the military of all blame. In the one-and-a-half-hour news conference, he did not acknowledge that soldiers might have acted improperly. No regret, apology, or admission of sorrow was given for the army's actions in addressing the crisis. The image of the young woman abused and stripped of her clothes aroused the deepest rage. As the video was broadcast around the world of soldiers mercilessly beating protesters, including women, Emara's casual response was that the incident needed to be investigated and no one should jump to conclusions. He made no mention of al-Azhar Sheikh Emad Effat or medical student Alaa Abd al-Hady, both of whom were killed by bullets. He did not explain why of the ten casualties tallied by the time of the press conference, the cause of death in nine was a bullet to the upper body, and in the tenth it was shotgun fire to the chest – according the government's own Ministry of Health.

Eighteen Egyptians ended up losing their lives in the clashes. The youngest was 14-year-old Islam Abd al-Hafiz Hamza, whose last moments of life were captured in a video circulated online.[36] Computer technician Ramy al-Sharqawy, 26, was shot dead by a bullet to the left side of his body: a long trail of his blood marked by stones on the ground of Tahrir became a temporary memorial.[37] A bullet punctured the chest of 20-year-old Muhammad Mustafa, an athlete, engineering student, and Ultras member. No one was reported dead from the ranks of the army.

In Emara's video presentation no armed protesters were shown. The evidence he offered was anything but conclusive for the army's case of a massive conspiracy to topple the foundations of the state. For the military council general, the media was a topic of considerable ire. 'The practices of some individuals, groups, and the media is a wrong implementation of democracy, an implementation that destroys and does not build. It is sometimes built on lies and deception, and on people's inability to know the truths,' Emara said.

Freed from incarceration a day earlier, activist and blogger Alaa Abd El Fattah, in his first studio interview on 26 December with Yosri Fouda on *Last Words*, described what it was like to have access only to the state-owned terrestrial channels as the violent clashes of Muhammad Mahmoud Street and the Cabinet took place. 'It presents a picture that is absurd even in its lack of completeness. Its problem is not only in its bias. For example, you find them responding to what was said on satellite channels. But what *was* said on satellite channels?' asked Abd El Fattah.

> *The picture has protesters throwing rocks at something, and they tell us that they are evil and thugs and they began it. They don't even say who is the other side. Then they tell us there are a number of deaths, all from the ranks of these protesters. And they don't tell you who the other party is. For 48 hours I didn't understand. Who is the other side? So I have one side that is resisting something, that is sabotaging and attacking something, and is sustaining deaths and injuries. And the other side is not known and is not sustaining deaths or injuries.*

Abd El Fattah was kept in the dark until he received newspapers reporting the events. It was not long before he noticed the official media narrative changing to a scenario that incriminated street children for the mayhem.[38] 'Egypt's history is burning before you', Major General Abd al-Moniem Kato, adviser to the armed forces on Morale Affairs, told a reporter for the daily *al-Shuruk*, 'and you are worried about delinquents who need to be placed in Hitler's incinerators.'[39]

The day following Emara's press conference, women staged protest marches, crying out, 'The girls of Egypt are a red line.'[40] The military has always asserted that *it* was the red line. The Supreme Council of the Armed Forces saw fit to issue Communiqué no. 91 expressing 'sincere regret to the great women of Egypt for the excesses of the last events in protests of the People's Assembly and the Cabinet'. The statement goes on to affirm the military council's 'complete respect and appreciation to the women of Egypt, their right to protest, and their active and positive participation in political life'.[41]

Beginning with Maspero and followed in succession by the casualties in Muhammad Mahmoud Street and the Cabinet, there was no longer the same cautiousness in speaking about the transgressions of the armed forces in the media that there had been in the weeks after the military council assumed the mandate of running the country. On 26 February 2011, the military police violently cleared the square of protesters objecting to the government of Mubarak-appointed Prime Minister Ahmed Shafik, confiscating camera equipment and detaining, torturing, and referring protesters to military trials. Egyptians and the media retained a belief and trust in the armed forces, overlooking abuses of a national army.

Strict laws against criticising the armed forces also played a role in quelling criticism. For its part, the military council categorically denied abuses of any sort had taken place: forced virginity tests, the systematic torture of detainees, the use of live ammunition, the crushing of protesters beneath the wheels of armoured personnel vehicles. Instead, blame was placed squarely on elusive 'hidden hands' or 'third parties' bent on driving a wedge between the army and the people.

Graffiti and protest slogans first began calling for the downfall of military rule, then for the downfall of Tantawi, and, notably with the events of Muhammad Mahmoud and the Cabinet, for the generals of the military council to be placed on trial and for Tantawi to be hanged. Official media continued to honour and embellish the role of the military in the revolution. In times of crisis state media proved to be an engine of propaganda for the men in power, just as it had been for Mubarak during the 18 days of revolution.

On her morning show *al-Youm* (The Day) on al-Tahrir satellite channel, Dina Abd al-Rahman brought on a career army general to discuss recent actions by the military. Five months earlier, Abd al-Rahman had been dismissed as a host on Dream TV because of her on-air criticism of a military council general. Following deadly clashes by the Cabinet, not only was the Supreme Council of the Armed Forces on the defensive, but so were the army's ranking officers.

'Did you see the videos of soldiers using guns and weapons?' Abd al-Rahman asked her military guest.

'I have not seen that,' he replied. 'The armed forces are part of the fabric of the Egyptian people; they are the sons of the Egyptian people. None of them can do any of the things that you talk about. Even if he is wearing army fatigues, he is not a part of the armed forces.'

'Does this mean that the ones we see hitting, dragging, urinating,[42] or using ammunition are not from the armed forces?'

Photographs of soldiers pointing firearms are presented on the screen.

'The pistol in his hand is his personal weapon,' responded the general. 'Show me that a shot was fired. . . . The gun is in his hand; he is protecting himself. Protection. Whoever attacks me, I will shoot.'

'So how did people get shot?' asked Abd al-Rahman.

'No one from the armed forces fired a shot and they swore an oath to this.'

'So what's the problem with having an investigation to affirm this?'

'That investigation is ongoing.'

'So why are we rushing to judgement and denying that firepower was used?'

'I know the military doctrine. The military doctrine is that an Egyptian soldier or officer cannot raise his weapon in the face of an Egyptian.'

A video of a soldier firing his pistol is shown for the general.

'See how a bullet was shot from the gun? And that's not a soldier, it's a ranking officer.'

'Listen, I want to tell you something. There is firing in the air,' suggested the flustered military defender.

'That is not in the air. That is at the level of the head.'

The video is played again.

'From the start of the interview you are concentrating on the death and the martyrs and the revolutionaries, and so on. We want to move on to other points,' said the cornered general.

'We will move on, but are these truths or are we inventing them?' asked Abd al-Rahman. 'Are there from 13 to 15 martyrs in the past days or not? Are there more than 300 injured or not? Are there people who were kidnapped and tortured or not?'[43]

Dina Abd al-Rahman found her morning show on al-Tahrir satellite channel abruptly suspended on 11 February 2012 by the order of the station's new owner, Suleiman Amer. 'There was a rumor that Amer was behind some of the original funders, who stood as front men until the time was right for him to make an appearance,' said Abd al-Rahman. 'Once Amer came on board, the management started to interfere with my show.'[44] Amer has had dubious business dealings, acquiring tracts of state-owned land for agriculture projects, which he used to build resorts and touristic ventures. Abd al-Rahman's contract gave her editorial independence in choosing topics and guests, a clause the owner wanted to revoke. To intimidate her, the station's management published her contract on their Facebook page, listing her salary, address, and other personal information.[45]

Mohamed Hashem, a democracy activist, writer, publisher, and founder of the Merit Publishing House, which first produced works like Alaa Al Aswany's 2002 novel *'Imarat Ya'qubyan (The Yacoubian Building)*, remained undaunted by attacks from the military rulers. 'There is no such thing as a ceiling to freedoms,' Hashem said at the offices of Merit, in a central Cairo building where the drab entrance was daubed with anti-security force slogans.

A press conference by a general on the ruling military council placed the bookseller in the crosshairs. An accompanying video clip showed the interrogation of a teenager, identified only as Mansour, who named Hashem as the owner of the Merit Publishing House, from which, the youth said, 'around 120 people' had distributed free helmets, goggles, gas masks, and food to the protesters. Hashem does not dispute that he handed out first-aid kits, blankets, and other supplies. He said he would continue to do so if needed, to help protesters facing bullets, shotgun pellets, and tear gas fired by the army and security forces. 'I will do anything that will prevent people from dying,' he said defiantly. 'I will not hold back on anything that I know to be right.'

Al-Hikma, an ultra-conservative Salafi satellite television channel, joined in the campaign against Hashem, labelling him an infidel because Merit published a book on the formative years of the Prophet Muhammad a decade before. Hashem said that it was these kinds of religiously toned media campaigns that posed the greatest threat to independent publishers. The decisions to censor often originate from publishers and are based on 'calculations', Hashem asserted. 'When they publish a book that upsets the president or powerful interests, they kill themselves with their own sword. We did not care about the sword or the gold.'

To Alaa Al Aswany it was no surprise the military rulers singled out Hashem, 'to intimidate and terrorise those who are faithful to the revolution'. The first edition of Al Aswany's *The Yacoubian Building* was released by Merit after being passed up by other publishers. The literary work, which went on to become an international bestseller, adapted into a blockbuster film and a television series, referenced an omnipresent 'Big Man', which readers could understand to mean Hosni Mubarak, the former president. 'You are up against an unlawful police state that has everything in its hands – the security apparatus, executive power, everything,' the novelist added. 'It can do anything to you.'[46]

Hashem was among the first members of the activist coalition Kifaya that would help make revolution possible in 2011. Being centrally located, Merit became the venue for literary and political gatherings as well as activism, including the Kifaya-affiliated group Writers and Artists for Change, which Hashem started. 'We are not afraid of anyone for the sake of Egypt's freedom. We will use the same tool of peaceful resistance, the loud voice and the brave chest,' he said.

Outside the Merit offices on a chilly evening on 30 December, eight speakers and a mixer were set up for a rally combining music, poetry, and politics to denounce the military rulers and support the revolutionary publisher. 'On 25 January, we will all go out in the millions and say the revolution continues and no one can steal this revolution,' Al Aswany boomed, referring to demonstrations planned to mark the anniversary of the start of the uprising.[47]

General Mohsen al-Fangary, when asked by a television reporter what his expectations were for 25 January, responded by admonishing the media: 'I hope, and we all hope, that we make a good start with teaching, and that the media is a media that is truthful because this media is like a fixed nuclear bomb; it is more than a nuclear bomb,' he said. 'So I appeal to the media, in respect for this day, that it fears God for Egypt's sake.'[48]

Opposition to military rule heightens

In the Coptic Christmas mass broadcast live on television, Pope Shenouda welcomed 'the distinguished and honourable number of military leaders present, those whom we love and who love us', as some churchgoers shouted, 'Down, down with military rule!'[49] Among the members of the military council was the despised Hamdy Badeen, commander of the military police. During the mass, Father Yuhana Fouad, pastor of the Virgin Mary Church in Old Cairo, was greeted and kissed by Badeen in what turned out to be a surprise photo op. In a Sunday sermon, Fouad apologised for greeting the general and allowing himself to be photographed with him. 'You have to know that your priest is someone respectable. He has to tell the truth. These are people who are oppressors and liars and thieves holding on to their chairs.'[50]

The military council even dealt with the inconvenience of bad press through confiscation. The weekly *Sawt al-umma* was pulled from newsstands on 15 January 2012 because of an exposé that featured an interview inside military prison with one of the dissenting army officers of 8 April, who charged top-ranking generals with corruption. *Sawt al-umma*'s publication of the story would otherwise have been considered publisher's suicide, given the callous laws on the books against any rebuke of the military. It was a risk the newspaper's editors took in challenging the sanctified role of the military and its immunity from critical scrutiny, with the reddest of red lines being discussion of military corruption.

Forgoing a press conference, presidential contender Mohamed ElBaradei disclosed that he was not seeking the position of head of state in post-revolutionary Egypt in a video on YouTube. In the 16-minute clip, shot somewhat clumsily at his home, he explained his decision.

'I will be more effective if in these circumstances I do not seek office, including the office of the presidency, and that I concentrate my goals on the big picture: How do we quicken the pace of change? How do we speed up building a new Egypt together?'

He has had strong reservations on the trajectory of the country's democratic transition. Nearly a year after the start of the revolution, legislative elections were not complete and no significant achievements were realised. 'We don't see any change in the media apparatus. It is the same as it was, a mouthpiece for the ruling regime,' said ElBaradei, adding that the judiciary also needed to be purged. But what is worse, he said, was the continued mistreatment, abuse, torture, and death of Egyptians.

'We have to realise that every revolution is not a straight line,' ElBaradei continued. 'We are transitioning from pharaonic rule that is based on a person to one that is based on institutions.' He said his major goal would be focused on working with young people who sparked revolution in organising politically so that their voice is heard in building Egypt's future. 'For them to rule they have to forget their divisions and return to the time when all of Egypt spoke of one thing: that we are all Egyptians. We all own this land.'[51]

As 25 January 2012 approached, fear-mongering and exaggerated predictions of doom were rife. Doaa Sultan, the host of *Talk Shows* on al-Tahrir satellite channel, charged the network's owner, Suleiman Amer, with banning an episode of her programme that was scheduled to air days before the revolution's first anniversary.[52] The nearly one-and-a-half-hour programme was uploaded on YouTube, where Sultan listed reasons for remembrance: virginity tests, women beaten and dragged in the streets, and protesters murdered or blinded. 'The Field Marshal Muhammad Hussein Tantawi says we will celebrate, which means we'll celebrate,' dryly commented Sultan. Amid lavish celebrations orchestrated by the military 'to commemorate failure' as the government reports dire budget shortfalls, she noted, cards will drop from planes with redeemable prizes – gifts that Egyptians need to bend down to receive. '25 January is a new revolution,' Sultan said, calling on the military to return to their barracks and fulfil their duty in guarding the nation's borders.[53]

On 24 January, Tantawi took to the airwaves for the second time since he assumed the role of de facto head of state. In a prepared speech that praised the army, police, judiciary, and the prime minister, he announced that emergency law would come to an end the following day except for crimes of thuggery, a qualified annulment that gave the military ruler enough latitude to determine who falls into that category. The concession was intended to take the wind out of the sail of mass protests against the military council on the revolution's first anniversary. 'It is certain that those who have degraded the role of the armed forces and its Supreme Council should review their nationalist standing,' chided Tantawi.[54]

Marches were organised in several neighbourhoods heading towards Tahrir on the morning of 25 January. In the lead up to this day, the media and the military council warned that there might be havoc as protesters took to the streets. Crowds nonetheless packed Tahrir Square to call for the end to military rule. Protesters also massed in front of the television and radio building at Maspero to protest the deceptive state media and its complicity with the military rulers. The Military Liars ('Askar Kazeboon) collective, in evening screenings, beamed images of army abuses from a projector onto the façade of the television and radio building.

Activist and blogger Alaa Abd El Fattah appeared on a programme called *Sawt Masr* (The Voice of Egypt) on state television on 27 January. He was one of the protesters outside the building when he was asked to join the programme. 'From the beginning of the revolution Maspero was shown to be one of the castles of the regime. This is one of the strongest institutions of control that the powers play with,' said Abd El Fattah on the programme. 'The biggest evidence is the systematic lies that come out of the news service specifically from inside this building,' he said. 'There was a concerted effort to smear the revolutionaries at every turn. There was lying using the methods of evading certain details or to avoid showing you the picture, like the video of the girl who was dragged in the streets,' he said. 'It was ignored, and with all the talk about it, they began talking about the video and about the girl but they did not show the picture at all.'

The interviewer asked whether he was referring to news programmes or talk shows and Abd El Fattah responded by saying that when we are talking about an institution, it might have variations that make one programme or host more commendable than others. 'What is more important is that I have a systematic crisis where this is clearly the media of the rulers. It is not the media of the people,' he remarked. While he admitted there had been some changes – he would not have been allowed inside the building during the Mubarak regime – they had not been sufficient. 'Is its administration independent or not? Is there methodical lying or not? Hosni Mubarak claimed that there were freedoms as evidenced by independent newspaper and satellite channels. So why did the revolution erupt if there were freedoms?' he asked.[55]

Through public screenings of videos displaying army and police violence, a grass-roots initiative called Military Liars brought the truth about the military council's crimes straight to the public.[56] The videos, stitched together from footage captured by citizen journalists, showed the crackdown against protesters since Tantawi and his posse of generals took over power, juxtaposing the shocking images with official statements. The visuals widely shared on social media networks were being broadcast on the streets, a laptop and projector beaming realities hidden from the public onto a makeshift screen.

The Mediterranean city of Alexandria, with a rich and cosmopolitan past, was a focal point of revolutionary fervour, expressed in a vibrant underground art and music scene. Direct, unfiltered, and delivering a brutally honest political and social message, Egyptian rap and hip-hop have their roots in this city. The message is written clearly in the name and songs of Alexandrian rap collective Revolution. 'Kazeboon', or 'Liars', is Revolution's signature rap, an unabashed tirade against the military rulers who have taken charge of Egypt since Mubarak's downfall. Revolution, in chorus, ripped into the song's signature refrain:

We say 'No' to a lying military
Whatever they say is nothing but lies
When we refuse, we're killed or thrown in jail
Nothing's changed. Stand up Egyptians![57]

'Kazeboon' became the anthem of the Military Liars campaign. Days away from presidential elections in May 2012 the struggle was far from over, said Revolution's rappers. 'The military council is Mubarak wearing a different mask,' said Ahmed Mabrouk, also known as Rock, interviewed with fellow crew-members at an alley café in downtown Alexandria's Raml Station that has become an underground musicians' hangout. 'Mubarak ruled over a cancerous regime,' added Amr Aboul Saoud, known to the rap world as C-Zar. 'It is not like a serpent, where you cut off the head and it's over.' Still, that is also true now of the revolution, said Mohamed Temraz, or teMraz. 'If the revolution fails, another revolution will come.'[58]

The football massacre

A football match in the seaside city of Port Said on 1 February 2012 descended into horrifying violence. As soon as the whistle ending the match was blown – with the home team, al-Masry, winning in a 3–1 upset against the top-ranked Cairo team, al-Ahly – stadium-goers invaded the pitch in a frenzied assault on visiting team players and fans. When the dust had settled that night the number of dead was counted at 74. The stands for the visiting fans were stained with blood as al-Ahly Ultras fans were beaten with clubs, knifed, robbed, and hurled down. With exit gates locked, many more died in the ensuing stampede.

Lax security set in motion a tragedy waiting to happen. In an expectedly tense match, ticket holders were not searched at entrances for weapons, and troublemakers in the crowd were intent on igniting a brawl. Captured in videos, riot police stood by idly, avoiding intervention in the melee. As matters escalated, stadium lights were shut off, with the darkness making the situation more volatile. To everyone watching at home, the massacre was either extreme negligence on the part of security officials or a sinister conspiracy to teach the football devotees known as Ultras, who have become a politically potent force, a harsh lesson. In a match four days earlier, al-Ahly Ultras had roared en masse for the downfall of military rule, the military police, and the Interior Ministry.[59] The fearless Ultras, out on the streets since day one of the uprising, were a force the military rulers may have wanted to cut down to size. The Ultras had been the revolution's front-line defenders and the Port Said massacre smacked of a plot to trigger a crackdown on those football 'hooligans'.

'Who did this? They are individuals from the Egyptian people,' said Tantawi at the airport in Cairo, receiving al-Ahly players and injured fans arriving aboard a military plane. 'Why are Egyptians silent? Everyone has to get involved. It's a must.'[60]

Past midnight and into the early morning hours, as enraged al-Ahly Ultras awaited the bodies of their friends at the Cairo train station in the massacre's aftermath, the chants were of anger and defiance against the military regime. Never has there been a more determined ground swell calling for Tantawi and military council generals to step aside and hand over power to a civilian government that can be held accountable. In the streets and on the airwaves, there was no fear in holding the military council responsible. Also being dismissed as a betrayal of the memory of the martyrs was the notion of a safe exit for the top military commanders or a special dispensation for the armed forces in the constitution. Months earlier those sentiments could hardly have been expressed on television.

The day after the massacre, Egyptian state and private television networks carried a live feed of the People's Assembly session with representatives in the newly elected chamber delivering strong condemnation of the Supreme Council of the Armed Forces.[61] 'What happened yesterday cannot be called an incident, but a conspiracy that the military council must be questioned about. The recommendations first are the downfall of military rule and expediting the handover of power to an elected civilian president. Secondly, the elimination of a safe exit; whoever bears the blood of Egyptians must be held accountable,' thundered MP Mohamed Abu Hamed.[62]

The political crisis, expressed MP Amr Hamzawy, is the loss of legitimacy for the military rulers as more Egyptian blood continues to be shed. 'A civilian president must be elected – and quickly – and without sidestepping or alleging that we are insulting the armed forces. We are not insulting the armed forces, instead the Egyptian citizen is the one being insulted.'[63] Hamzawy demanded that the People's Assembly pass a law determining when presidential elections would take place, overhauling the Interior Ministry and purging it of corruption, calling for questioning of the prime minister and other government officials, and commissioning an investigation of the massacre that would not stop at holding civilians to account but also probe the military ranks.

On 2 February a protest rally of thousands marched from al-Ahly Club in the Cairo district of Zamalek to the Interior Ministry building downtown. Protesters vowed that the fortress walls erected by the military at Muhammad Mahmoud Street and nearby roads would come down. Clashes started at 6:40 pm, with security forces and army firing volleys of tear gas on protesters, followed by the sound of gunfire. Soon motorcycles began ferrying the injured and ambulances rushed to the scene. Yet another battle had begun in downtown Cairo. Days later, more military-sanctioned walls would rise near the Interior Ministry.

In a communiqué, the Supreme Council of the Armed Forces warned of an escalation instigated by 'external and internal parties targeting the nation.'[64] The state's 24-hour news channel, Nile News, candidly talked about the pressing issue of the day with discussions centring on calls for the military council to step aside and the purging of the state-owned media.[65] Not only was censure being directed at the security apparatus, a lynchpin of Mubarak-style authoritarianism, demanding its overhaul, but former regime collaborators in Tora Prison were accused of sowing chaos by financing bands of trouble-makers. A common refrain was that the only thing that was secure in Egypt was Mubarak, who resided comfortably in a hospital and was transported to and from court in a helicopter.

For days the tense street battles dragged on, and each day the list of dead and injured grew.

Civil disobedience and the spin offensive

Initiated by university students, a nationwide civil disobedience campaign was announced to start across Egypt on 11 February, one year after Mubarak stepped down. 'In the beginning you said you protected the revolution. We believed you and forgave you. We said, "Let's begin anew." The days and months passed and the tyrant is still talking from inside palaces,' went one video, as we hear Mubarak saying how pained he was at the attacks levelled against him. 'Innocents were imprisoned, blinded, degraded, killed, and suffocated,' the voice-over on the video explained. All the while the military council and its cohorts have run the country for 60 years. 'You have your land, clubs, and hospitals. May God be praised! And you hold 40% of the economy – fertiliser, chemicals, metals, armaments, ammunition, planes, trains, armoured vehicles, televisions, and laptops. You, of course, will say that your factories operate for the sake of *the protection and building of the nation*.'[66]

On 10 February thousands marched from downtown and other points in Cairo to converge in front of the Ministry of Defence, winding past barricaded thoroughfares, to demand an end to military rule. In front of the ministry were rows of tanks, armoured vehicles, and troops stationed behind barbed wire; an army marching band drowned out protesters' slogans. The civil disobedience campaign of 11 February did not generate the anticipated effect and the front page of *al-Ahram* the following day boasted, 'The Strike Has Failed'.

'In Egypt there is no safe exit for a criminal,' MP Ziyad al-Eleimy bellowed at a political rally to applause. 'The criminal who killed the people in the stadium is the same criminal who later said, "I don't understand why Egyptians are silent." The criminal is known to us. . . . We know the criminal is a jackass. And the jackass is Field Marshal Tantawi.'[67] The parliamentarian for the Social Democratic Party was referred to a special parliamentary committee to investigate his unflattering comparison after he refused to apologise directly, only saying that he did not intend to offend any public figures. Social media witnessed a flurry of cartoons and jokes about the donkey and the field marshal. 'Can we request a hearing for the donkey to find out his opinion on the insult directed against him?' tweeted

Mona Seif, activist and campaigner against military trials for civilians, who added a hashtag in Arabic, 'I am sorry, donkey', a play on the 'I am sorry, Mr President' expressed by Mubarak's supporters.[68]

The day after ten protesters in a sit-in outside the Defence Ministry were killed in the district of Abbasiya, three generals of the military council scheduled another spin offensive three weeks before the start of presidential elections.[69] 'Our hands are clean. They are not stained with Egyptian blood, and there will not be Egyptian blood, God willing, until we transfer power,' said Muhammad al-Assar, assistant defence minister, to applause from some journalists in the hall. 'Disregard the images and the films. The Egyptian army, which belongs to the people, did not kill anyone. It won't happen. Do not believe.'

General Mukhar al-Mulla advanced the narrative that the protesters sought to storm the heavily fortified Defence Ministry. 'I urge you to use phrases correctly: We do not have bloodbaths or massacres,' he told journalists. 'Whoever approaches military installations should bear responsibility *(applause)*.' He added cryptically, 'We all know and I know and you know who is behind this.' For his part, General Mamdouh Shaheen assured a reporter that the military does not demand special dispensation in the constitution. At the close of the conference, al-Mulla thanked the applauding journalists for their show of support and in raising morale. This was the first military council press conference where the generals' words were punctuated by applause, leading to speculation that the audience was packed with sympathetic participants.[70]

The following day, a Friday, soldiers forcibly cleared a zone far beyond the Defence Ministry. Army personnel assaulted protesters and bystanders, raided hospitals and mosques, and arrested some 320 individuals, referring them to military prosecution on charges of assaulting army staff and assembling in a military area. Findings of a partially leaked fact-finding commission report revealed that hired ruffians worked in concert with the army, protesters were assaulted and trapped inside a military hospital, and army doctors were commanded to operate on their injuries without anaesthetics or sterilisation.[71]

The verdict

On the morning of 2 June 2012, Egyptians awaited the verdict in the much-hyped 'trial of the century'. In a live broadcast of the ruling, presiding judge Ahmed Rafaat demanded silence in the courtroom. In a flowery introduction, Refaat described 25 January 2011 to be a 'new dawn' following the 'dark nightmare' of Mubarak's long reign. He recounted how Egyptians peacefully rose up 'to ask for the basic necessities of existence from rulers raised on the throne of luxury and riches – a demand to make available for them a piece of bread to staunch their hunger, a drink of clean water to quench their thirst, and to live in dwellings that gather their families instead of the dehumanising filth of the slums'. Their rulers offered no mercy from the oppressiveness of poverty, continued Refaat. The judge's words were a damning rebuke of Mubarak's administration that 'committed the gravest of evil, tyranny and corruption with no accountability or oversight'.[72]

Then came the first ruling: a life sentence for Hosni Mubarak for his complicity in the killing of protesters in the first days of revolution. While no evidence was presented to the court that proved the former head of state sanctioned the executions, the judge reasoned that by virtue of his position he bears foremost responsibility. Live ammunition could not have been used in crowd control without his authorisation – or by doing nothing Mubarak had given the green light. Inside the metal dock, his sons stood over their father, who hid behind sunglasses, sported a pricey Blancpain Fifty Fathoms timepiece, and reclined, as he always had during proceedings, on a hospital gurney. Mubarak's 74-year-old interior minister, Habib al-Adly, was given a life sentence based on the same logic. His six associates, who allegedly supervised deadly force against protesters by police forces under their command, were acquitted due to insufficient evidence. The judge dismissed the illicit gain indictment against Mubarak and his sons because the ten-year statute of limitations had expired. Mubarak was also acquitted on bribery and squandering public funds in relation to the natural gas export deal with Israel brokered through a no-bid deal with a company set up by businessman and political ally Hussein Salem.

As soon as the judge finished announcing the ruling, Mubarak was quickly wheeled out of the courtroom dock. The courtroom erupted in pandemonium with lawyers in attendance standing on benches, wailing 'null and void'. Alaa and Gamal Mubarak remained in custody for insider stock trading, charges filed by the public prosecution three days earlier. The prosecutor's office ordered that the 84-year-old Mubarak be transferred to Tora Prison after his sentencing, where the hospital facilities had been refurbished at a cost of 6 million Egyptian pounds ($1 million) for his arrival.

No serious effort was made to hold senior Interior Ministry officials accountable for systematic human rights violations, including torture and deaths in custody. The military rulers ignored repeated calls for reform of the public prosecution office, which proved its inadequacy in going after police abuses or obtaining convictions of officers implicated in the death of protesters. The Interior Ministry officers stonewalled criminal investigations by destroying evidence and intimidating witnesses. No cases were filed against soldiers caught on tape beating and assaulting women.

Egyptians took to the square to protest the verdict, especially against top Interior Ministry officials who were set free. Some demanded revolutionary trials for the powerbrokers of Mubarak's regime. An effigy of the ousted president hanging by its neck from a traffic pole made its reappearance in the square. The harshest slogans were directed against Mubarak protégé and presidential candidate Ahmed Shafik. Protesters sensed that their revolution could slip their grasp if an old regime cohort were to be elected president with the tacit help of the military rulers.

The People's Assembly passed a disenfranchisement law disqualifying Shafik from running for president.[73] The Presidential Election Commission allowed him to run anyway, pending a review of the law's constitutionality. Calling Mubarak his role model, Shafik had been campaigning on a pledge to restore order. Another surge of revolutionary protest coalesced, yet it was marred by incidents of sexual harassment and assault, spontaneous or by malicious design, targeting women in the square.[74] Violence and the threat of violence have always been the greatest threat to freedom of expression and the highest form of censorship.

On 20 June, a couple of days after Egypt's first true presidential elections, Mubarak was transferred to a military hospital, either because he went into cardiac arrest before suffering a stroke (and pronounced 'clinically dead', as the state wire service reported) or because he fell in the prison bathroom (as his lawyers claimed). His alleged near-death, some speculated, may just have been a state media ruse to gain him sympathy for the move out of prison. The generals of the military council later confirmed that Mubarak was not clinically dead and that he would be moved back to the prison hospital when his health improved. Surveying the Egyptian political scene on *The Daily Show*, American satirist Jon Stewart quipped, 'Egyptian democracy is dead, in a coma, or trying to get a better room.'[75]

It was later discovered by a fact-finding commission investigating the 18 days of revolution that Mubarak watched the uprising unfold via an encrypted satellite channel that broadcast live feeds from video cameras positioned around Tahrir. The commission's report also directly implicated the army in the detention, torture, disappearances, and death of civilians during the revolution – confirming that the military had Mubarak's back while openly declaring its neutrality.[76] (The full 1,000-page report was not made public.) The judiciary on 13 January 2013 ordered a retrial of Mubarak and his ten co-defendants. In settlements reached with prosecutors, the former president and his family were required to repay 20 million Egyptian pounds ($3 million/£1.9 million), the cost of lavish gifts bestowed by al-Ahram, the largest state-owned publishing enterprise, from 2006 until the revolution. The Mubarak clan agreed to return another 11 million Egyptian pounds ($1.6 million/£1.1 million) and 1.4 million Egyptian pounds ($200,000/£133,000) to publishing houses al-Akhbar al-Youm and al-Gumhuriya respectively.

5

Fall of Military Rule and the Islamists

> *Man is condemned to be free. Condemned, because he did not create himself, yet is nevertheless at liberty, and from the moment that he is thrown into this world he is responsible for everything he does. . . . Man is nothing else but what he purposes, he exists only in so far as he realises himself, he is therefore nothing else but the sum of his actions, nothing else but what his life is.*
>
> (Jean-Paul Sartre, philosopher, playwright, novelist[1])

The scene begins with a man entering a café, the foreboding music adding to the drama. He expertly surveys the patrons, eyeing a table where two young women and a man are seated. 'He knows why he's coming and has outlined his goal. He won't exert any effort to get to know people,' says the narrator. 'He will infiltrate your heart as if you've known him for ages. Useful information, he'll receive for free.' The friends at the table tell their guest about overhearing a plot targeting the army and complain about gasoline shortages and escalating prices. 'Really?!' says the interested spy as he busily texts the information to his handlers. The narrator warns, 'You don't know who he is and who is behind him. *Weigh your words before you say them. Every word has a price. A word can save a nation.*'[2]

Reminiscent of Secord World War propaganda campaigns against aiding the enemy, the controversial public service spots were admonished for sending the wrong message: instructing Egyptians to engage in vigilante spy hunts. It was never disclosed who was behind the xenophobic ads, widely believed to be the General Intelligence Service, headed for 18 years by Omar Soliman. The campaign brought to mind the grand foreign conspiracy theory pushed by regime backers during the revolution, where journalists and travellers were fingered in espionage schemes to topple the state by making use of naïve and unsuspecting protesters. For the security state commandeered by generals, it seemed little has changed.

For the first time since President Anwar Sadat's assassination, emergency law was allowed to expire on 31 May 2012. But four days later, the minister of justice issued a decree – later revoked in a court challenge – authorising army intelligence and military police to arrest civilians. The new powers of the military went into effect on 14 June 2012, the day the Supreme Constitutional Court, the highest legal body, ruled to immediately dissolve the revolution's first democratically elected People's Assembly and struck down as unconstitutional a law that would have disqualified Mubarak's former premier from contesting the presidency.[3] In addition to reinstating the military rulers' legislative powers, the judiciary ensured that there would ultimately be no complete handover to civilian rule.

The presidential race

Egypt's first presidential debate took place on 10 May 2012 between Amre Moussa, the former foreign minister and secretary-general of the Arab League, and Abd al-Moneim Aboul Futouh, a leading opposition figure who had belonged to the Muslim Brotherhood. The event was eagerly anticipated among viewers in cafés and living rooms in Egypt and across the Arab world – where among the region's entrenched autocracies it was only the second presidential debate to take place.[4] Moussa and Aboul Futouh were chosen because they were seen as leading in opinion polls. The live debate began a few minutes past 9 pm and lasted until 2 am. Subtracting the copious advertisements and television promos, the verbal sparring lasted slightly less than four hours, with questions being posed to the candidates by seasoned journalists Mona al-Shazly and Yosri Fouda. Moussa and Aboul Futouh were questioned on a range of topics: how they would manage strikes and protests; the responsibilities of the president under a new constitution; the relationship between religion and the state; the role of the armed forces and the military council; tax policy, subsidies, and the minimum wage; health care and education reform; restoring security and protecting freedoms; foreign affairs; the candidates' health and personal fortunes; and how they were financing their campaigns.

Aboul Futouh challenged Moussa on why he did not stand up to the crimes of the Mubarak regime of which he was part. Moussa hammered Aboul Futouh on his ties to the Muslim Brotherhood. The career diplomat emphasised his political experience in the international arena while Aboul Futouh underscored his message of unity and his appeal to broad swathes of the population – revolutionaries, Islamists, and liberals. When presidential elections were held on 23–24 May, Abd al-Moneim Aboul Futouh and Amre Moussa finished in fourth and fifth places respectively among 13 candidates vying for the top job. Muhammad Morsi, chief of the Muslim Brotherhood's Freedom and Justice Party, and Ahmed Shafik, Mubarak's one-time prime minister, ranked in first and second place respectively, moving on to the 16–17 June runoffs.

As vote counting was underway at the close of the second day of polling, the Supreme Council of the Armed Forces unilaterally issued amendments to the constitutional declaration that diminished the duties of the president and expanded the role of the military council, giving them control of the legislative process (including approval of the national budget), autonomy in all matters related to the military, and the power to override a declaration of war. The unelected generals of the military council also acquired the role of selecting the 100 members of the Constituent Assembly tasked with drafting the new constitution if the delegation arranged by the dissolved People's Assembly reached an impasse. The amended constitutional document carved out a fourth branch of power – the military – devoid of oversight by the three branches of power.

All this was happening as the backdrop to Egypt's first truly contested presidential elections. This time, the winner and next president was not known before the votes were counted. Television stations, newspaper websites, and social media were key to informing an electorate about political developments and reported a running vote tally throughout the night and into the early morning. Morsi's campaign delegates live tweeted the voting results, compiled from 13,067 polling stations throughout the country. Just after 4 am on 18 June, Morsi gave a victory speech at his party headquarters, later going for a victory lap in Tahrir Square. This was a couple of hours before most media outlets, waiting for district-by-district tallies from judges, confirmed him as the unofficial winner. Not to be outdone, Shafik's campaign went on to announce that their candidate had won the popular vote to become Egypt's next president.

The newly issued interim constitutional framework hardly went unnoticed. The *al-Masry al-youm*'s headline the day after the elections aptly read: 'The Military Hands Over Power to the Military'. Described as the 'deep state', the military-dominated rule of the last six decades showed no intention of surrendering power. Old regime loyalists had sizeable influence within the security apparatus, judiciary, military, and state-run institutions, including the media. The military rulers advocated conspiracy theories and shrewdly exploited the Islamist–secular fault line in order to uphold a favoured status and divide the ranks of the broad coalition of citizens and political forces supporting the revolution and its goals.

On 24 June, amid heightened army and security presence around the country, Farouk Sultan, chair of the Presidential Election Commission and the Supreme Constitutional Court's outgoing chief justice, in an eagerly awaited midday press conference, officially declared Muhammad Morsi the democratically elected head of state with 51.73% of the vote.[5] Along with hundreds of Muslim Brotherhood members, Morsi, an engineering professor and opposition parliamentarian from 2000 to 2005, was jailed for seven months in 2006 for supporting an independent judiciary. He was again detained on the night of 27 January 2011, hours after the Brotherhood backed the uprising that would lead to Mubarak's downfall.[6]

Morsi gave his first address as president-elect from a studio in the state television and radio building, standing behind a podium, a flag draped on a pole behind him. 'The Egyptian people have in the past waited tolerantly. They have suffered illness, hunger, oppression, defeat, marginalisation, and the forgery of elections and the people's will,' Morsi told viewers. 'We looked at the world around us and asked, "What will become of Egypt? When will the people of Egypt be the source of power?" Today, *you* are the source of power.'[7] It was a revealing moment for Egyptian state television, which not too long ago barred anyone affiliated with the Muslim Brotherhood from appearing on air.

To a packed Friday crowd in Tahrir Square on 29 June, a day before officially pledging the oath of the presidency before the Supreme Constitutional Court and delivering an inaugural address at Cairo University, Morsi vowed to uphold the civil and constitutional state, fight oppression and corruption, and serve the interests of the people and the nation. 'Today I have come to the Egyptian people and everyone now hears me,' he thundered. 'All the people hear me, the ministries and the government, the army and the police, the men and women of Egypt, within the country and abroad: There is no power above the power of the people.' He stepped from behind the podium and repeated the refrain closer to the audience. He opened his jacket to show them he was not wearing a bulletproof vest. 'Our appointment, whenever we need each other,' he said as he was about to leave the platform, 'is the square of the revolution and the martyrs.'[8]

From the 1952 Free Officers' coup to the popular revolution of 2011, one unquestioned military-backed power centre controlled the political system. A new dynamic of power emerged in post-Mubarak Egypt.

Vying for influence and dominance in a tug of war were the military establishment, protective of its political and economic interests; the broad spectrum of Islamist forces, foremost among them the Muslim Brotherhood; old regime loyalists, who wanted to protect their privileged position; and the often-discordant supporters of the revolution – activists, students, trade unionists, human rights campaigners, and civil society.

A president's coup

It was no secret that the 76-year-old Field Marshal Tantawi, Mubarak's long-serving defence minister, held a certain loathing for President Muhammad Morsi and the organised power of the Muslim Brotherhood. During a visit to Egypt, US Secretary of State Hillary Clinton met with Tantawi on 15 July to nudge the head of the military council to concede political power to civilian authority. In statements reported by the state news agency following the meeting, the top military commander hinted that the army would prevent the Brotherhood from dominating the political process. 'Egypt will not fall,' Tantawi remarked at a military ceremony, in apparent response to Washington's envoy. 'It is for all Egyptians, not for a certain group – the armed forces will not allow that.'[9]

On 5 August, militants ambushed and killed 16 Egyptian soldiers stationed at a border post in Sinai after sunset as they broke their Ramadan fast. Morsi seized on conflicting loyalties within the military institution to make his boldest moves. On 8 August he sacked the intelligence chief, the heads of the Republican Guard and Central Security forces, the governor of North Sinai, the president's chief of staff (a military council appointee), and requested the replacement of the chief of the military police, Hamdy Badeen. On 12 August, just over a month into his presidency, Morsi annulled the supplementary constitutional declaration that empowered Tantawi and the Supreme Council of the Armed Forces, and sent the field marshal and army chief of staff Sami Anan into retirement. The new president also dismissed commanders of the air force, navy, and air defence forces.

Abd al-Fattah al-Sisi, head of military intelligence, was promoted two military ranks to colonel general and tapped to become the defence minister; he sent army officers who outranked him into retirement, including top brass on the Supreme Council of the Armed Forces. By removing the military generals from the political arena, Morsi's surprise shakeup caught

Tantawi and Anan – given top state honours as consolation – off guard. The move extended a safe exit for the commanders, who were let off scot-free for the deaths of protesters under their rule and faded from public view. Assuming full executive as well as legislative powers, including authority in shaping the nation's constitution, Morsi consolidated vast powers that many feared could be used against his opponents and critics.

New loyalties for state media

On 8 August 2012 the Islamist-dominated Shura Council appointed the editors-in-chief of 44 state-owned newspapers, magazines, and a wire service. The following month parliament's upper house appointed six new board chairmen for the state-owned publishing houses. The editorial and executive hires kept the state press in the grip of the governing power. The new chief editor of *al-Ahram*, Abd al-Nasser Salama, had lambasted protesters in his columns during the revolution, parroting the regime's line of nefarious plots by foreign-financed provocateurs. Salama's first task as the head of the flagship state-owned daily was to terminate a section of the paper assessing Morsi's first hundred days in office.[10] While some of the top editors of the state press may have lacked overt Islamist leanings, they displayed an opportunistic and pliable relationship with power, qualities as useful in Mubarak's Egypt as they were under the Brotherhood's political hegemony. The editorship of *al-Akhbar*, the second largest state-owned daily, was given to Muhammad Hassan al-Banna, who moved to censor opinion pieces critical of the Islamist president and shrink the number of editorial pages.[11]

Salah Abd al-Maqsoud, Morsi's campaign spokesman and a journalist with Muslim Brotherhood-affiliated publications and websites, was appointed minister of information in August 2012, a position where loyalty to the regime is a prerequisite.[12] His job was to redirect the compass of the state media establishment to favour the designs of the head of state. Abd al-Maqsoud lifted an unwritten ban on women wearing the hijab from being news presenters on Egyptian state television. Yet he turned heads when he inappropriately called a Lebanese presenter 'hot' during an interview.[13] And during a speech where the information minister lauded press freedoms under President Morsi, journalist Nada Muhammad asked, 'Sir, where is this freedom when journalists are being killed and injured?' 'Come and I'll tell you where it is,' Abd al-Maqsoud replied with a grin, brushing off the question with a sexual innuendo.[14]

Using his new legislative powers, Morsi on 23 August amended an article of the press law that ended pre-trial detentions of journalists yet he did not go as far as abolishing jail sentences for publishing crimes. The order released *al-Dustur* editor-in-chief Islam Afifi, who was charged with insulting the president, falsifying news, and fuelling sedition in a front-page editorial warning of a Brotherhood 'emirate' and urging support for the military against the Islamists.

Media wrangles with the President

On 12 October 2012 clashes broke out during a Friday rally when Brotherhood members destroyed a stage of opposition factions in Tahrir because they disapproved of the speakers' rhetoric. The ensuing confrontation led to scores injured and the torching of three buses used to transport Brotherhood members to the square. In official statements, the Brotherhood claimed that it was thugs wearing party insignia who destroyed the platform.

'Those who were breaking the stages were saying, "Freedom and Justice, Morsi has men behind him." Those are words recorded on television,' said Jihan Mansour, presenter of the programme *Sabahak ya Masr* (Your Morning, Egypt) on Dream TV, speaking by phone with Brotherhood party leader Essam al-Erian. 'The other parties totally condemn the burning of the Muslim Brotherhood's buses and want to know who are the perpetrators. Why doesn't the Muslim Brotherhood and the Freedom and Justice Party admit some mistakes so that there is agreement and compromise with all. Why always denial, denial, denial?'

'Great, you don't want to listen. What should I do to get you to listen?' replied al-Erian, annoyed because he was being interrupted.

'You have all the time and complete freedom,' said Mansour.

Instead al-Erian berated her for her supposed lack of journalistic ethics. 'See what you have done? Find someone who understands the profession to tell you whether you were right or wrong. Jihan, it's a shame for me to tell you those words on the air!'

'Sir, I am giving you the time for you to talk.'

'I am not going to ask how much you get paid to say and do these things,' retorted al-Erian, suggesting Mansour receives payouts to assail the Brotherhood. 'I am talking to you as a respectable professional. You asked a question. Does it equate those pretending to be from the party, or may have been from the party and broke a stage in anger, with people coming with Molotovs and firebombs and burning buses, which could have cost lives. Is this justice? Is this equality?' The Brotherhood organiser added that Egyptians understand very well what is going on.

'They see the pictures, too,' said Mansour. 'The media, which is always blamed, broadcasts the images as they are. We do not invent images. We do not make charges or haphazard accusations, as you have done, accusing me of an allegation of which I am innocent.'[15]

The edgy exchange seemed to have vexed the minister of information, who took punitive action. Dream TV owner Ahmed Bahgat was informed in November 2012 that within five days he must halt live transmission from studios in his real estate development compound called Dreamland. On 15 November, Dream was off the air. Six years earlier, the Egyptian Radio and Television Union gave Bahgat permission to build studios outside Media Production City, a television and film complex where the state holds a controlling stake.

'Our station is upsetting the ruling regime. It is not just our station, it's all the stations. I heard that most of the people meeting with the president are telling him that the media is the problem,' Bahgat said at a press conference. 'But in reality, the media is not the problem. The media clarifies where the problem is. The problem is that we are not doing anything to solve the problems that exist.'

Dream TV was a trailblazer among Egyptian satellite broadcasters while shunning the bravado of Qatari news channel Al Jazeera. The station's talk shows took risks in hosting guests from the Muslim Brotherhood. 'All the people who were sidelined, we gave them a platform where they could express their point of view. And once they reached power, the first thing they want to do is to shut us up,' said Bahgat, pointing out that his network had been operating for a decade under Mubarak and its signal was never blocked.[16]

This was not the first time that broadcasters were in the crosshairs of the new rulers. Al-Fara'in (Pharaohs) satellite channel is owned by the brash and bellicose Tawfiq Okasha, an old regime hack and vehement revolutionary and Brotherhood foe, who hosts his own show called *Masr al-youm* (Egypt Today). He used his platform to imaginatively dish out conspiratorial monologues linking Zionists, Freemasons, and the Brotherhood, which often came across as comedic. In a 6 August episode of his programme, he came dangerously close to calling for the president's murder by exclaiming, 'Well, I declare it permissible to spill your blood. And if you think you have supporters willing to implement, you don't know what I have. Beasts and lions come out with me.'[17] Within 48 hours the channel was off the air.[18]

The media's criticism of Morsi did not subside. On the morning of 17 November an oncoming train collided with an overcrowded school bus in the village of al-Mandara in the southern province of Assiut when a railroad worker failed to close the manually operated road crossing. The accident claimed the lives of 51 children, the driver, and a woman, strewing mutilated bodies and schoolchildren's belongings across the tracks. With shoddy maintenance and non-existent safety standards, train accidents have been an all too frequent occurrence.

In a hastily arranged television statement that lasted barely two minutes, Morsi said he accepted the resignation of the transportation minister and the chief of the railway authority. Waiting hours before departing for Assiut, Prime Minister Hesham Kandil was jeered and chased out of the public hospital by grieving villagers. The president did not consider it necessary to pay a visit to families of the children who perished. Amr Adeeb, host of the evening talk programme *al-Qahira al-youm* (Cairo Today) ranted against the failures of the country and its leadership. 'Egypt is too big for you, Mr President,' yelped the broadcaster. 'The former regime was negligent and you too are negligent. The former regime was a failure and you are also a failure.'[19] The train disaster was media fodder for critics of Morsi, who as a parliamentarian in 2002 hotly demanded the prime minister and his Cabinet resign when a fire engulfed a Luxor-bound train, charring to death hundreds of third-class passengers returning to their towns and villages for the Eid holiday.

Protesters and security personnel again clashed on 19 November, the one-year anniversary of the street battles of Muhammad Mahmoud Street. Ahmed Gaber Salah, nicknamed Jika, a 16-year-old activist with the April 6 Youth Movement, died of injuries from shotgun fire to his head, neck, and chest. Overlooking Tahrir Square, the first floor offices of Al Jazeera Live Egypt were firebombed by a mob on the third day of fighting. For days, round-the-clock clashes persisted between security forces armed with an arsenal of tear gas, rubber-coated bullets, and shotguns and enraged young protesters hurling rocks and Molotovs.

The making of a pharaoh

On 22 November 2012, a day after brokering a cease-fire in Gaza between Israelis and Palestinians for which he was showered with accolades, the president gave himself extraordinary constitutional powers, without recourse to a referendum or seeking political consensus. The constitutional decree's most contentious clause immunised all decisions the president had made and would make from any sort of legal or judicial challenge until a new constitution was approved in a referendum *and* a new House of Representatives was elected. The president's decree also barred the dissolution of the Constituent Assembly and the Shura Council by the courts and further bypassed the separation of executive and judicial powers by sacking the prosecutor general and allowing Morsi to appoint his own.[20]

The election law on which the legislative chambers were elected was deemed unconstitutional by the Supreme Court five months earlier and it was expected that the court would dissolve the Shura Council, initially a consultative body not elected to have law-making functions. The highest court was also expected to review the constitutionality of the law forming the Constituent Assembly. Civil and church representatives withdrew from the committee drafting the constitution, protesting a charter with Islamist overtones that marginalised the rights of women and religious minorities.

The Brotherhood's leadership called on its rank and file to go to the streets and support the president's decree before it was even announced. In taking his decision, Morsi did not seek the counsel of his vice president or his justice minister, both former judges, strong advocates of an independent judiciary, and brothers. Seven of the president's 21 advisers and top aides resigned, including the only two Christians. The president's power grab received wide condemnation, with detractors christening him Morsilini.

Dozens of buses transported the party faithful to a rally the day after the issuance of the decree, a Friday, in front of the presidential palace. Opponents of the president's measures headed to Tahrir. In a 45-minute speech before thousands of supporters on 23 November, Morsi, flanked by bodyguards, his oversized campaign headshot in the background, struck a decidedly defiant tone. He claimed to have foreknowledge of a constitutional court ruling dismantling institutions of government: 'I see with all of you that the ruling of the court is announced two, three weeks before the session: We will dissolve the Shura Council and we will dissolve the whole nation, it seems.' The fervent crowd hollered, 'The people want the implementation of God's law' and 'The people support the president's decree.'

Morsi spoke of conspiracies and lurking threats imperilling the nation yet submitted no concrete evidence. 'Some people have decided to cover themselves with the cloak of the judiciary. I will uncover them. The five, six, seven, three, four who try to conceal themselves with the cloak, don't think I don't see you. You cannot affect the path of the revolution,' roared Morsi, declaring himself a guardian of Egypt's popular uprising as the military council had done before him.[21]

Demonstrations flared up against the president and the Brotherhood. The cries in the squares were 'The people want the downfall of the regime' and 'Down with the rule of the supreme guide'. Morsi's Islamist base grouped for its own mass protests. With a president unwilling to reconsider his dictum, national discourse became polarised. Pro-Morsi champions condemned critics as infidels and regime remnants who sought Egypt's destruction, while anti-Morsi crowds depicted the president as a tyrant and his supporters as sheep, the mindless herd of the supreme guide. Over the coming weeks, dozens of Freedom and Justice Party offices were vandalised or torched, including the Brotherhood's headquarters.

Morsi's supporters dismissed the numbers on the ground. Ikwanweb, the official Twitter account of the Muslim Brotherhood, offered its own spin on the 27 November rallies in Tahrir and across the country: 'opposition thinks the significance of today is # of Tahrir protestors (200–300k), they shld brace for millions in support of the elected prez'.[22] The highest appeals court, the Court of Cassation, suspended work nationwide to protest Morsi's decree. A cascade of appellate courts in various governorates voted to do the same. On 2 December, as the nation's highest court was set to review the constitutionality of law governing the formation of the Constituent Assembly and the election law for the Shura Council, Morsi's supporters besieged the court building, preventing the justices from entering the chamber and issuing a ruling.

As a candidate for president, Muhammad Morsi insisted that he had a duty to obey the law, and if he failed to do so, the people should remove him from power. In an interview with Mahmoud Saad on his programme *Akhir al-nahar* (Day's End), Morsi said, 'The people are aware, Muslims and Christians, and they know that the one who comes [to rule] and does not respect the laws and the constitution, the people will revolt against him. I want the people to revolt against me right away if I do not respect the laws and the constitution.'[23]

Khairy Ramadan on the CBC network asked the candidate Muhammad Morsi the hypothetical question: 'After you have assumed the presidency, huge mass rallies took to the squares, shouting "The people want the downfall of the president." How would you respond?'

'I see that this cannot happen because the president, if it were me, would act according to the will of the people. And if this occurred, I am the first to obey the will of the people.'[24]

A few short months after assuming the presidency, Morsi succeeded in deepening divisions, giving citizens the choice of accepting the constitution in a referendum or the continuation of his unchallenged powers. 'The Muslim Brotherhood received their [election] votes under dubious circumstances,' Mohamed ElBaradei, who led an opposition coalition called the National Salvation Front, told *Der Spiegel*. The group won elections with the help of handouts to the poor and religious sermonising urging a vote for religious parties as a duty towards God. 'The country is fractured. If the moderate forces no longer have a voice, a civil war threatens to erupt in Egypt,' added ElBaradei.[25]

The president and the Brotherhood lost a sizeable chunk of their political capital in the power grab. Wael Ghonim, who started the 'We are all Khaled Said' Facebook page, voted for Morsi and supported his decision to cancel the military council's constitutional declaration making the army a co-ruler, but he staunchly opposed the president's controversial decree. 'This unconstitutional declaration surpasses the notion of "protecting the revolution" to one of "protecting power",' he posted on his personal Facebook page. 'What some of his supporters call a temporary dictatorship is illogical, for all dictatorships begin as temporary and then persist.'[26]

Before runoff elections, Morsi promised to rebalance the Constituent Assembly to make it more representative of Egyptian society, Ghonim explained. The president did not follow through with his pledge and his position did not change when a quarter of the members withdrew from the constitution drafting body. The president also broke a vow that a referendum on the constitution would not be called without first commencing a nationwide dialogue on the charter. Morsi had pledged to use his newfound legislative powers sparingly and then went on to issue a declaration 'that prevents an Egyptian citizen from the right to litigate against his decisions'. The Constituent Assembly, which Morsi promised to rebalance, became immune from dissolution by the court, forfeiting the chance to create 'a constitution befitting the revolution', wrote the activist. The president has pledged to go back on any decision made in error, but then decided to mobilise crowds of supporters and considers those who oppose him to be 'revolutionaries who have sold the revolution for personal gain', expressed Ghonim. 'When you wanted our votes, you told us, "Our strength is in unity", and today you say that we are the few who cannot change society: "Die of your frustration."'[27]

Imams during Friday mosque sermons urged support for the president's decree. The Ministry of Religious Endowments, whose top bureaucrat is a Cabinet appointee, is charged with assigning preachers to the nation's 100,000-plus state-controlled mosques. Mosques have frequently been employed to rally the faithful behind the Islamist president for the sake of the nation and Islam. On 30 November 2012, Morsi attended Friday noon prayers at the Hassan al-Sharbatli Mosque in New Cairo. The iman defended the president's constitutional decree by drawing comparisons with revered Muslim caliphs. Pandemonium broke out, with mosque-goers furious as the imam waxed poetic of the president seated cross-legged in the front row, guarded by his security entourage.[28]

The Muslim Brotherhood marshalled supporters from Greater Cairo and the provinces for a rally the next day. The Brotherhood-affiliated Masr 25 satellite channel broadcast an aerial view of the crowds. The headline of *al-Ahram*, the flagship state-owned daily, on 2 December was 'Millions Mass in Cairo and the Governorates to Support the President'. Above the masthead was the headline, 'The President Invites the People to a Constitutional Referendum on 15 December'. Several independent and party newspapers on 3 December printed front-page images of an imprisoned figure mummified in newsprint and bound with a ball and chain. The caption read 'No to Dictatorship'. Protesting against Morsi's diktat and the restrictions on the press in the new constitution, a dozen newspapers decided not to publish an edition of their papers the following day.

The rumble at the presidential palace

Demands of the opposition were for a cancellation of the decree and postponing the referendum on the constitution until a national consensus on the document was reached. For two weeks Egyptians peacefully protested; tens of thousands converged on the presidential palace on 4 December. Demonstrators scrawled their proclamations of anger on the gates of the palace, covering them in graffiti. A band of protesters climbed atop a security van and waved flags. Despite the dearth of security – after police, vastly outnumbered, retreated – the crowds did not breach the palace walls.

As mass protests unfolded across Egypt, no statement was issued by the president, whisked safely home through a back entrance. Al-Azhar's

Islamic Research Academy, which issues fatwas, called on the president to suspend the constitutional declaration and embark on a national dialogue. Yet escalation by Morsi's backers continued. A day later, the president's Islamist defenders called for counter-demonstrations before the gates of the presidential palace where a sit-in of revolutionary opponents had assembled. Descending on them in combat drill, Morsi's supporters tore down tents and pillaged possessions.

Propaganda became a useful weapon. Brotherhood members claimed they found drugs, alcohol, dollars, and contraception with protesters and among their belongings. Pro-Morsi protesters whitewashed graffiti etched on the walls the night before. With tensions at a boiling point, the crisis spiralled into violence. Street battles lasted into the dawn hours, leaving ten dead. A chant of the Islamists was, 'Our dead are in heaven and your dead are in hell.' Brotherhood members detained and abused at least 49 anti-Morsi protesters on 5–6 December, holding them by the presidential palace gates and forcing them to confess to being paid to foment strife.[29]

CNN journalist Mohamed Fadel Fahmy tweeted: 'Muslim Brotherhood supporters attack a number of journalists around palace, chase them down streets, destroy cameras.'[30] Camera in hand, Al-Husseini Abu Deif, photo-journalist for the daily *al-Fajr* (The Dawn), was shot in the head by an alleged Morsi supporter. The 33-year-old slipped into a coma and was pronounced dead a week later.

Morsi avoided addressing the public after announcing a referendum on the constitution, with the Constituent Assembly hurriedly approving the articles of the charter in a marathon all-night session. In interviews as a presidential candidate Morsi stayed on message, promising to be the model leader who would respect freedoms, assimilate political forces, consult with broad sections of the political class, and rule with the will of the people. Before the runoffs, talk show host Yosri Fouda interviewed Morsi, who when referring to campaign promises stated, 'What I say is a contract; it is a collar around my neck. What I say is a commitment to the people.'[31] In that interview he promised to reconstitute the Islamist-weighted Constituent Assembly – one of several pledges he violated after assuming the presidency. As confrontations flared by the presidential palace, Fouda issued an apology to his viewers 'for any vote that could have passed through me during that interview' to elect the Brotherhood's candidate as the president of Egypt. 'It is my obligation to apologise,' said the broadcaster.[32]

If the expectation was that Muhammad Morsi would rise to the occasion and bridge divisions, it was not to be – a sharp contrast to the promise of a soon to be president taking the oath of office in Tahrir and travelling the globe as Egypt's first democratically elected head of state following a revolution. In office, Morsi and his backers skilfully enlisted the mechanisms of authoritarianism: consolidating power, intimidating media outlets, defaming his opposition, and retaining the trappings of the security state.[33]

Whereas the opposition held Morsi ultimately responsible for the bloodshed, the Brotherhood fingered Mohamed ElBaradei and Hamdeen Sabahy, the founder of a political party called the Popular Current, for the 'escalation of violence' and 'inciting their supporters',[34] in addition to Mubarak loyalists who are 'arming thugs to attack protestors'.[35] As clashes took place between the president's supporters and opponents, vice chair of the Freedom and Justice Party Essam al-Erian in a phone interview with the Brotherhood channel Masr 25 beseeched Islamists to head to the presidential palace and engage in vigilante justice by arresting the illusive and troublesome third parties:

> *What's happening now are skirmishes between supporters of the revolution and the rules of legitimacy, and the counter-revolution and those who seek to overthrow legitimacy. That is the true description of what is happening. That is what is happening between peaceful demonstrators who want to convey their opinion and say this is the opinion of the people, and between people who seek chaos, who want to practise political thuggery, force their opinion on others, and usurp power with a civilian presidential council that displaces an elected president. That is what's happening and that is the truth. I believe the people surpassed the invitation of the popular forces [i.e. Islamist political parties]. I invite them to go in the tens of thousands to surround these thugs because this is the opportunity to arrest them and expose the third party that fires bullets and buckshot.*[36]

Those who stridently opposed the president's actions were enemies of the revolution, subversive regime remnants, provocateurs, instigators, or agitators – a common smear strategy used by defenders of the ruling order, past and present. 'What is regrettable is that some of those arrested have work and communication ties with some of those who belong to the political powers,' alleged Morsi in a televised address the night after the bloodshed. 'Some of those with weapons were hired in exchange for money paid to them. This is what was revealed by the investigations and confessions.'[37] (When Morsi made those statements, prosecutors had not begun investigations.) He promised neither to rescind the constitutional declaration nor postpone the referendum on the constitution – demands of the National Salvation Front in order to engage in dialogue.

Khairy Ramadan, the host of *Mumkin* (Perhaps), bowed out after executives at his private satellite station, CBC, barred Hamdeen Sabahy, former presidential candidate and a leader in the National Salvation Front, from appearing as an in-studio guest to respond to the president's speech. 'During the break, the management of the channel called and requested that Hamdeen Sabahy not appear because I did not inform the station manager,' Ramadan told viewers. 'I did in fact inform the station manager. I respect the management of the station. I respect its reasons and justifications. I understand that many things that are happening in the country are not understood. But I am not a politician but a professional. With respect to my profession and my respectable guest who came tonight, I also announce my withdrawal.'[38] Sabahy wrote in a Facebook post: 'This incident proves beyond a reasonable doubt that the notions of democracy Dr Morsi speaks about in his speech and in his calls for dialogue with national and opposition forces have been put to death – in restraining the freedoms of expression and the press, and preventing those who oppose his policies and decisions from addressing our great public.'[39]

Minister of information Salah Abd al-Maqsoud, who hailed from the Muslim Brotherhood, was said to have issued instructions during the clashes that opponents of Morsi not be allowed to appear on state television. Abd al-Maqsoud went as far as to tell the state daily *al-Ahram* that he possessed documents and evidence confiscated from armed thugs in front of the palace that proved that Egypt was the target of a conspiracy by political forces to sow chaos and thwart the measures of the president towards stability.[40]

Concerning the violent turn of events, satirist Bassem Youssef had this to say on *al-Bernameg?*: 'This programme is more than just laughs. This programme chronicles what has happened and what is happening,' he said, deriding those who 'transgress in the name of religion in order to beat and harass, then they pray the evening prayers with a clear conscience'.

> *What has happened in the country the last few days – hatred, killings, and attacks on sit-ins or even the offices of the Brotherhood – is because of a leadership that only listens to its group, and traders in religion, who after mixing religion with politics are now mixing hatred with religion. They have no connection with the laws of God that they're exploiting.*

Youssef pronounced that every death on either side of the conflict is a liability 'of the person who says he is the president of the whole country'. He concluded the segment with:

> *We are not the ones who made it: us against them. We are not the ones who turned a political feud into heaven versus hell. Other people turned it into Muslims versus infidels, Islam versus the age of ignorance. With that kind of demeanour, only God knows which one of us is delusional. For those who think they are living in this country by themselves:* wake up! *If you think it's about numbers:* wake up! *If you think Egypt will be ruled by one group:* wake up! *If you think Egypt is a small child that needs guidance:* wake up! *Wake up because others were smarter.* Wake up![41]

The Brotherhood offensive

On 8 December, a new constitutional declaration replaced the 22 November declaration, dropping an article that blocked the judiciary from reviewing all executive orders, but still barred the courts from challenging or nullifying any of the president's constitutional declarations. It was not much of a compromise. Morsi's die-hard supporters had the Supreme Court cordoned, thwarting any ruling on the validity of the Constituent Assembly or the Shura Council until the referendum vote.

The main criticism of the Brotherhood for decades has been a distrust of its commitment to democratic principles. Decades of being an insular and officially banned group has translated into a doctrine that shuns cooperation and compromise with divergent parties. In power, the Brotherhood sought to monopolise the political process. In chants and rally speeches Morsi's impassioned supporters framed the political conflict in terms of shari'a and jihad, and conjured up myriad conspiracies against their embattled president. Khairat al-Shater, the Muslim Brotherhood's top strategist and deputy supreme guide, argued that what was happening in the aftermath of Morsi's power-grabbing decree was nothing short of a high-level global and regional conspiracy:

> *A period of time after the revolution a number of specific meetings took place between global and regional sides, and within Egypt, assessing the situation after Mubarak stepped down. They put in place a recognised*

> *strategy called 'disabling the Islamists and any true revolutionary force from reaching power in Egypt' and attempting to steal the revolution and drain it of its real objectives in order to maintain the hegemony of regional and global powers over our country, as had been the case for long periods of time.*

And if the Islamists reached power, the plan was to ensure their failure, he continued, by creating economic havoc, leading Egyptians to disavow the revolution. 'When they realised that the constitution was nearing a referendum vote, they used many methods,' al-Shater stated. 'They escalated and escalated until we reached the final weeks, so the final card they are working with is to instigate the greatest amount of sabotage and chaos in the country.' This, he said, was expected to shake the confidence of Egyptians in the regime and its stability. He also harped on the shortcomings of the media, which he said deliberately concealed the facts. 'Some of the corrupt people in the media, the media of corrupt money, are present and they're working and conniving and they attempt to distort the facts.'[42]

Hardline Islamists have laid periodic siege to Media Production City, vandalising vehicles and threateningly announcing their displeasure with Egypt's private satellite broadcasters. The Brotherhood's channel, Masr 25, rarely accepted opposing viewpoints or guests on their programmes, as ruling party officials accused other satellite broadcasters of failing to be neutral, objective, or abide by journalistic ethics. Media restrictions were locked in place with a constitution that was unsatisfactory to broad sectors of the population. Morsi had not made an appearance in Tahrir Square since the day he took the oath of office and brazenly unbuttoned his jacket to display to the crowds that he was not wearing a bulletproof vest.

The constitution and a free press

The Journalists' Syndicate, objecting to how press freedoms and the activities of workers' and professional unions were being restricted, voted to withdraw from the body charged with drafting the constitution.[43] As during the era of Mubarak, media outlets could still be shut down and journalists jailed for what they reported or published. The constitution allowed for the closure or confiscation of media outlets when a court order was obtained and the imposition of censorship during times of war and public mobilisation (article 48). While newspapers no longer needed to be licensed, the establishment of digital media and radio and television stations 'are regulated by law' (article 49). The charter mandated the press 'respect the sanctity of the private lives of citizens and the requirements of national security' (article 48) and prohibited 'insulting or showing contempt towards any human being' (article 31), making defamation an offence that could be skilfully used against journalists, bloggers, and dissidents. Additionally, blasphemy lawsuits were expected to rise with a prohibition on 'insult or abuse of all religious messengers and prophets' (article 44). Other vaguely worded articles could have potentially chipped away press freedoms.[44]

Critics point to a number of other pitfalls in the 236-article constitution. The advice of al-Azhar was sought in matters pertaining to shari'a on which legislation is based (article 4), giving a group of non-elected religious scholars jurisdiction over matters of governance, which could conceivably form the basis of theocratic rule. The authoritarian foundations of the state remained in place. The military institution retained a high degree of autonomy, devoid of oversight by an elected legislature, whose representatives had no say in the budget of the armed forces (article 197). Civilians could still be tried in military tribunals for 'crimes that harm the armed forces' (article 198) and the constitution left it up to the law to regulate protests and strikes (article 63).[45]

Voters waited in queues for hours to cast their vote. The referendum vote took place amid a boycott by judges in supervising the vote as Islamists laid siege to the Supreme Court. Irregularities during the referendum vote, which took place on 15 and 22 December, included attempts to influence voters and prevent Christians from casting their ballots, particularly in provinces where Islamists have a forceful presence. The prosaic and uninspiring constitution passed with a yes vote of 63.8%; only a third of eligible voters showed up to the polls.

After the vote a video surfaced of Salafi preacher and member of the constitution drafting body Sheikh Yasser Borhami assuring adherents that language inserted in the constitution in fact 'completely restricts' rights and freedoms in a manner unprecedented in any previous Egyptian constitution. One instance he cited is article 10: 'The family is the basis of society and is founded on religion, morality, and patriotism. The state is keen to preserve the genuine character, cohesion, and stability of the Egyptian family, and to instil and protect its moral values, all as regulated by law.' 'This article is very, very important because it restrains [individual] freedom of thought, belief, expression, creativity, and all these things,' said Borhami, especially when combined with other articles of the charter on shari'a.[46]

Suing the satirist

Media personality Emad Eddin Adeeb threatened a slander suit against Bassem Youssef for poking fun at the soporific Adeeb – famous for a lauding three-part interview with Mubarak in 2005 – and other talk show presenters on the CBC satellite network on which *al-Bernameg?*'s second season aired. Youssef rolled a clip of Adeeb alleging that 'President Mubarak – and I say this with certainty and I hope you and the viewers believe me – is the most important ruler to govern Egypt since Muhammad Ali.' A baffled Youssef then played another clip of Adeeb gushing over the present holder of the office: 'The decisions Dr Morsi took in 40 days of his rule,' he emphatically stated, 'are like 40 years in the life of Egypt.'[47]

Adeeb devoted an entire segment of his programme to lambasting the satirist, who delivered a hilarious dissection of Adeeb's melodrama in his next episode. Youssef concluded with the words:

> *In the hundred episodes that we've done, we've talked about ministers, the military council, the Brotherhood, Salafis, liberals, the owner of the station I was on, and in the future the owner of this station if I remain on* (applause). *And if we are still alive, God willing, we will talk about the ruling party and the president of the republic. We did not have a revolution so that we could talk about the president of the republic and not talk about someone else.*[48]

Suits filed with the public prosecutor against the host piled on – accusing him of contempt of religion, ridiculing the pillars of Islam, and defaming the president.

Youssef has poked fun at a crop of sheikhs who talk politics on religious-based satellite stations and who use their television pulpits to spitefully attack Morsi's critics, including the popular satirist. Youssef played a clip of Khaled Abdullah, one such tele-sheikh, who appeared on al-Nas satellite channel justifying his foul and hateful taunts against compatriots by claiming to wage a 'jihad against the infidels and hypocrites'.

'And that is the source of the problem – their explanation and understanding of religion,' wryly remarked Youssef. 'They don't see us as Muslims and Christians. They see us as infidels, hypocrites, the enemies of religion and God. That is why we deserve being cursed and demeaned, and if it extends to beatings and torture and, God forbid, even murder, all this is permissible.' He added:

> *Just as you don't consider us Muslims. For us, you are neither sheikhs nor scholars* (applause). . . . *Why are most of our episodes on a particular political current? Because they have the power, they have dominated the writing of the constitution, and they have the majority in parliament. All this and they don't want us to bring them up? . . . The former regime used to say: you are against the nation. Now they say you are against shari'a. No one believes those words. Stop playing on the emotions of people by saying to those who oppose or expose you that they are against religion. Or to cover your failures by saying that your opposition is against Islam. Islam is wide, welcoming, and better than you who have expropriated its name.*[49]

In another segment of his programme, Youssef aired clips of the president's advocates likening him to the Prophet Joseph, claiming that he is supported by God, has the miraculous ability to convert Christians to Islam, and is so refreshingly pure as to be 'translucent white'. 'God has chosen him, or God is testing us with him. Either way, whatever God brings is good,' quipped Youssef, who then broadcast a clip where a television sheikh warned that those criticising Morsi 'are waging war on Islam'.

> *I would like to say to anyone who thinks of filing a lawsuit against us for contempt of religion or insulting the president, look again at the videos and see who is in contempt of religion and insulting religion, along with the president. Long ago, it was known that Egyptians manufacture their pharaoh. Now we are manufacturing prophets.*[50]

Bassem Youssef's popularity and brand of satire was a formidable strike against the demagoguery, chauvinism, and Tartufferie of a band of tele-sheikhs.

The lawsuits continued to flood in. So it was little surprise that on 30 March 2013 Morsi's appointed prosecutor general, Talaat Abdullah, ordered Youssef's arrest and questioning for insulting the president, denigrating Islam, and spreading false news with the intent of disturbing public order. Greeted by crowds of supporters and the press, Youssef showed up the next day for five hours of questioning in downtown Cairo's

High Court of Justice and was released on bail of 15,000 Egyptian pounds ($2,200/£1,450).[51]

News of the arrest warrant against Bassem Youssef and his interrogation made headlines around the world. 'By the way, without Bassem and all those journalists and bloggers and brave protesters who took to Tahrir Square to voice dissent, you, President Morsi, would not be in a position to repress them. For someone who spent time in jail yourself under Mubarak, you seem awfully eager to send other people there for the same non-crimes,' Jon Stewart noted on *The Daily Show*. 'I am going to let you in on a little secret: The world is watching. No one wants Egypt to plunge into darkness. Democracy isn't a democracy if it only lasts until someone makes fun of your hat.'[52] In a later appearance on Stewart's programme, Youssef remarked, 'When religion ceases to be a spiritual guidance and turns into a way of governance it turns into a tool of tyranny.'[53]

On his first show since his interrogation Youssef described a ruse used by the people in power: the creation of convenient distractions. 'Let's get people riled up about something fictitious: a silly programme, a clown of a presenter. And people will sympathise and shriek, and then the matter fades.' This will happen again and again until people get bored, fed-up, and eventually turn against the trouble-maker. 'Are you surprised? Do you think that won't happen?' asked Youssef. 'I am someone who hosts a programme that people know, so it is natural that when something happens you find all this commotion. But what about the activists, journalists, and bloggers who are arrested, jailed, beaten, and perhaps tortured each day?'

He goes on to name individuals ensnared by the regime and the countless others who face a similarly uncertain fate. 'And it will all be done by law,' he says. Television channels will be shut down until what is left is a servile and obedient media. The men in power will appoint their brethren, craft laws to suit their whim, and entrench their rule, as the people are caught up in illusionary battles and contrived distractions. 'Before we used to complain that what ruled this country was a gang. Now my fear is that we have replaced a gang with a mafia.'[54]

Additional legal complaints prosecutors were investigating Youssef for included propagating homosexuality and obscenity, inciting violence and civil strife, and insulting the nation of Pakistan. 'If your regime can't handle a joke then you don't have a regime,' Jon Stewart, a guest on *al-Bernameg?* said to applause. 'What Bassem is doing . . . is showing that satire can still be relevant, that it can carve out space in a country for people to express themselves because that is all democracy is: the ability to express yourself and be heard.'[55]

The crime of insulting the president

The number of lawsuits filed for defaming the ruler were greater during Morsi's first 200 days in office than for all of Egypt's monarchs and presidents from 1892 until Mubarak.[56] Litigation against press and dissident voices had become a form of censorship through intimidation, intended to restrain a noisy press as Egyptians failed to see tangible accomplishments from the president and his party. Prosecutors interrogated popular talk show presenters and newspaper editors over charges of slandering the judiciary, contempt of religion, insulting the president, and disseminating false news likely to disturb public peace.

The president's office issued legal complaints with prosecutors against journalists and columnists, such as Ola al-Shafei. In an opinion piece in the daily *al-Youm al-sabi'* (The Seventh Day) she assailed the defenders of the president who talk about conspiracies and traitors funded from abroad as Morsi 'lets loose the militias of his group in the streets and squares of Egypt'.[57] In another complaint the presidency charged television presenter Mahmoud Saad and his guest, psychologist Manal Omar, with insulting the head of state for discussing how repression affects prisoners, referencing the incarceration of Morsi and Brotherhood leaders. Omar explained the psychological theory where the victimised learn in turn to be victimisers, linking it to the episode of the president's power grab. She noted that when the pressure is suddenly released, 'the beast comes out'. 'Why should they believe they're wrong?' asked Omar, adding that because they believe themselves to be pious they ignore detractors, who they view as lacking in religious belief. She added that when power is concentrated in the hands of one person with a legion of supporters, an attack on the unruly media is inevitable. Saad asked how such a psychological case could be treated. 'Leave,' responded Omar in an obvious reference to Morsi. 'Leave the scene.'[58] The show's popular presenter had advocated voting for Morsi against his rival Ahmed Shafik, only to join the president's growing list of critics.

The lawsuits hardly fazed the media or safeguarded the president from reproach. Facing censure for clamping down on the media, in April 2013 Morsi requested the withdrawal of nine criminal complaints of insulting the president his office had filed with the public prosecutor. Yet private citizens and regime allies still filed complaints with the office of the prosecutor charging media personalities, opposition leaders, and critics with a host of crimes, including insulting the president and contempt of religion.[59]

Two years after revolution

The enigmatic anarchist youth group Black Bloc burst on the scene, a new element of resistance in battles with police. Set to action-themed music, a video for the group, first appearing on YouTube days before the revolution's second anniversary, shows a band of young men cloaked in black, faces concealed, waving an anarchist flag in night-time Alexandria. They claim their mission is to 'face off against the regime of fascist tyranny – the Muslim Brotherhood – with its military wing'.[60]

The revolution's second anniversary was commemorated with rallies, marches, and clashes with police across the country, with protesters expressing frustration at a regime that had not lived up to the revolution's aspirations. In a number of provinces, protesters surrounded municipal offices and demanded that governors belonging to the Brotherhood step down. Spray-painted on the tile walls of the Tahrir Metro station was the pronouncement, 'Morsi is Mubarak with a beard.' 25 January 2013 was also marred by frequent and methodical incidents of sexual assault on women in Tahrir Square.

By day's end nine protesters were dead: eight in Suez and one in Ismailia – cities that tallied the first casualties of the uprising against Mubarak. No word came from the president until 1:11 am, on 26 January, when Morsi offered his condolences on Twitter, affirming that state agencies would prosecute offenders and bring them to justice. 'I call on all citizens to uphold the noble principles of the Egyptian revolution to express their opinion freely and peacefully, renouncing violence in word and deed,' he wrote.[61] Critics roundly scorned the president for conveying his message to Egyptians via a 140-character social networking site. ElBaradei followed with a tweet: 'What we see so far from the president and his government in dealing with the tragedy in which we live is the epitome of irresponsibility.'[62]

With a leadership unprepared to respond, the violence only worsened. Clashes with police and residents of Port Said – in the aftermath of a 26 January verdict sentencing 21 defendants to death in connection with a football rampage a year earlier – claimed 32 lives in a single day. To the people of Port Said the death sentences were unjust and politically motivated. By contrast, for the hundreds of civilians killed during the revolution, only two police officers of 172 charged were imprisoned, and none were sentenced to death. One of Morsi's many campaign promises was to secure the rights of the revolution's martyrs. Yet he took no action when a fact-finding commission on the deaths of protesters delivered to him its report, which was never made public.

The death toll in Port Said rose by eight a day later when police opened fire on a funeral procession and protest march calling for the downfall of the regime. On the night of 27 January, Morsi addressed the public, announcing strict orders: the deployment of the army, a month-long state of emergency in the canal cities of Port Said, Suez, and Ismailia, and a 9 pm to 6 am curfew.[63] With an offending wag of his index finger, he threatened that he would not hesitate to take further action. As a candidate for president Morsi had promised never to resort to emergency measures.

As Morsi thanked the police and army and blamed the 'ugly face of the counter-revolution' for sowing havoc and destroying property, live television and internet videos showed security forces smashing cars in Suez and beating protesters in Cairo. Officers expelled the interior minister, Muhammad Ahmed Ibrahim, from the funeral prayer of a fallen comrade. In Port Said, police snipers occupied rooftops and security forces fired tear gas and live ammunition on mourners. Morsi ended his 12-minute speech by offering political forces an invitation for a national dialogue at the presidential palace the next day, a call rejected by the National Salvation Front if the president was not willing to take political responsibility for the deaths of protesters, agree to a national unity government, and form a committee to amend the constitution.

In bold defiance, residents of Port Said, Suez, and Ismailia violated the curfew and organised rallies and football tournaments. With the Black Bloc becoming an overnight media obsession, the prosecutor general pronounced the shadowy vigilantes a terrorist group and ordered the arrest of all members. In addition to the media and the opposition, the Black Bloc was the new focus of fury and angst for the administration, which called them the opposition's militia.

Civil disobedience campaigns in Port Said spread across the country, blocking roads and train tracks, shutting down government offices, and orchestrating work stoppages. Police strikes in 12 governorates called for the toppling of the interior minister amid anti-government protests. Thirty police stations closed their doors in one day, as police revolted against inhumane and degrading work conditions and prolonged confrontations with protesters. In an address to military cadets, minister of defence Abd al-Fattah al-Sisi, warned of dire consequences, including the 'collapse of the state', if the unrest continued. The message was read as a hint that the military might reassert itself in political affairs.

Mona al-Shazly, on her nightly programme *Gumla mufida* (Meaningful Sentence), was in the middle of a phone interview with an Interior Ministry spokesperson describing clashes outside the presidential palace when a video feed displayed the revolting scene, broadcast concurrently on several private Egyptian satellite channels. A reporter on the scene explained that security forces charged one of the side streets near the palace, firing shotguns at protesters. The naked man in the video had been captured by police, dragged, stripped of his clothing, and beaten.[64]

Caught on live camera, the jolting images were proof positive that the security agencies had forfeited none of their bad habits. The beating shone the media spotlight not only on the common practice of police abuse, arbitrary arrests, and disappearances, but on the general disregard for the rule of law. 'The nation of laws collapses with a scene like this one,' declared al-Shazly, as viewers saw the gruesome footage of an unclothed man being clubbed and humiliated.

> *The nation of law collapses when the Supreme Constitutional Court is besieged, while the president of the republic and the ruling party resort to this practice and defend it. The nation of laws collapses when people at the presidential palace torture others without authority, evidence, or conscience and silence reigns. The nation of laws has collapsed in Egypt a thousand times in the past two months, a thousand times the nation of laws has fallen and no one's lifted a finger.*[65]

The victim of the assault, 48-year-old Hamada Saber, a labourer who resided in a one-room dwelling with his wife and three children, was rushed to a police hospital when it became apparent that television cameras were rolling.

The following day, Saber, appeared in television interviews from his hospital bed, where he bafflingly claimed that it was protesters and not police who shot him in the leg with buckshot and stripped him of his clothes.[66] Saber, a staunch Mubarak supporter previously filmed battling protesters in league with security forces, reversed his testimony a day later and acknowledged to prosecutors that it was in fact the police that had victimised him, apologising to protesters in Tahrir and at the presidential palace in a phone interview to a satellite channel. 'I ask every Egyptian to forgive me,' he said, denying that he had accepted money, an apartment, or a job to exonerate the police.[67]

Fifty-seven protesters lost their lives in a bloody week of unrest; two of them shot outside the presidential palace on the night Saber was assaulted. Security forces beat back protesters with tear gas and shotguns and set fire to tents. Protesters threw Molotovs, fireworks, and rocks into the grounds of the presidential palace. Arrested by Tahrir Square on 27 January, 28-year-old tour guide and activist Mohamed ElGendy died eight days later after slipping into a coma from sustaining blows to the head, his body bearing signs of torture. The alternative narrative advanced by the authorities when ElGendy surfaced at a public hospital was that the injuries were the result of a hit-and-run accident.

Sheikh Mahmoud Shaaban, a Salafi professor of rhetoric at al-Azhar University who appeared regularly on the al-Hafiz religious satellite channel, issued an edict, announced on the air, that shari'a makes it permissible to assassinate leaders of the opposition National Salvation Front because they have gone against the ruler, seek his downfall, and their actions have led to corruption and bloodshed.[68] Another Egyptian television sheikh, Ahmed Muhammad Mahmoud Abdullah, who goes by the moniker Abu Islam and sports a long white beard, staunchly defended Shaaban's ruling and went a step further by justifying the rape and sexual assault of female protesters, identifying 90% of them as Christian with the rest including widows who do not have men to keep them in line.[69] On his nightly television programme Abu Islam delivered plodding invectives against democracy, the West, Zionism, Christianity and the Coptic Church, and communism, all wrapped in the guise of religiosity.

Prime Minister Hesham Kandil briefly visited the periphery of Tahrir in a chauffeured 7 Series BMW flanked by a convoy of vehicles and security detail armed with automatic weapons. He quickly got back in the car and sped off.[70] In a speech he gave later in the day, a highly strung Kandil derided the masses in Tahrir and the presidential palace as 'neither protesters nor revolutionaries'.[71] Voicing displeasure at the current regime, marches and rallies commemorated the day, two years earlier, when Mubarak fell from power. Rallies called for Morsi's downfall, the departure of his ineffective government, and the demise of an unpopular constitution. By 8 pm on 11 February, as a few hundred protesters massed outside the presidential palace, the presidential guard and security forces doused the crowds with water cannons then fired volleys of tear gas. Protesters, including Black Bloc members, hurled fireworks and Molotovs, and lobbed tear gas canisters back at police.

Economic and political woes were laid at the doorstep of the media. To a group of businessmen, Morsi accused the media of having a negative affect on the investment climate. Yet critical media and street action were the main line of defence against the formation of a remodelled authoritarianism under the rule of the Muslim Brotherhood. The Ministry of Insurance and Social Affairs recognised the Muslim Brotherhood as a non-governmental organisation as of 19 March 2013, but this did not resolve the group's longstanding legal conundrum since NGOs cannot operate as political movements. 'A new experience to suddenly have Egypt ruled by a charity organisation!' wrote television presenter Jihan Mansour on Twitter. 'Is this why they distribute cooking oil, sugar, and rice during elections? But is it possible to examine the budget and sources of funding for the organisation?'[72]

Revolt

Morsi missed the chance to bridge the political divide in April 2013, when the European Union negotiated a compromise, endorsed by Washington, which bridged the rift between his party and the opposition. The deal, brokered by EU envoy Bernardino Leon, would have required six opposition parties to recognise Morsi's legitimacy as president, in question since his controversial fiat five months into his rule, and to take part in elections they had threatened to boycott. In turn, Morsi would substitute his prime minister and five key ministers with technocrats, dismiss the prosecutor general he appointed in violation of the separation of powers, and negotiate an election law meeting constitutional standards.

A contentious election law, passed by the Islamist-dominated Shura Council and signed into law, was mired in court challenges, seen as favouring an Islamist advantage in elections by gerrymandering districts and skirting around the principle of equal representation. Saad al-Katatni, chief of the Brotherhood's political party, helped negotiate the EU deal, ignored by Morsi, which would have buoyed Egypt's $4.8 billion International

Monetary Fund loan to restore confidence in a shattered economy.[73] As a campaign demanding early presidential elections gained momentum in May and June, the chance for reaching a middle ground disintegrated.

Officially established on 22 April the petition drive called Tamarod, 'rebellion' in Arabic, embarked on collecting endorsements calling for President Muhammad Morsi to step down and early elections to be held. The campaign aimed to exceed 15 million signatures by the end of June – beating the 13,230,131 votes Morsi received to win office – and a lead-in to nationwide rallies one year after the president's inauguration, with protesters raising red penalty cards. Asem Abd al-Magid, a leading figure in al-Jama'a al-Islamiya, a one-time jihadist group that renounced violence in the late 1990s, spearheaded a counter-initiative called Tagarud (meaning 'impartiality', and ironically also 'nakedness') to support Morsi completing his four-year term and asserting his right to constitutional legitimacy.

Infusion of Brotherhood stalwarts in high positions of government and the pursuit of ineffective policies solidified opposition to Morsi's rule. A new minister of culture, Alaa Abd al-Aziz, was appointed in a May 2013 Cabinet reshuffle and went about dismissing one official after another, first replacing the directors of the National Library and Archives and the state book publisher. When he fired Opera House director Ines Abd al-Dayem, a renowned flautist, the artistic community was up in arms.

Thirty-one prominent writers, artists, and intellectuals – including novelists Sonallah Ibrahim and Bahaa Taher, film director Khaled Youssef, painter Mohamad Abla, author and journalist Sakina Fouad, and publisher Mohamed Hashem – took over the minister of culture's office in an open-ended sit-in. They accused the minister of reorienting the institutions of state culture to the designs of the Islamists all in the guise of fighting corruption. The occupants of the ministry quickly went from demanding the minister's resignation to demanding Morsi's impeachment.

Cameras broadcast an afternoon meeting between Morsi and political leaders to review Ethiopia's Grand Renaissance Dam project and its effects on Egypt's water security. Unaware their comments were being aired live on television, attendees seated around an oval conference table in a discussion chaired by the president suggested sordid schemes to sow conflict and violate Ethiopia's sovereignty, including sabotage, hinting at a military strike, orchestrating rivalries among Ethiopian tribes, pressuring or destabilising the country with the aid of neighbouring countries, and using Egypt's intelligence agencies for political machinations.[74] For a president who had sternly warned in a speech that he would 'cut off' the 'fingers reaching inside' Egypt,[75] he did not seem to mind recommendations of interference in the affairs of another country. The farcical and troubling gaffe displayed the arrogance and inexperience of the elected leadership in addressing matters of vital importance to Egypt and upstream nations sharing the Nile's liquid lifeline.

President Muhammad Morsi met with Sheikh Ahmed al-Tayib, the grand imam of al-Azhar, and Coptic Pope Tawadros II (whose papal inauguration the president declined to attend) as the day of the protest rallies approached. Both religious figures refused to issue statements discouraging adherents from taking to the streets on 30 June. Coptic Christians had become acutely concerned about a sharpened sectarian divide during the Islamist president's rule.[76] In a television interview Salafi preacher and Nour Party leader Sheikh Yasser Borhami said, 'If millions went to the streets like the millions that went to the streets during the Egyptian revolution and demanded the downfall of the president, I would call on the president to resign because that is the constitutional method.' But he did not think the numbers on the street would reach 13 million and he favoured Morsi completing his term. The Nour Party announced they would not join protests for or against Morsi.[77]

To solidify his base and shore up his popularity, Morsi held a rally at Cairo stadium on 15 June in support of Syrian resistance to Bashar al-Asad, announcing that Egypt was shutting down the Syrian Embassy and severing ties with the Arab nation, a decision he took without consultation with the military, raising apprehension the president might rashly involve the armed forces in an Arab state's civil conflict. One speaker after another urged opening the doors of jihad in Syria and spoke in strident, sectarian tones pitting Sunnis against Shias as the president looked on. The supplications of Salafi preacher Muhammad Abd al-Maqsoud were directed pointedly against Morsi's rivals: 'I ask God Almighty to make Islam victorious and bring glory to Muslims, and to make the 30th of June the glory for Islam and Muslims and to break the backbone of the infidels and hypocrites.' The crowds responded with wild cheers.[78]

Radical Islamist sheikhs banded around Morsi on religious satellite channels and in street rallies, pillorying the opposition and Tamarod campaigners as former regime remnants, infidels, Christians, criminals, communists, drug addicts, and devil worshippers waging a war against Islam. In a challenge to the president and the sheikhs he surrounded himself with, al-Tayib, al-Azhar's highest religious authority, issued a declaration affirming that peaceful opposition to the ruler is acceptable and religiously permissible, and has nothing to do with belief or non-belief.[79]

The day after the stadium rally, Morsi appointed 17 new governors by presidential decree, many from the Muslim Brotherhood or factions allied with them. Chosen to be the governor of the tourist city of Luxor was Adel al-Khayat, a member of al-Jama'a al-Islamiya and its political arm, the Building and Development Party. The decision was met with alarm within Egypt and abroad because the group was responsible for the November 1997 massacre of 58 foreign tourists and four Egyptians at the Temple of Hatshepsut, a pharaonic mortuary temple in Deir al-Bahari. Demonstrations erupted, particularly in Luxor, to prevent newly appointed governors from entering their offices. Under pressure, al-Khayat resigned a week later.

Leading Brotherhood figures have resolutely maintained that the constitution outlined a process for electing the president and he cannot be removed through a petition campaign. The office of the presidency initiated a website, Facebook page, Twitter account, and YouTube channel to laud the accomplishments of Morsi's first year.[80] With 30 June approaching, Morsi's supporters planned their own set of rallies as the president prepared to dig in his heels. Brotherhood leaders directed harsh words at al-Azhar's grand imam and the army at a Friday rally.

On 23 June, days after Morsi's infamous stadium rally, a mob purporting to uphold Islam surrounded the home of a Shia family in the Giza village of Zawyat Abu Musalam, screaming angry slogans, and viciously struck with sticks and pipes a group of Shia believers assembled for a worship ceremony. The raving mob, cheered on by onlookers, attempted to demolish and storm the dwelling. Four men were dragged out, including prominent Shia spiritual leader Hassan Shehata. They were whipped, beaten, stabbed, and their bloody corpses dragged through the streets as crowds rejoiced. The homes of other Shia families were torched; tens were injured. What set off the madness was the divisive, sectarian language of local Salafi sheikhs during Friday mosque sermons, berating the Shia Muslim community for insulting the Prophet and his Companions and then leading enraged marches through the village in the weeks prior to the lynchings.[81]

The National Salvation Front, the April 6 Youth Movement, and former presidential candidate and Brotherhood castaway Abd al-Moneim Aboul Futouh, leader of the Strong Egypt Party, endorsed the Tamarod campaign. 'Dr Morsi, stop the strife at our doorstep for the sake of God and nation, and announce your resignation before 30 June,' Wael Ghonim admonished in a YouTube video.[82] Bolstered by millions of petition signatures, the main opposition coalition no longer demanded a national unity government, the replacement of the top prosecutor assigned by Morsi, or a committee to amend the constitution. The demand was for new presidential elections. 'We did not give him a blank cheque,' said Khaled Dawoud, journalist and spokesperson for the National Salvation Front. 'We did not elect a president so he could do with us what he wants.'[83] Unlike the start of revolution two and a half years earlier, the fear factor dissipated as the agencies of state oppression could not be counted on to stand by the ruler.

Morsi had asserted that the people are the source of political power and invited Egyptians to rise up against him if he violated the law and the constitution. In a television interview when campaigning for the presidency, he intoned, 'If they are patient for a year, they may not be patient for two.'[84] In office Morsi had not proven to be a man of his word. Swathes of the population wanted him out.

6

An Overthrow, a Revitalised Police State, and the Military Presidency

> *And one of the most potent remedies that a prince has against conspiracies, is that of not being hated by the mass of the people; for whoever conspires always believes that he will satisfy the people by the death of their prince; but if he thought to offend them by doing this, he would fear to engage in such an undertaking, for the difficulties that conspirators have to meet are infinite. . . . A prince need trouble little about conspiracies when the people are well disposed, but when they are hostile and hold him in hatred, then he must fear everything and everybody.*
>
> (Niccolò Machiavelli, *The Prince*[1])

Engaged youth and a diverse political collective – from leftists to Islamists – contributed to a popular revolt against Mubarak. Overestimating its own power and insulated by a trust network, the Muslim Brotherhood failed to see the need to preserve a diverse coalition, since the larger battle was against the abuses and institutionalised corruption of the Mubarakist state. It considered there to be two ascendant political factions: the Mubarakists and the Brotherhood; everyone else was too trivial and unorganised to matter. Liberal, leftist, and revolutionary forces that tacitly or overtly backed Morsi in elections against his old regime rival endorsed mass protests against him, a surge of popular discontent that combined with interests supportive of the Mubarak regime. The aspiration of the 30 June protests was to see Morsi ejected from office.

Over the year of his rule, Morsi racked up detractors, unconvinced that he had the requisite leadership qualities – his gaffes delivering critics and comedians ample fodder for ridicule. Morsi's inflexible and partisan stance in responding to crises convinced one-time revolutionary partners that not only was the Brotherhood untrustworthy, it was usurping the political system. Unable to communicate beyond his Islamist electoral base, Morsi understood democracy to be the ballot box, remaining ever loyal to the insular organisation that funded and propelled his presidential bid.

Toughened by decades of repression and bonded by the conformity demanded of its members, the Brotherhood's structure and operating manual were not reformed by the transparency and accountability the democratic process required. According to his detractors, Morsi got his marching orders from the group's Guidance Council, and especially the influential, shrewd, and moneyed deputy supreme guide, Khairat al-Shater. By doling out government appointments to political allies, Morsi turned politics into patronage, just as Mubarak had done. His supporters dismissed the groundswell of opposition as a conspiracy of the Mubarak business and political elite in an alliance with opportunistic parties, who wished to see the Brotherhood fail.

Many of Morsi's adversaries openly welcomed the military's return as saviour. On 23 June, defence minister Abd al-Fattah al-Sisi issued a cryptic statement urging all sides to reconcile before 30 June, pledging that the armed forces would protect the nation from 'sliding into a dark tunnel of conflict, internal killings, civil war, sectarianism, or the collapse of state institutions'. 'The will of the Egyptian people alone is what rules us,' declared the general to an audience of military men. He received a standing ovation when he proclaimed, 'We would rather die than for the Egyptian people to be frightened or threatened.'[2] Morsi's opponents read the message as a clear sign that the military was distancing itself from the president's divisiveness. The presidency chose to interpret the message as a shot across the bows of a cantankerous opposition. An uneasy relationship lingered between the executive branch and the military, which scorned Morsi's leniency of jihadists infiltrating northern Sinai.

Khairat al-Shater, the Brotherhood's second-in-command, and Saad al-Katatni, chairman of the group's political party, arranged a meeting with al-Sisi the following day. Al-Shater reproachfully lectured the general, telling him the Brotherhood was incapable of reining in militant Islamists, who will target Egypt's armed forces, according to al-Sisi's account. The top general described how the chief Brotherhood ideologue irritatingly squeezed an imaginary trigger, warning of the ensuing mayhem should the military be seen as acting against the wishes of the president. Al-Sisi said he erupted after al-Shater had finished speaking, telling him how the Brotherhood leadership had wrecked the country, made Egyptians ashamed of their Muslim faith, and warned that whoever assassinates citizens or military personnel will be hunted down. The deputy supreme guide's haughty and patronising demeanour hardened al-Sisi's resolve to knock Brotherhood leaders off their dais once the opportunity arose.

The Supreme Council of the Armed Forces held a meeting the same day and agreed to side with the president's opponents should millions take to the streets in protest. For its part, the presidency contacted the field army commander based in the Suez Canal, Major General Ahmed Wasfi, exploring the option of naming him defence minister. Wasfi immediately briefed al-Sisi on developments. In a meeting with Morsi, al-Sisi urged the president to propose solutions to the stalemate, suggesting he mend fences with the judiciary, al-Azhar, the Coptic Church, and opposition parties. The defence minister felt he had got through to the president only to be dismayed by the content of Morsi's 26 June speech as he sat in the front row, hand resting on chin, in a conference hall packed with government officials and the president's enthusiastic supporters.[3] In the evening address that lasted an inordinate two and half hours, Morsi showed no signs of changing course. He lashed out at adversaries and accused satellite television owners Ahmed Bahgat of Dream TV and Muhammad al-Amin Ragab of CBC, which airs Bassem Youssef's *al-Bernameg?*, with tax evasion and broadcasting content that 'harasses us'. 'No one will escape justice,' scoffed Morsi. The president announced that 'one year was enough' to put up with potshots from the media and his rivals, signalling his tolerance had reached its limit.[4]

Al-Sisi again pressed Morsi to make concessions a day before protests started, including changing the Cabinet, but the Islamist president balked. In an interview with the *Guardian* the same day, Morsi rejected calls for early elections as being an antithesis to the constitution and a formula for instability, claimed he was 'very' certain the army would not intervene, and blamed the private media for magnifying incidents of violence.[5] Morsi braced for a showdown, viewing politics not as an art, but a battle. The Islamist president had weathered other protest action, and the Brotherhood believed the 30 June protests would be no different.

Yet Tamarod gained notoriety because its petition campaign communicated with citizens, the kind of on-the-ground organising that had propelled Islamists into elected office. Seen as an effective mobilisation campaign, Tamarod was stealthily monitored by security informants, with funding channelled by the Mubarak-era business class. The military formed indirect links with campaign organisers via retired officers, who advised abandoning anti-military protest slogans.[6] Tamarod activists foresaw the army's intervention as the surest route to oust Morsi from the presidential palace. While at the time organisers dismissed the notion that they were naïvely manipulated by elements hostile to the revolution, the campaign proved a useful conduit for the designs of the behemoth military and police establishments in toppling Morsi and embedding a security-backed order with public acquiescence.

Days 1–3: 30 June–2 July

A stagnant economy, frequent power outages, and long queues for gasoline fed into frustrations with Morsi's rule. In Cairo on Sunday, 30 June, anti-Morsi marches and rallies converged at the presidential palace and Tahrir Square. Across the country millions of Egyptians poured unto the streets in impassioned protest – blaring horns, whistling, clapping, dancing, chanting, drum beating, fireworks, and revelry – ordering Morsi to leave. Unlike the uprising that ousted Mubarak two and a half years earlier, the element of fear was absent. Yet marring the protest spirit were frighteningly routine incidents of sexual assault on women in Tahrir Square. The armed forces announced that they would protect demonstrators – helicopters dropped flags on the crowds in Tahrir, hardly concealing whose side the army was on – and the police, largely absent from the streets, said they would not confront protesters. In the provinces, demonstrators blockaded government buildings and cut off roads. Once the rallies got started, it seemed a foregone conclusion that an oblivious and slow-to-react president would find himself the loser.

Fuel shortages eased and electricity cuts subsided, feeding suspicion by Brotherhood supporters that calamities were set in motion to undermine the president and draw protesters onto the streets.[7] The pro-Morsi contingent gathered at Rab'a al-Adawiya Square in the Cairo neighbourhood of Nasr City days before the 30 June protests got started, and later occupied Nahda Square by Cairo University, to defend the legitimacy of an elected leader. The president's aides assured him that his defenders outnumbered the masses on the streets calling for him to step aside. Clashes erupted outside the Brotherhood's Muqattam headquarters between armed disciples inside the building and angry opponents massed outside, killing 11. Sections of the building were set ablaze, then looted and gutted in the ensuing days.

On 1 July the army's central command, which deployed around the country without presidential orders, issued a 48-hour ultimatum directed at Morsi and political players, ordering them to meet the people's demands, or the army, fulfilling its national duty, would intervene to impose a roadmap and oversee its implementation. The presidency rebuffed the ultimatum, demanding its withdrawal. The National Salvation Front issued a statement that it did not endorse a coup. Hours later a military spokesman clarified that the warning was not an attempt at a coup and the military had no intention of orchestrating an overthrow.

The Brotherhood's Guidance Council met to consider the option of backing a referendum on Morsi's presidency and decided against it. Al-Shater and other hardliners viewed such a move as certain defeat for the organisation. From the stage of the pro-Morsi sit-in, a speaker spoke of visions from Mecca of the archangel Gabriel praying at the Rab'a al-Adawiya Mosque as crowds wildly rejoiced in the omen.[8] President Obama telephoned Morsi, informing him that a commitment to the democratic process involves more than elections and that he should ensure 'the voices of all Egyptians are heard and represented by their government'.[9] In the next couple of days two presidential spokesmen, 11 ministers, and three governors resigned.

The defining blunder of Morsi's administration can be traced back to a surprise constitutional diktat where he bestowed himself dictatorial powers – a move the opposition regarded as a forfeiture of his democratic legitimacy. Following public dissension, al-Sisi invited political factions, including the presidency, for a dialogue session. Opposition groups accepted, believing the forum to be on more neutral ground. The office of the presidency, presumably on instructions from the Guidance Council, scrapped the session before it began after initially accepting to participate. Morsi spurned international prodding for compromise and did not appreciate lectures on democracy.[10]

In a 2 June meeting with the defence minister, Morsi, faced with mounting pressure, accepted the proposal to change the Cabinet. Al-Sisi later informed the president that the opposition rejected the offer as too little, too late. That night, Morsi appeared in his first televised address since the outbreak of protests. He denounced his detractors and struck a defiant chord of 'legitimacy' – constitutional, electoral, and legal – a phrase he repeated ad nauseam, saying that he would 'give his life' to protect it and reminded Egyptians that he was chosen in free and fair elections.[11]

Again demanding the army retract its ultimatum, an agitated president blamed failures on remnants of the Mubarak regime. He finally accepted a coalition government, the selection of a prime minister who had the approval of all political factions, altering the public prosecutor chosen by him, and forming an independent committee to propose constitutional amendments – all of which had been the opposition's demands for months. Morsi rejected a referendum on early presidential elections, and the opposition refused dialogue now that nationwide rallies were demanding the president's departure. Some of his supporters at Rab'a al-Adawiya Square trained in mock combat drill, apparelled in construction helmets and clutching sticks, in defence of Morsi's right to rule and vowing martyrdom for their cause. Armed clashes by Cairo University, where Morsi supporters organised a sit-in, claimed 17 lives.

Day 4: 3 July 2013

Abd al-Fattah al-Sisi and top generals convened a four-hour meeting with political and religious leaders at military intelligence headquarters on the day the ultimatum was due to expire. Saad al-Katatni, head of the Brotherhood's Freedom and Justice Party, was invited to attend negotiations but did not show up.[12] Through intermediaries the army pressed Morsi to bow to the will of the street for early elections and be guaranteed a safe exit, or to resist and have the army strip him of his authority. Al-Sisi waited until 4 pm for Morsi to accept a referendum on his rule or relinquish executive power to the speaker of the Shura Council. Tamarod organisers vigorously rejected a transition plan that included a referendum on whether Morsi should continue in office.[13]

The US State Department along with National Security Advisor Susan Rice worked behind the scenes to get Morsi to make concessions that would avert a military takeover. As the final hours of his administration ticked away, Morsi received a call from an Arab foreign minister, an emissary of Washington, with an offer to end the stand-off. The compromise involved appointing a new prime minister and Cabinet, which would take over legislative powers until parliamentary elections were held. He flatly refused. US ambassador to Egypt Anne W. Patterson, al-Sisi later disclosed, requested an additional day or two before the decision was made to oust Morsi.

By 7 pm the generals informed Morsi he was no longer the president. On al-Sisi's orders the chief of the Republican Guard placed Morsi and top aides in military custody and blocked their communications. With the armed forces granted autonomy in the 2012 constitution, Morsi felt he had reached an understanding with the military institution to safeguard their fiefdom in exchange for their exit from the political sphere.[14] When it came down to choosing between a referendum on his rule (which could have been held alongside parliamentary elections), early presidential elections, or a military overthrow, Morsi wilfully opted for a coup – a perilous choice for Egypt's nascent democratic experiment.

Just before his arrest Morsi delivered a livid address spoken in the manner of an unrehearsed homily, shot on a handheld video recorder, and uploaded to a president's YouTube channel before being removed shortly afterwards. 'There are desperate attempts to steal this revolution so that we return to square one,' intoned Morsi. 'I am the elected president of Egypt and the constitution should be respected by all.' He said he accepted a proposal to change the Cabinet and to move forward with parliamentary elections. 'Many media outlets destroy what we've built,' he asserted, warning that there would be 'bloodshed' if the path of constitutional legitimacy were thwarted. 'This is the will of the Egyptian people and you cannot cancel this will after only a year has passed. How can this happen?' he asked in astonishment. He said that, while he encouraged a strong opposition, he knew he had a strong base of support. 'No one can impose their will on us.'[15]

In a 9 pm television address al-Sisi announced Morsi's removal and the implementation of a military-backed roadmap endorsed by political forces – save the Brotherhood and its Islamist allies – that suspended the constitution and dissolved the Shura Council, called for constitutional revisions, followed by elections for the legislature and presidency. The chief justice of the Supreme Constitutional Court was tapped to become the interim president. Flanking al-Sisi were Mohamed ElBaradei, al-Azhar's Grand Imam Ahmed al-Tayib, Coptic Pope Tawadros II, secretary-general of the ultra-conservative Nour Party Galal Morra (which tried to mediate between the opposition and the Brotherhood), and Tamarod organisers Mahmoud Badr and Mohammed Aziz.[16] While al-Sisi stressed that the armed forces had no interest in politics, the military deftly choreographed Morsi's removal: an unelected civilian government under the leadership of a jurist was the face of transition. The military, an institution powerful enough to steer the nation's course, was back in a position of dominance.

The revitalised power centre of the military and the security agencies were calling the shots. Military police took over the state television and radio building and stormed the offices of the Brotherhood's satellite channel Masr 25, Al Jazeera Live Egypt, and pro-Morsi Islamist channels, shutting down their broadcasts, seizing communications equipment, and detaining presenters and crew.[17] Talk show hosts on private Egyptian satellite channels rejoiced in the news of Morsi's removal, shawled in Egyptian flags, crying tears of joy, singing along as the national anthem was played, and uttering words of praise to the valiant public guardians – the army and police.

As anti-Morsi protesters erupted in euphoric celebration, military troops in riot gear and armoured vehicles ringed Rab'a al-Adawiya Square, where the president's supporters vowed to continue protesting, calling the army's intervention on behalf of one group of demonstrators a subversion of the people's will and a call for civil war. The White House cautioned against 'arbitrary arrests of President Morsy and his supporters' yet refrained from using the word 'coup'.[18] In a sign of disapproval as turmoil engulfed the country in the coming weeks, the US cancelled joint military exercises, suspended cash transfers of economic aid, and halted the delivery of four F-16 fighter jets, Apache helicopters, and large-scale military systems.

The Brotherhood demanded the restoration of the constitution and Morsi's return to power, so he could transfer power to an interim Cabinet before presidential election slated for two months' time. Morsi had rejected a similar eleventh-hour proposal, and the military-backed government ruled out his return, insisting there was no going back on the roadmap. The country's dire financial travails were alleviated by billions in aid flowing from the Gulf monarchies of Saudi Arabia, the United Arab Emirates, and Kuwait, which have sought to stave off turbulent Arab uprisings and especially the Brotherhood's brand of political Islam.[19]

Revolution or coup?

The uprising was on the verge of achieving its goal – without the backing of the most powerful institutions of the state Morsi could not have lasted as long as Mubarak's 18 days – when the military stepped in, expelled the president, and announced a roadmap going forward. Brotherhood foes went along with the generals, putting their faith in a patriotic military, which forced Morsi's compliance. The day after Morsi's ouster, chief justice of the Supreme Constitutional Court Adli Mansour was sworn in before the nation's highest court as interim president, bestowed with the power to legislate and issue constitutional declarations. Even with Mansour as placeholder president, the defence minister was seen as the true arbiter of power. Prosecutors issued warrants for the arrest of senior Brotherhood officials – including supreme guide Muhammad Badie, his deputy Khairat al-Shater, and former supreme guide Muhammad Mahdi Akef.

'Let me make one thing clear: This was not a coup,' ElBaradei told *Der Spiegel*. 'Without Morsi's removal from office, we would have been headed toward a fascist state, or there would have been a civil war. It was a painful decision. It was outside the legal framework, but we had no other choice.' Probed further on the undemocratic turn of events, he responded, 'You cannot apply your high standards to a country burdened with decades of autocratic rule. Our democracy is still in its infancy.'[20] An internationally recognised figure, ElBaradei worked on selling to world leaders the need to depose Morsi. He called the military takeover 'the least painful option', and justified the closure of Islamist channels and arrest of Brotherhood leaders, arguing the measures were a security precaution against violence.[21] Morsi's ouster was not dressed as a coup, but a restoration of the democratic path derailed by an Islamist president. 'You see Sissi's picture everywhere, and it's good that he is not thinking of running for president. It's good that he does not want to have the army run the country,' ElBaradei told the *Washington Post*. 'But people in a national emergency look for power, and the power rests with the army right now.'[22]

A constitutional declaration issued by Adli Mansour placed the power to legislate and call for a state of emergency in his hands. In one of his first legislative decisions Mansour amended the penal code to eliminate jail sentences for the crime of insulting the president, swapping it for a fine of between 10,000–30,000 Egyptian pounds. ElBaradei was named vice president for international relations and economist Hazem Beblawi was appointed prime minister. Al-Sisi held the post of deputy prime minister along with being minister of defence and military production.

Islamists, particularly in Egypt's southern provinces, unleashed their anger against Christians. Nine Copts were murdered within a week following Morsi's ouster. Militants in the restive Sinai Peninsula stepped up their attacks. Tens of thousands of pro-Morsi protesters descended on Rab'a al-Adawiya Square. Hundreds massed outside the Republican Guard compound, where the former president was believed to be held captive. On that first Friday following his ouster, troops guarding the complex shot dead five of his supporters. In Alexandria the same day Islamists were filmed by eyewitnesses shoving two teenagers shouting anti-Morsi slogans from a building's rooftop; one bearded assailant waved a black jihadist flag.[23]

Images of Morsi were all over the Rab'a encampment, situated along intersecting boulevards, the entrances lined with sandbags and barriers fashioned from pavement slabs. Metres away from one entrance was the reviewing stand where President Anwar Sadat was assassinated by al-Jama'a al-Islamiya militants in 1981. Tents and makeshift shelters gathered supporters from the provinces. Clinics and pharmacies were set up, volunteers sprinkled protesters with water in the stifling heat, blocks of ice were sold from pickup trucks. Crowds swelled by evening, assembled around a stage, a battery of organisers keeping order, partitioning sections for women and ensuring pathways were clear. Protesters were adamant on staying for the long haul, disregarding security threats to forcefully evict them. They persisted in the summer heat and throughout the fasting month of Ramadan.

Demanding Morsi's return to power, speeches from the Rab'a stage projected anti-coup and pro-democracy appeals – contradicted by sectarian and bellicose rhetoric – along with sermonising urging martyrdom and supplications for God's wrath to befall the coup general. Crowds cheered the rumoured news of US warships near Egypt's shores, their intended aim to restore the legitimate president. A jingoistic, pro-military media exploited those pronouncements from Rab'a to denigrate defenders of the former president, branding them traitors and deriding their pleas for international involvement. For Brotherhood antagonists, Rab'a was a breeding ground for terrorists seeking to hold the country hostage. Protest sites were depicted as dangerous, scabies-infected tent cities packed with brainwashed minions. The Interior Ministry announced that 11 bodies of alleged captives, which bore signs of torture, were found in the vicinity of the sprawling sit-ins.[24]

Announcers brandished their support of the military and its top commander on public and private channels. With the alarmist media and its pundits in tow, the groundwork was being laid to transform the Muslim Brotherhood into more than a nuisance or a strong-willed rival, but a murderous terrorist network. A swirl of media-fuelled rumours advanced theories of foreign-financed plots to carve Egypt into pieces, instigate turmoil and strife, and undermine national security. A web of contradictions, the conspiracies weaved the malevolent designs of the Brotherhood, Hamas, America, Israel, Qatar, and hapless Syrians fleeing civil war. A few voices were seeking reasoned political discourse. A defender of Morsi's ouster, Bassem Youssef, in a newspaper column, called for reopening Islamist channels and sounded the alarms on the tide of xenophobia. 'Don't you see that with your incitement of Palestinians and Syrians that it is no different from their incitement of Shias, Baha'is, Christians, and Muslims who objected to the Brotherhood and Salafis? We replaced their bogeyman of "enemies of the Islamic project" with the bogeyman of "betrayal and enmity for the nation".'[25]

In the early hours of 8 July, soldiers stationed outside the headquarters of the Republican Guard opened fired on Morsi supporters – 61 protesters, an army and a police officer were killed.[26] State media reported the death of an officer and scores of 'armed' individuals captured. Only later during the six-hour assault was it mentioned that dozens of civilians also lost their lives. News presenters interviewed security officials who lent credence to the story of a coordinated strike by Islamist instigators on the Republican Guard compound. An armed forces spokesman denied the army killed peaceful protesters and alleged the shootings started when assailants on motorcycles attempted to storm the officers' club and soldiers fired in self-defence. Al Jazeera Live Egypt, which plainly labelled the events of 3 July a military coup, offered a conflicting storyline, focusing on the civilian casualties among the ranks of Brotherhood supporters. Survivors say they were attacked with tear gas, buckshot, and live ammunition immediately after dawn prayers and pointed to videos of shots fired by army snipers on rooftops.

The mandate

Attired in full military regalia and sporting pitch-black, wraparound shades, Abd al-Fattah al-Sisi at a 24 July graduation ceremony of the naval and air defence academies, broadcast live, warned that national security was in peril and summoned nationwide rallies two days later. 'I urge the people to take to the streets this coming Friday to prove their will, and give me, the army, and police a mandate to confront violence and possible terrorism,' invited the general. The night before, an explosion outside the security directorate in the Nile Delta city of Mansoura took the life of a police conscript. Al-Sisi used the platform to defend his decision to remove Morsi from power. 'Don't ever think I tricked the former president.' The army, he stressed, does not betray or conspire.[27] With his demand for a 'mandate' al-Sisi made the populace complicit in his designs – as if authorities required popular approval to confront acts of terrorism.

Pageantry of the military and adulation of its commander became a craze. Fighter jets streaked cartoonish-shaped hearts in the sky. Patriotic songs and aerial footage of the 30 June protests with al-Sisi's words as voice-over blared on Egyptian television screens: 'This great civilization will show the world that they are all – people, army, police – behind one man.' The charismatic and chivalrous general loomed larger than the president he installed. 'If al-Sisi tells us to take to the streets, that's what we'll do,' enthused columnist Ghada Sherif in *al-Masry al-youm*. 'To be honest, he doesn't need to ask or cajole. A wink or a flutter of those eyelashes is enough for all of us to comply. Egyptians adore this man! Should he wish to round out his stable of four wives, we're at his beck and call, and if he desires us as captured sex slaves, by God we're at his command!'[28]

Satellite networks announced the cancellation of dramas and entertainment shows on 26 July – during the ratings-driven month of Ramadan – to deliver wall-to-wall coverage of the pro-military rallies and motivate a larger turnout. Crowds flocked to the squares, music blaring, fireworks lighting the sky, laser beams trained on army helicopters overhead. Morsi supporters organised their own rallies and marches, roundly ignored by the state and pro-government media. It was on that day that Morsi and Brotherhood leaders were formally charged with espionage for allegedly conspiring with Hamas to break out of prison during the revolution.

In an on-air phone interview, interim president Adli Mansour demanded Morsi supporters vacate their sit-ins and return to their homes and workplaces, pledging that police would not pursue them. The government, he chided, 'cannot accept security disorder, blocking roads and bridges, and attacks on public buildings. The state has to impose order by all force and decisiveness.'[29] The army gave the Brotherhood a 48-hour ultimatum, ending on 27 July, to endorse the roadmap as a way out of the impasse. Beginning in the early hours of the 27th, police shot dead 95 Morsi supporters, many in the head and chest, when they marched from the Rab'a sit-in and approached the Sixth of October Bridge, with the intention of bringing traffic on the thoroughfare to a standstill. One policeman lost his life. In a press conference that morning, interior minister Muhammad Ibrahim argued the Brotherhood was provoking bloodshed in a bid to win sympathy and insisted the pro-Morsi encampments represented a public danger and would soon be cleared. Ibrahim announced he was reconstructing the loathed State Security directorate, which kept tabs on the political opposition and had supposedly been disbanded under military rule.

Ibrahim Eissa made heaping scorn on the Brotherhood a staple of his nightly programme. He lavishly called al-Sisi a 'historic hero' who 'demolished their temple': 'If anything happens to this man it will be with the knowledge of America and the execution of the Brotherhood,' he proclaimed as he urged the break-up of what he deemed the terrorist sit-ins.[30] The one-time Mubarak gadfly also had disparaging words for idealist revolutionary youth, depicting them as callow and combative. Riding the al-Sisi bandwagon was newspaper editor and former parliamentarian Mustafa al-Bakry, who warned that Americans would be hunted down should the military commander be targeted in an US-choreographed assassination plot. 'It will be a revolution to slaughter the Americans in the streets,' he told the programme host. 'If anything happens to Colonel General al-Sisi, there will not be an American on the face of the earth, here or abroad.'[31] Media personalities frequently warned of devious plots to assassinate the military commander.

The killing field

Weeks of shuttle diplomacy by the European Union's foreign policy chief Catherine Ashton failed to bring both sides closer. Flown by military helicopter to a naval base on the evening of 29 July, Ashton was allowed to hold a two-hour conversation with Muhammad Morsi in confinement. He refused to call an end to street protests and accept the roadmap in exchange for a safe exit and the release of Brotherhood detainees. 'The mood right now is, "Let's crush them, let's not talk to them,"' ElBaradei told an interviewer. 'I hope the Brotherhood understands that time is not on their side. I'm holding the fort, but I can't hold it for very long.'[32] The vice president worked to broker reconciliation talks, rebuffed by the Brotherhood if Morsi was not reinstated or freed to engage in negotiations. Press editorials scorned ElBaradei for his efforts to stall a dispersion of the sit-ins. In a Twitter message he lamented, 'It seems that none of my efforts to save the country from slipping into a cycle of violence reaches the government papers except articles about "my danger to the people".'[33]

United States and European Union mediators counselled Egyptian officials, principally al-Sisi, against the use of force in favour of a diplomatic solution, beginning with freeing two imprisoned Islamist leaders in exchange for the Brotherhood shrinking the size of its sit-ins and disavowing violence. In regular calls to his Egyptian counterpart, US Secretary of Defence Chuck Hagel advised steps towards inclusive governance. Yet the Cabinet on 31 July authorised the interior minister to take all necessary measures to clear pro-Morsi encampments, referencing the mandate given by the people to the state to combat terrorism. A week later Adli Mansour announced that negotiations had come to an end.[34]

National reconciliation efforts were abandoned in favour of a security solution, which came with predictable and devastating consequences on 14 August. In hyper-nationalist mode, Egyptian state and pro-government media backed the operation, citing weapons caches, torture, and terrified area residents. The harrowing forced evacuation of pro-Morsi sit-ins in Rab'a and Nahda Squares began in the dawn hours. In the sustained assault on the camps, security forces alongside military personnel stormed the area, employing snipers, armoured vehicles, helicopters, and bulldozers.

Security forces announced a safe exit. From the Rab'a stage, Brotherhood leaders told protesters to stay put since exits were a security ambush. When tear gas canisters and bullets started flying, and security forces advanced through the five main street entrances to the square, safe passages were all but nonexistent. Armed pockets of resistance inside the camp were in two areas: in the vicinity of Rab'a al-Adawiya Mosque and inside a high-rise under construction overlooking the square. During the 12-hour siege of Rab'a, security forces had free reign to use deadly force, assured that they would not be prosecuted for any deaths.[35] Ambulances and medics were prevented from reaching the injured.

Scores of bodies covered in melting bags of ice filled the nearby al-Iman Mosque. The number of civilian casualties was in the untold hundreds – at least 627 lives, revealed the state medical examiner three months later. The actual number may be upwards of a thousand or more; some bodies did not make a detour to the morgue before burial.[36] Ten officers lost their lives in the clearance of the two pro-Morsi sit-ins. The interior minister announced after the dispersal that the armaments found in the square totalled nine automatic weapons, a pistol, five homemade guns, and ammunition. As protests and violence spread to other parts of the capital, state television showed images of vigilantes mired in street battles and masked gunmen firing automatic rifles.[37] Train services traversing the country came to a standstill, an effort to scuttle Morsi defenders from reinforcing protests. The militarised state and its supporting media deemed the massacre as due punishment of a dehumanised opponent.[38]

ElBaradei resigned hours after the forced eviction began. In his resignation letter he refused to be held accountable for a decision he did not approve, believing peaceful methods for resolving the conflict had not been exhausted. 'I cannot bear responsibility before God, my conscience, or citizens for a single drop of blood,' he wrote, deploring the polarisation that threatened to tear the national fabric, and asserted that the only beneficiaries of the bloodshed were extremists and proponents of terrorism.[39] ElBaradei departed for Vienna days later, eliciting contempt in the media and among the political elites.

The backlash

A spasm of madness gripped the country on that tragic day in August. Less than 36 hours after the police and military raid on protest camps, no less than 31 churches, two monasteries, four schools, an orphanage, and a museum were looted and partially or completely torched. The majority of attacks were in the southern provinces of Minya, Assuit, Sohag, and Beni Suef, where hardline Islamists have a strong presence. The interim president declared a three-month state of emergency and a 7 pm to 6 am curfew. Sectarian violence against Christians surged since the start of nationwide protests against Morsi. Anti-Christian graffiti was scrawled on walls and flyers condemned Christians for waging a war on Islam. Islamists marching through Christian districts chanted sectarian slogans and pelted homes with rocks. As armed mobs associated with right-wing religious currents and criminal elements rode roughshod, security forces were nowhere in sight.

Razing pro-Morsi encampments with such calamitous results may have set off the Islamist backlash the security apparatus sought all along – setting in motion a state of lawlessness that would make it possible to resurrect the police state, capable of striking with impunity at a moment's notice. Its function was not the protection of citizens, but to hammer into submission opponents of the military-backed order behind a ruling façade that dispensed with political solutions, the rule of law, pluralist democracy, and revolutionary demands. Amid a polarising political climate mirrored in an ideological media, shrill cries for retribution were mixed in a witch's brew of apathy, distrust, anger, and hatred. Egyptians were again brought to cower in manufactured fear, this time in the name of imagined security. In response to the killings at Rab'a, the anti-coup National Alliance to Support Legitimacy called for protests after Friday noon prayers on 16 August, heading towards downtown Cairo's Ramses Square; 120 people and two policemen lost their lives in clashes, hundreds more were arrested.[40] State and private television broadcast images of armed gunmen accompanying pro-Morsi protesters and blocking bridges in central Cairo.

Faced with mounting international criticism for the bloodshed, presidential adviser Mostafa Higazy argued during a news conference, simultaneously translated into English, that security forces used utmost restraint, listing 57 officers killed and citing foreign terrorist elements that included Pakistanis, Syrians, and Palestinians. He alleged the Brotherhood used women and children as human shields, dismissed the notion that protests were peaceful, and frequently referenced the terms 'terrorism' and 'religious fascism'. He cited facts he said the foreign press was ignoring: church burnings, al-Qaeda's backing of the violence, and the slaughter of 14 policemen during a militant siege of a station in the Kirdasa district of Giza.[41] Egyptian channels announced on their screens in English, 'Egypt fights terrorism'. Al Jazeera Live Egypt focused its coverage on pro-Morsi rallies simulcast on the internet, where protesters shouted, 'The caliphate is coming', 'The people want the implementation of God's law', and 'Down with military rule, down with all the dogs of the military'.

In a speech on 18 August, al-Sisi defended the bloodletting, reminding his military audience of the mandate given to the armed forces by the people to root out terrorism. 'Protecting the will of the people, and their freedom in choosing what they want, and to live as they wish, is more precious and honourable to me, I swear to God, than ruling Egypt,' said al-Sisi.[42] Within days, militants murdered 26 police conscripts in the Sinai town of Rafah, one in a chain of attacks targeting police and military personnel; *al-Ahram*'s bureau head in the Nile Delta province of Beheira was shot dead at an army checkpoint; Brotherhood supreme guide Muhammad Badie was arrested in an apartment near Rab'a and filmed in custody;[43] 37 detainees, most of them Morsi supporters, died of asphyxiation when police fired a hot tear gas canister into an overcrowded security truck outside Abu Zaabal Prison on Cairo's outskirts; and following two years on remand, a court ordered the release of ousted former president Hosni Mubarak, who left the medical wing of Tora Prison the next day and checked into a military hospital overlooking the Nile.

Leading Brotherhood figure Salah Soltan castigated al-Sisi as a traitor, murderer, and liar on the Rab'a stage. A month after the dispersal he apologised to God and Egyptians for the Brotherhood's mistakes in an article – quickly removed – on the Freedom and Justice Party's website, and counselled the group to listen to criticism and accept responsibility. Brotherhood officials, known to have little tolerance for internal recrimination, dismissed the sentiment as a personal viewpoint, arguing that it was not the time for reflection and assessment. Soltan's son Mohamed, shot in the arm in Rab'a, was picked up on 25 August when security officials came in search of his father, later arrested. A dual Egyptian–US national, Mohamed Soltan staged a long-running hunger strike in prison. The court delivered an emaciated Soltan a life sentence. After renouncing his Egyptian nationality, he was deported to the US after serving 643 days behind bars. His father was sentenced to be executed, as were senior Brotherhood leaders in various trials. Multiple death sentences hung over the head of supreme guide Muhammad Badie.

25 January's revolutionaries

With the massacre at Rab'a, Tahrir Square was cordoned off by the military with barbed wire and armoured vehicles. The Metro has skipped the Tahrir stop for fear the landmark would be taken over by anti-government protesters.[44] In the stand-off between army and Morsi supporters, Abdelazim Fahmy, better known as Zizo Abdo, found no room on the street for secular revolutionaries like himself. 'The death of unarmed civilians cannot be a justification for confronting terrorism,' he said. He found just as much danger in the rhetoric of division: 'The language prevalent in society cannot be the language of blood and violence; either I convince you or I kill you.'

After revolution Abdo joined the April 6 Youth Movement, gathering activists of sundry political trends. During Morsi's reign the group organised a protest outside the home of interior minister Muhammad Ibrahim, waving women's underwear, suggesting that the top security official was the administration's harlot. Abdo was arrested and jailed for 33 days in a maximum security prison. He was one of 78 revolutionaries who comprised the June 30 Front, a collective that planned nationwide protests and marches to begin on the anniversary of Morsi's inauguration as president. When massive street demonstrations got started, he was not surprised when the army intervened to expel the Brotherhood from power and set a new course for the country.[45]

The Islamist president had avoided dismantling the authoritarian structures of the state, perhaps thinking he could use them to his benefit. His interior minister would remain in his post to lead the massacre and crackdown on Morsi's supporters. Islamist extremists, jihadists, and criminal gangs that thrive on havoc and disorder became ostensibly allied with the former president's backers. The Muslim Brotherhood's rallies and sit-ins to restore Morsi to power coincided with church burnings, sectarianism, and terror strikes rocking Sinai, a mountainous peninsula that has become a favoured hideout and training ground for insurgents. Days after Morsi's ouster, prominent Brotherhood leader Muhammad al-Beltagy told a reporter, 'What's happening in Sinai is a response to the military coup. It will stop the second Abd al-Fattah al-Sisi announces that he has gone back on this coup.'[46] When security forces cleared out Rab'a, they gunned down al-Beltagy's 17-year-old daughter, Asmaa.

On 23 September 2013 an Egyptian court ordered a ban of the Muslim Brotherhood, including its charitable network, and the seizure of assets. Two months later, on 25 December, the government officially designated the Brotherhood a terrorist organisation, a day after a car bomb outside the security directorate in the city of Mansoura in the Nile Delta killed 16, almost all policemen. An al-Qaeda-inspired group claimed responsibility.

The trial of Muhammad Morsi along with other Brotherhood leaders began on 4 November. Shown escorted from a white van, it was the former president's first public appearance since being toppled. State television displayed scenes of the trial, none broadcast live, believing that Morsi would use the forum to send coded messages to followers. During proceedings, the ex-president shouted from his caged dock that he was the legitimately elected president and refused to recognise the court. After the hearing he was flown by helicopter to the maximum security Borg al-Arab Prison near Alexandria. In later sessions Morsi and his co-defendants were placed in soundproof docks so they would not disrupt the trial.

The former head of state faced a host of charges that could spell life imprisonment or a death sentence: plotting acts of terrorism, conspiring with terrorist organisations, relaying state secrets to national powers, murdering protesters, and colluding with Hamas and Hezbollah to break out of jail. In white jailhouse overalls, Morsi, emulating Brotherhood leaders during their capture, was photographed smirking in a mugshot, splashed on newspaper front pages, appearing to be unfazed by the predicament of going from president to prisoner.

Adli Mansour, a president inducted through demonstrations, approved a protest law on 24 November prohibiting public gatherings of more than ten people – including election-related activity, outdoor cultural events, and labour strikes – without a three-day prior security approval. Jail sentences of up to seven years and hefty fines of up to 300,000 Egyptian pounds were imposed. The Interior Ministry was given broad discretion to bar gatherings deemed a threat to public safety and to use force to disperse them.

A couple of days after the law was issued, organisers of No Military Trials for Civilians held a protest before parliament demanding the cancellation of an article in the draft constitution allowing civilians to be tried before military tribunals. In the first application of the protest law, security forces broke up the demonstration, beating, sexually molesting, and arresting dozens of participants minutes after the rally got underway.[47] The next day prosecutors ordered the arrest of April 6 co-founder Ahmed Maher and revolution activist Alaa Abd El Fattah for inciting protest. On the night of 28 November police broke down the front door, cuffed, and hauled a barefoot Abd El Fattah from his home, confiscating laptops and mobile phones. With the issuance of the protest law, the April 6 Youth Movement withdrew its support for the roadmap. Maher turned himself in to prosecutors, and along with April 6 leader Mohammed Adel and activist Ahmed Douma, was sentenced to three years in jail for unauthorised protest and assaulting police, and fined 50,000 Egyptian pounds. Douma was handed a life sentence in another case concerning the Cabinet clashes of December 2011, where he was tried with 268 other defendants.

Alaa Abd El Fattah and 24 co-defendants were sentenced in absentia to a 15-year prison term for protesting without a permit, blocking traffic, threatening public safety, and assaulting police. (He and two defendants were taken into custody at the courthouse after their lawyers and the media were not informed the session had begun.) Calling for the release of political detainees, Abd El Fattah's youngest sister, Sanaa Seif, and 22 other activists were arrested at a protest march to the presidential palace, which was attacked by thugs working in concert with security forces.

Imprisoned siblings Alaa and Sanaa were only allowed to see their ailing father, distinguished human rights lawyer Ahmed Seif al-Islam, after he had slipped into a coma and lay in the intensive care unit following complications of open-heart surgery. After leaving his father's bedside and landing back in Tora Prison, Abd El Fattah decided to call attention to the absurdity of his incarceration and of others unjustly locked behind bars by embarking on a hunger strike. Scores of political prisoners have done the same in an elusive battle for justice. 'My days in prison are not bringing us any closer to a state committed to its laws or to courts committed to justice,' he wrote. 'Prison gives me nothing now except hatred.'[48]

The indomitable rights defender Seif al-Islam passed away on 27 August 2014 at the age of 63. Arrested during the revolution when military police raided the Hesham Mubarak Law Center, a legal advocacy group he co-founded, Seif al-Islam was interrogated at military intelligence headquarters, where he encountered al-Sisi. Mubarak and the army leadership ought to be respected, admonished the general, and protesters needed to vacate Tahrir Square. When Seif al-Islam spoke up and said Mubarak was corrupt, al-Sisi became enraged, recalled the lawyer.[49] A court sentenced Sanaa Seif and other activists to three years in jail, reduced to two years on appeal. Abd El Fattah was handed a five-year sentence in a retrial, plus another five years on probation, and fined 100,000 Egyptian pounds.

The satirist, again

Bassem Youssef's third season returned to the airwaves four months following the tumultuous events of July 2013. On his show he reacts with mock outrage at talk that smacks in the face of press freedoms in a leaked video of al-Sisi and military officers discussing ways of influencing the media.[50] Youssef changes course when a hand, representing the government's minders, creeps up from his desk, swaps his script, and knocks sense into him. He lampoons the fawning over the defence minister, his images decorating chocolates and pastries. A skit uses the tune of 'Old McDonald Had a Farm' to chronicle the former president's misfortunes, where one of the revellers is shushed up for uttering the word 'coup' in the sing-along. In another skit comedian Khaled Mansour plays the part of Gamaheer (the 'public'), a giddy young woman calling a radio show, enthralled by her new suitor, a military man, after a failed romance with her former love interest, a man with an autocratic streak espousing piety. Youssef, in more serious tone, concludes the show by expressing, 'We fear that fascism in the name of religion is replaced with fascism in the name of patriotism.'[51]

Soon thereafter the public prosecutor received a flurry of complaints filed against the satirist for fomenting chaos, defaming the military, undermining Egypt's dignity, and disrupting national peace. The next day, the CBC satellite channel issued a statement acknowledging the disapproval the network had received over the content of *al-Bernameg?* and affirmed that it was against 'mocking national sentiment or symbols of the Egyptian state'. The following Friday the network refused to air *al-Bernameg?* minutes before airtime and announced its suspension. The show lasted

30 episodes under Morsi and was shut down after one episode following his ouster.

'I agree that we might've gone a bit too far. Perhaps our Eastern society rejects some of the things we do,' says a not-so-apologetic Youssef in the banned episode of *al-Bernameg?*, which surfaced on video sharing sites months later. 'I promise we'll abide by the same rules and moral standards the station has got you used to,' he says, alluding with a grin to a saucy drama series broadcast on the channel during the holy month of Ramadan. He shines a spotlight on the outlandish assertions of military supporters on talk shows, saying it undermines the credibility of the case they are defending. Another segment dissects Al Jazeera's questionable reporting. During the 25 January revolution the Qatari news channel proclaimed two million people packed Tahrir. But in protests that unseated Morsi, Al Jazeera posited the square could only hold 518,000 'according to international standards.'

Youssef ends the programme by bringing up the controversy surrounding his previous episode, which set off diatribes in the media, a slew of court petitions, and gathered fuming protesters outside his theatre. Others would have relished the trappings of fame, he says. Instead he felt saddened to see the country's pressing problems being ignored over a weekly, hour-long satire show. 'I am not a political leader, a hero, a freedom fighter, or even a media personality. I host a programme where I try to get people to laugh under very difficult circumstances,' professes Youssef.

> *If the decision-makers see that it's best for the programme to end – that Egypt, its security, army, and people cannot handle it – let us know. Send us a message, a missed call: 'Bassem, your programme is a danger to the nation.' Then fine, we'll stay at home. There's no need for pressure, trumped up charges, character assassination, or arrests. Just tell me. I don't think the country is that fragile and weak that it cannot tolerate a programme. But if you see differently, just tell us, and we're at your command.*[52]

Three years after revolution

Speaking in a lisp that ordinarily would have sidelined him from a job in television, the host of the night-time talk show *al-Sanduq al-aswad* (Black Box), Abd al-Rahim Ali, has woven an elaborate tale of how the

25 January revolution was a plot to bring Egypt to ruin. On the private Egyptian satellite channel al-Qahira wa-l-Nas (Cairo and the People), he played recorded phone conversations of revolutionary activists – no doubt obtained from the security agencies – reading into them sinister motives to tar and sully their reputations. He posited that the 25 January revolution was an aberration seized upon by the Muslim Brotherhood and foreign-backed operatives – especially the April 6 Youth Movement – who were all the while orchestrating the fall of the nation. They colluded to torch police stations, he goes on, and break open prisons, leaving criminals to roam the streets and terrorise citizens into submission. It is a narrative that has gained considerable traction.

The true revolution, Ali asserted, began on 30 June 2013 and culminated with the defence minister's removal of President Muhammad Morsi four days later, recalibrating the military's dominion over the state. Devotees of al-Sisi in the media alleged Morsi's electoral win was a hoax – he was handed the presidency to prevent his group from carrying out threats to burn down the country. The vilification went beyond Morsi's undemocratic tendencies and absence of political savvy to sow a visceral loathing of the Brotherhood, considering the group a danger to the very essence of Egyptian identity. Had the military not intervened, they argue, Egypt would have become another Syria, Libya, or Iraq. The true revolution of 30 June eclipsed the 25 January ruse, relegated for many to a grand conspiracy against Egypt.[53] Propaganda that was laughably futile during the 2011 uprising was repurposed with masterful and weighty consequences. In talk show after talk show, guests alleged that non-profit organisations working in the field of human rights were fifth columnists; the so-called Arab Spring was a plot hatched by the Americans and their allies to carve up the Middle East and weaken Arab armies; and what seemed to be revolutions in the Arab world were staged in studios in Qatar.[54]

During the Islamist president's rule critics enjoyed a wide margin of freedom. 'Control of the media was not in the hands of Muhammad Morsi or the office of the presidency, but in the hands of the security agencies, and with instructions from them there was an attack on the Muslim Brotherhood,' conceded activist Zizo Abdo. Three years after a popular uprising to oust Egypt's authoritarian regime the revolutionary youth who started it all have found themselves back at square one. Their ranks have thinned. Well-known activists who organised for revolt languish in prisons. Others have stayed away from the political fray, like Wael Ghonim, who rejoined Google, later venturing out to form a social media startup.

The 'We are all Khaled Said' Facebook page fell silent after posting the military chief's 3 July announcement.

'We see the Muslim Brotherhood as a wing opposed to the revolution, like the military is now,' said Abdo. He accused the Brotherhood of selling out the revolution in its bid for power, and with its political failures and reluctance to compromise ushering the military back onto the political stage. 'The revolutionary wave of June 30 was taken over by the military council once again,' he said. 'We see that it is going in the path of an overthrow of the principles and goals of the 25 January revolution; it was a coup on the Muslim Brotherhood.'

The reviled practices of the security apparatus have returned with unrestrained tenacity. The state and its media cheerleaders have marshalled the masses in a war on terror, stirring patriotic fervour against all enemies of the state, internal or external, real or imagined. Dissidents, students, and journalists were jailed, beaten, or harassed in a broad mandate by the security apparatus to quell political unrest. Tens of thousands have been detained for political reasons, including hundreds of women and minors. 'We see that we are going towards the consecration of a despotic state,' warned Abdo. 'Unfortunately, the consecration comes with a blessing from the people and a blessing from the civil forces that allied with the military.'[55]

The constitution passed overwhelmingly in January 2014, garnering 98% of the vote; 39% of the electorate participated in a referendum that witnessed a low turnout of young voters. Arrests ensured that no one was campaigning for a 'no' vote. The constitution bans political parties based on religion, enshrines the autonomy and privileges of the military institution (the military budget remains a state secret), and allows military trials for civilians.[56] While a dozen people lost their lives in clashes during the two days of voting, state and private media honed in on the celebrations surrounding the new charter, featuring middle-aged women dancing in the street.

On the eve of the third anniversary of the 25 January revolution, four explosions rocked Greater Cairo, killing six. Fifteen more anti-government protesters lost their lives in clashes with security forces. In addition to a string of bombings over the ensuing days, a military helicopter was shot down in Sinai with a surface-to-air missile, a natural gas pipeline was again blown up, and a top-ranking security official was gunned down on his way to work. Army and police officers, including the interior minister himself, were the targets of bombings and assassinations carried out by militants. A jihadist group calling itself Ansar Bayt al-Maqdis, or Champions of Jerusalem, claimed responsibility for these and other attacks, with the frequency and sophistication of their operations on the rise. Other militant cells, including Ajnad Masr, or Soldiers of Egypt, have emerged, targeting police installations, businesses, and infrastructure, and carrying out bombings.[57]

The square was snatched from the revolutionaries and turned into a venue that extolled the military and the state. Pursuing a zero-tolerance policy, security forces broke up revolutionary and anti-military protests on 25 January 2014, firing off volleys of tear-gas canisters and shotguns to disperse crowds. Ahead of the uprising's anniversary the Brotherhood sought reconciliation with the revolutionary youth it had alienated. Yet the only actual mistake the Brotherhood publicly admitted was in trusting the military council, and apologies by the group were not forthcoming.[58] Secular revolutionaries had as much faith in the Brotherhood as they did in military generals, having been deceived by the group's earlier promises, and unsettled by their demand for Morsi's reinstatement and recourse to sectarian rhetoric. Strata of society not only turned against the Brotherhood, they disowned the revolution and the activist youth who started it.

Inside the symbolic heart of revolution three years on, security checkpoints, bag searches, and metal detectors blocked entrances to Tahrir Square. Singing and cheering filled the square as military helicopters dropped flags and redeemable coupons. Street vendors briskly sold posters of the defence minister, pictured in military attire, in a suit, with the head of a lion in the background, and flanked by venerated past presidents and military commanders Gamal Abd al-Nasser and Anwar Sadat. Nationalist hymns blared from speakers set up on stage. Banners, facemasks, and memorabilia exalted the cult of a military man. Bombings a day earlier stirred rising anger against the Muslim Brotherhood, with crowds chanting, 'The people want the execution of the Brotherhood.'

Clashes between police and demonstrators erupted blocks away and across cities and provinces. By nightfall, 64 Egyptians were dead in confrontations with security forces; more than a thousand were arrested. Labour organisers and secular political dissenters were swept up along with Islamists and remanded in custody for months without charges or trial. Rights groups documented dozens of cases of forced disappearances, secret detentions, and torture in military camps.[59] Public universities remained a hotbed for anti-government activism. The Cabinet authorised security forces to enter university grounds without permission from administrators, leading to 15 student deaths in the space of a few weeks. Security forces carried out waves of arrests, student groups were frozen for having political leanings, and student union elections cancelled. Campus demonstrations were not only in support of the Brotherhood, but to condemn security crackdowns and restrictions on academic freedoms.

The Brotherhood was blamed for myriad catastrophes, in addition to the death of protesters during the 25 January revolution, conveniently vindicating the police, whose abuses ignited the uprising in the first place. Anything evoking the Rab'a massacre – especially the four-fingered hand sign (Rab'a means 'fourth' in Arabic) – became profane in the eyes of military advocates. While disavowing bloodshed in official statements, the Brotherhood has not denounced jihadist militants, often suggesting they were State Security creations to defile Islamists. With a leadership in jail or exile, a faction of Brotherhood scouts, enraged at seeing colleagues murdered, tortured, and imprisoned, had sanctioned or adopted vengeful retaliation. Resistance to the coup became the Brotherhood's singular goal: extremism and instability became the price the military-led state paid for staging a putsch. Security forces ensured Rab'a al-Adawiya Square was not reoccupied, the memory of the tragedy that took place there papered over with a revisionist memorial – an orb cradled by two minimalist hands, symbolising the army and police safeguarding the people – and fenced with tarpaulin to keep vandals away.

Interim president Adli Mansour made the decision to hold presidential elections ahead of parliamentary elections, contrary to the arrangement in the roadmap, favouring a victory for al-Sisi. Mansour anointed the defence minister the highest military rank of field marshal – despite possessing no actual battlefield experience – and the Supreme Council of the Armed Forces gave their top commander the green light to run for president. 'General Sisi is coming after a revolution that rejected oppression by any regime. It is a revolution that has toppled two presidents, one after the other,' argued Amre Moussa, career diplomat and chairman of the Constituent Assembly. 'The constitution has called for a civil state,' he emphasised, placing full faith in the charter's guarantees. 'We cannot leave the country in the hands of any group – without specifying a group – that would use violence and terrorise people.'[60]

In February the military made the stunning announcement that its scientists had developed a handheld diagnostic device affixed with a moving antenna that remotely signals when persons are infected with such viruses as hepatitis and HIV. A second dialysis-type contraption – aptly called Complete Cure (CC) – treats patients by bombarding the virus with electromagnetic waves to form proteins. 'I take AIDS from the patient, and feed the patient on AIDS. I give it to him as a kofta skewer for him to eat. I take the disease, and I give it to him as nourishment, and that', emphatically declared Major General Ibrahim Abd al-Ati, 'is the pinnacle of scientific discoveries.'

The honorary general thanked the field marshal for his devotion to the research. 'We cannot walk like others are walking. We need to leap,' said Abd al-Ati, quoting al-Sisi. 'And this is the first leap, God willing, conquering AIDS around the world *(applause)*.'[61] Media cheerleaders rhapsodised on how the scientific discovery would reap the nation a windfall in medical tourism. The cure was planned for a 30 June 2014 rollout to coincide with the anniversary of protests deposing Morsi, but when that day approached the Defence Ministry acknowledged the devices required additional testing.[62] Nothing more was officially spoken about these miraculous inventions.

The general seeks the presidency

General Abd al-Fattah al-Sisi managed to keep a low profile as the youngest member of the Supreme Council of the Armed Forces. He first prominently appeared in the news when he admitted to Amnesty International in 2011 that the military had subjected female protesters to virginity tests to 'protect' soldiers from rape allegations.[63] Known for his piety, al-Sisi was the military council's liaison with the Brotherhood, the reason he was selected by Morsi to be defence minister. A prayer mark of devout Muslims can be seen upon his forehead.

Al-Sisi delivers speeches extemporaneously and in the vernacular, couched in nationalist mottos, catchy colloquialisms, and occasional Islamic parlance. In an audio section leaked from his interview with *al-Masry al-youm*'s chief editor Yasser Rizk, al-Sisi professed seeing visions in his dreams foretelling the future. In one dream he is speaking to Anwar Sadat, who predicts, 'I know you will be president of the republic.' 'I, too, know I will be president,' al-Sisi confidently replies.[64]

On 26 March the defence minister who toppled a president resigned his post to run for the nation's highest office. In a televised address the newly promoted field marshal, seated behind a desk, proclaimed his candidacy by stating that this would be the last time he would wear his military attire, adding that he was honoured to have donned his uniform in defence of the nation. 'Today, I set aside this uniform also in defence of the nation,' he mentioned, speaking his words rather than reading prepared remarks. 'Egypt is not a playground for internal, regional, or international factions,' he continued. 'We are threatened by terrorists, from parties that seek to destroy our lives, to destroy our peace and security.'[65]

His first long-form televised interview was broadcast jointly on the CBC and ONtv satellite channels with hosts Lamees al-Hadidi and Ibrahim Eissa. 'I won't sleep and I won't let you sleep,' al-Sisi envisaged, honing in a statist, roll-up-your-shirt-sleeves ethos, reliant on military-owned enterprises to be the economic engine. He criticised religious speech that 'has robbed Islam of its humanity' and confessed to having survived two assassination attempts, yet offered no details. He alleged the Brotherhood operate behind jihadist militants.

'An Egyptian citizen voting for you will know that you'll end the Muslim Brotherhood?' asked Eissa.

'Yes,' answered al-Sisi, slicing the air with an open hand, affirming that there would be nothing called the Brotherhood during his tenure.

He staunchly defended the protest law. Whoever does not see the necessity of following the letter of the law 'wants to destroy Egypt', he proclaimed. 'I say you have the right to ask to protest and it will be considered. But for us to allow this country to fall apart from us, no.'

'It will fall apart with protests?' Eissa wondered.

'Yes, with the state of chaos we're living in,' scoffed al-Sisi, the tone of his voice rising.

'With violence and terrorism, not protests,' ventured Eissa.

'And protests that are not responsible,' added al-Sisi. 'You have a country that's being lost. You have a nation that's threatened. How could you speak to me about protests? Even the fuel for the vehicles to protect a protest is a burden on us, Mr Ibrahim.'

In response to a question on the demands of striking workers, he exclaimed, 'I cannot give you!'

'And if they block roads?' quizzed al-Hadidi.

'There's a law. I am not playing around. I cannot give you. You do not have to tell me, "give". If I could give you, I would. But I cannot. Will you devour Egypt?'

His solutions relied on the military taking the lead. 'The army, Mr Ibrahim, is a great institution in a way you cannot imagine, O Egyptians. Until we can see the whole of Egypt at this level,' said the former military chief, waxing poetic.

'The value of the army in the sentiments of Egyptians is great and deep,' interjected Eissa, sceptical of al-Sisi's ideal depiction and questioning whether there should be a state body 'that is separate and independent'.

'We have to stand next to this institution, not to monitor it, but to value it,' said al-Sisi. 'Before 25 January, no one could write the name of an officer in the newspaper or circulate it in the media. We don't do this rejecting oversight. This is a closed society that is extremely sensitive. Any insult hurts it deeply despite being powerful and able to kill.'[66]

Al-Sisi's campaign was vague when it came to specifics, yet promised to restore stability and make 'leaps' in development. Viewed as a candidate born of necessity, he did not release a detailed electoral programme, declined to debate his challenger, and did not do live television interviews or attend campaign rallies. Al-Sisi's presidential campaign was flush with money, buying hours of commercials and pockmarking the skyline with billboards emblazoned with his image and the slogan 'Long live Egypt'. Al-Sisi placed national interests above what he considered quixotic notions of democracy. He has said it might take up to 25 years to realise full democracy in Egypt.

Al-Sisi's sole contender in presidential elections was leftist politician Hamdeen Sabahy, who tailored his message to revolutionary youth, workers, farmers, and underserved populations. In a live, three-and-a-half hour interview with journalists Khairy Ramadan and Magdy al-Gallad, Sabahy said he had been a champion of the oppressed from his days as a student activist in the 1970s. Since then he was jailed 17 times and served in parliament for a decade. 'This revolution did not arise so that we return to the corruption and tyranny that we rose against on 25 January.' 30 June would not have occurred if not for 25 January, Sabahy argued, considering the protests that culminated in Morsi's ouster to be a revolutionary wave, not a separate revolution. He said he did not seek the votes of those who consider 25 January a conspiracy or 30 June a coup.

'The army supported us,' he proclaimed. 'No one places the Egyptian people in second place.' He challenged the line that the military 'rescued' the country from Brotherhood rule. 'I'm a believer that the one who leads in this country is the Egyptian people. The army is the patriotic institution of the people,' remarked Sabahy. 'I say that it is *with* the people, not before the people, above the people, or leading the people.' He confirmed the Brotherhood would not have a presence as a movement or a party if he were elected president.[67]

Religious discourse was in the grasp of authorities for reasons, they insisted, of quelling extremism and keeping houses of worship removed from politics. The Ministry of Religious Endowments under the leadership of Sheikh Muhammad Mokhtar Gomaa, dean of al-Azhar's Department of Islamic Studies and a Brotherhood antagonist, brought independent, privately run mosques under the ministry's umbrella. The ministry prohibited sermonising in unregulated prayer areas, unlicensed imams were barred from preaching, and the ministry determined the topic and script of each week's oration.[68]

On 21 May, days ahead of presidential polls, the courts handed Mubarak a three-year sentence and his sons were given a four-year sentence for embezzling over 100 million Egyptian pounds ($14 million) in state funds for remodelling their homes and offices, fined 125 million pounds ($17.5 million), and ordered to reimburse the state 21.2 million pounds ($3 million). The Mubaraks fraudulently billed the expenses as maintenance work for the president's secure communications network.[69] A member of the influential Policies Committee of Mubarak's National Democratic Party, the presiding prime minister, Ibrahim Mehlab, spent a 42-year career at the Arab Contractors, 11 of them as chairman. During his tenure the state-owned construction company was the conduit for millions in public funds siphoned for renovations and furnishings of the Mubarak family's mansions.

In ten and a half months leading to presidential polls, 41,163 arrests were made, 1,250 persons were tried in military tribunals, and 53 detainees died in police custody.[70] Opponents splattered red paint on al-Sisi's campaign billboards. Exam schedules at public universities were pushed back to ensure classes were not in session when elections took place on 26–28 May 2014, following less than a month of campaigning. Voting was extended for a third day to shore up lower-than-expected turnout, despite the prime minister declaring the second day of elections a public holiday. News announcers joined in the drive to get voters to the polls, echoing the government's hollow warning of a 500 Egyptian pound fine imposed on any eligible citizen who does not cast a ballot. A weak turnout would be chalked up as a victory for the boycotting Muslim Brotherhood.

Presidential elections were little more than a coronation. When the vote tally was announced on 3 June, al-Sisi was crowned the winner with 96.9% of the vote. The number of spoiled ballots (over a million) exceeded the votes obtained by his cash-strapped challenger; turnout stood at 46%.[71] Al-Sisi would wield executive and legislative powers until a parliament was finally elected a year and a half later.

In a letter supposedly penned in prison and released after al-Sisi was declared the next president, Morsi said the revolution would stand victorious after the world heard the voters' 'rumbling silence'. He called elections a 'charade' that only convinced those who were 'deceived, slapped of their consciousness, and demeaned'. 'God knows that I have spared no effort to fight corruption and criminality through the law at times, but more often through revolutionary measures,' Morsi wrote, justifying controversial decrees that toughened opposition to his rule. 'I made mistakes but I have not and will not betray your trust.' The letter was signed 'Muhammad Morsi, President of the Arab Republic of Egypt'.[72]

The war on creativity

The Vodafone commercial has the comic and light-hearted puppet widow Abla Fahita rambling on the phone with her friend Mama Tutu while her daughter Caro Carcoura searches for her late father's old SIM card.[73] The pro-Mubarak campaigner known by the moniker Ahmed Spider parsed the dialogue and scenery to unravel a wild and sordid scheme. By his imaginative reckoning, Abla Fahita's idle chitchat was code for the Brotherhood to carry out terror campaigns that included church bombings on Coptic Christmas. The conspiratorial accusations were actually taken seriously when prosecutors opened an investigation. Khairy Ramadan gave Abla Fahita an opportunity to face her accuser live on his programme via Skype. 'It is the fertile tree that gets pelted with stones,' the puppet groused, remarking how a comely widow always has admirers. 'The whole world fights ignorance and poverty and we're fighting the sweet laugh.'[74]

Entertainment genres were mired in a political tempest. Bassem Youssef's *al-Bernameg?* found a home on the Saudi-owned MBC network, where the satirist touched on al-Sisi's awaited presidential bid. The station elected to place the programme on hiatus during the month-long campaigning and election cycle for the stated reason of not influencing the outcome. But in a press conference at his downtown

Cairo theatre on 2 June Youssef announced that the show would not be returning to the airwaves. Under pressure MBC was forced to drop Egypt's and the Arab world's highest rated programme after 11 episodes. 'The decision to ban came without the officials in charge of censoring seeing what the episode was about,' Youssef explained. 'That means the problem wasn't the content but the programme itself. The programme in its current form would not be allowed to continue, not on MBC or any other Egyptian or Arab channel.'

Although fans urged him to soldier on, he knew 'a hashtag and retweet' was about all the support he would have when faced with ramifications. 'I got tired – tired of the insecurity, tired of being afraid for my personal safety, that of my family, and the people around me,' said the surgeon-turned-satirist after he and his team reviewed their options. 'We were fed up with hopping from one channel to the next, under emotional and financial stress until we're stopped again.' European and American stations offered to carry the programme, but Youssef felt that would lead naysayers to denounce *al-Bernameg?* and its crew for being agents in the pay of foreign governments. Broadcasting the show from abroad would erase its credibility, he concluded, and webcasting on YouTube would not generate the revenues needed to cover production costs. Angry demonstrations were staged outside *al-Bernameg?*'s downtown studios, despite the promulgation of a protest law. 'God only knows when they would've received instructions to barge in,' speculated Youssef.

On his Friday night show he unveiled the outlandishness of Egypt's politics and media scene, always prone to melodrama, hyperbole, inventive rumours, and conspiracy theorising. But it was Morsi's clumsiness, rambling speeches, and missteps that made for enlivened satire. 'It's not like the Brotherhood didn't want to stop the programme. They wanted to, but they couldn't,' he said. 'It was only a matter of time.' Each week the doctor-satirist reminded viewers of the countdown to the military's sensational cure-all gadgets. The end of *al-Bernameg?* in its third season opportunely shielded al-Sisi – the candidate and the president – from Youssef's artful wit. 'We're living in the glorious era of democracy,' he joked. 'Off with the tongue of anyone who says otherwise!'

He faced a stream of lawsuits, prosecutors hauled him in for questioning, the programme's broadcast signal was jammed, and the show twice cancelled. 'I'm proud of the amount of effort people have exerted to stop us,' he said. 'And for the people who're happy the programme has ended and consider this a victory, the truth is the cancellation of *al-Bernameg?* is in fact a victory. But it's a victory for the programme, a victory for us.' Youssef said he was not willing to compromise the show's quality or distort its message just to keep it on the air. *Al-Bernameg?*'s demise, he said, 'is a stronger, clearer, and louder message than its continuation'.

When pressed on the exact reasons for the cancellation, he said, 'I know everyone wants me to give more details, but *I can't give you! (audience laughs)*. It's not that I don't *want* to, I just can't give you *(applause)*.' Eliciting guffaws, Youssef was mimicking al-Sisi's outburst in one of his interviews when asked how he would meet the demands of strikers. Reading between the lines of Youssef's statement it seemed evident that the master censors of the military and security agencies were behind the programme's closure, in alliance with Saudi royals having an ownership stake in the MBC Group.

Satire pushes the envelope of public scrutiny, challenges the sanctity of power, reveals absurdities, and breaks down barriers of fear. In a 'new Egypt' expected to fall behind the will of 'one man', the jester was deemed annoyingly troublesome. Ratings for Youssef's programme had never been higher precisely because the Egyptian media were shunning honest debate for a format that espoused propaganda and ridiculed adversaries.[75] An essential function of the press is to connect citizens in a public conversation that goes beyond 'I'm right' and 'you're wrong'.

'Perhaps our disappearance is a way for people to think of other methods that are more creative, and more useful to their cause, instead of depending on a programme or person,' reflected Youssef.

'If you were to direct a message to the person responsible for stopping the programme,' a reporter asked, 'what would you say?'

'I would tell him, "Why are you afraid?"' replied Youssef.[76]

Soon after *al-Bernameg?*'s cancellation, two satellite networks turned down the drama series *Ahl Iskindiriya* (Alexandrians), scheduled to air during their Ramadan line-up, under Interior Ministry pressures. Penned by screenwriter and polemicist Belal Fadl, the mini-series, approved for filming by the censorship authorities, centred on police corruption and abuse before the revolution.[77]

Journalism and justice

The Interior Ministry adopted a policy of forcing press censorship, confiscating publications (including pro-government newspapers), referring reporters to prosecution, and imprisoning journalists.[78] After a police raid on the offices of Al Jazeera English in September 2013, the network set up a temporary base in two suites at the nearby Marriott Hotel. Reports by Al Jazeera English were aired on the court-banned Al Jazeera Live Egypt, which provided Brotherhood activists with video equipment and paid them for footage of demonstrations. When the Muslim Brotherhood was deemed a terrorist group in December, security forces stormed the rooms at the five-star hotel, filming the operation – televised to an action movie soundtrack – and arresting bureau chief Mohamed Fadel Fahmy and correspondent Peter Greste.[79]

Convicted with conspiring with the Brotherhood, spreading false news, and endangering national security, the two journalists and producer Baher Muhammad were handed seven-year prison sentences on 23 June 2014. An additional three years for weapons possession was tacked on to Muhammad's prison term – the proof being a spent bullet casing he recovered as a souvenir during a protest.[80] None of the evidence presented during the five-month trial corroborated the serious charges against the journalists. Demanding the outrageous sum of 1.2 million Egyptian pounds, prosecutors blocked defence lawyers from accessing a trove of supposedly incriminating videos privately viewed by the judge.

Local media lined up to defend bizarre judicial verdicts against those deemed agitators against the state. 'Al Jazeera's journalists are all Brotherhood,' alleged Ibrahim Eissa. 'I prefer to call them employees of Al Jazeera, not journalists, so my gallbladder doesn't rupture. Is Al Jazeera a news channel? It's the same as Israel Radio. No, Israel Radio is better because it is the broadcast of the clear enemy, the Zionists, our enemy. But Al Jazeera is a broadcast of our enemies produced by our sons. It's a channel that incites, forges, falsifies, deceives, lies,' he said, preferring to liken the Qatari news channel to jihadist outlets.[81]

Al-Sisi defended the ruling by an 'independent judiciary' in an address the next day to military academy graduates. Internationally acclaimed barrister Amal Alamuddin agreed to represent Mohamed Fadel Fahmy in his appeal, describing the proceedings as 'a travesty of justice'. She went on to describe some of the hallmarks of a show trial: 'antiquated laws that criminalize ordinary (and necessary) speech', 'the right judge', 'some sort of evidence so that it looks like a real case', and 'the use of religious references to demonize the defendants'.[82] Vocal in his support of Morsi's ouster, Fahmy lashed out against Al Jazeera Arabic for waging a media war against Egypt and called out the network for failing to protect its journalists or securing for them press accreditation.

A day before the verdict, US Secretary of State John Kerry paid a visit to Egypt's military president, promising the restoration of military aid and the delivery of Apache helicopters. Jihadists have captured towns and cities along a vast stretch of Iraq and Syria, controlling oil fields, supply routes, and military installations, declaring the territory the Islamic State. Its combatants, recruited from far-flung corners of the globe, have been on the march, seizing armaments caches and financed through taxation, extortion, and smuggled oil. Militias in a smattering of countries have sworn allegiance to the self-styled caliphate.[83] The US-led military intervention against the expansionist menace in the Middle East required al-Sisi's cooperation, overshadowing Egypt's worrying human rights record and slow democratic advance. Kerry expressed disquiet over the journalists' conviction, yet the Apaches were delivered. After being imprisoned for 400 days, Australian national Peter Greste was deported, following presidential approval and ahead of an economic development conference meant to attract billions in foreign investment. The two other Al Jazeera journalists were released on bail for the retrial (but then later sentenced to three years in prison). In late March 2015, Obama telephoned al-Sisi to let him know the US freeze on military aid was being lifted. The warming in US–Egypt relations underscored the global superpower's longtime commitment to regional stability and counterterrorism over democratisation.

Egypt and Gulf allies seemed to acquiesce in Israel's July–August 2014 bombing and invasion of Gaza. Al-Sisi withheld condemnation of Israel, seeing the deadly military campaign as a way to cut Hamas, a Brotherhood offshoot, down to size. The Egyptian press joined in reprimanding the Palestinian resistance group as Israel shelled to rubble the densely populated enclave. Despite media diatribes of Zionist conspiracies, relations between Egypt and Israel had never been closer. Al-Sisi admitted he talks to Netanyahu often, and Israeli reconnaissance and intelligence have been valuable for Egypt's armed forces in tracking militants in Sinai.[84]

Local media went overboard to burnish the president's image as he vied for a role on the international stage as a bulwark against Islamic fundamentalism. In his first address before the United Nations General Assembly, Abd al-Fattah al-Sisi concluded by triumphantly chanting to applause, 'Long live Egypt!' 'More than any change in his standing abroad, however, what the event demonstrated was the strength of the cult of personality that Mr. Sisi's allies are building around him at home as he consolidates his power,' wrote David Kirkpatrick in the *New York Times*. 'What viewers back in Egypt could not see was that during the General Assembly, almost all of the diplomats present watched in amused silence as Mr. Sisi's small entourage did the clapping in response to his chant. But the Egyptian media's applause was sustained and unanimous, dramatizing a monopolization of power under Mr. Sisi.'[85]

'Kirkpatrick pointed out that all the diplomats were in a state of silence and enjoyment throughout al-Sisi's speech,' enthused *al-Ahram*.[86] The *New York Times* challenged the daily for publishing a story that intentionally misrepresented the article by its Cairo bureau chief, providing the original article alongside the rosy version published in *al-Ahram*. 'There is no such thing as bad press for President Abdel Fattah el-Sisi, at least not if it is translated by Al Ahram, Egypt's flagship state newspaper,' the *New York Times* opined.[87] *Al-Ahram* explained that the story was taken from the state wire service, the Middle East News Agency, and published in other press outlets. The paper rebuked the *New York Times* for singling it out for criticism and took a swipe at its correspondent. 'It is known that the *New York Times* correspondent rejects the political path in Egypt after the 30 June revolution, vigorously defends the terrorist group, always promotes the notion that there is a repression of freedoms and a lack of respect for human rights, and calls into question the political will that extracted the Brotherhood from power.'[88]

Al-Sisi instructed the media to highlight dangers faced by the nation and complained about the press focusing on the negatives. Days after militants in Sinai killed 33 army troops in coordinated attacks, the chief editors of 17 state and private newspapers vowed to stop publishing content criticising the performance of state institutions, astonishingly forfeiting an essential function of the press.[89] Rancorous opinions cluttered the media landscape and facts of a debate became amorphous. A gaggle of television hosts harangued al-Sisi's critics and swaggered their presidential connections. 'Your men, sir, are the ones who created a monster – and no one else!' decried columnist Ghada Sherif, who had gushed over al-Sisi when he commanded Egyptians to the streets. 'You are the ones who plant them on satellite channels by command, and they use you, and they become intoxicated with grandeur, and they persist in their media obscenities.'[90]

Without a legislature, the press had much to scrutinise. Al-Sisi decreed that public university presidents and deans would be appointed and dismissed by the president, as they were under Mubarak, turning back one of the revolution's minor gains, where the selection was made by the faculty through internal elections. University presidents were granted broad powers to suspend or expel students for violations and refer professors to disciplinary committees for their political activity. Another one of al-Sisi's edicts referred students charged with sabotaging educational facilities to military prosecution.

The president announced the construction of a 72-kilometre addition to the Suez Canal to increase shipping capacity. Surrounded by foreign dignitaries, Abdel al-Fattah al-Sisi inaugurated the extension, completed in a year's time, with nationalist pomp and pageantry. Favouring economic revival over democratic freedoms, he envisioned the project to be the cornerstone of an industrial and maritime hub along the Canal Zone. Unaudited and untaxed, military businesses were handed billions in no-bid contracts to oversee these megaprojects. Still, bombings have become all too frequent occurrences and jihadists hold sway in north Sinai. In a drastic preventive measure, al-Sisi ordered the displacement of thousands of families and the demolition of homes along a one-kilometre stretch on Egypt's border with Gaza. Ruling by presidential fiat owing to stalled parliamentary elections, al-Sisi signed into law a revision to the penal code imposing life imprisonment for receiving foreign funds, equipment, or arms to harm national interests. He decreed a stringent law that broadly outlined acts of terrorism and granted prosecutors, with the approval of a panel of judges, the authority to list persons or entities as terrorists. This was followed by a draconian counterterrorism law expanding the arsenal of the state in dealing with dissent by empowering police and prosecutors in pursuing suspects and levying exorbitant fines on journalists who deviate from official statements on militant attacks. When issues of constitutionality were brought up, al-Sisi alleged the constitution was 'ambiguous' and 'would take time to implement'.

Republic of fear

Abd al-Fattah al-Sisi framed the confrontation with militants as a war of survival against an enemy that seeks to thwart the nation's advancement. Jihadist strikes delivered the state an excuse to label opposition as subversion, justifying censorship, the killing of hundreds of protesters, the arrest of thousands, and wholesale life and death sentences doled out in mass trials that lack due process. Led to believe they could not have both freedom and security, citizens were lulled into surrendering rights for the promise of stability.

In his moment in the spotlight following three-and-a-half tumultuous years, a seemingly vindicated Mubarak, donning the blue attire of a convict, read prepared remarks during his retrial that burnished his legacy and highlighted his service to the nation. He spoke of his long tenure of 'allowing for unprecedented spaces for freedoms of the media and the press, and freedoms of opinion and expression'. He blamed 'traders of religion' and their allies, externally and internally, with transforming peaceful protests to violence and killings.[91]

On 29 November 2014, criminal court judge Mahmoud Kamel al-Rashidi dismissed charges against Mubarak for the death of protesters on procedural grounds; on all other counts he, his sons, the former interior minister, top security chiefs, and a billionaire associate were acquitted. Prosecutors added Mubarak to the trial docket in a case charging security officials with killing protesters only after mass demonstrations forced the former president's arrest. For the judge this lapse represented an implicit admission that he was not culpable. Al-Rashidi offered a mild rebuke of the former president, yet assigned the final judgement to history and the 'Judge of judges'.[92]

The court ruling was elaborated in a wordy 1,430 pages, which surmised an American–Zionist conspiracy at work that threatened to divide the nation, basing the assertion on the testimony of state, military, and security officials, in addition to lead witness and media personality Ibrahim Eissa. In the first trial, Eissa testified that the former president was responsible for all that happened in the country, including the protesters killed and injured. He redacted his testimony during the retrial, admitted that he did not witness security personnel shooting protesters, and commended Mubarak's patriotism. The Muslim Brotherhood was an agent in fomenting violence and bringing down the state in league with Hamas and Hezbollah, concluded the judge. He pointed to the acquittals of police officers in the death of protesters on self-defence grounds or lack of evidence to absolve their commanders. The testimonies of the injured and family members of those who died were cast side and security excesses were deemed isolated cases when so many protesters were on the streets.

Reclining on a gurney, Mubarak was transported by helicopter to a military hospital, where well-wishers had gathered, cheering his arrival. In a phone interview with the exonerated autocrat, television host Ahmed Musa, who advances the 25-January-is-a-conspiracy reading of events, asked Mubarak if he was optimistic about an acquittal. 'I felt I didn't do anything, at all,' he responded, adding that he laughed at the original guilty verdict against him.[93] The judiciary has handed prominent symbols of the Mubarak era get out of jail free cards. In short order, Mubarak's sons and his interior minister Habib al-Adly, acquitted of corruption charges, were released from prison.

The military closed off Tahrir Square ahead of the ruling. Thousands came out to demonstrate beyond the armoured vehicles and barbed wire fortifications, shouting slogans against the military and the Brotherhood, and demanding, 'The people want the downfall of the regime!' Security forces fired tear gas and shotguns to disperse the crowds, on the pretext that they were infiltrated by Brotherhood supporters, killing two protesters.

'It's my right as a citizen and as an announcer on state radio to also feel hurt and aggrieved from a ruling like this,' said Aida Seoudy on the music station Radio Hits a day after the verdict exonerating Mubarak. 'It shouldn't be that when people protest the acquittal of those who killed their friends, the same killers kill them again.' Seoudy noted how rallies by celebrants were not broken up like the rallies of those expressing their anger and grief – both being in violation of the protest law.[94] She was promptly suspended, reinstated only under presidential orders when young journalists meeting with al-Sisi brought up her case. Television talk shows expressed the resignation that the nation should move on and look to the future.

The justice system was more efficient in punishing those who challenged state power. Non-violent protesters, democracy advocates, and journalists were imprisoned for years on end, yet security officials ordering or carrying out the death of hundreds of Egyptians have walked free. Mubarak would not be held accountable for decades of despotism, corruption, and human rights violations. The process of instating judicial independence, reining in the extraordinary powers of the security state, and ending repression of citizens' basic freedoms has a long way to go.

Hope for an open, free, and democratic society has been extinguished by a retooled and more experienced police state that penetrates the media, the judiciary, and the state bureaucracy. The law gives the military and security agencies unrestricted access to phone calls and messages through direct links to the networks of telecom companies. Private communications may be intercepted without the control or oversight of a court, the company, or the telecommunications regulator.[95] Awash with secret slush funds and accorded unchecked powers, the Interior Ministry has commenced the mass surveillance of social media and electronic communications.[96]

The security agencies' obsession with eavesdropping was made plain when a Brotherhood-affiliated channel outside Egypt broadcast recordings from a listening device in the office of General Abbas Kamel, al-Sisi's office manager and top aide, supposedly planted by the General Intelligence Service to spy on the military. One leak had top generals, the interior minister, and the public prosecutor elaborately plotting to forge evidence to show that ousted president Muhammad Morsi was not being held incommunicado at a naval base – the legality of which was being challenged by his lawyers – but in an Interior Ministry holding facility. The plan had military engineers build a hangar fitted to be an exact replica of Morsi's quarters, identifying it as an Interior Ministry prison, complete with torture chamber and forged ledgers.[97] The leaks exposed collusion among the pillars of the deep state: the military, the interior ministry, and the judiciary. Another recording revealed that the United Arab Emirates bankrolled the anti-Morsi Tamarod campaign via Egypt's military, revealing behind-the-scenes intrigues that culminated in the Islamist president's toppling.[98] Officials professed the wiretaps were fabricated by the Brotherhood using 'advanced technology'.

In the mid-afternoon of 24 January 2015, a band of party members from the Socialist Popular Alliance, chanting the revolutionary slogan 'bread, freedom, social justice', made their way to downtown's Talaat Harb Square, a stone's throw away from Tahrir. They planned a procession to place a wreath of flowers in the landmark square to commemorate the revolution's martyrs. Seconds later and without warning, on their commander's orders, masked police stationed in force in Talaat Harb opened fire to scatter the crowd; arrests followed. Thirty-two-year-old Shaimaa Elsabbagh, a poet, activist, and mother to a five-year-old boy, collapsed and died, her lungs and heart lacerated by shotgun pellets. Videos of the police strike and photographs of a male colleague clutching and carrying her, as blood streaked down her face, circulated around the world, evoking horror.[99]

Prosecutors promised an investigation. Police officials denied responsibility for the death, maintaining only tear gas was used in crowd control – a routine lie – and blame was pinned on Brotherhood interlopers seeking to damage the reputation of law enforcement. A day later and four years after the start of an uprising, the military sealed off Tahrir and main squares to prevent the masses from assembling. Clashes erupted; at least 20 were counted among the dead, including a Coptic Christian boy of ten. The woman with flowers was laid to rest that day in the same Alexandria cemetery as Khaled Said, whose police death became a catalyst to revolution.

With the nationalisation of political discourse, spaces where differing points of views could be expressed and debated in a civil and respectful manner all but vanished. It resembled how historian Ami Ayalon, in *The Press in the Arab Middle East*, described the media under Gamal Abd al-Nasser, who abolished multiparty politics and took over the private press:

> *In many ways the press regressed to its starting point, becoming little more than official bulletins extolling state leaders, fighting the state's domestic and foreign verbal propaganda battles, and 'educating' the public according to dictates from above. The press became an echo rather than a voice, and journalists, little more than bureaucratic functionaries, were forced back into docility.*[100]

From those heady days of popular uprising, when dreams of a just and democratic society seemed within grasp, the struggle has turned to one of small victories – lobbying for the release of incarcerated journalists and political detainees, shaming officials on social media for their dereliction, batting in the courts to roll back a clause in restrictive legislation, and gradually squeezing open spaces for expression and dissent.

Egyptians await their revolution.

Epilogue: Media Matters

In this epilogue I set out 14 observations based on a review of the role of Egyptian media in politics and society to illustrate how access to and limits on information have led to both revolutionary activism and the forces working to preserve the status quo.

The state information regime has collapsed

Egypt was taken by surprise when Israel struck in June 1967. During the Six Day War broadcast outlets aired invented reports of fabulous victories against the Zionist foe. It was only later that Egyptians could comprehend the true extent of a humiliating defeat that left the whole of Sinai under occupation. At no other moment did state media prove so complicit in deepening a sense of public betrayal. Egyptians tuned to the shortwave transmission of the BBC World Service and French Monte-Carlo to find out what was *not* being reported in the official press. Three decades later, Qatari news channel Al Jazeera served a similar role, becoming the station the Arab public tuned to first during periods of crises. Satellite communication and the internet rendered it impossible for the state to manage the information grid and set the media agenda. One party cannot propel a narrative of truth, determine the authority of the debate, or completely control information and its dissemination. Preserving the sanctity of the state, its rulers, and institutions of power by insulating them from censure is no longer a tenable option.

Information sharing empowers citizens

Traditional news media – print, radio, and television – offer one-way channels of communication. Censorship controls attempt to regulate information transmission to the audience. Decentralised social networks deliver a different kind of protocol, opening up spaces to analyse and debate at a cost far less than publishing a periodical. Breaking down the psychic isolation central to a regime's power, the internet and social media have served as equalisers in an information battle against despotism, forming centres of influence and amplifying the public's voice. Yet digital communication tools are simply enablers: a nexus linking citizens and driving a message. They are not substitutes for the laborious work of grass-roots outreach and mobilisation needed to engage marginalised sectors of the population in the arena of decision-making, thereby turning information into power.

Never underestimate the power of the press

With international and local pressures on Hosni Mubarak's Western-allied regime to at least give the appearance of moving towards democratic reform, the regime made the calculation that allowing a modicum of liberty to the press was a way of acquiescing to those demands without surrendering political power. A widening gap was exposed between the hardships citizens faced and a government that was *not* acting to remedy endemic problems. With a more vibrant media in the lead-up to revolution, the public was better informed and involved, political action was escalating, and a collective national will for change was taking shape. Invented truths of state media, the dominance of the security apparatus, and all other forms of repression were inadequate against an uprising against Mubarak's rule.

Expression and the arts adapt to restricted political environments

Creativity has found ways around the impasse of censorship. Literature, film, comedy, and politics have been inextricably linked in Egyptian popular culture. The realities of the Arab world's despotic regimes and long-reigning rulers have been the subject of parodies like the 1989 comedic play *Takharif* (Delusions), about a lunatic dictator reigning over the fictional land of Antika. At first he vows to rule for no more than 20 years and announces plans to govern democratically – by declaring a dictatorship and imprisoning opponents. In the 2006 comedy film *Zaza*, the aim of the autocratic ruler is to implement a veneer of democracy by announcing contested presidential elections, but the state uses heavy-handed tactics to ward off any real opposition. A simple, virtuous man reluctantly joins the race, promising to address the needs of the masses – and wins. Satire, humour, and the arts are valuable devices for reproach because they get audiences to think, poke fun at venerated leaders and official dogma, start conversations and shatter illusions, and expand the boundaries for other forms of expression. For a time, spaces for expression during and following the 25 January revolution unleashed a creative energy – in street murals, song, stand-up comedy, and performance art. But when the security-minded state was reinstated, Bassem Youssef's satire on the Arab world's top-rated programme was deemed so threatening to entrenched power that it was forced to shut down. Singers and artists who did not fall in line were banished. Creative outlets chip away at the castles of a ruling order over time.

Freedoms of expression that have been gained have also been lost

Authorities tightened press controls in the run-up to Egypt's fraudulent 2010 parliamentary elections, and cut off communication links months later in a far-reaching attempt to quash the popular uprising that would end Mubarak's 30-year reign. After his downfall the ruling military council was shown to be intolerant of criticism, routinely referring civilians accused of insulting the army to military trials, jailing bloggers, assaulting and detaining journalists, raiding the offices of broadcasters, engaging in misinformation campaigns that target activist groups, and blaming failings on conspirators, agitators, and foreign hands. That response hardly changed under a democratically elected president, and a military-backed government following his ouster went further in restricting the press, pressuring the cancellation of a television drama and a popular satire programme, and jailing journalists under the guise of waging a war against terrorism. As the security state regained its footing after revolution, a critical press was being caged in and dissident voices hounded. Press freedom remains a constant demand.

The larger the media audience, the greater the censorship

In the setup of Egypt's censorship regime, books have had the widest spectrum of freedom, while reaching the comparatively smallest audience, followed by the local print press, where no official censorship mechanisms – save instructions from security officials and confiscations – apply. Formal censorship requiring permits and licences – coupled with directives from the security services – remains in place for theatre, cinema, and television. The government has sought to control the imagery transmitted from Egypt, restricting the practice of journalism on the streets in covering elections, demonstrations, and revolution. Television is vulnerable because it is a more involved method of conveying information than the written press. Following Mubarak's fall, the military council maintained pressure on broadcasters, fearful of the power of the moving image. The administration of President Muhammad Morsi, who hailed from the Muslim Brotherhood, exercised restrictions on the press using litigation to intimidate critics. Finally, an army-backed government and military president have been more brazen, shutting down satellite broadcasters, killing and jailing journalists, rejuvenating the fear of the security agencies, and closing off arenas for expression in the media and on the streets.

Censorship walls fall when psychological barriers are broken

Censorship barriers are breached when citizens dare to protest, dare to speak up, dare to challenge authority in the public space. By 2005 Hosni Mubarak, no longer quite as untouchable as he once was, faced more direct criticism in the press. On 25 January 2011 the most important psychological barrier of fear came crashing down as tens of thousands of Egyptians took to the streets calling for the downfall of the regime, and in 18 days the second Arab despot within a month saw his demise. After an uprising Egyptians gave themselves the right to criticise their rulers, including generals and presidents, despite efforts to quell dissent through military prosecution, violent crackdowns, sexual assault, and intimidation. Spaces for expression open up because of the willingness of an active public to defy the limits and accept the risks that come with it. Still, there can be no genuine freedoms, for citizens or the press, within a military or police state.

Censorship cannot work in the absence of fear

Unpopular regimes rule by instilling a paralysing fear. Fear is an essential component of censorship – fear of the security agencies, fear of being beaten, jailed, or detained, fear of being sued, fear of being fired, ostracised, or branded traitors. Fear coupled with paranoia is a coercive brew for ingraining groupthink and preserving an adherence beyond the censor's red lines. In Mubarak's Egypt an immense security apparatus interlaced with the office of the presidency and the ruling party maintained his hold on power, rigged elections, controlled the press, and quashed protests. Taking risks became necessary to overcome barriers of censorship and push the limits of expression. The renewed dominance of the military and security agencies has worked to re-establish the fear factor, seduced by nationalist rhetoric in a war on terrorism.

Indirect censorship controls work as effectively as direct controls

Indirect censorship is sustained through judges that produce rulings favourable to the government, stifling and time-consuming bureaucracy, and the refusal to license, distribute, or issue press and filming permits. The state has leverage to control the private press, often involving pointed messages to media owners, who have interlocking interests with the state. They were well aware that owning a piece of the media pie requires financing, and they were not going to risk investing without government backing. Media owners know they could face harassment from government regulators and tax authorities, or be subjected to restrictive rules on their business ventures. Controls were also present in favourable and beneficial relations cultivated between security agencies and journalists.

Censorship of the streets can be more perilous than official censorship

A social censorship has emerged when ideologues have vied for political and societal influence, desiring to become the upholders of nationalist identity or public morality. Censorship of the street is advanced by religious commentators, lawyers, politicians, media personalities, or any self-appointed protector of fundamental values or the state's higher interests. They hold no official authority, yet are able to galvanise a following. Under the rule of Islamist president Muhammad Morsi, a crop of television sheikhs gained notoriety spewing hatred against liberals, secularists, Christians, and anyone considered a critic of political Islam; they framed differences in religious tones. After Morsi's downfall, vigorous patriotic fervour was the modus operandi for silencing and assailing regime critics – opponents were traitors, fifth columnists, and terrorists who did not belong to the nation.

Freer expression enables action

It has often been said that, in the absence of any kind of true democratic representation, a relatively freer press merely amounted to the right to bark – newspaper editorials and talk shows on satellite television served as nothing more than a catharsis rather than a catalyst for action. While the pace of change was frustratingly slow, it was having a measurable – and in the long term, a cumulative – effect. Social media created a new arena for networking, activism, and political engagement through which Egyptians were overcoming their fears. As power gave rise to hubris, rulers undervalued the organised power of the masses, and conversely citizens underestimated their own collective strength. Egyptians have grown accustomed to hearing different perspectives and viewpoints, and accessing various news sources. All this has led to greater civic involvement, especially among a generation of youth, setting in motion an uprising that would attract the world's attention, although it has yet to spawn a vibrant democracy or a credible and trustworthy media. The promise of revolution dissolved to be replaced by the repression that has ruled the lives of Egyptians for so long. The powers are now aware that narrowing the arena for expression, coupled with restrictive security practices, diminishes the potential and threshold for constructive action.

The immediacy of information amplifies its influence

Immediacy has been the major freedom gain of technology. Transmitting news and information in real time gives it greater authority in influencing a public and policy reaction. There is no relying on gatekeepers to decide what is and what isn't news or how and when it should be covered. In blogs, tweets, photographs, audio recordings, and videos, citizens have become information contributors. That trend will deepen as crowdsourced and integrated digital tools come online and reach wider populations, feeding into news ecosystems particularly in under-reported communities.

Propaganda and conspiracy theories have lost none of their efficacy

When the ruler, his party, and security apparatus cannot dismiss or prohibit media discussion, they invent and push competing narratives. With individuals sharing first-hand information and forming their own conclusions, they provide a picture of events that responds to the propaganda. Yet even in the age of open communications, skilful propaganda remains a potent stratagem and conspiracy theories find a believing public. Propaganda involves repeating and fortifying a falsehood and appealing to base emotion over reason. Media find it convenient to fall into line when external dangers are reinforced and dissenting voices muzzled, enabling the state to reclaim the dominant narrative and channel public frustration against opponents. Propaganda is a means to insulate authoritarianism and facilitate the reinvention of repression. Those techniques have worked to stifle the reach and popularity of those who question or challenge the ruling order.

Citizens are forming their own personal truth narratives

With atomised outlets for news and information, the version of events people choose to believe is the one they *want* to believe. Fiction has become as attractive as fact. It has never become easier to fashion myths out of whole cloth, theorise about conspiracies mired in a crazy web of contradictions, or espouse new parallel realities. In the echo chamber of the media and cyberspace, it is generally the loud, pugnacious voices that are heard over the din of clashing narratives. Initiating dialogue and finding areas of common ground have become more of a quandary when each side operates based on its own set of truths. Credible and trustworthy media outlets fostering a national conversation are more in demand than ever. What needs to happen, particularly in the media, is a reasoned and ongoing conversation between people of differing viewpoints, a sincere effort to determine the facts and work through solutions. In the heart of the public square during 18 days of revolution, Egyptians were actually talking to one another: Islamists with liberals, Christians with Muslims, rich with poor. Not only were they having a dialogue, they were willing to make the ultimate sacrifices for one another knowing that, whatever their differences, they wanted to live in a nation of justice, freedoms, tolerance, and dignity.

Timeline

	2005
7 September	Hosni Mubarak wins 88.6% of the vote in Egypt's first contested presidential elections.
	2007
26 March	Judicial supervision of elections comes to an end with amendments to the constitution.
	2008
6 April	The April 6 Youth Movement begins as a Facebook group in solidarity with a factory workers' strike. Organisers call for a general strike to protest corruption, political stagnation, and economic hardships.
	2010
19 February	Mohamed ElBaradei, retired chief of the UN's atomic energy watchdog, announces his intention to run for the presidency if reforms are made to open the political process. He returns to Egypt, greeted by throngs of supporters at Cairo airport.
1, 8 June	The ruling National Democratic Party sweeps elections for the upper house of parliament, amid claims of vote buying and election rigging.

6 June	Plain-clothes police beat 28-year-old Khaled Said to death in Alexandria. Graphic photos of Said, bloodied and disfigured, surface on social media. He becomes the symbol of national anger against the practice of police torture.
November–December	Mubarak's National Democratic Party secures a crushing win in People's Assembly elections.
17 December	Vegetable seller Mohamed Bouazizi sets himself ablaze in Tunisia's provincial town of Sidi Bouzid after authorities confiscate his vegetable stall. Dying of his burns, Bouazizi emerges as a martyr to Tunisians who take to the streets protesting high unemployment, lack of political freedom, and rampant corruption.

2011

14 January	Tunisia's 23-year reigning president Zine el-Abidine Ben Ali flees the country.
25 January	A popular uprising starts against the rule of Hosni Mubarak. Nationwide protests are publicised on the 'We are all Khaled Said' Facebook page.
28 January	In the Friday of Rage, millions of Egyptians take to the streets calling for Mubarak's downfall.
2–3 February	In the Battle of the Camel, pro-Mubarak ruffians attempt to dislodge revolutionaries from Tahrir Square.
11 February	Mubarak relinquishes executive power to the Supreme Council of the Armed Forces, led by defence minister Muhammad Hussein Tantawi.

19 March	Amendments to Egypt's 1971 constitution are approved in the first democratic vote following Mubarak's downfall, paving the way for parliamentary elections.
9 April	In the pre-dawn hours, army commandos and security forces charge Tahrir Square, shooting volleys of gunfire and detaining dissenting army officers who joined protesters.
10 April	Al Arabiya broadcasts an audio speech made by Mubarak where he responds to critics who said he had plundered the nation and amassed a huge fortune.
13 April	Hosni Mubarak and his sons, Gamal and Alaa, are placed under arrest.
3 August	Criminal court proceedings begin for Mubarak, his sons, and senior security officials.
9 October	Coptic Christians stage a rally in front of the state television and radio building, demanding a redress of grievances. 27 protesters are shot or crushed beneath the wheels of military vehicles. State television is accused of fuelling violence.
19 November	Security forces and army troops break up a Tahrir Square sit-in, escalating into an all-out confrontation that claims the lives of 51 protesters.
15 December	Clashes erupt when a protester is abducted and beaten by soldiers inside the parliament grounds, leading to days of street fighting between army troops and protesters. 18 Egyptians lose their lives.

2012	
1 February	74 fans die when a football match in seaside city of Port Said descends into violence.
2 June	A criminal court hands Mubarak and his interior minister a life sentence for their complicity in protester deaths.
14 June	The Supreme Constitutional Court dissolves the democratically elected People's Assembly, reinstating the military rulers' legislative powers.
23–24 May	In Egypt's first free presidential elections, Muhammad Morsi, chief of the Muslim Brotherhood's Freedom and Justice Party, and Ahmed Shafik, Mubarak's one-time prime minister, rank in first and second place respectively, moving on to the 16–17 June runoffs.
17 June	As votes are being counted, the military council issues amendments to the constitutional declaration that diminish the duties of the president and expand the role of the military council.
24 June	Morsi is officially declared the democratically elected head of state with a slim majority.
30 June	Morsi takes the oath of the presidency.
5 August	Militants ambush and kill 16 Egyptian soldiers stationed at a border post in Sinai. Morsi uses the crisis to sack top security officials.

12 August	Morsi annuls the supplementary constitutional declaration that empowered Tantawi and the military council. Morsi assumes full executive and legislative powers. Abd al-Fattah al-Sisi, head of military intelligence, is tapped to become the defence minister.
22 November	Morsi grants himself extraordinary constitutional powers. The power grab receives wide condemnation.
4 December	Tens of thousands of protesters converge on the presidential palace protesting Morsi's decree.
5 December	The president's Islamist defenders call for a rally before the gates of the presidential palace, where a sit-in of revolutionary opponents had assembled. Street battles last into the dawn hours, leaving ten dead.
8 December	A new constitutional declaration drops an article that blocks the judiciary from reviewing all executive orders, yet the president's supporters blockade the nation's highest court.
15, 22 December	The Islamist-backed constitution passes with a yes vote of 63.8%; only a third of eligible voters show up to the polls.

2013

13 January	An appeals court nullifies Mubarak's conviction and orders a retrial.
April	Morsi misses the chance to bridge the political divide when the European Union negotiates a compromise between his party and the opposition.

22 April	A petition drive called Tamarod embarks on collecting endorsements calling on Morsi to step down and early elections held. The campaign culminates in nationwide rallies on 30 June 2013.
15 June	Morsi holds an Islamist rally in support of the Syrian resistance, announcing that Egypt is shutting down the Syrian Embassy.
23 June	Defence minister Abd al-Fattah al-Sisi issues a cryptic statement urging all sides to reconcile before 30 June.
24 June	The Supreme Council of the Armed Forces agrees to side with the president's opponents should millions take to the streets.
29 June	Morsi rejects calls for early elections as being a formula for instability.
30 June	Huge anti-Morsi rallies mass at the presidential palace, Tahrir Square, and across the country.
1 July	The army's central command issues a 48-hour ultimatum ordering Morsi and political players to meet the people's demands.
3 July	Al-Sisi announces Morsi's removal and the implementation of a military-backed roadmap. The chief justice of the Supreme Constitutional Court becomes the interim president. Morsi supporters continue protests and sit-ins.
8 July	Soldiers outside the headquarters of the Republican Guard open fire on Morsi supporters, killing 61.

26 July	Egyptians take to the street in rallies after al-Sisi calls on Egyptians to give the military and the police the mandate to confront terrorism.
27 July	Police kill 95 Morsi supporters as they attempt to block a major Cairo thoroughfare.
14 August	Security forces and army personnel violently disperse two pro-Morsi sit-ins, killing hundreds of protesters. The massacre sets off a wave of vendetta attacks by Islamists.
16 August	120 mostly pro-Morsi protesters are killed by downtown Cairo's Ramses Square.
23 September	An Egyptian court orders a ban of the Muslim Brotherhood and the seizure of its assets.
25 December	The government officially designates the Brotherhood a terrorist organisation.
6 October	57 people die in clashes between Morsi supporters and police on a national holiday commemorating 40 years after the 1973 War.
4 November	Muhammad Morsi faces trial, his first public appearance since his ouster.
24 November	Interim president Adli Mansour approves a draconian protest law that prohibits public gatherings of more than ten people without prior security approval.

2014

14–15 January	A referendum on the constitution garners 98% of the vote, with a 39% turnout.

25 January	64 Egyptians are killed in confrontations with security forces on the revolution's third anniversary.
27 January	Mansour anoints al-Sisi the highest military rank of field marshal and the Supreme Council of the Armed Forces endorses their top commander's presidential bid.
26 March	Al-Sisi resigns as defence minister to run for president.
May 21	Mubarak is handed a three-year sentence for embezzling state funds.
26–28 May	Presidential elections are held following less than a month of campaigning.
2 June	Satirist Bassem Youssef announces that his top-rated programme has been cancelled under pressure.
3 June	Abd al-Fattah al-Sisi is declared the president in a landslide win.
8 June	Al-Sissi is sworn in as president for a four-year term.
23 June	Three Al Jazeera English journalists are sentenced to long prison sentences on charges of conspiring with the Brotherhood, spreading false news, and endangering national security.
29 November	A criminal court dismisses the charge against Mubarak for killing protesters during the revolution on procedural grounds. He is acquitted on the other corruption counts.

	2015
24 January	Poet and mother Shaimaa Elsabbagh is shot and killed by police as she and a group of activists resolve to lay a wreath of flowers in Tahrir Square to commemorate the revolution's martyrs.
24 February	The presidency decrees an anti-terrorism law that broadly defines terrorism to include any threat to public order.
21 April	In the first verdict against him, Morsi is sentenced to 20 years in prison for the death of protesters outside the presidential palace in December 2011.
16 May	A court sentences Morsi and five senior leaders of the Brotherhood to death for prison breaks during the 2011 revolution.
16 June	Morsi receives a life sentence for conspiring with foreign groups to destabilise the country.
19 June	WikiLeaks begins releasing over a half million cables and documents from the Saudi Foreign Ministry, revealing the kingdom's active manipulation of the media and intrigues of regional power.
29 June	Egypt's prosecutor general Hisham Barakat, is assassinated in a car bombing, marking an escalation in an insurgency that has targeted the army, police, and judges.
6 August	Amid national fanfare, al-Sisi inaugurates an extension to the Suez Canal, underscoring a commitment to military-led megaprojects over democratic freedoms.

Notes

Chapter 1 Prologue to Revolution

1 Ami Ayalon, *The Press in the Arab Middle East: A History* (New York and Oxford: Oxford University Press, 1995), 59.

2 Abdalla F. Hassan, 'As War Continues, Tensions Rise in Egypt', *World Press Review*, 31 Mar. 2003, www.worldpress.org/Mideast/1029.cfm (accessed Jan. 2011).

3 Alaa Al Aswany, 'Why the Muslim World Can't Hear Obama', tr. from Arabic by Geoff D. Porter, *New York Times*, 8 Feb. 2009, WK11, www.nytimes.com/2009/02/08/opinion/08aswany.html (accessed Feb. 2009).

4 Interview with Miral al-Tahawy (Arabic), 19 Sept. 2011, Cairo. In her novel *al-Badhinjana al-zarqa' (Blue Aubergine)*, she chronicles the melancholy childhood, adolescence, and adulthood of a woman named Nada, who in her search for identity dons the niqab, joins a secret religious society, and eventually loses hope in the possibilities of political Islam.

5 The original Arabic text of Sonallah Ibrahim's unacceptance speech is available at ow.ly/FTsdV (accessed Feb. 2012). Abdalla F. Hassan, 'Black Humor in Dark Times: Egyptian Novelist Sonallah Ibrahim', *World Press Review*, 19 June 2003, www.worldpress.org/Mideast/1205.cfm (accessed Jan. 2011).

6 Interview with Gamal Bekheet (Arabic), 25 Oct. 2012, Giza.

7 Interview with Hany Ramzy (Arabic), 21 May 2013, New Cairo.

8 Kifaya held its first protest rally on 12 Dec. 2004 before the High Court of Justice in downtown Cairo in support of an independent judiciary.

9 '05CAIRO2280, Codel Pelosi March 19–20 visit to Cairo: Mubarak on Israel/Palestinians, Iraq, Iran, Egypt's presidential election, and Darfur', 23 Mar. 2005, wikileaks.org/cable/2005/03/05CAIRO2280.html (accessed Aug. 2011).

10 Hesham al-Bastawissy was a candidate in the May 2012 presidencial elections. Mahmoud Mekki served as vice president from Aug. to Dec. 2012.

11 Interview with Wael Abbas (Arabic), 17 Jan. 2011, New Cairo.

12 Protesters and striking workers in the factory town of al-Mahalla al-Kubra set fire to the offices of the National Democratic Party and shouted slogans against Hosni Mubarak. The city remained a centre of worker strikes and labour organising leading up to the revolution and afterwards.

13 Interview with Mahrusa Salem Hassan (Arabic), 4 Apr. 2010, Cairo.

14 Interview with Hossam Bahgat (Arabic), 12 Aug. 2009, Cairo.
15 'Hal Hosni Mubarak diktatur?' (Is Hosni Mubarak a Dictator?), *al-Dustur*, 20 Sept. 2006, 5.
16 *Al-Dustur*, 30 Mar. 2006.
17 Ibrahim Eissa, 'al-Ilahiya la tamrad' (Gods Don't Get Sick), *al-Dustur*, 27 Mar. 2008, 1.
18 Mohamed ElBaradei, 'Harb Uktubar . . . ma huwa akbar min al-intisar?' (The October War: What Is Bigger than Victory?'), 5 Oct. 2010.
19 Ibrahim Eissa returned to television following the revolution. He also became the editor-in-chief of the daily *al-Tahrir* newspaper, whose inaugural issue rolled off the presses on 3 July 2011.
20 Following the revolution, Hamdy Kandil returned to television with *Qalam rusas* (Pencil) on al-Tahrir satellite channel, but his programme was again cancelled.
21 In July 2011 Lamis al-Hadidi started a talk show called *Huna al-'asima* (Here Is the Capital) on the satellite channel CBC.
22 The interview with Mubarak was broadcast on 24–26 Apr. 2005. Al Arabiya also aired the four-hour interview.
23 Amr Adeeb's talk show returned to the airwaves after the revolution.
24 Interview with Naglaa El Emary (Arabic), 29 July 2010, London.
25 Interview with Hussein Abdul Ghani (Arabic), 6 Apr. 2010, Cairo. He left Al Jazeera and for a time hosted his own talk and current affairs show on the Egyptian private satellite channel al-Nahar. In Nov. 2012 Abdul Ghani became the media spokesperson of the National Salvation Front, a coalition of political parties and activist groups formed in opposition to Islamist-dominated rule under President Muhammad Morsi.
26 It was not just Arab governments that were concerned about what influences the hearts and minds of the Arab public. The US set up its Arabic-language news channel Al Hurra (The Free One) in 2004. France created an Arabic-language France 24 in 2007. State-run Russia Today launched an Arabic channel in 2007. Germany's Deutsche Welle started with three hours of Arabic programming in 2002, which expanded to 12 hours in 2008 and 17 hours in 2014. The BBC World Service began a 24-hour Arabic news channel in 2008 and China began an Arabic news and entertainment channel, CCTV, in 2009.
27 Interview with Alaa Al Aswany (Arabic), 9 Apr. 2010, Cairo.
28 The Photoshopped image was published online (front page) and in print (p. 6) on 14 Sept. 2010.
29 Osama Saraya was appointed editor-in-chief of *al-Ahram* on 4 July 2005, replacing Ibrahim Nafei, who led the flagship state-owned daily since 1979 and was criticised for mismanaging the paper and using his position for self-enrichment.
30 Osama Saraya, 'Sani' al-mustaqbal' (The Maker of the Future), *al-Ahram*, www.ahram.org.eg/archive/The-Writers/News/18722.aspx (accessed Aug. 2011).
31 '06CAIRO1351, Next steps for advancing democracy in Egypt', 6 Mar. 2006, wikileaks.org/cable/2006/03/06CAIRO1351.html (accessed Aug. 2011). Francis J. Ricciardone's fluency in Arabic (a unique talent for a US ambassador) and his willingness to discuss the US position on probing television interviews made him popular among Egyptians.
32 Abd al-Halim Kandil also authored *al-Ayam al-akhira* (The Last Days) in 2008 and *Did al-rayis* (Against the President) in 2005, both books directed criticism at Mubarak.

33 Andrew Hammond, *Popular Culture in the Arab World: Arts, Politics, and the Media* (Cairo: The American University in Cairo Press, 2007), 229.
34 Interview with Abd al-Moneim Aboul Futouh (Arabic), 4 Apr. 2010, Cairo.
35 '09CAIRO874, Scenesetter: President Mubarak's visit to Washington', 19 May 2009, www.wikileaks.org/cable/2009/05/09CAIRO874.html (accessed Dec. 2010).
36 Interview with Gamal Ellatif (Arabic), 28 July 2010, London.
37 Interview with Awatef Abdel Rahman (Arabic), 30 Mar. 2010, Cairo.
38 Interview with Abd al-Moneim Aboul Futouh (Arabic), 4 Apr. 2010, Cairo.
39 Interview with Alaa Al Aswany (Arabic), 9 Apr. 2010, Cairo.
40 Alaa Al Aswany, 'Mata yadruk al-ra'is Mubarak hadhhi al-haqiqa?!' (When Will President Mubarak Grasp This Truth?), *al-Shuruk*, 6 Apr. 2010, 16, ow.ly/Jbw4p.
41 After Egypt's 18-day revolution, Alaa Al Aswany's weekly columns, 'Parenthetically', became regular features in the top-selling daily *al-Masry al-youm*. On 23 June 2014, Al Aswany announced that he would no longer be publishing his columns in the paper. 'It is no longer acceptable but to have one opinion, one thought, and one word,' he tweeted. 'It is not permitted to criticise or to have differing viewpoints. It is no longer acceptable but to praise at the expense of truth.' Alaa Al Aswany, 23 June 2014, twitter.com/AlaaAswany/status/481185067650539521 (accessed June 2014).
42 Interview with Max Rodenbeck, 7 Apr. 2010, Cairo.
43 *The Economist*, 'A Tantalizing Return', 6–12 Mar. 2010, 64–5, www.economist.com/node/15612471 (accessed Mar. 2010).
44 Dream 2, 21 Feb. 2010. Mona al-Shazly's interview with Mohamed ElBaradei on *Ten at Night* can be seen online in 15 parts (all 22 Feb. 2010, accessed May 2010): part 1: youtu.be/CLdNdAChY7A; part 2: youtu.be/tbT8W3K5u0g; part 3: youtu.be/Jti1uYk-bIw; part 4: youtu.be/sQn2o_qGxWs; part 5: youtu.be/mv1Xu8R1ilk; part 6: youtu.be/cN5ony6cT70; part 7: youtu.be/ibjaplV7kxs; part 8: youtu.be/k_1AmsyF_G4; part 9: youtu.be/Gc04geDQ-Dw; part 10: youtu.be/o-RHSlzUqlM; part 11: youtu.be/4PBpDTeI0D0; part 12: youtu.be/HYDH2V4QyXM; part 13: youtu.be/gFaxAN2CEc4; part 14: youtu.be/D_UPmMXCJ3Q; part 15: youtu.be/YjEF8Qf0thg.
45 Mohamed ElBaradei's page on Facebook is www.facebook.com/Elbarad3i, his Twitter account is twitter.com/ElBaradei, and his YouTube channel is www.youtube.com/ElBaradeiOfficial.
46 'The possibility that Gamal might succeed his father remains deeply unpopular on the street – a sentiment often echoed by commentators in the independent and opposition press,' wrote former US ambassador to Egypt Francis J. Ricciardone Jr in a leaked 2006 embassy cable. '06CAIRO2010, Egypt: Actions louder than words – Gamal Mubarak and the presidency', 3 Apr. 2006, www.wikileaks.org/cable/2006/04/06CAIRO2010.html (accessed Dec. 2010).
47 The Earl of Cromer, *Modern Egypt* (2 vols. London: Macmillan and Co., 1908), ii, 565.
48 Interview with Muhammad Mahdi Akef (Arabic), 6 Apr. 2010, New Cairo.
49 'A message from ElBaradei', 7 Dec. 2010, youtu.be/ZLtrrK_z0jk (accessed Dec. 2010).
50 Days before his death, Khaled Said had reportedly posted online a seven-minute video of narcotics officers sharing out confiscated drugs among themselves. 'The

video that killed the martyr Khaled Said', 11 June 2010, youtu.be/35t58GFfMbo (accessed Sept. 2011).

51 The young man's full name was Khaled Muhammad Said Muhammad Sobhi. Tamir Amin mixed the order in stating his name.

52 Channel Two, 13 June 2010. '*Masr al-naharda*: The death of a youth in Alexandria', 14 June 2010, youtu.be/F8viKU5ac74 (accessed Sept. 2011).

53 An Alexandria criminal court sentenced Mahmoud Salah Amin and Awad Ismail Suleiman, the officers accused of the beating to death of Khaled Said, to seven years in prison on 26 Oct. 2011. In a retrial after the conviction was overturned, the pair were given a ten-year prison sentence in Mar. 2014.

54 Channel Two, 12 Oct. 2010. The broadcast can be seen in three parts: '*Masr al-naharda* and the benefits and faults of Facebook, part 1', 13 Oct. 2010, youtu.be/Vk8dT6SSVyI; part 2: youtu.be/xWcst7HgqBc; part 3: youtu.be/fOkS_nu8u_k (accessed July 2012).

55 'Zine el-Abidine Ben Ali's final televised address', 14 Jan. 2011, youtu.be/3vvjSILioOE (accessed Jan. 2011). Ben Ali vowed reductions in the price of basic commodities, the formation of an independent commission to investigate corruption, support for democracy and pluralism, and called for civil rule and national dialogue. Promising that he would not remain president for life, he announced that he would not run in the 2014 elections.

56 Anthony Shadid, 'Joy as Tunisian President Flees Offers Lesson to Arab Leaders', *New York Times*, 14 Jan. 2011, nyti.ms/fBGNKp (accessed Jan. 2011).

57 '08TUNIS193, President Ben Ali meets with A/S Welch: Progress on counter-terrorism cooperation, regional challenges', 3 Mar. 2008, www.wikileaks.org/cable/2008/03/08TUNIS193.html (accessed Jan. 2011).

58 Rania Al Malky, 'Tunisia Leads the Way', *Daily News Egypt*, 14 Jan. 2011, 7, www.thedailynewsegypt.com/editorial/editorial-tunisia-leads-the-way.html (accessed Sept. 2011).

59 Interview with Rania Al Malky, 13 Apr. 2011, Giza. The *Daily News Egypt* is licensed in Dubai and as a foreign publication it is subject to control by the state censors.

Chapter 2 Eighteen Days

1 Gene Sharp, *From Dictatorship to Democracy: A Conceptual Framework for Liberation* (4th edn. East Boston, MA: Albert Einstein Institution, May 2010), 4, www.aeinstein.org/wp-content/uploads/2013/09/FDTD.pdf (accessed Sept. 2011).

2 We are all Khaled Said, 'Details for 25 January', bit.ly/Egypt25 (accessed Jan. 2011).

3 Asmaa Mahfouz, 18 Jan. 2011, youtu.be/SgjIgMdsEuk (accessed Aug. 2011).

4 Asmaa Mahfouz, 'A last word before 25 January', 24 Jan. 2011, youtu.be/hKgN6A0UWCU (accessed Sept. 2011).

5 Interview with Laila Muhammad and protesters (Arabic), 25 Jan. 2011, Giza. 'Day one of Egypt's Freedom Revolution', 24 Jan. 2012, youtu.be/Co-oJUk_P_A (accessed Jan. 2012).

6 Channel Two, 25 Jan. 2011. '*Masr al-naharda* programme introduction, part 1 of 3', 26 Jan. 2011, youtu.be/ihh6KssuvqU; part 2: youtu.be/pY4dNPU_RCA;

part 3: youtu.be/O6h1t1eQsxo; '*Masr al-naharda* and the news bulletin, part 1 of 2', 26 Jan. 2012, youtu.be/1bQocNpm1-A; part 2: youtu.be/jBLZqvlMnrA (accessed Mar. 2012).

7 Evolving into a news website, Rassd's model for citizen journalism spawned similar social media initiatives in Egypt and in covering the Arab uprisings.

8 'Egypt's Freedom Revolution, day 2', 26 Jan. 2011, youtu.be/ElQV6nCzH30 (accessed Jan. 2011).

9 'Protest on the tracks at the Gamal Abd al-Nasser Metro station', 26 Jan. 2011, youtu.be/fXSuOE8lUbI (accessed Jan. 2011).

10 'Egyptian Tank Man', 25 Jan. 2011, youtu.be/kWr6MypZ-JU (accessed Oct. 2011).

11 Al Jazeera, 26 Jan. 2011. 'We will continue until we hear, "I have understood you"', 27 Jan. 2011, youtu.be/eE2itEB__v8 (accessed Oct. 2011).

12 Dream 2, 26 Jan. 2011. '*Ten at Night* with Mona al-Shazly: A report on the absence of Mahmoud Saad on *Masr al-naharda*', 27 Jan. 2011, youtu.be/eJ3wSA31hY8 (accessed Feb. 2011).

13 According to security sources, hundreds had been arrested in the past two days of protests. Human rights groups claimed the number was over a thousand.

14 A physician, Hossam Badrawi was appointed the secretary-general of the ruling party on 5 Feb. in an effort to recast its image. He resigned on the morning of 11 Feb., before Vice President Omar Soliman announced that Mubarak was stepping down.

15 Dream 2, *Ten at Night* with Mona al-Shazly, 26 Jan. 2011. Online in six parts (6 Feb. 2011 and 27 Jan. 2011) – part 1: youtu.be/IBoYmzQgE5o; part 2: youtu.be/ykllNhPo8Hk; part 3: youtu.be/vsy7Yqd0V-k; part 4: youtu.be/g4Req_Q3Vi4; part 5: youtu.be/Bfxv9fpHl3s; part 6: youtu.be/706a5TsU6Io (accessed Feb. 2011).

16 Mohamed ElBaradei, 'A Manifesto for Change in Egypt', *The Daily Beast*, 26 Jan. 2011, www.thedailybeast.com/articles/2011/01/26/mohamed-elbaradei-the-return-of-the-challenger.html (accessed Jan. 2011).

17 Anonymous threatened to attack Egyptian government websites and to make sure that the international media saw the horrid realities of oppression. 'Operation Egypt – Anonymous press release', 26 Jan. 2011, youtu.be/yOLc3B2V4AM (accessed Jan. 2011).

18 Wael Ghonim, 27 Jan. 2011, twitter.com/Ghonim/status/30748650980249600 (accessed Feb. 2011).

19 Salon with Alaa Al Aswany (Arabic), 27 Jan. 2011, Cairo.

20 *Sawt al-umma*, 29 Jan. 2012. The paper, printed on Thursdays, was on news-stands on 28 Jan.

21 Video clips can be seen at youtu.be/t4OSMFYc9Mc (28 Jan. 2011), youtu.be/PujwO_iY5BU (30 Jan. 2011), and youtu.be/2ExW3vxFMig (4 June 2011) (accessed Aug. 2011).

22 Eighteen days of revolution resulted in more than 840 officially recorded deaths and hundreds missing.

23 'Hosni Mubarak's address on 28 Jan. 2011', 2 Jan. 2012, youtu.be/dVZ8wvvuiBw (accessed Feb. 2012).

24 Al Jazeera, 30 Jan. 2011.

25 Ibid.

26 Ibid.

27 Emad Eddin Adeeb landed his own show, *Bihudu'* (Quietly), on CBC in Jan. 2012. The owner of the network, wealthy businessman Muhammad al-Amin Ragab, enjoyed close ties with the Mubarak clan.

28 BBC Arabic, 1 Feb. 2011.

29 Sayed Ali and Hanaa al-Simary interviewed Shaymaa by phone on 1 Feb. 2011. She appeared as an in-studio guest on 2 Feb.: youtu.be/CUD8eX8seBw (accessed Mar. 2013).

30 'Hosni Mubarak's address on 1 Feb. 2011, the night before the Battle of the Camel', 31 Jan. 2012, youtu.be/hieZso8dSeg (accessed Feb. 2012).

31 The White House, 'Remarks by the President on the Situation in Egypt', 1 Feb. 2011, www.whitehouse.gov/the-press-office/2011/02/01/remarks-president-situation-egypt (accessed Aug. 2014).

32 The lead headline in *al-Ahram* the next day read, 'Millions Go Out in Support of Mubarak'. Mid-way down the front page was the headline, 'Violent Clashes between Supporters and Opponents in Tahrir Square'.

33 Anthony Shadid, 'Street Battle Over the Arab Future', *New York Times*, 2 Feb. 2011, nyti.ms/gjkehk (accessed Feb. 2011).

34 On 10 Oct. 2012, a criminal court acquitted all 24 defendants, including pro-regime businessmen, politicians, ministers, and National Democratic Party officials, for inciting and financing the attacks on protesters in Tahrir Square, citing insufficient evidence.

35 'Police car running over protesters in Egypt', 3 Feb. 2011, youtu.be/Lug41HbhC0s (accessed Sept. 2011).

36 Christiane Amanpour, 'Mubarak: "If I Resign Today There Will Be Chaos"', ABC News, 3 Feb. 2011, abcn.ws/dV5IOE (accessed Feb. 2011).

37 Al Jazeera's Cairo bureau chief and one of the network's journalists were also detained on 4 Feb. A Twitter update from Al Jazeera English said: 'Al jazeera Arabic's Cairo office has been stormed by unknown men and the office has been trashed #Egypt #tahrir'. Al Jazeera English, 4 Feb. 2011, twitter.com/AJELive/status/33503612671893504 (accessed Feb. 2011).

38 Al Jazeera, 4 Feb. 2011.

39 Rania Al Malky, 'Lies, Damned Lies', *Daily News Egypt*, 5 Feb. 2011, www.thedailynewsegypt.com/editorial/editorial-lies-damned-lies.html (accessed Sept. 2011).

40 Interview with Rania Al Malky, 13 Apr. 2011, Giza.

41 The White House, 'Remarks by President Obama and Prime Minister Stephen Harper of Canada in Joint Press Availability', 4 Feb. 2011, www.whitehouse.gov/the-press-office/2011/02/04/remarks-president-obama-and-prime-minister-stephen-harper-canada-joint-p (accessed Mar. 2011).

42 'Mubarak is high', 30 Jan. 2011, youtu.be/kCBFHo0_PPA (accessed Feb. 2012).

43 'Mubarak is high 3', 9 Feb. 2011, youtu.be/jbyg2Ej1uDY (accessed Feb. 2012).

44 Ramy Essam was among those arrested and tortured by the army on 9 Mar. 2011 as soldiers along with vigilantes swept into Tahrir Square to clear out protesters. He was beaten and stunned with a Taser in the Egyptian Museum and his long hair was hacked off with broken glass. After his release, he posted images of his scarred and

bruised body on Facebook. This was his online testimony after his release: 'Ramy Essam: A protester, not a thug', 10 Mar. 2011, youtu.be/xiRu8bZBXfM (accessed Feb. 2012). Essam continued to sing dissident songs against successive regimes, but under security pressures found it problematic to hold concerts after the 3 July 2013 coup. He moved to Malmö, Sweden in Oct. 2014.

45 Farrag Ismail, 'Ex-minister suspected behind Alex church bombing', Al Arabiya News, 7 Feb. 2011, www.alarabiya.net/articles/2011/02/07/136723.html (accessed Feb. 2011).

46 Dream 2, 7 Feb. 2011. '*Ten at Night* with Mona al-Shazly and Wael Ghonim, part 1', 7 Feb. 2011, youtu.be/K689F4PNvVo; part 2: youtu.be/njwPw7hdCPc; part 3: youtu.be/WfnSuRUGPKo; part 4: youtu.be/uKyNUIlxo9Q (accessed Feb. 2011).

47 Interview with Alaa Al Aswany, 10 Feb. 2011, Cairo.

48 'Hosni Mubarak's address on 10 Feb. 2011', 10 Feb. 2011, youtu.be/XOiXKqPiPVw (accessed Feb. 2012).

49 'Speech by Omar Soliman on 10 Feb. 2011', 10 Feb. 2011, youtu.be/x-WCWNsX1mw (accessed Feb. 2012).

50 Sharp, *From Dictatorship to Democracy*, 13.

51 'Soliman: Hosni Mubarak is stepping down', 11 Feb. 2011, youtu.be/ph8e11KR8mk (accessed Feb. 2012).

52 Interview with Gamal Bekheet (Arabic), 25 Oct. 2012, Giza.

Chapter 3 Politics and the Press under Military Rule

1 *Relix* magazine, Nov. 1979.

2 BBC Arabic, 16 Feb. 2011. 'Osama Saraya erupts in anger at a BBC correspondent', 16 Feb. 2011, youtu.be/JfOJTPvE58w (accessed Oct. 2011). Prime Minister Essam Sharaf dismissed Saraya, an NDP and Mubarak loyalist, on 30 Mar. 2011 along with the chief editors of the other state-owned dailies and the chairmen of the state-owned media houses.

3 The Qatari-owned Al Jazeera added Al Jazeera Mubashir Masr (Al Jazeera Live Egypt) to its bouquet of news, documentary, sports, and children's channels. The Egypt-focused news channel ceased broadcasting in Dec. 2014. Rotana, a media and entertainment conglomerate owned by Saudi billionaire Prince Alwaleed Bin Talal, started Rotana Masry (Rotana Egyptian) for its Egyptian audiences. In Nov. 2012, the MBC Group, owned by Saudi royals, launched an Egyptian channel, MBC Masr (MBC Egypt).

4 Naguib Sawiris sold ONtv in Dec. 2012 to Tunisian media mogul and film producer Tarak Ben Ammar.

5 Egyptian Prime Minister Ahmed Shafik on CNN's *State of the Union* with Candy Crowley, 6 Feb. 2011, cnnpressroom.blogs.cnn.com/2011/02/06/egyptian-prime-minister-ahmed-shafiq-on-cnns-state-of-the-union (accessed Mar. 2011).

6 The 2 Mar. 2011 episode of *Baladna bil-masry* hosted by Reem Magued and Yosri Fouda with guests Ahmed Shafik, Alaa Al Aswany, Hamdy Kandil, and Naguib Sawiris can be seen online (accessed Mar. 2011) – part 8: youtu.be/Ijr6HCiPD3w; part 9: youtu.be/rrOGOGxM8yQ; part 10: youtu.be/CJCuDOEkLeo; part 11: youtu.be/jo61wpG_9i4; part 12: youtu.be/Jw4xeDwuYHs; part 13: youtu.be/

uzYiwLGXIJI; part 14: youtu.be/7uyCpZcwsPM; part 15: youtu.be/d17Xivs4I6w; part 16: youtu.be/KuOl1b9sNus; part 17: youtu.be/ZBXNkP2kJhU. Abdalla F. Hassan, 'Fearless Egyptian Author Both Jubilant and Cautious', *International Herald Tribune*, 9 Mar. 2011, nyti.ms/tXpxGR (accessed Mar. 2011).

7 'Communiqué no. 1 of the Honorable Army Officers', 9 Apr. 2011, youtu.be/Mq6wePlcWFI (accessed Apr. 2011).

8 Omar Kamel, 'What Happened Yesterday Night/This Morning . . . April 8/9', 9 Apr. 2011, ow.ly/C7bI9 (accessed Apr. 2011).

9 'Army raid on the sit-in protesters of Tahrir, 8–9 Apr. 2011', 9 Apr. 2011, youtu.be/k4I0Q5jLXFs (accessed Apr. 2011).

10 Supreme Council of the Armed Forces, Communiqué no. 34, 9 Apr. 2011.

11 Al Arabiya, 'al-Na'ib al-'amm talab al-tahqiq ma' al-ra'is al-sabiq wa najlay' (The Prosecutor General Demanded an Investigation with the Former President and Both His Sons), 10 Apr. 2011, www.alarabiya.net/articles/2011/04/10/144947.html (accessed Apr. 2011).

12 The programme's YouTube channel is www.youtube.com/albernameg.

13 '*The Bassem Youssef Show* with Tamer from Ghamra, episode 5', 23 Mar. 2011, youtu.be/OgCjpA03mOI (accessed Apr. 2011).

14 Interview with Bassem Youssef, 14 Apr. 2011, New Cairo.

15 '*The Bassem Youssef Show*, episode 7', 6 Apr. 2011, youtu.be/NRSQqawnStU (accessed Apr. 2011).

16 Interview with Bassem Youssef, 14 Apr. 2011, New Cairo. Abdalla F. Hassan, 'Surgeon Using Parody to Dissect the News in Egypt', *International Herald Tribune*, 28 Apr. 2011, nyti.ms/PB7L9n (accessed Apr. 2011).

17 Interview with Bassem Youssef, 14 Apr. 2011, New Cairo.

18 Maikel Nabil Sanad, 'The army and the people wasn't ever one hand', 8 Mar. 2011, www.maikelnabil.com/2011/03/army-and-people-wasnt-ever-one-hand.html (accessed May 2011).

19 'Message to Israel Calling for Solidarity with the Egyptian Revolution', 4 Feb. 2011, www.maikelnabil.com/2011/02/message-to-israel-calling-for.html (accessed May 2011).

20 Mahfouz charged the military rulers with corruption in an interview on Al Jazeera on 23 July, as protesters attempted to stage a rally in front of the Ministry of Defence, where the Supreme Council of the Armed Forces is headquartered. Leila Fadel, 'Asmaa Mahfouz, Egyptian youth activist, is charged by military prosecutor', *Washington Post*, 14 Aug. 2011, wapo.st/pCdEPH (accessed Aug. 2011).

21 Supreme Council of the Armed Forces, Communiqué no. 72, 18 Aug. 2011.

22 Bothaina Kamel fell short of collecting the required number of endorsements – 30,000 voter proxies from at least 15 of Egypt's 27 governorates – to make it on the ballot for the 23–24 May 2012 presidential elections.

23 Interview with Bothaina Kamel (Arabic), 9 May 2011, Cairo. Abdalla F. Hassan, 'Muslim Woman Seeks Egyptian Presidency', *International Herald Tribune*, 15 June 2011, nyti.ms/iKcSgX (accessed June 2011).

24 Nile Culture, 10 May 2011. The *Shari' al-kalam* interview with Bothaina Kamel can be seen online in four parts (13 May 2011, accessed May 2011) – part 1: youtu.be/yHZO2aU07QE; part 2: youtu.be/3BL-VDnKBL0; part 3: youtu.be/CVX-S-541VA; part 4: youtu.be/DxQ46Hnouko.

25 ONtv, 1 June 2011. '*Akhir kalam*: Mahmoud Sharaf and Bothaina Kamel face Sami al-Sherif', 1 June 2011, youtu.be/xjXWysJAVKU (accessed June 2011).

26 ONtv, 26 May 2011. '*Baladna bil-masry*: Citizens and revolutionaries . . . the second Friday of Rage', 26 May 2011, youtu.be/NWaiY4KdNzQ (accessed May 2011).

27 Shahira Amin, 'Egyptian general admits "virginity checks" conducted on protesters', CNN, 31 May 2011, on.cnn.com/msw5Di (accessed May 2011). Amin later disclosed that the unnamed general was Ismail Etman of the Surpreme Council of the Armed Forces. 'Declarations on forced virginity tests', 25 Feb. 2012, youtu.be/VHV4lKc5gL4 (accessed Feb. 2012). On 19 June, *al-Fajr* (The Dawn) journalist Rasha Azab and editor-in-chief Adel Hammouda were asked to come for questioning about an article Azab wrote that discussed incidents of torture by the military and details of a meeting between the Supreme Council of the Armed Forces and activists opposing military trials.

28 Hassan al-Roweiny admitted spreading rumours in an on-air telephone interview with Dina Abd al-Rahman on *Sabah Dream*. Dream 1, 23 July 2011. '*Sabah Dream*, Dina Abd al-Rahman: Phone-in with General al-Roweiny, commander of the central military region, part 1', 25 July 2011, youtu.be/T_b3Rn439Yg; part 2: youtu.be/h2Da_m3F4os; part 3: youtu.be/NXsD4CNHSYU (accessed July 2011). Al-Roweiny resigned from the Supreme Council of the Armed Forces on 14 Aug. 2012 in a shakeup of the military ranks by President Muhammad Morsi.

29 Dream 1, 24 July 2011. '*Sabah Dream*, Dina Abd al-Rahman and Khaled al-Balshy: The details of the important phone-in of General Abd al-Moneim Kato', 25 July 2011, youtu.be/9Vq6AqWwOIA (accessed July 2012).

30 Dina Abd al-Rahman moved on to host *al-Youm* (The Day), the morning show on al-Tahrir satellite channel.

31 State television news crews were not allowed inside Tahrir Square by protest organisers. Protesters have called for the state media establishment, which was complicit with Mubarak and his rule during the revolution, to be purged of former regime loyalists.

32 The officer convicted in absentia of murdering 18 protesters, Muhammad Abd al-Moneim Ibrahim, known as Muhammad al-Sunni, turned himself in after 11 months on the run and was retried. A criminal court sentenced him to five years in prison on 30 May 2012. He was acquitted on appeal on 12 Feb. 2014.

33 A tense and violent stand-off between police and protesters outside the Interior Ministry and in Tahrir Square began on the evening of 28 June 2011 and continued into the following day, reigniting a vendetta against the security forces, their tactics, and the lack of justice.

34 Mohsen al-Fangary's stern and parental video statement, where he frequently gestured with his index finger, can be seen at: 'Announcement of the armed forces, Tuesday, 12 July 2011', 12 July 2011, youtu.be/CqpgsqPggH0 (accessed July 2011). Al-Fangary gained notoriety – and a Facebook fan page – for his salute to the revolution's martyrs. The creators of the fan page took it down following his overbearing public statement on behalf of the ruling military council.

35 Mosireen's videos can be viewed on their website (mosireen.org) and YouTube channel (www.youtube.com/Mosireen).

36 Alaa Al Aswany, 'Kayf taqdi 'ala al-thawra fi sit khatawat?!' (How to End the Revolution in Six Steps), *al-Masry al-youm*, 2 Aug. 2011, www.almasryalyoum.com/node/482397 (accessed Dec. 2011).

37 Surat Ali 'Imran (The House of 'Imran), verse 26. Tr. Arthur J. Arberry in *The Koran Interpreted* (Oxford and New Yew York: Oxford University Press, 1998), 48.

38 Surat Yunus (Jonah), verse 92. Tr. Muhammad Taqi-ud-Din Al-Hilali and Muhammad Muhsin Khan, *Interpretation of the Meanings of the Noble Qur'an in the English Language* (4th rev. edn. Riyadh: Maktaba Dar-us-Salam, 1994), 329.

39 'MK Ben-Eliezer: Israel offered political asylum to Mubarak', *Haaretz*, 3 Aug. 2011, www.haaretz.com/news/diplomacy-defense/mk-ben-eliezer-israel-offered-political-asylum-to-mubarak-1.376721 (accessed Aug. 2011).

40 Mohamed ElGarhey, twitter.com/mohamedelgarhey, 25 Sept. 2011 (accessed Sept. 2011). Breaching a gagging order may result in penalties of 5,000 to 10,000 Egyptian pounds and a year in prison, according to article 190 of the penal code.

41 Al-Masriya, 26 Sept. 2011.

42 Created to manage public information and serve as a quasi-censoring authority, the minister of information post had remained vacant until Osama Heikal, former editor of the centrist Wafd Party's newspaper, was sworn in as minister before Field Marshal Tantawi on 9 July 2011 and charged with reorganising the Egyptian media. Heikal was the information minister during October's Maspero massacre.

43 In People's Assembly elections, the Muslim Brotherhood's Freedom and Justice Party secured 47% of the seats, the largest bloc, followed by the ultraconservative Salafist Nour Party with 25% of the seats. In elections for the Shura (Consultative) Council, the upper house of parliament, the Freedom and Justice Party won 58% of the seats.

44 Al-Hayat and Nile News, 30 Sept. 2011. 'The governor of Aswan denies reports on the burning of al-Marinab Church', 30 Sept. 2011, youtu.be/N5eJEYpXQs0 (accessed Oct. 2011).

45 'Clashes between the army and protesters in front of Maspero', 9 Oct. 2011, youtu.be/tzRpdcqV0gU (accessed Oct. 2011).

46 Sarah Carr, 'A firsthand account: Marching from Shubra to deaths at Maspero', *Egypt Independent*, 10 Oct. 2011, www.egyptindependent.com/news/firsthand-account-marching-shubra-deaths-maspero (accessed Oct. 2011).

47 ONtv, 10 Oct. 2011. '*Baladna bil-masry*: The events of Maspero, where will it take us?', 10 Oct. 2011, youtu.be/kXHgkOW-Mw4 (accessed Oct. 2011).

48 Al Hurra, 9 Oct. 2011. '*Birnamig al-youm*: The military police ends live transmission', 9 Oct. 2011, ow.ly/C7bUe (accessed Oct. 2011).

49 ONtv, 10 Oct. 2011. '*Akhir kalam*: The state media and the events of Maspero', 10 Oct. 2011, youtu.be/ZG1Sdeik6B0 (accessed Oct. 2011).

50 Wael Mikhael, a cameraman for the Coptic broadcaster al-Tareeq (The Way) was shot dead, as was Mina Danial. 'The victims of the Maspero events at the Coptic Hospital', 9 Oct. 2011, youtu.be/CNHnMZyojho (accessed Oct. 2012).

51 ONtv, 11 Oct. 2011. 'Vivian Magdy tells how Michael Masaad was killed on *Headlines*', 11 Oct. 2011, youtu.be/xV6nsBiutAg (accessed Oct. 2011).

52 'The military council press conference on the events of Black Sunday', 12 Oct. 2011, youtu.be/BPkhFC-6ksM (accessed June 2012).

53 Dream 2 and al-Tahrir, 19 Oct. 2011. The broadcast can be seen in six parts: '*Ten at Night* with Mona al-Shazly: An exclusive interview with representatives of the military council on many important issues, with Ibrahim Eissa, part 1', 20 Oct. 2011, youtu.be/Un-jnb0OBfs; part 2: youtu.be/HDLv4E4JvqI; part 3: youtu.be/KbWh2OUJzh4; part 4: youtu.be/AGFJxvQDiv8; part 5: youtu.be/QMkHVwrCzWA; part 6: youtu.be/3uitP_oqNjM (accessed Oct. 2011).

54 Three officers were convicted in military court of manslaughter in Sept. 2012 for the deaths of 14 protesters at Maspero and given sentences of two to three years in prison. A civilian court sentenced two Coptic activists to three years in jail for looting armaments from military vehicles.

55 Alaa Abd El Fattah, 'Ma' al-shuhada' dhalik afdal jiddan' (To Be with the Martyrs Is Far Better), *al-Shuruk*, 20 Oct. 2011, ow.ly/B5mvw (accessed Feb. 2012). Alaa Abd El Fattah, along with 50 other activists from Kifaya, was detained on 7 May 2006 and held for 45 days for activism in favour of an independent judiciary. His father, Ahmed Seif al-Islam – who was tortured and served five years in prison in the 1980s for membership in a clandestine communist organisation – co-founded the human rights advocacy group, the Hesham Mubarak Law Center. Seif al-Islam and other lawyers and activists were arrested by military police during a raid on the centre on 3 Feb. 2011, as the revolution was unfolding, and interrogated by military intelligence.

56 Al-Tahrir, 30 Oct. 2011.

57 Alaa Abd El Fattah, 'After Egypt's revolution, I never expected to be back in Mubarak's jails', *Guardian*, 2 Nov. 2011, gu.com/p/3343t/tw (accessed Nov. 2011). The article was also published in Arabic by the daily *al-Shuruk*.

58 Yosri Fouda, 'Press Release', 21 Oct. 2011, ow.ly/C7c8f (accessed Oct. 2011).

59 Yosri Fouda, 'Yosri Fouda yaktub li-l-*Masry al-youm*: qabl an yakum haqan . . . *Akhir kalam*' (Yosri Fouda Writes in *al-Masry al-youm*: Before It Truly Becomes the *Last Words*), *al-Masry al-youm*, 29 Oct. 2011, www.almasryalyoum.com/node/509988 (accessed Oct. 2011).

60 Alaa Al Aswany, 'Ma lam yasma'hu al-majlis al-'askari' (What the Military Council Does Not Hear), *al-Masry al-youm*, 25 Oct. 2011, www.almasryalyoum.com/node/508270 (accessed Oct. 2011).

61 ONtv, 13 Nov. 2011. '*Akhir kalam*: Nine months – where we've been and where we've gone', 13 Nov. 2011, youtu.be/RZ-e7QLqjUs (accessed Nov. 2011).

Chapter 4 Revolutionaries versus the Generals

1 John Stuart Mill, *On Liberty* (London: John W. Parker and Son, 1859), 52–3.

2 Interview with Miral al-Tahawy (Arabic), 19 Sept. 2011, Cairo. Abdalla F. Hassan, 'Making the Life of a Modern Nomad Into Literature', *International Herald Tribune*, 4 Jan. 2012, nyti.ms/y3CLxi (accessed Jan. 2012).

3 'Tahrir: After the attack', 20 Nov. 2011, youtu.be/Fr2-VlldcuE (accessed Nov. 2011).

4 'Security forces and the army soldiers drag Tahrir protesters', 20 Nov. 2011, youtu.be/zJ7FHUtxePw (accessed Nov. 2011).
5 'An officer fires at the eyes of protesters', 20 Nov. 2011, youtu.be/lqfP2LL3SPk (accessed Nov. 2011).
6 'New victims fall in the clashes at Tahrir', 20 Nov. 2011, youtu.be/P9Nrr0vktcY (accessed Nov. 2011).
7 'Tantawi accepts the resignation of Essam Sharaf's Cabinet', 22 Nov. 2011, youtu.be/DNwGfABOuQQ (accessed Feb. 2012).
8 A short-lived truce brokered by sheikhs from al-Azhar was broken – a hint that the centuries-old religious establishment was not siding with the country's rulers.
9 'Scenes condemn the killers of revolutionaries in Muhammad Mahmoud', 22 Jan. 2012, youtu.be/KEqBS6Dc_fc (accessed Jan. 2012).
10 Al-Hayat, *al-Hayat al-youm* (Life Today) programme, 23 Nov. 2011. 'Mansour al-Essawy, minister of interior, by phone, part 1', 23 Nov. 2011, youtu.be/IuQ9hWYs_KI; part 2: youtu.be/bpHzbnK41G0; part 3: youtu.be/g6hOLWaz8ss (accessed Feb. 2012).
11 Al-Hayat 2, 26 Nov. 2011.
12 Robert Springborg, 'Is Tantawi reading the public's pulse correctly?' Original opinion piece in the unpublished 1 Dec. 2011 edition of *Egypt Independent*.
13 Alastair Beach, 'Censorship row fuels public's fears over Egyptian election', *Independent*, 5 Dec. 2011, ind.pn/sdgVkY (accessed Dec. 2012).
14 '*Independent* al-britaniya tanshur taqriran mukhtaliqan 'an *al-Masry al-youm*' (The British *Independent* Publishes a Fabricated Report about *al-Masry al-youm*), *al-Masry al-youm*, 5 Dec. 2011, www.almasryalyoum.com/node/535411 (accessed Dec. 2012).
15 Robert Springborg, 'What Egypt's Military Doesn't Want Its Citizens to Know', *Foreign Policy*, 9 Dec. 2011, j.mp/rNQM6E (accessed Dec. 2011).
16 The modified version of the article was posted online. Robert Springborg, 'Is Tantawi reading the public's pulse correctly?', 6 Dec. 2011, www.egyptindependent.com/node/536236 (accessed Feb. 2012).
17 'Time for an independent conversation', *Egypt Independent*, 7 Dec. 2011, www.egyptindependent.com/node/537776 (accessed Mar. 2012).
18 Magdy al-Gallad, 'Ishrabu min al-bahr!' (Drink from the Sea!), *al-Masry al-youm*, 12 Dec. 2011, www.almasryalyoum.com/node/544201 (accessed Mar. 2012).
19 The owner of *al-Watan* is Mubarak-linked businessman Muhammad al-Amin Ragab, who also owns the CBC satellite network, where Magdy al-Gallad hosts a programme.
20 The final issue appeared online: *Egypt Independent*, 25 Apr. 2013, www.scribd.com/doc/137896360/Egypt-Independent-s-50th-and-final-print-edition (accessed Apr. 2013). *Egypt Independent* began in 2009 as the English-language edition of the daily *al-Masry al-youm*. The English-language website was reduced to wire service reports and select translations from *al-Masry al-youm*. Staff members of *Egypt Independent* went on to found the news website *Mada Masr*.
21 'Violations of the military council', 17 Dec. 2011, youtu.be/4iboFV-yeTE; 'Breaking up the Cabinet sit-in by force', 16 Dec. 2011, youtu.be/5pI0UpU2XnQ (accessed Dec. 2011).

22 A video on YouTube shows just how viciously he was beaten: 'The military police abducts and beats Aboudy', 16 Dec. 2011, youtu.be/WGyZmTZ7vY0 (accessed Dec. 2011).
23 'The testimony of Aboudy: The spark for the events of the Cabinet', 16 Dec. 2011, youtu.be/MChw2kqlRG8 (accessed Dec. 2011).
24 'The army above the people', 16 Dec. 2011, youtu.be/3a8akplbudQ (accessed Dec. 2011).
25 Video of Sheikh Emad Effat as he was taken by ambulance after being shot in the chest: 'The martyrdom of Sheikh Emad Effat with an Egyptian army bullet', 16 Dec. 2011, youtu.be/0anjC2mE4tc (accessed Dec. 2011). Video of Alaa Abd al-Hady being taken into an ambulance moments after he was shot: 'The martyrdom of Alaa Abd al-Hady with an Egyptian army bullet', 16 Dec. 2011, youtu.be/dqhPu2QuMyA (accessed Dec. 2012).
26 'Tens of thousands mourn the martyr of al-Azhar', 17 Dec. 2011, youtu.be/W6YeyBZwc_Q (accessed Dec. 2012).
27 Al-Azhar Mosque, Cairo, 17 Dec. 2011. Citizens have the power to bear witness, documenting the struggles on the ground in images that circulate online and in the media. Twenty-eight-year-old Ghada Abd al-Khaliq, a pharmacist and activist with the April 6 Movement, described how she and others were detained by soldiers in a parliament building and abused. One of the soldiers slapped her around and threatened her with rape. 'Ghada: Beaten and assaulted by the army', 17 Dec. 2011, youtu.be/lU_0SEGnCRY (accessed Dec. 2011).
28 'The events of the Cabinet', 20 Dec. 2011, youtu.be/D-DjKZTxP78 (accessed Dec. 2011).
29 'The Egyptian army storms Tahrir', 17 Dec. 2011, youtu.be/fF8SwqlWlqk (accessed Dec. 2011).
30 'The crimes of paratroopers during the storming of Tahrir', 17 Dec. 2011, youtu.be/DtPFFkCEyIQ (accessed Dec. 2011).
31 'Communiqué no. 90 from the Supreme Council of the Armed Forces', 17 Dec. 2011, youtu.be/8grDc-iz5wg (accessed Dec. 2011).
32 Al-Tahrir, *Qalam rusas* with Hamdy Kandil, 17 Dec. 2011.
33 A conscript, Ahmed Sayid Abd al-Hay, was held on 15 Dec. by protesters and released after he gave a video confession. He had infiltrated the sit-in by claiming to be a soldier who wanted to defect to the ranks of the protesters. Instead Abd al-Hay, who joined the sit-in for five or six days, was working for military intelligence. The 34-minute video confession was posted on YouTube. 'Confessions of military movements in the Cabinet sit-in', 16 Dec. 2011, youtu.be/gPnxUsJ844M (accessed Dec. 2011).
34 'Scenes shown for the first time from atop the Institut d'Égypte', 24 Dec. 2011, youtu.be/mMDERCoKJc0 (accessed Feb. 2012); 'The moment thugs were let out on the roof of the Institut d'Égypte', 23 Dec. 2011, youtu.be/tS-PqL0PqXc (accessed Feb. 2012); 'SCAF', 9 Jan. 2012, youtu.be/vrtO-sXwHZg (accessed Jan. 2012).
35 'The military council's press conference on the events of the Cabinet', 19 Dec. 2011, youtu.be/GTyjBmdlZP0 (accessed Feb. 2012).
36 'The moment the child was martyred in Tahrir, part 1', 20 Dec. 2011, youtu.be/-Fodbnhikl8; part 2: youtu.be/hG6LnyuGtDg (accessed Dec. 2011).

37 'The path to Ramy is still long', 20 Dec. 2011, youtu.be/lF9Pmqeh_M8 (accessed Dec. 2011).

38 ONtv, 26 Dec. 2011. '*Akhir kalam*: Alaa Abd El Fattah is free, and the hero Ahmed Harara', 26 Dec. 2011, youtu.be/CrD6bKMnaH4 (accessed Dec. 2011).

39 Ahmed Adly, 'Kato: 'Unf junud al-jaysh raddan 'ala muhawlat ihraq al-barlaman' (Kato: The Violence of Soldiers Is a Response to Attempts to Burn the Parliament), *al-Shuruk*, 19 Dec. 2011, ow.ly/B5n7H (accessed Feb. 2012).

40 'Women's march', 20 Dec. 2011, youtu.be/8iMphaogjdY (accessed Dec. 2011).

41 Supreme Council of the Armed Forces, Communiqué no. 91, 20 Dec. 2011.

42 A photo circulated on social media showed a soldier atop the Cabinet building relieving himself on the street (and protesters) below.

43 Al-Tahrir, 21 Dec. 2011.

44 Sherif Awad, 'Straight Talk: Dina Abdel-Rahman on being off the air', *Egypt Today*, May 2012, 100–1.

45 Dina Abd al-Rahman later moved to the CBC satellite channel as a regular presenter, then as the host of the morning show *Zay al-shams* (Like the Sun) in Sept. 2012. She left the network, which had become stridently pro-military, in Apr. 2014.

46 Interview with Alaa Al Aswany (Arabic), 30 Dec. 2011. At the time prosecutors called in for questioning prominent revolutionary activists, bloggers, and public figures, linking them with the recent violent clashes.

47 Interview with Mohamed Hashem (Arabic), 25 Dec. 2011, Cairo. Abdalla F. Hassan, 'A Loud Voice for Egyptian Resistance Movement', *International Herald Tribune*, 11 Jan. 2012, nyti.ms/y6wvRH (accessed Jan. 2012).

48 The interview with the general was broadcast on the satellite station 25. 'General al-Fangary: What do they want from Egypt?', 15 Jan. 2012, youtu.be/KBWQdB0pDFY (accessed Jan. 2012).

49 'Shouts of "Down with military rule" as the Pope greeted members of the military council during Christmas mass', 6 Jan. 2012, youtu.be/gWhOSAgfSfY (accessed Jan. 2012). Pope Shenouda III's Coptic Christmas mass was held at the Coptic Orthodox Cathedral in Abbasiya. Pope of the Coptic Orthodox Church since 1971, he passed away on 17 Mar. 2012.

50 'The most courageous Christian man of religion', 8 Jan. 2012, youtu.be/0D2sjg-_HTY (accessed Jan. 2012).

51 'A message from Dr Mohamed ElBaradei', 14 Jan. 2012, youtu.be/Nv5l6295Jn8 (accessed Jan. 2012). ElBaradei launched the Constitution Party on 28 Apr. 2012.

52 On Dina Abd al-Rahman's morning programme *al-Youm* on al-Tahrir network, Doaa Sultan made the claim that the station's owner was behind banning the episode of *Talk Shows*. The incident led to both Abd al-Rahman and Sultan being pushed out of the station. 'Doaa Sultan's response on the ban of an episode of *Talk Shows* on al-Tahrir channel', 21 Jan. 2012, youtu.be/2lr3Lme02co (accessed Jan. 2012).

53 'Doaa Sultan's *Talk Shows* that was banned by al-Tahrir Channel', 22 Jan. 2012, youtu.be/W15JSaSIRWM (accessed Jan. 2012).

54 'Field Marshal Tantawi's speech to the Egyptian people', 24 Jan. 2012, youtu.be/yIhgrmJ3dqQ (accessed Feb. 2012).

55 Al-Masriya, 27 Jan. 2012.

56 Inaugurated on 16 Dec. 2011, the campaign 'Askar Kazeboon is on Facebook at www.facebook.com/3askar.Kazeboon, on Twitter at twitter.com/3askarkazeboon, and on YouTube at www.youtube.com/3askarKazeboon.

57 'Kazeboon: Revolution Records', 22 Jan. 2012, youtu.be/4h0KPtc-Dqc (accessed Jan. 2012).

58 Interview with Revolution crew rappers (Arabic), 24, 28 Mar. 2012 and 2, 6 Apr. 2012, Alexandria. Abdalla F. Hassan, 'Rap Group at the Leading Edge of Egyptian Rebellion', *International Herald Tribune*, 17 May 2012, nyti.ms/IZNvJF (accessed May 2012).

59 'Al-Ahly Ultras chant, "Down, down with military rule"', 31 Jan. 2012, youtu.be/cPvQvbk2X_4 (accessed Jan. 2012).

60 'Field Marshal Tantawi's statement after al-Ahly and al-Masry match', 2 Feb. 2012, youtu.be/QgFh53B_7TY (accessed Feb. 2012).

61 The first session of the newly elected People's Assembly was on 23 Jan. 2012, two days before the one-year anniversary of the revolution. A protest march was organised on 31 Jan. 2012, called the 'Tuesday of Determination', from Maspero to the buildings of parliament, demanding the handover of power to civilian rule. The Muslim Brotherhood youth created a human cordon to block the demonstration from reaching parliament, which set up clashes between the Brotherhood youth, security forces, and protesters, who charged the dominant political party with striking deals with the military rulers.

62 'Mohamed Abu Hamed: The military council must be overthrown and tried', 2 Feb. 2012, youtu.be/11g-D9cwp5w (accessed Feb. 2012).

63 'Amr Hamzawy: The military council has lost legitimacy', 2 Feb. 2012, youtu.be/_z12gbVYvMo (accessed Feb. 2012).

64 Supreme Council of the Armed Forces, Communiqué no. 3, 3 Feb. 2012.

65 In an on-air call, Mahmoud al-Ghazaly, a Nile News reporter, told how he had been struck in the face with buckshot fired by police, sustaining an eye injury. Nile News, 4 Feb. 2012 (12:50 am).

66 'Where did you get this? An accounting of the military institution', 6 Feb. 2012, youtu.be/hmy6lSPaO3M (accessed Feb. 2012). On the military's vast economic holdings, see Shana Marshall and Joshua Stacher, 'Egypt's General's and Transnational Capital', *Middle East Report (MER)*, 262/42 (spring 2012), www.merip.org/mer/mer262/egypts-generals-transnational-capital (accessed Apr. 2012).

67 'Ziyad al-Eleimy in Port Said says the field marshal is a jackass', 17 Feb. 2012, youtu.be/uPT9ksqLxic (accessed Feb. 2012).

68 Mona Seif, 20 Feb. 2012, twitter.com/Monasosh/status/171637841292562432 (accessed Feb. 2012).

69 The sit-in was staged by supporters of Salafi lawyer and preacher Hazem Salah Abu Ismail, who was disqualified from the presidential race by the election commission on grounds that his late mother held US citizenship. According to the election law, presidential contenders and their parents cannot be dual nationals.

70 'Military Council press conference to discuss the events of Abbasiya', 3 May 2012, youtu.be/vr-n87mKAhI (accessed May 2012). In a shakeup of the military ranks, Mukhtar al-Mulla was sent to retirement in Sept. 2012 by President Muhammad Morsi's defence minister, Abd al-Fattah al-Sisi.

71 Patrick Kingsley and Louisa Loveluck, 'Egyptian doctors "ordered to operate on protesters without anaesthetic"', *Guardian*, 11 Apr. 2013, gu.com/p/3f44n (accessed Apr. 2013).
72 'The verdict for Mubarak, his sons, Habib al-Adly, and his associates', 2 June 2012, youtu.be/ubwHg7lRqPE (accessed 2 June 2012).
73 The law forbid Mubarak's vice president, prime ministers, and top ruling party officials for the last ten years from holding political office.
74 Sarah El Deeb, 'Alarming assaults on women in Egypt's Tahrir', *Associated Press*, 6 June 2012, bigstory.ap.org/article/alarming-assaults-women-egypts-tahrir; Sarah El Deeb, 'Mob attacks women at Egypt anti-sex assault rally', *Associated Press*, 8 June 2012, bigstory.ap.org/article/mob-attacks-women-egypt-anti-sex-assault-rally (accessed June 2012). Also see the Unreported World documentary *Egypt: Sex, Mobs and Revolution*, series 2012, episode 14, www.channel4.com/programmes/unreported-world (accessed Dec. 2012).
75 *The Daily Show* with Jon Stewart, 'The People Rose in Cairo', 21 June 2012, on.cc.com/1sGRQfU (accessed June 2012).
76 Evan Hill and Muhammad Mansour, 'Egypt's army took part in torture and killings during revolution, report shows', *Guardian*, 10 Apr. 2013, gu.com/p/3f3v2/stw; 'Egyptian army's role in torture and disappearances – leaked document', *Guardian*, 10 Apr. 2013, gu.com/p/3f2n8/tw (accessed Apr. 2013).

Chapter 5 Fall of Military Rule and the Islamists

1 Jean-Paul Sartre, *Existentialism is a Humanism*, tr. Philip Mairet (1946).
2 'The commercial that frightened the spies 1', 7 June 2012, youtu.be/_1yj5IlyZqo (accessed June 2012).
3 The Supreme Constitutional Court declared unconstitutional a provision in the law organising parliamentary elections that allowed party members to run in one-third of the seats in the People's Assembly contested by individual candidates. Since two-thirds of the legislative chamber was elected through a party list system, this granted party-backed candidates the right to contest all the seats (and thus a greater opportunity to win office), a right unavailable to independent candidates.
4 The Arab world's first presidential debate was in 2007 in the West African nation of Mauritania, whose elected president was overthrown in a military coup the following year. Broadcast on air and online, the debate between Moussa and Aboul Futouh was sponsored by private satellite channels Dream TV and ONtv, and independent newspapers *al-Shuruk* and *al-Masry al-youm*.
5 Voter turnout was 51.85%. The number of spoiled ballots in the runoff elections was 843,252. Ahmed Shafik, Omar Soliman, and their families left Egypt for the United Arab Emirates less than 48 hours after the election results were announced. Soliman died the following month while undergoing medical tests in the United States.
6 Held in Wadi al-Natrun Prison along the Cairo–Alexandria desert highway, Muhammad Morsi and other jailed members of the Muslim Brotherhood were

freed allegedly by area residents after Interior Ministry personnel were withdrawn on 28 Jan. 2011. Security agency accounts assert that Hamas and Hezbollah fighters were involved in their release.

7 'The speech of Dr Muhammad Morsi, president of the Arab Republic of Egypt', 24 June 2012, youtu.be/CRZ6VphJrXE (accessed June 2012).

8 'President Muhammad Morsi takes the oath and gives a speech in Tahrir Square', 29 June 2012, youtu.be/RHmZTFsevf8 (accessed July 2012).

9 Kareem Fahim, 'After Meeting With Clinton, Egypt's Military Chief Steps Up Political Feud', *New York Times*, 15 July 2012, nyti.ms/O4e5F1 (accessed July 2012).

10 In the lead-up to anti-Morsi protests on 30 June 2013, Abd al-Nasser Salama counselled that change must come through the ballot box, a president's year in office was not enough time to undo decades of corruption, and that protests would come at the expense of safety and security. As *al-Ahram*'s editor-in-chief following Morsi's ouster, Salama penned a front-page article in Aug. 2013 outlining a sordid scheme where fifth columnists infiltrated the media and liberal political parties in a conspiracy sponsored by US ambassador to Egypt Anne Patterson in cahoots with the Brotherhood's point man Khairat al-Shater, prior to his timely arrest. The armed forces, Salama revealed, had come to the rescue and terminated this foreign-funded plot before it could be carried out. Despite his best efforts to curry favour with the new system of power, he found himself out of a job in Dec. 2013. 'Mu'amra jadida li-za'za'it al-istiqrar bi-tawatur siyasiyin wa sahafiyin wa rijal a'mal' (A New Plot for Destabilisation Involving Politicians, Journalists, and Businessmen), *al-Ahram*, 27 Aug. 2013, www.ahram.org.eg/NewsQ/228698.aspx (accessed Oct. 2014).

11 Columnists in the private press protested the Shura Council's control over publicly owned media by leaving their columns blank in the next day's edition. Gamal Abd al-Rahim, appointed editor-in-chief of the third largest state-owned daily, *al-Gumhuriya* (The Republic), was dismissed for running a front-page story in the 17 Oct. 2012 issue incorrectly reporting that a travel ban would be imposed on military council generals Muhammad Hussein Tantawi and Sami Anan pending the outcome of corruption investigations. Abd al-Rahim has been known for his caustic attacks against believers of the Baha'i faith in Egypt.

12 Salah Abd al-Maqsoud's brother is the prominent Muslim Brotherhood lawyer Abd al-Moneim Abd al-Maqsoud.

13 Zeina Yazijy's interview with Salah Abd al-Maqsoud on Dubai Media, 24 Sept. 2012.

14 'Salah Abd al-Maqsoud, minister of information: Egypt is moving in the direction of freedoms of opinion and expression in the era of President Morsi', 13 Apr. 2013, youtu.be/zbWN7h6CyKc (accessed Apr. 2013).

15 '*Sabahak ya Masr* with Jihan Mansour: Phone-in with Essam al-Erian', 14 Oct. 2012, youtu.be/HsQRRbklZJ4 (accessed Jan. 2013). Mansour filed a defamation suit against al-Erian. The court's verdict in Apr. 2013 fined the Brotherhood leader 15,000 Egyptian pounds, suspended for three years, for defaming Mansour.

16 'Press conference for Ahmed Bahgat on halting the transmission of Dream', 17 Nov. 2012, youtu.be/hBXdNVeJLdM (accessed Nov. 2012). On 24 Nov. an administrative court ordered Dream's broadcasts to resume pending a review of the case.

17 Al-Fara'in, 6 Aug. 2013. 'Tawfiq Okasha deems it permissible to spill the president's blood and says he has beasts', 6 Aug. 2012, youtu.be/m4Wp1FIgHpk (accessed Aug. 2012).

18 Mired in debt and numerous lawsuits, Tawfiq Okasha's station remained closed. He was acquitted in criminal court on 8 Jan. 2013 on charges of insulting the president and inviting his assassination. An administrative court in Feb. 2013 ordered al-Fara'in back on the air. A month later, Okasha's station was again operational under Morsi's rule – but not without obstructions. Prosecutors issued an arrest warrant for the television host on 28 June, a couple of days before nationwide rallies calling for Morsi to step down.

19 Orbit Showtime Network, 17 Nov. 2012. 'Amr Adeeb: President, you are a failure and so is Hesham Kandil', 17 Nov. 2012, youtu.be/oh0iQ0yve4s (accessed Nov. 2012).

20 The president's spokesman, Yasser Ali, announced the decree. 'Constitutional declaration', 22 Nov. 2012, youtu.be/yBBv7pNqN5Y (accessed Nov. 2012).

21 'President Morsi's speech in front of the presidential palace', 23 Nov. 2012, youtu.be/QkEtIKfbJ1k (accessed Nov. 2012).

22 Ikhwanweb, 27 Nov. 2012, twitter.com/Ikhwanweb/status/273472456902180864 (accessed Nov. 2012).

23 Al-Nahar, 26 May 2012. 'Morsi: I want the people to revolt against me if I violate the laws and the constitution', 27 Nov. 2012, youtu.be/vmKQ_TXRP6g; '*Akhir al-nahar*: Mahmoud Saad interviews Muhammad Morsi', 27 May 2012, youtu.be/hhLfBD3Kwg4 (accessed Dec. 2012).

24 'Morsi before the presidency: I will follow the desires of the people if they protest against me', 25 Jan. 2013, youtu.be/gAbgMfKj2-Y. The original interview was broadcast on CBC+2 on 9 May 2012: 'Egypt elects a president: Muhammad Morsi complete interview, part 1', 11 May 2012, youtu.be/iq2UzNmbufM; part 2, youtu.be/nZLnHuJyjPA (accessed Jan. 2013).

25 'ElBaradei Speaks Out against Morsi: "Not Even the Pharaohs Had So Much Authority"', *Der Spiegel*, 26 Nov. 2012, spon.de/adOjh (accessed Nov. 2012).

26 Wael Ghonim, 27 Nov. 2012, ow.ly/C7e4S (accessed Nov. 2012).

27 Wael Ghonim, 3 Dec. 2012, ow.ly/C7erb (accessed Dec. 2012).

28 'The response to Morsi after the events of Friday prayers', 30 Nov. 2012, youtu.be/URhbt0Cs9pk; 'Shouts of "null and void" in the mosque in the face of Morsi', 1 Dec. 2012, youtu.be/h338l8H8w20 (accessed Dec. 2012).

29 Videos, photos, and testimonials were posted on social media of the abuse inflicted by zealous members of the Muslim Brotherhood. 'The Brotherhood to protesters: Say you belong to the National Democratic Party and we will stop hitting you', 6 Dec. 2012, youtu.be/NgtMtHB4Kj0; 'The Brotherhood strip the clothes off a protester and drag him on the ground', 6 Dec. 2012, youtu.be/d1UPFvkrUx0; 'Exclusive: The confessions of suspects against the backdrop of the presidential palace events', 6 Dec. 2012, youtu.be/rI8K1xNHGO4; 'A confession of a thug at the presidential palace', 5 Dec. 2012, youtu.be/aVP3XzdisD4 (accessed Dec. 2012).

30 Mohamed Fadel Fahmy, 5 Dec. 2012, twitter.com/MFFahmy11/status/276344423036624897 (accessed Dec. 2012).

31 ONtv, 30 May 2012. 'Brotherhood candidate for president Dr Muhammad Morsi on *Last Words*', 30 May 2012, youtu.be/NFgcNI_p6Bg (accessed June 2012). Morsi

again made the pledge to have a consensus on the makeup of the Constituent Assembly in an interview with Emad Eddin Adeeb. '*Bihudu*': Morsi respects judges and the judiciary', 7 June 2012, youtu.be/HBRpgnHESso (accessed June 2012).

32 ONtv, 5 Dec. 2012. '*Akhir kalam*: Who is responsible for the blood of the presidential palace', 5 Dec. 2012, youtu.be/lFKLvfSTHZo; '*Akhir kalam*: Egypt and the blood of the presidential palace . . . what now?', 5 Dec. 2012, youtu.be/kBzRNc_K444 (accessed Dec. 2012).

33 The image of a dignified statesman imploded when videos surfaced on social media in Jan. 2013 that have Morsi speaking disparaging of Jews and Zionists, labelling them 'descendants of apes and pigs' in an interview in 2010, then unconvincingly arguing the words were taken out of context.

34 Ikhwanweb, 5 Dec. 2012, twitter.com/Ikhwanweb/status/276377294854041600 (accessed Dec. 2012).

35 Ikhwanweb, 5 Dec. 2012, twitter.com/Ikhwanweb/status/276391444426682368 (accessed Dec. 2012).

36 Masr 25, 5 Dec. 2012. 'Dr Essam al-Erian invites everyone to go down and arrest thugs and bring them to justice', 5 Dec. 2012, youtu.be/1LQcs3vMgWc (accessed Dec. 2012).

37 'President Muhammad Morsi's speech', 6 Dec. 2012, youtu.be/uN2iu-8_Ss8 (accessed Dec. 2012).

38 CBC, 6 Dec. 2012. 'Khairy Ramadan withdraws from CBC', 7 Dec. 2012, youtu.be/uAPFGDtl1wk (accessed Dec. 2012).

39 Hamdeen Sabahy, 7 Dec. 2012, ow.ly/C7boi (accessed Dec. 2012).

40 Ismail al-Fakharany, 'Wazir al-i'lam: amtalik wath'iq 'ala wujud al-mu'amra' (Information Minister: I Possess Documents on the Presence of a Conspiracy), *al-Ahram*, 8 Dec. 2012, www.ahram.org.eg/archive/The-First/News/187230.aspx (accessed Dec. 2012).

41 '*Al-Bernameg?*: We are the revolution of underwear, episode 3, part 1', 7 Dec. 2012, youtu.be/nEN8M87-xhU (accessed Dec. 2012).

42 'Khairat al-Shater: We won't allow the revolution to be stolen again', 8 Dec. 2012, youtu.be/bZrCZVo2OYg (accessed Dec. 2012).

43 Mamdouh al-Wali, then-head of the Journalists' Syndicate, attended a final vote on articles of the constitution on 29 Nov. 2012, even after the syndicate's vote to secede from the constitution drafting body. Al-Wali was elected to lead the syndicate in Oct. 2011 with the support of the Brotherhood. The Islamist-dominated Shura Council appointed him the chairman of al-Ahram Publishing House in Sept. 2012 and President Morsi appointed him to the Shura Council after the constitution was ratified. Al-Wali was removed as chairman of the largest state publisher following Morsi's ouster.

44 This included e.g. article 11: 'The State shall safeguard ethics, public morality, and public order.'

45 Egypt's 2012 constitution: ow.ly/JCHiJ; 'Unofficial English Translation of Egypt's Draft Constitution', Atlantic Council, 30 Oct. 2012, www.acus.org/egyptsource/unofficial-english-translation-egypts-draft-constitution; 'Egypt's draft constitution translated', *Egypt Independent*, 2 Dec. 2012, www.egyptindependent.com/news/egypt-s-draft-constitution-translated (accessed Dec. 2012). After the constitution was approved in a referendum, the Shura Council, bestowed with legislative

functions, went on to draft controversial legislation that sought to impose a restrictive protest law, severely regulate the work and funding sources of non-governmental organisations, and rein in the judiciary.

46 The video was taken at a Salafi conference on 22 Nov. 2012, the day Morsi gave himself sweeping powers, which among other things insulated the Constituent Assembly from being disbanded by the courts. 'The most dangerous 18 minutes', 26 Dec. 2013, vimeo.com/56330681 (accessed Dec. 2012).

47 '*Al-Bernameg?*: The return of the prodigal son, season 2, episode 1', 23 Nov. 2012, youtu.be/PS0aWlYCVB0 (accessed Nov. 2012).

48 '*Al-Bernameg?*: Your blankets, tiger – episode 2, part 1', 3 Dec. 2012, youtu.be/wCVqTCTN_50 (accessed Dec. 2012).

49 '*Al-Bernameg?*: episode 5, part 1', 21 Dec. 2012, youtu.be/DonuZolkeuE (accessed Dec. 2012).

50 '*Al-Bernameg?*: On the margins of the presidency, episode 6, part 2', 28 Dec. 2012, youtu.be/0-bFQz73zOY (accessed Dec. 2012).

51 Stand-up comedian Ali Kandil, hosted on *al-Bernameg?* on 22 Feb., was also questioned by prosecutors on charges of insulting Islam and released on 5,000 Egyptian pounds in bail. '*Al-Bernameg?*: Ali Kandil, episode 14, part 3', 22 Feb. 2013, youtu.be/wiHm_bmnGSg; 'Ali Kandil on being summoned by prosecutors', 2 Apr. 2013, youtu.be/8blHVOUPAXs (accessed Apr. 2013). Khaled Mansour, comedian and a writer for *al-Bernameg?*, was called for questioning by prosecutors on 2 May, also on charges of contempt for religion and insulting the president. Mansour was interrogated for a mock commercial on the show inviting mobile users to guess where the president would be attending next Friday's prayers. For a small fee participants would have the chance to be one of ten winners to pray with the president, while revenue from the service would go to covering the costs of his motorcade and security entourage. Contest guidelines disqualified Copts and anyone who voted 'no' on the constitutional referendum from participating. '*Al-Bernameg?*: The jinn of the asphalt, episode 6, part 1', 28 Dec. 2012, youtu.be/sDawDzeoFeY (accessed May 2013).

52 *The Daily Show* with Jon Stewart, 1 Apr. 2013, 'Morsi "Viva Hate" – Egyptian Democracy', on.cc.com/1Ai47qO (accessed Apr. 2013).

53 *The Daily Show* with Jon Stewart, 24 Apr. 2013, 'Bassem Youssef', on.cc.com/1qdf5Lz (accessed Apr. 2013).

54 '*Al-Bernameg?*: Look, the bird, episode 20, part 3', 5 Apr. 2013, youtu.be/8M-8CmWVzX4 (accessed Apr. 2013).

55 '*Al-Bernameg?*: Jon Stewart with Bassem Youssef in Egypt', 21 June 2013, youtu.be/kEO2Rd3sJbA (accessed June 2013).

56 Arab Network for Human Rights Information, 'Jarimat ihanat al-ra'is, jarimat nizam mustabid' (The Crime of Insulting the President Is a Crime of a Despotic Regime), 20 Jan. 2013, ow.ly/E1NT6 (accessed Jan. 2013).

57 Ola al-Shafei, 'Jawaz Morsi min Fu'ada batil' (The Marriage of Morsi to Fu'ada Is Null and Void), *al-Youm al-sabi'*, 8 Dec. 2012, www.youm7.com/News.asp?NewsID=870596 (accessed Dec. 2012).

58 Al-Nahar, *Akhir al-nahar* (Day's End) with Mahmoud Saad, 23 Nov. 2012. 'Manal Omar: Morsi is psychologically ill and should leave', 3 Dec. 2012, youtu.be/dIQpGfUiH4w (accessed Jan. 2013).

59 Alone, the penal code offence of defaming the head of state carried a penalty of up to two years in prison and a fine of 5,000–10,000 Egyptian pounds.
60 'Black Bloc Egypt', 23 Jan. 2013, youtu.be/L8IyRkEKywY (accessed Jan. 2013).
61 Muhammad Morsi, 25 Jan. 2013, twitter.com/MuhammadMorsi/status/294946596318228480 (accessed Jan. 2013).
62 Mohamed ElBaradei, 25 Jan. 2013, twitter.com/ElBaradei/status/294949808672755712 (accessed Jan. 2013).
63 'The president's speech on the events of Port Said and Suez', 27 Jan. 2013, youtu.be/H96WRAKRoS0 (accessed Jan. 2013).
64 MBC Masr and ONtv, 1 Feb. 2013. 'Dragging and stripping of a protester at the presidential palace', 1 Feb. 2013, youtu.be/P0-Foz6r5X8; 'Stripping, dragging, and arresting a protester by the presidential palace', 1 Feb. 2013, youtu.be/LJBFYEt859A (accessed Feb. 2013).
65 MBC Masr, 1 Feb. 2013. "The emotional reaction of Mona al-Shazly after the scene of the citizen being dragged', 1 Feb. 2013, youtu.be/MSgLxWybcW8 (accessed Feb. 2013).
66 Al-Hayat, 2 Feb. 2013. 'Interview with Hamada Saber', 3 Feb. 2013, youtu.be/LeyWZzw0Mg8 (accessed Feb. 2013).
67 Al-Hayat, *al-Hayat al-youm* (Life Today) with Sherif Amer, 3 Feb. 2013.
68 'A fatwa permitting spilling the blood of leaders of the National Salvation Front', 7 Feb. 2013, youtu.be/HBxXKTLEIk0 (accessed Feb. 2013). The declaration came as Chokri Belaid, Tunisian opposition politician and a vocal leftist critic of the Islamists' rule, was fatally shot in the neck and head on 6 Feb. as he left his home in Tunis.
69 Al-Umma, 7 Feb. 2013. 'Abu Islam justifies the rape of women in Tahrir Square', 7 Feb. 2013, youtu.be/ZksLzsStcFs (accessed Feb. 2013).
70 ONtv, 2 Feb. 2013. 'Hesham Kandil inspects the security situation in Tahrir', 2 Feb. 2013, youtu.be/dwMpEH4VAF4 (accessed Feb. 2013).
71 'The prime minister's statement on the events happening in the country', 2 Feb. 2013, youtu.be/YEfakGtZGso (accessed Feb. 2013).
72 Jihan Mansour, 21 Mar. 2013, twitter.com/Jimansour/status/314704489166823424 (accessed Mar. 2013).
73 Paul Taylor, 'Exclusive – Egypt's "road not taken" could have saved Mursi', *Reuters*, 17 July 2013, reut.rs/12UHzvw (accessed July 2013).
74 'President Muhammad Morsi's meeting with national forces on the crisis of the Grand Renaissance Dam', 3 June 2013, youtu.be/kdyMi1hrpoA (accessed June 2013). In an ironic twist, the Ethiopian dam project shares the same name as the Muslim Brotherhood's ill-fated electoral platform – Renaissance (Nahda).
75 'President Morsi's speech during the launch of the women's rights initiative', 24 Mar. 2013, youtu.be/CihcaXsJCCM (accessed Mar. 2013).
76 Sectarian violence in the town of Khosus claimed the lives of five Christians and one Muslim on 5 Apr. Two days later, during the funeral for the victims at Cairo's St Mark's Cathedral, the seat of the Coptic papacy, police failed to halt the escalation of clashes between Christian protesters and vigilantes, and fired tear gas and shotguns inside church grounds.
77 Al-Tahrir, *al-Sha'b yurid* (The People Want) with Ahmed Musa, 4 June 2013.
78 'President Muhammad Morsi at the Egyptian nation conference in support of the Syrian revolution', 17 June 2013, youtu.be/4gv_is7hO-o (accessed June 2013).

79 Al-Azhar, 'Bayan ham min al-Azhar al-sharif bi-sh'n takfir al-muslimin' (An important announcement from al-Azhar regarding calling Muslims infidels), 19 June 2013, www.alazhar-alsharif.gov.eg/Item/1123/2 (accessed June 2013).

80 Flashing in a red box at the top left of the website were reminders of the excuses: '7,709 strikes', '5,821 protests and clashes', 'more than 50 smear campaigns against the president', '24 invitations to million people rallies'. The website is www.morsifirstyear.com, the Facebook page is www.facebook.com/MorsiFirstYear, and the Twitter account is twitter.com/MorsiFirstYear.

81 'The slaughter of Shia in Zawyat Abu Musalam', 23 June 2013, youtu.be/satudpo5xWQ (accessed June 2013).

82 'Wael Ghonim calls on the president of the republic to resign', 23 June 2013, youtu.be/m6g2b_by1MI (accessed June 2013).

83 Interview with Khaled Dawoud (Arabic), 15 June 2013, Cairo. Dawoud resigned as a spokesman for the National Salvation Front in Aug. 2013, the day after the group praised the security forces' violent dispersal of pro-Morsi protest camps in a statement he was involved in drafting. He was pulled from his car in downtown Cairo, beaten, and stabbed by Morsi supporters on 4 Oct., with attackers trying to slice his wrist.

84 Al-Nahar, *Akhir al-nahar* with Mahmoud Saad, 26 May 2013.

Chapter 6 An Overthrow, a Revitalised Police State, and the Military Presidency

1 Niccolò Machiavelli, *The Prince and the Discourses*, tr. Luigi Ricci, rev. E. R. P. Vincent (New York: The Modern Library, 1950), ch. xix, 67–9.

2 'General Abd al-Fattah al-Sisi assures Egyptians', 23 June 2013, youtu.be/n6Wxg8_Okk4 (accessed May 2014).

3 'Egypt elects the president: Field Marshal al-Sisi in his first televised interview', 7 May 2014, youtu.be/eotGq0j9LzM (accessed May 2014); Yasser Rizk, 'Al-Sisi . . . al-ladhi a'rafu' (The al-Sisi I Know), *al-Masry al-youm*, 26 July 2013, ow.ly/ENrbT (accessed July 2013).

4 'Morsi's speech on 26 6 2013', 26 June 2013, youtu.be/uMEb4aTOvcI (accessed June 2013). Following the speech, minister of investment Yehia Hamed, a Brotherhood member and Morsi protégé, who in his former job was a sales manager at a mobile phone operator, dispatched missives to private channels informing them that they risked being shut down if they continued criticising the president and threatened closures for stations that disseminated false information.

5 David Hearst and Patrick Kingsley, 'Egypt's Mohamed Morsi remains defiant as fears of civil war grow', *Guardian*, 30 June 2013, gu.com/p/3hx79/tw (accessed June 2013). Before the interview with the *Guardian*, Morsi was meeting with his defence minister, Abd al-Fattah al-Sisi.

6 Mike Giglio, 'A Cairo Conspiracy', *The Daily Beast*, 12 July 2013, thebea.st/16wgWON (accessed July 2013); Sheera Frankel and Maged Atef, 'How Egypt's Rebel Movement Helped Pave The Way For A Sisi Presidency', *BuzzFeed*, 15 Apr. 2014, bzfd.it/1gCl88E (accessed Apr. 2014).

7 A gasoline crisis could have been manufactured. Subsidised gasoline was being smuggled, and fuel distributers and owners of petrol stations could have restricted supply or limited imports to produce chronic shortages. A manufactured electricity crisis was less probable. Egypt lacked sufficient power generation capacity and natural gas and mazut supplies to run power plants during the peak summer months when outages lasted hours per day. Qatar promised to gift Egypt natural gas shipments in May to meet the demand, which reduced the power cuts after Morsi had already been toppled.

8 Masr 25, 1 July 2013. 'Earthquake in Rab'a al-Adawiya Square after the omen', 1 July 2013, youtu.be/tu9Wcudw5WA (accessed July 2013).

9 The White House, 'Readout of the President's call with President Morsy of Egypt', 2 July 2013, wh.gov/lcdiJ (accessed July 2013).

10 In an Oval Office meeting with Morsi's foreign policy adviser Essam El-Haddad in Dec. 2012, in the fallout of the Egyptian president's poorly conceived decree, President Obama offered to intervene with opposition leaders Mohamed ElBaradei or Amre Moussa to reach a working solution, a gesture that was rebuffed.

11 'The president's 2 July address to the Egyptian people', 2 July 2013, youtu.be/O0Uqap-cX8Y (accessed July 2013).

12 Saad al-Katatni was placed under arrest following the announcement of Morsi's removal from power.

13 Yasmine Saleh and Paul Taylor, 'The Egyptian rebel who "owns" Tahrir Square', *Reuters*, 8 July 2013, reut.rs/16hUvNe (accessed July 2013).

14 David D. Kirkpatrick and Mayy El Sheikh, 'Morsi Spurned Deals, Seeing Military as Tamed', *New York Times*, 6 July 2013, nyti.ms/16VI6Rf (accessed July 2013).

15 'Deleted video message from Mohamed Morsi', 3 July 2013, youtu.be/6tN6g9AiR_Q (accessed July 2013).

16 'The Egyptian armed forces' announcement of a roadmap', 3 July 2013, youtu.be/gj93wlRwxy0 (accessed July 2013).

17 Al Jazeera Live Egypt was on air the next day, cameras recording the Rab'a protests. On 8 July 2013, 22 staff members resigned en masse, citing the network's biased news coverage. A court banned the news station from operating in Egypt in Sept. 2013. Qatar delivered billions of dollars in assistance to Morsi's government and was seen as favouring regional Islamist movements. Following rapprochement between Cairo and Doha, Al Jazeera Live Egypt stopped broadcasting on 22 Dec. 2014.

18 The White House, 'Statement by President Barack Obama on Egypt', 3 July 2013, www.whitehouse.gov/the-press-office/2013/07/03/statement-president-barack-obama-egypt (accessed July 2013).

19 In a wiretap recording leaked to anti-coup media outlets, al-Sisi as defence minister reportedly tells a top aide to request additional tens of billions from Saudi Arabia, the United Arab Emirates, and Kuwait to be deposited into the military and state accounts because 'they have money like rice'. 'Al-Sisi despises the Gulf', 7 Feb. 2015, youtu.be/uy0D-nz4Br0 (accessed Feb. 2015). Turkey's Islamist politician Recep Tayyip Erdoğan was a vocal critic of Egypt's coup. In Nov. 2013, Egypt expelled the Turkish ambassador and downgraded its diplomatic relations with Turkey to the level of chargé d'affaires in retaliation for Ankara's interference in internal affairs.

20 'The generals are aware that they are historically partly to blame for the disaster in which the country now finds itself,' ElBaradei said. 'But the military doesn't get a free pass from me, either. My red line is this: I don't align myself with anyone who ignores tolerance and democracy. And they know that.' 'Interview with Egyptian Politician ElBaradei: "This Was Not a Coup"', *Der Spiegel*, 8 July 2013, spon.de/adYTc (accessed July 2013).

21 David D. Kirkpatrick, 'ElBaradei Seeks to Justify Ouster of Egypt's President', *New York Times*, 4 July 2013, nyti.ms/16REa3W (accessed July 2013).

22 Lally Weymouth, 'An interview with Mohamed ElBaradei, who hopes for reconciliation in Egypt', *Washington Post*, 2 Aug. 2013, wapo.st/1cvParF (accessed Aug. 2013).

23 Footage of the incident gained much airtime on Egyptian television to illustrate the vindictiveness of the former president's backers. 'Teens pushed off rooftop in Sidi Gaber, Alexandria', 6 July 2013, youtu.be/ig8uyGygLGE (accessed July 2013). Sixteen people were killed in clashes in Alexandria that Friday.

24 Amnesty International documented cases of torture by Morsi supporters of individuals endorsing political rivals or suspected informants as a form of retribution and reprisal. Eight bodies arrived at morgues bearing signs of torture in the space of a month, at least five were found near areas of pro-Morsi sit-ins. Amnesty International, 'Egypt: Evidence points to torture carried out by Morsi supporters', 2 Aug. 2013, ow.ly/K8WPv (accessed Aug. 2013).

25 Bassem Youssef, 'Ma 'ad ya'ish biha ahad' (No One Lives Here Anymore), *al-Shuruk*, 16 July 2013, ow.ly/B5jxB (accessed July 2013).

26 Among the dead was photographer Ahmed Assem al-Senousy, who worked for the Brotherhood's party newspaper. His last footage was of an army sniper aiming at him. 'Details of the Republican Guard massacre', 7 July 2013, youtu.be/ZLo6H89kxKk (accessed July 2013).

27 'Colonel General al-Sisi's speech to naval and air defence students', 24 July 2013, youtu.be/ZpuuCqXhhFw (accessed July 2013).

28 Ghada Sherif, 'Ya Sisi . . . inta taghmiz bi-'aynak bas!' (O Sisi, All You Need to Do Is Wink), *al-Masry al-youm*, 25 July 2013, www.almasryalyoum.com/news/details/198680 (accessed July 2013).

29 Al-Hayat, 26 July 2013.

30 Al-Qahira wa-l-Nas, 28 July 2013. 'Ibrahim Eissa: *Here in Cairo* during Ramadan', 28 July 2013, youtu.be/clqSEN9KjWc (accessed July 2013).

31 CBC, *Bihudu'* (Quietly) with Emad Eddin Adeeb, 13 Jan. 2014. In a document leaked by WikiLeaks, Mustafa al-Bakry, who harangues revolutionary activists as being in the pay of foreign governments, asked Saudi Arabia for funds to set up a daily newspaper, a political party, and a pro-Saudi, anti-Shia satellite channel, a request endorsed by the Saudi foreign minister; wikileaks.org/saudi-cables/doc97297.html (accessed June 2015).

32 Lally Weymouth, 'An interview with Mohamed ElBaradei, who hopes for reconciliation in Egypt', *Washington Post*, 2 Aug. 2013, wapo.st/1cvParF (accessed Aug. 2013). ElBaradei was ready to resign after the police shootings of Morsi supporters by Rab'a on 27 June, but was talked out of it by US Secretary of State John Kerry, who saw him as the only voice of restraint in the government.

A Mubarak appointee, General Muhammad Farid al-Tohamy scuttled corruption investigations when he headed the Administrative Oversight Authority, a military-run auditing agency useful in the Mubarak era for threatening adversaries and keeping allies in check within the state bureaucracy. Dismissed by Morsi, he was chosen by al-Sisi to run the powerful General Intelligence Service, the post once occupied by Omar Soliman. The slighted general, now intelligence chief, became a hawkish proponent for the dispersal of the pro-Morsi sit-ins and the crackdown on Islamists and secular activists. Al-Sisi sent al-Tohamy into retirement in Dec. 2014, after bugged recordings in the offices of top generals surfaced on Brotherhood-affiliated satellite channels.

33 Mohamed ElBaradei, 6 Aug. 2013, twitter.com/ElBaradei/status/364690136430166016 (accessed Aug. 2013).

34 The decision came a day after US senators John McCain and Lindsey Graham were in Cairo for talks with the country's interim leadership, including Colonel General Abd al-Fattah al-Sisi. At a press conference, the Arizona lawmaker called Morsi's removal a 'coup' despite being told by al-Sisi to convey to members of Congress that the events of 3 July were not a military takeover. When asked by a reporter to define a coup, McCain retorted, 'I'm not here to go through the dictionary. If it walks like a duck and quacks like a duck, it's a duck' – a statement the ruling echelon found infuriating. Paul Taylor, 'Exclusive – West warned Egypt's Sisi to the end: don't do it', *Reuters*, 14 Aug. 2013, reut.rs/16lm8Kq; David D. Kirkpatrick, Peter Baker, and Michael R. Gordon, 'How American Hopes for a Deal in Egypt Were Undercut', *New York Times*, 17 Aug. 2013, nyti.ms/1aeYocB (accessed Aug. 2013).

35 Hamza Hendawi, Maggie Michael, Sarah El Deeb, and Lee Keath, 'A year later, protest's bloody end divides Egypt', *Associated Press*, 10 Aug. 2014, bigstory.ap.org/article/year-later-protests-bloody-end-divides-egypt-0 (accessed Aug. 2014). 'Rab'a massacre', 15 Aug. 2013, youtu.be/x6Mnm9neSLc; youtu.be/ZCgsh5HfctQ (accessed Jan. 2015).

36 The government's National Council for Human Rights listed 624 civilian deaths during the dispersal of the pro-Morsi sit-ins; the non-profit advocacy group the Egyptian Center for Economic and Social Rights counted 932 deaths; and Human Rights Watch documented a minimum of 817 protesters killed in Rab'a and another 87 in Nahda Square. Three journalists lost their lives: Sky News cameraman Mick Deane, Ahmed Abd al-Gawad of the state-owned daily *al-Akhbar*, and Mosaab al-Shaami of the online Rassd News Network. Al Jazeera journalist Abdullah Elshamy was arrested in Rab'a and jailed for ten months without charge, released by prosecutors only after a prolonged hunger strike. Photojournalist Mahmoud Abou Zeid, known as Shawkan, was also arrested and jailed without charge or a trial. Adli Mansour amended the criminal procedures law to allow for indefinite administrative detention.

37 'The Brotherhood carrying automatic weapons in a face-off with security', 14 Aug. 2013, youtu.be/OkXdoasAVik (accessed Jan. 2015).

38 Staunch military defender and television host Wael Elebrashy urged celebrating the anniversary of the dispersal of pro-Morsi sit-ins. 'I told al-Sisi in the meeting he had with media personalities that he should transform this day into a day of celebration. The day of the clearing of the Rab'a sit-in is the day of restoring the

eminence of the state. The bloody, armed sit-in in Rab'a and Nahda was a statelet inside the state,' he said. 'We regained Egypt from the Brotherhood occupation.' Dream 2, 12 Aug. 2014. 'Wael Elebrashy asks President al-Sisi to make Aug. 14 an official holiday', 12 Aug. 2014, youtu.be/X2tzkoZlNZE (accessed Aug. 2014).

39 Mohamed ElBaradei's resignation letter, 14 Aug. 2013, gate.ahram.org.eg/News/382972.aspx (accessed Aug. 2013).

40 Amaar Muhammad Badie, the supreme guide's 38-year-old son, and Khaled al-Banna, the 30-year-old grandson of the Brotherhood's founder, were killed in a scene of urban warfare involving police, army soldiers, anti-coup supporters, and pro-military vigilantes.

41 'Egyptian presidency international press conference about the situation in Egypt', 17 Aug. 2013, youtu.be/6Cxwrtz9nrY (accessed Aug. 2013). The Ministry of Information's State Information Service complained, 'Egypt is feeling severe bitterness towards some Western media coverage that is biased to the Muslim Brotherhood', adding the group 'exceeded all red lines regarding common humanitarian rules.' State Information Service, 17 Aug. 2013, ow.ly/EAB6g (accessed Aug. 2013).

42 'The speech of Abd al-Fattah al-Sisi, minister of defense', 18 Aug. 2013, youtu.be/Z27UzrhZHxc (accessed May 2014).

43 'First footage of the arrest of Badie, the Brotherhood's supreme guide', 19 Aug. 2013, youtu.be/G56ZcgKStE8 (accessed Aug. 2013).

44 The central Tahrir Square Metro station remained closed for 672 days, finally reopening in June 2015, on the eve of Ramadan. It was temporarily closed 13 days later, after the assassination of Egypt's top prosecutor.

45 Interview with Zizo Abdo (Arabic), 18 Aug. 2013, Cairo. Abdalla F. Hassan, 'Activists Find No Place on Egypt's Streets', *VICE*, 26 Aug. 2013, www.vice.com/read/activists-find-no-place-on-egypts-streets (accessed Aug. 2013).

46 'Al-Beltagy: What is happening in Sinai will stop when al-Sisi rescinds', 8 July 2013, youtu.be/mrqdr-qNgq4 (accessed July 2013). Muhammad al-Beltagy was apprehended on 29 Aug. 2013.

47 'Arrest of activists at the Shura Council protest', 26 Nov. 2013, youtu.be/QoCaZfaQeOg; youtu.be/-r11u205QlM (accessed Nov. 2013).

48 Alaa Abd El Fattah, 'An open letter', tr. Ahdaf Soueif, *Mada Masr*, 26 Aug. 2014, www.madamasr.com/content/open-letter (accessed Aug. 2014).

49 Patrick Kingsley, 'Abdel Fatah al-Sisi: behind the public face of Egypt's soon-to-be president', *Guardian*, 22 May 2014, gu.com/p/3pc7q/tw (accessed July 2015).

50 'Al-Sisi: the military spokesman is attractive to women, and the army's plan to control the media', 2 Oct. 2013, youtu.be/WB9MVTR02YE (accessed Oct. 2013).

51 '*Al-Bernameg?*: episode 1', 25 Oct. 2013, youtu.be/4dIlb5Q4vDI (accessed Oct. 2013). Youssef was awarded the Committee to Protect Journalists' 2013 Press Freedom Award.

52 *Al-Bernameg?* found a new home on MBC Masr in Feb. 2014 and was simulcast on Deutsche Welle's Arabic transmission.

53 The controversial *Black Box* programme aired from Dec. 2013 to Aug. 2014 on al-Qahira wa-l-Nas. The satellite channel's owner, advertising mogul Tarek Nour, announced the programme's cancellation on 18 Aug., a day after Abd al-Rahim Ali in his final episode ripped into billionaire businessman

Naguib Sawiris, who days earlier tweeted, 'Watching another episode for that informant Abd al-Rahim Ali is enough to make me empathise with the Muslim Brotherhood's anger!' Ali accused Sawiris, a Copt, of bankrolling the Muslim Brotherhood to the tune of billions of Egyptian pounds and aired a nondescript telephone conversation between Sawiris and Mohamed ElBaradei, reading into the exchange another one of his ludicrous collusions. Ali promised a trove of other security tapes that supposedly incriminated Sawiris in the epic Brotherhood conspiracy. *Black Box* and its ranting host were pulled off the air ten minutes before the programme's conclusion. Naguib Sawiris, 13 Aug. 2014, twitter.com/NaguibSawiris/status/499672951600709633 (accessed Aug. 2014). Article 57 of the 2014 constitution clearly states, 'Telegraph, postal, and electronic correspondence, telephone calls, and other forms of communication are inviolable, their confidentiality is guaranteed, and they may only be confiscated, examined, or monitored by causal judicial order, for a limited period of time, and in cases specified by the law.' Abd al-Rahim Ali and his programme *Black Box* moved to al-'Asima (The Capital) satellite channel.

54 As one example, see the programme *Tis'in daqiqa* (Ninety Minutes) on the Mehwar satellite channel for 7 Nov. 2014, where these claims are made by the two guests and unchallenged by the presenter. '*Ninety Minutes*: Al Jazeera's black dossier and civil society organisations and their involvement in dividing the Arabs', 7 Nov. 2014, youtu.be/G2LKEeldMZ8; '*Ninety Minutes*: The truth of the funding for April 6 and the methodology of American organisations to destroy Egypt', 7 Nov. 2014, youtu.be/PMG6Wqf5qQ8 (accessed Nov. 2014).

55 Interview with Zizo Abdo (Arabic), 19 Jan. 2014, Cairo.

56 The preamble of the constitution states, 'our patriotic army delivered victory to the sweeping popular will in the 25 January–30 June revolution'. The right to peaceful strike 'is organised by law' (article 15); the law regulates 'ownership and establishment procedures for radio and television broadcast stations and online publications' and newspapers may be issued upon notification 'as regulated by law' (article 70); media outlets may be censored or shut down 'in time of war or general mobilisation' (article 71); citizens may peacefully protest 'upon providing notification as regulated by law' (article 73); civilians may face military trials 'for crimes that represent a direct assault against military facilities, armed forces barracks, or whatever falls under their authority' (article 204); a National Media Council 'regulates the affairs of broadcast, print, and digital media' and ensures that 'press and media outlets adhere to professional and ethical standards, and national security requirements as set out by law' (article 211). Egypt's 2014 constitution, ow.ly/HGy0S (Arabic); ow.ly/HGy8e (English) (accessed Jan. 2014).

57 Many of these clandestine groups have adopted overt Islamist rhetoric in their statements and claims of responsibility, while others, like al-'Iqab al-Thawri, or Revolutionary Punishment, launched on the uprising's fourth anniversary, purport to defend the revolution against a despotic regime.

58 'Muslim Brotherhood Calls for Unity on January 25 Revolution Anniversary', Ikhwanweb, 22 Jan. 2014, www.ikhwanweb.com/article.php?id=31536 (accessed Jan. 2014).

59 Amnesty International, 'Egypt: Dozens of disappeared civilians face ongoing torture at military prison', 22 May 2014, ow.ly/KcOzG (accessed May 2014); Tom Stevenson, 'Sisi's Way', *London Review of Books*, 19 Feb. 2015, 3–7, www.lrb.co.uk/v37/n04/tom-stevenson/sisis-way (accessed Feb. 2015); Human Rights Watch, 'Egypt: Dozens Detained Secretly', 20 July 2015, www.hrw.org/news/2015/07/20/egypt-dozens-detained-secretly (accessed July 2015).

60 Interview with Amre Moussa, 28 Jan. 2014, Cairo. Abdalla F. Hassan, 'How Egypt's 25 January Revolutionaries Became Enemies of the State', *VICE*, 10 Feb. 2014, www.vice.com/read/how-egypts-january-25-revolutionaries-became-enemies-of-the-state (accessed Feb. 2014).

61 'The armed forces: Invention of devices to detect and treat the hepatitis and AIDS viruses', 23 Feb. 2014, youtu.be/rdSshvqgy6c (accessed Feb. 2014).

62 Meanwhile, the Health Ministry contracted with the pharmaceutical company that manufactures the hepatitis treatment Sovaldi for the importation of the drug, invented by Raymond Schinazi, born in Alexandria of Italian-Jewish heritage, who fled Gamal Abd al-Nasser's Egypt with his family in the early 1960s.

63 Amnesty International, 'Egypt: Military pledges to stop forced "virginity tests"', 27 June 2011, ow.ly/K8WAV (accessed May 2014).

64 'The new al-Sisi leak reveals his dreams of reaching the presidency of Egypt', 11 Dec. 2013, youtu.be/L8Lwyf_4ydc (accessed Dec. 2013).

65 'Field Marshal al-Sisi's resignation and presidency speech', 26 Mar. 2014, youtu.be/8ZpmDBL7Xv4 (accessed Mar. 2014). On 28 Mar., the Friday following al-Sisi's announcement, 23-year-old reporter Mayada Ashraf was killed by gunfire to the head as she covered protests and clashes in the eastern Cairo district of Ain Shams.

66 CBC and ONtv, 5–6 May 2014. 'Egypt elects the president: Field Marshal al-Sisi in his first televised interview', 7 May 2014, youtu.be/eotGq0j9LzM (accessed May 2014).

67 CBC, 8 May 2014. 'Egypt elects a president: The complete interview with presidential candidate Hamdeen Sabahy', 9 May 2014, youtu.be/dZgqKFaKIHQ (accessed May 2014).

68 Adli Mansour's 7 June presidential decree set out a three-month to one-year prison term and a fine of 20,000–50,000 Egyptian pounds for unauthorised sermonising in mosques. The Ministry of Religious Endowments also prohibited the sale of religious videos, audio recordings, or books without government permission.

69 On 13 Jan. 2015, an appellate court reversed Mubarak's only conviction on embezzlement charges and ordered a retrial. In May, the judge in the case upheld the verdict, but reduced the sentence of Mubarak's sons to three years.

70 The figures were tallied by WikiThawra, an initiative of the Egyptian Center for Economic and Social Rights, from 3 July 2013 to 15 May 2014. WikiThawra, 'Tally of Those Arrested and Prosecuted during the Rule of al-Sisi/Adli Mansour', May 2014, wikithawra.wordpress.com/2014/01/09/sisi-mansour-detainees (accessed May 2014). In the year since the military ousted Morsi, police raided the offices of ECESR twice, seizing computers and documents and arresting staff and activists. The centre was founded by human rights lawyer and former presidential candidate Khaled Ali.

71 Election observers from the European Union noted the biased media coverage in favour of al-Sisi (private media gave al-Sisi more than twice the media coverage),

undocumented spending by his supporters that exceeded campaign funding limits, and a general atmosphere that quashed dissent, narrowed media freedoms, and lacked political inclusion. 'EU election observation mission to Egypt in 2014', eeas.europa.eu/eueom/missions/2014/egypt/index_en.htm (accessed Sept. 2014).

72 Official page of President Muhammad Morsi, 4 June 2014, ow.ly/C7aCp (accessed June 2014).

73 'Abla Fahita and her late husband's SIM card', 26 Dec. 2013, youtu.be/EQm694L7ByY (accessed Dec. 2013).

74 CBC, 1 Jan. 2014. '*Mumkin*: For the first time Abla Fahita faces Ahmed Spider', 1 Jan. 2014, youtu.be/YGwr5xWDfUc (accessed Jan. 2014). A billboard advertising Pepsi with the catchphrase, 'Now is our chance' and footballers with T-shirts that have the numbers 14, 1, and 25 was investigated by prosecutors for inciting youth to revolt on the third anniversary of revolution.

75 Some presenters, like ONtv's Reem Magued, refused to play along, choosing silence as 'the most honest news'. Magued, opted not to renew her contract with ONtv, which expired on 30 June 2013, believing the station's orientation contradicted her convictions. Reem Magued, 25 Aug. 2013, twitter.com/Reemmagued/status/371657362702340096 (accessed Aug. 2013). Magued returned to television in May 2015 with a women-focussed programme on Deutsche Welle Arabia. Local production partner ONtv suspended her programme under security pressures. Yosri Fouda, another critical journalist, suspended his ONtv programme from 9 July to 25 Nov. 2013, and ended *Last Words* in Sept. 2014.

76 'Press conference for *al-Bernameg?* at the Radio Theatre', 2 June 2014, youtu.be/3DL5Gtp_JcU (accessed June 2014).

77 On 1 Feb. 2014, *al-Shuruk* refused to publish Belal Fadl's daily column, instead publishing an apology on his behalf, as it did the following day. He refused to pen his columns after the censorship, saying the paper was placing increasing pressure on writers to self-censor.

78 As of June 2015, 18 journalists were behind bars because of their reporting, more than a third were sentenced to life in prison, ranking Egypt among the world's top jailers of journalists. Committee to Protect Journalists, 'Egypt's imprisonment of journalists is at an all-time high', 25 June 2015, cpj.org/x/64aa (accessed June 2015).

79 Peter Greste, an Australian, arrived in Egypt 17 days before his arrest, and Mohamed Fadel Fahmy, a Egyptian-Canadian national, was appointed bureau chief three months earlier. On 2 Feb. 2014, television host Ahmed Musa broadcast the security raid on his programme on al-Tahrir satellite channel. The pro-military, pro-government network was renamed TEN TV in Mar. 2015.

80 British journalists Sue Turton and Dominic Kane, and Dutch journalist Rena Netjes were convicted in absentia and sentenced to ten years in prison.

81 ONtv, 23 June 2014. '*25/30*: The controversy around the trial of journalists in Egypt', 23 June 2014, youtu.be/OwA85LL-eGI (accessed June 2014).

82 Amal Alamuddin, 'The Anatomy of an Unfair Trial', *Huffington Post*, 18 Aug. 2014, huff.to/1AsSsqS (accessed Aug. 2014).

83 In Nov. 2014 Sinai-based Ansar Bayt al-Maqdis swore allegiance to the Islamic State in an audio message and renamed themselves Wilayat Sina (Province of Sinai).

84 Lally Weymouth, 'Egyptian President Abdel Fatah al-Sissi, who talks to Netanyahu "a lot," says his country is in danger of collapse', *Washington Post*, 12 Mar. 2015, wpo.st/xT1N0 (accessed Mar. 2015).

85 David D. Kirkpatrick 'As Egyptians Grasp for Stability, Sisi Fortifies His Presidency', *New York Times*, 7 Oct. 2014, nyti.ms/1xnbDAB (accessed Oct. 2014); 'President Abd al-Fattah al-Sisi's speech before the UN General Assembly', 24 Sept. 2014, youtu.be/EXXkohl29zM (accessed Sept. 2014).

86 'Katib Amriki: al-Sisi rajul dawla yahza bi-l-ihtiram wa-l-taqdir' (American Writer: al-Sisi Is a Respected and Appreciated Statesman), *al-Ahram*, 9 Oct. 2014, www.ahram.org.eg/NewsQ/330119.aspx (accessed Oct. 2014).

87 'Misstated Excerpt of Times Article Offers Fresh Take on President Sisi of Egypt', *New York Times*, 15 Oct. 2014, nyti.ms/1sRY8ZP (accessed Oct. 2014).

88 'Al-Haqiqa al-gha'iba wara ma nasharitu *al-Ahram* wa *New York Times*' (The Hidden Truth behind What Was Published in *al-Ahram* and the *New York Times*', *al-Ahram*, 16 Oct. 2014, www.ahram.org.eg/NewsQ/331647.aspx (accessed Oct. 2014). *Al-Ahram* did not credit the original story to the Middle East News Agency.

89 'Bayan ru'asa' tahrir al-suhaf al-masriya' (Statement of the Editors-in-Chief of Egyptian Newspapers), *al-Wafd*, 26 Oct. 2014, ow.ly/DpEUa (accessed Oct. 2014).

90 Ghada Sherif, "Afwan sayidi al-ra'is . . . man yasna' al-wahsh?!' (Sorry Mr President, but Who Creates the Monster?), *al-Masry al-youm*, 13 Oct. 2014, www.almasryalyoum.com/news/details/543322 (accessed Oct. 2014). A top aide to al-Sisi, General Abbas Kamel, is heard in a leaked wiretap recording telling the military spokesman to instruct certain media personalities to rally behind al-Sisi's presidential bid, mentioning how the benevolent field marshal 'sacrificed everything' for the sake of the nation. Mekameleen, 19 Jan. 2015. 'Al-Sisi office leaks and the media arms', 19 Jan. 2015, youtu.be/YzYQLTtZ5Mk (accessed Jan. 2015).

91 'Mubarak before the judges', 13 Aug. 2014, youtu.be/lHMbcS-0U8E (accessed Aug. 2014).

92 'The sentencing of Mubarak, his sons, al-Adly, and his aides', 29 Nov. 2014, youtu.be/AV1Nv0YPV28 (accessed Dec. 2014). Mubarak faces a second and final retrial over the killing of protesters during the Jan. 2011 uprising after the prosecution appealed the verdict.

93 Sada al-Balad, 29 Nov. 2014. 'Mubarak's first statement after his acquittal: By God, I did not do anything at all', 29 Nov. 2014, youtu.be/-1yDrK6I3Hk (accessed Dec. 2014). Three days before the revolution's fourth anniversary, the courts ordered the release on bail of Mubarak's sons.

94 Radio Hits, 30 Nov. 2014. 'The segment that caused the suspension of announcer Aida Seoudy for her remarks on Mubarak's acquittal', 2 Dec. 2014, youtu.be/EgFblSXir0g (accessed Dec. 2014).

95 Vodafone, 'Law Enforcement Disclosure Report', Feb. 2015, ow.ly/K93xp (accessed Feb. 2015).

96 The Interior Ministry was in the market for technologies to monitor and trace internet communications. *Al-Watan* published a copy of the interior ministry's tender. Magdy al-Gallad, 'Infirad: al-Dakhiliya tafrid "qabda iliktruniya" 'ala jara'im shabakat al-tawasul al-ijtima'i' (The Interior Ministry Imposes an 'Electronic Grip' on Social Media), *al-Watan*, 1 June 2014, www.elwatannews.com/news/

details/495659 (accessed June 2014); Sheera Frankel and Maged Atef, 'Egypt Begins Surveillance Of Facebook, Twitter, And Skype On Unprecedented Scale', *BuzzFeed*, 17 Sept. 2014, bzfd.it/1uHvzNL (accessed Sept. 2014); Mohamed Hamama, 'Monitoring communication: Where will the state's attempts to control "space" lead?', *Mada Masr*, 21 June 2015, www.madamasr.com/sections/politics/monitoring-communication-where-will-states-attempts-control-space-lead (accessed June 2015). On the ministry's secret slush funds see Nizar Manek and Jeremy Hodge, 'Opening the black box of Egypt's slush funds', *Africa Confidential*, 26 May 2015, www.africa-confidential.com/angaza-file (accessed May 2015).

97 Mekameleen, 4 Dec. 2014. 'Leaks from al-Sisi's office', 4 Dec. 2014, youtu.be/hkCNg6B3VRI (accessed Dec. 2014).

98 Mekameleen, 1 Mar. 2015. 'Leaks from al-Sisi's office reveal the role of the Emirates in exhausting the Arab Spring', 1 Mar. 2015, youtu.be/3mlacrYZobs (accessed Mar. 2015).

99 'A march in Talaat Harb for the Socialist Popular Alliance', 24 Jan. 2015, youtu.be/ftL06ZYUGY8; 'Last moments before the death of Shaimaa Elsabbagh', 24 Jan. 2015, youtu.be/ftL06ZYUGY8; 'The death of the activist Shaimaa Elsabbagh', 24 Jan. 2015, youtu.be/cHW4bnP28Uo. An examination of photographs and videos show Elsabbagh was shot by security forces: 'A masked officer killed Shaimaa Elsabbagh', 29 Jan. 2015, youtu.be/JqvcWTjwMvA; 'Video shows police shot Shaimaa al-Sabbagh', 31 Jan. 2015, youtu.be/uMBvbIojtWU (accessed Jan. 2015). In June, a court found 24-year-old police lieutenant Yasin Hatim Salahedeen guilty of manslaughter and sentenced him to 15 years in prison.

100 Ami Ayalon, *The Press in the Arab Middle East: A History* (New York and Oxford: Oxford University Press, 1995), 245.

Index

25 January 2011, 35, 37–42, 45, 47, 48, 56, 69, 71–3, 81, 85–6, 94, 99, 115, 123, 131–4, 140, 166, 191, 195–9, 202, 217, 218, 224, 230
30 June 2013, 117, 172–4, 175–8, 186, 196, 200, 202, 209, 226, 228, 249 n10

Abbas, Mahmoud (Palestinian Authority president), 22
Abbas, Wael (blogger), 13
Abd al-Dayem, Ines (Opera House director), 171
Abd al-Hady, Alaa (murdered medical student), 122–3, 127
Abd al-Magid, Asem (al-Jama'a al-Islamiya leader), 171
Abd al-Maqsoud, Muhammad (Salafi preacher), 172
Abd al-Nasser, Gamal (president), ix, 29, 43, 198, 214, 260 n62
Abd El Fattah, Alaa (activist, blogger, programmer), 111–13, 127–8, 134, 193–4, 243 n55
Abdel Rahman, Awatef (journalism professor), 25
Abdo, Zizo (activist), 191, 196–7
Abdullah II, King (Jordon), 22
Abla Fahita (puppet), 204
Aboudy (activist, Ultras member), 122–3
Aboul Futouh, Abd al-Moneim (politician, formerly in the Brotherhood), 24–5, 144–5, 173
activism, 12, 15, 25, 30–2, 35, 49, 76, 112, 131, 198, 215, 220, 243 n55
activists, 11–16, 22, 34, 37–9, 43, 46–8, 50, 54, 56, 58, 63–4, 68–70, 74, 78, 81, 85–90, 94, 105, 111–13, 115, 121–3, 127–8, 130–2, 134–5, 138–9, 147, 151, 154–5, 164, 169, 173–4, 177–8, 191–4, 195–8, 202, 207, 213, 217, 231, 234 n25, 241 n27, 243 n54–5, 245 n27, 246 n46, 256 n31, 256–7 n32, 260 n70
actors
  Ramzy, Hany, 6–11
  Sobhi, Muhammad, 4–6
  Waked, Amr, 45
Adel, Mohammed (April 6 Youth Movement), 193
al-Ahram Publishing House, 142, 251 n43, *see also* newspapers
Ajnad Masr (Soldiers of Egypt, jihadist group), 198
Akef, Muhammad Mahdi (Brotherhood supreme guide), 29–30, 58, 183
al-Akhbar al-Youm Publishing House, 142
Alamuddin, Amal (human rights barrister), 207
Alexandria, 14, 31, 37, 38, 41, 67, 79, 93, 116, 135, 166, 183, 192, 213, 224, 260 n62
Ali, Khaled (human rights lawyer, presidential candidate), 260 n70
Amnesty International, 200, 256 n24
Anan, Sami (military chief of staff), 86, 119–20, 147–8, 249 n11
Anonymous (hacktivists), 48–9
Ansar Bayt al-Maqdis (Champions of Jerusalem, jihadist group), 198, 261 n83
April 6 Youth Movement, 13–14, 32, 37, 45, 56, 90–1, 123, 151, 173, 191, 193, 196, 223, 245 n27
Arab Spring, x, 34, 196
armoured personnel carriers (APCs), 52, 102, 107, 129, 138, 182, 188, 191, 212
al-Asad, Bashar (Syria), 172
Ashton, Catherine (EU foreign policy chief), 187

assassination, 9, 144, 187, 201, 250 n18, 258 n44
Aswan, 79, 102
Al Aswany, Alaa (novelist, polemicist), 3, 21–2, 25–7, 50, 71, 77–80, 94–7, 113–14, 130–2, 235 n41
authoritarian, x, 19, 21, 23, 26–7, 30, 76, 115, 137, 157, 161, 191, 196, 221
Ayalon, Ami (press historian), 1, 214
al-Azhar (centre of Sunni Islamic learning), 2, 122, 127, 155–6, 161, 169, 172–3, 177, 181, 203, 244 n8
Aziz, Mohammed (Tamarod organiser), 181

Badie, Muhammad (Brotherhood supreme guide), 183, 190–1
Badr, Mahmoud (Tamarod organiser), 181
Badrawi, Hossam (politician in Mubarak's ruling party), 44–6, 237 n14
Baha'i, 185, 249 n11
Bahgat, Hossam (human rights campaigner), 15, 104–5
Baring, Evelyn (Lord Cromer, British agent and consul-general), 21, 29
The Bassem Youssef Show, 83
al-Bastawissy, Hesham (advocate for an independent judiciary), 12, 233 n10
Battle of the Camel, 61, 66, 224
BBC, *see* news channels
Bekheet, Gamal (poet), 4, 74
al-Beltagy, Muhammad (Brotherhood leader), 192
Ben Ali, Zine el-Abidine (Tunisia), 33–4, 38, 39, 53, 58, 65–6, 224, 236 n55
Ben-Eliezer, Benjamin (Israeli politician), 99
al-Bernameg? (The Programme?), 83, 158–9, 162–5, 177, 194–5, 204–6, 252 n51, 258 n52
Black Bloc (anarchist youth group), 166–7, 170
blog, 13, 22, 42, 43, 49, 85–6, 89, 99, 102, 111, 127, 134, 161, 164, 217, 221, 246 n46
Borhami, Yasser (Salafi sheikh), 161, 172
Bouazizi, Mohamed (Tunisian vegetable seller, sparked Arab uprisings), 33–4, 224
boycott, 30, 85, 161, 170, 203
Bush, George W., 23

Cabinet, 8, 53–4, 57, 68, 78–80, 92–3, 100, 107–8, 117, 151, 155, 171, 177, 179–82, 187–8, 198–9
Cabinet clashes (December 2011), 121–32, 193, 246 n42
cafés, 1–2, 25, 41, 66, 106, 135, 143, 144
Cairo, 1, 9, 12–14, 25–6, 33, 40–2, 44, 47–8, 52, 55, 57, 60, 63, 65, 83, 94, 99–100, 116, 122, 130, 132, 136–8, 155, 163–4, 167, 172, 178, 189–90, 197, 204–5, 229, 238 n37, 248–9 n6, 253 n76, 254 n83, 257 n34, 260 n65
Cairo International Airport, 27, 136, 223
Cairo University, 25, 76, 146, 178, 180
caliphate, 190, 208
censorship, 2, 13, 21, 33, 34, 49, 131, 141, 160–1, 165, 210, 215–16, 218–20, 259 n56
  film, 6–7, 9–11
  press, 35, 118–21, 148, 261 n77
  television, 18, 63, 76, 113–14, 205–6, 242 n42
Christians, 37, 49, 67, 78, 84, 103–4, 107, 152, 153, 161, 162–3, 169, 172, 183, 185, 189, 213, 220, 222, 225, 253 n76, *see also* Coptic Christians
churches, 49, 132, 152, 169, 177, 189, 190, 192, 204
  Church of the Virgin Mary (Giza), 87
  St George Coptic Orthodox Church (Aswan), 182
  St Mark's Cathedral (Cairo), 253 n76
  Two Saints Church (Alexandria), 37, 41, 67
CIA (US Central Intelligence Agency), 23, 56
CitizenTube, 61
civil disobedience, 13–15, 30, 47, 138–9, 167–8
civilian presidential council, 81, 157
Clinton, Hillary Rodham (US secretary of state), 67, 147
columnists, 165, 186, 209
comedians, 175, 194, 152 n51
comedy, 4–11, 83–5, 216–17
communiqués
  armed forces, 71, 81, 86, 123, 128, 137
  dissenting army officers, 80
conspiracy, 120, 127, 136–7, 143, 145–6, 150, 152–3, 158–9, 165, 175, 176, 184, 196, 202, 204–5, 208, 211, 217, 221, 249 n10, 258–9 n53
Constituent Assembly, 145, 152–61, 199, 251 n43

constitution, 6, 56, 66, 93, 109, 136, 139, 144, 153
1971 (and amendments), 3, 11–13, 16, 26, 28, 30, 54, 57, 59–60, 63, 68, 72–3, 79, 83–4, 86, 101, 223, 225
2012, 160–1, 145, 148, 152–8, 160–1, 163, 167, 173–4, 177, 180–82, 227, 251 n43, 251–2 n45, 252 n51
2014, 193, 197, 199, 210, 229, 258–9 n53, 258–9 n53, 259 n56
constitutional declarations, 145, 147, 151–9, 179, 182–3, 226, 227
Coptic Christians, 37, 67, 78, 87–8, 102–7, 132, 169, 172, 177, 181, 183, 204, 213, 225, 242 n50, 243 n54, 246 n49, 252 n51, 253 n76, 258–9 n53
corruption, 2–4, 13, 16, 20, 25, 31, 33, 34, 39–40, 49, 53, 57, 66, 76–7, 81–2, 132, 137, 140, 146, 169, 175, 202, 204, 206, 212, 223, 224, 230, 236 n55, 240 n20, 249 n10–11, 256–7 n32
counter-revolution, 157, 167
coup, 5, 9, 35, 38, 71, 118–21, 146, 147, 179, 181–5, 189, 192, 194, 197, 199, 202, 238–9 n44, 248 n4, 255 n19, 257 n34, 258 n40
curfew, 48, 52, 54–5, 57, 66, 167, 189

Danial, Mina (murdered activist), 105, 112, 242 n50
Dawoud, Khaled (Constitution Party spokesperson), 174, 254 n83
al-Deeb, Farid (Mubarak's lawyer), 98, 101
detention, 66, 69, 81, 111, 120, 142, 149, 198, 257 n36
disappearances, 142, 168, 198
dissidents, 2–3, 23, 78, 86, 161, 165, 197, 217
Douma, Ahmed (activist), 193
drama series, 131, 186, 195, 206, 217

Effat, Sheikh Emad (murdered al-Azhar scholar), 122–3, 127
Egyptian Center for Economic and Social Rights, 257 n36, 260 n70
Egyptian Initiative for Personal Rights, 15, 104
Egyptian Movement for Change, *see* Kifaya (Enough)
Egyptian Museum, 51, 55, 238–9 n44
Egyptian Radio and Television Union, 88, 150
Egyptian Stock Exchange, 44, 48, 78
ElBaradei, Mohamed (democracy advocate, politician), 17–18, 27–30, 48, 50–1, 56, 63–4, 66, 132–3, 154, 157, 166, 181, 183, 187–9, 223, 225 n10, 226 n20, 226–7 n32, 258–9 n53
elections, 12, 25, 26–7, 28–9, 33, 56, 61, 63, 72, 77, 86, 93, 109, 111, 122, 146, 154, 170–1, 179, 192, 210, 217–19, 223, 236 n55
parliamentary, 18, 30, 42, 45–6, 54, 57, 58, 63–4, 68, 87, 93, 101, 109, 117, 121–2, 133, 152–3, 170, 180–1, 199, 223, 224, 225, 242 n43, 248 n3
presidential, 3, 7–8, 9, 11–12, 16, 18–19, 23, 28, 54, 59, 64, 72, 86, 91, 93, 109, 135, 137, 139, 141, 145–6, 154, 171, 174, 175, 177, 179–82, 199, 202–4, 217, 223, 226, 228, 230, 233 n10, 240 n22, 247 n69, 248 n5, 260–1 n71
student union, 16, 199
ElGendy, Mohamed (murdered activist), 169
Elsabbagh, Shaimaa (murdered activist), 213, 231
emergency law, 2, 3, 15, 28, 31, 38, 47, 54, 63, 72, 79, 82, 101, 112, 133–4
al-Erian, Essam (Brotherhood leader), 149–50, 157, 249 n15
Ethiopia, 171–2, 253 n74
European Union (EU), 170–1, 187, 227, 260–1 n71
Ezz, Ahmed (powerbroker in Mubarak's ruling party), 56, 62, 76–7

Facebook, 15, 28, 31, 32–3, 42, 44, 45–7, 48, 49, 50, 65, 69, 81, 85, 108, 113, 130, 154, 158, 173, 238–9 n44, 241 n34
April 6 Youth Movement, 13–14, 32, 223
'We are all Khaled Said', 32, 37–8, 49, 69, 154, 196–7, 224
Fadl, Belal (screenwriter, polemicist), 206, 261 n77
fatwa (religious edict), 122, 156, 169
field hospitals, 117, 122
fifth columnists, 196, 220, 249 n10
films, 6–11, 94, 131, 216–17
'Ayiz haqi (I Want My Rights), 10
al-Diktatur (The Dictator), 9
Gawaz bi-qarar gumhuri (Marriage by Presidential Decree), 9–10

Zaza, 6–11, 217
football, 39, 261 n74
Port Said massacre, 135–8, 167, 226
Former Internet Junkies Yahoo! Group, 13
freedom of speech, 27, 49, 59
Friday of Rage (28 January 2011), 47–53, 59, 71, 79, 99, 101, 224

Gaza, 151, 208, 210
General Intelligence Service, 25, 143, 213, 256–7 n32
general strike, 13–14, 93, 223
generals of the military council
Anan, Sami, 86, 119–20, 147–8, 249 n11
al-Assar, Muhammad, 106–11, 139
Badeen, Hamdy, 89, 132, 147
Emara, Adel, 105–6, 124–8
Etman, Ismail, 89, 113, 241 n27
al-Fangary, Mohsen, 93, 132, 241 n34
Hegazy, Mahmoud, 105–11
al-Mulla, Mukhtar, 139, 247 n70
al-Roweiny, Hassan, 90–1, 94, 241 n28
Shaheen, Mamdouh, 118, 139
al-Sisi, Abd al-Fattah, 194, 200, 227
Tantawi, Muhammad Hussein, 55, 81, 99–100, 109, 110, 116–21, 129, 133–9, 147–8, 224, 227, 242 n42, 349 n11
Ghonim, Wael (activist), 46–7, 50, 68–70, 154–5, 173–4, 196
Giza, 39, 51, 173, 190
governors, 10, 47, 50–1, 93, 102, 147, 166, 173, 179
al-Gumhuriya Publishing House, 142

Hagel, Chuck (US secretary of defence), 187
el-Hamalawy, Hossam (activist, blogger), 89
Hamas, 12, 41, 56, 58, 101, 184, 186, 192, 208, 211, 248–9 n6
Harb, Osama al-Ghazali (Democratic Front Party leader), 44–6
Hashem, Mohamed (publisher), 126, 130–2, 171
Hesham Mubarak Law Center, 63, 194, 243 n55
Hezbollah, 56, 101, 192, 211, 248–9 n6
High Court of Justice, 13, 154, 233 n8
hip-hop, 15, 135
honourable citizens, 59, 92, 93, 101, 104, 123
House of Representatives (formerly People's Assembly), 152
human rights, 3, 6, 12, 15, 23, 26, 27, 52, 63, 78, 82, 89, 104, 141, 147, 193, 196, 208, 209, 212, 237 n13, 243 n55
Human Rights Watch, 257 n36
Hussein, Saddam (Iraq), 2

Ibrahim, Sonallah (novelist), 4, 171
incitement, 35, 40, 59, 64, 102–6, 119, 185
informants, 177, 256 n24, 258–9 n53
Institut d'Égypte, 124–6
insurgency, 231
intellectuals, 20, 21, 86, 171
International Monetary Fund (IMF), 170–1
internet, ix, 13, 20, 31, 34, 44–50, 61, 68–9, 83, 167, 190, 215, 216, 262–3 n96
Iran, 26, 56, 101
Iraq, 1–2, 18, 42, 196, 208
Islamic State, 208, 261 n83
Islamist satellite channels, 172, 181–2
al-Hafiz, 169
al-Hikma, 131
al-Nas, 162
al-Umma, 253 n69
Islamists, 2, 3, 12, 29, 62, 67, 121, 145–9, 152–3, 155–7, 159–63, 170–2, 175–7, 181–92, 196–9, 213, 220, 222, 227, 228, 229, 234 n25, 251 n43, 253 n68, 255 n17 n19, 256–7 n32, 259 n57
Ismailia, 37, 48, 166–7
Israel, 6, 18, 22, 41, 56, 58, 85, 98–9, 101, 103, 106, 107, 140, 151, 184, 207, 208, 215

al-Jama'a al-Islamiya (one-time jihadist group), 171, 173, 184
Jasmine revolution, 33–5
Al Jazeera, 1–2, 20, 24–5, 34, 40–1, 48, 51, 55–7, 63–4, 150, 195, 215, 234 n25, 238 n37, 240 n20, 257 n36
Al Jazeera English, 51, 207–8, 230
Al Jazeera Live Egypt, 100–1, 151, 181–2, 185, 190, 239 n3, 255 n17
jihad, 40, 159, 162, 172, 176
jihadists, ix–x, 171, 183, 191, 198–9, 201, 207–8, 210
journalists, 12, 14, 16, 20, 24, 42–3, 49, 57, 61, 62, 70–1, 75, 78, 86, 89, 117, 122, 125–6, 135, 139, 143, 148–9, 156, 160–1, 164–5, 197, 206–8, 212, 214, 217–19, 238 n37
Abd al-Gawad, Ahmed (murdered journalist), 257 n36

Abd al-Rahim, Gamal (*al-Gumhuriya*), 249 n11
Abd al-Rahman, Nagat (*24 Sa'a*), 58
Abdul Ghani, Hussein (Al Jazeera), 20, 234 n25
Abou Zeid, Mahmoud (photojournalist), 257 n36
Abu Deif, Husseini (murdered photojournalist), 156
Afifi, Islam (*al-Dustur*), 149
Amanpour, Christiane (ABC News/ CNN), 62
Amin, Shahira, 89
Ashraf, Mayada (murdered journalist), 260 n65
Azab, Rasha (*al-Fajr*), 241 n27
al-Banna, Muhammad Hassan (*al-Akhbar*), 148
Beach, Alastair (*Independent*), 119
Bedair, Naglaa, 90–1
Carr, Sarah, 102–3
Crowley, Candy (CNN), 78
Deane, Mick (murdered cameraman), 257 n36
Eissa, Ibrahim, 17–18, 106–14, 186–7, 201–2, 207, 211
ElGarhey, Mohamed (*al-Tahrir*), 99
Ellatif, Gamal (BBC Arabic), 25
Elshamy, Abdullah (Al Jazeera), 257 n36
El Emary, Naglaa (BBC Arabic), 20
Ezz al-Arab, Khaled (BBC Arabic), 75
Fahmy, Mohamed Fadel (CNN/Al Jazeera), 156, 207–8, 261 n79
Fouad, Sakina, 171
al-Gallad, Magdy, 44–6, 118–21, 202–3, 244 n19
al-Ghazaly, Mahmoud (Nile News), 246 n65
Greste, Peter (Al Jazeera), 206–8, 261 n79
Hammond, Andrew, 24
Hammouda, Adel, 17, 241 n27
Kandil, Abd al-Halim, 17, 24, 234 n32
Kandil, Hamdy, 18, 77–80, 123, 234 n20
Kirkpatrick, David D. (*New York Times*), 208–9
Al Malky, Rania (*Daily News Egypt*), 34–5, 64
Mikhael, Wael (murdered cameraman), 242 n50
Muhammad, Baher (Al Jazeera), 206–8
Muhammad, Nada, 148
Rizk, Yasser, 113, 200
Rodenbeck, Max (*The Economist*), 27
Salama, Abd al-Nasser (*al-Ahram*), 148, 249 n10
Saraya, Osama (*al-Ahram*), 22–3, 70–1, 75, 234 n29, 239 n2
al-Shaami, Mosaab (murdered journalist), 257 n36
Shaban, Akram (BBC radio), 64
Shadid, Anthony (*New York Times*), 34, 61
al-Shafei, Ola (*al-Youm al-sabi'*), 165
Sherif, Ghada (*al-Masry al-youm*), 186, 209
Zayda, Gamal (*al-Ahram*), 100
Journalists' Syndicate, 12, 44, 76, 160, 251 n43
judges, 12–13, 95, 98–9, 112, 124, 139–40, 145, 152, 161, 207, 210, 211, 219, 231, 260 n69
judiciary, 12–13, 30, 53, 79, 85, 97, 112, 133, 142, 144, 145–6, 152–3, 159, 165, 177, 207, 212, 213, 227, 233 n8, 243 n55, 251–2 n45

Kamel, Abbas (al-Sisi's office manager), 213, 262 n90
Kamel, Bothaina (media presenter, presidential candidate), 86–9, 240 n22
Kamel, Ibrahim (pro-Mubarak businessman), 64
Kamel, Omar (video producer, musician, blogger), 81
al-Katatni, Saad (Brotherhood leader), 170, 176–7, 180, 255 n12
Kato, Abd al-Moniem (military advisor), 90–2, 128
Kerry, John (US secretary of state), 208, 256–7 n32
Khaled, Amr (religious reformer), 54
al-Khayat, Adel (al-Jama'a al-Islamiya), 173
Kifaya (Enough), 11–12, 23, 90, 131, 233 n8, 243 n55
Kuwait, 12, 182, 255 n19

Leon, Bernardino (EU envoy), 170
liberals, 78, 84, 145, 162, 175, 220, 222, 249 n10
Libya, 113, 196
literature, 17, 25, 216
live ammunition, 52, 105–6, 115–16, 129, 140, 167, 185

Lord Cromer, *see* Baring, Evelyn
Luxor, 151, 173

Machiavelli, Niccolò, 175
magazines
24 Sa'a (24 Hours), 58
Der Spiegel, 154, 183
The Economist, 17, 28
Foreign Policy, 119, 121
Liwa' al-Islam (Banner of Islam), 3
Magdy, Rasha (newscaster on state television), 103
Magdy, Vivian (protester), 105
al-Mahalla al-Kubra (Nile Delta industrial city), 13, 116, 233 n12
Maher, Ahmed (April 6 Youth Movement), 193
Mahfouz, Asmaa (activist), 38–9, 85–6, 240 n20
Mansour, Adli (interim president), 182–3, 186, 188, 192–3, 199, 229, 230, 257 n36, 260 n68
Mansour, Khaled (comedian), 194, 252 n51
Mansoura (Nile Delta city), 42, 66, 116, 185, 192
march of millions, 57, 71, 93, 254 n80
martyrs, 31, 33, 45, 68, 72, 78–9, 84, 92, 103, 111–12, 115, 130, 136, 146, 167, 213, 224, 231, 241 n34
Maspero, 102–7, 111–13, 127–8, 134, 242 n42, 243 n54, 247 n61, *see also* television and radio building
Maspero massacre, 102–8, 111–13, 127, 128, 242 n42, 243 n54
Media Production City, 19, 150, 160
Merit Publishing House, 128, 130–2
Metro, 43, 166, 191, 258 n44
Middle East News Agency (state wire service), 141, 148, 209
militants, 147, 183, 184, 190, 197–8, 201, 208, 210, 226, *see also* jihadists
al-'Iqab al-Thawri (Revolutionary Punishment), 258 n 57
military aid, 208
military businesses, 138, 210
military council, *see* Supreme Council of the Armed Forces
Military Liars ('Askar Kazeboon) campaign, 134–5
military police, 80, 89, 105, 112, 115–16, 128, 136, 144, 147, 181–2, 193–4, 243 n55
military trials, 7, 82, 85–6, 112, 128, 139, 193, 197, 217, 241 n27, 259 n56
Mill, John Stuart, 115
Miloševic, Slobodan (Serbian and Yugoslav politician), 14
minister of culture, 4
Abd al-Aziz, Alaa, 171
minister of foreign affairs
Aboul Gheit, Ahmed, 54, 79
minister of information, 48
Abd al-Maqsoud, Salah, 148, 150, 158, 249 n12
al-Fiqqi, Anas, 40, 51, 55, 57, 75–6
Heikal, Osama, 100, 242 n42
minister of interior, 7, 78
al-Adly, Habib, 2, 25, 38, 52, 56, 67, 76, 93, 98–100, 140, 212, 226
al-Essawy, Mansour, 117
Ibrahim, Muhammad Ahmed, 167–8, 186–8, 191, 197, 213
minister of religious endowments
Gomaa, Muhammad Mokhtar, 203
ministries
Communication, 46
Culture, 171
Defence, 138–9, 199–200, 240 n20
Health, 123, 127, 260 n62
Information, 16, 258 n41
Insurance and Social Affairs, 170
Interior, 7, 22, 31–2, 40–1, 42, 44, 51–2, 67, 80, 92–3, 116–17, 124, 126, 136, 137, 141, 168, 184, 192–3, 206–7, 212–13, 241 n33, 248–9 n6, 262–3 n96
Investment, 254 n4
Justice, 79, 144
Religious Endowments, 155, 203, 260 n68
Morale Affairs Directorate (armed forces), 89, 90–1, 128
Morra, Galal (Nour Party secretary-general), 181
Morsi, Muhammad
Brotherhood leader, parliamentarian, 146, 151, 248–9 n6, 251 n33
presidential candidate, president-elect, 145–6, 226, 250–1 n31
as president, 147–81, 200, 205, 218, 220, 226, 227, 228, 234 n25, 241 n28, 247 n70, 249 n10, 250 n18, 251 n33 n43, 252 n46, 254 n80 n4, 255 n10 n12 n17, 256–7 n32

after his ouster, 181–92, 194–200, 202, 204, 207, 213, 220, 228, 229, 231, 249 n10, 254 n83, 255 n7, 256 n24, 256–7 n32, 257 n34 n36, 257–8 n38, 260 n70
Mosireen (activist media collective), 94, 241 n35
mosques, 49, 51, 77, 102, 139, 155, 173, 188, 203, 260 n68
al-Azhar Mosque, 2, 122
Hassan al-Sharbatli Mosque, 155
Rab'a al-Adawiya Mosque, 179, 188
Sayeda Zeinab Mosque, 1
Mossad (Israeli spy agency), 56, 58
Moussa, Amre (politician, presidential candidate), 144–5, 199, 248 n4, 255 n10
Mu'alim, Ibrahim (newspaper publisher), 27
Mubarak, Alaa, 10, 48, 82, 98–9, 140, 203, 211–12, 225, 260 n69, 292 n93
Mubarak, Gamal, 10, 16, 21, 48, 62, 68, 76, 82, 98–9, 140, 203, 211–12, 225, 260 n69, 262 n93
Mubarak, Hosni
as president, ix, 2–35, 106, 109, 111–12, 117, 119, 131, 134–5, 150, 160, 162, 164–6, 176, 187, 209, 216, 219, 223, 224, 233 n12, 234 n32, 256–7 n32
during revolution, 37–74, 123, 129, 141–2, 166, 175, 178, 182, 194, 216, 217, 224, 237 n14
after downfall, 75–94, 113, 115, 128, 135, 137–9, 144–8, 157, 159–60, 169, 177, 179, 190, 204, 212, 218, 225, 226, 238 n27, 239 n2, 241 n31, 244 n19, 248 n73
trials, 98–101, 110, 139–42, 203, 211–12, 225, 226, 227, 230, 260 n69, 262 n92
Mubarak, Suzanne, 17, 21, 76
Muhammad Mahmoud Street, 117, 127–8, 137, 151
Muslim Brotherhood
opposition to Mubarak, 3–4, 16, 24–5, 29–30, 34, 78, 144–5, 146
during revolution, 40–3, 45, 48, 50, 58, 62–4 66–7, 69, 123, 128, 146, 248–9 n6
after Mubarak's downfall, 76, 84, 147, 226, 251 n43
in power, ix–x, 146–82, 218, 250 n29, 253 n74, 249 n12 n15, 251 n43, 253 n74, 254 n4
after Morsi's ouster, 182–92, 196–213, 229, 230, 231, 249 n10, 256 n26, 256–7 n32, 258 n40–1, 258–9 n53
Freedom and Justice Party, 145, 149, 153, 157, 170, 176, 180, 190, 226, 242 n43, 247 n61
Guidance Council, 48, 176, 179
youth, 62, 247 n61
Muslims, 1, 37, 49, 84, 153, 155, 159, 162–3, 172–3, 176, 185, 200, 222, 253 n76

Nagati, Loai (activist, blogger), 86
Nasser, *see* Abd al-Nasser, Gamal
National Alliance to Support Legitimacy, 189
National Coalition for Change, 28
National Democratic Party (NDP, Mubarak's ruling party), 3, 11, 17, 30, 43–6, 48, 51, 54, 57, 61, 63, 68, 77, 81, 122, 203, 223, 224, 233 n12, 238 n34, 239 n2
National Salvation Front, 154, 158, 167, 169, 173–4, 179, 234 n25, 254 n83
national security, 32, 121, 161, 184–5, 207, 230, 259 n56
Negm, Ahmed Fouad (poet), 43, 55, 94–5
Negm, Nawara (activist, blogger), 43
Netanyahu, Binyamin (Israeli prime minister), 22, 208
news channels
Al Arabiya, 82, 225, 234 n22
BBC, 20, 25, 51, 56, 64, 75, 215, 234 n26
CCTV, 234 n26
CNN, 51, 78, 89, 156
Deutsche Welle, 51, 234 n26, 258 n52, 261 n75
EuroNews, 51
France, 24, 51, 234 n26
Al Hurra, 51, 103–4, 234 n26
Al Jazeera, *see main entry for* Al Jazeera
Nile News, 137, 247 n65
Russia Today, 51, 234 n26
Sky News, 257 n36
news sites
Mada Masr, 244 n20
Rassd News Network (RNN), 42, 237 n7, 257 n36
newscast, 23, 55, 76, 86, 87–8
newscasters, 51, 103

newspapers
  al-Ahram (The Pyramids), 12, 21–2, 50, 70–1, 75, 98, 100, 138, 148, 155, 158, 190, 209, 234 n29, 238 n32, 249 n10
  al-Akhbar (The News), 12, 101, 148, 257 n36
  Daily News Egypt, 34–5, 64
  al-Dustur (The Constitution), 16–17, 149
  Egypt Independent, 118–21, 244 n20
  al-Fajr (The Dawn), 17, 156, 241 n27
  Guardian, 177, 254 n5
  al-Gumhuriya (The Republic), 249 n11
  Independent (UK), 119–21
  al-Masry al-youm (The Egyptian Today), 44, 94, 114, 118–21, 145, 186, 200, 235 n41, 248 n4
  New York Times, 3, 34, 61, 209
  Sawt al-umma (The Nation's Voice), 12–13, 17, 50, 132
  al-Shuruk (Sunrise), 26–7, 90, 98, 111, 128, 248 n4, 261 n77
  al-Siyasa (Politics), 12
  al-Tahrir (Liberation), 90, 98, 99, 234 n19
  al-Usbu' (The Week), 125
  al-Wafd (The Delegation), 242 n42
  Washington Post, 183
  al-Watan (The Nation), 121, 244 n19, 262–3 n96
  al-Youm al-sabi' (The Seventh Day), 165
Nile Delta, 13, 42, 66, 116, 185, 190, 192
NileSat, 51, 55, 57, 63
No Military Trials for Civilians campaign, 193, 241 n27
novelists, 3, 4, 21, 25, 77, 97, 115, 131, 143, 171
novels, x, 17, 130, 233 n4

Obama, Barack, 22, 60, 62, 64, 179, 182, 208, 255 n10
Omar, Manal (psychologist), 165
Opera House, 171
Otpor! (Serbian youth movement), 14

parliament, 3, 14, 30, 43, 45, 54, 58, 63, 68, 70, 73, 78, 122–3, 148, 163, 193, 204, 223, 225, 242 n43, 245 n27, 246 n61, *see also* People's Assembly; Shura (Consultative) Council
parliamentarians
  Abu Hamed, Mohamed, 137
  al-Bakry, Mustafa, 187, 256 n31
  al-Eleimy, Ziyad, 138
  Hamzawy, Amr, 137
  Morsi, Muhammad, 146, 151
  Mustafa, Hesham Talaat, 98–9
parliamentary elections, 64, 68, 180–1, 199, 210
  2005, 87
  2010, 18, 30, 42, 45–6, 58, 217
  2011–12, 93, 101, 109, 114, 117, 225, 248 n3
parody, 5, 216
patronage, 63, 68, 120, 178
Patterson, Anne W. (US ambassador to Egypt), 180, 249 n10
penal code, 15, 16, 183, 210, 242 n40, 253 n59
People's Assembly, 3, 10, 14–15, 16, 26, 30, 45–6, 72, 85, 101, 117, 124–8, 136–7, 141, 144, 145, 224, 226, 242 n43, 247 n61, 248 n3
photojournalists, 156, 257 n36
plays
  Mama Amrika (Mother America), 6
  Takharif (Delusions), 4–6
poets, 4, 43, 55, 65, 74, 77, 93–4, 131, 213, 231
police brutality, 13, 31, 168, 224
political Islam, 182, 220, 233 n4
political parties, 43, 70, 157, 197, 234 n25, 249 n10, 256 n31
  Building and Development Party, 173
  Constitution Party, 246 n51
  Democratic Front Party, 44
  Freedom and Justice Party, 145, 149, 153, 157, 170, 176, 180, 190, 226, 242 n43, 247 n61
  Karama Party, 26, 50
  National Democratic Party (NDP), 3, 11, 17, 30, 43–6, 48, 51, 54, 57, 61, 63, 68, 77, 81, 122, 203, 223, 224, 233 n12, 238 n34, 239 n2
  Nour Party, 172, 181, 242 n43
  Popular Current Party
  Social Democratic Party, 157
  Strong Egypt Party, 173
  Wafd Party, 242 n42
Pope Shenouda III, 132, 246 n49
Pope Tawadros II, 172, 181
Port Said, 135–6, 166–7, 226
poverty, 7, 22, 26, 28, 38, 40, 50, 53, 57, 60, 70, 87, 92, 140, 204
presidential debates, 12, 144–5

presidential decrees, 5, 9–10, 30, 72, 151–5, 159, 173, 204, 209–10, 227, 231, 255 n10, 260 n68
presidential palace, 47, 67, 73, 152, 155–8, 167, 168–9, 170, 178, 193, 227, 228, 231
press law, 149
prime minister, 151, 170, 179–80
  Beblawi, Hazem, 183
  al-Ganzoury, Kamal, 117, 122–3, 133, 137
  Kandil, Hesham, 151, 169
  Mehlab, Ibrahim, 203
  Shafik, Ahmed, 54, 57, 77–80, 128, 141, 145, 165, 226, 248 n5
  Sharaf, Essam, 80, 93, 107–8, 116, 239 n2
prisons, 23, 52, 56, 132, 196, 213
  Abu Zaabal Prison, 190
  Borg al-Arab Prison, 192
  Tora Prison, 76, 137, 140–1, 190, 193
  Wadi al-Natrun Prison, 248–9 n6
propaganda, ix, 129, 143, 156, 196, 206, 214, 221
prosecutor general, 32, 152, 162, 166, 167, 170, 174, 180, 194, 258 n44
  Abdullah, Talaat, 162, 163–4, 166, 167, 170, 174, 180
  Barakat, Hisham, 194, 231, 213, 258 n44
prosecutors, 32, 158, 164, 165, 169, 183, 193, 204, 205, 207, 210, 211, 213, 246 n46, 250 n18, 252 n51, 257 n36, 261 n74
  military, 111–13, 139, 210, 218
protest law, 192–3, 201, 205, 212, 229, 251–2 n45

al-Qaddafi, Muammar (Libya), 113
al-Qaeda, 67, 190, 192
Qasr al-Nil Bridge, 37, 51, 65
Qatar, 1, 20, 40, 56, 58, 63, 150, 184, 195, 196, 207, 215, 239 n3, 255 n7
Qur'an, 98

Rab'a massacre, 187–92, 199, 229
radio, 64, 87, 99, 161, 194, 207, 212, 215, 259 n56
Ramadan, fasting month of, 83, 94, 98, 147, 184, 186, 195, 206, 258 n44
rap, 135
red lines, 10, 15, 20, 128, 132, 219, 256 n20, 258 n41
referendum, 3, 11, 12–13, 86, 96, 109, 117–18, 152, 154–6, 158–9, 161, 179–81, 197, 229, 251–2 n45, 252 n51
Republican Guard, 147, 180, 183, 185, 228
revolutionaries, 47, 61–2, 65, 67, 89, 94–7, 116, 130, 134, 144–5, 154–5, 169, 191–4, 198, 224
Revolutionary Socialists, 123
Ricciardone Jr, Francis J. (US ambassador), 23, 234 n31, 235 n36
Rice, Susan (US national security advisor), 180
rule of law, 26–7, 168, 189

Sabahy, Hamdeen (leftist politician, presidential candidate), 157–8, 202–3
Sadat, Anwar (president), 5, 144, 184, 198, 200
Said, Khaled (young man murdered by police), 31–2, 37, 112, 213, 224, 235–6 n50, 236 n53
Salafi, 84, 102, 131, 161, 169, 172–3, 247 n69, 252 n46
Salah, Ahmed Gaber (Jika, murdered activist), 151
Salem, Hussein (pro-Mubarak businessman), 140, 211
Sanad, Maikel Nabil (blogger), 85–6
Sartre, Jean-Paul, 143
satellite channels/networks
  25 (satellite channel 25), 103, 246 n48
  Al Arabiya, 82, 225, 234 n22
  al-'Asima, 258–9 n53
  CBC, 76, 83, 153, 158, 162, 177, 194, 201, 234 n21, 238 n27, 244 n19, 246 n45, 250 n24, 251 n38, 256 n31, 260 n66–7, 261 n74
  Dream, 18, 19, 54, 68–70, 89–92, 106–11, 129, 149–50, 177, 235 n44, 237 n12 n15, 239 n46, 241 n28–9, 243 n53, 248 n4, 249 n16, 257–8 n38
  al-Fara'in, 150, 250 n11
  al-Hafiz, 169
  al-Hayat, 117, 242 n44, 244 n10–11, 253 n66–7, 256 n29
  al-Hikma, 131
  Al Hurra, 51, 103–4, 234 n26
  Al Jazeera, *see main entry for* Al Jazeera
  Masr, 25, 76, 155, 157, 160, 181, 251 n36, 255 n8
  MBC, 204–6, 239 n3, 253 n64–5, 258 n52
  Mehwar, 58, 259 n54
  Mekameleen, 262 n90, 263 n97–8
  al-Nahar, 234 n25, 250 n23, 252 n58, 254 n84

al-Nas, 162
Nile Culture, 88, 240 n24
ONtv, 18, 77, 83, 89, 104, 105, 113, 201, 239 n4, 241 n25–6, 242 n47 n49 n51, 243 n61, 246 n38, 248 n4, 250–1 n31, 251 n32, 253 n64 n70, 260 n66, 261 n75 n81
Orbit Showtime Network, 18, 88, 250 n19
al-Qahira wa-l-Nas, 196, 256 n30, 258–9 n53
Rotana, 239 n3
Sada al-Balad, 262 n93
al-Tahrir, 106, 112, 129–30, 133, 234 n20, 241 n30, 243 n53 n56, 245 n32, 246 n43, 253 n77, 261 n79
al-Tareeq, 242 n50
al-Umma, 253 n69
satellite station owners
Amer, Suleiman (al-Tahrir), 130, 133
Bahgat, Ahmed (Dream TV), 19, 92, 150, 177
Ben Ammar, Tarak (ONtv), 239 n4
Nour, Tarek (al-Qahira wa-l-Nas), 258–9 n53
Okasha, Tawfiq (al-Fara'in), 150, 25 n18
Ragab, Muhammad al-Amin (CBC), 76, 177, 238 n27, 244 n19
Sawiris, Naguib (ONtv), 18, 77–80, 239 n4, 258–9 n53
satire, 6, 83–5, 163–4, 195, 205–6, 217, *see also al-Bernameg?*
Saudi Arabia, 18, 88, 182, 204, 206, 231, 239 n3, 255 n19, 256 n31
secular, 2, 146, 191, 198, 220, 256–7 n32
security apparatus/agencies, 3, 12, 19, 24–6, 29–31, 38, 42, 47, 49–50, 58, 61, 63, 67–9, 77, 79–80, 115, 131, 137, 145, 168, 181, 189, 196–7, 206, 212–13, 216, 218, 219, 221
Seif, Mona (activist), 139
Seif, Sanaa (activist), 193–4
Seif al-Islam, Ahmed (human rights lawyer), 193–4, 243 n55
Seoudy, Aida (radio announcer), 212
Shafik, Ahmed (pro-Mubarak politician, presidential candidate), 54, 57, 77–80, 128, 141, 145, 165, 226, 248 n5
shari'a, 159, 161, 163, 169
Sharm al-Sheikh, 22, 72, 76, 92, 98–9
Sharp, Gene (nonviolence advocate), 14, 37, 73
al-Shater, Khairat (Brotherhood deputy supreme guide), 159–60, 176, 179, 183, 249 n10
Shehata, Hassan (Shia spiritual leader), 173
al-Sherif, Safwat (secretary-general of Mubarak's ruling party), 48
al-Sherif, Sami (Egyptian Radio and Television Union), 88–9
Shia, 173
Shura (Consultative) Council, 30, 126, 148, 152–3, 159, 170, 180–1, 242 n43, 249 n11, 251 n43, 251–2 n45
Sinai, 18, 72, 147, 176, 183, 190, 192, 197, 208–10, 215, 226, 261 n83
singers/musicians, 81, 99, 135
Abd al-Hakim, Reham, 121–2
Eissa, Sheikh Imam, 93–94
Essam, Ramy, 66, 238–9 n44
al-Sisi, Abd al-Fattah
military intelligence chief, 194, 227
military council general, 200
defence minister, 147–8, 168, 176–7, 179–81, 183, 185–7, 190, 192, 194, 196, 199–200, 213, 227, 228, 229, 230, 247 n70, 254 n5, 255 n19, 256–7 n32, 257 n34
presidential candidate, 200–6, 230, 261–2 n71, 262 n90
president, ix, 205, 207–12, 230, 231, 256–7 n32, 257–8 n38
snipers, 9, 51, 71, 78, 167, 185, 188, 256 n26
social media, ix, 13, 15–16, 22, 31–33, 34, 42, 45, 48–9, 51, 73, 81, 87, 98, 105, 122–3, 126, 135, 138, 145, 196, 212, 214, 216, 220, 224, 237 n7, 246 n42, 250 n29, 251 n33
Soliman, Omar (intelligence chief, vice president), 25, 54, 57, 62, 67, 71, 73, 101, 143, 237 n14, 248 n5
Soltan, Mohamed (protester), 190–1
Soltan, Salah (Brotherhood leader), 190–1
songs, 9, 15, 54, 66, 95, 185–6, 194, 217, 238–9 n44
'Bil-waraqa wa-l-qalam' (With Paper and Pen), 121–2
'Guevara maat' (Che Guevara Died), 94
'Kazeboon' (Liars), 135
Spider, Ahmed (pro-Mubarak campaigner), 204
spies, 80, 91–2, 98, 123, 143, 213
Springborg, Robert (military historian), 118–21

squares, 2, 49, 88, 92–3, 153, 165, 186, 198, 213, 222
  Abbasiya Square, 94
  Giza Square, 51
  Mustafa Mahmoud Square, 61, 77
  Nahda Square, 178, 188, 257 n36, 257–8 n38
  Rab'a al-Adawiya Square, 179–80, 182–4, 186–192, 199, 257 n36, 257–8 n38
  Ramses Square, 189, 229
  Tahrir Square, 1–2, 32, 38, 40, 42–4, 51–2, 55–8, 60–74, 76–84, 90, 93–4, 115–16, 122, 125–6, 128, 134, 141, 145–6, 149–50, 151, 160, 164, 166, 196, 178, 191, 194, 195, 198, 212, 213, 224, 225, 228, 231, 238 n32 n34, 238–9 n44, 241 n31 n33, 258 n44
  Talaat Harb Square, 213
state of emergency, 167, 169, 183, 189
State Security, 2, 14, 17, 27, 30, 35, 54, 68–9, 76, 78–80, 86, 112, 126, 186, 199
state television, 11–12, 18–19, 21, 31–3, 40–1, 51–2, 54, 55–7, 61–2, 70–3, 75, 82, 86–9, 94, 98, 100, 102–5, 122–3, 134, 146, 148, 158, 181, 188, 192, 225, 241 n31
  Channel One, 19, 21, 76
  Channel Two, 31–3, 236 n52 n54, 236–7 n6
  al-Masriya, 242 n41, 246 n55
  Nile Culture, 88, 240 n24
  Nile News, 137, 247 n65
Stewart, Jon (satirist), 141, 164
Stockholm Syndrome, 77
Storyful, 61
Suez, 45, 48–50, 93, 116, 166–7
Suez Canal, 177, 210, 231
Sunni, 172
Supreme Constitutional Court, 144, 146, 152, 159, 161, 168, 181–2, 226, 228, 248 n3
Supreme Council of the Armed Forces, 71, 73, 80–82, 85–94, 98–101, 106–41, 144–8, 153, 154, 162, 177, 197–200, 217, 218, 224, 226, 227, 228, 230, 240 n20, 241 n27–8 n34, 249 n11, *see also* generals of the military council
surveillance, 80, 125, 212
Syria, 172, 184–5, 190, 196, 208, 228

Tagarud (pro-Morsi petition campaign), 171
al-Tahawy, Miral (novelist), 3, 115, 233 n4
Tahrir Square, *see* squares
Tamarod (anti-Morsi petition campaign), 171–3, 177–8, 180–1, 213, 228
Tantawi, Muhammad Hussein (defence minister, head of the military council), 55, 81, 99–100, 109, 110, 116–21, 129, 133–9, 147–8, 224, 227, 242 n42, 349 n11
al-Tayib, Sheikh Ahmed (al-Azhar's grand imam), 172–3, 181
tear gas, 42, 51–2, 94, 116–17, 131, 137, 151, 167, 169–70, 185, 188, 190, 212–13, 253 n76
tele-sheikhs , 162–3, 219–20
  Abdullah, Khaled, 162
  Abu Islam, 169
  Shaaban, Mahmoud, 169
television and radio building, 47, 55, 70, 73, 88, 102–3, 134, 146, 181, 225
television hosts
  Abd al-Rahman, Dina, 89–92, 129–30, 241 n28 n30, 246 n45
  Adeeb, Amr, 18–19, 151, 234 n23
  Adeeb, Emad Eddin, 18–19, 56–7, 162, 238 n27, 250–1 n31, 256 n31
  Ali, Abd al-Rahim, 195–6, 258–9 n53
  Ali, Sayed, 58, 238 n29
  Amin, Tamer, 31–2, 40–1
  Eissa, Ibrahim, 17–18, 106–14, 186–7, 201–2, 207, 211
  Elebrashy, Wael, 17, 257–8 n38
  Fouda, Yosri, 88–9, 104, 113–14, 127–8, 144–5, 156
  al-Gallad, Magdy, 44–6, 118–21, 202–3, 244 n19
  al-Hadidi, Lamis, 18, 201–2, 238 n21
  Kandil, Hamdy, 18, 77–80, 123, 234 n20
  Khalil, Amr, 103–4
  Magued, Reem, 89, 113, 261 n75
  Musa, Ahmed, 211–12, 253 n77, 261 n79
  Muslim, Mahmoud, 118
  Okasha, Tawfiq, 150, 25 n18
  Ramadan, Khairy, 40–1, 153–4, 158, 202–3, 204
  Saad, Mahmoud, 44, 153, 165, 254 n84
  Sharaf, Mahmoud, 44, 153, 165, 254 n84
  al-Sharqawy, Mona, 32–3
  al-Shazly, Mona, 19, 28, 43–7, 68–70, 106–11

al-Simary, Hanaa, 58, 238 n29
Sultan, Doaa, 133, 246 n52
television programmes/talk shows
48 Sa'a (48 Hours), 58
Akhir al-nahar (Day's End), 153, 252 n58, 254 n84
Akhir kalam (Last Words), 88–9, 104–5, 113–14, 127–8
'Ala al-hawa (On the Air), 18–19
Arguk ifhamni (Please Understand Me), 88
al-'Ashira misa'an (Ten at Night), 19, 43–7, 68–70, 106–11, 113
Baladna bil-masry (Our Country . . . in Egyptian), 18, 77–80, 89, 113–14
al-Bernameg? (The Programme?), 83, 158–9, 162–5, 177, 194–5, 204–6, 252 n51, 258 n52
Bihudu' (Quietly), 238 n27, 250–1 n31, 256 n31
Birnamig al-youm (The Today Show), 103–4
Fi-l-midan (In the Square), 112
Gumla mufida (Meaningful Sentence), 168
al-Hayat al-youm (Life Today), 244 n10, 253 n67
Huna al-'asima (Here Is the Capital), 234 n21
Manshet (Headlines), 105
Masr al-naharda (Egypt Today), 31–3, 40–1, 44
Masr taqarar (Egypt Decides), 118
Masr al-youm (Egypt Today), 150–1
Min qalb Masr (From the Heart of Egypt), 18
Mubashir min Masr (Live from Egypt), 100
Mumkin (Perhaps), 158
al-Qahira al-youm (Cairo Today), 18–19, 151
Qalam rusas (Pencil), 123, 234 n20, 245 n32
Ra'is al-tahrir (Editor-in-Chief), 18
Sabah Dream (Dream Morning), 89–92
Sabahak ya Masr (Your Morning, Egypt), 149–50
al-Sanduq al-aswad (Black Box), 195–6, 258–9 n53
Sawt Masr (The Voice of Egypt), 134
Shari' al-kalam (The Street of Words), 88–9
Talk Shows, 133, 246 n52
terrorism, ix, 38, 72, 185, 188, 190–2, 201, 208, 210, 217, 219, 229, 231
text messaging, 14, 48, 54, 61, 66
theatre, x, 3, 4, 75, 195, 205, 218
thuggery, 86, 88, 96, 133–4, 157
Tunisia, 33–5, 37, 39, 53, 58, 66, 224
Twitter, 28, 42, 44, 46, 48–50, 65, 85, 87, 99, 108, 153, 166, 170, 173, 187, 238 n37

Ultras (hard-core football fans), 39, 62, 122–3, 127, 136
underground music, 15–16, 135
United Arab Emirates, 182, 213, 248 n5, 255 n19
United States, 1, 6, 16, 18, 23, 57–8, 90–1, 105, 119, 121, 182, 184, 187, 191, 196, 208, 211, 235 n26, 248 n5
embassy cables, 11–12, 23, 25, 235 n46
universities, 1–3, 15–16, 25, 76, 78, 138, 146, 169, 178, 180, 198–9, 203, 209–10

wars, 22–3, 59, 82, 143, 145, 160, 259 n56
in Iraq, 1–2, 18, 42
October 1973 War, 17–18, 299
Six Day War (1967), 215
Wasfi, Ahmed (general), 177
Welch, David (US assistant secretary of state), 34
WikiLeaks, 231, *see also* United States, embassy cables
WikiThawra, 260 n70
Writers and Artists for Change, 131

Yemen, 65
Youssef, Bassem (satirist), 83–85, 158–9, 162–5, 177, 184–5, 194–5, 204–6, 217, 230, 258 n51
YouTube, 13, 15, 28, 30, 39, 42–3, 48–9, 61, 83–5, 121–3, 132–3, 166, 173–4, 181, 205

Zappa, Frank, 75
Zewail, Ahmed (Nobel Prize-winning chemist), 54
Zionist, 58, 150, 207, 208, 211, 215, 251 n33

RISJ/I.B.TAURIS PUBLICATIONS

CHALLENGES

Innovators in Digital News
Lucy Küng
ISBN: 978 1 78453 416 5

Journalism and PR: News Media and Public Relations in the Digital Age
John Lloyd and Laura Toogood
ISBN: 978 1 78453 062 4

Reporting the EU: News, Media and the European Institutions
John Lloyd and Cristina Marconi
ISBN: 978 1 78453 065 5

Women and Journalism
Suzanne Franks
ISBN: 978 1 78076 585 3

Climate Change in the Media: Reporting Risk and Uncertainty
James Painter
ISBN: 978 1 78076 588 4

Transformations in Egyptian Journalism
Naomi Sakr
ISBN: 978 1 78076 589 1

BOOKS

Media, Revolution and Politics in Egypt: The Story of an Uprising
Abdalla F. Hassan
ISBN: 978 1 78453 217 8 (HB); 978 1 78453 218 5 (PB)

The Euro Crisis in the Media: Journalistic Coverage of Economic Crisis and European Institutions
Robert G. Picard (ed.)
ISBN: 978 1 78453 059 4 (HB); 978 1 78453 060 0 (PB)

Local Journalism: The Decline of Newspapers and the Rise of Digital Media
Rasmus Kleis Nielsen (ed.)
ISBN: 978 1 78453 320 5 (HB); 978 1 78453 321 2 (PB)

The Ethics of Journalism: Individual, Institutional and Cultural Influences
Wendy N. Wyatt (ed.)
ISBN: 978 1 78076 673 7 (HB); 978 1 78076 674 4 (PB)

Political Journalism in Transition: Western Europe in a Comparative Perspective
Raymond Kuhn and Rasmus Kleis Nielsen (eds)
ISBN: 978 1 78076 677 5 (HB); 978 1 78076 678 2 (PB)

Transparency in Politics and the Media: Accountability and Open Government
Nigel Bowles, James T. Hamilton and David A. L. Levy (eds)
ISBN: 978 1 78076 675 1 (HB); 978 1 78076 676 8 (PB)

Media and Public Shaming: Drawing the Boundaries of Disclosure
Julian Petley (ed.)
ISBN: 978 1 78076 586 0 (HB); 978 1 78076 587 7 (PB)

Caer
The Celtic Night Sky

Michael Bayley

Caer Sídhe
The Celtic Night Sky

ISBN 1 898307 74 1

Cover design by Paul Mason

Published by:

Capall Bann Publishing
Julia & Jon Day
Auton Farm, Milverton
Somerset, TA4 1NE
Tel 01823 401528
Fax 01823 401529
www.capallbann.co.uk

Contents

Foreword 1

Chapter 1 The Celtic Night Sky **3**

The Star Maps 12

Chapter 2 The Twenty-one Northern Constellations **23**

Andromeda xx 26

Aquila xvi 27

The Fawcon Hath Born My Mak Away 27

Auriga xii 31

Bootes v 33

Cassiopeia x 41

Cephus IV 55

Corona Borealis vi 57

Cygnus ix 62

Delphinus xvii 65

Draco iii 67

Equuelus xviii 73

Hercules vii 75

Lyra viii 89

Pegasus xix 90

Perseus xi 103

Sagitta xv 105

Serpens xiv 106

Serpentarius xiii 109

Triangulum xxi 112

Ursa Major II 113

Ursa Minor I 129

Chapter 3 The 12 or 16 or 27 Constellations of the Zodiac **131**

The Year and The Twelve Zodiacal Constellations 132

Aries I 137

Aquarius XI 141

Cancer IV 143

Capricornus XI 145

Gemini II 149

The Hyades 152

Leo V 153

Libra VII 159
Pisces XII 161
The Pleiades 163
Sagittarius IX 169
Scorpio VIII 170
Taurus II and the Pleiades 173
Virgo VI 177
Corn Dollies 179
Chapter 4 The Seven or Fifteen Southern Constellations 184
Ara XIII 185
Argo VII 185
Canis Major V 187
Canis Minor VI 189
Centaurus XI 189
Cetus I 189
Corona Australis XIV 190
Corvus X 191
Crater IX 192
Eridanus III 193
Hydra VIII 193
Lepus IV 195
Lupus XII 197
Orion II 199
Piscis Australis XV 204
The Galaxy or Milky Way 205
The Moving Stars 207
The Moon (Luna) 211
Mars 217
Mercury 219
Jupiter 221
Venus 223
Saturn 229
The Sun (Sol) 233
The Earth 237
Bibliography 238
Index 239

Foreword

The Celtic tribes of ancient Western Europe saw nearly the same night sky as we do, only it was clearer, with no industrial haze or light pollution. The constellations were the same, but they were interpreted in a different way with different names.

We can re-create their night sky if we can give their names to the constellations we know. There are four ways that this can be done.

The first and most obvious way is from ancient manuscript sources, telling of the legendary deeds of ancient kings - heroes and gods. The glosses added by early scribes and commentators help us here.

The second way is by noting the alternative names of constellations and the way classical writers equated their gods to those of the Celts.

The third way is by the interpretation of the acts and descriptions of Celtic and other Deities.

The fourth way is by linking stars or constellations with Deities through certain dates or times of the year and astronomical events.

However, since the astronomical knowledge of ancient Britain had as many sources as Britain had invaders, refugees, travellers, immigrants and traders, there is often more than one name or story connected with each constellation.

One must remember that Britain was not an isolated backwater. Some two to three thousand years ago Britain sent her Hyperborean priestesses to serve in the temple at Delos in Greece. The great Greek mathematician Pythagoras travelled to France to study with the Gaulish Druids, who told him that the source of their knowledge was in Britain. This shows that there was an exchange of scientific knowledge and of religious ideas between Britain and the Mediterranean in antiquity.

It has been suggested that Druidical astronomy evolved its very accurate calendar from their observations from Dene Holes. In legend these are described as Merlin's airy tower, in which he was imprisoned. They are deep vertical holes, 20ft to 40ft deep, that an agile man may climb into and out of by bracing his back one side and walking up or down the tube. Merlin was imprisoned as he was too old to climb out unaided, having descended to explain the mysteries of the heavens to Nimue. At this depth all reflected light is excluded, and stellar observations can be made in daylight. They must have evolved from the flint mines. Such an observatory would scan a different sweep of the heavens every night, repeating the same sweep twice a year. Hence the Celtic calendar was split into two halves - the light half and the dark half, divided by the Solstices. It was a stellar year set by annual meteor showers, and was therefore more accurate than any other early calendar. This idea survived into modern times as a cog almanac.

Chapter 1

The Celtic Night Sky

This is a study of the Astronomy and Astrology of Pre-Classical north western Europe, from surviving records and artefacts, archaeology, folklore, and the pursuit of logical answers to awkward questions. It includes star maps of both the traditional classical constellations, and of the known and probably pre-Classical or Celtic constellations. It also shows how the wandering pole has altered the area of night sky visible from any particular place over the last few thousand years.

The first awkward question is, why do all our pictorial representations of the constellations of the night sky show the Great or Little Bears with huge tails, when anyone who has seen a bear knows that bears don't have tails? To put it down to the general ignorance of the population won't do, as bears were almost as well known predators across Europe as wolves, and remained so with the help of bear-baiting and dancing bears until at least the end of the medieval period.

The answer to this awkward question is to be found in Greek myths. Isn't that a bit far away from the Celts of western Europe; you may ask? The answer here must be no. The Doric Greeks were part of the great wave of Celtic tribes that swept westward and southward over Europe during the two millennia BC. Even today the Welsh and Greek languages have many words in common and in the ancient world there was relatively rapid communication by boat from the Aegean Sea to the Atlantic coasts and Britain, so that a first century writer could recall that in the 5th century BC Hyperborean priestesses from Apollo's shrine, at what we now call Stonehenge in Wiltshire, regularly visited another of Apollo's shrines at Tempe in a valley near Mount Olympus, home of the Greek gods. In later times, Tempe became a centre for Pythagorean learning, which included mathematics, magic or perhaps religion, and astrology. The Athenian Greeks held a festival in honour of Artemis called the Brauronia, in which a big girl of ten, and a small girl of 5, dressed in saffron yellow robes, played the part of the Moon Goddesss attendant bears, and savagely chased boys from the festival procession.

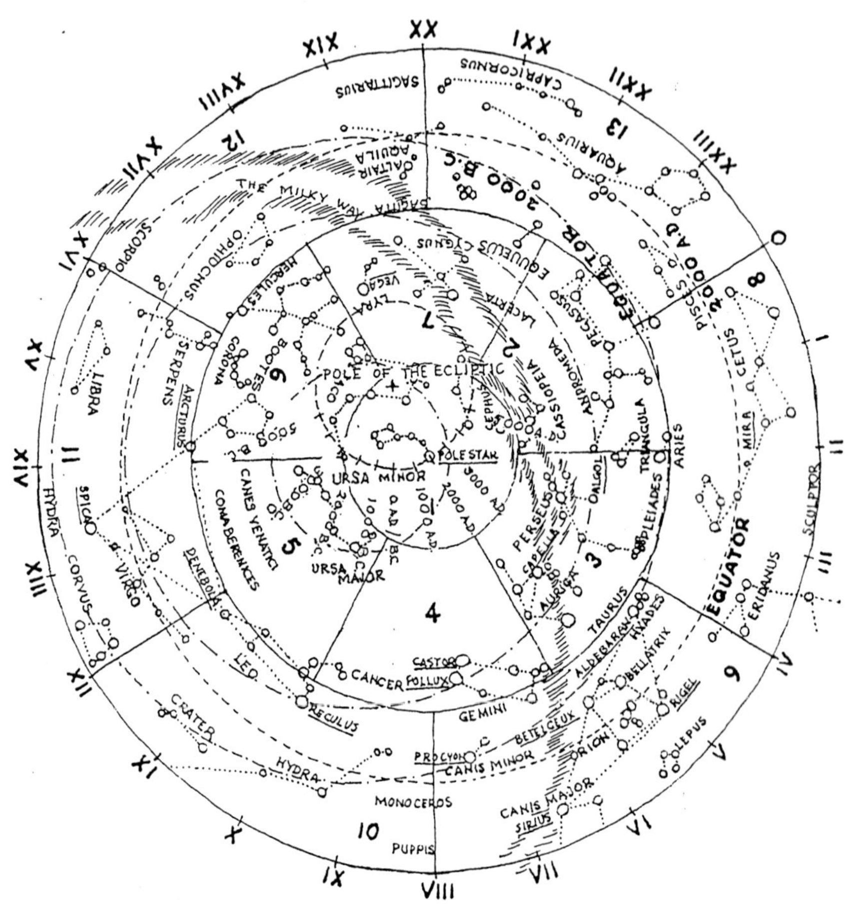

THE NORTHERN SKY EXTENDED 25° SOUTH OF THE EQUATOR

Arabic numerals denote regions

Roman numerals denote Right Ascention.

Map 4. How the moving pole alters the area of sky visible

The origin of these two bears is told in the Arcadian legend of Callisto, daughter of Lycaon the king of Arcadia. Her name means Most Beautiful, and she had sworn to remain a maiden and to serve the goddess Artemis as one of her companions in the hunt. However, her beauty attracted Zeus and he lay with her against her will and she conceived a son. Some say that it was to conceal her from Hera's notice that Zeus changed her into a bear. Others say that Hera, jealous of her beauty, changed Callisto into a bear herself. Anyhow, Hera was not to be fooled, and she encouraged Artemis to shoot Callisto in the form of a bear. However, Hermes, the conductor of dead souls, was instructed by Zeus to save Callisto or to change her into the constellation of the Great Bear. He also saved the life of her son, who in turn became King Arcas of Arcadia, but was later changed into the Constellation of the Little Bear. It was King Arcas who introduced the art of agriculture to the people of Arcadia, as Bootes did elsewhere in Greece and Hu Gadarn did in Wales.

These Arcadian legends at least start us off on the quest for clues as to the original nature of the polar constellations. The Great Bear was originally a beautiful nubile woman called Callisto, and was also connected with the introduction of agriculture. We can, therefore, take it that it was the priesthood of the Olympian Gods who organised the acceptance of the northern polar constellations as bears, even if their form made it necessary to invent tails to use up the stars available. But the peasantry in Arcadia coming from the stock of early inhabitants, still knew that those same stars had once represented a woman or goddess.

Our next clue comes from nearer home with the legend of the Gaulish corn goddess Berecynthia, who is sometimes equated with Cybele the Great Mother goddess of Phrygia. She came west with those pre-Dorian Greek settlers from the Aegean, the Milesians, between 1200 and 1500 BC. Irish legend tells us the Milesians sailed west to Spain and then to Britain, and that Queen Bera came from Spain. Queen Bera is otherwise known as the Hag of Beara or the Old Woman of Bere who had seven periods of youth. Bere is a primitive form of Barley which gives us another link with agriculture, at least in the languages of Britain. Perhaps there is a link between BERE and BEAR.

The earliest legends we have of Berecynthia tell us that her name derives from the mountain Berecyntus in Phrygia, the country in Asia Minor of the legendary Trogian War. She was the goddess of the Berecynthians, and was also called Cybele.

To complicate matters, it was on another mountain with nearly the same name as Cybele, Mount Cynthus in Delos, that Apollo and Diana were born, which is

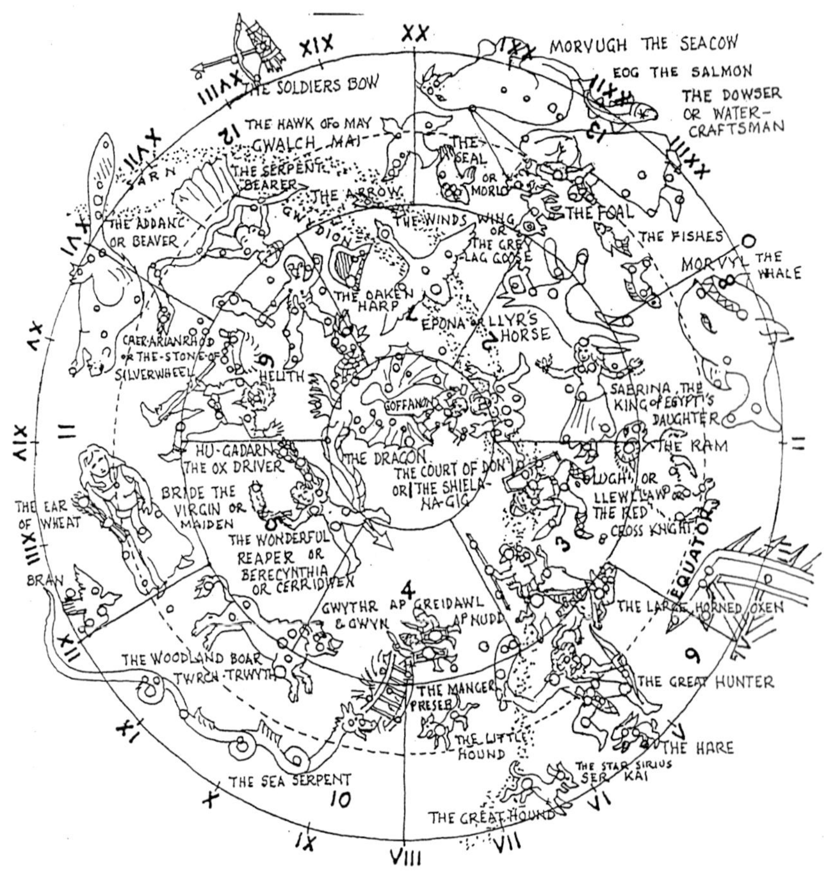

THE NORTHERN SKY EXTENDED 25° SOUTH OF THE EQUATOR

Arabic numerals denote regions

Roman numerals denote Right Ascention.

Map 2. The Celtic Constellations seen from Britain

why Diana is also called Cynthia, as a moon goddess. Diana was the Latin or Roman name for Artemis whose companion became the constellation of the Great Bear in Arcadian legend.

Fortunately, the people of the ancient Greek world were good at producing lifelike representations of their gods and goddesses and heroes, so that even today after millennia of religious wars and suppressions we still know how Berecynthia or Astante was pictured. She was said to ride round the heavens every night on the back of her dragon - or in her chariot drawn by dragons, and as Cybele she was the Great Mother of all gods and men of all life. In the Roman world she was equated with the Bona Dea and Demeter, the corn goddess. Now the constellations that ride round the night sky every night on the back of the Dragon Constellation are the constellations of the Great Bear and Little Bear, so if the Great Bear was once a woman, she was Berecynthia.

Here we must make a round trip via the British calendar to Imperial Rome and Asia Minor, and the town of Bethlehem in Palestine, to show how the Great Goddess has shaped our world as is still there for all to see.

To any agricultural community it is important to be able to keep track of the seasons, and the passage of time, in spite of unseasonable weather, so that seeds are planted at the correct time. Before the advent of printing, or even of writing on parchment, men still had to have some method of counting the days of the year accurately. In Britain this was done with the aid of a cog almanac, a squared up billet of wood with notches cut down the four arises, one for each day of the year, with a system of numbering, and carried pictorial signs to denote important feast days and festivals. Since the name Cog Almanac means The Almanac of our grandfathers or ancestors in Cornish, it probably originated in Celtic speaking times. Further, since none of the feast days or festivals marked coincide with the solstices or equinoxes, it is unlikely to be a solar calendar. Since at least half of the feasts and festivals shown fall on the eve, or day or morrow of an annual meteor shower, the calendar is shown to be based on stellar observations, which incidentally makes it more accurate than the Christian Gregorian Calendar, or of the Roman Julian one that preceded it.

Most surviving cog almanacs date from the 18th century, which was one thousand three hundred years after the introduction of Christianity to this country, and 1400 years after the end of the Roman Empire, yet only 62% of the signs denote Christian feast days alone and 71% denote Roman or Pagan Celtic feast days. Some signs of course show days which were both Christian and Pagan feasts.

This suggests that the cog almanac has been in use for a very long time. One sign in fact suggests that it dates back to at least Roman times, and this is the sign that can be interpreted as an empty bed frame, to mark St Lawrence's day on 10th August. This has been explained by the apocryphal story that St Lawrence was martyred by being roasted alive on a brass bedstead outside the gates of Rome. The Church has rightly disowned this story, as St Lawrence being a Roman Citizen would have been put to death by the sword. But the 10th August was the day of the annual holiday of the Prostitutes of Rome, when the bed of Venus was left empty, hence the sign on the Cog Almanac, which doubtless gave rise to the apocryphal story.

The start of the year as shown by our modern calendars is 1st January throughout the world. Conveniently it lies in the dead and uneventful part of the year when the celebration of Christmas is over and cleared up. It is only the Celts of this island, the Scottish ones, that still insist on celebrating at new year. They also insist on calling Christmas Little Nativity Day, and Lady Day Great Nativity Day, but tactfully they only do this in the Gaelic. Until the calendar reform of the 18th century the year started on Lady Day throughout Britain. In fact, in the City of London, and in every financial establishment of this country even today, it still does so. The financial year runs not from January 1st but from April 5th which, allowing for the eleven days lost in the calendar reforms, is 25th March or Lady Day Old Style.

Of all the days in the year, surely new years day must have been one of the most important, and 25th March is probably the easiest day in the year to fix from an annual meteor shower. There is a one night meteor shower from the direction of the forefoot of the Great Bear or between the thighs of Berecynthia/Cybele or Cerridwen on the night of 24-25 March, which is probably why the Scots still call it Great Nativity Day. This is the time of the Phrygian festival Cybele, and the re-birth of Attis Adonis, also celebrated in Rome. It was about the time of Passover to the Jews, and of the Greater Dionysia for the Ancient Greeks and of the Annunciation of the Blessed Virgin to Christians. It is probable that it was also celebrated as Easter in the early British Church.

Having shown that the start of the year throughout the Old World was marked by a one day meteor shower from the direction of the constellation, we have shown to represent Berecynthia and Cybele, the Mother of the Gods, which the Scots call Great Nativity Day, we shall now look at what fixes Little Nativity Day. Actually Christmas, 25th December, is not marked by any meteors, but there is a two night meteor shower between December 20th and 22nd from the direction of the Constellation of the Little Bear, and this period covers the Winter Solstice and the Roman Saturualia and the Opelia in honour of the goddess Ops, who we earlier saw that the Romans equated with Cybele and therefore Berecynthia and the Cailleach. This is obviously why the Scots called this time of the year Little Nativity Day long before the birth of Christ was declared to have happened on 25th December.

In the pages that follow we have listed the classical constellations, and related their stories and have shown, where possible, how these are related to Celtic stories, gods and heroes, some of which may pre-date the Celts. In some cases we have been able to reconstruct the figures that the constellations represented to the eyes of our ancestors two millennia and more ago. But as the stories evolved, and religions changed, so the pictures in the stars have changed, and some constellations were pictured in more than one way, the Plough or Great Bear in particular.

One of the later Welsh bards whose works have survived went by the name of Taliesin. In one of his poems he refers to his original country as the region of the summer stars. Some commentators have suggested that this refers to the other world, or the stars of the southern skies. But it could also mean that he felt at home in the lands where the stars only seen in Britain in the summer are seen all the year round, and that he had travelled to the south of France, or Spain or Greece.

Alternatively, and perhaps more likely, it may be that the phrase translated as the region of the summer stars, that is "*bro ser hefin*", by one authority, and as "*bro Gerubim*", the region of the Cherubim by another, may actually have been intended to be read as something like BRO GER UGHE BEN, that is "the region of the high head or chief". This could be interpreted as the region below the Great goddess of the pole, and which recognised her. That is, the lands that recognised Don, the Cailleach or Cerridwen in all her phases.

From various ancient books of Celtic history, myth or folklore, we know the names of the constellations that Merlin and Taliesin saw in the sky, and we know the classical names of some of them, but not all of them. The following list shows the usual Welsh or English translation of these names, but of course some may have been mis-translated for one reason or another. After this the classical name follows where it is known, or can be guessed at.

1 Caer Arianrhod or The Court of Silver Wheel - Corona Borealis or The Northern Crown.
2 The White Throne - the star Spica in Virgo the Virgin
3 Telyn Idris or Arthur's Harp - Lyra
4 Caer Gwydion or The Court of Gwydion - The Milky Way or Galaxy

5 Arthurs Plough Tail - The Great Bear or Ursa Major
6 The Little Ploughtail - the Little Bear of Ursa Minor
7 The Great Ship or Prydwen or Arthur's Ship Navis
8 The Bald Ship
9 Arthur's Yard or Wain - Orion
10 Twr Tewdws or Theodosus Groups - The Pleiades
11 The Triangle - Triangulum
12 Llys Don or The Palace or Court of Don - Casseopea
13 The Grove of Blodeuwedd - possibly the Milky Way
14 The Chair of Teyrnon
15 The Court of Eiddionydd
16 Caer Sidi or the revolving castle - The Zodiac
17 The Conjunction of 100 circles
18 The Camp of Elmar
19 The Soldiers Bow - Sagittarius
20 The Hill of Dinan or the tumulus of Dirinon or the grave of St Non
21 The Eagles Nest
22 Bleiddyd's Lever or Bleidad's Lever
23 The Winds Wing - Cygnus - the Grey Lag Goose
24 The Trefoil
25 The Cauldron of Cerridwen - possibly the constellations of the pole
26 Teivis Bend
27 The Great Limb
28 The Small Limb
29 The Large Horned Oxen - The Twins or The Bull
30 The Great Plain or Sarn Gwydion - The Milky Way
31 The White Fork - The Pole Star
32 The Woodland Boar - Twrch Twyth - Leo
33 The Muscle
34 The Hawk - Aquila
35 The Horse of Llyr - Pegasus
36 Elphin's Chair
37 Olwen's Hall

It is the purpose of this book to try to show us more of the night sky as Taliesin may have pictured it, and to show how he and his predecessors may have acquired their knowledge, how they kept track of time, and organised their calendar, and how they passed their knowledge on to other parts of the world and other times.

Map 4 at the front of this chapter shows how the pole, the point about which the heavens appear to revolve, has moved through the constellation we call Draco the dragon from about 5000 BC until some 2500 BC, since when it has passed by the length of Ursa Minor, and is now near the tip of its tail. This has altered the number of constellations visible from this country over the millennia.

Map 1, which follows this chapter, shows the relative positions of the constellations with their traditional names derived from classical mythology. Map 2 shows the same map of the stars of the heavens, but with the names by which the Celtic tribes of Britain probably knew them. Lists of the names of the Celtic constellations have survived, but how accurate these are, and whether all the attributions are correct, we will probably never know. The possibilities and probable origins of each name are set out in the following chapters under the traditional classical name of the constellation. It is probable that the names of constellations, and the way they were pictured varied over time and with the movement of tribes and also the development of their technology religion and forms of government, but some of the stories are shared by peoples half a continent and a millennia or more apart.

The classical star maps of Europe appear, from omissions in the southern areas, to have been mapped out by about 2400 BC.

In around 370 BC Eudoxus, a pupil of Plato, brought a celestial globe to Greece, presumably from the Middle East or India.

By 260 BC a Cilican poet called Aratus tells us in his writings that most of the constellations had their present classical names and that the northern constellations were known as The Bears.

It, therefore, seems likely that the Celtic constellations date from before the Celts arrived in the British Isles.

The Star Maps

Map	1	The Traditional Constellations seen from Britain	13
	2	The Celtic Constellations seen from Britain	6
	3	The Celtic Constellations of Hu-Gadarn	14
	4	How the moving pole alters the area of sky visible	4
	5	The Traditional Constellations in Winter	15
	6	The Celtic Constellations in Winter	16
	7	The Traditional Constellations in Spring	17
	8	The Celtic Constellations in Spring	18
	9	The Traditional Constellations in Summer	19
	10	The Celtic Constellations in Summer	20
	11	The Traditional Constellations in Autumn	21
	12	The Celtic Constellations in Autumn	22

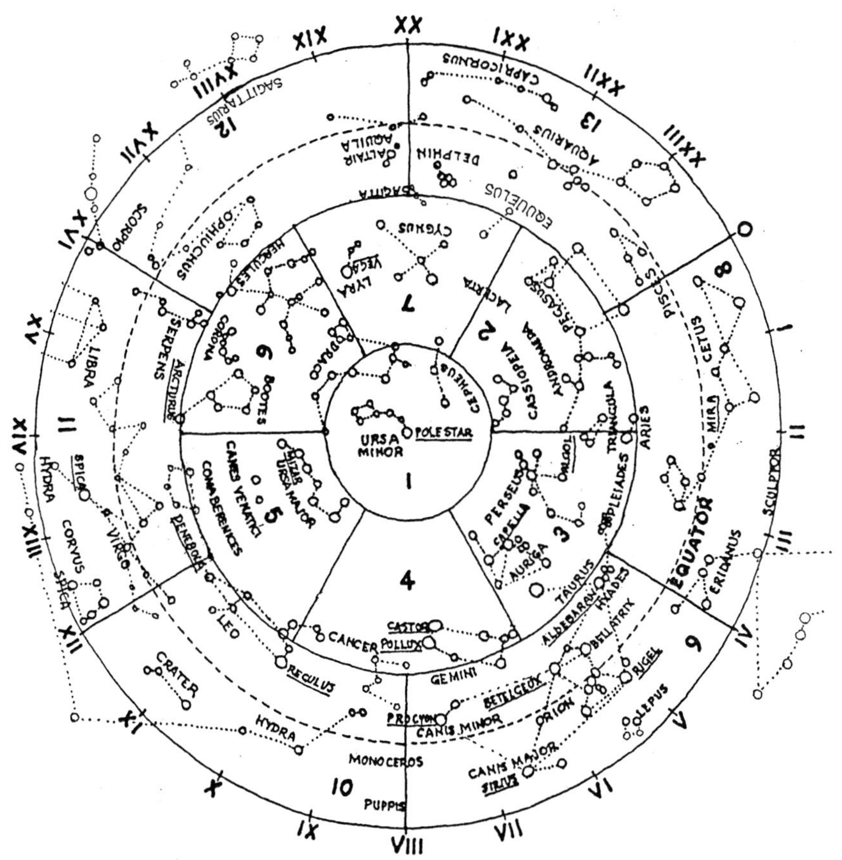

THE NORTHERN SKY EXTENDED 25° SOUTH
OF THE EQUATOR

Arabic numerals denote regions
Roman numerals denote Right Ascention.

Map 1. The Traditional Constellations seen from Britain

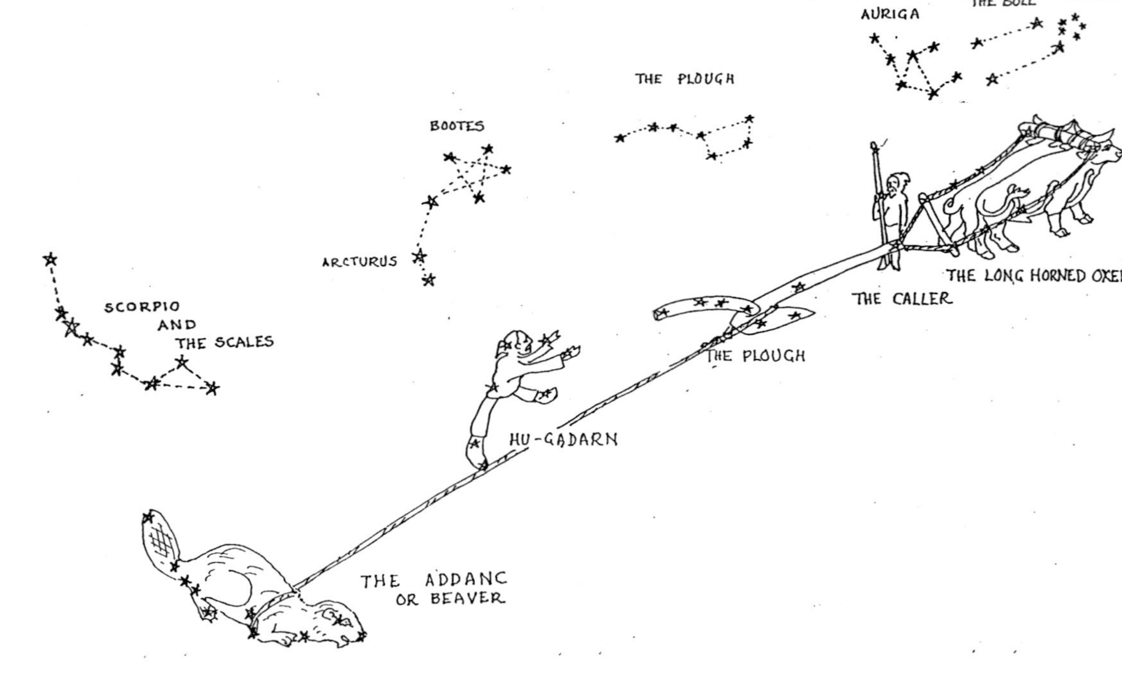

Map 3. The Celtic Constellations of Hu-Gadarn

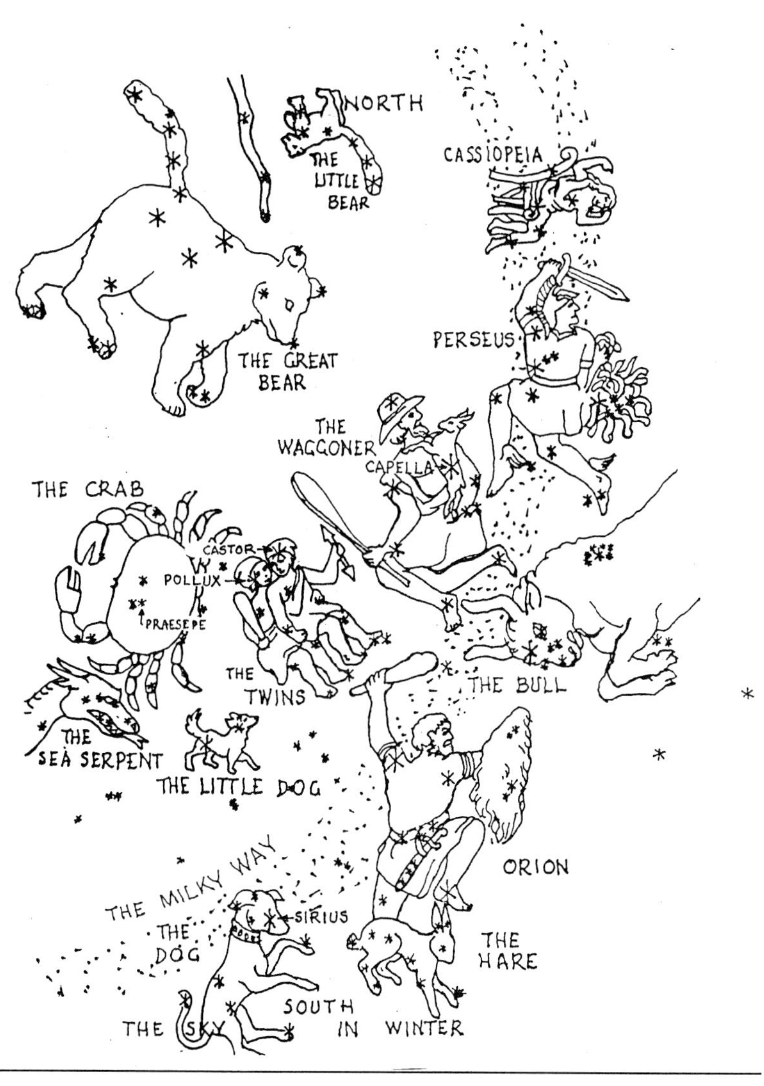

Map 5. The Traditional Constellations in Winter

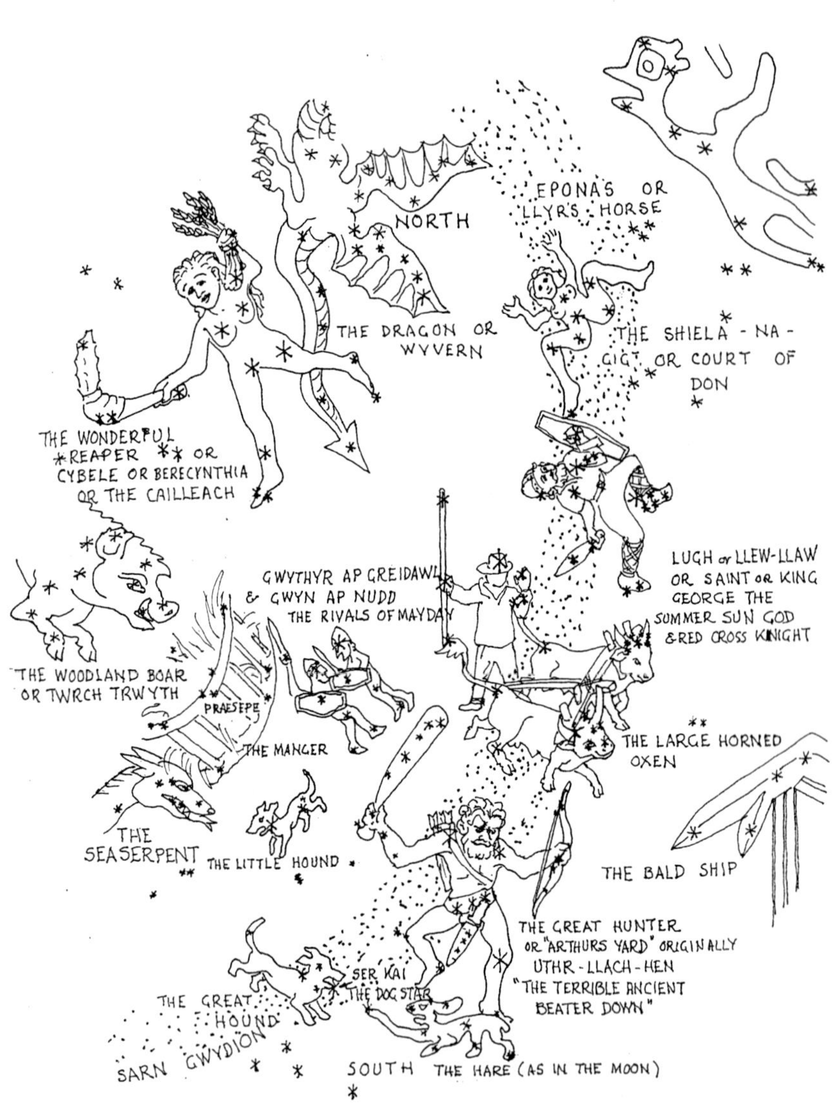

Map 6. The Celtic Constellations in Winter

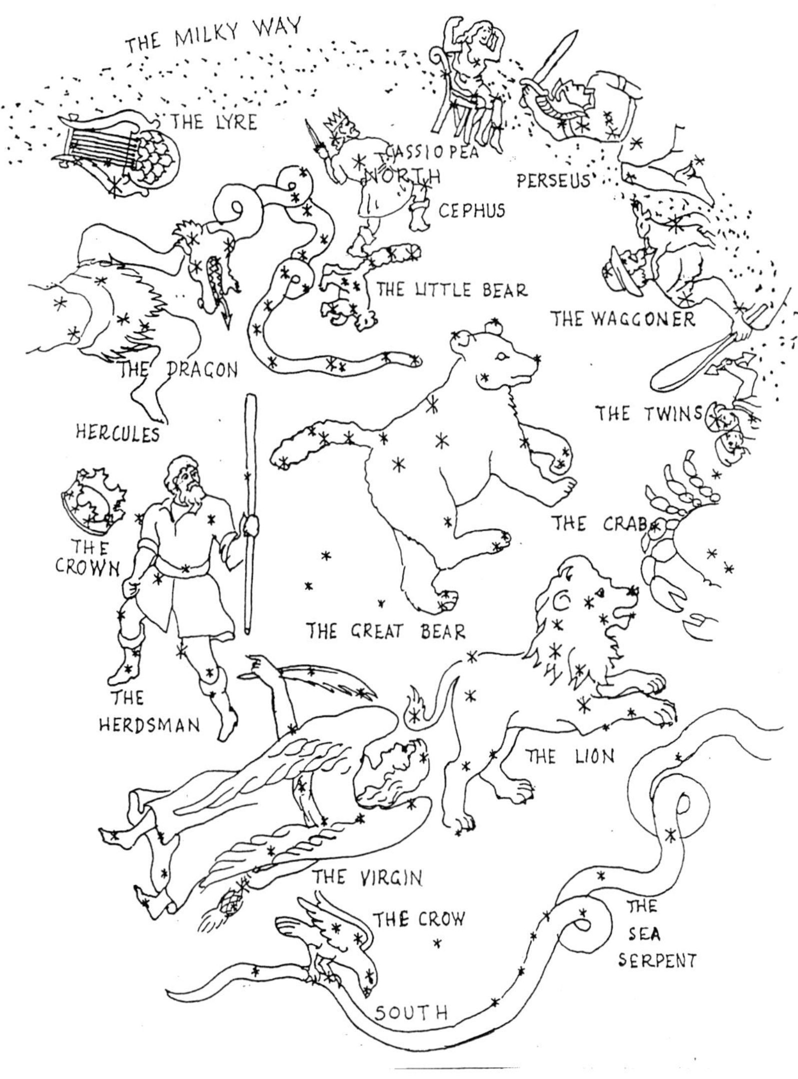

Map 7. The Traditional Constellations in Spring

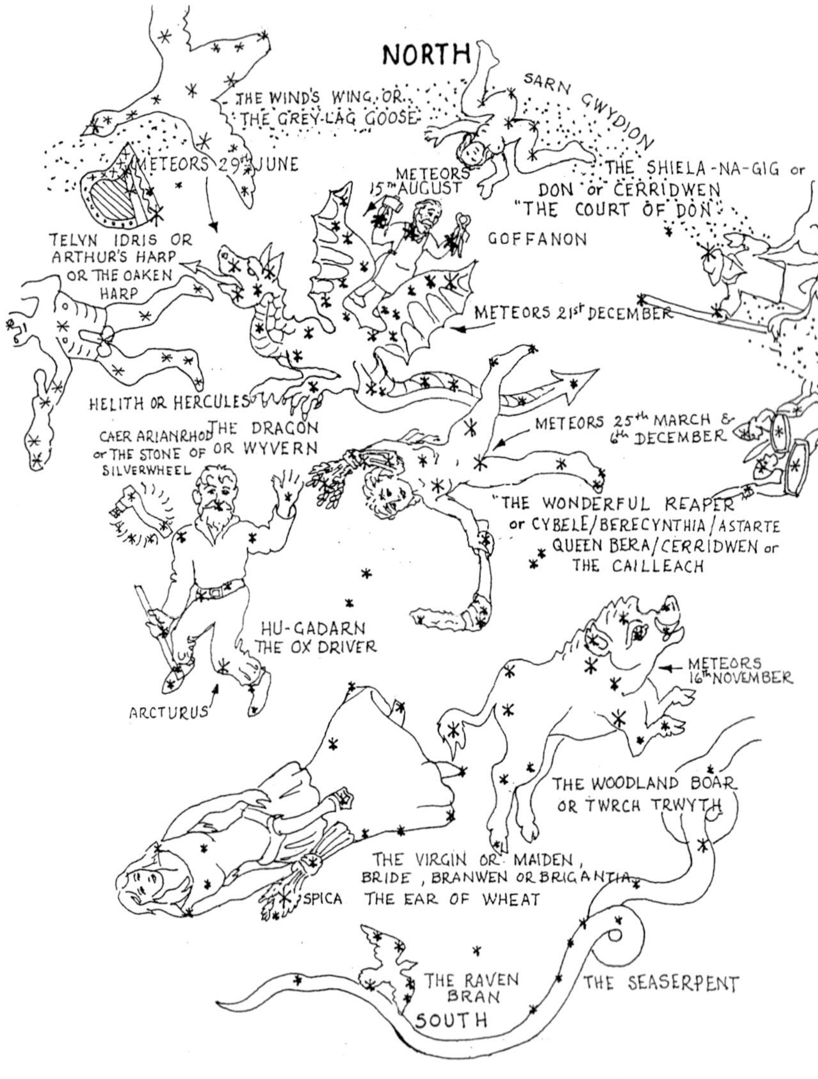

Map 8. The Celtic Constellations in Spring

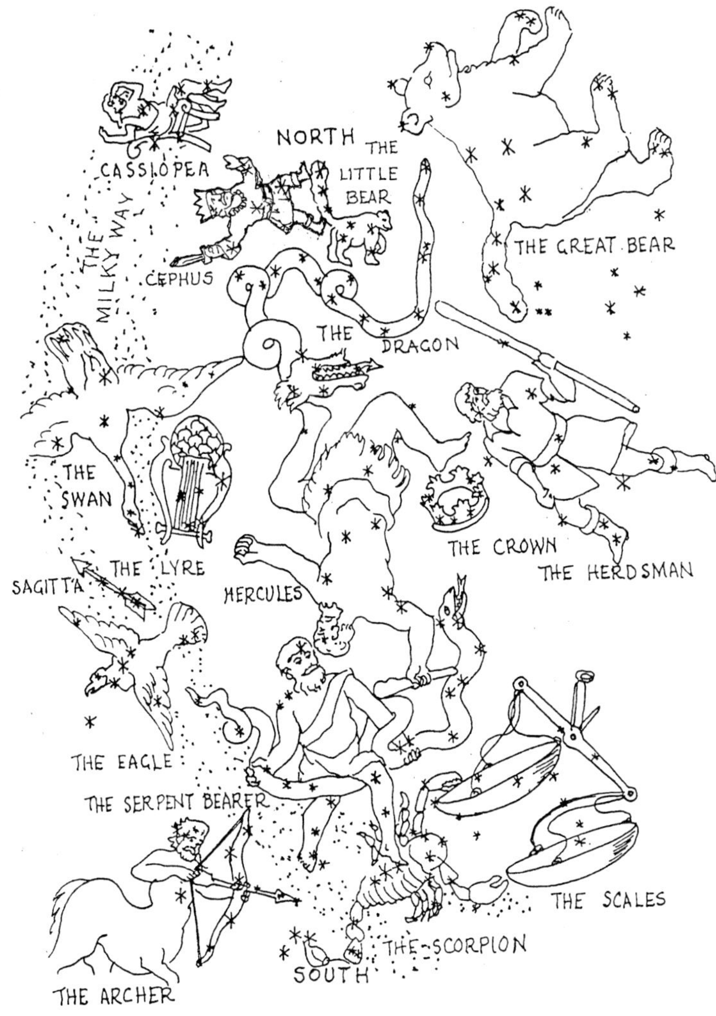

Map 9. The Traditional Constellations in Summer

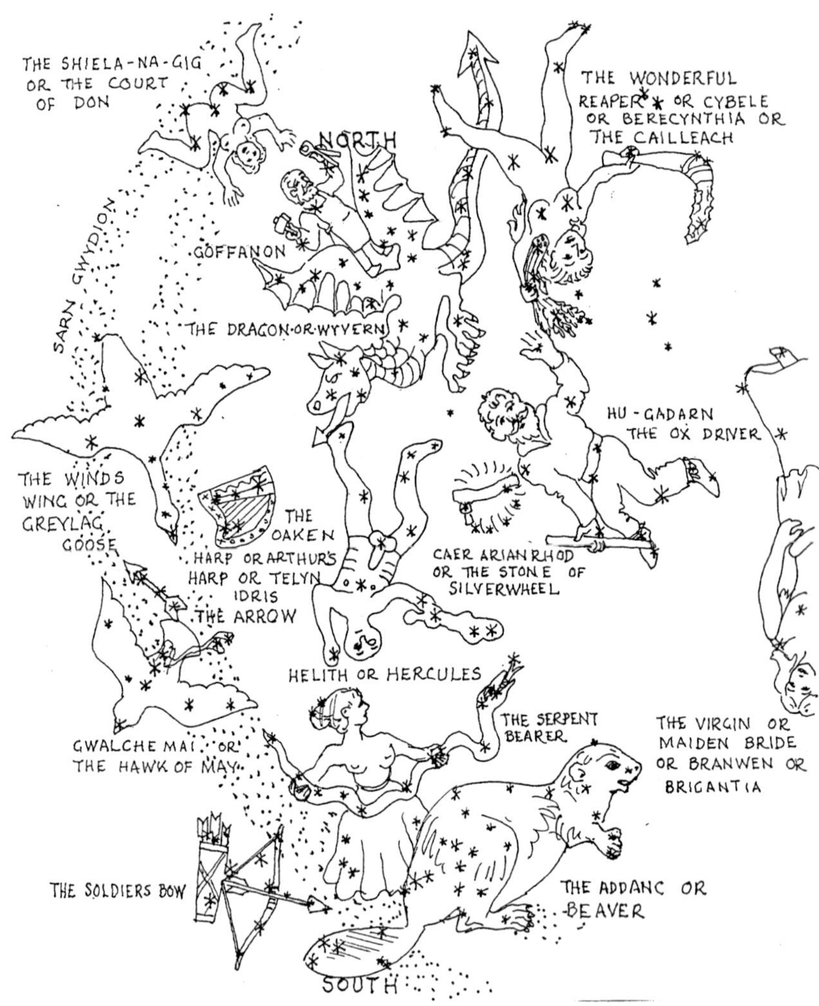

Map 10. The Celtic Constellations in Summer

Map 11. The Traditional Constellations in Autumn

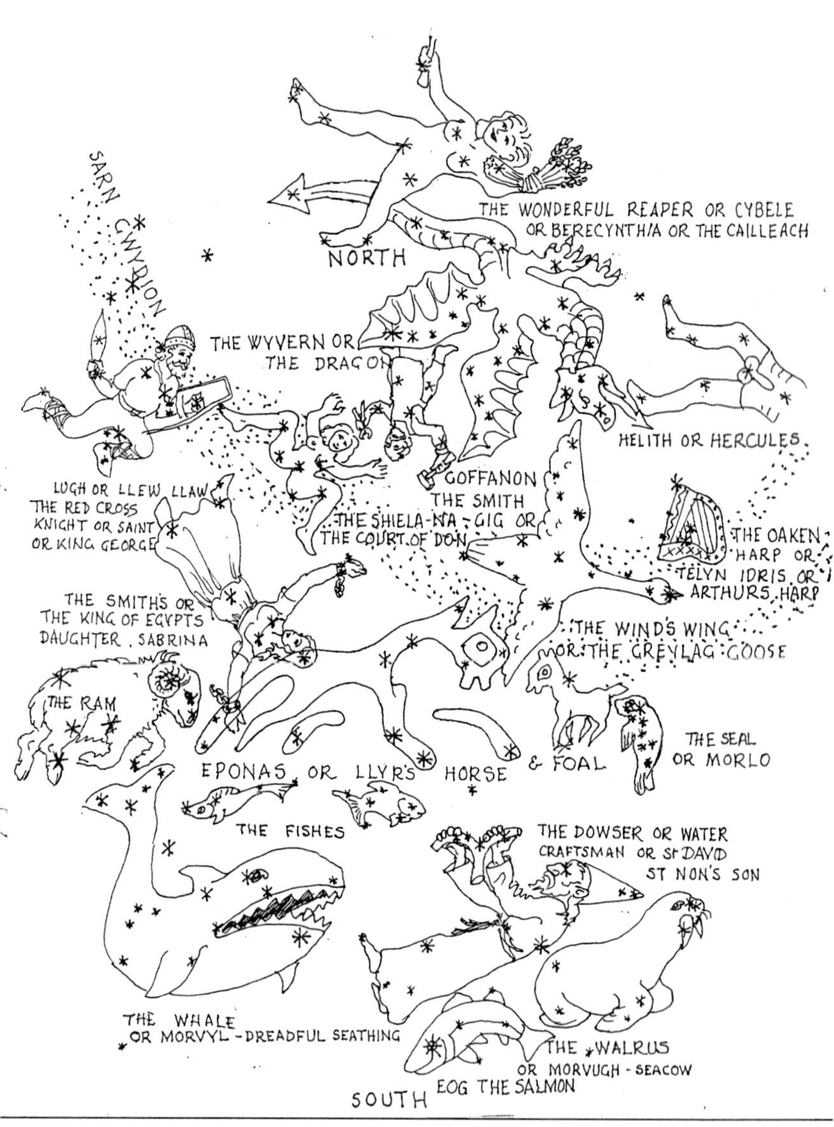

Map 12. The Celtic Constellations in Autumn

Chapter 2

The Twenty-one Northern Constellations

These constellations are listed alphabetically under their normal modern names. This is followed by the names used by earlier astronomers, as these sometimes show a different name. The first name being the name used by Ulugh Beg, the second that used by Tycho Brahe. Then follows the English translation of the name. The number given after the name signifies the position of the constellation in the normal list of constellations. In the alphabetical list as follows, the Arabic numrals denote the region, the Roman numerals the Right Ascension on the circular star maps.

The Location	The Traditional Name	The English Translation
2 - I	Andromeda	The Maiden or Princess
12/13 - XX	Aquila	The Eagle
3 - V	Auriga	The Charioteer or Wagoner
6 - XV	Bootes	The Ploughman
2 - I	Casseopea	The Seated Queen
1/7 - XXI	Cyphus	The King and Husband of Casseopea
6 - XVI	Corona Borealis	The Northern Crown
1/7 - XXII	Cygnus	The Swan
13 - XXI	Delphinus	The Dolphin
1/6 - XVII	Draco	The Dragon
7/13 - XXII	Equuelus	The Colt
6 - XVII	Hercules	The Kneeling Man
7 - XIX	Lyra	The Lyre
2/13 - XXIII	Pegasus	The Horse
3 - IV	Perseus	The Warrior
7/13 - XX	Sagitta	The Arrow
11 - XVI	Serpeus	The Serpent

THE MILKY WAY
CASSIOPEA OR THE SHIELA-NA-GIG OR THE COURT OF DON
SARN GWYDION
ANDROMEDA OR THE KING OF EGYPT'S DAUGHTER SABRINA
PERSEUS OR LUGH OR LLEW LLAW OR THE RED CROSS KNIGHT SAINT OR KING - GEORGE

12 - XVII	Serpentarius	The Serpent Bearer
2/3 - II	Triangulum	The Triangle
5 - XII	Ursa Major	The Great Bear
1 - XVI	Ursa Minor	The Little Bear

Andromeda XX

Mulieris catenatae
Andromeda

Andromeda is the Maiden or Princess daughter of Queen Casseopea and King Cephus (see Cephus for the story). She was rescued from Cetus the sea monster by Perseus. This story is re-told in British Mummers plays as the rescue of the King of Egypt's daughter Sabrina by Saint or King George who killed the dragon in a dreadful fight.

The name given to The Maiden or Andromeda in Britain, Sabrina, is probably just a description of her in the old British language. Saben Rhiain Nare which sounds similar and means "The fir tree queen on high". In the Irish Ogham alphabet of trees, Ailim is the tree of the winter solstice, the silver fir tree, which is sacred to the Greek goddess Artemis and the Roman Diana, goddess of the hunt. In bird Ogham it is the tree of the magpie, the black and white bird that gives omens of good and ill.

In the ceremonies of Cybele on Lady Day a fir tree bole was wrapped and carried reverentially as the body of Attis Adonis for his burial, before his annual re-birth. So this is one of the many starry constellations which has an earthly counterpart in Britain, not carved in a hillside as at Cerne Abbas, but acted out in the Mummers plays. She has been revered as a moon goddess since the beginning of mythologies.

Aquila xvi

Aquilae
Aquila or Vultrur Volans
The Eagle

In the classical story this was the eagle that carried off Ganymede to serve the Olympians, the gods of ancient Greece.

To the Celt, the eagle constellation is probably the soul of Llew Llaw, son of Gwydion, for whom he searched among the stars of the Milky Way (see Cygnus). The Hawk was the Celtic name for a constellation, perhaps the classical one of the eagle, in which form Gwydion found the soul of Llew and was able to restore him to life. Thereafter he was known as Gwalchmei, that is The Hawk of May. The constellation Aquila still flies along the edge of the Milky Way, Sarn Gwydion, The Causeway of Gwydion to the Celt.

To later Celts of the Christian era, old beliefs still lingered and the hawk or falcon remained the personification of the soul of the hero or god who was sacrificed for the good of all. This is shown clearly in the pre-reformation 16th century poem *The fawcon hath born my Mak away*, which survived in North Staffordshire and Scotland. The poem appears to have been Christianised with an extra two verses and a little alteration.

The Fawcon Hath Born My Mak Away

Lully Lulley, lully lulley;
The fawcon hath born my mak away.

He bore hym up, he bore hym down;
He bore hym into an orchard brown.

In that orchard ther was an hall,
That was hangid with a purill pall.
And in that hall ther was a bede,
Hit was hangid with gold so rede.

A MEDIEVAL KNIGHT OUT HAWKING (from a floor tile)

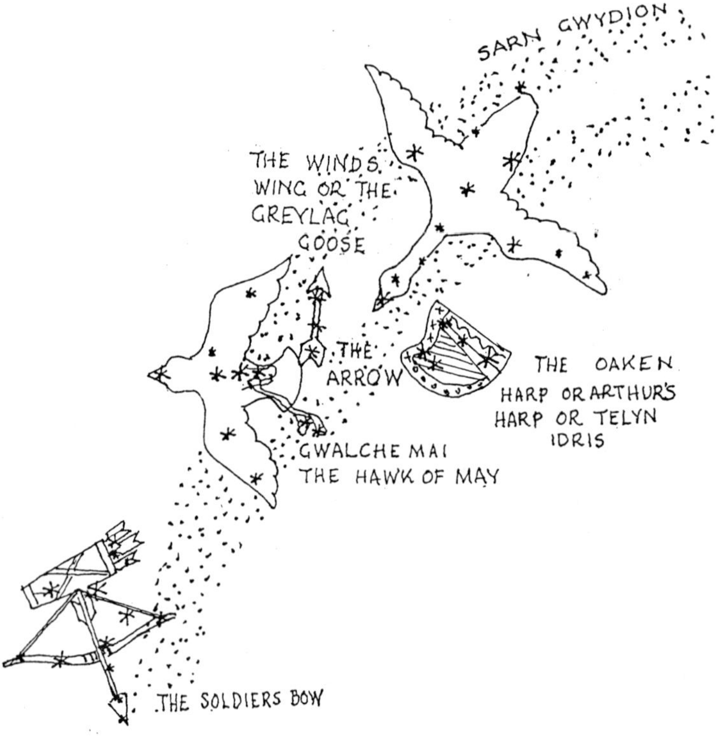

SARN GWYDION

THE WINDS WING OR THE GREYLAG GOOSE

THE ARROW

THE OAKEN HARP OR ARTHUR'S HARP OR TELYN IDRIS

GWALCHE MAI THE HAWK OF MAY

THE SOLDIERS BOW

And in tht bed the lythe a knyght,
His wowndes bledying day and nyght.

By that bedes side ther kneleth a may,
And she wepeth both nyght and day.

With silver needle and silken thread,
Stemming the wowndes where they did bleed.

And by that beddes side ther standeth a stone
Corpus Christos wretyn theron.

At the bedsfood ther grows a thorn
Which blows blossom since he was born.

Over that bed the moon shines bright
Denoting Our Saviour was born this night.

See Chapter 13 in Volume II The Applewell.

Although the poem seems to be written in Old English, it is probably derived from a Celtic origin in the British Celtic kingdom of Strathclyde, because it was a Celtic belief that one of the souls of the dying hero or man went into the form of a bird. For a chief-petty-officer in the British navy they still hold that his soul becomes a gannet, always ready to swallow another fish. For a dark age Celtic knight or noble it would be into a falcon, the bird used in falconry by an earl - see the medieval floor tile of hawking.

The time of year is shown by the orchard being brown, as the leaves turn in the autumn. This shows that apples are available, for the five pointed star of a cross-cut apple is the Seal of the Virgin, the passport of the departing soul of the hero to the seventh heaven, the heaven of the Virgin, the Court of Don behind the north wind.

To present day Christians, purple is a rich and sombre colour suitable for mourning, but anciently the colour Tyrian purple was derived from the murex shellfish sacred to Aphrodite, so it is also a promise of resurrection or re-birth after death. This resurrection after death was the promise - fulfilled for Llew Llaw in Celtic lands, and for Attis Adonis in the Roman Empire and Middle East, and for Jesus Christ in Palestine for Christendom.

It may be that in this poem there is little difference between the meaning of the Anglo Saxon *bede* meaning bed, and the Welsh or Cornish *bedd*, meaning a grave or tomb. The gold shows rank.

The poem doesn't specify what the bleeding wounds were, nor how they were acquired, but the context would fit in with the ancient emasculation and sacrifice of a young lord by the Queen of Elphame, or for Cybele or Anna at the hands of his lover and mistress, the priestess of a long barrow. The word *mak* in the poem is usually interpreted as the Anglo Saxon *make* meaning mate, husband wife or euqal, but it would make more sense if *mak away* derived from the Old Welsh *macwy* meaning a youth or young lord. One is reminded of a very similar poem called *Down in the Fores*t, and that the folk hero Robin Hood was reputedly bled to death by a lady caring for him.

The companion of the knight is variously described as a May or a leal maiden or The Virgin Mary. The latter is obviously a later gloss. A May must mean a maiden or a maiden who has gone A Maying in the woods. May is the flower of the hawthorn, so maybe the maiden is Blodeuwedd, which means flower face, the wife of Llew Llaw.

The inscription on the stone has been read rather unhistorically as "the body of Christ", but it can also be read just as well as "the body of the annointed one". The blooming thorn can suggest May and Christmas and Glastonbury. May blossom should never be used inside houses or sacred Christian buildings for fear of ill luck. But it was used for sweeping out temples in Roman times in honour of Cardea, the hag aspect of the great White Goddess, the Welsh Cerridwen, during the month of May; a time when men were expected to refrain from sexual intercourse. That the thorn tree is blooming by the dying knight suggests that though he is laying on a bed beside a maiden he will not - and probably can never again - have sexual intercourse, because of the nature of his wounds.

The promise of re-birth from the Wonderful Reaper, Berecynthia Cybele or Cerridwen took place on Lady Day with the shower of meteors from between the thighs of the constellation representing the Great Goddess. Shooting stars were one of the multiple souls of heroes or gods going to heaven, or returning to earth to be re-born for another life. It was up to the priests and priestesses to divine which child would grow to take the place of the previous sacred king and lover of the priestess who was the incarnation of the goddess.

Auriga xii

Tenentis habenas
Auriga, Heniochus, Erichthonius
The Charioteer or Wagoner

The Constellation Auriga is adjacent to that of the Bull. In Celtic eyes this may be the yoke by which the culture hero Hu Gadarn, Hu the Mighty, first harnessed the long horned oxen to the plough. Auriga as the wagoner is near to the Bull constellation representing the draught oxen. The she goat on the Charioteer's or Wagoner's shoulders is called Capella, and the stars below in his lap are called 'the kids' in some illustrations of the constellations. In early ploughing, one man manoeuvred the plough, while another called or drove the oxen. It may well be that Auriga was the caller or ox driver of the group consisting of Bootes, The Plough, Auriga and The Bull. (see Bootes)

One of the main feats of Hu Gadarn was to use his yoked team of oxen to drag the water monster, the Afanc or beaver out of lake Llion Lyon and so prevented it flooding the surrounding country and drowning the people.

There is an annual meteor shower from the direction of Auriga, for about four days, which is the number of increase. It runs from 10th February, which to the Jews would be the feast of Esther when Passover is 24th March, or Lady Day like the old Celtic Christian festival of Easter. Esther was the successor of Ishtar or Cybele, and equivalent of the Celtic goddess-cum-saint Bridget or Bride.

The meteor shower from Auriga lasted until St Valentine's Day - 14th February, also known as The Birds Wedding day and the Roman Lupercalia. Ostensibly this Roman festival was in honour of the she-wolf that suckled Romulus and Remus, but it was also a fertility promoting festival, which is probably connected with Auriga seen as the ox driver or caller who tends the team pulling the plough.

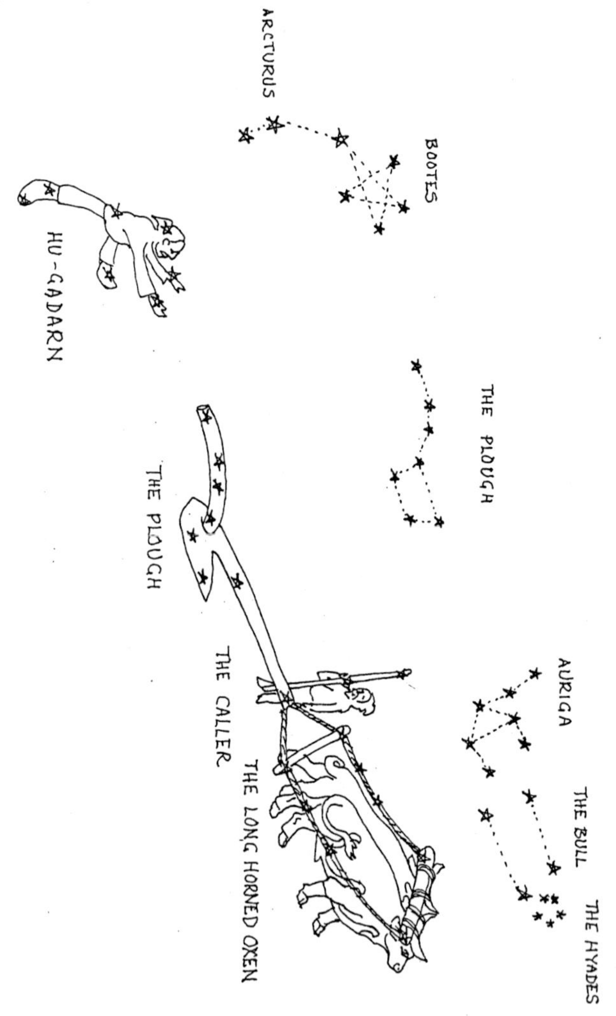
ARCTURUS
BOOTES
HU-GADARN
THE PLOUGH
THE PLOUGH
THE CALLER
THE LONG HORNED OXEN
AURIGA
THE BULL
THE HYADES

Bootes υ

Vociferatoris

Bootes (the Ox Driver) or Arctophylax (the Bear Driver) in Greek. The Ploughman or Herdsman or Ox Driver or Good Shepherd. The name Arctophylax meaning the Bear Driver was given to the main five star constellation, because the sixth star in the constellation, a little way off, is called Arcturus which denotes King Arthur. The name is probably Celtic deriving from Arth-Ter meaning "the bright clear high place".

Bootes is a group of five stars in the form of a pentacle. The Pentacle is called the Seal of the Virgin (see the constellation Virgo) and also the Druids footprint and Fuga Daemonam because it protects you from all evil. It lies next to the Corona Borealis, the British Celts Llys Arianrhod, the Court of the Moon Goddess Arianrhod, a pagan northern heaven. It was necessary to have the seal of the virgin before entering the seventh heaven, the Heaven of Maidens and therefore Llys Arianrhod, the Court of the Virgin Moon Goddess. This five pointed star is found naturally as fossilised sea urchins, and in this form has been found with Neolithic burials in long barrows, as the key to heaven for those buried there, see the illustrations. For the living, it is found in the cross-cut apple or central square section of the Applewell (see) which carries the secret of procreation and of reincarnation as explained to the sacred king victims before they were bled to death as described in the poem *The Fawcon hath born my mak away*, the falcon being one of the sacred kings souls (see Aquila.)

Because this sign is sometimes called the Herdsman or Good Shepherd it is associated by some with Jesus Christ as he was The Good Shepherd of the Christians. The constellation Bootes, the Ox Driver, reaches its most northern limits around Martimmass, 11th November, disappearing over the horizon towards the Northern heaven at dusk and returning at dawn.

There is an annual meteor shower from the direction of the Bull constellation from October 25th until November 16th. The last four days of this meteor shower is concurrent with another from the area of the Sickle in the constellation Leo on 13th, 14th, 15th and 16th November, the woodland boar to the Celts.

CAER ARIANRHOD
OR THE STONE OF
SILVERWHEEL
HU-GADARN
THE OX DRIVER

The legend of the Scottish Celtic Saint Martin holds that he was martyred there in Scotland by being cut up and eaten in the form of an ox at Martimmass, because SANCT MAIRT TIENE in Gaelic, or SANCT MARTH TAN in the lowland British Celtic language, both mean "The Holy One of the Ox Fire". Bootes reaches its northernmost point about Martinmass 11th November.

This was the time of year when surplus stock for which there was not enough fodder to keep them alive over winter, were slaughtered.

The Greek story of Bootes the Ox Driver tells of how Bootes' brother robbed him of all his goods, but how, after many wanderings and hardships, he invented the plough drawn by two oxen, and with this he tilled the land better than had ever been done before, and so made a good living. His mother was so pleased with him that she placed him and his ox team and plough in the heavens for all to see. Other Greek sources say this constellation is Icarius who brought wine to men as a gift from Bacchus.

Bootes the Ox Driver, the plough Ursa Major, Auriga the yoke or perhaps the Ox Caller, and The Bull constellation, all lie in a straight line across the heavens.

The story of the Greek Bootes is paralleled by our own Welsh stories of their culture hero Hu Gadarn, Hu the Mighty. The Welsh claim that Hu Gadarn lead the Cymry out of the Summer Country, called Delphrobani or Constantinople, over the hazy sea to Britain and Amorica (see chaper on the Celts and their tribal gods). It was he who first taught the Cymry (Cambrians) to plough as he was the first to yoke oxen to a plough. He was, therefore, called constable of the golden corn. He used his team of oxen to drag the Aranc, a water monster, from lake Llion Lyon so that it did not flood the surrounding land.

Since the Avanc was presumably an afanc or beaver, he probably demolished a beaver dam threatening to flood nearby farmland. To this day the Adanc or beaver, which takes the place of the constellations Scorpio and Libra is in a line behind Hu Gadarn, the plough, the caller and the oxen (see illustration).

By 1538 Hu Gadarn had become the idol Saint Darvell Gadarn of the diocese of Saint Asaph to whom offerings of cattle and horses were made, but he was arrested together with his attendant friar, and both were burnt at the stake in Smithfield. As a saint, his feast day was 5th April, which as a god was the date of his first birthday in heaven, as the first fruit of the tree guarded by a serpent, where he was nursed by a woman as beautiful as the moon. However, to a people who believed in multiple souls and reincarnation it was quite possible to

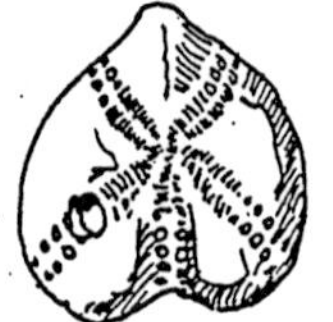

A HEART SEA URCHIN
OR FAIRY LOAF

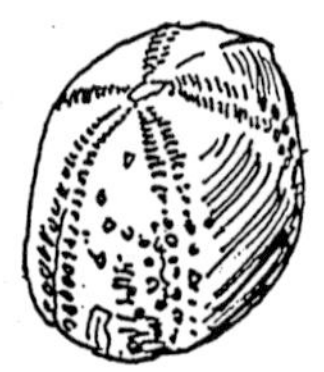

SEA URCHIN
FAIRY CROWN

FOSSILS FROM THE
CHALK & GRAVEL

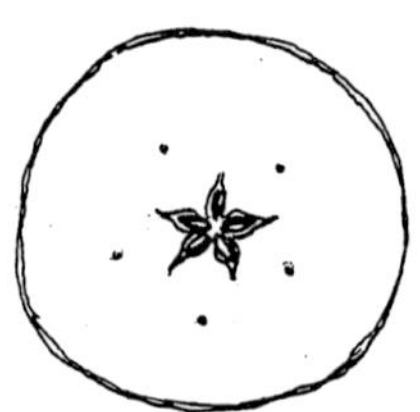

THE CROWN

THE APPLE

CUT ACROSS THE MIDDLE

A PENTACLE
OR DRUIDS FOOTPRINT
OR FUGA DAEMONUM

A PENTALPHA
(FIVE ALPHAS)

THE "MAYOR" OF CHALVEY & WASHERWOMEN WITH THE BANNER AT THE STAB-MONK CELEBRATIONS

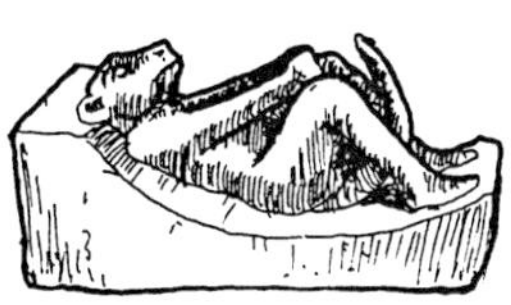

THE CHALVEY STAB MONKEY LAYING IN THE CURVE OF A WINNOWING BASKET

SABAZIAN DIONYSUS THE BARLEY BEER GOD OF THE GREEKS & ROMAN ARMY, BORN IN A COWSTALL WITH A CALF HEAD. SURVIVES AS THE CHALVEY STAB-MONK IN 20TH C.

A KING ADORING A CALF HEADED CHILD - DIONYSUS SABAZIUS - ON A 13C FLOOR TILE IN NEAR BY HITCHAM CHURCH (BUCKS)

A SIDE VIEW OF A WINNOWING BASKET, USED IN CLEANING GRAIN

A MASK OF DIONYSUS REPRESENTING THE CALF HEADED CHILD IN A WINNOWING BASKET ON A GREEK PAINTED VASE.

GRAPHITI IN CHURCHES

CASSIOPEA IN SUMMER ~ WINTER ~ AND ~ AUTUMN

LITTLE MARLOW LALEHAM

GRAPHITI IN BENGEO CHURCH . HERTS

A CARVING IN WHITTLESFORD CHURCH

THE CONSTELLATION CASSIOPEA SEEN AS
A SHIELA NA GIG

have more than one birthday, and so Hu Gadarn was reborn, a second time on 22nd December the winter solstice (see Ursa Minor) from Cerridwen, the hag who renewed her youth annually.

The pentacle or five pointed star was "the symbol at your door" in the carol *Green Grow the Rushes Oh.* It kept evil spirits and witches away, hence it was scratched on the door moulding to the south porch of Little Marlow, Bucks, church of St John (see Hercules). In a carving of the assumption of the Blessed Virgin Mary in Sandford Church in Oxfordshire the Virgin is shown crowned and in glory standing on a five sided figure supported by two angels.

The legend of Hu Gadarn, the Welsh Bootes, is as follows: Hu Gadarn, was reborn on 22nd December, the shortest day, out of Keridwen or Cerridwen the wife of Celi. On earth this was contrived by Druids or priests at the burial mound called Pentre Ifan in the Nevern valley, which is still known locally as The Womb of Cerridwen. This is shown in the heavens on that day, by the last day of a three day meteor shower from the Little Bear. The meteors on this day are the soul of the deity returning to earth for reincarnation, as they were the soul of the earthly hero leaving for his heavenly home earlier in the year. Cerridwen was the same deity as Berecynthia, who flew round the pole every night as the constellations Ursa Major and Ursa Minor. Hu Gardarn's first birthday on 5th April must be seen as the date of his conception. The 5th April is Lady Day old style, old New Years Day and still the start of the Financial Year.

In another set of parallel legends Bootes can be equated with Dionysus Sabazius who was born in a cowstall. Diodonus Siculus tells us that it was Dionysus who first yoked oxen to the plough. Sabazian Dionysus was the son of Rhea, and was also called Sabazian Zeus. The name Sabazius derives from Saben meaning of the fir tree. Sabazius was placed in a winnowing basket to be shown to the public. He has survived in Britain in the shape of a plaster cast of the original idol called the Chalvey Stab Monkey. Chalvey is a village in the flood plain just north of Eton and Windsor in south Bucks. His ceremony is identical to that of Dionysus Sabazius in Greece, and was doubtless brought to Britain by the Roman army, in which the cult of the Beer god Sabazius was very popular. The villages of Chalvey claimed their four industries were drinking beer, making babies, working down the treacle mines, and taking in washing.

It is necessary to yoke oxen to the plough to till the soil to sow the grain to yield a crop of barley from which beer is made. Hence it is possible to equate the Constellation of Bootes with the deity who first yoked oxen to the plough. Whether this deity is called Bootes as in the classical world, or Hu Gadarn as in

Wales or Sabazian Dionysus as in ancient Greece doesn't matter. He is the original of the Chalvey Stab Monkey in the present day Thames Valley. It is probable that anciently the stab monkey was born in a cowstall of Queen Anne by Long John, when Queen Anne was not just the name of a local beer house but was QUIDDEN UN ANNER, that is "the white fair holy and blessed one of the heifer", and lived in the ancient timber framed cottage called Queens Cottage, and Long John was not just the mock mayor of the village who had to lie in the grave dug for the stab monkey to measure it, but was LON ION that is "the Lord of the young oxen".

The illustrations show male washerwomen carrying Chalveys banner in the Stab Monkey procession with Long John the major, on the left. On the right is the plaster model made from the original stab monkey, and below it the side view of a winnowing basket showing the same curve the stab monkey rests on, and below that an illustration from an ancient Greek vase.

To the left at the bottom is the design from a 13th century floor tile fom Hitcham Church, some three miles only from Chalvey, showing a king adoring a calf-headed child. It is the oldest local representation of the Stab Monkey, which must have come over with the Roman army. In the original, the very thick tail of the Monkey which was lengthened to hide its origin in Victorian times, was a phalus. (see under Serpens).

As a footnote to the three stories of the first man to yoke oxen to the plough, it is worth pointing out that none of the stories tell us how the oxen were yoked. It is probable that the first way was to lash the plough beam to a straight yoke or bar of wood lashed to the horns of the oxen across their foreheads. In Ireland it is said that it was the men of the elf mounds who first yoked oxen at the shoulder to a shaped yoke. This may mean that it was the Tuatha da Dannan, the Bronze Age colonists who came by sea from the Mediterranean who called themselves Milesians that introduced this more efficient way of harnessing oxen.

Cassiopeia x

Inthronatae
Cassiopeia

Cassiopeia is the Lady seated in this chair, the wife of the King of Ætheopea called Cephus. For the classical legend see under Cephus.

Perhaps the Latin name derives from Casa, the hut or home of Ops, the goddess of corn and wealth. This derivation would fit most ladies of this constellation.

In classical Greece the court of the goddess was the Dromos or forecourt of the tomb of the hero, just as the horns of the long barrow was in Britain. In one sense these were the earthly representations of Cassiopeia or Llys Don, the Palace of Don or the Court of Don. It is also the chair of Cerridwen. Mallory tells us of King Arthur's dream, in which he sat in this chair fixed to a wheel. Far below him lays a hideous black water wherein were all manner of serpents and worms. Suddenly the wheel turned, and he fell out of the chair as it turned upside down, and he fell among the serpents. It is, therefore, sometimes called Arthur's Seat. As with many constellations there is an earthly equivalent. The highest peak of the Breckonshire Beacons in Wales now called Pen-y-Fan; used to be called Cadair Arthur, or Arthur's Chair. The relevance of the serpents was that to the Celts when a man dies his soul separates, part returns to heaven as a star, sometimes seen as a shooting star or meteor, part becomes a bird, and part becomes a serpent or worm. The dream was a portent of Arthur's coming death and that he would fall among the dead heroes whose souls become serpents, not just little worms. But the Chair that he sat in, is also known as St Swithin's Chair. Sir Walter Scott recorded an old verse about it which ran:

He that dare sit in St Swithins Chair
When the night hag rides the troubled air
Questions three when he speaks the spell
He may ask and she must tell.

The night hag who rides the troubled air is the Christian description of the Lady who rides round the pole of the heavens each night on the back of a dragon, the constellations of Ursa Major and Ursa Minor with Draco. She is sometimes called Cybele or Berecynthia. But in Christian iconography the Lady with the

THE SHIELA-NA-GIG FROM ST. MICHAEL'S CHURCH TOWER

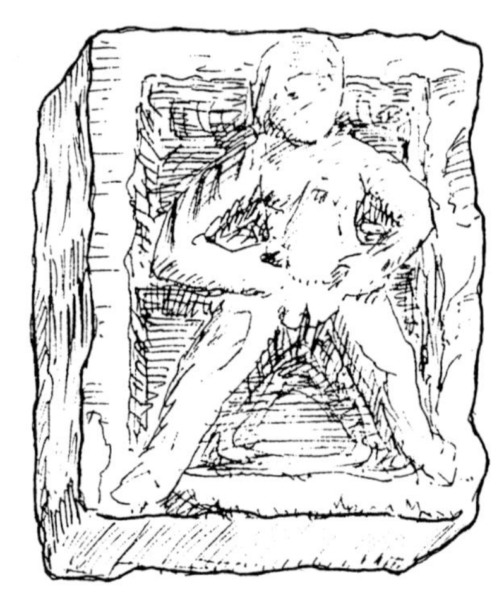

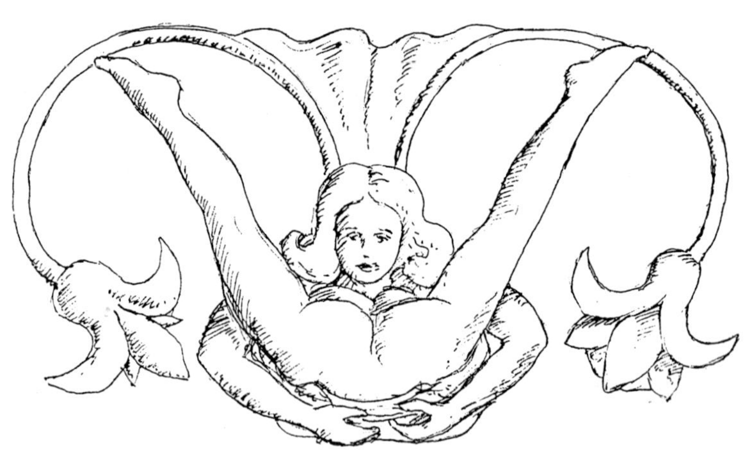

THE "TUMBLER" FROM MAGDALEN COLLEGE CHAPEL

MEDIEVAL SCULPTURE & CARVING AT OXFORD

Dragon is Saint Margaret. Her connection with Saint Swithin is that her feast day varies from 13th to 20th July while his feast day is on 15th July. And there is an annual meteor shower from the area of the head of the swan constellation the nearest to Casseopea, from St Swithin's Day to the last celebration of St Margaret's Day. Although Saint Margaret was one of the most popular saints in the west in medieval times, there is no evidence that she even existed. It would appear that the Lady with the dragon was worshipped so widely that the only way the Christian church could deal with the cult was to claim it as its own.

In celebration of the meteor shower from the head of the swan on St Swithin's Day, we have "Swan Upping" on the river Thames.

The sign for the start of this meteor shower on the cog almanac is a cross in a circle, the Celtic cross that was formerly a sun symbol.

The sign for the end of this shower on St Margaret's Day is a line of three diabolos XXX, presumably to show that the night hag Cerridwen who owns this chair has, like the moon, three aspects of maiden, nymph and crone, each formed of the two Vs point to point that form Casseopea. The name Cerridwen shows us from its origin that she was not just an old crone, KERYADES-WEN means "the white fair holy beloved female lover".

Having found that St Swithin is connected with this constellation, and also with a rather dubious lady saint, it poses the question of how did this happen to a very respectable historical councillor of the kings of Wessex. The answer must be sought after his translation into the Cathedral in 962 AD, in the city of Winchester of which he was bishop, the ancient capital of Wessex. Even the Norman kings usually went to Winchester to wear their crowns at Easter. In the early Celtic church it appears that Easter was fixed and coincided with Lady Day 25th March, on the eve of which there was a one night meteor shower from the forefoot of the Great Bear, which was seen as either the propitious right hand of the Great Goddess of the dragon, or her vagina, depending on how the stars were viewed. In the latter case it represented the re-birth of Attis Adonis, or Dionysus Sabazius.

In Roman times, Winchester was Venta Belgarum, perhaps from the Celtic VEN-TIR, that is the chief territory of the Belgae. It was reputed to have been founded in 854 BC, by Ludor Rous Hudibras. This appears to be a title or description rather than a name, for as the founder of a great city Ludor Rous was probably originally either LLU-D-IOR ROUS that is "the lord or leader of the army of the fertile country" or possibly LUIT IOR ROUS, "the grey and hoary lord of the host of the fertile country". The name Hudibras is found

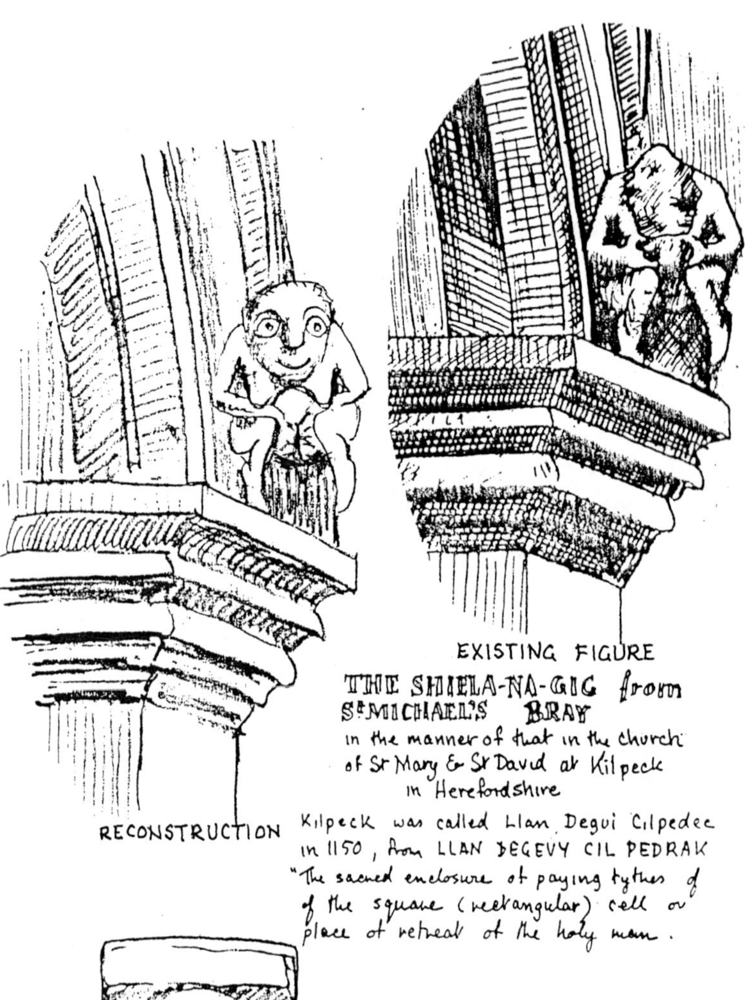

THE KILPECK FIGURE

elsewhere, and could derive from Hudol Bras that is the fat wizard or enchanter, but most probably came originally from Huan dew bras and that is" the fat god of the summer sun". This is where the cog almanac sign for St Swithin of Winchester came from. He must have acquired it from his association with the City of Winchester.

It may be significant that Saint Swithin was consecrated bishop by Archbishop Ceolnoth, as the Archbishop's name appears to be a description in the, by then, old fashioned British language, COEL NOOTH meaning "of the new belief". This suggests that the old beliefs were still alive at the time. To the pagan Celts of his flock, St Swithin would have been SANCT YS WY TER NI, that is "the holy one of the clear water of heaven". That is why St Swithin is associated with rain. Traditionally, if it rains on his feast day it will rain for the next forty days. An alternative sign for St Swithin's Day on the cog almanac represents a shower or rain.

Apart from sharing the same annual meteor shower as marker for their feast days, is there anything else that links St Margaret with St Swithin? The main thing is of course her name, since *margarite* means daisy in French, and a daisy is so called because of its yellow disc of a centre. It opens at dawn, closes at evening, and follows the course of the sun. It is in fact the days eye watching the sun all day. As we have seen, St Swithin had acquired a sun symbol as his own. St Margaret's Day, 20th July, is also Saint Elias' day in Greece, where his hill top church was built on top of the Temple of the sun god Helius.

In Latin and Greek St Margaret's name means pearl, and in Gaelic a pearl is *neambnaid* or *leus-sul*. The latter word means "blister of the sun". In the same language the vegetable equivalent of the pearl is the mistletoe, *an-t-uil-ioc*, that is "the all heal". Here it is relevant to remind ourselves that it was to St Margaret that St Frideswide of Oxford prayed, to effect the cure of her rejected suitors blindness. Her well still stands by the church at Binsey, just outside Oxford. Just as St Frideswide's name shows that she was a corn goddess SANCT FRAID DELWES YDD ie "the Holy One Bride of the Corn Dolly", so her patroness St Margaret is said to put the Sickle to the corn on her feast day.

The animal equivalent of the pearl is semen. This may prove relevant when we consider the shape of the constellation Casseopea, and its use in graphiti in churches as a symbol of the passing seasons, and its connection with another lady saint whose feast day is also fixed by the same annual meteor shower. This is St Mary Magdalene whose feast day on 22nd July is just two days after St Margaret's.

SAINT MARGARET

St Margaret is pictured leading a chained Dragon and can be equated with Astarte, Cybele and Berecynthia, who as the Great Reaper of the heavens rode round the pole each night on the back of her dragon. She may also be equated with The King of Egypt's daughter of the English mummers plays, who also lead the dragon that St George defeated on a chain. This is but another version of the tale of Perseus saving the life of Andromeda, Casseopeia's daughter. All the actors in this play are to be found among the constellations.

St Mary Magdalene is the penitent prostitute of the Bible who, to show her trade, wears a red dress. However, one must remember that in Roman times, and even in early medieval times, a red dress was the dress of a bride, since it showed that the wearer was nubile. That is why the ox on the coat of arms of the City of Oxford is red, because it was originally the symbol of the patron saint of the city, the maiden St Frideswide, when it was a red and therefore nubile cow.

As the Lady in red she can be equated with the Gay Ladye in the nursery rhyme about London Bridge. Gay in ancient times very definitely meant heterosexual, not homosexual as it does in the late 20th century. The Lady in the red dress of London Town in ancient Celtic literature, or story, was Credyladd, Shakespeare's Cordelia, the daughter of King Lear, or Lud of Ludgate in the City of London.

To the French the Lady in Red has become another saint; Notre Dame, de la Lorette or Our Lady of easy virtue.

In medieval romance St Mary Magdalene was said to have been betrothed to St John the Evangelist, just as Christ was to St Katherine. St John's symbol is an eagle, so in this legend St Mary Magdalene is being compared to Blodeuwedd, the wife of Llew Llaw who had taken the form of an eagle when killed, or to Arianrhod wife of Gwalchinai, the falcon of May.

It appears that St Mary Magdalene is the Christian equivalent of the classical goddesses Aphrodite or Venus. (see Venus in The Moving Stars).

A study of graphiti in English churches at first sight suggests that most of the people who have an urge to carve their initials on the walls and door jambs are called William or Mary, and that a lot of them do the carving when laying down on a trestle table. A moments thought then suggests that this cannot be the real reason for the preponderance of the signs M or W upright or laying on their sides.

THE FIGURE FROM THE EXTERNAL NORTH WALL OF THE CHANCEL OF SAINTS MARY & PETER, WILMINGTON SUSSEX ~ BECAUSE OF THIS FIGURE PRESUMABLY IT IS ST MARY MAGDALENE F. D. 22 JULY & ST. PETER F.D. 29 JUNE

Most business was transacted in or by churches, not only marriage contracts, the reading of wills and payment of heriots, but also buying and selling, renting and payment of rents. Thus is became useful to make some record of the due date for rents agreed to be paid in some public place, and where could be more holy and safe than the walls of the church itself.

It therefore seems probable that some at least of the Ms and Ws are drawings of the constellation Casseopea and denote the seasons or quarter days when rent was due. At mid-summer Casseopeia is in the W position, in the autumn it is in the position of a W fallen over to the left (say at Michaelmas), in winter it is in the M position, and in the spring (at Lady Day) it is like an M fallen to the left. The W represents a lady squatting with her legs apart, as can be seen in a few surviving figures in churches known as shiela-na-gigs. They are crude representations of a fertility goddess. Their purpose was to bring fertility to the crops and cattle and cottagers of the parish. They were normally only to be found on the outside of churches, so their influence radiates to the fields of the parish. That on St Michael's church tower at the entrance to the city of Oxford by Cornmarket Street, remained high on the tower from its building until the middle of the 20th century, when a kind-hearted vicar brought it inside to preserve it from the then corrosive atmosphere. The very vandalised figure at Bray on Thames and the better preserved one at Kilpeck are nearer to the graphic figures shown. The summer position W at Little Marlow has an extra line that shows what this lady is waiting for.

Referring back to the dream of King Arthur as he sat in this chair, one must remember that besides his wife Gweynevere, he also coupled with one of the three Queens who were his aunts. This was Queen Morgause whose name means "she who breeds in August", and so he fathered Mordred. It puts another dimension onto the story of his dream that when his seat turned over he fell off and followed the fate of all sacred kings.

Breeding in August has further connections with the Cog Almanac and Celtic mythology.

The first of August, which falls two days after the end of an annual four day meteor shower from the fore foot of Pegasus, was the day of the great Fair or Games at Taillten in Ireland, founded by the god Lugh himself in honour of his mother Tailltiu, beside her funeral mound. The first and second of August are marked on the Cog Almanac with a Bow and a Bird Arrow respectively, to remind us that this is when the sparrow, Bran's sparrow, the goldcrest wren, shot cock robin. And this set all the birds of the air 'a-sighing and a-sobbing'. The sparrow was the soul of the winter sun god, taking revenge on the soul of

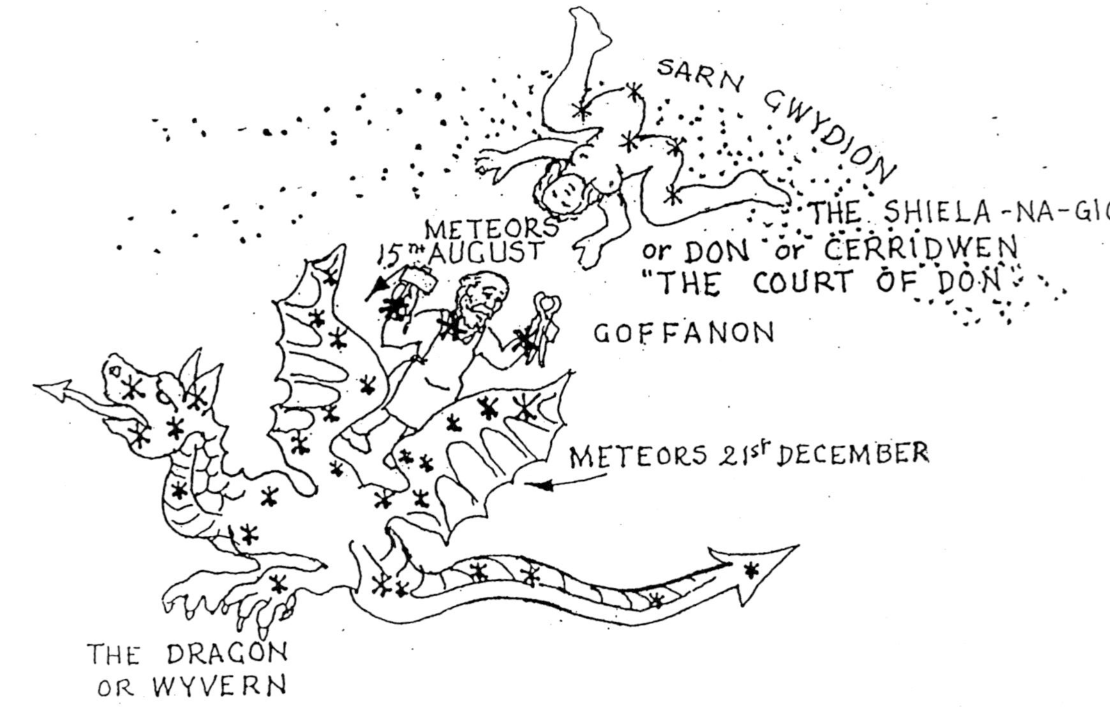
SARN GWYDION
THE SHIELA-NA-GIG
or DON or CERRIDWEN
"THE COURT OF DON"
METEORS
15th AUGUST
GOFFANON
METEORS 21st DECEMBER
THE DRAGON
OR WYVERN

the summer sun god, cock robin, for the mid-winter wren hunt on St Stephen's Day.

The Roman second Cerealia, a Harvest Festival, started on 6th August. The Roman day of Venus was heralded by the start of a five day meteor shower on 9th August from the direction of Perseus. This was the day of the coupling in August. It is marked on the Cog Almanac on the following day by the sign of an empty bed frame. After the exertions of the 9th this day, the 10th, was a holiday for the prostitutes of Rome and of the Roman empire, hence the sign of an empty bed.

Later Christians claimed it was a brass bedstead on which St Lawrence was roasted to death, and made 10th August St Lawrence's Day, but the church has now consigned this tale to the stock of unhistorical legends.

Perhaps the prettiest of the representations of the lady who epitomised the Celtic idea of the constellation Casseopeia is still to be found in that home of lost causes, the City of Oxford. It is in the form of a 15th century miserecord in Magdalene College Chapel, though it is no longer in its original position. In guide books it is prudishly referred to as a tumbler, but the position, holding up her skirts and flanked by two yellow water irises, the symbol of the west European fertility and cattle goddess, makes the insinuation quite clear. Magdalene's ante chapel, its present site, is an appropriate setting, as St Mary Magdalene was a Lady in Red, a prostitute, and they still sing carols on the top of the college chapel to welcome in the pagan Mayday morning, with the flowers of the White Goddess, May Blossom, which may be propitious on cottage and byre, but should never be seen in church.

The church of St Mary and St Peter, Wilmington, the parish that contains the Long Man of Wilmington (see Hercules) also has a much damaged shiela-na-gig that probably looked like the illustration a few centuries back. This figure suggests that the church was originally dedicated to St Mary Magdalene, and not to St Mary the Virgin.

But the old gods and goddesses do not just live on in stone and wood carvings, they also live on in song, especially in the first songs we sing, in the nursery.

It is the last, and safest refuge of the old gods and goddesses. Who has not heard that:

There was an old woman tossed up in a basket
Seventeen times as high as the moon;

Where she was going I couldnt but ask it,
For in her hand she carried a broom.

Old woman, old woman, old woman, quoth I
Where are you going to up so high?
To brush the cobwebs off the sky!
May I go with you?
Aye bye and bye.

This nursery rhyme can be sung to the rollicking tune of *Lillibolero*. Some authorities tell us that the tune of *Lillibolero* was originally called "*Old Woman Wither So High*", and that it was an anti-Jacobite song, or one composed to ridicule the French wars of Henry V. Other authorities hold that it is even older and was an old Morris dancing tune used for step dancing and was a harvest song. In a Scottish version the wee wifee is tossed up in a blanket to push the clouds away from the sun.

Nursery rhymes have survived for hundreds of years because they were assumed to be nonsense and of no historical, theological, or social value! Literary records tell us that this rhyme is over 300 years old, and if it has connections with Morris Dancing and Harvest Time it may go back a lot farther among the native British peasantry.

If one wants to know who this old woman was, one only has to picture the scene. It is a night sky because the moon is there. Who else could be going up in the sky with a broom but a witch?

Now in Welsh, basket is *cawell* which also means cradle. Blanket is *gwrthban.* owing to the Welsh habit of changing the initial letter of words in certain circumstances, a blanket or *gwrthban* can also be spelt *cwrthban*, which could be derived from *cwrt-ban* , which would mean "the court on high".

Since the old lady is at least seventeen times as high as the moon, she must be among the stars. And if she is in a *cwrt-ban* rather than a *gwrthban* there are only two Courts among the stars, Llys Arianrhod and Llys Don.

Since it is suggested that the rhyme and tune, are connected with harvest time and chasing the cold clouds away from the sun, the lady in the blanket or in the basket would appear to be in the *cwt-ban*, that is the Court on High, Llys Don, the Court of Don, the constellation we call Casseopeia; which turns around the pole and never sets. She is Don, the mother of the gods, and she is the

Christians Night Hag, the Britons' Calleach or Cerridwen, or Berecynthia of the late Roman Empire. The cradle is also a suitable accompaniment to this lady, the mother of many deities.

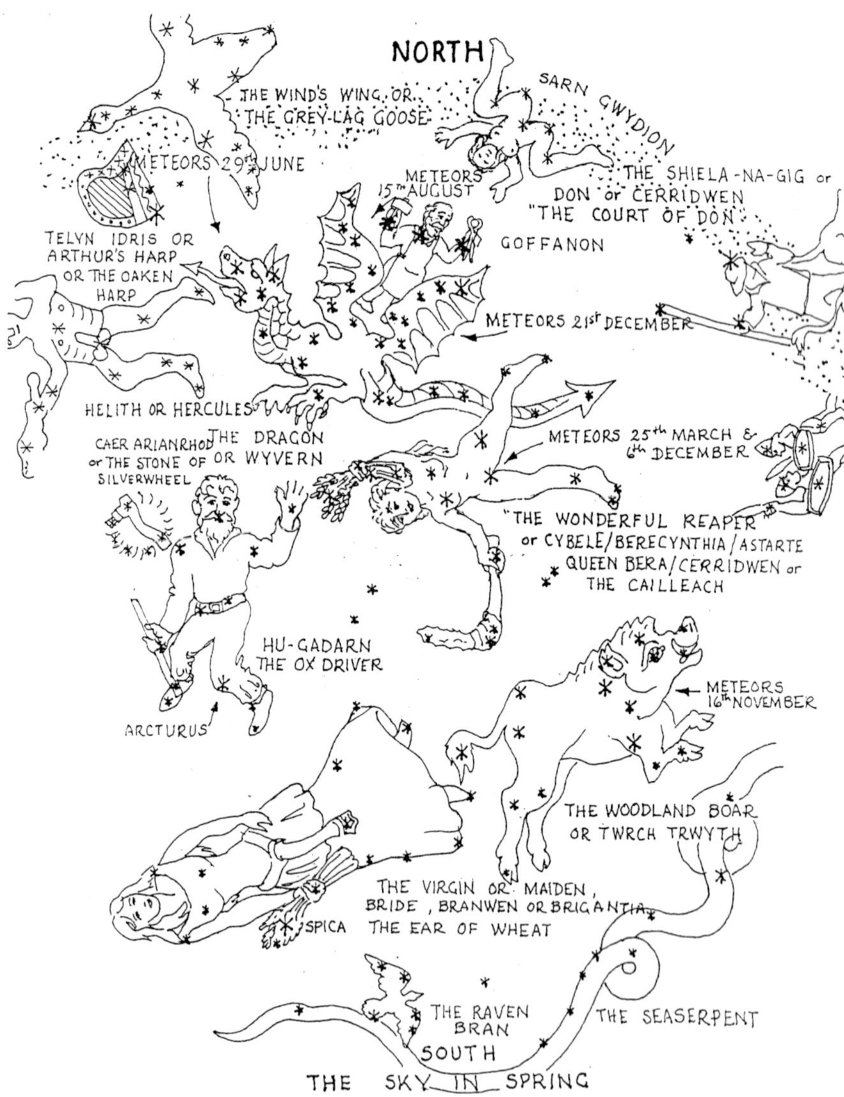

THE SKY IN SPRING

Cephus IV

Cephei
Cephus
Cepheus, King of Aetheopia

The Legend of Andromeda and Perseus with that of Casseopeia and Cephus

There was once an Aetheopian King, Cephus, whose wife Casseopeia boasted of the great beauty of her daughter Andromeda. The Nereids, the nymphs of the Mediterranean, were jealous and got their father, Nereid, to send a great flood and a sea monster or dragon to devastate the kings land. The king sent to the oracle of Ammon to ask how he could get rid of this plague, and was told to sacrifice Andromeda. She was chained to a rock for the monster, but was rescued by Perseus, fresh from his labour of killing the Gorgon. Andromeda is supposed to have been chained to the rocks of the cliffs of Jaffa, the port of Tel Aviv in Israel (Palestine).

Athene eventually put Perseus and Andromeda and her mother and father and the sea monster into the sky as constellations. The sea monster, Cetus, is a southern constellation.

In British mummers plays Cephus, the king of Aetheopia, survives as the King of Egypt, and his daughter Andromeda as Sabrina the King of Egypt's daughter. Her rescuer Perseus survives as the Red Cross knight Saint George or sometimes King George, while Cetus the sea monster is the dragon that Saint George slew on dragon hill below Uffington Castle, within sight of the White Horse.

If King Cepheus named in the British mummers plays The King of Egypt meant anything to the Celtic Britons, in the same way as this daughters name Sabrina appears to have derived from SABEN RHIAIN NARE meaning the fir tree queen on high, then it may have been derived from CYN-COF-Y- JY -EP which means the first blacksmith of the horse house or stable.

Since he stands just the other side of the Milky Way from Pegasus, the white horse of the sky, which has its earthly counterpart on the downs above

Uffington in Berkshire, this derivation is possible. The long barrow of the Saxon fairy smith Weyland lies not very far from the White Horse along the Ridgeway.

Maybe it was the burial place of a much earlier smith which the Iron Age Celts took to be the first blacksmith to shoe horses, "the first blacksmith of the stable". The smith god of the Irish Celts was Goibnu and his Welsh equivalent was Gofannon or Gavida, so perhaps that is the British name for The King of Egypt, if he is not the sun god Lug or Llew who was also a smith. Another Irish hero, similar to Lug, was Finn, and he wed a smith's daughter. Smiths were akin to magicians and druids, and were important people, even in historical times. In Brittany it is said that our William the Conqueror was the offspring of Robert the Devil and the daughter of the smith of Falais.

Corona Borealis vi

Coronai, Phecca
Corona borea
The Northern Crown or The Seven Stars

The name we use is Latin, where Corona means a crown, a garland or circlet, something curved worn on the head. Certainly Boreas was the North wind and the constellation lies in the northern part of the sky, but Boarius means relating to cattle, like the Forum Boarium in Rome. Since to the Celts the constellation belonged to the moon goddess, perhaps the constellation was thought of as a crescent or a pair of cow horns, like a croissant roll.

Llys or Caer Arianrhod means The Court of Arianrhod, whose name means Silverwheel because she was a goddess of the moon. There may be some connection with the "Shepherds rhod", which was a lightweight throwing axe, so called because when thrown the honed iron blade shone as a circle or silver wheel as it spun through the air. It was the iron age successor to the neolithic axe, bedded in deer horn set within the growth rings of a fork off a branch (to prevent splitting), and this was a development of a throwing club that has survived to this day in Ireland as a Conemara Shillelagh. In other mythologies this was Thor's Hammer or the Thunderbolt and in later times became the Francisca of the Franks.

Arianrhod appears to have been the maiden aspect of Cerridwen. As the maiden huntress perhaps she used a stone throwing axe and this constellation was Carreg Arhianrhod, the stone of Arianrhod.

In classical astronomy the northern crown is Ariadne's chaplet. It is the source of occasional meteor showers between the 10th and 18th May, around the Christian Whitsun when Easter is Ladyday and the Caelic Caingeir (13th May) from CAIN, the tribute and GEIR = fat fallow or grease. The Welsh or British name for the festival is Beltane or *Latha Beall Tuinn* deriving from the words BELU = to kill and TAN = by fire. These festivals marked the death of the winter sun god and the rebirth of the summer sun god which is represented by the shooting star, one of the gods souls, returning to earth from the northern heaven of Llys Arianrhrod, the Court of the Moon goddess.

THE EVOLUTION OF THE SHEPHERDS RHOD OR THE THROWING AXE OR FRANCISCA

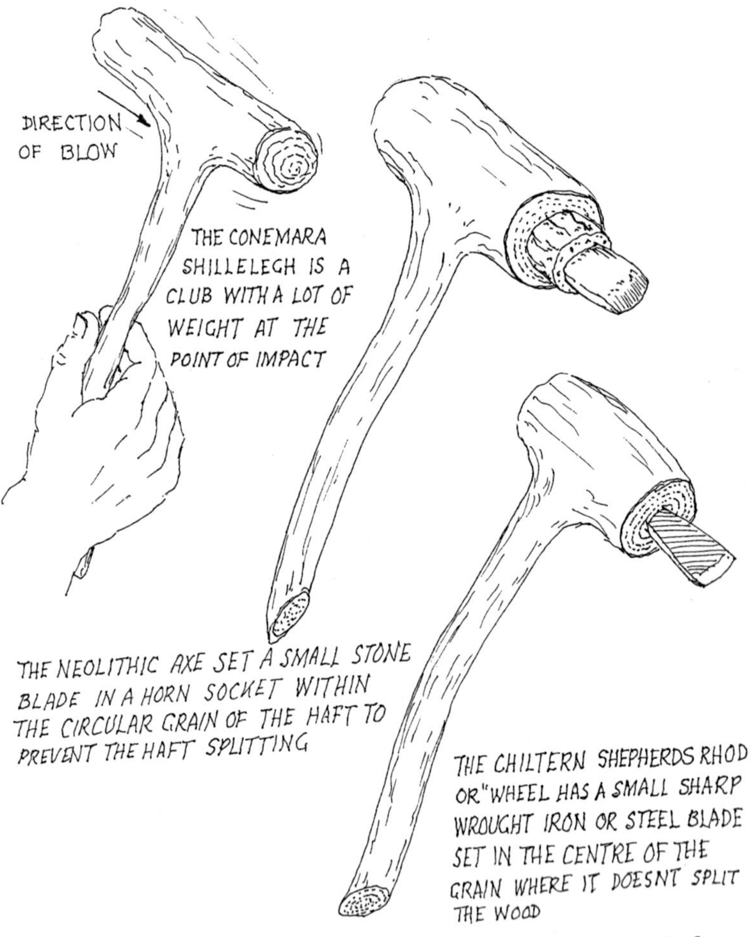

THE FRANCISCA WAS A DARK AGE MILITARY DEVELOPMENT OF THIS ANCIENT THROWING WEAPON BY THE 3RD-5TH C. FRANKS.

Up until the 16th or 17th century large banners were paraded at Whitsuntide fairs around England showing the wide grinning face of the Bugabo, with rows of sharp teeth as used in the inn signs of "The Bull and Mouth" or as used to decorate the boiled eggs of this time of year in South Bucks and East Berkshire. The Bugabo was, from its name, both a cow devil and a cow protector, as the name derives from BUGELYA - BOO that is "to guard the cows" or, the cowherd or stockman.

The Bugabo as the winter sun god, the Great Hunter, is known as Herne the Hunter in south Bucks or East Berks. He was known in Shakespeare's time to be able to raise a murrain on cattle. At this time of year when his powers had wained it was safe to open his egg head with a knife and eat his brains, in the ancient British head hunting manner. In Sussex, harvesters, the loyal men of the summer sun god, were called Mouth Men.

The Gaulish god Esus who was associated with the horned god Cernunos, had a Latinised name probably derived from the word EDO = to eat. In the form ESUS we have a past participle meaning 'has eaten'. This was, therefore, a title of the summer oak tree gods Jupiter or Mars in the Roman World, and the Dagd in Irish mythology. They were all voracious eaters. In Rome, a white wether was sacrificed to Jupiter on his day. In Kingsteignton in the Dartmoor area of Devon, there is still a ram roasting at Whitsun, the Christian successor festival, which falls on this day when Easter falls on Ladyday as it did in the early Celtic Church and on the Cog Almanac.

Some say that it is the Arianrhod whose name means "silverwheel" who spins the lives of men. Her court is in the shape of a crescent moon, her sign as the chaste huntress and new moon goddess. Caer Arianrhod is also in the form of the horns at the entrance to a Neolithic long barrow, where the resident priestess, lover, and killer of the successive sun god reincarnations, would hold court, hence its name Llys Arianrhod. Arianrhod is the daughter of Don, whose constellation is Casseopeia or Llys Don.

In another sense Arianrhod, "silverwheel" is just one of the names of the goddesses of the wheel. Fortuna is another, and so is Gwynevere who brought the round table, a very large solid wheel to Camelot, and for that matter Kulwich's bride Olwen, daughter of Giant Hawthorn, Yspaddaden Penkawr, whose name may derive from Olwyn meaning wheel. Later barrows of the Bronze Age and Iron Age were circular like wheels and like Caer Arianrhod.

THIS GRAPHITO OF A GREY LAG GOOSE OVER DOTS SHOWING THE STARS OF THE CONSTELLATION CYGNUS IS ON THE NORTH FACE OF THE SECOND PIER FROM THE WEST END, FACING THE NORTH AISLE OF THE 12c CHURCH OF WALTHAM SAINT LAWRENCE, BERKSHIRE.

THE CONSTELLATION CYGNUS AS A GOOSE IN FLIGHT FLYING ALONG THE MILKY WAY "THE CAUSWAY OF GWYDION

THE DEVIL PREACHING AT THE NORTH DOORWAY
OF HAMBLEDON CHURCH

Cygnus ix

Gallinae
Olor, Cygnus
The Swan or Bird

The constellation of the Swan represented the Grey Lag Goose to the Celts. These birds migrated north in the direction of Llys Don, the Court of Don the great goddess (Casseopeia) along the line of the Milky Way on or about St Gabriel's Day, Ladyday, the Spring Equinox or Beltain, and returned around Hallowe'en or Michaelmas, the Autumn Equinox. It was the grey lag goose that carried the souls of the pagan dead to the northern heavens behind the north wind. This is why in the medieval period Christians buried criminals, heretics and pagans on north facing unconsecrated land and the lower orders in general on the northern side of the churchyard, outside the north or devils door of the church. If you go to Hambledon Church in the Buckinghamshire Chiltern Hundreds you will find a devil in clerical garb preaching, carved on the door jamb of the north door. Those who the church deemed unworthy of Christian burial, such as heretics and men who offended the Bishop of Lincoln and died in his private prison at his abbey at Wooburn in South Bucks were buried in unconsecrated ground on a northern slope of Northend Woods, just west of Wooburn Abbey. In Waltham St Lawrence church in Berkshire there is a graphito of this constellation of the goose on a column facing the north or devils door.

To the British Celts this constellation may also represent Gwydion as lord of the Goose, that is GWYDD-ION, flying along his track in the heavens, Sarn Gwydion "The Milky Way", looking for the soul of his son Llew among the stars. He eventually found it as a hawk (the constellation of Aquila the eagle) before restoring him to life in his former shape. This was probably as the constellation Hercules, just off the Milky Way, as Llew or Lugh was the summer sun god.

There is an annual five day meteor shower from the head of the swan constellation starting on the 15th July, St Swithin's feast day. It is also the day when Swan Upping starts on the river Thames, that is the marking of swans as the property of various London City Guilds or Companies.

THE OAKEN
HARP OR
TELYN IDRIS
ARTHURS HARP
THE WIND'S WING
OR THE GREYLAG GOOSE
THE SEAL
OR MORLO
THE FOAL
THE DOWSER OR WATER
CRAFTSMAN OR St DAVID
ST NON'S SON
THE WALRUS
OR MORVUGH - SEACOW

Belief in the northern heaven seems to have survived at least in the Scottish borders into the 16th century, if Robert Graves is correct in his reconstruction of an old fragment of a ballad recording the death of King James 4th of Scotland and his lords in battle with the English at Flodden Edge on 9th September 1513. It goes:

Grey goose and ganer
Wap your wings togidder
And bear ye the guide kings banner
Owre the ane strand river.

The king and his court had been ex-communicated by the Pope for taking up arms against the English king Henry VIII, the defender of the faith. Therefore, they could not go to the Christian heaven, so the grey goose would take his banner to notify those in the pagan northern heaven that the souls of the king and his men were on their way there, so they could make ready for them.

There may be some connection between this constellation, seen as a grey lag goose, and the arrow Sagitta flying towards one of its outstretched wings, as the flights of the Celts arrows were made of the feathers of the grey lag goose. While the weapon of the Saxon was the seax, a long stabbing knife or short sword, the weapon of the Celt and the later Welsh was the long bow.

Julius Caesar records that the Britons revered the goose and the hare and would not normally eat them. This disinclination survived into the 19th century in Wales, South West England and Brittany, except at Ladyday or Easter when jugged hare or hare pie was the traditional dish, and at Michaelmas when goose was the traditional dish.

Delphinus xvii

Delphini
Delphinus
The Dolphin
(In the classical story the dolphin was sent by Neptune to bring his bride Amphtrite to him).

The dolphin doesn't seem to have figured in Celtic myths. This is probably because it frequents warmer seas than those around the Celtic lands. Its place, as a sea creature that is sometimes friendly to man is taken by the seal, *marlo* in Welsh, that is the sea calf, or perhaps the porpoise, in Welsh the *morhogh* or sea pig.

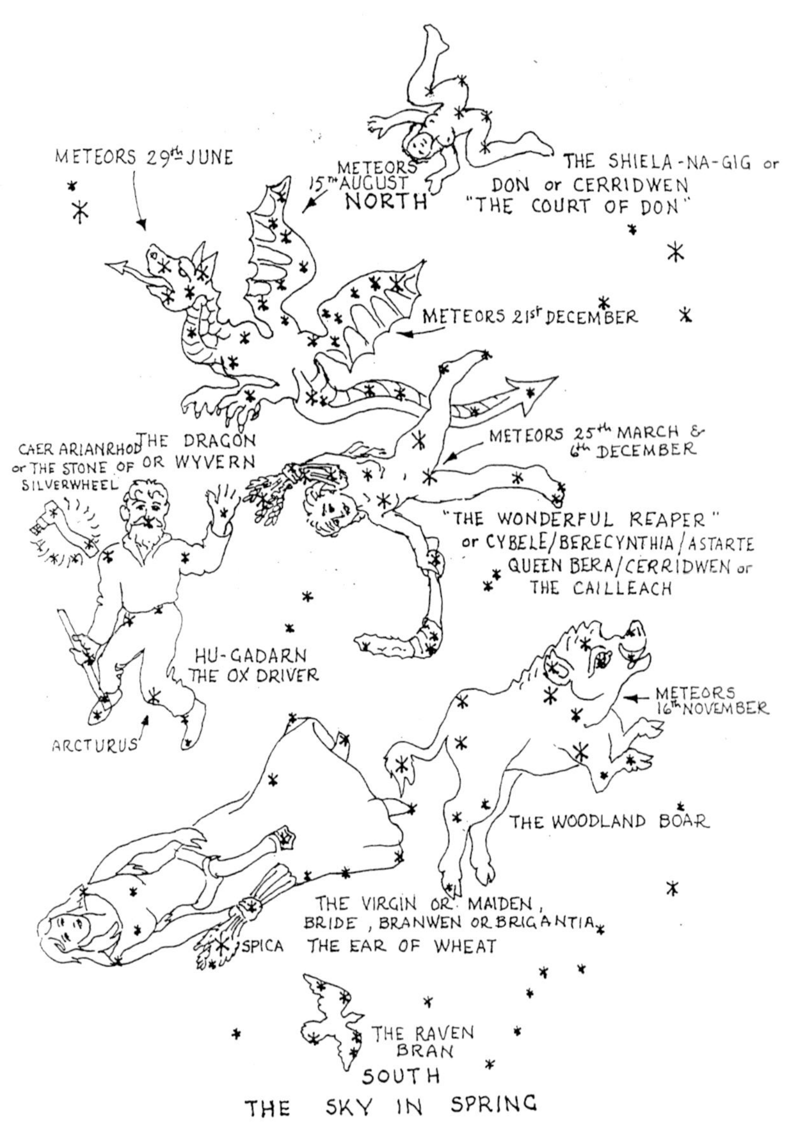

THE CELTIC CONSTELLATIONS

Draco iii

Draconis
Draco
The Dragon

There may be some connection here with King Arthur's father Uthr Pendragon, as his name can be translated as the wonderful head of the dragon. It ceased to hold the pole star in about 1900 BC. In Celtic eyes it must be seen as a wyvern, the Welsh Dragon, upon which Cybele/Berecynthia/Astante/Cerridwen or the Cailleach rides round the heavens every night. In Christian eyes it must, therefore, be the dragon of St Margaret of Antioch or the one defeated by St George.

On another plane The Dragon can be seen as Y-DRAEN-ION The Hawthorn Tree Lord, in other words Giant Hawthorn, Yspaddaden Penkawr, Hawthorn Chief of the Giants. He was the father of Olwen who wed Kulwch, and seems to be similar to Balor, and to Ogyr Vran, Queen Guinevere's father, all associated with the older gods of the matriarchal period.

Since among the Celtic Britons, and other early peoples, attempts were made to link heavenly events and constellations with earthly constructions, times and places, we must now consider the annual meteor showers that appear to emanate from the constellation Draco.

On 29th June there is a meteor shower from the mouth of Draco as seen as a classical Dragon. This marks the feast of St Peter and St Paul in the Christian calendar. This feast day had been celebrated since time out of mind at St Paul's Cathedral in London, by a forester leading in a live buck to be slaughtered upon the high altar, while the keeper who brought it sounded the mort on his hunting horn. The practice was only discontinued in 1557. It forms no part of Christian worship but of course the meat provided was a welcome supplement to the living expenses of the clergy of the cathedral. It would seem that this offering had survived from the former use of the site, which legend tells us was the site of a Roman temple to Diana. Certainly an altar with a relief of Diana was dug up nearby, and the crypt of the temple is supposed to have survived as vaults up into the medieval period, called the Camera Dianae.

THE HERALDIC
WYVERN OR WIVERN
THE HERALDIC
DRAGON

There is no obvious connection between the deer or the Goddess Diana, and Draco the Dragon. But if the constellation was not seen as a dragon or wyrern but as DRAEN-ION The Thorn Lord, Draco may have been seen as a man crowned with thorns, not as a thorny wreath as in Christian iconography, but with a thorny head-dress of deers horns, like Cerrunnos. The meteor shower of 29th June would then emanate from Cerrunnos propitious right hand holding the luna torque, bestowing blessings on men, and recording the death of a buck whose horns were still in velvet, quarry to Dianas hounds like Actaeon, her unwanted suitor. This may be why the great goddess Diana at the pole of the sky would appear to have her back to Draco when seen as Cerrunnos with a luna torque in his right hand and a ram headed snake in his left hand.

Since both these deities live on in the traditions of Windsor Forest as The Lady Huntress and Herne the Hunter, it is reasonable to suppose that they were important enough gods in the past to have equivalent status in the night sky to that enjoyed by King George and the King of Egypt's daughter in the surviving mummers plays. As a god and goddess of northern Europe, they must date back to the hunter gatherers age of Mesolithic/Neolithic times or earlier.

There is another meteor shower from 20th to 22nd December from the direction of Ursa Minor. This is marked in the Cog Almanac as the Christian feast day of St Thomas, on the eve of which children and workmen went Thomasing, begging for alms. Formerly to nordic peoples this was Tundermans Eve in honour of Thor, and when Easter is Ladyday as it probably was in the Celtic calendar, it was a Thursday, Thor's day. 22nd December is the Winter Solstice, called AN FHEILL SHLINNEIN, in Gaelic, that is "the Feast of the Shoulder Blade". This may have been because the shoulder blade was the part of the sacrifice burnt as the portion offered to the gods, but if the constellation Draco is seen as the god Cerrunos, then this meteor shower emanates from his left shoulder blade, the shoulder of his left hand which holds the ram headed serpent, perhaps the original dragon of Draco.

It may well be that the endowed bull baiting at Wokingham, the only town in Windsor Forest, on St Thomas' Day, may have had pagan origins, as both the stag and bull were sacred to Herne the Hunter or Cerrunnos.

Perhaps more importantly, the Romans celebrated the Augeronalia on 21st December when the ancient goddess Augerona gave birth to the reborn sun. Perhaps one of these meteors represented the return to earth of the soul of the sun god for his physical rebirth. The Celtic parallel is the birth of Hu Gadarn at the Winter Solstice from Kerridwen whose name can be interpreted as KER-YD-WEN OR "of the holy corn enclosure". Hu Gadarn was the first to harness oxen to the plough in Wales, so he must be equated with Saturn who was reckoned as the deity who introduced agriculture to Italy. Saturn's Consort was Ops the goddess of agriculture, one of whose festivals, the Opalia, started on December 19th and culminated on 20th or 21st at the solstice. The name Ops means plenty, and she can be equated with Demeter or Ceres, and as Demeter was the mother of Dionysus, Dionysus can be equated with Hu Gadarn, which may explain the survival of the worship of Calf headed Dionysus Sabazius as a child born in a cow stall and presented to the people in a winnowing basket in the Village of Chalvey, just north of Windsor, in the form of the Chalvey Stab Monkey. The present Stab Monkey is a plaster cast of the original, reputedly of a monkey, but having the appearance of a very virile calf-headed child laying in a hollow the shape of a winnowing basket.

There is also a meteor shower on 15th August from the area between the harp (Lyra) and The Wings of the Dragon or Cernunnos right hand antler. It is a common day for village feasts, and is the Christian Assumption of the Blessed Virgin. This was the Christian substitute for the Roman festival of the Mother Goddess Diana of 13th August. In Celtic Brittany 15th August is celebrated as the Pardon of Notre Dame de la Clarte, that is Our Lady of the Dawn, a title of the amorous nymph goddess Aradia of the witches, daughter of Lucifer and Diana. In the context of the constellations if Cernunnos as the horned god is taken to be Lucifer, the Christian devil, and Ursa Major the terrible reaper as the goddess Diana, meteors emanating from near them might bc interpreted as the soul of Aradia, their child returning to earth for reincarnation.

Before leaving Draco there are just two more tales about him among the classical constellations. The two main stars near the end of his tail are called The Guards. It is their job to prevent Ursa Major swallowing the Pole Star and making it part of the Great Bear constellation. This story notes how the pole of the heavens is moving.

The other story of Draco probably links him with Ladon, the dragon guarding the apples of The Hesperades. When Hercules, whose name means beloved of Hera, killed the dragon, it was Hera who set it in the heavens as a reward for his services. However, others claim that Draco fought on the side of the Titans in their war against the Olympian gods, but that after ten years of warfare Minerva, who was Athene to the Greeks, threw Draco up into the sky where he froze stiff. A third version of the story claims that Draco is really Typhon, the fire spitting demon son of Gaia the Earth Goddess. He has fire spitting from the meteor showers emanating from him around the end of June and the middle of August.

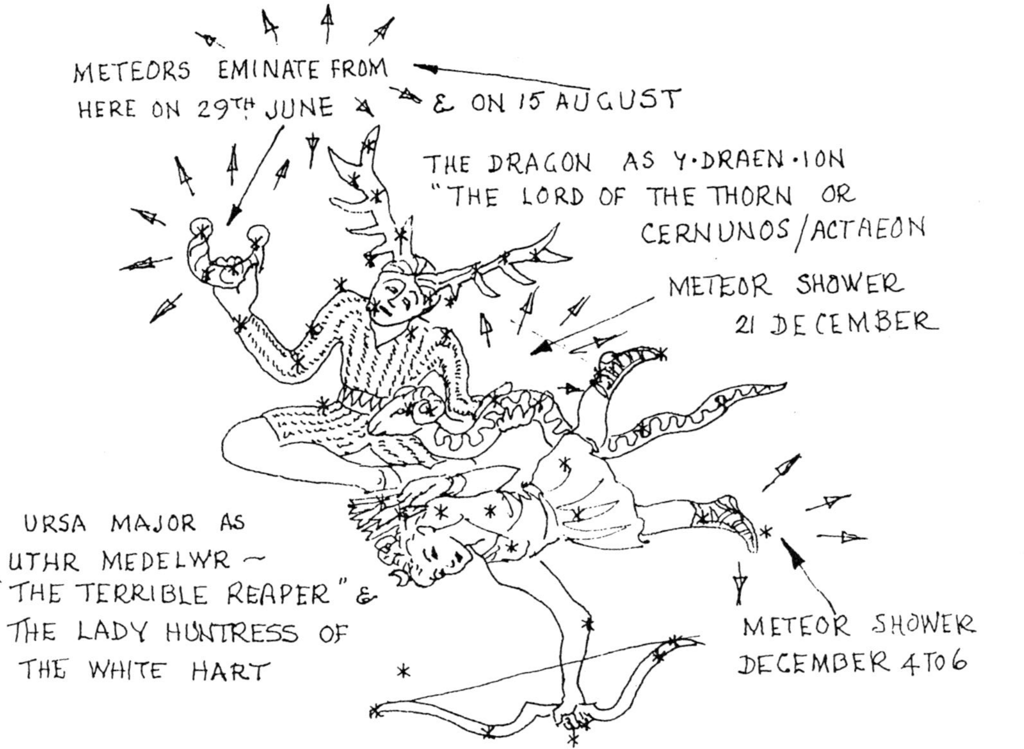
METEORS EMINATE FROM
HERE ON 29TH JUNE
& ON 15 AUGUST
THE DRAGON AS Y·DRAEN·ION
"THE LORD OF THE THORN OR
CERNUNOS/ACTAEON
METEOR SHOWER
21 DECEMBER
URSA MAJOR AS
UTHR MEDELWR ~
"THE TERRIBLE REAPER" &
THE LADY HUNTRESS OF
THE WHITE HART
METEOR SHOWER
DECEMBER 4 TO 6

EPONA'S OR LLYR'S HORSE & FOAL

Equuelus xviii

Sectionis equi
Equuleus, Equi sectio
The Colt

To the Celts, Equuelus is the foal to the White Horse, that is the goddess Epona's Mare (see Aegaseus).

The White Horse at Uffington is traditionally supposed to have had a foal, but archaelogists have not yet found any trace of one. It may well be that the Berkshire White Horse was anciently known to be the earthly representation of the constellation Pegasus and so, as the constellation had a foal, and as Epona's mare had a foal, logically there must be a foal upon White Horse Hill, somewhere, at least in the minds of the people of the Vale of the White Horse, if not on the ground.

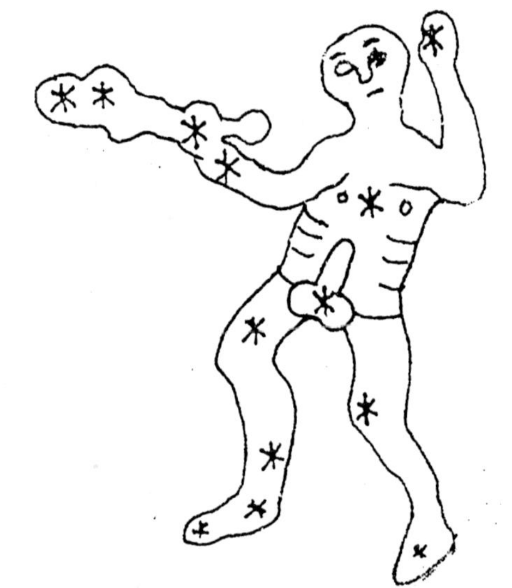

HERCULES OR HELITH

Hercules vii

Incumbentis genubus
Engonasi, Hercules
Labouring man kneeling - with his right foot on the dragon, according to the Scilican Avantus in 270 BC
The Babylonians called this constellation The Great Dog

Hercules may for some purposes be equated with the oak gods Jove, Zeus, and the Dagda (the cattle god of Ireland) or his son Ogimus or Ogma Sunface. Like the Cerne Giant, the 180 foot long hill figure in Dorset, Hercules carried an oaken club in his right hand, and a lion skin over his left arm. The lion skin is sometimes shown as a shield and in mummers plays in England it has become a dripping pan or frying pan - like the maypole enclosure above the left arm of the Cerne Giant.

Locally the Cerne Giant is called Helis or Helith and is held to be an earthly representation of the constellation Hercules. The name of the village of Cern probably derives from the giants name, as in Welsh or Cornish SER-NER means "the Lord of the Stars". The village name dates from at least the early 12th century. There is a rectangular enclosure called the frying pan on the hilltop above him where a maypole is erected and used on 1st May, to celebrate the start of his reign.

Hercules may have been Gwalch Mai the restored form of Llew, the son of Gwydion, which his father found among the stars in the form of an eagle (the constellation of Aquila). Llew Llaw, like Lugh, was the summer sun god. The summer sun is Huan in Welsh, and is feminine in gender, as opposed to Haul, the winter sun, which is masculine. The constellation Hercules is rising at Ladyday, just as the constellation of Orion on the opposite side of the pole is dipping below the horizon. They stand one either side of the lady at the pole, Arianrhod, Berecynthia, or Creudyladd the lady in red. In one sense Hercules and Orion are rivals for the favours of this lady, and one Gwythur ap Griedawl and Gronw Pebyr who fight for her favours every first of May.

The constellation Hercules disappears from the sky in the winter, appearing in the east in the spring, and setting in the west in the autumn. The Long Man of Wilmington may be another representation of Hercules or Helith.

THE LONG MAN OF WILMINGTON
AS HE STANDS ON THE HILLSIDE

There are, or were until the interior of the church was whitewashed, a series of graphiti in the 13th century church of St John the Baptist at Little Marlow, Bucks; which explain the relationship of both Helith at Cerne in Dorset and the Long Man of Wilmington with the constellation of Hercules. The feast day of St John the Baptist is on 24th June, just after the summer solstice on 22nd June. It is denoted on the cog almanac by a smiling sun face. The Christian interpretation of this is that it is the head of St John the Baptist on a dish as presented to Salome, but this feast is of St John's birth. His decollation, beheading, was in the winter. A saints day normally celebrates his death.

Graphito A shows how the constellation was seen as an H for Hercules in the 13th century and in B how it was seen as Hercules himself. Drawings F & G show these two graphiti drawn over the constellation. Graphito D shows the letter H in the form of the giant Hercules holding his club in his left hand. The M shaped graphito cannot represent casseopea here, as it is in the W position at midsummer. But the rather misshapen M shown in E, may perhaps represent a figure like the Long Man of Wilmington, standing with his legs apart and holding two long poles. Or perhaps it shows the summer sun god or his earthly representative with his hands tied up to two poles at his execution at midsummer. Certainly this was when the sparrow, Bran's sparrow, the goldcrest wren, shot Cock Robin, as told in the nursery rhyme, when all the birds of the air fell a-sighing and a-sobbing. This was the time of the Celtic AN FHEILL EOIN, The Festival of Birds, when Celtic Bale Fires were lit.

An Fheill Eoin, The Festival of Birds, is the Gaelic name for the midsummer feast day. Its connection with birds, which one must remember can hold one of the multiple souls of the earthly incarnations or representations of the gods, is explained in the nursery rhyme of *Who Killed Cock Robin*?

1 *Who killed Cock Robin?*
I said the Sparrow
With my bow and arrow
I killed Cock Robin.

Cock Robin is so called because in Welsh or Cornish the name COCH or GOCH means red, and RHI-BEN means the Chief King, so the robin is The red chief king of birds. The sparrow is not the common house or hedge sparrow, but is Bran's sparrow, which is a name for the Goldcrest Wren. But it seems that the arrow was shot on 1st or 2nd of August, which is marked on the cog almanac with a bow on 1st August, and a crescent headed bird arrow on the 2nd August. This period covers the feast of the sungod Lugh. Archery contests are traditionally held at this time.

A PIECE OF CASTOR WARE
FROM ROMAN WELNEY
SHOWING HERCULES

2 *Who saw him die?*
I said the Pie,
With my little eye,
I saw him die.

The magpie is a bird of ill omen or death.

3 *Who caught his blood?*
I said the fisher
With my little disher
I caught his blood.

Since the robin is a royal bird, its blood must not be allowed to fall on the ground - hence the dish. According to Pliny midsummer is one of the three times in the year where the halcyon or kingfisher is seen.

4 *Wholl make the shroud?*
I said the eagle
With my thread and needle
Ill make the shroud.

The eagle is the bird of the winter solstice, near the time of the midwinter wren hunt and triumph of the robin again, when Arianrhod gave her son Llew Llaw a bow and arrow so he could shoot Gronw Pebyr, Lord of the Lake, his rival in love.

5 *Wholl dig his grave?*
I said the owl
With my pick and shouell
Ill dig his grave.

Or

Wholl dig his grave?
The owl with the aid
Of mattock and spade
Will dig robins grave.

The word shouell is the 14th century spelling of shovel. Llew Llaw's wife Blodowedd was turned into an own as punishment, for betraying him and was therefore implicated in his death like this owl.

6 *Wholl be the parson?*
I said the rook
With my little book
Ill be the parson.

The rook is the bird of the unlucky intercalanary 13th month of the Colingy Calendar.

THE CERNE GIANT & THE "FRYING PAN"

7 *Who'll be the clerk?*
I said the lark
If its not in the dark
I'll be the clerk.

The lark is the bird of the sun god Apollo or Beli and of the summer solstice, sacred to the Queen of the Pentad the goddess of death in life. The tree of midsummer is heather which is sacred to Venus.

8 *Who'll carry the link?*
I said the Linnet
I'll come in a minute
I'll carry the link.

A link in this sense is a torch made of tow and pitch used for illumination. The connection with the linnet is that this birds name derives from the old French *linette*, from *lin* meaning flax, from which tow is made, and upon the seeds of which linnets feed. The linnet also has a pinkish red breast suggesting the fire of the link.

9 *Who'll be chief mourner?*
I said the dove
I'll mourn for my love
I'll be chief mourner.

Or

Who'll be chief mourner?
I said the swan
I'm sorry he's gone
I'll be chief mourner.

The Pleiades which rise in May are supposed to be Hera's doves or the attendants of Artemis, who were the seven daughters of Atlas. The verse about the swan appears to be modern.

10 *Who'll carry the coffin?*
I said the kite
If its not through the night
I'll carry the coffin.

Or

Who'll carry him to his grave?
I said the kite
If its not in the night
I'll carry him to his grave.

The kite is a carrion eater and scavenger, and in the days when corpses were exposed before burial would have frequented the area and carried away bits of the bodies.

11 *Who'll bear the pall?*
We said the wren
Both cock and hen
We'll bear the pall.

There is the possibility that if the song is really old it may have been translated from the British language in which *pal* means spade. In some traditions the wren is the wife of the robin, in others it is the goldcrest wren, Brans Sparrow, that kills Cock Robin.

12 *Who'll sing a Psalm?*
I said the thrush
As she sat in a bush
I'll sing the psalm.

13 *Who'll toll the bell?*
I said the bull
Because I can pull
I'll toll the bell.

Since all the other mourners are birds, the bull here probably refers to the bullfinch.

14 *Who'll lead the way?*
I said the martin
When ready for starting
I'll lead the way.

15 *All the birds of the air*
Fell a-sighing and a-sobbin
When they heard of the death
Of poor Cock Robin.

There is a 15th century stained glass window in Buckland Rectory in Gloucestershire which shows a robin pierced through the heart by an arrow. In 1508 John Skelton wrote a similar story about Phyllup Sparrow. In a German version the cuckoo is the gravedigger. The cuckoo is the bird of the Cailleach, the old woman who lets it loose as a harbinger of Spring.

Superstition or belief in the older gods must have survived at Little Marlow long after the church was built for the explicit graphiti there to have been scratched on its walls. There is also a pentacle cut on the south door moulding. This is the 'symbol at your door' of the carol *Green Grow the Rushes Oh*. It is often found on the latches and hinges of church doors also, as it will keep out evil spirits and witches (see the constellation Bootes).

The tower of Little Marlow church was built on a foundation of long thin sarsen stones, actually a good damp proof course, but they look as if they were from a circle of standing stones. No legend has survived at Little Marlow as it has at nearby Penn, where the tower has similar foundations which legend tells were taken from a druid circle at Penn Bottom, whence many of the stones hauled up to the church during the day, returning the following night. Since to the Celts the name of Little Marlow, which lies on the flood plain of the Thames, probably derives from LLI DOL MA LLEW, that is "the flood meadows of the place of Llew Llaw", that is the summer sun god, it is quite possible that there was a circle of standing stones here, perhaps aligned to predict the summer solstice. This would account for the dedication of the church to the saint with a feast day near the previous gods feast day.

Before leaving the constellation of Hercules, one of the few direct links between ancient Greece and ancient Britain, we should perhaps look at the classical legends of Hercules, or Heraclese as the Greeks called him.

Heraclese, we are told, was the son of Alcmene the wife of Amphitryon by Zeus, while she and her husband were in exile in Thebes. Aclmene was known as The Lady of the light footsteps, and was the daughter of Electryon and Perseus, king of Mycenae. With this parentage it is no wonder we see him among the stars, as his mother's name is said to mean The Might of the Moon and his father's The Bright Sky.

His original name appears to have been Alcides, a name suggesting might and justice, his grandfather's name. But the name Heraclese was given to him when he visited the great holy centre of Greek religion at Delphi. Curiously it means the Glory of Hera, for Hera was the normally very jealous wife of Zeus.

As befits one of the immortals invoked in matters of fertility, and the traditions of the Cerne Giant in Britain which have survived into the 20th century show the strength of this link. Heraclese did not confine the fathering of sons to his wife Megera, daughter of the king of Thebes. She bore him three sons.

Whether it was during his twelve Labours, when he hunted the Cerynitian hind to the Land of the Hyperboneans and back, or later when he visited Italy as Hercules, somewhere he lay with a Hyperborean girl and fathered Latinas, later king of Latium, on her. Whether it was before or after the birth of Latinas, his Hyperborean mother was taken to wife by Faunus, the god of pastures and woods, protector of herds, and promoter of fertility, hence he is sometimes claimed as the father of Latinus.

It was when Latinus reigned as King of Latium that Aeneas arrived from Troy, where Latinus granted him land and the hand of his daughter Lavinia. It was by this marriage that Aeneas came to rule Latium as its next King.

The Romans worshipped Hercules as Invictus, that is as the Victor, and also as Salutaris, the averter of evil and protector of the home and house. Merchants therefore worshipped him as their protector and offered him a tenth of their profits. Similarly, travellers honoured him as their protector too.

His twelve Labours link him with some other constellations, as will be seen under their histories. Briefly the twelve Labours of Hercules were as follows:

The First Labour was the slaying of the Nemean Lion, whose skin he is said to wear or carry over his left arm as a shield. The Lion survives as the constellation Leo.

The Second Labour was the slaying of the Hydra of Lerna. Hercules used its blood to poison his arrows. In this contest Hera wished Heracles to lose so she sent the constellation of the Crab to help the Hydra.

The Third Labour was the capture, alive and unharmed, of the fifth Cerynitian Hind. These beasts were deer with golden horns and brazen hooves. They were sacred to Artemis, who had captured four of them to pull her chariot. From the practical and natural history point of view, the only deer whose hinds carry horns are reindeer; and reindeer are the only deer that have been domesticated to work in harness. This is perhaps why it was to the Land of the Hyperboreans that Hercules had to travel in this quest for the last Cerynitian hind. While in the rest of Europe the reindeer retreated north to the tundra as the ice retreated after the last ice age, in the land that was to become Britain, the land of the Hyperboreans, they were cut off by the sea and the flooding of North Sea land. It is probable that Britain was the most southerly and accessible land where reindeer still lived known to the ancient world. They are supposed to have survived in Scotland into the medieval period, and their horns have survived into this century as those carried by the Abbots Bromley Horn Dancers. The medieval chapel of Our Lady in the Forest, that once stood in the valley now flooded as Virginia Water in Windsor Great Park, was decorated with Cerynitian Hinds. It was of course a Royal Peculiar, that it not under the rule of any bishop. Perhaps Sir Thomas Mallory actually knew that Artemis or Diana was still worshipped by those who hunted deer in the Forest of Windsor, when he recorded the tale of the Lady Huntress of Windsor Forest in Arthurian Britain.

The Fourth Labour was the capture of the Erymanthian Boar of Arcadia. This ferocious wild beast had been one of the sons of Apollo, who was turned into this form as punishment for watching Aphrodite bathe. It is a similar story to that of Actaeon who was turned into a stag by Artemis for the same crime. Perhaps this legend came from north west Europe where Leo was seen as a wild boar.

The Fifth Labour was the cleaning of the Augean Stables.

The Sixth Labour was the driving away of the Stymphalian birds. These birds feathers were used like arrows, and they had brazen claws and beaks. They ate humans and destroyed their crops with their droppings.

The Seventh Labour was to bring the Cretan Bull to Mycenae. Hercules did this by riding it over the sea.

The Eighth Labour was to bring the man-eating Mares of Diomedes of Thrace to Mycenae.

The Ninth Labour was to fetch the girdle of Hypolyte the Amazon.

The Tenth Labour was to fetch the cattle of Geryon of Erythia, an island in the far west beyond the pillars of Hercules, in the Atlantic Ocean. Since Erythia means the red land, perhaps this land was Devonshire, the red land of red cattle even today.

The Eleventh Labour was to fetch the Golden Apples of the Hesperades, again from a land in the far west guarded by Ladon the Dragon and the three maidens, the Hesperades. The orchard belonged to Hera - in Norse myth apples gave immortality. In Britain the ceremonially cut apple forms the applewell, and this is the well at the bottom of which truth can be found. It confers immortality because it contains the secret of procreation, as explained to the sacred king by the priestess of the mound. Megalithic tombs like New Grange in Ireland have stones decorated with spirals, symbols of life, which originated as the peel of the apple offered to the sacred king. This is explained in the last chapter of Volume II. New Grange, our name for the Brugh-na-Boyne was the Sidh of Angus the Gaelic god of love and beauty.

The final and **Twelfth Labour** was to bring up Cerberus from Hades. Since other constellations are connected with the Labours, perhaps this is connected with the Dog Star Sirius.

GRAPHITI FROM THE 13THc CHURCH OF St. JOHN THE BAPTIST, LITTLE MARLOW

FROM THE NORTH SIDE OF THE PILLAR IN THE NORTH WEST CORNER OF THE CHURCH

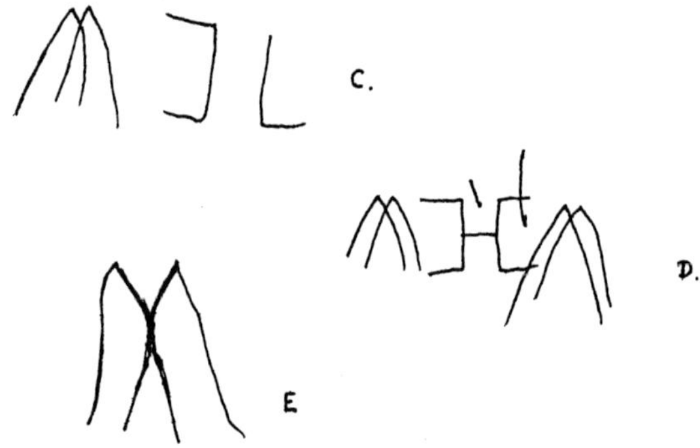

FROM THE NORTH SIDE OF THE ARCH FROM THE NAVE TO THE TOWER ON THE WEST END, WHICH IS BUILT ON A BASE OF LONG THIN TRIMMED SARSENS. POSSIBLY A STONE CIRCLE AS AT PENN.

THE CONSTELLATION AS THE GRAPHITI IN SUMMER

The classical gods gave Hercules or Heracles presents. Although he made his own oaken club, it was Hephaestus who made him his golden breastplate; Apollo who provided him with his bow and arrows; Hermes who gave him his sword and Poseidon his horses. Among the goddesses, Athena gave him a robe, but Hera sent the Crab against him during his Labours.

It is rare to have a firm date for the introduction of the worship of any ancient god into the British Isles. But probably as a result of early Christian annalists among the holy men of Ireland, we have a date of 1267 years BC, that Heremon the High King of Ireland introduced the worship of Hercules or Apollo or Ogma to Ireland. We, therefore know that Ogma or Ogminus Sunface was the local name of the sungod elsewhere called Apollo or Hercules, whose representation has probably survived to this day in the countless inn signs of The Sun or The Rising Sun.

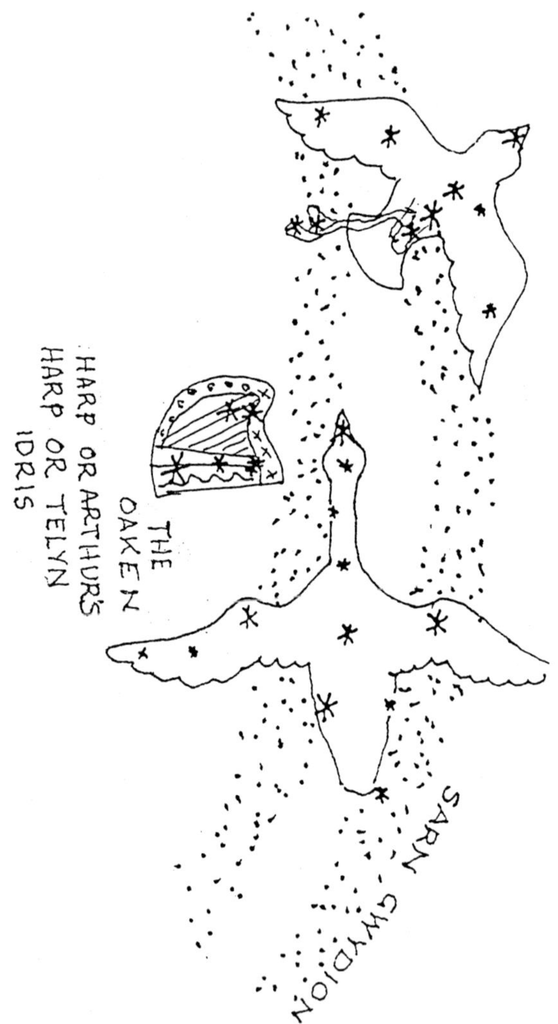
THE OAKEN
HARP OR ARTHUR'S
HARP OR TELYN
IDRIS
SARN GWYDION

Lyra viii

Shelyak, Testudo
Lyra, Vultur cadens
The Lyre (in classical astronomy the Lyre was made by Mercury)
The Babylonians called the constellation Lyra the Goat

Telyn Idris or Arthur's Harp is the Welsh name for this constellation, but the only reason for translating Idris as Arthur's would seem to be because either the constellation was also called *Telyn Arth Seren* that is "The Harp of the High Stars", or because it was described by Idris Gawr one of the famous Gwyn Serenyddion or Happy or Blessed Astronomers of Wales. He was said to have observed the heavens from the top of Cader Idris (the seat of Idris), a mountain in north Wales. Because it lays adjacent to the constellation Hercules, the giant wielding an oaken club, it may also have been considered to be the oaken harp of the Dagda, the cattle god of Ireland.

Pegasus xix

Equi majoris
Pegasus, Equus alatus
Pegasus or The Horse

As this is the only other white horse to be seen in Britain, apart from the Uffington White Horse, all others being greys or albinos, the Uffington White Horse must be the terrestrial equivalent of the constellation Pegasus, the heavenly white horse. Equuelus must, therefore, be the white horses foal, just as the Ufflington one is said to have had a foal at one time.

It is possible that Pegasus is the constellation called "The Horse of Llyr", the sea god of the Celts though the crests of waves are the white horses of the sea. The constellation is also Epona's mare to the Celts and Equuelus is her foal.

There are many springs around Britain that are said to have burst forth from the front hoof print made by a white horse. Such a spring is the one made by the horse of "Saint" Anne Bolyn at Carshalton in Surrey, and also the one made by Uffington's White Horse at Woolstone wells in the hamlet that lays below the hollow in the hillside under the White Horse, called the Manger. That is why the Well dressing of springs in Derbyshire is done between the 28th and 30th July, when the Aquarids (339^0 - 11^0). An annual meteor shower, appears to emanate from the front foot of Pegasus, the White Horse of the heavens. There is another meteor shower from (338^0 - 2^0) in nearly the same area from the 1st to the 3rd May which covers other well dressings in Derbyshire and near Chertsey in Surrey and from 1st to 2nd August at (338^0- 11^0) and about July 15th at (339^0- 11^0), but these are less visible.

Since it appears that the White Horse at Uffington is an earthly representation of the White Horse in the sky it may be useful to look into Uffington's situation and nearby place names. Recently scientific research by Optical Stimulated Luminescence has shown that the White Horse of Uffington was first cut into the hillside around 1400 to 600 BC, that is 3000 years ago in the late Bronze Age. Early spellings of Uffington like that of 1080, Offentone, suggest an origin from OP-PEN-TONE or OP PEN DUN that is from "the horse of the hill top permanent pasture" or "the horse of the hill top fort". It lies just below the Iron Age hill fort of Uffington Castle. Woolstone Wells, the spring of the White

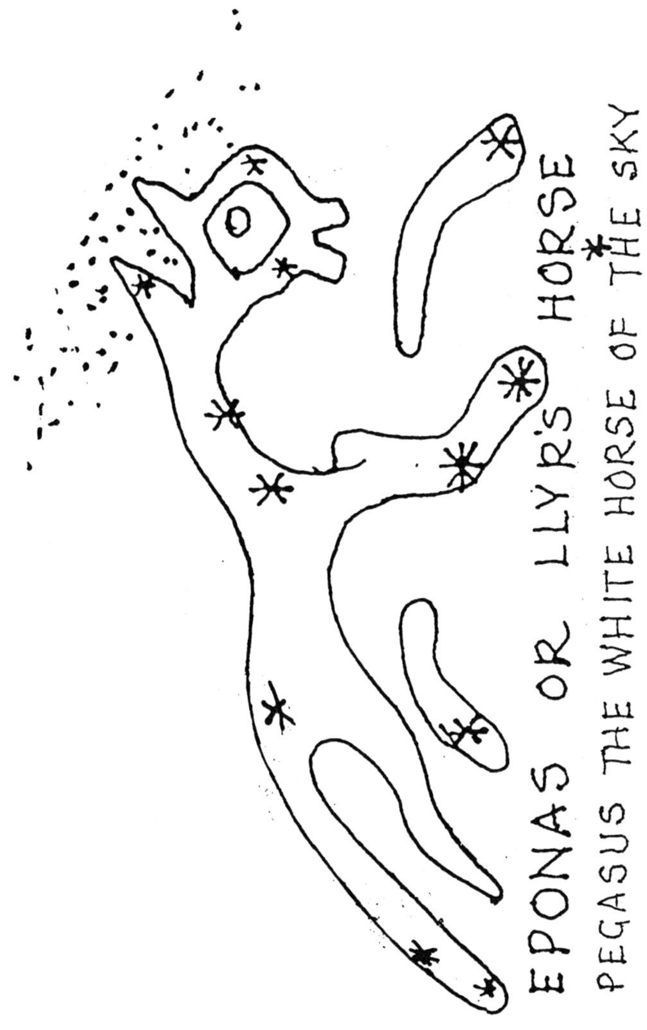
EPONAS OR LLYR'S HORSE
PEGASUS THE WHITE HORSE OF THE SKY

Horse, was spent WLSIESTON in 1080, which probably derives from WY OLVA SERTH YS TON, that is "the weeping waters of the steep place below the permanent pasture". The stream that flows from these wells is "Holywell Brook". It is not connected with any Christian saint, so the name here probably derives from OLVA WY LEE that is "the weeping water place".

Local tradition tells us that the White Horse used to dance upon Dragon Hill, the flat topped hill just below Uffington's Castle and White Horse, and that this is where St George killed the Dragon. The White Horse vale mummers play still shows a version of the story of Perseus rescuing Andromeda from the sea monster or dragon, and many of its so-called nonsense words are just words of the old lowland British language. Dragon Hill was almost certainly what the Welsh call a *Twmpath Chwarae*, "a mound of the games" where ceremonies and mummers plays took place. St George like St Michael and St James, the other red cross knights, all rode white horses. Throughout the Ancient World, from Scandinavia to Etruria and Greece, heroes and gods rode white horses to take them to heaven. That is why Etruscan tombs show the soul of the deceased riding to heaven on a white horse. And the frieze round the Parthenon on the Acropolis in Athens shows the 190 souls of those who fell as foot soldiers at Marathon riding to heaven on horses.

The name Dragon Hill really derives from its ancient use at the time of the May 1st to 3rd meteor shower from the forefoot of the heavenly White Horse. DRAENEN HEL LE that is the congregating place of the May tree (Hawthorn, which can mean the Maypole, at the Celtic feast of Beltain - "the fire of the summer sun god Bel". BELLAN TAN means the "circle of fire"; through the embers of which stock were driven to preserve them from disease in the coming year. Saint George in this context was the successor to Lugh or Llew Llaw the summer sun god whose symbol was the Celtic cross, a cross in a circle. He survives under the name of Bel in the White Horse mummers play as Old Betsy Bubb or Ol Belzebub deriving from OL BEL SYBER, meaning "the Sun God, proud and generous". Elsewhere in Britain this god has survived as Helith or Hercules. It is even possible that there was once a hill figure like the Cerne Giant on the steepest part of the hill at Uffington which is called The Manger. Perhaps this was once TIR MAEN GWYR, that is "The Stone Man".

The tradition is that the horse, or the castle, at Uffington was made in the time of the Danes, and therefore by Saxon King Alfred, is purely a linguistic misunderstanding. The hill fort was certainly made at the time of the D'ANES, not the Danes or people from Denmark, but the Celtic British D'ANES meaning "the time of the troubles", a term still used today for a time of insecurity and civil warfare, as in Northern Ireland.

THE GODDESS EPONA ON HER WHITE HORSE
WITH ITS FOAL

The connection with Epona probably occurred when the Roman cavalry evolved the cataphract. Cataphracts were heavy cavalry using stirrups from the Scythians, but using the heavier European forest horse. The first highly mobile armoured cavalry fulfilled the role of our recent tank and armoured car regiments. Cataphracts survived into the dark ages as King Arthur's Knights of the Round Table, the Marchion or Horse Lords of the Celts. Epona was a popular deity with the Roman Auxiliary and possibly Celtic cavalry. Her white horse has survived into the 20th century as the badge of the Berkshire Yeomanry, the cavalry raised from farmers sons and men of the county of the White Horse. Pre Roman British coins showed horses similar to the Uffington horse on them, like the gold states of Commius (see drawing).

The Romano British Horse Lords survived into the time of the Heptarchy in central Britain in Mercia, the land of the Mercians where one of our countrys most famous lady horse-riders and her husband came of the Mercian nobility. The Lady Godifu who rode in the nude through Coventry, was actually called Godgifa. She was the wife of Leofric, the Earl of Mercia in the time of King Canute.

Lady Godiva's fame may be due to her name being spelt GODGIFU by the Saxon scribe, as GODISER is the Breton word for "the coaxer", and she certainly coaxed her husband to do what she wanted. But the existence of other fine ladies who rode upon horses in other Mercian towns, like Southam and Banbury, suggests the survival of the worship of Epona, or Rhiannon of Welsh legend, Macha of Gaelic legend, and Creudyladd or Cordelia of London, well into the Christian era of only a thousand years ago. The fine lady with rings on her fingers and bells on her toes who rode a white horse to Banbury Cross, is shown carved on a medieval misericord as the symbol of lechery. Perhaps the link between fine ladies riding white horses and Lady Godiva, and the carving symbolising lechery derives from the Celtic work GODINEBWRAIG. meaning "adulteress", which sounds not dissimiliar to the name Godiva and its variations. Both the horse, of which Pegasus is the heavenly representation, and its lady rider, pervade ancient Celtic myth and legend, and medieval and modern folklore.

Whatever traditional local folklore customs she took part in in Coventry, history records that Lady Godiva and her husband Leofric founded a monastery there.

Leofric also supported Harold against Hardicanute, and mediated between Edward the Confessor and Earl Godwine in 1051. He was succeeded by his son Aelfga.

A GOLD STATER OF COMMIUS

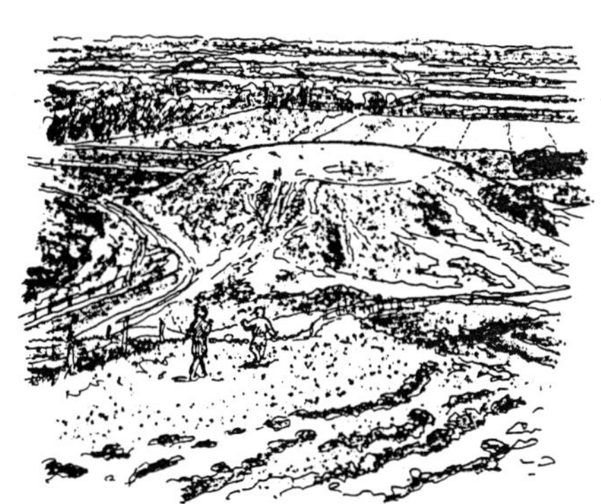

DRAGON HILL FROM UFFINGTON CASTLE & THE WHITE HORSE

THE BERKSHIRE WHITE HORSE AT UFFINGTON

THE SOUL OF THE ETRUSCAN MAN ON THE TOOMB IS SHOWN BELOW RIDEING TO HEAVEN ON A WHITE HORSE .

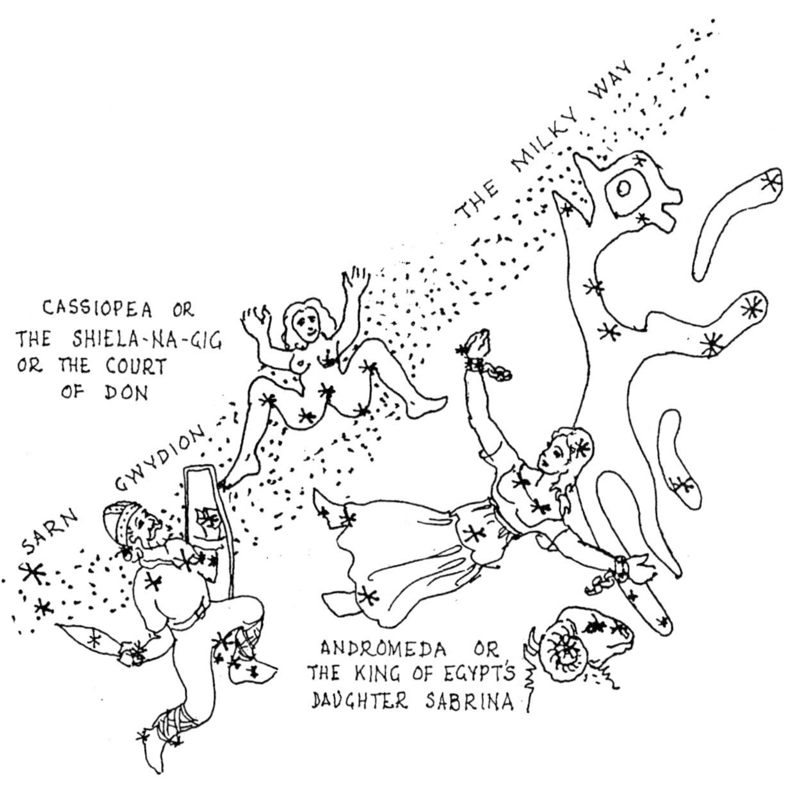
THE MILKY WAY
CASSIOPEA OR
THE SHIELA-NA-GIG
OR THE COURT
OF DON
SARN GWYDION
ANDROMEDA OR
THE KING OF EGYPT'S
DAUGHTER SABRINA
PERSEUS OR LUGH OR
LLEW LLAW OR THE RED
CROSS KNIGHT SAINT OR
KING - GEORGE

His title of Earl is a modern translation of the term Ealdorman used in his time. While the translation is correct in showing that Leofric was a high ranking noble, it leaves out the nature of his wealth, importance and position. What the Saxons termed an ealdorman or earl the Celts termed an EAL-DOR-MARGHION, that is "The Horse Lord of the heads of cattles land". He was the civic officer and military guard of all the cattle of a town. EAL is still the Cornish term for "head of cattle" or "yoke oxen", and DOR means earth or ground or land.

The name Epona is said to be the Gaulish for Mare. She is the White Goddess of the White Horse. She appears in the Mabinogian as Rhiannon the "Queen Lady and Virgin of the Stream", hence the connection of white horses with springs.

The British legend of the gift horse, a white horse that brought gifts, but would take them away again if you looked in its mouth, derives from the practice of looking in the mouth of a horse at its teeth to tell its age before buying it. But if the horse is a gift, this precaution is unnecessary, as the whole horse is a profit anyhow.

There is also the saying that if wishes were horses, beggars would ride. Wishes are also part of the tradition of the Uffington White Horse. If you stand on its eye (or tail) and wish, your wish will be granted.

Scandanavian chiefs were buried with their horses so that they could ride to Valhalla. The god Odin rode the eight-legged grey horse Sleipnir between this world and the next. This horse was a helhurst or death horse, hence dreams or ghosts of horses are premonitions of death.

The Nightmare was a frightening creature like the Lamia. Horses troubled with bad dreams, the nightmare, were covered with lather as if they had been ridden hard all night. To stop horses being so troubled, or as the saying was, being "hagridden", the stable man would hang a flint with a hole in it over the centre of the back of the affected horse on a bit of iron wire. This would keep evil spirits and witches away.

In medieval Wales, rich families would give a horse to be sacrificed to Saint George at the shrine of Llan Sant Sior, by St George's Well near Abergele in Denbighshire, in order to obtain the saint's blessing on all their other horses.

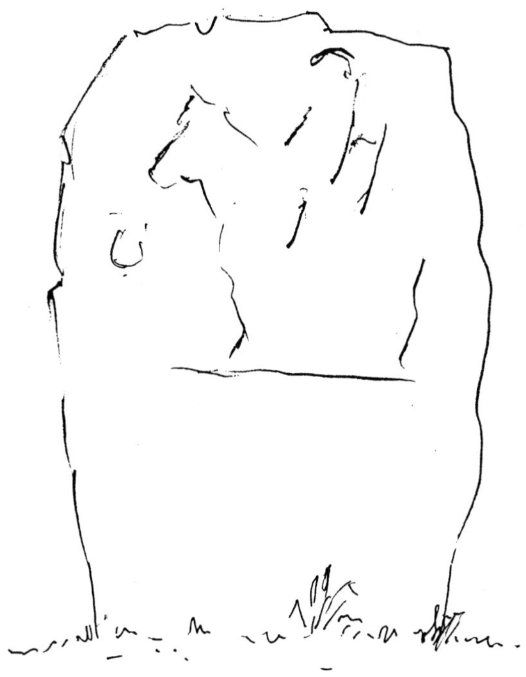

A sculpture on one of the stones at Carnac – perhaps a later drawing of an iron age mounted cattleman or shepherd, forerunner of the EAL-DOR-MARGHION, the "Horse lord of the cattle lands".

At nearby Parc-y-Meirch (The Park of the Stallions) a hoard of Bronze Age horse trappings were found, suggesting that the horse sacrifices had been going on since the Bronze Age. The horse and its sacrifice became a link with the spirit of fertility or the Great Goddess. She was variously known as Rhiannon, Artemis, Diana, Hecuba, the Great Mother, Hecate, Epona, Lucippe, Demeter, Ceres, Berecynthia and The White Lady in every other English village. In our nursery rhymes and ballads she is the Lady of Banbury Cross, of the Luckenbooths and of Coventry.

"Crying the Mare" in Herefordshire is a relic of ancient religion. The last patch of corn was tied half way up into four bunches, and then into one bunch a little higher up. This was known as The Mare. The reapers tried to cut it down by throwing their sickles at it. The successful reaper sat opposite his master at the harvest home feast. The mane itself was then plaited and kept until the next year.

In Wales, the mummers horses were the Hodening Horse or the Mari Llwyd. The latter name means The Grey Mare. It was a horse skull on a stick worked by a man under a white sheet. He accompanied Christmas Wassailing Parties singing songs and requesting alms, from house to house.

The old classical stories about the White Horse and horses are as follows;

The astronomers' name for the white horse of the heavens is Pegasus, and it comes from Greek mythology. But just as in Celtic mythology the horse is a mare with a foal, so it is with the Greeks.

Poseidon, who was the god of both inland water and of the seas, was the father of two famous horses. He was father of the winged black maned wild horse ARION on Demeter, or some say on the nymph Despoena. Arion was eventually tamed and ridden by Heraclese.

In the form of a white stallion Poseidon was the father of Pegasus the white horse of the wells, and of Chrysaor, on Demeter in the form of the white mare Lucippe.

However Lucippe or Leucippe, which means "White Mare" was one of the three daughters of Minyas. Her sisters were Alcithoe and Arisippe or Arisnoe. The three sisters refused to join in the revels of Dionysus, so he drove them insane by changing shape, and Lucippe offered her own son Hippasus, the horseman, chosen by lot, as a sacrifice, and the three sisters tore him to pieces and ate him while roaming the mountains in their frenzy, until either Hermes changed them into birds or Dionysus changed them into bats. This murder was commemorated annually in the festival of Agrionia when women devotees of Dionysus sat in a circle asking riddles until the priest of Dionysus rushed out of the temple and killed the first woman he caught.

THE WHITE HORSE ON THE BERKSHIRE YEOMANRY BADGE

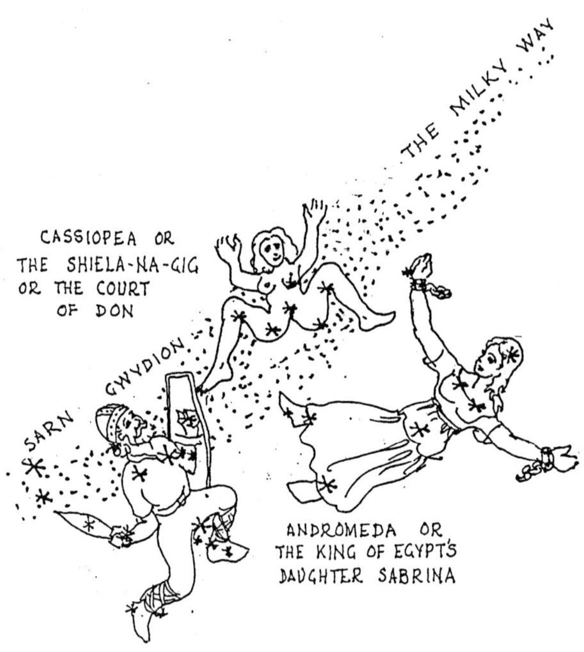
THE MILKY WAY
CASSIOPEA OR
THE SHIELA-NA-GIG
OR THE COURT
OF DON
SARN GWYDION
ANDROMEDA OR
THE KING OF EGYPT'S
DAUGHTER SABRINA
PERSEUS OR LUGH OR
LLEW LLAW OR THE RED
CROSS KNIGHT SAINT OR
KING - GEORGE

Perseus xi

Bershausk, Portans
Perseus

Perseus was the hero who rescued Andromeda, daughter of Casseopea and Cephus the King and Queen of Aetheopia from the sea monster.

This story was re-enacted in British mummers plays by Saint George killing the dragon on Dragon Hill before the White Horse at Uffington, and so winning the King of Eygpt's daughter, Sabrina's, hand in marriage.

These parallel stories show that Perseus must be equated with the three champions of Christendom who rode white horses and carried red crosses, St George, St Michael and St James. The red cross is the sun symbol inherited from Lugh the sun god of western Europe, and champion of the herdsman on the high summer pastures, who was succeeded by the Saints. They rode white horses to show that they were dead heroes or demigods, as it was their privilege to ride to the next world on horseback, and back again to earth if they chose.

The classical constellation Perseus depicts him holding the Gorgon's head which contains the star Algol (the ghoul or mischief maker) (see the story of Perseus and Andromeda under her mother and father's constellation Casseopeia and Cephus). To the Celt he must have been Lugh or Llew Ll aw the patron and protector of the herdsmen on the high summer pastures, the mounted herdsmen who used the iron age hill forts as overnight cattle pens in the summer when the lowland meadows were growing the winter feed of hay.

This may explain the connection between the hill fort of Uffington, the Mummers Play of the Vale of the White Horse, and the story that the white horse once pranced upon Dragon Hill, which still has patches where no green will grow on its flat top as a result of being poisoned by the dragons blood.

Dragon Hill is just an outsized Mound of the Games, a TWMPATH CHWARAE in Welsh. It was the place where the mummers plays, originally religious dramas, were enacted, and doubtless St George or Llew Llaw, the hero, once rode around the area of Dragon Hill upon a white hobby horse. In Celtic lands it is St Michael, who is the protector of the flocks and herds on the high summer pastures, not St George. Even in southern England the path up to the high summer pastures from Burchetts Green and Bisham in Berkshire is still known as Michael's Path. Just as it was St Michael who was in command of heavens military forces, so the chief herdsman of a village or town, who guarded its most precious possession, its flocks and herds, was the military commander of the village or tribe or towns cavalry. Such a post easily became an inherited title, or at least an inherited position.

This is demonstrated in the history of the Buckinghamshire city of Aylesbury, a Roman British town in the lush pastures of the Vale of Aylesbury. It is only logical to attribute the largest iron age hill fort in the Chilterns, the Grim's Ditches that surround the hilltop settlements of the Hambdens, as the hill fort of the largest town of the Vale. We know that the Saxons took Aylesbury in the summer, when the citizens cattle would have been up in the Chiltern hills, and the Chilterns remained an independent kingdom for at least another couple of centuries. The British city of Aylesbury's chief herdsmen and their cavalry remained safe in the Chilterns with their cattle. This probably accounts for the wealth of the Hambden family whose family seat and lands lay at the centre of this huge hill fort. They never held any title other than Hambden of Hambden. One son and heir of this family beat the Black Prince in a joust, and the family provided the cavalry for Edward III's invasion of Scotland. They must have been worthy followers of the role of St Michael and Lugh or Llew Llaw, as protectors of herdsmen on the high summer pastures of the Chilterns, whose heavenly counterpart was the constellation we call Perseus.

The transition from the sun god Lugh to St Michael was helped by the nearest sounding Celtic words to the saints name SANCT MAG CAE HAUL which can be translated as "The Holy One of the feeding fields of the summer sun", a poetic description of Lugh. Just as Perseus was associated with Andromeda and a sea monster that devastated the land, and St George was associated with Sabrina and a dragon, so St Michael in Celtic North Britain is associated with St Margaret - another lady with a dragon, who is but another version of the goddess Berecynthia who flies round the sky on her dragon, the constellation Draco, every night.

Just as when one studies the histories of the early Celtic saints one finds that some of them were related to each other, so among the constellations of the heavens we find that some of them are related. Hercules for instance was the son of Alcmene by Zeus, and Alcmene was the daughter of Perseus and Electryon. It is curious that Hercules should have been Perseus's grandson when one would have thought that Hercules was the older deity.

Sagitta xv

Sagittae
Sagitta, Telum
The Arrow

It is curious that this single arrow is usually shown as flying in the opposite direction to the one in Sagittarius, the archer's bow. It may be significant that it has passed by the eagle or hawk and may miss the swan or goose, but is flying directly towards the colt. Since it was grey goose feathers that provided the flights of Celtic arrows, there may be some significance to the proximity of Sagitta, the arrow and Cygnus the swan - or goose to the Celt.

Serpens xiv

Serpentis
Serpens opkiuchi
The Serpent

The head and neck of the serpent marks the position of the sun at the Autumn Equinox. It seems possible that to the Celts Serpens represents the monster Addanc (possibly afanc or beaver) that Hu Gadarn's yoked oxen pulled out of the lake of Llyon Llion to stop it causing a flood (see Bootes). If it was not part of the beaver, it was near it and still associated with Hu Gadarn who was born as the first fruit of a tree guarded by a serpent and nursed by a woman as beautiful as the moon. To the Celt the soul of a dead hero or king split into at least three parts. One part was a shooting star that carried the soul to its heaven in the sky, one part became a bird, and one part became a worm, snake or dragon. The serpent guarding the tree of Hu Gadarn's first birth may well have been one of the souls of his predecessor in office.

The spotted snake on a hill is associated in the Ogham alphabets with the vine or blackberry in the month of September when the fruit is ripe. The picture of a snake is from a Pictish Celtic drawing.

However, this serpent is associated with a serpent bearer (see Serpentarius), so maybe it is the serpent soul of the great man whose star soul was the meteor that came to earth at Porth Lisky Bay near St David's in south west Wales. His mother had attributes in common with the Mother of Hu Gadarn, and was known as Saint Non. She gave birth to St David during a storm in the centre of a circle of standing stones. Her baby was St David or Dewi (see the constellation of Aquarius).

We have noted that the serpent is connected with the birth of Hu Gadarn of the Welsh, the first in Wales to yoke oxen to the plough. A serpent is also linked with the birth of Dionysus, who according to the Greek Diodorus Siculus, was the first in Greece to yoke oxen to the plough.

It was as a serpent that Zeus visited Persephone, and so begot Zagreus who was the horned infant Dionysus, shown to the people in a winnowing basket. In this form he was known as Sabazian Dionysus, the beer god, very popular with the later Roman army. He has survived in this form as The Stab Monkey, until Victorian times presiding over a beer drinking orgy in the village of Chalvey, between the industrial town of Slough and Windsor Castle. The form of the ceremony following that recorded for him in pre-Roman Athens in Greece (see under Bootes). Sabazian Dionysus also survives in the town of Slough as the ghost of a large white shaggy calf that haunts Shaggy Calf Lane there, and is inclined to chase those who have drunk too much beer. In ancient Greece Sabazian Dionysus was hunted to death and torn limb from limb by frenzied maenads. Whether the ghost of the Shaggy Calf arrived in Britain in post Celtic times with the Roman army, or in pre Celtic times as the white bull god of the Danaans with seabourne colonists from the Mediterranean is anyone's guess. Whether he was still actively worshipped in 13th century Buckinghamshire when a floor tile was made showing a king kneeling before him, or whether this was only a representation of a curious old folk custom of the time, again is anyone's guess.

THE SNAKE
OR SERPENT
NEIDR

THE SERPENT BEARER

AND THE SERPENT.

Serpentarius xiii

Serpentarii
Ophiuchus, Serpentarius
The Serpent Bearer

In Celtic traditions when a man dies his soul divides into at least three parts. One part becomes a worm, one part becomes a bird and one part becomes a star in the night sky. The more important the person, the bigger and more important their souls, so that the soul of a king or hero, buried in a fine tumulus, will become a large snake or even a dragon to guard the treasure buried with him. His bird soul will become a hawk or even an eagle, and his star soul will become a shooting star or meteor. Hence the priestess of a long barrow could well have been a serpent bearer, caring for a snake that might well decide to live in an open long barrow, which would give shelter and warmth in winter, and small vermin attracted by human refuse and bones, to prey upon. The most ancient European earth goddess whose name we know is Gaia, she was associated with snakes.

However, if we want to put the earliest classical name to Serpentarius and Serpens, it must be that of the mother goddess of all things, Eurynome, who appeared from chaos and divided the waters from the sky danced southwards over the waves. She caught the turbulent eddies that formed behind her and created Ophion or Boreas the North wind and formed him into a serpent with whom she coupled, and from which came the world egg that hatched into all creation.

This story must be very ancient as it seems to be reflected in the way the Egyptians saw their goddess Nu or Nun, as a person standing in the waters with both arms raised like Serpentarius. It may be no accident that in Britain a pagan princess by the name of Nun or Non, whose name may means the streamlet, was raped by Sant, and also wandered southwards by the Prescelly hills following a star through bad weather, and finally as the star came to earth found shelter within a stone circle where flowers grew and birds sang, and gave birth to St David or Dewi Sant. A spring appeared there to quench her thirst and has continued to this day as a curative spring.

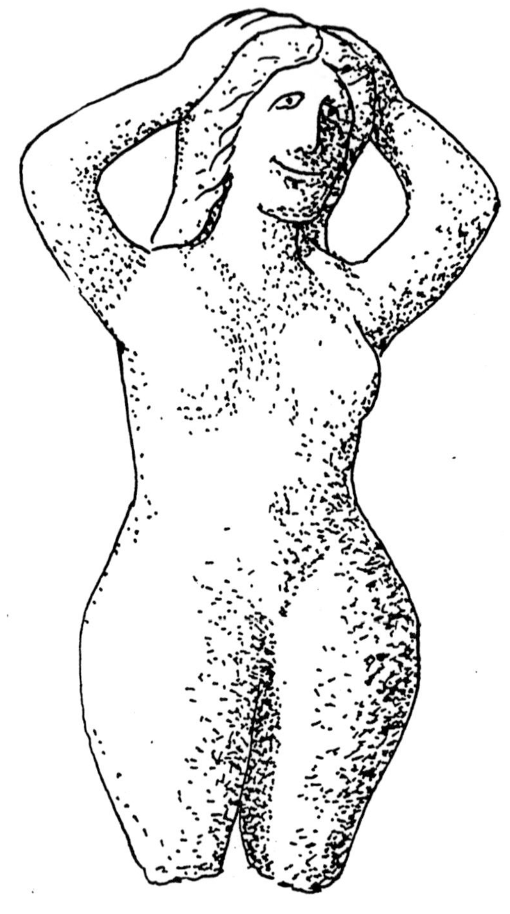

GAIA from Tanagra

Some say Sant was the son of a Cardigan Chieftain, but it is also the name of a north Welsh river falling into the Menai Straits.

The star she followed towards Duwies Llan Hundred, that is the Hundred of the sacred enclosure of the goddess came to earth in about 520 AD as a meteorite, and may still be seen at porth Lisky Bay, just to the west of St Non's stone circle near St Davids. It was one of the annual shower of meteors that lasts from St David's Day on March 1st until St Non's Day on March 3rd of 4th.

This meteor shower appears to originate near the left hand of Serpentarius, the serpent bearer. In Cornwall, St Non's Well cures madness, which suggests that she was originally a moon goddess. Perhaps she was the goddess Rhiannon, the Great Queen whose name can be interpreted as RHAIN-NON, that is Queen Non or the Queen of the streamlet.

If this is the case then the Celtic name for Serpentarius should be Rhiain Non or Sanct Non "The Holy One Non or Holy One of the Streamlet", perhaps the streamlet that still flows from St Non's spring within the stone circle near St Davids. Her son certainly had magical powers, making springs appear and commanding the ground to rise up to provide him with a pulpit. His name Sant Dewi in Welsh is very similar to Sanct Dewin which is just The Holy Magician.

There is one other goddess who was worshipped in her own name and also under other names in Britain, who could lay claim to being the Serpent bearer. She was Astarte the lady who rode the dragon around the polar skies every night. She was also called Cybele or Berecynthia. As Astarte she held a viper in her left hand (see Ursa Major and Draco).

Triangulum xxi

Trianguli
Triangulus, Deltoton
The Triangle

This was also known by the Celts as the Triangle. Certainly the constellation consists of three stars. It may be that the constellation was named after the magic triangle with sides measuring three, four and five units, which gives a true right angle, which is exactly a quarter of a circle, and the angle between vertical and horizontal.

This knowledge was necessary before truly square buildings could be built. But these three stars do not form a triangle of the right dimensions, they look more like a pair of dividers, also used in measuring, and in constructing the intersecting arcs necessary to form a right angle. The narrow triangle of stars is more like a spearhead. However, in Welsh triangle is Triongl, so the original name could have been Tri-ion-gu-al meaning perhaps "The three of the lords spear white and shining".

Ursa Major II

Ursi Majoris

Ursa Major, or Helice according to the Scilican Aratus in 270 BC. The Great Bear or The Plough or Charles' Wain or the Dipper. The Anglo Saxons called it Carles Wagen; from *Carl* their version of Charlemagne. The Babylonians called this constellation The Wagon too. The Welsh called the Plough Y Saith Seren, The Seven Stars.

Like Corona Borealis, Ursa Major as the plough is called The Seven Stars. In England, Charles' Wain refers to King Charles I or King Charles II, not to Charlemagne.

To the British Celts Ursa Major was called Arthur's Plough Tail, but as with most stellar references to Arthur it really has nothing to do with the Latin Arturus (for King Arthur) or Arctos or Ursa (for bear), but derives from the Celtic Arth-ter (the bright or clear high place). It may have a connection with Arddwr meaning Ploughman, since the first ploughman of the Celts was either Amathon or Hu Gadarn.

Alternatively, since both classical and Welsh legends tell us of a plough being set among the stars, the name Arthurs plough tail could either derive from "*Uthr-ys-pel-o-tal*" meaning "The wonderful distant place of the end". The end being the north star Theuban, or from "*Aradr-beili-tir-le*" that is "the plough of the courtyard and of the place of the tumulus". It may be that the curve of the handle of the plough was likened to the horns of a tumulus, forming a courtyard at its entrance; or it may be because of the use of a plough with a mould board being tethered to a post set in the ground over a grave in bronze age times, being driven round and round to throw up a mound of spiral furrows. It was also symbolically ploughing the land in which a man had been sown, like corn for rebirth. Besides forming a low mound, this would also form a spiral, symbol of a life. The name Helice is from the helical or spiral ploughing, which survived as turf cut mazes and maze patterns in Cathedral paving in the Middle Ages. Mazes on the village green are known as Troy Town mazes, that is Troy-tir-wen-maes, meaning "the ploughing of the holy land enclosure".

The Cornish word for sickle is Cromman, originally cro-maen that is "bent stone" which is explained by examples A & B

A a sickle or pruning knife from Windmill Hill

B a flint sickle from Grovehurst in Kent c 2400 B.C.

C & D sculptured stones reused as roofing slabs at Collorgues, France c. 2500 B.C.

E an early Bronze Age idol of chalk from Folkton, Yorkshire.

The classical Greek story of why this constellation of Ursa Major is called The Great Bear, relates that Callisto, a daughter of Lycaon King of Arcadia, who had sworn to remain a maiden and companion of Artemis, was caught by Zeus. He lay with her against her will. To escape the wrath of Hera, Zeus turned Callisto into a bear, but Hera saw all and contrived that Artemis should hunt and shoot her. Hermes saved her by changing her into the constellation of the Great Bear. The name Callisto means "most beautiful" Artemis Calloste was the goddess to whom the she bear was sacred in Arcadia.

In Athens, at the Libyo-Thracio-Pelasgian festival of Artemis Brauronia, one girl of 5 and one of 10 years of age dressed in saffron robes in honour of the Moon played the part of bears, and savagely chased boys at the festival. Callisto was also called Helice from the willow branch sacred to the Moon Goddess. The great and little bears are said to turn the mill of heaven around the pole, the hinge of heaven; Cardea the White Goddess was the goddess of hinges, and Janus the god of hinge sockets.

In the north of England, where Norse traditions are strongest, and in north Germany, Ursa Major is called the Hellwain. Herlewin's troop or Hurlewain's Kin accompany the hell wagon or Woden's Wagen in the wild hunt - to the Celt hell is the word for 'to hunt' and Her-Lergh-Gwaen would mean "the hunt trail of the level plain", so there seems to have been some mixing or misconceptions between cultures. Herian was the leader of the host of Valhalla, and he seems to have become King Herla, leader of the wild hunt, and eventually Harlequin of the pantomimes! Similar names can be most muddling. To the Saxons, The Herlingas were the heavenly twins Castor and Pollux, in the constellation Gemini. But to Celts Harlequin was probably just Har-Lu-Cun which is "the Great Leader of the Host".

The name Ursa Major is Latin, and probably the nearest sounding Latin words, that were inoffensive to the establishment priesthood at the time, that sounded like the Celtic name or description of the northern constellation Uthr Medelwr. To the Celts this name meant "The Terrible and Wonderful Reaper". In later times and places this goddess was called Berecynthia, Cybele and Astante. She is probably the lady with a flint sickle shown on the roofing slabs of the Neolithic Long Barow at Collargues in France, and the other similar Megalithic sculptures shown in drawings C, D and J. she is the goddess of agriculture.

There is an annual meteor shower on Ladyday, 25th March, from the direction of the forefoot of the Great Bear constellation if we look at the heavens as seen on a traditional classical star map. But this was from between the legs of Great Goodess as seen by the Celts and their predecessors in Britain.

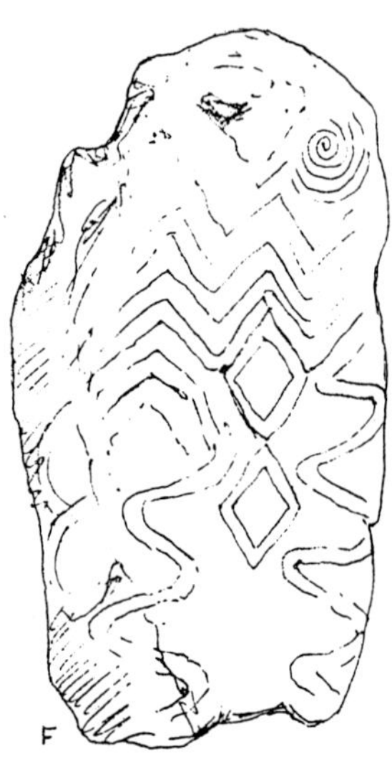

F A carved stone figure from Barclodiod passage grave near Holyhead Anglsey.

G A carved stone from the entrance of the chambered tomb of New Grange in Ireland. The sidh of Angus Mac Oc

H The reputed coffin lid from Christ Church Oxford, formerly the Priory of St. Frideswide. Sanct Ffraid Delwes Ydd is the Old British "The Holy One of the Corn Image of St Bride."

I. A carved stone support from Locmariaquer in Brittany called "the merchants table" showing a hedged field of corn with the sun shining over it

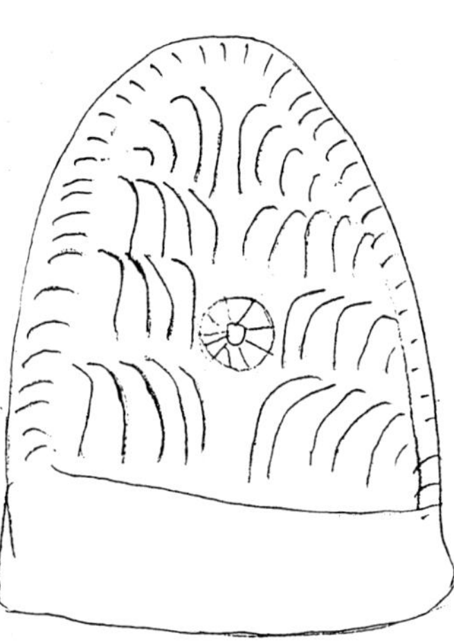

J.

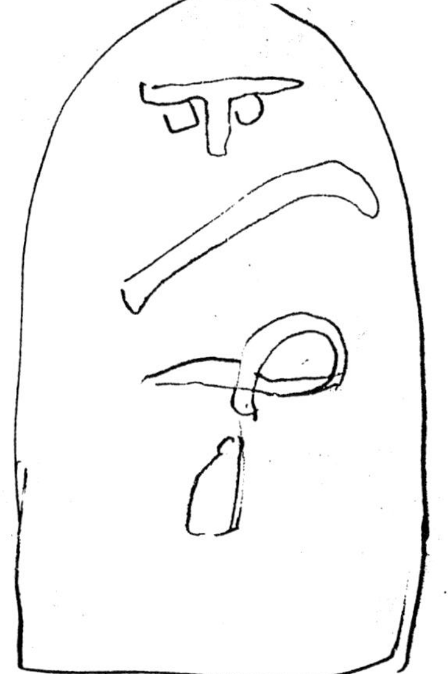

Another carved stone of the Megalithic Period from Brittany showing the great goddess of agriculture with her stone sickle or reaping hook.

K

In a hunting society where the constellation Draco was seen as the horned god, the Great Goddess of the pole was seen as the Lady Huntress or Diana. Here on a Megalithic stone from Brittany is the Lady with bow & arrow & short hunting dress

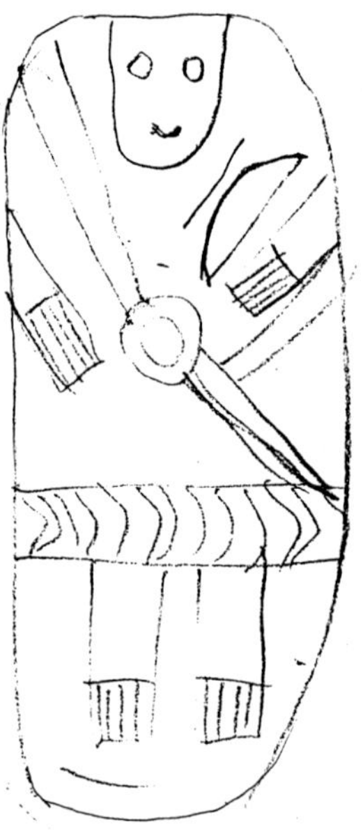

L

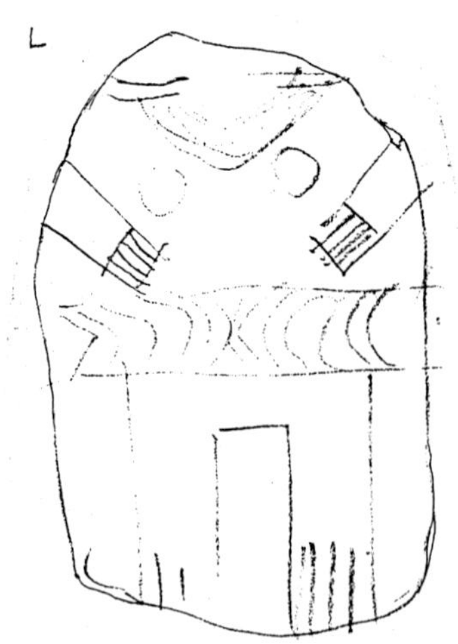

This figure is female as it has breasts. It also wears a necklace & a girdle or belt.

M

This Megalithic carving must be female because of the breasts. The marks across the face may be tattoos.

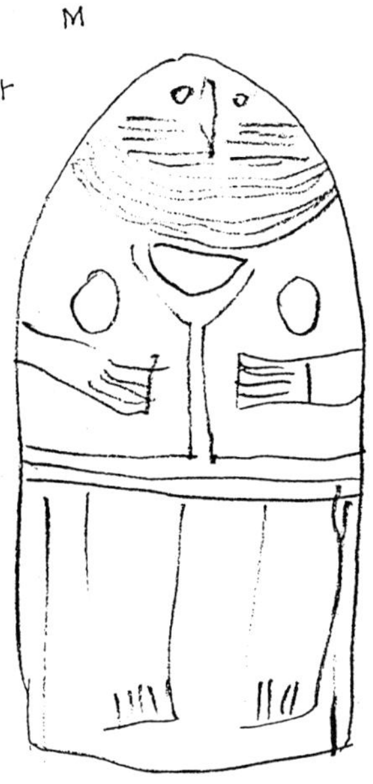

N

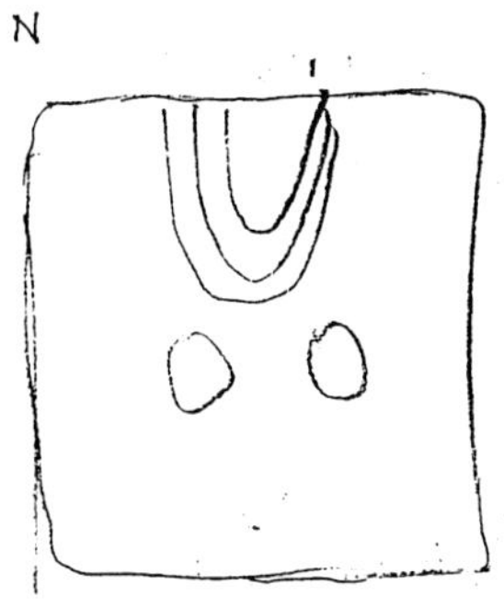

This stone probably represents a woman or priestess as it has breasts & a necklace

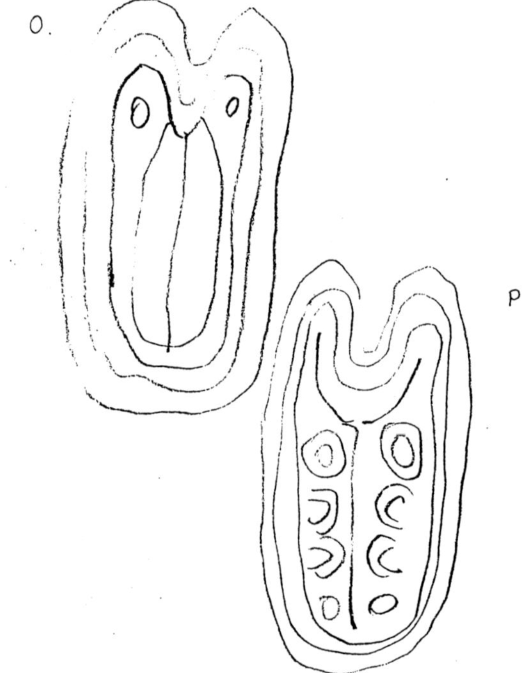

These two Megalithic stone carvings from Brittany are virtually styalised artistic shorthand for a woman. O has reduced representation to two breasts & a vigina, while P is similar but with eight breasts, an embrionic Diana of the Ephescians, a mother to all.

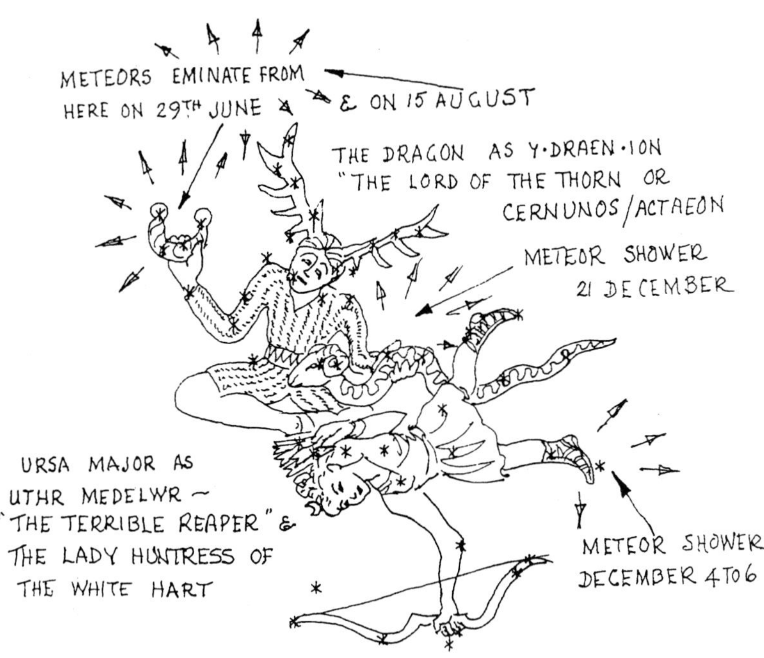

THE CONSTELLATIONS URSA MAJOR & MINOR & DRACO AS DIANA & ACTAEON OR THE LADY HUNTRESS OF WINDSOR FOREST & HERN THE HUNTER

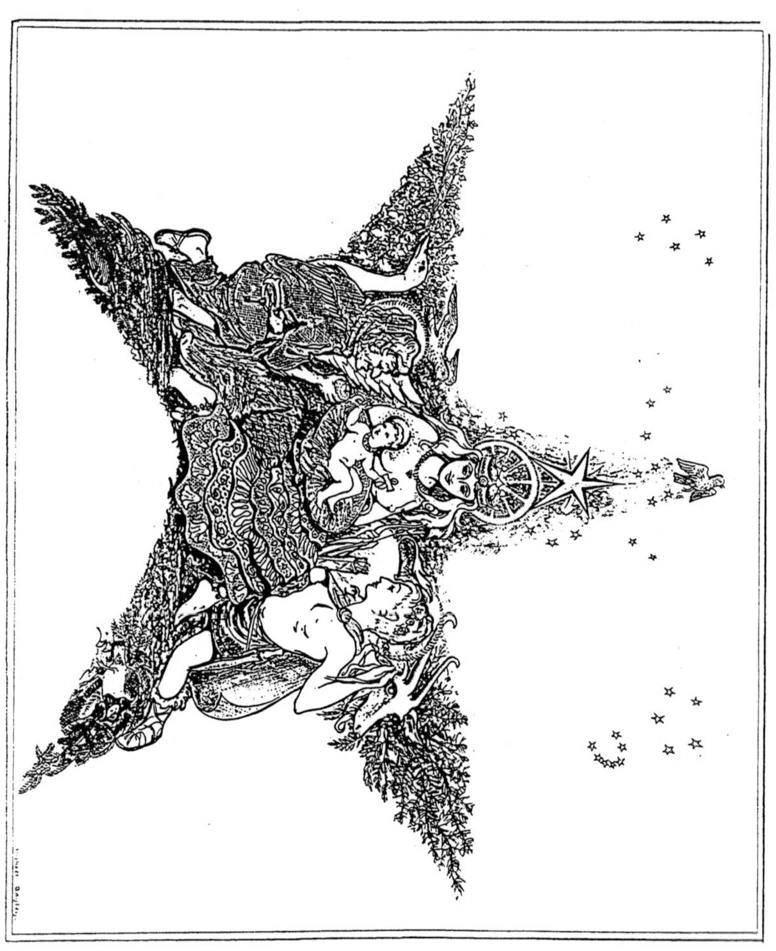

Since shooting stars were considered by the Celts and other peoples before the Christian era, as the souls of gods and goddesses, or dead heroes going to heaven, or descending to earth from heaven for a reincarnation, this particular shower would include the soul of Attis Adonis returning to earth for his annual reincarnation.

It, therefore, seems that the Neolithic interpretation of the northern constellation evolved with the mysteries or science of agriculture, perhaps fused with or adapted from the myths of the Ice Age or Mesolithic hunters of Northern Europe.

In Middle Eastern myth Astarte rode a dragon like Berecynthia, and she, like Cybele was worshipped from Gaul to the Levant in Roman times. Astarte also held a viper in her left hand.

There is a Palestinian legend that on Lady Day, 25th March, the New Year's Day, old style, the goddess Cybele descended from heaven herself in the form of a shooting star, to seek out and bring to life again her dead lover the corn king Attis Adonis, that is Attis the Lord. Violets and anemones sprang from his blood. Attis was born in Bethlehem in Palestine. The name of the place means "the city of Bread". The Garden of Adonis still stands on a hill just outside Bethlehem. The historical fact that Bethlehem was the birthplace of the pagan lord god, whose body was bread, even before the Christians claimed that the communion wafer was the body of their God, was explained by medieval theologians as an example of how the devil had interfered with time by inventing a sacrilegious parody of the nativity before it had actually happened! Media manipulation and propaganda are older than civilisation!

Berecynthia was worshipped in Gaul as the goddess of the harvest, and of ploughing and sowing, and so must be equated with the classical Ceres and Demeter, as well as with Cybele and Astarte.

The Irish have a story of a Queen Bera who came to Ireland from Spain with the Milesian colonists from the Greek islands. In mainland Britain the same lady survives as the hag Beara, and as the Old Woman of Bere who had seven periods of youth. Her image was the corndolly or corn idol. Bere, which forms a component of all these names is a form of primitive barley.

Berecynthia was said to ride around the heavens every night on the back of her dragon like Astarte, or in a wagon or chariot drawn by dragons, the dragon being the constellation Draco. In later Christian times she was demoted by priests, but still recognised as the Night Hag on her broomstick.

SAINT MARGARET

In her heyday it is probable that the handle of the Plough constellation was viewed as a sheaf of corn in the left hand of the goddess, from which grain in the form of meteors fell to mark the Roman Opiconsivia grain storage ceremony about the 24th of August, while her right hand holds a flint sickle. This is shown on the Megalithic tomb sculptured stones as pictured in drawings C, D and J.

The source of the Ladyday meteor shower is from near Theuban, the pole star in about 2000 BC, that was in Neolithic farming times. This meteor shower represents the rebirth of the god of vegetation and of corn, the Lord Adonis, or whatever the local name was, for the New Year or Hogmanay child, reborn from the womb of the goddess Berecynthia, Astarte, Cerridwen or the Cailleach, the sower or reaper of human lives. This suggests another possible origin for the classical name Ursa Major. It may have been "politically correctly" translated from the Celtic Arth Seren Mam Ior, that is "The High Stars of the Mother of the Lord".

In some English counties a new flowering spray of blackthorn was hung over the kitchen hearth on New Years Day. This was New Years Day Old Style 25th March, by which time the blackthorn was "out". The old blackthorn bush was then set alight and carried blazing over thirteen new ploughed furrows, for luck and prosperity. In France the blackthorn is called La Mere du Bois, the mother of the woods. It was the witches rod for blasting and cursing, the rod of the House of Lords messenger to the House of Commons, and of the verger leading the bride to the altar. It is the wood of the swingle of the flail that broke John Barleycorn's bones.

The connection with meteors that have survived entry into the earths atmosphere is shown by the fact that the image of Cybele the Great Idean Mother of the gods, the Mountain Mother of Phrygia, was a black meteoric stone. Diana of the Ephesians, Venus in Cyprus, and St Non near St David's in Wales, are all associated with meteoric stones, and a similar stone lays at the heart of the holy place of the Muslims in Mecca, once representing the Mother Goddess Allat.

In Greek mythology the Great Bear started as Callisto, one of the nymphs or maidens of Artemis (Diana to the Romans), the huntress. She was got with child by Zeus and was then changed into a bear. This appears to have been a theological change when the male sungod superseded the mother goddess. Megalithic carvings not only show the Great Goddess with a sheaf of corn and a flint sickle in drawings C, D and J, they also show a cornfield protected by a hedge with the summer sun shining over it in drawing I from Locmariaques in Brittany, and also the Great Goddess as Huntress in carvings K and L. In

British Celtic legend she has survived as The Lady Huntress of Windsor Forest, whose medieval Chapel of Our Lady in the Park was decorated with paintings of horned hinds, sacred to Diana, which must have been reindeer, as it is only among reindeer that the hinds carry antlers. This is probably why the horns used in the Abbots Bromley Horn dance are reindeer horns.

The reindeer did actually survive in Britain into the historic period, cut off here by rising sea levels.

This ability to see the polar constellations of the Great and Little Bear both as the Great Goddess of Agriculture and as the Lady Huntress seems to have been around since the time of the Megalith builders as both goddesses appear in their sculptures. The patterning of megalithic stones from Anglesey and New Grange in Ireland, shown in drawings F and G have similarities with the reputedly Dark Age coffin lid from St Frideswide's church in Oxford. This may be no accident as the name Oxford's saint derives from *Sact Ffraid Delwes Ydd*, that is "The Holy One Bride of the Corn Idol", or as we would put it today Saint Bride or Bridget of the Corndolly. Some representations of the Goddess by the Megalith builders, as in drawings M, N, O and P, show a figure with many breasts, like Diana of the Ephesians.

The modern drawing of the triple goddess in the form of a five pointed star, is an attempt to illustrate the British Celtic legends associated with the birth of the child born in a cowstall on Ladyday, whether he is Hu Gadarn, Attis Adonis, Jesus Christ or Dionysus Sabazius. He is horned and virile and gives the blessing of fertility, as he lays in a winnowing fan. His mother wears a pink and green seven-layered skirt and is crowned with hearts and pearls under a solar wheel symbol and the five pointed star that is the seal of the Virgin, all below a skylark. To the left or sinister side kneels Cerridwen who holds a pruning knife in her left hand, but presents the child with an applewell, that holds the secret of immortality. The goose which will take his soul to paradise stands behind Cerridwen. To the right of the child kneels the Virgin Huntress, and behind her is the mythological Hiccafrith or Sidehill Winder. The starry constellations belong to the three goddesses as do the birds and trees forming the design.

In the classical world the Great Mother of the Gods was called Rhea, who was the daughter of Uranus and Ge, that is Heaven and Earth. She was equated with Cybele and was reckoned to be the wife of Cronus or Saturn, and mother of the Olympian gods and goddesses and their Roman equivalents. In Rome she was equated with Ops. Her priests were known as Corybantes in Phrygia and Galli in Rome. She is pictured as enthroned with or without a red and mural crown, guarded by Lions who sometimes pulled her chariot.

CYBELE

As the Lady of the polar constellations who rode around the skies as Astarte or Berecynthia on a dragon, this great goddess is also represented as the Christian saint of the Dragon, St Margaret of Antioch in Pisida.

Her legend tells that she was the daughter of a pagan priest Aedesius who put her in the care of a foster mother in the country to be brought up as a shepherdess. Her beauty attracted the Roman prefect Olybrius who wished to marry her, but in the course of his enquiries he found that she was a Christian and had her seized and tortured. While in prison she was tempted by the devil in the form of a dragon which swallowed her. However, she made the sign of the cross upon which the dragon disappeared, hence she is shown in art accompanied by a dragon which she overcomes by thrusting her long staffed cross down its throat. In the eastern Mediterranean she is associated with Marina, Aphrodite, Venus and Pelagia, as Margarita is the Greek for a pearl. She was reckoned as the guardian of women in childbirth. Her feast day varies from 17th to 20th July with variations to 4th May and 8th October. Her cult came to western Europe with returning crusaders who attributed their safe return to her. Her name, Margaret, had many variants as Madge, Meg, Maggie, Margot and so is associated with the Magpie the prophetic bird of Aphrodite. Among her titles are Pearl of Heaven and Daisy of Paradise, with the heart of gold and crimson tipped white petals that always looks to the sun. Her British counterpart is the Welsh St Brynwyn of Anglesey, the old goddess Branwen whose symbol was the black and grey hooded crow in Ireland, and the black and white magpie in Lowland Britain.

In North Britain it is St Margaret who accompanies Saint George the rider of the white horse and successor of Lugh as patron of the herdsmen of the high summer pastures. As the dragon slayer and consort they can also be equated with Perseus and Andromeda.

Saint Margaret inherited the scallop shell from Aphrodite. This connection came to Western Europe via the Crusades and the pilgrimages to Compostella in Spain. It was in this connection that the title Stella Maris as a guiding star of voyagers came to be associated with the Pole Star and the Virgin Mary and St Mary Gypsy. She was pictured robed in blue with a pearl necklace inherited from the pagan Sea Goddess Marian or Myrrha, the mother of Adonis.

In Norse mythology the northern constellations were still connected with corn and three, four and five units, which gives a true right angle, which is exactly a quarter of a circle, and the angle between vertical and horizontal.

Ursa Minor I

Uris Minoris
Ursa Minor, or Cynosura according to the Scilian Aratus in 270 BC
The Little Bear or the Dipper. A dipper was a measure of corn.

The Little Plough Tail or sometimes Arthan. Caer Pedryvan - the four-cornered castle, in legend belonging to King Ban of Benwick, ie king of the high place of the head of the wood. The Iron Age Celts were in the ascendency in western Europe about the time of the start of the Christian Era, which was at the time that the pole star lay in the constellation of Ursa Minor. The four-cornered castle of the four main stars of this constellation contained the pole from about 600 BC until about 600 AD.

More anciently the Little Bear together with the Great Bear formed the constellation of the Great Goddess Berecynthia, Cybele, Cerridwen or the Cailleach as described under Ursa Major. Hence the Welsh culture hero god or Saint Derfel Gadarn, whose first birthday was on 5th April (see under the constellation of Bootes) was reborn of Cerridwen at the Winter Solstice, An Fheil Shlinnern, that is "The Feast of the Shoulder Blade". This event is commemorated annually in the heavens by a meteor shower for three days from the direction of the Little Bear, between Cerridwen or Berecynthia and the Dragon as in Celtic eyes a shooting star was the soul of a god or hero returning from heaven to earth to be reborn.

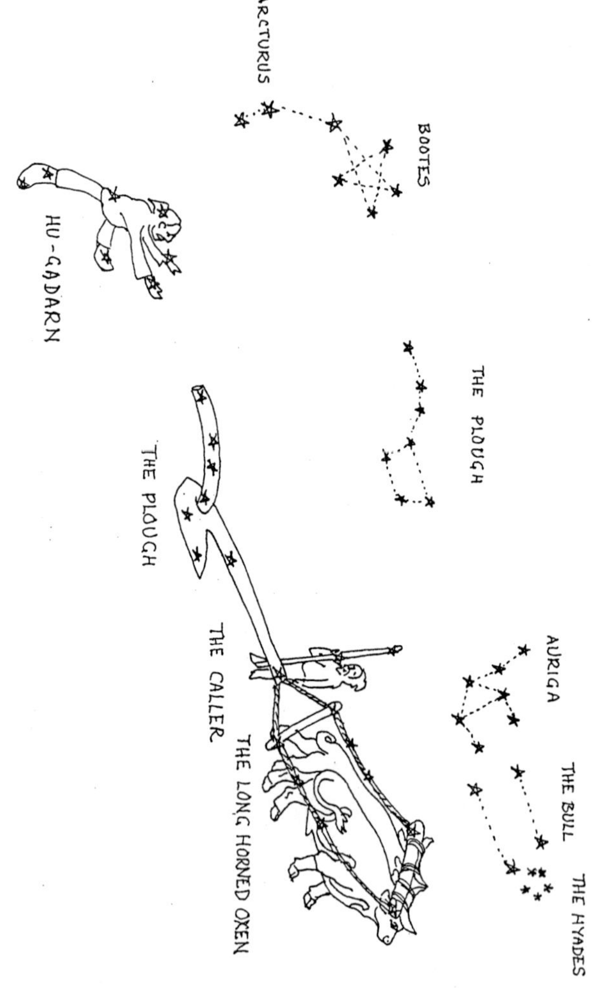
ARCTURUS
BOOTES
HU-GADARN
THE PLOUGH
THE PLOUGH
THE CALLER
THE LONG HORNED OXEN
AURIGA
THE BULL
THE HYADES

Chapter 3

The 12 or 16 or 27 Constellations of the Zodiac

The Constellations of the Zodiac arranged alphabetically are as follows, the Arabic numeral denotes the Region and the Roman numerals the Right Ascension on the circular star maps.

The Location	The Traditional Name	The English Translation
2/3 - II	Aries	The Ram
13 - XXII	Aquarius	The Water Carrier
4/10 - VIII	Cancer	The Crab
13 - XXI	Capricorn	The Sea Goat
4 - VIII	Gemini	The Twins
9 - IV	Hyades	Part of Taurus the Bull
5/10 - X	Leo	The Lion
11 - XV	Libra	The Balance
4/10 - VIII	The Manger	Part of Cancer
13 - XXIIII	Pisces	The Fishes
3 - III	Pleiades	Part of Taurus
12+ - XVIII	Sagittarius	The Archer, Centaur, or Horseman
11/12+ - XVI	Scorpio	The Scorpion
4/5 - X	The Sickle	Part of Leo
3 - V	Taurus	The Bull and The Pleiades
11 - XIII	Virgo	The Virgin

The cardinal points of the compass are marked by the following constellations at specific times of the year. These positions are also associated with the four Gospel writers of the Christian Bible, the four Royal Stars and the four Archangels (see Stars and Angels in volume 2).

South is in the constellation Taurus the Bull from the spring equinox until June - St Luke.

West is in the constellation Leo the Lion from midsummer until September - St Mark.

North is in the constellation the Eagle of Scorpio from the autumn equinox until December - St John.

East is in the constellation the Man of Aquarius from the winter solstice until March - St Matthew.

The Year and The Twelve Zodiacal Constellations

These constellations are seen as ruling the months of the year, and the number of these months in the Old Year starting at Lady Day is given after the name. They are arranged alphabetically.

In c1627 Julius Schilles attempted to replace pagan mythological names with Christian ones for the Constellations. He named the signs of the zodiac after the twelve apostles, and as this either resulted in, or resulted from, popular connections with these saints, the appropriate saint's name is added below the English version of the name of the sign.

The Zodiac itself was known to the Celts as Caer Sidi (the revolving castle) since from the earth the panorama of stars appeared to turn, revolving once every year. The word 'zodiac' means "the ring of animals" in Arabic and refers to all twelve signs.

There were many attempts in antiquity to devise a rigid calendar that was astronomically accurate, but they all developed faults eventually, that had to be corrected. The early Roman calendar was in just such a state when it was obviously out of step with the seasons, at the time when Julius Caesar became the first emperor. He used his new sweeping powers to reform the calendar. The most learned men of his day devised the Julian calendar for him. It consisted, so they had calculated, of 365.25 days so they decreed that every fourth year should be a leap year of 366 days, and the normal year should have 365 days. This system was approximately correct, but actually exceeds the solar year by 11 minutes, or one day every 131 years.

The result of this was that by the dawn of the 18th century, the year was so obviously out of step again with the solar year, that many European countries decided that a revision was required. At the Diet of Ratisbon in 1700 it was decreed that 11 days should be omitted from the year to put the calendar right with the sun. This was effected between September 2nd and 14th of that year, and so began The Gregorian Calendar. England did not adopt the new calendar until the day after September 2nd of 1752.

The Old Style Julian New Year's Day was 25th March, Ladyday, and this was 6th April New Style, which even today remains the financial New Year's Day. The Gregorian year therefore consisted of 365 days five hours and 49 minutes as opposed to 365 days and 6 hours of the Julian Calendar.

Although for financial purposes new year still remains on 25th March, Old Style, for the rest of the country the year started on 1st January, which became New Year's day in 1599.

However, the countrymen of Britain who used the wooden Cog Almanac, which means grandfather's or our ancestor's almanac in Welsh and the Celtic languages, were able to keep their year for agricultural purposes, exact by the sun with a year of 365 days only. This was done by setting the calendar right every new year's day, 25th March or Lady Day, as this was the day of a single day's annual meteor shower from the direction of what in conventional astronomy would be the front foot of the Great Bear Constellation. This would have been the region of the pole star in about 2500 BC. But to the eyes of the Pagan Celts of the old religion, this would have been between the legs of Cerridwen or the Caillach or The Great Goddess Berecynthia herself, the original Lady of Lady Day, at least up to the time of the Battle of the Trees. After the Battle of the Trees, when the Sun God Apollo became supreme, this same annual meteor shower marked the end of the festivities of the Vernal Equinox and of the god Apollo's visit to Stonehenge. It also marked the period of the Phrygian festival of Cybele which was adopted by the Romans in 204 BC. It celebrated the annual death and rebirth of Attis/Adonis in the Levant. In Scotland, to Gaelic speakers, Lady Day, the 25th March, is known as Great Nativity Day (Nollaig Mhor) to celebrate the rebirth of the deity or Hu Gadarn from the Great Goddess who was Cybele or Berecynthia to the ancients, the Cailleach in Scotland and Carridwen in Wales. Cerridwen was said to have bean the second mother of Hu Gadarn, the sun god, born at midwinter on December 22nd, and therefore conceived at the Vernal Equinox, Lady Day. Merlin's mistress Vivien, Nimue or Nyere was the Whire Lady of Lady Day, also known as the White Serpent and the Lady of the Lake. The term White Serpent is used because when an ancient British Celt died, his or her soul divided and part went into a star, part into a bird and part into a worm, of a standing similiar to the earthly importance of their human incarnation. The various annual showers of meteorites or shooting stars were seen as the souls of heroes and heroines going to heaven, or returning to earth for reincarnation.

The twelve signs of the Zodiac which rule the twelve months of the year, and the year which waxes and wanes, may be represented on the sacred hill at Locronan in Brittany. Here there is a path that may be followed from the base of the hill, which starts going west, but gradually climbs the hill as it veers north. From its highest point the path proceeds diseal eastwards, gradually descending as it turns south towards its start. The path is marked with 12 stones at 12 stations equidistant from each other. Tradition has it that this path was walked every seven years, and at the end of the walk the participants climbed the hill again and descended westward, and in doing so circled a large rounded stone said to represent the moon that stands by the wood of Nevert, that is the wood of ìthe sacred place. Since the moon was a goddess the stone was a goddess too.

However, to the Celts there are said to have been 27 constellations in their zodiac. This may be explained by the importance the Celts attached to the fact that every day consisted of a light and a dark half. The number of 27 constellations can be achieved if we consider each of the 12 signs has a light and a dark half, which gives us 24, plus one for each of the three phases of the moon, which gives us the 27 and all these are represented at Locronan.

If one adds in the hill as well, one gets 28, the number of nights of the age of a moon. Here we get a connection with the seven independent moving bodies of the heavens known to the ancient world, after which our days of the week are named. Four seven day weeks comprise one 28 day month, which is why both the moon and the number four are held to represent growth. Even in the enlightened and scientific 18th century, when the agricultural revolution was taking place, four grains of corn were sown in each dibbed hole, which was explained "scientifically" as "one for the rook, one for the crow, one to rot, and one to grow".

The grouping of twelve signs of the zodiac with the sun in the center, has been copied by Asian and European societies in their mythologies and government both in heaven and upon earth, as groups of thirteen. King Solomon had under him twelve officers making 13. Jesus Christ had twelve apostles - made 13. Joseph's dream of the sun and moon and eleven stars makes 13. The Roman god Mars was worshipped with the Salii, twelve warrior priests, on the Palatine Hill, and Qurinus, that is Mars' son Romulus after his death, was similarly worshipped with twelve Salii on the Collini Hills, both being groups of 13, as was Romulus in life with his twelve lictors.

In Romanesque times Charlemagne was supported by his twelve Peers or Paladins.

Norman London was governed by the Lord of the City or mayor, supported by twelve echevins or skivini in 1191. The arrangement was also maintained in Roman and other continental cities, giving a group of thirteen. This still exists in British law courts with a judge and a jury of twelve men.

In cards there is a king and twelve other cards in each suit.

In Norse mythology we have Odin and twelve other gods and goddesses in Asgard, Thor, Frey, Freyja, Loki, Baldur, Iduna, Heimdall, Sif, Frigga, Bragi, Gerda and Nana. There was also Hrolf and his twelve Beserks.

In English history there were two groups of thirteen around King Edward III and the Black Prince in the knights of the Garter. In folklore we have Robin Hood and his twelve merry men; Little John, Will Scarlet, Friar Tuck, Alan-a-Dale, Much the Miller, Maid Marian, Gamble Gold, Sir Richard of the Lea, The Jolly Pinder who was the keeper of the Pound, and The Three Foresters. In mythology there was King Arthur and his knights of the round table.

On a more local level there was the Devil or Warlock or witch master and the coven of twelve, ideally six men and six women. The word coven is Celtic *Corven*, "the little circle" as opposed to the great circle of the Sabbath.

THE RAM

Aries I

a Spring sign
starts 21st March finishes 19th April

Arietis
Aries
The Ram

Saint Peter, to the Celt Sanct-Pel-Ter, that is "the Holy One of the Bright Sphere (the summer sun)", since the spring equinox marks the start of the light half of the year ruled by the summer sun god, the lord of the harvest. St Peter's feast day is on 29th June and his first day is the third day of a four day meteor shower from the mouth of the dragon constellation, the mount of the Great Goddess Berecynthia. However, if the goddess becomes the Lady Huntress, the dragon becomes Cernunnos and the dragon's mouth becomes his Lunar Torque.

But if the constellation Orion is seen as the Celtic Great Hunter god Cernunnos, Cetus becomes his serpent and Ares becomes the serpent's Ram's head. His antlers are Gemini and Auriga, the sickle of Leo becomes his lunar torque and Lepus his feet. However, this spreads the god over a lot of sky, so it is unlikely that Orion was ever pictured this way.

The astrological sign for Aries represents a ram's head with its two spiral horns: These in twin represent the spirals of the past and of the future. This sign or house contains the vernal equinox, the rebirth day of the Lord of the Harvest, the start of one year and the death of the old year.

Astrologically the sign is that of the Pioneer, the starter of all things new and of the head. Its ruler is the planet Mars and the element of fire.

The spirals of the ram's horns in one sense herald the waxing of the year and coming fruitfulness, but the second spiral denotes withering and death at the end of the summer, and Aries marks the great Celtic feast of Samhain, Hallowe'en on 31st October by an annual meteor shower.

It is significant that to the Romans it was the feast of Pomonia, and we still bob for apples and tell fortunes from them at this time, and to the initiated the secret

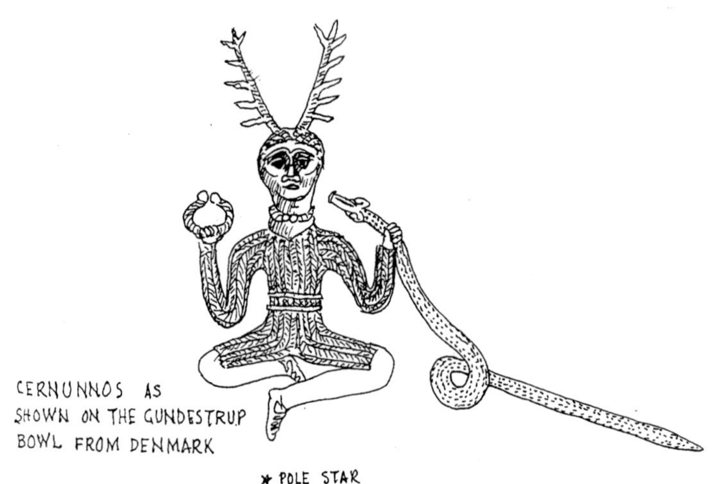

CERNUNNOS AS SHOWN ON THE GUNDESTRUP BOWL FROM DENMARK

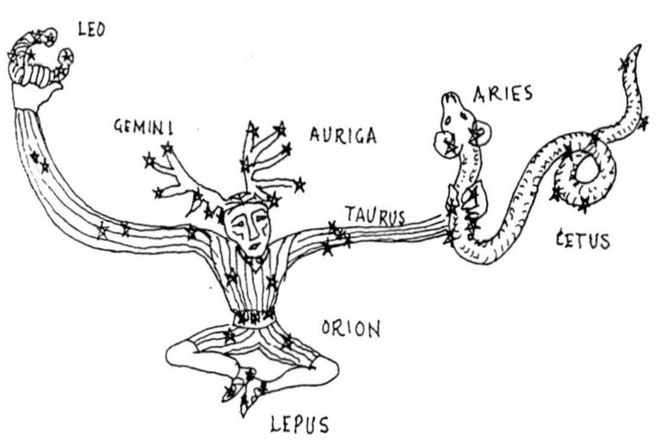

CERNUNNOS BASED ON THE GREAT HUNTER ORION BUT INCLUDING LEO GEMINI AURIGA TAURUS ARIES & CETUS.

truth at the bottom of the well is told not in words but with the apple well (see Volume 2). To the Celts the following day is Cailleach Day.

It should be remembered that the Roman goddess Pomonia carried a pruning hook or knife, which had other uses. As a beautiful maiden she courted and won the Red God Mars. Samhain falls at the full moon of the Hunter's moon, the red moon, when Easter falls on Ladyday, at the vernal equinox.

THE WATER CARRIER AQUARIUS AS THE DOWSER OR WATER CRAFTSMAN

Aquarius XI

a Winter sign
starts 20th January finishes 17th February

Effusoris aquae, Situla
Aquarius

The Water Pourer or Water Man, hence perhaps St David who was called the waterman. Saints Thaddeus and Jude whose feast day is 28th October are also associated with this sign. This is the house of parliamentarians, of loyalty and of intercession and of The Air element. Its stones are sapphire, jade and ruby, and its colour is indigo. Its planet used to be Saturn, shared with Capricorn, but in modern times it is Uranus. This constellation is said to affect the legs. The star Formhaut, near the southern fish's mouth, is in the constellation of Aquarius and marked the winter solstice about 1500 BC. It is associated with St John and the eagle and also with the angels Raphael or Suriel.

In Celtic terms "The Water Man" would have meant a dowser, which as Dowr-saer means "The Water Craftsman". Traditionally the dowser used a forked hazel rod to devine where water could be found, because hazel is the tree of knowledge and is associated with a salmon in a pool. Hazel is called coll in Welsh. However in the Thames Valley ash is also used, perhaps because in the Ogham alphabet it is the symbol of "wind on the water", and is a charm against drowning, perhaps because oars are made of ash wood. Ash is also the tree of the Celtic god Gwydion and the Gaulish goddess On Niona. One can prove that the green ash stick is really being forced to turn because the bark slips over the wood and the bark becomes twisted around the arms of the rod. It is called 'rod' because it "turns" like a wheel. Over water the downward stalk of the Y moves forward and up. Witches broomsticks and pitchfork handles are made of ash.

In the Celtic calendar the ash month was from 18th February to 18th March, just a month removed from the Sign of Aquarius, but covering 1st March, birthday of St David, who is called The Waterman (see Serpentarius). To the Welsh, St David is also Sant Dewi, which sounds very similar to Sanct Duw Wy, that is "The Holy One of the God of Water", and to Sanct Dewin, that is "The Magician Holy One". So if Serpentarius was Rhiannon or St Non, Aquarius may have been her son St David who used his magic skill to discover springs.

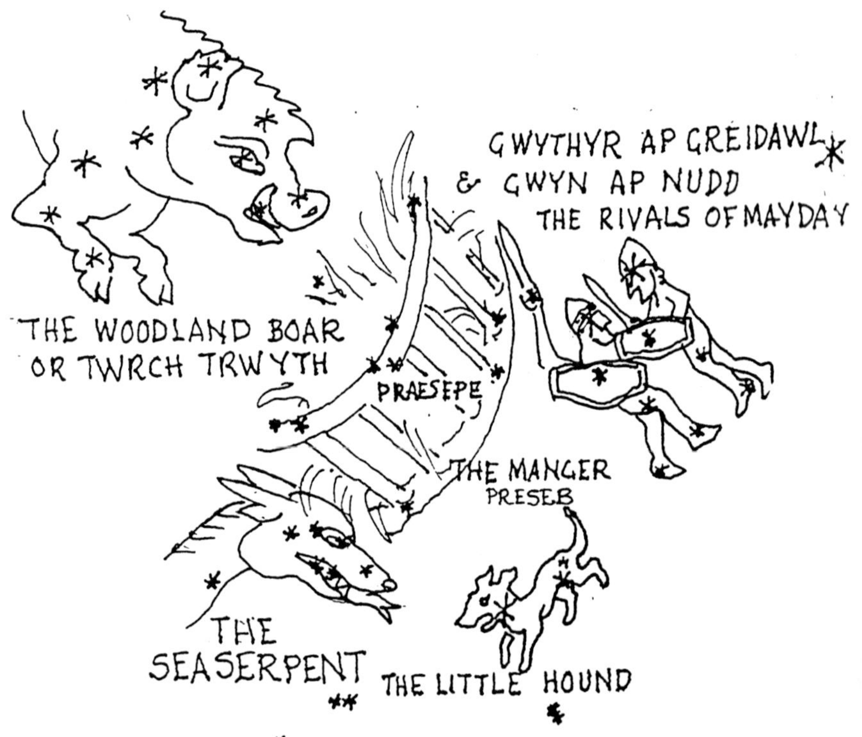
GWYTHYR AP GREIDAWL
& GWYN AP NUDD
THE RIVALS OF MAYDAY
THE WOODLAND BOAR
OR TWRCH TRWYTH
PRAESEPE
THE MANGER
PRESEB
THE
SEASERPENT
THE LITTLE HOUND

Cancer IV

a Summer sign
starts 21st June finishes 22nd July

Cancri
Cancer
The Crab

Saint Andrew the Apostle. To the Celt, Saint Andrew was Sanct-Anad-Drew. The Holy One of the especial wren. The especial wren was the goldcrest wren, refuge of the soul of the winter sun god Bran or Mabon, which was therefore called Bran's Sparrow.

It was this sparrow that shot and killed poor cock robin at midsummer according to the popular old ballad of the death of cock robin. The robin being the refuge of the soul of the summer sun god who died from midsummer onwards. Saint Andrew's feast day is on 30th November, which is the feast day of the Celtic god Mabon, the god of winter, who hunted the Woodland boar which may be the constellation Leo, the lion.

Astrologically this house of the zodiac controls farms, land, property and buildings and, therefore, home makers. The stones are aquamarine, sapphire, chrysoprase and the colour yellow-orange. It rules the water element. Its ruling planet is the moon.

There is a small group, said to be of eight stars, called Praesepe in the constellation Cancer, also called The Manger. Appropriately eight is the number of increase. Cancer lies mid-way between Orion the hunter and Virgo the Virgin. The Welsh for manger is *preseb* - very similar to the Greek name, perhaps from *Pras-ep* that is "the meadow of the horse" or "the horse's eating place".

The Babylonians called the constellation we call Cancer, The crab "The Bow and Arrow" the weapon of their Lady, The Great Huntress.

Within the constellation Cancer, the small group called Praesepe or the Manger is set in an arrangement of stars reminiscent of the courtyard in front of a long barrow. The nearest animal constellations which might be interested in a manger, are Pegasus the White Horse, and Taurus the Bull. There is in fact a hollow in the hillside below the only British White Horse at Uffington, where it is much nearer to the horse than is this Manger.

To the classical world Cancer is the crab that was sent by Hera to assist the Hydra in its battle against Hercules in the second of his twelve Labours.

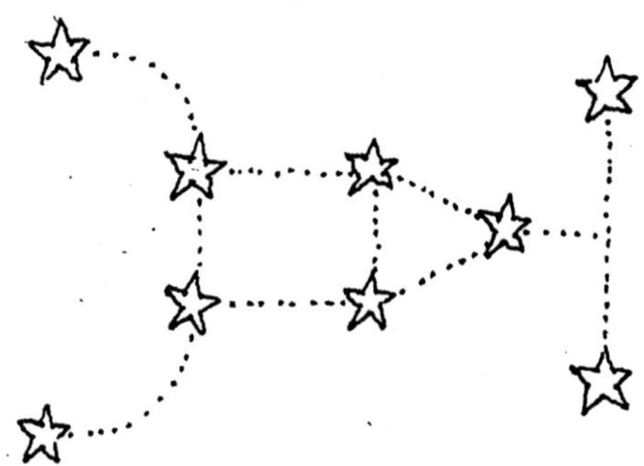

THE SMALL GROUP OF STARS CALLED PRAESEPE OR THE MANGER. LIES WITHIN THE CONSTELLATION CANCER

Capricornus XI

♑

A Winter sign
starts 21st December finishes 19th January

Capricorni
Capricornus
The Goat or The Sea Goat

Saint Matthew whose feast day is 21st September. This house is the house of the governor, or planning and strategy and of the earth element. Its stones are white onyx, garnet and ruby, and it is ruled by Saturn. It is the sign of knees and its start marks the Winter Solstice.

If the sea goat was a sea creature with two straight horns, it must have been a walrus, *morvugh* or sea cow to the Welsh. Although known to seafaring lands of north west Europe, it would be a fabulous animal best described as a sea goat to peoples of the Mediterranean and near east. The Welsh name of sea cow may have been given as much for its call, somewhere between the low of a cow and the bay of a dog, as for its horns! Maybe it is the creature of Midwinter, as it is probably that it only appeared off the coasts of southern Britain when walruses came south in the winter.

However, there is a goat-like creature in the realms of Heraldry and medieval natural history called a Hirco-cervus or goat-stag, and sometimes an antelope, which also occurs in the possibly Celtic mythology of the forest of Windsor as a Sidehill Winder. This British beast may be seen once in a blue moon on the seven hills at Ascot. The seven hills were round barrows now under a housing estate just south of the railway station for Ascot racecourse. According to the local tradition it was a beautiful mid-white creature with big eyes and the legs on one side of its body shorter than on the other from running round hills. And the blue moon, when it occurs, is normally the one before the red Hunters Moon, caused by dust in the atmosphere, and after the Harvest Moon.

The association of this creature with circular tumuli may account for its name, since in Welsh SIDELLU GWYNDER means winding or spinning whiteness, and in Cornish SEDHA LLE GWYN DIR would mean "of the place to be seated of the holy blessed white tumulus". All the meanings of the word

THE WALRUS
OR MORVUGH - SEACOW
OR CAPRICORNUS THE SEAGOAT

THE CONSTELLATION CAPRICORNUS & TWO STARS OF AQUARIUS AS A HIRCO-CERVUS OR SIDEHILL-WINDER

A "SAXON" CARVING FROM NEAR ST. PAULS IN LONDON

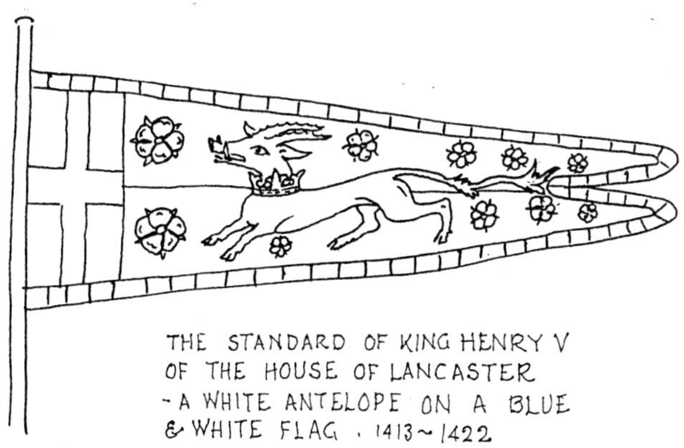

THE STANDARD OF KING HENRY V OF THE HOUSE OF LANCASTER - A WHITE ANTELOPE ON A BLUE & WHITE FLAG . 1413~1422

GWYN are used to describe the Sidehill Winder, as it is white, fair and beautiful, pale, bright, holy and blessed.

The connection of an early carving of the creature with St Paul's Cathedral in London, which in mythology is said to be built on the site of a temple to Diana, who appears in Arthurian legend in Windsor Forest as the Lady Huntress of Windsor Forest, suggests that there was a mythological connection here too. It is, therefore, possible that this creature may have been pictured as the constellation Capricornus, the sort of webbed back feet of the St Paul's version of the creature having been interpreted as a fishy end. The British Heralds revived the creature in the time of King Henry V, as his standard. Some authorities link Capricornus with the god Pan because of the goat horns.

Gemini

II

a Spring sign
starts 21st May finishes 20th June

Gemellorum
Gemini
The Twins, Castor and Pollux. The Discori

Saint James the Lesser or St Thomas the twin, the Apostle. His feast day is 1st May in the Anglican church and 11th May to Catholics.

Astrologically this house of the zodiac rules teachers, education and communication. Its stones are tourmaline, emerald and lapis, its colour orange, its ruler is the planet Mercury and it is associated with the armsand legs and the element of Air.

This was probably the Celts' Long Horned Oxen, perhaps one of the pair, the other being Taurus the Bull, that Hu Gadarn and Amaethon harnessed to the plough.

To the Saxons, the Discori or Heavenly Twins were sometimes called the Herelingas, which suggests some connection with Herlewin's troop or Hurlewain's Kin, who followed Woden's Wagon in the Wild Hunt. And Woden's Wagon is another name for Charles Wain or the Great Bear Constellation (see Chapter 2).

The classical Heavenly Twins Castor and Pollux also known as the Dioscuri were the twin sons of Tyndaceus king of Sparta, the husband of Leda. They are shown on star maps as armed with a club and a double-ended arrow, ready to fight each other. In this context they can be interpreted as The Rivals in the carol *Green Grow the Rushes Oh*, and as Sir Gawain and the Green Knight or Gwyn and Gwyrthur son of Greidawl, contending every first of May for the hand of the Lady in Red, Creudyladd. The twins shows them in their paired form while alone as the champions of the light and dark halves of the year they are represented by the constellations Orion and Hercules.

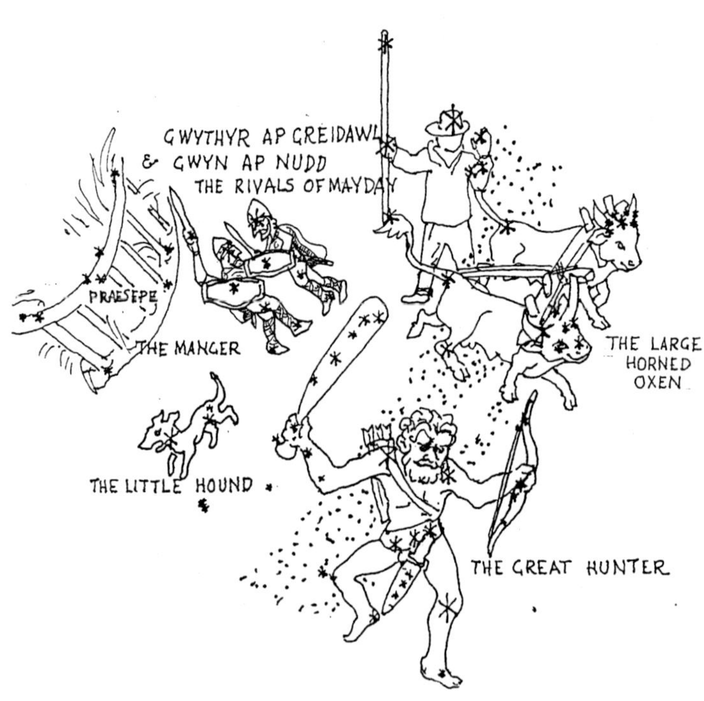
GWYTHYR AP GREIDAWL
& GWYN AP NUDD
THE RIVALS OF MAYDAY
PRAESEPE
THE MANGER
THE LARGE
HORNED
OXEN
THE LITTLE HOUND
THE GREAT HUNTER

The Saxons had another story about the constellation Gemini. They told of the Giant of Winter called Waendel, or Orwaendel, who stole away the spring. The gods caught him and threw him up into the sky, where his eyes became the two starts Castor and Pollux.

The forest of Windsor was anciently called Waendels Frith as Saxon scribes assumed it was called after the Fyrth or wood of their giant god of Winter. However, this is probably a misunderstanding of the original Celtic name, which was probably WAUN DA LES OR FFRITH that is "The meadow of the cattle bushes of the border or edge of the rough hill pasture".

THE GIANT OF WINTER WAENDEL OF WINDLESHAM & WAENDELS FRITH OR WINDSOR FOREST WAS THROWN UP INTO THE SKY FOR STEALING THE SPRING. HIS EYES STILL SHINE AS CASTOR & POLLUX

The Hyades

The Hyades lay near Taurus the Bull as a star cluster in its head.

The Hyades to the classical world were the eight nurses of Dionysus. They lay close to the head of The Bull and are called the Eight April Rainers in the song *Green Grow the Rushes Oh.* In the Mediterranean area they herald the rainy season which starts there in mid May. Their number varies in different traditions from two to eight. Together with the Seven Pleiades they were the fifteen daughters of Atlas and sisters of Hylas who was killed by a snake while out hunting with them in Lybia.

The Hyades were brought by Zeus to Dodona, and cared for the infant Dionysus Hyes, they took him to Ino the sister of Semele his mother at Nysa.

Meteor showers emanate from their area between the 16th and 28th November, a fact that is marked by a jug of water on the Cog Almanac against the 21st November, presumably because their rising brought water to the rains of April six months later.

Leo V

♌

a Summer sign
starts 23rd July finishes 22nd August

Leonis
Leo
The Lion

Saint John (the beloved disciple) whose symbol is an eagle and whose feast day is 27th December.

To the Celt, the name Saint John was SANCT ION that is "the Holy One of the Lord", perhaps the Lord of the Harvest?

Astrologically this is the sign of heterosexual love and children and of the Fire element. Its stones are the emerald, ruby and black onyx, and the colour yellow. The ruling planet is the sun (and therefore the sun god Apollo). It is the sign of the innovator, of recreation, courage and companianship.

The bright star Regulus in Leo marked the summer solstice in 2450 BC. It, therefore, marked the conception of the Lord of the Harvest, reborn at the Spring Equinox nine months later. The sign of Leo the Lion is associated with St Mark (whose symbol was a winged lion) and with the angel Gabriel, who is associated with Orion. The name of the star Regulus is the same as that given to the Goldcrest Wren otherwise called Bran's Sparrow, probably thought of as the soul of the gian god Bran.

Since the hounds of the Great Hunter Orion are going towards the constellation of Leo, and wild lions were unknown in north west Europe in the Iron Age, it is probable that to the Celts the constellation Leo represented the fiercest and most dangerous beast that they hunted, the wild boar. One was hunted by the Celtic Great Hunter, Mabon. It, therefore, appears that Leo is the Celtic constellation called The Woodland Boar. Its name was TWRCH-TRWYTH and it was hunted and of the land off-Cornwall by King Arthur, for the sake of Kulhwch, and Olwen the daughter of giant Hawthorn.

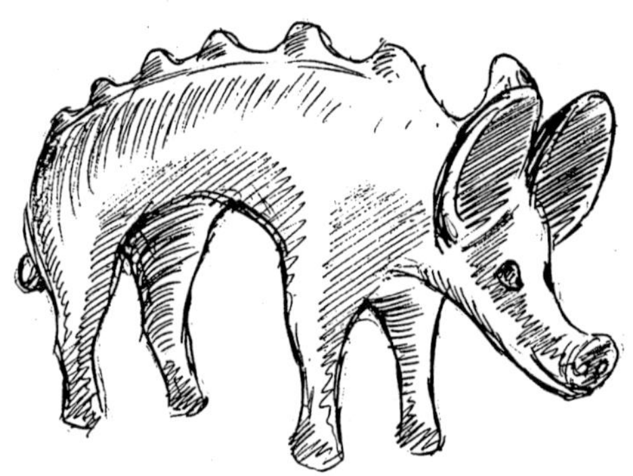

Bronze Boar from Hounslow

A MEDIEVAL FLOOR TILE

A BRONZE BOAR FROM COLCHESTER ESSEX
LATE IRON AGE

There is an annual meteor shower over the three or four nights from November 14th to November 16th from the centre of the ring of stars above Regulus in the constellation of Leo. This is sometimes called the sickle. Regulus is also the name of the goldcrest wren, in mythology Bran's Sparrow. This is the spirit of the Winter Sun God, as it was the sparrow who shot Cock Robin dead with his bow and arrow at midsummer. In revenge, the wren, in fact any ordinary wren, was hunted by country people on St Stephen's Day, 26th December. See the medieval floor tile of an archer shooting at a very small bird, perhaps a wren.

TWRCH TRWYTH the king of all boars kept a magical comb and razor and scissors between his ears, which were the objects for which he was hunted.

The Great Goddess of the polar region of the heavens, when pictured as the goddess of the chase and protector of wild things, Diana or Artemis, she is shown either seated on a stag, or standing bow in hand on a hill that was surmounted by a boars head.

This picture of the goddess associated with a boar or pig is shown in the local traditions of the Berkshire Chiltern Hundreds. The parish of Cookham lies on the south bank of the river Thames as it breaks out of the Chilterns. Between the riverside winter homestead village and its old hilltop summer shieling and fort of Cookham Dean lies the haunted Whyte Ladys Lane. The White Lady was reputed to ride down the lane mounted on a white horse from Spencers Farm to Cookham Dean Bottom at Hallowe'en. There she would dismount and walk up to the Hallowe'en bonfires on Winter Hill. A crude chalk-carved figure of a Lady was found in the remains of the early medieval hall at Spencers Farm.

If this White Lady was the same person as the Welsh Ladi Wen, and the cottagers and some yeomen of the area still spoke the Celtic British language in the area in the 1850s, then she was accompanied to the Hallowe'en bonfires by her tailess black sow. One or other of them would take the hindermost when the assembled people around the bonfires turned tail and ran down the hill when the White Lady appeared at the end of the celebrations. To reach the bonfires on Winter Hill from Cookham Dean Bottom the White Lady would have to walk up the lane past Swineshead Farm, now called Hillgrove Farm. If the White Lady is the same deity of the northern pagan heaven as Anne, Anner, Diana, Artemis, Dana and Don and the Cailleach, then here is the hill surmounted with the boars or swines head, of the Lady with the magic wand. This magic wand may also have been a hammer, or double axe, the Labrys in Crete or the throwing axe or Shepherds rhod in the Chilterns. When thrown, like a thunderbolt, it could strike someone dead.

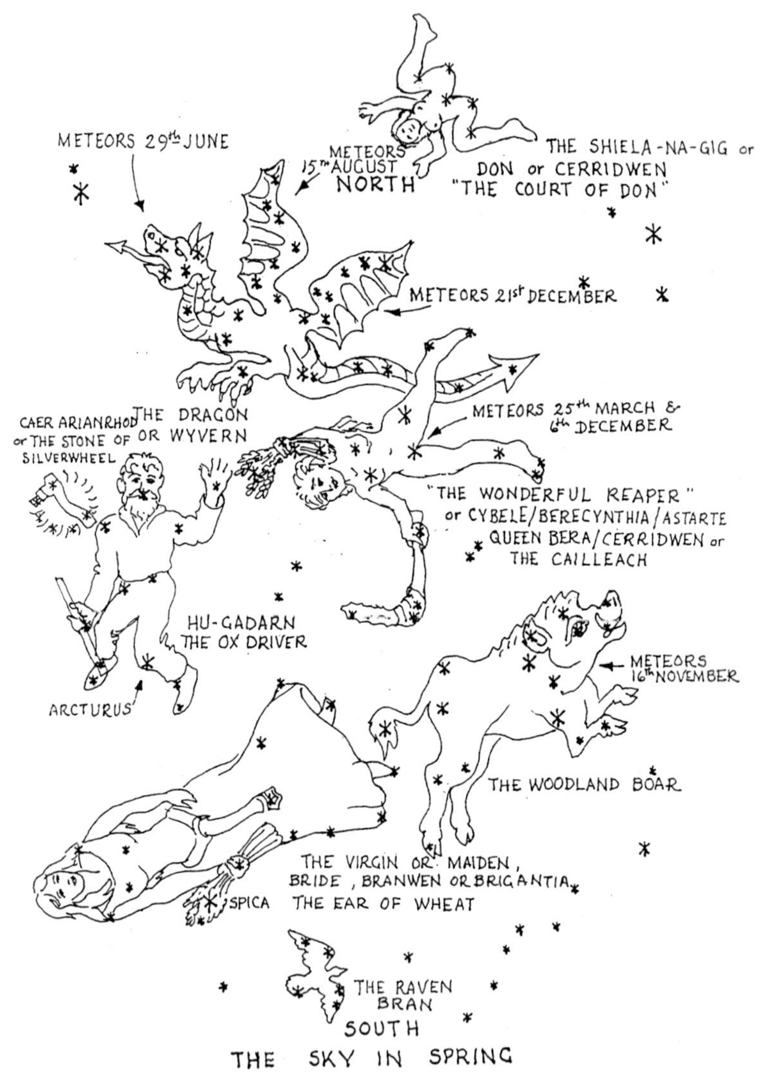

THE SKY IN SPRING

THE CELTIC CONSTELLATIONS

There is an annual meteor shower from the area of the head of the constellation Leo, the Woodland Boar to the Celts, from 4th to a maximum on 16th November, when a second three day meteor shower starts from the hounds that Mabon used to hunt the boar. Some authorities claim the meteor shower from the hounds lasts twelve days. To the Greeks and Romans they were the hounds of Orion with which he hunted Leo the lion. But rather confusingly Leo is said to be the Nemean Lion which Hercules slew, and whose skin he wore or carried over his left arm, as is related in the story of the first of Hercules' Labours. However, in the fourth of his Labours he captured the Erymanthian Boar of Arcadia alive, and so as traditional representations of the constellation Hercules show him carrying the skin of the Nemean lion, and Leo still has his skin, perhaps the early Greeks still thought of the constellation Leo as a boar, the Erymanthian Boar.

This beast was the result of a son of Apollo being caught watching Aphrodite bathing. He was turned into a boar as punishment just as Actaeon was turned into a stag for watching Artemis bathing.

A MEDIEVAL FLOOR TILE
PERHAPS SHOWING THE MIDWINTER
WREN HUNT

THE THREE STARS FORMING THE CLAWS OF THE SCORPION OR FRONT PAWS OF THE ADDANC ARE THE CONSTELLATION LIBRA. VERY NEARLY A 3:4:5 RIGHT ANGLE TRIANGLE

Libra VII

an Autumn sign
starts 23rd September finishes 22nd October

Librae
Libra
The Balance of the Scales (and therefore the sign of justice)

Saint Bartholomew (also called Nathaniel) the Apostle with a feast day on 24th August. His symbol is a butchers knife or falchion and on the Cog Almanac a gutted carcass as he was martyred by being flayed alive. His feast day ends a five day meteor shower from the wings of the dragon constellation. This meteor shower links the saint back to Berecynthia the lady who rides the dragon. Also, the falchion, which is a short broad sword rather like a sickle, probably gets its name from the Celtic or Welsh FALS-ION, "the sickle of the lord".

To the Celt, Saint Bartholomew would sound like SANCT BAGH TORRI MEUGH that is "the Holy One of the reaping hook guarantee". Perhaps this suggests that at the Autumn equinox or Michaelmas the Great Goddess who gave birth at the Spring equinox took a life back with a falchion at the Autumn equinox.

The sign for Michaelmas, just a week into the sign of Libra, is the scales which St Michael used for weighing good and evil in souls. The House of Libra is the house of the Lawyer, of the Air element, and of the stones pink jasper, opal, chrysolite and the colour green. Its ruler is the planet Venus.

In the first century BC this constellation was reckoned to be the claws of the Scorpion, and not a separate sign of the zodiac. To the Celts it appears to have been the front feet of the Addanc or Beaver, the creature who taught the Celts how to build their pre-Roman type of bridge, like a beaver dam. Grand Pont still stands at Oxford as a bank of black soil across the flood plain of the Thames, where once the British brush wood dam formed a bridge. The beaver still stands on Oxford's coat of arms, though few understand why.

Perhaps the very name of this sign is Celtic not Latin. It could derive from the Welsh and Cornish LLI BRAS that is "of the great wide flood", as created by beaver dams and man's imitations of them. The sign of the zodiac for Libra is a pictogram of such a dam, connecting side to side but letting water through!

The constellation of three stars forming Libra are very nearly the magic right angled triangle with sides respectively of three, four and five units in length. It is perhaps appropriate that the paws of the only other mammal to build large structures, and to alter the course of nature to serve his needs, the beaver, should contain the secret that enabled man to build truly rectangular buildings himself.

Písces XII

a Winter Sign
starts 18th February finishes 20th March

Piscis
Pisces
The Fishes

Judas Iscariot because he was the 12th Apostle.

This sign is depicted as two fishes facing in opposite directions tied together by the tails. It is the house of nurses, hospitals, prisons and all closed societies. Its stones are pearl, opal and moonstone, its element Water and its colour violet. It is ruled by Neptune and is associated with the feet. The Babylonians called this constellation The Great Swallow.

So far as we know the Celts also saw two fishes in the sky, between two other watery signs, of the Dowser and the Whale. We do not know what sort of fishes

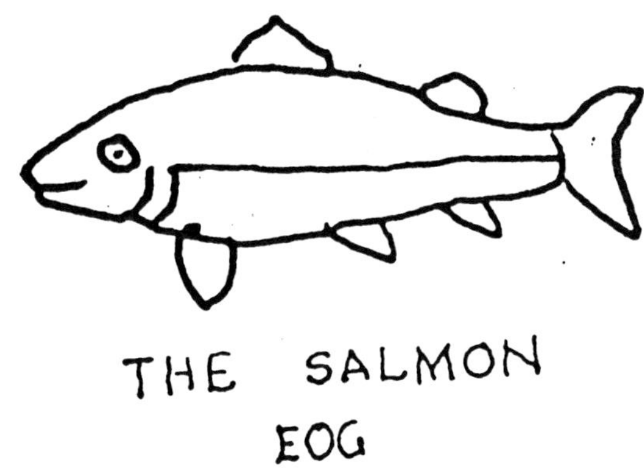

THE SALMON
EOG

were represented, but to the Celts of Britain and Ireland, probably the most important was the salmon, the fish of wisdom and of sacred pools. The drawing of a salmon to mark this sign is from a Celtic Pictish carving. The sea fish most likely to be immortalised among the stars would be the mackerel, for sea shanties tell us that it is the king of the sea. Since the first century BC The Fishes have contained the equinoxial point.

The Pleiades

The Pleiades lie near Taurus the Bull. They are a group of seven stars, in classical astronomy, said to be the daughters of Atlas, who were changed into doves by Venus. They are, therefore, Venus birds, but are also known as Hera's doves. Their names are Celeno, Maia, Merope, Taygete, Asterope, Electra and Alcyone, the brightest central star of the group. The name Pleiades in Latin means a squall or sudden storm, which the rising of the Pleiades about May appeared to herald, like our March winds.

They are also called the Sailing Ones, as the fresher winds and calmer summer seas marked the start of the sailing season in the ancient Meditteranean sea.

They are known as the seven sisters and sometimes as the hen and chickens.

The constellation sets about Hallowe'en. The Hyades are their eight sisters.

The Pleiades are called Y Saith Seven Siriol, "the seven cheerful stars", and also Y twr-ser "the heap of stars" in Welsh. But their most important name is Twr Tewdws and this is usually translated as "Theodosius Group", but seems more likely to derive from Twr Tew Dywys "the great thick tower of ashes". In astrology they are favourable and fortunate.

The god Beli or Hyperhorean Apollo came to Britain (perhaps Stonehenge) every great year when solar and lunar time coincided, that is every 19 years, at the spring equinox. He danced and played his harp until the setting of the Pleiades in early November, according to the Greeks of Delos. The second half of the Great year had seven months not six, in order to equate solar and lunar time.

Today only six Pleiades can be seen, and many nations have stories about how the seventh was lost. It exploded in about 1081 AD lighting up the night sky, and now forms the crab nebulae.

It is just possible that this constellation is the one referred to in Welsh records as Caer Ludd, the celestial representation of London.

THE PLEIADES

Y TWR SER ~ TWR TEWDWS

GRIOGLACHAN

In Gaelic, they are just called Grigirean or Grionlachan meaning "the cluster". They are one of the groups of stars called "the seven stars" along with the Plough. However, being seven in number it is possible that they represent the seven periods of youth of the Cailleach in the form of the Gruagch, her maiden aspect.

The Greek story about them was that they were companions of the Lady Huntress Artemis and were fleeing from Orion the Hunter from Boetia. They were, however, not really maidens as three of them lay with Zeus, two with Posiedon, one with Aries and one with Sysphus of Corinth. One of them, Merope, deserted her sisters. It was Maia who bore Zeus son Hermes. Her name is the same as that of the old earth goddess, and the name means grandmother. Their leader was Alcyone who gave her name to the kingfisher, which was supposed to build its nest to float on the sea during the Halcyon days, when it lay calm. Maia is said to be the Goddess of Spring, the Queen of May, the Hawthorn, or Quickthorn. She is, therefore, the White Goddess. Groups of seven ladies have a very long ancestry. They occur as cave paintings near Lerida in Spain.

To discover the place of these stars in Celtic mythology, one must bear in mind their Welsh name which we have seen meant "the great thick pile of ashes". We also know that the constellation set or ceased to be visible in early November which must have been about Martinmass, that is on the 11th November, when surplus cattle, for which there was no winter food, were slaughtered. The meat was dried or salted, but there was also feasting. In the heavens, there were meteor showers from the direction of the Bull and the Pleiades, from St Crispen's Day on 25th October over Hallowe'en until St Edmund of Abingdon's feast day on 16th November. Martinmass is marked on the Cog Almanac with a pollaxe, to show it is the time of slaughter. Meteors to the Celts were the souls of the departed leaving for heaven or returning to earth from heaven. Whose soul would those meteors represent? Obviously someone who died at this time of year.

While the Saint Martin of most of Christendom was St Martin of Tours, the Roman soldier who shared his own cloak with a beggar by cutting it in half with his sword, they have another tale in Scotland. There they say that St Martin was martyred by being killed and roasted and eaten in the form of an ox. In Germany the festival of Martinsfeur appears to have had pagan origins as it is mentioned by the Roman commentator Tacitus. In Belgium it is St Martin not St Nicholas, who brings children presents, and he rides a grey horse. We should probably call it a White Horse, as it is a white horse that transports the holy hero to and from heaven. In Welsh or the British language St Martin would be Sanct Marth

An Aurignacian Cave painting at COGUL in north east SPAIN near Lerida.

Tan, that is "The Holy One the Marvel of the Fire", and in Gaelic the Scottish version of St Martin's legend is explained as the nearest sounding words would translate as "The Holy One of the Ox Fire".

The explanation of why St Martin's symbol is a goose, is because this is the time of year when the wild grey lag goose returned for the winter from its northern breeding grounds, and it was the grey lag goose that transported pagan souls to and from their heaven behind the north wind.

Latterly Martinmass has got its traditions rather muddled with those of Hallowe'en or Samhain, because Martinmass is Hallowe'en Old Style, before we lost our eleven days.

"The Great Fat Tower of Ashes", twr tew dywys, was the remains of the great fire that roasted the ox sacrifice made by the Celts, and possibly the human one too, at Martinmass, when the Pleiades set.

The Greek story that the Pleiades were seven sisters, companions of the Lady Huntress Artemis, who the Romans called Diana, suggests that they were at least priestesses of the hunt way back in the Mesolithic or even Paleolithic period. If this is so then the wall paintings in a cave at Cogul near Lerida in north east Spain may show the seven Pleiades dancing round the St Martin of those days, the man who was to be slaughtered and eaten like St Martin whose soul would be a star in the meteor showers in the sky at this time of year. Maybe the small animal in the centre foreground is a young deer substitute - and maybe the shape falling from under the skirt of the lady on the right is the reincarnation of the sacred king who will be slaughtered and is his child whose soul has returned to earth as a meteor in a shower from the Pleiades.

There is, however, one Christian legend associated with the Pleiades. The seven stars here are said to be the bakers wife and her six daughters who gave bread to Christ when the baker refused it. The baker was then turned into Dusty Miller the cuckoo!

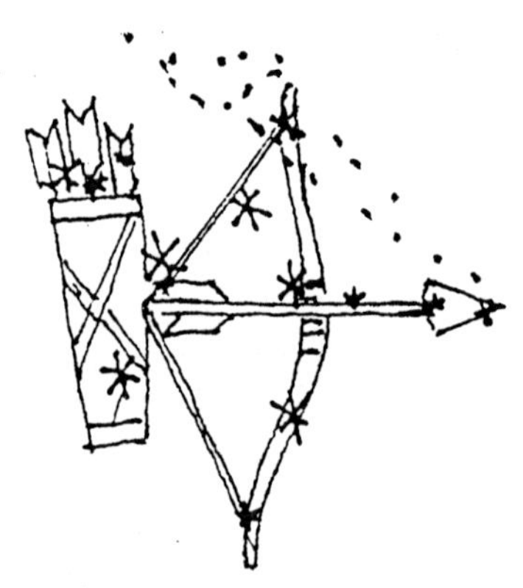

THE SOLDIERS BOW

Sagittarius IX

an Autumn Sign
starts 20th November finishes 20th December

Sagittarii Arcum
Sagittarius
The Archer, Centaur or Horseman
St James the Greater

This is the house of judges, religion and the legal profession, it is associated with the Fire element and its stones are turquoise, moonstone and chrysolite and its colour is blue. It is ruled by Jupiter and is associated with the thighs.

The connection with St James probably dates from the legendary appearance of St James mounted on a white horse riding to assist the kings of Spain against the Moors, and Sagittarius is depicted as a horseman.

In classical myth this constellation represents Chiron, the noblest of the Centaurs. Centaurs had mens bodies, arms and heads set on horses bodies and legs. Chiron was the son of Saturn or Cronus and Philyra, and was instructed by Artemis and Apollo on mount Pelion, becoming most learned in medicine, hunting, gymnastics, music and prophecy. He in turn instructed distinguished Greek youths, and was a friend of Hercules. He gave his immortality to Prometheus and so died and Zeus set him among the stars.

To the Celts it is reasonable to assume that this was the constellation they referred to as "the soldiers bow", since even in the classical interpretation it is really only the bow and arrow of the archer centaur, that is outlined in stars.

It is curious that the small constellation Sagitta, the arrow, is shown flying away from the archer in the opposite direction to that which the archers arrow is pointing. The bow was especially the weapon of the Celts and the Welsh, as the spear and shield was of the Romans and the Seax was of the Saxons.

Scorpío VIII

an Autumn Sign
starts 23rd October finishes 19th November

Scorpionis
Scorpius
The Scorpion

Saint Thomas (Didynus ie the twin) feast day 21st December or St James the Less (see Gemini).

This is the house of surgeons or detectives and the Water element. Its stones are malachite, topaz and beryl and its colour is green/blue and it is ruled by Mars. The scorpion is like the serpent and signifies wisdom, sex and evil.

The star Antares in Scorpio marked the autumn equinox in about 3000 BC and is associated with Saint Matthew and St Michael, and by the Romans with Rural Mars.

As late as the first century BC the constellation Libra was considered to be part of the constellation Scorpio.

In north west Europe scorpions are unknown so the constellations of Scorpio and Libra must have had another name. Some animal associated with preparations for winter would be appropriate.

In the Welsh story of their folk hero Hu Gadarn, he harnessed oxen to the plough, and used this team to drag the monster Addanc from his lair. If we look at his oxen in the heavens, the constellation Taurus, and then to the Plough, and then to Hu Gadarn as the constellation Bootes, behind him lie the constellations Scorpio and Libra, so they probably formed the monster Addanc, the beaver. Beaver dams can cause floods, as is mentioned in the story of Hu Gadarn. The beaver prepares for winter by stacking young branches of the trees that it eats under water, so that it can feed below the ice of winter. It is said that the European beaver does not build vast beaver dams like the American beaver, but this is probably because its environment was changed quicker in Europe by the advance of agriculture and forestry than in America. The European beaver must have built dams in the past, because the Celtic BRIVA or bridge, still built by Chiltern shepherds in Burnham Beeches in the 19th century, was based on the engineering principles of the beaver dam. The rotted remains of such Celtic bridges built on bundles of water preserved brushwood still exist as The Causeway at Bray on Thames and as Grand Pont causeway south of Oxford. The beaver still forms part of the coat of arms of the City of Oxford, because it taught the engineering skills necessary to build the first Grand Pont.

In modern Welsh the word for beaver is Llostllydan, literally "wide tail". It is a name used by a people who have nearly forgotten the proper name - it is completely descriptive.

THE BULL
TARW

Taurus II and the Pleiades

a Spring Sign
starts 20th April finishes 20th May

Tauri
Taurus
The Bull

St Simon Zelotes, whose feast day is the 28th October, is associated with Saint Jude. They were the brothers of Saint James the Less. Saint Simon was martyred by being sawn in half, and St Jude by being killed with a halberd. St Simon's feast day is the middle day of a seven day meteor shower from Taurus the Bull constellation. The Bull represents the oxen needed at this time of year to plough the land for seed time. This sign or house is ruled by the planet Venus, and the colours red and orange, and the gemstones amythest, diamond and moss agate. Astrologically it rules the neck and throat, and the producers of money and power, endurance and the working population.

The sign of Taurus is associated with Saint Luke, whose symbol is a bull with wings. It is also associated with the angel Ariel. When the zodiac was first recognised in Babylon, some 3000 years BC, the bright star Aldebaran in Taurus marked the Spring Equinox and the Bull was occupied by the sun at the start of the year. Even in Roman times this was not true, but the tradition prevailed, and Vigil wrote, the Bull opens the year with his golden horns. For most European countries the year started at the Spring Equinox until the coming of industrialisation. The Hyades are a star cluster in the Bulls head (see the separate sections on the Pleiades and the Hyades).

The constellation we call The Bull was to the Celts the Large Horned Oxen. They were the team of oxen that Hu Gadarn or Huw the Mighty yoked together to draw the first plough, just as in the Greek story it was Bootes the ox driver who first yoken oxen to the plough. This story has been told under the sign of Bootes, and also under the sign of Ursa Major and of Scorpio. It is one of the few constellations that was seen in the same way from Snowdon to Salamis. The Bull was an important animal to the Celts, and like all cattle was in one sense an animal of the moon as all cattle wore a crescent on their heads in a pair of horns, just as the Moon Goddess wore a crescent moon in her hair.

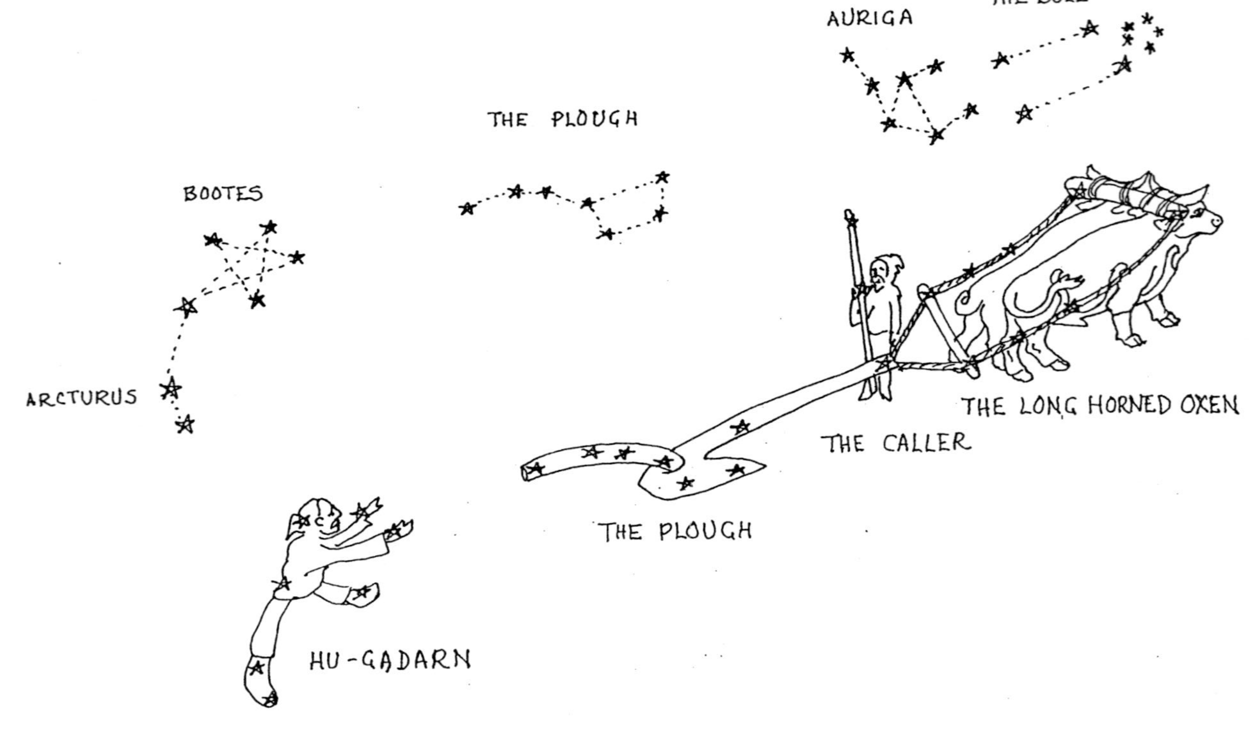
THE HYADES
THE BULL
AURIGA
THE PLOUGH
BOOTES
ARCTURUS
THE LONG HORNED OXEN
THE CALLER
THE PLOUGH
HU-GADARN

The picture of a grazing bull is from a Pictish Celtic drawing. The statuette of a three horned bull from Colchester in Essex is British and roughly of the Roman period. The fact that it has three horns suggests an even closer connection with the triple moon goddess.

AN IRON AGE TRIPLE HORNED BULL
FROM COLCHESTER, ESSEX

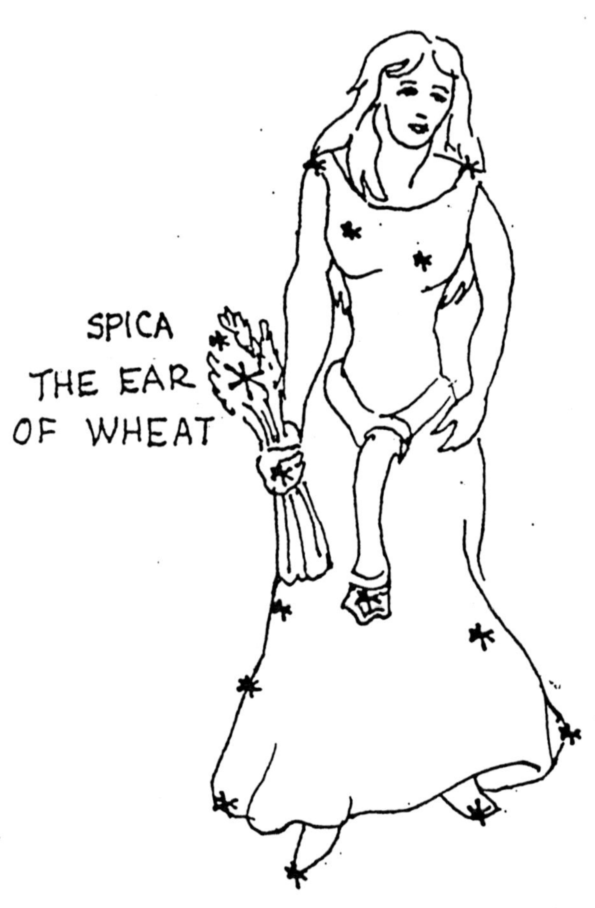

THE VIRGIN OR MAIDEN,
BRIDE, BRANWEN OR BRIGANTIA

Vírgo VI

a Summer Sign
starts 23rd August finishes 22nd September

Virginis, Sumbela
Virgo the Virgin or Astraea
The Virgin or Maiden

Saint Philip (whose feast day is 1st May)

To Christians The Virgin is the mother of Our Lord, and so she was to the Pagan Britons as Briget, Brigantia and Branwen. Some said The Virgin was Nell Gwynn! Bernice's Hair lies just above this constellation.

"The White Throne" is said to be the Celtic name for the Star called Spica in the constellation Virgo. This name was something like TYWYS-SEDD-GWYN which can also be translated as The Holy, white, fair, and blessed seat that guides. However, in classical astronomy Spica is called the ear of corn, so the real name of the star in Welsh is TYWYSEN-GWENITH which is the ear of wheat.

The sign of Virgo is like the sign of Scorpio, a sex sign, but in this case with a cross not an arrow, so is therefore feminine. Some say it denotes a Virgin holding a sheaf of wheat, the star Spica, perhaps the virgin Bride to the Celt. It is the sign of mathematicians, health workers, food production and armies. It is associated with the Earth element, the stones sardonix, diamond, and jasper, the colour yellow/green. It rules the abdomen, and its ruler is the planet Mercury.

In classical astrology, Virgo is Ceres the goddess of corn and crops. Alternatively, she was Proserpina to the Romans and Demetes or Persephone to the Greeks, though some claimed her to be Erigone daughter of Icarus. This constellation is visible in western Europe only between March and August, the growing season for corn crops. This connects it with Saint Frideswide of Oxford whose name proclaims her to be the British "Corn Image of Bride" or Brigit, "The Corn Dolly in fact". Bride or Briget, who became Saint Bridget, is described in Celtic literature as "The Mother of Our Lord, the King of Glory" and "The Mary of the Gaels", "The ever virgin, mother of God".

Since The Virgin was the title of the mother of the Lord to both British Pagans and Christians the constellation was taken to represent the Virgin of both faiths. The acceptance of Briget and/or Saint Bridget as the mother of the Lord was explained by the monks of Ireland by a tradition that St Bridget had been whisked away to Palestine by a miracle so that she could act as the midwife and/or foster mother of Christ.

The title of "The Virgin" could in certain circumstances be claimed equally by Bridget, Bride, Brigantia or Branwen, and curiously in Restoration times in Britain by Nell Gwynn!

If one slightly mixes one's mythology, which seems permissible, as old world mythologies are but variations on one theme, the key to the heaven of the Virgin Sophia, the seventh heaven, is the pentacle, also called the seal of the Virgin or the Druids footprint. Astronomically this is the constellation Bootes, the group of five stars that was adjacent to Llys Arianrhod, the Court of Arianrhod (see Bootes and Corona Borealis). One needed the key, Bootes, before entering the court of the Virgin Arianrhod, in other words Llys Arianrhod (Corona Borealis).

The sign of the Virgin was the lily or flag - originally the yellow water iris, as its curving petals as shown in the fleur de lys is reminiscent of cows horns. A red heifer was the symbol of Saint Frideswide (later changed to Oxfords Ox).

In Christian art blue is the colour of the Virgin, and this colour is connected with cattle. The muslin covers to milk jugs and churns was weighted down by blue beads to prevent the milk from turning sour - and a string of blue beads tied round a cows horn would cure it of diseases affecting its milk.

The constellation Virgo is sometimes called Astraea, who was the goddess of Justice (as shown in the pack of Tarot Cards).

The star that astronomers call Epsilon Virginis was called Protrygetor, that is "forerunner of the vintage". So the Virgin is connected with both the corn and the grape harvest, and with justice. If she was Bride or Briget to the Celts, then she was also Vesta to the Romans, and she has survived until the present day in the form of the corn idol that we now call a Corn Dolly.

Corn Dollies

Corn Dollies are the European Pagan or countryman's representation of Demeter or Ceres, they are Corn Idols, pagan images of a deity which are made as objects of worship. To the classical mind the image is that of Ceres the goddess of corn. To the lowland British Celt it is SANCT FFRAID YS YDD that is "the Holy One Bride of the Corn". In Welsh the word for religion is CREFYDD, which is derived from CREFU = to implore for, and YDD = corn, or CREFFT-YDD which is corn craft.

The first ploughs were little more than hoes pulled by hand. Later they were pulled by oxen, and various culture heroes were credited with this innovation; Hu Gadarn being the name of the Welsh hero who first harnessed oxen to the plough. In the heavens, this is commemorated by the constellation Bootes, the Plough and Auriga and Taurus the Bull (see all).

In early times with the primitive ard-plough, it was necessary to cross plough a plot in order to break up the soil surface enough to form a seed bed for broadcast sown grain. Hence the early neolithic and bronze age fields were small and square. Where these are still visible on the downs and other high pastures, they are known as Celtic fields. With the iron age came the mould-board to turn the sods right over on heavier lands and from the carvings on the Trajan column in Rome we know that in that emperor's time Britain produced the first combine harvester, a cart with a wooden comb on its open side, that was pushed though the fields of wheat and barley, and combed off the ripe heads of the corn.

It was only in the 18th century in this country that lighter steel ploughs were made to be pulled by quicker horses, to speed up corn production for the industrial revolution. In 1731 Jethro Tull advocated sowing seeds in rows to allow hoeing between rows. A man with a dibber made lines of holes and a child followed dropping four seeds of corn into each hole with the chant of:

One for the rook
One for the crow
One to rot and
One to grow.

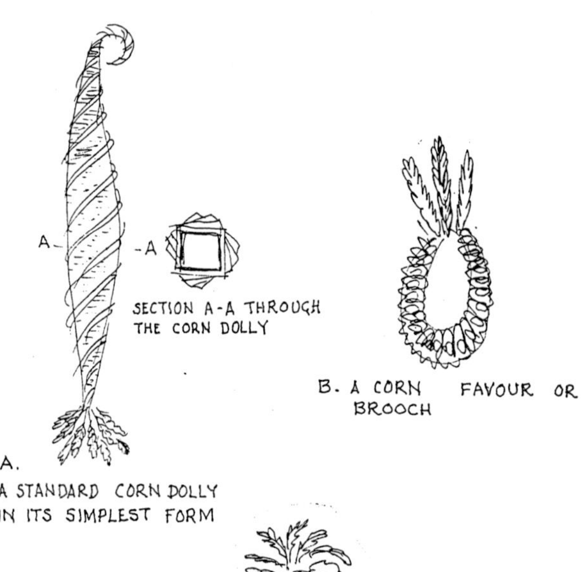

A.
A STANDARD CORN DOLLY
IN ITS SIMPLEST FORM

B. A CORN FAVOUR OR
BROOCH

C. THE OLDER FORM OF CORN MAIDEN
OR CORN DOLLY OR KERN BABBY

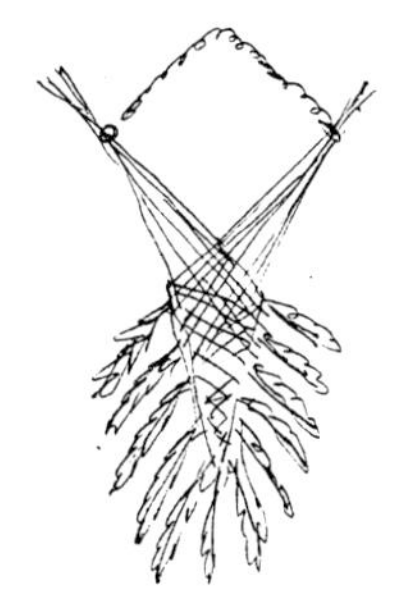

D. THE YORKSHIRE FAN - OR FERN LEAF (THE FERN IS SAID TO DROP ITS SEEDS ON MID-SUMMERS NIGHT)

E. THE WELSH CORN DOLLY (REPRESENTING A PENIS & A VAGINA)

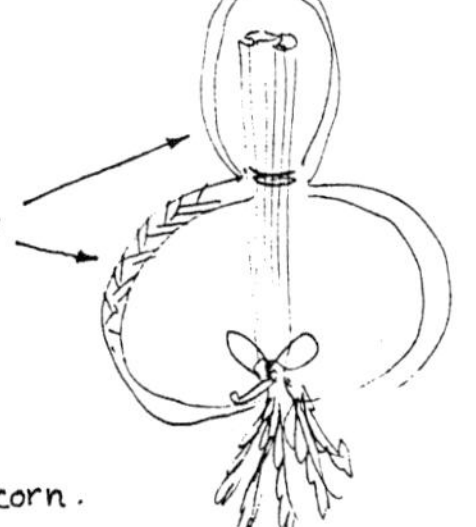

F. A SIMPLER FORM OF THE WELSH CORN DOLLY FROM HEREFORDSHIRE

The seed barrow with brushes followed, and then the first seed drill. Experimental work at this time produced a tenfold or hundredfold increase on the corn planted, and an increase to 4850 fold in one case! Reaping machines started in 1826, with cutters and binders by 1890 and the first combine harvester in 1907. The latter could cut 120 acres a day but needed 36 horses or a traction engine to pull it.

The forms of corn dollies, corn decorations for men and women, corn ricks and harvest wains, tend to differ from country to country, but the following are typical, and the Kern Babby or Corn Maiden in human form is usually about four foot high and was a very widespread custom.

Corn Dollies are common to all counties in Britain. They are known by many names, such as: The Knack, The Kern Babby (corn baby), The Maiden, The Hag, The Cliack, The Doll, The Mare and The Harvest Queen.

In the standard form of Corn Dolly (A) the square space is now filled with cut lengths of straw, but used to be filled with grain, perhaps even seed corn. It was made square with four equal sides because four is the number of increase. It was really for the same reason four grains of corn were planted in each dibbed hole.

There were nine heads of corn hanging down, the number of the triple moon goddess who controls the growth of the corn.

Favours or brooches were also made from corn B. They were pinned to a mans shirt or womans dress and a bunch of flowers or acorns was set in the loop. The one shown is of the type made in Northumberland and Scotland, where they were made of rye straw, with two or three and sometimes four, five, six or seven split straws in the plait.

In Cambridgeshire and elsewhere the last load of corn from the fields to the stackyard was accompanied by handbell ringers so everyone would know that the harvest was in. It was accompanied by the Harvest Lord and his lady, usually the captain of the reapers, and the prettiest girl on the farm who rode the lead horse of the wagon. She represented the goddess Ceres, or the local variation. Probably because of the use of handbells to signal the Harvest Home corn dollies were also made in the shape of bells too.

In Kent the Ivy Girl is made from the last corn cut. At Whalton in Northumberland the same image is called the Kern Babby, from Cornish *kerghn meaning* oats, or just Corn Baby. There it is made the height of a sheaf of corn (approximately four feet six inches) and is fixed to a pole for carrying in the procession home and so it will stand to preside over the harvest supper table where it is chief guest. In this instance it is sat in the back pew at the Church Harvest Festival where is stays until the next harvest.

C. This figure is also called:

Mother Earth	Queen
Dame	Ceres
Berecyntha (in Gaul)	

Berecynthia at least was carried round the fields in the spring to awaken the winter sown seeds.

The older form of Corn Dolly is shown in sketch C.

It has long been the custom to clothe the Corn Dolly in contemporary clothing of as gorgeous a nature as was possible.

The Lord of the Harvest was normally the best, strongest and quickest reaper. Those who broke his rules (and he was the best fitted to command the reapers) were fined by him - and his Lady collected the fines and passed them on to the Lord! He was elected by the labourers and saw they were fairly paid - he was of course first served at mealtimes and was addressed as 'My Lord' by other workers. The fines were not always in money and were sometimes just in fun.

In the 1600s Moresin complained of the Roman Popery of the people who made chaplets of corn which were carried on poles in the harvest thanksgiving processions. He also mentions straw images likewise being carried. This practice continued at least up until 1959 when country dancers in the Wishech area of the Isle of Ely also carried a crude straw dolly on a pole in their dance. The corn image of c1600 was carried home in a cart - around which people danced, sang and played.

Brand, in his *Popular Antiquities* quotes from *A Journey into England* by Paul Hentzner in 1598. Speaking of the Moor north of Windsor he says "*As we were returning to our inn, we happened to meet some country people celebrating their Harvest Home; their last load of corn they crown with flowers, having besides an image, richly dressed, by which they would signify Ceres;this they keep moving about, while men and women, men and maidservants riding through the street in the cart, shout as loud as they can until they arrive at the barn.*"

Chapter 4

The Seven or Fifteen Southern Constellations

The number given after the name of the constellation signifies its position in he normal list of constellations. Alphabetically they are as follows, the Arabic numeral denotes the Region and the Roman numerals the Right Ascention on the circular star maps.

Location	The Traditional Name	The English Translation
. - .	Ara	the Censer or Altar
. - .	Argo	the Ship
9 - vi	Canis Major	the Great Dog
9 - viii	Canis Minor	the Little Dog
12+ - xviii	Centaurus	the Centaur
8 - i	Cetus	the Whale or Sea Monster
11 - xii	Corvis	the Crow
10 - xi	Crates	the Bowl
8+ - iii/iv	Eridanus	the River
10/11 - ix/xiv	Hydra	the Sea Serpent
9 - v	Lepus	the Hare
9 - v	Lupus	the Wolf or Wild Beast
9 - v	Orion	the Hunter or Giant
13+ - xxii	Piscis Australis	the Southern Fish

and also the Galaxy the Milky Way
which stretches from 9 - vii/vi to 3 - vi/vii to 2 - ii/xxii to 7 - xxii/xix to 12 - xx/xvi.

Ara XIII

Thuri buli
The Censer or Altar

This constellation is not seen from north west Europe.

Argo VII

Navis
Argo Navis
The Ship

This could be the Celtic constellation known as The Great Ship Llong Mawr, or Prydwen that was Arthur's ship. This constellation is not really one that was familiar to the Celts of ancient north west Europe so far as we know, though it is possible that seafaring Celts of ancient north west Europe knew it from voyages to the Mediterranean. It was certainly visualised as a boat with a sail, perhaps a trading ship rather than a raiding vessel, to differentiate it from the Bald Ship, Llong Moel which was probably the constellation Eridanus, and named in the second millennium BC.

Some authorities split Argo up into its component parts:- MALUS is the mast, VELA is the sails, CARINA is the keel, and PUPIS is the stern of the ship. However, this was probably done in medieval times when ships had very high sterns carrying the owners standard or flag, while the original ship is more likely to have been seen as a Greek or Roman merchant ship.

A large and a small hound or dog shown on a medieval floor tile

Canis Major V

Canis Majoris
Canis Major
The Great Dog

This constellation contains the star Sirius which in classical times was reddish in colour. Its name means Sparkling.

As the hound of Orion it is one of the Yell Hounds, Wish Hounds or Gabriel Raches that go with the Wild Hunt.

However, to the Celts the name the Dog Star was SEREN CI which sounds very similar to the Arthurian hero SIR KAI. Sir Kai was King Arthur's foster brother who killed his second son (and presumably heir) Llachlu, and at one time tried to abduct Gwynevere. Since Llachlu survives in our mummers plays as Bold Slasher or the Turkish Knight, the opponent of Saint or King George, Sir Kai must be equated with the red god Mars or Bran the winter sun god, and in the mummers play with Saint George (or King George), the red cross knight. In some circumstances a Celtic cross is a sun symbol.

In mythology, the Great Hunter Orion is equated with Herne the Hunter of the Thames Valley, who is equated with the stag horned god Cernunnos. Canis Major and Minor are, therefore, the Great Hunters hounds and also the hounds of Actaeon in classical mythology, and the Wish Hounds or Gabriel Raches of our northern mythologies.

If all of Hercules' Labours were recorded among the constellation as some of them are. like the slaying of the Nemean Lion and the Hydra and its helper the Crab, then Canis Major or the dog star should be Cerebus the hound that Hercules brought up from Hades in his twelfth labour.

THE WHALE CETUS OR MORVYL - DREADFUL SEA-THING

Canis Minor VI

Canis Minois
Canis Minor Procyon
The Little Dog

Like Canis Major this is one of Orion's hounds, the Yell Hounds or Gabriel Raches that run with the Wild Hunt. All the mythological connections with Canis Major apply also to Canis Minor.

Centaurus XI

Centauri
Centaurus, Chiron
The Centaur

The Centaur is Chiron, who carries the beast (now called Lupus the Wolf) for sacrifice on the Altar, Ara. The Milky Way is the smoke from this altar. But like Ara, Centaurus is probably too far south to have appeared in the mythology of north west Europe, and would have been unknown to all but the more adventurous seafaring Celts.

Cetus I

Ceti or Cetus
Cete
The Sea Monster or The Whale

This is the sea monster sent to devour Andromeda, and from whom she was rescued by Perseus.

The story of Perseus and Andromeda has entered into British folklore as the nummers play of St George and the King of Egypt's daughter. In this context the whale has become the Dragon that Saint George, or Lugh or Llew Llaw slaughtered upon Dragon Hill at Uffington in the vale of the White Horse in Berkshire. However, as we saw when considering the constellations Draco and Ursa Major and Minor, The Dragon in the mummers play may well once have been the DRAEN-ION, that is Giant Hawthorn or the Lord of the Thorn, which may be a reference to Cernunnos with his thorny horns. As the Winter Sun God and Lord of the dark half of the year he would be the natural adversary of St George/Lugh/Llew Llaw, the Summer Sun God and ruler of the light half of the year. Early pictures of St George in which the dragon is depicted as a crocodile are responsible for our mythological picture of what he is like.

Corona Australís XIV

Coronae Australis

The Southern Crown, is too far south to have been brought to Celtic Mythology.

Corvus X

Corvi
Corvus
The Crow

This constellation is a small square of stars on the opposite side of Virgo to Bootes.

The Crow is associated with the corn crop as crows traditionally followed the plough, and nested in the elm trees near to farmyards.

In Welsh the word for rook or crow is Bran or Brain, which was also the name of a great god, the British equivalent of the classical Uranus or Cronos, and in a sense god of the underworld, whose soul survives in Celtic fashion as a bird. It is said that Bran's soul lives as one of the ravens at the Tower of London, which

was built on the site of Bran's tumulus. He survives as a raven, to keep watch over Britain and save it from invasion by being reincarnated to lead its people in its defence in its hour of need. He was also associated with the magical Alder tree, a tree of riverside swamp land, as would have been land east of the City of London in the late Bronze Age. The Welsh name for the tree is GWERN.

At the Battle of the Trees Bran was defeated by the sun god Hercules or Lugh, the Celtic Apollo. Bran was a mighty giant whose sister Branwen married Matholwch king of Ireland and bore him a son called Gwern. Matholwch slighted Branwen and war between Ireland and Britain ensued with great slaughter on both sides.

Bran was mortally wounded, so his followers cut off his head at his bidding and brought it back to Britain to protect it from invasion. Bran appears to be equated with another Celtic sun god Belinus, in some places and had an important temple in Normandy at Bayeux. He would have been the winter aspect of the sun god and therefore also connected with Orion.

Crater IX

Craterae
Crater
The Bowl

This constellation is too far south to appear in any Celtic myth and lies well south of Virgo.

Eridanus III

Fluminis
Eridanus Fluvius
The River

The River flows between Orion and the Sea Monster and is too far south to appear in Celtic myths, except perhaps for seafaring Celts.

The name Eridaan was an old name for the river Po in Italy. Some authorities trace the river Eridanus to a pre-Babylonian town called Eridu in Mesopotania on an island in an inland sea. It had a temple to the god of the deep called Ea.

However, from the surviving list of Celtic constellations there is one called The Bald or Bare Ship, that is LLONG MOEL, which is mentioned in the list near to The Great Hunter or Orion. It is, therefore, possible that Eridanus is the Bald Ship that is the ship with no sail, one usually propelled by oars. The outline of the constellation is very similar to that of a ship shown on a Minoan seal. This must have been the sort of east Mediterranean boat that carried the Milesian Colonists across the seas to Spain and to the British Islands. Primarily it was rowed by the warriors on board, but with a sail to assist if the wind was favourable. This was long before the Celts reached the Atlantic coast of Europe, but would be part of the maritime history they acquired as they learned about the sea.

Hydra VIII

Hyrdi
Hydra
The Sea Serpent

The sea serpent appears in Norse myths and legends but not in Celtic ones. Perhaps the Scandinavians had better boats and ventured further south.

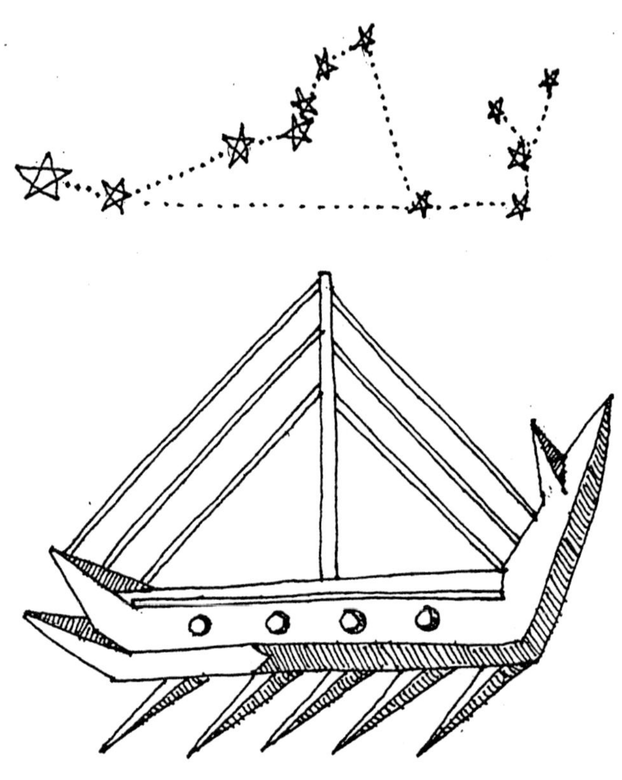

Top: the constellation Eridanus, probably the Celtic bald ship, that is one being rowed, not just sailing.
Bottom: A ship shown on a Minoan seal, showing the sort of ship the Milesians could have used to come to Britain in the second millenium B.C.

Lepus IV

Leporis
Lepus
The Hare - this constellation lies below Orion

The Hare is the animal into which witches habitually changed. It is also the form in which the soul of the corn crop escapes from the mill. As a messenger of the Moon Goddess, its outline can be seen in a full moon, just as a face can be imagined. Its fancied form on the moon is shown in 13th or 14th century encaustic floor tiles in the church at Cookham in Berkshire. A Teutonic legend tells us that the hare was once a bird, and was changed into a hare by the goddess Ostara of the spring. However, she still allowed it to lay eggs again once a year on her festival at the spring equinox, which we still call Easter from her name. The hares eggs are now our Easter Eggs, but people have forgotten the Mad March Hares of Easter which disappeared from our celebrations and have been replaced by a cuddly Easter Bunny!

The constellation Lepus is persued by Orion's hounds, so it may once have represented the roe deer. The description of CI-N-IEIRCH meaning "the roebuck of the hound" may have been misread as CEINACH meaning the hare.

Hares go mad in mating on about Lady Day which was probably the Celtic Christian Easter. It was certainly their Great Nativity Day, when there was a meteor shower denoting the return to earth of the soul of the god of corn and vegetation for rebirth from the great goddess Ceridwen or Berecynthia. The name Berecynthia suggests that she was also the moon goddess Cynthia of the corn or bere.

That the hounds of Orion, the Gabriel Raches or Wish Hounds have not yet caught the hare, suggests that they are dogs, as only a spayed bitch can actually catch a hare. Hares belong to the Moon goddess, because they tend to be nocturnal. The Round dances performed at Ladyday were in imitation of the dance of fighting or courting hares.

The last stand of corn in a field is known by the reapers alternatively as the hare or the hag.

THE HARE IN THE MOON ON A MEDIEVAL TILE

A ROE DEER

A ROE DEER ON A TILE

The herb hares eye is also called red campion. The word campion is the same as champion, and Red Champion is a name given to the god of the witches.

Lupus XII

Ferae

The Wild Beast or Wolf

The picture is from a Pictish Celtic drawing of a wolf, still a wild animal in Britain until at least medieval times. However, it may be that the constellation we know as Lupus was part of the constellation known as Orion or the Great Hunter to the Celts. After all the wolf is a great hunter itself. The Welsh for wolf is *blaidd*, and the Cornish *blyth* and Breton *bleiz*.

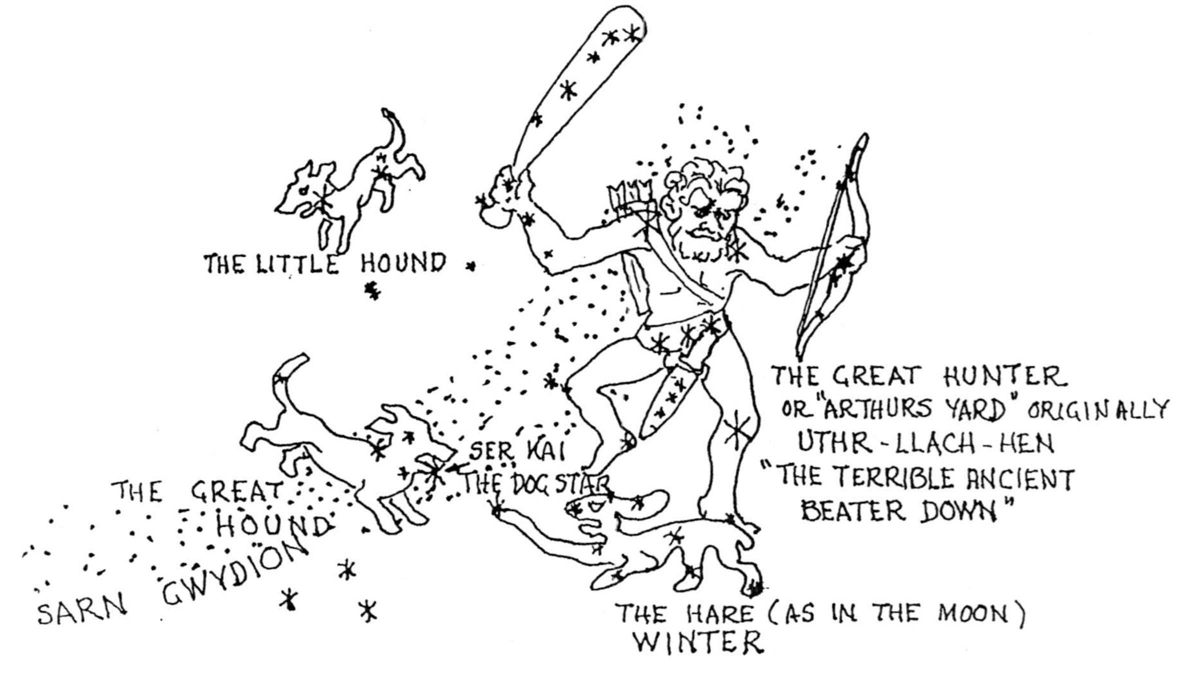
THE LITTLE HOUND
THE GREAT HUNTER
OR "ARTHURS YARD" ORIGINALLY
UTHR-LLACH-HEN
"THE TERRIBLE ANCIENT
BEATER DOWN"
SER KAI
THE DOG STAR
THE GREAT
HOUND
SARN GWYDION
THE HARE (AS IN THE MOON)
WINTER

Orion II

Gigantis
Orion
Orion

Orion may well be equated with the horned god Cernunnos and therefore with Actaeon, Herne the Hunter, St Nicholas and the Angel Gabriel.

This constellation rises high in the southern sky at midwinter, and represents the Winter Sun God. It is only visible in Great Britain from late autumn to early spring.

Arthur's Yard or Arthur's Wain was supposed to be the Celtic name. Here the term Arthur must derive from the Cornish ARTH-UN-HER the High One to Challenge. In other cultures Orion is the same person as Marduk, or as Gabriel, the archangel who announced the coming birth of Christ to the Virgin Mary at the Annunciation. Since the hounds of the Wild Hunt are known as Gabriel Raches, the hunting dogs of Gabriel, and also as the Cwn Annwn, or Hounds of Hell, Orion must be the Great Hunter, Le Grande Vernier in France and Herne the Hunter in lowland Britain, and in times past the giant Bran.

In classical stories Orion was the son of Hyrieus or of Euryale and Neptune. He too was a giant, and Diana the Huntress goddess fell in love with him, and so did Aurora (Dawn) who carried him away.

In Norse mythology this constellation was the great giant of winter Orvandel or Waendel, whose eyes were the stars Castor and Pollux. In Welsh the winter sun is Haul and is masculine, as opposed to the summer sun which is Huan which is feminine. Orion is the winter sun god, Maponus or Mabon to the Celts. The constellation Orion is setting and the constellation of Hercules is rising at Ladyday, the start of the year.

Other sources tell us that Orion was the son of Jupiter, and that it was Diana who killed him and put him in the sky. In British Arthurian legend it is Diana who appears in the legend about Sir Lancelot getting the Fair Elaine's brother, Sir Lavine, trained to be a knight by Sir Brastas at St Leonards Hill near Windsor. She is referred to there as The Lady Huntress of Windsor Forest, where she wounded Sir Lancelot accidentally with her arrow.

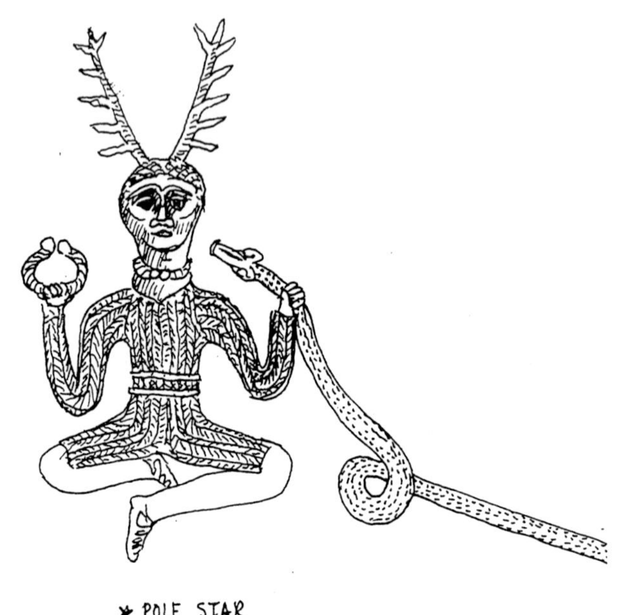

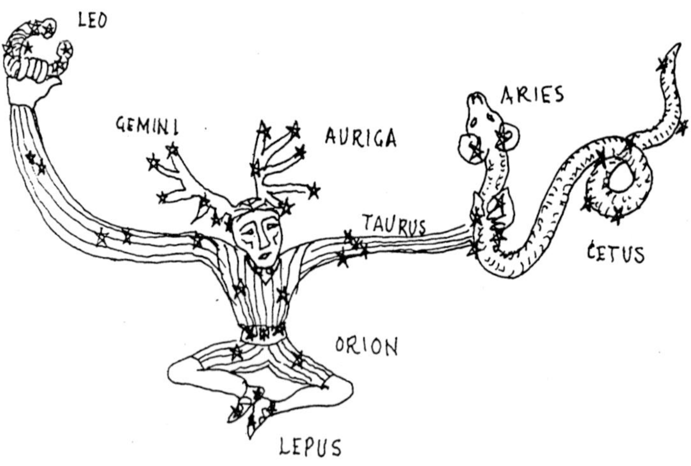

Top: Cernunnos as shown on the Gundestrup bowl from Denmark
Bottom: Cernunnos based on the great hunter, Orion, but including Leo Gemini Auriga, Taurus, Aries and Cetus

Orion may also be equated with Rural Mars, a red god like Bran of the British. He is equated as a great hunter with the angel Gabriel and Zagreus and Zeus the father of Dionysus.

Rigel is the brightest star in the constellation, and in Norse mythology is called Orwaendel's toe. The Scandinavians say that he was originally called DAZE and could take the shape of any bird or beast he chose. He stole a roast ox from Loki (or Odin or Thor) and make Loki steal the apples of Iduna to give him everlasting youth, but Loki retrieved the apples for the gods who then caught him, and as he was the giant of Winter they killed him with fire, pulled out his eyes and set them in the heavens as Castor and Pollux and threw him up among the stars by his big toe - Rigel. Orwandle was Grow's husband. Orion too was blinded at one time by Dionysys and Enopion, the father of Merope who he lay with. It is said that Orion hunts Taurus the Bull with his hounds the big and little dog stars, but in Celtic eyes he was the Great Hunter Mabon pursuing the great wild boar TWRCH TRWYTH which is the constellation Leo the Lion of classical astronomy.

Mabon, known as the chief of the glittering west perhaps because he was the winter sun god like Llew Llaw and Gwalchemei. He was the son of Modron. He was the only huntsman able to hunt with the hound Drudwyn (perhaps DROED-GWYN the ability to make a choice that is blessed and holy) the whelp of Greid son of Eri. Also he alone could ride the horse of Gewddw (perhaps GEW-DU of the dark enclosure, or GEW-DEW of the enclosure of god). In Gaul, Mabon was called Maponus. He may even have survived into the Christian period in Cornwall as Saint Mabyn or Mebena, recorded as early as 1266. Near Penzance there was a Saint Madron, who had a church and his own well by a hawthorn grove which was used for baptisms and for bathing in to cure nightmares or various bodily afflictions. To complete the cure the patient had to sleep on St Madron's bed, a nearby rock, perhaps once the capstone of the saints tomb or *bedd* in Cornish. The best time for a cure is at or around the 3rd of May, the middle of a meteor shower from the forefoot of Pegasus. To cure a child of rickets it must be dipped in the saints well thrice and all present must circle the well nine times sunwise while the childs parents face the rising sun. St Madron used to have a second well, the doom well for divinations.

The name of this god may derive from MAB-ION, the son of the Lord, since sun gods were reborn annually. A similar sounding saint is Saint Mabene, whose name may derive from SANCT MAB BENYW, the holy one, the son of the woman.

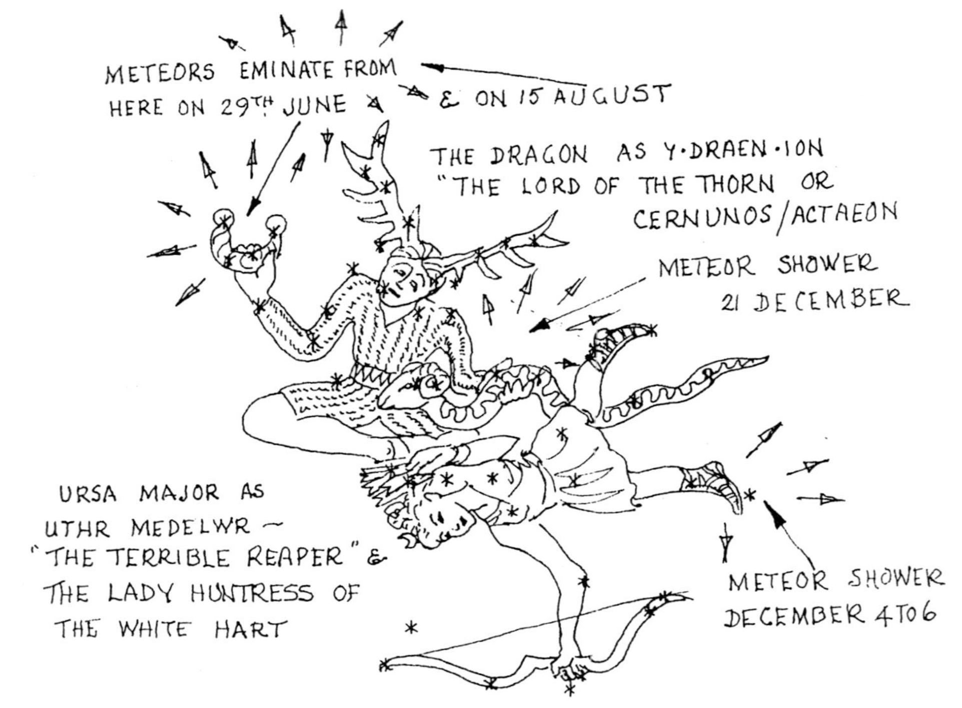
METEORS EMINATE FROM
HERE ON 29TH JUNE
& ON 15 AUGUST
THE DRAGON AS Y·DRAEN·ION
"THE LORD OF THE THORN OR
CERNUNOS/ACTAEON
METEOR SHOWER
21 DECEMBER
URSA MAJOR AS
UTHR MEDELWR ~
"THE TERRIBLE REAPER" &
THE LADY HUNTRESS OF
THE WHITE HART
METEOR SHOWER
DECEMBER 4 TO 6

Orion as a classical constellation carries a club and a lion skin as shield, and sometimes a sword and a girdle, though this can be taken as his penis and girdle.

The constellation rises about the beginning of November, the season of rain and storms, hence he is sometimes called nimbosus or aquosus and imbrifer.

As a Celtic great hunter he must carry a bow and arrows, but he must also carry a club. The reputed Welsh name of this constellation that has been translated as Arthurs Yard, may actually have been UTHR LLACH HEN which would translate as something like The Terrible Ancient Beater Down, which must refer to Orions club.

The fact that Orion was known as the Great Hunter, a title of Cernunnos and Herne the Hunter, and the fact that Herne and Cernunnos are depicted as holding a lunar torque in their right hand and a ram headed snake in his left hand, does suggest that the constellation Orion may have been pictured by the Celts as Cernunnos. In which case, the sickle of Leo must become the lunar torque, Gemini and Auriga, Cernunnos' horns, and a combination of Aries and Cetus become the Ram Headed Serpent. The illustration opposite shows how this would look, compared with an illustration of Cernunnos on the Gundestrup bowl and the layout of the stars.

However, it must be remembered that the Great Hunter and the Lady Huntress probably date back to Mesolithic times, and the polar start may have been interpreted as Cernunnos and Diana. See for this possibility under Draco and Ursa Major. If Draco was ever interpreted as Cernunnos, as shown in the following picture, then Orion was just a club-swinging giant and great hunter of the winter sun, and in late Celtic times perhaps he was Gwyn ap Nudd, when he is said to ride out of his land under the hill of Glastonbury to hunt mens' souls across the winter skies in a Great Hunt, as Herne the Hunter is said to do in Windsor Forest.

Píscís Austealís XV

Piscis australis

The Southern Fish lies below the Water Carrier and the Sea Goat, or to the Celts the Dowser and the walrus. Being a southern constellation it is only seasonally visible, like the salmon, in British Waters. The salmon being as prominent in Celtic legend surely must have a stellar counterpart and this seems the most likely constellation. Salmon were supposed to be of a great age and gifted with knowledge, for it was known that they travelled great distances, and returned from their travels. The illustration is of a Pictish Celtic drawing of a salmon.

THE SALMON
EOG

The Galaxy or Milky Way

There are many names for the dense band of stars across the sky that we call the Milky Way. From Norse mythology we get the name Watling Street, from the elf smith, Wate or Vate or Wald, but in Britain this name belongs to the Roman road to the north, which before that was one of the Four Roads of Britain. In Italy the Milky Way is called La Strada di Roma, in Germany it is the road to Aachen or Cologne or Frankfurt, and in Friesland and Lancashire it is called The Cow Path. It is also the pilgrims path to Walsingham or Compostella or Santiago, and other similar shrines. In ancient Rome it was said to have been caused by a spurt of milk from the breast of Rhea, the mother of Romulus, hence it is also known as the Via Lacta in Italy. In classical astronomy it was the mortals road to heaven and the court of Jupiter. The myriad of stars were the souls of mortals on their journey to the court of the gods.

In this country since Tudor times it has been known as the Fairies Path, perhaps since it leads to the pagan heaven behind the north wind. But also perhaps since the name Caer Sidhe, sometimes applied to the Milky Way can be translated as The Castle of the Fairies. The Sidhe were the Gaelic gods who became the fairies of later folklore and dwelt in the fairy mounds or long barrows and tumuli.

The banshee were the ghostly women or fairies of the tumuli, the hills of the dead. So Caer Sidhe can also mean the castle of the women of the mound of the banshees.

Another spelling of the name as Caer Sidi is normally translated as the turning castle from the Welsh root *SID* meaning "to turn", which gives us the words Sidellu, "to wind or whirr" and sidle, "a flywheel".

The Irish name for the Milky Way is Siog na speire, which is translated in everyday Irish as "the streak or stripe of the (night) sky". However, *siog*, besides meaning "streak or stripe", also means "fairy". It derives from the root *SI* meaning "fairy or magic". So the Milky Way was The Path of the Fairies or Gods to all the later Celts.

In Wales the Milky Way has several names. It is Sarn Gwydion the causeway of Gwydion, along which he searched for the soul of his son Llew Llaw, which is nearer to the general idea that it is a road than another of its names Caer

Gwydion, the Court or Castle of Gwydion, the son of Don, whose own court Llys Don lies beside the Milky Way.

To the Irish and Scottish Celts it is either The Great Plain or Lugh's Chain. More romantically the Welsh also say that it is the white track of Olwen, daughter of Yspaddaden Penkawr, or Hawthorn Chief of the Giants.

The Greeks, whose legends of Perseus survive as the legends of St George in English mummers plays, had further legends to account for the Milky Way. They explained that it was the cloud of dust kicked up by Perseus, from the speed of his exploits.

Another of their legends claims that it is the smoke from the constellation Ara the Altar when the constellation Centaurus sacrificed the constellation Lupus the wolf or beast upon it.

The Moving Stars

If the fixed stars were conceived as representations of supernatural beings, gods and goddesses and their abodes, then the regularly moving stars were even more important deities, and the seasonal really fast moving stars, the meteors, meteorites and comets were messengers, or the souls of gods and heroes.

The most important visible objects in the sky after the sun and moon, throughout most of human history, have been those stars to whom men have dedicated the days of the week.

In the following list of the planets and the sun and moon, the Latin names have been used followed by the days of the week, the associated metal, colour and attributes. Then follows the astronomical sign and its usual derivation.

After this follow the pair of Titans associated with the day, then the Norse gods, and the Christian angels, followed by the Babylonian gods and then a host of Christian Saints, classical and Celtic gods and goddesses, and finally the trees and birds and numbers associated with the days of the week and the planets, as derived from the Ogam alphabet of the Irish Celts.

After this more or less formal list, come the associated stories.

From this will be seen that seven was a very special number. Not only were there the seven planets of the days of the week, but there were seven heavens, the seventh being the heaven of the Virgin. To the pious Christian this was the heaven of the Virgin Mary, to the pious Muslim it was the heaven of the faithful and pious man where he would be waited upon by heavenly virgins, the houries. This was no doubt associated with the seven dances of women and the seven ecstasies of man, and possibly the seven devine days. There were also the seven divine words, the seven human words, the seven human members and the Seven Seals of the Apocalypse. There were also said to be seven climates, seven regions, seven oceans, seven abysses and seven constellations. The seven continents are of quite recent observation.

In the folklore of many countries there are Seven Sleepers, doomed to sleep in a cave below the hills until the end of time. In Ireland it is Finn-mac-Coul with his dog called Bran and the Fians or Fingalians.

In Scotland they are said to sleep below Craig-a-how on Black Isle, or in Ossian's cave in Glencoe, and below Smith's Rock on Skye. At Tomnahurich in Inverness the chief of the sleepers is Thomas the Rhymer, but he also sleeps below the Eildun Hills.

As we know from the story of Thomas the Ryhmer, the men who became one of the seven sleepers were lovers of the Queen of the Fairies. They ruled beside her for seven years, and at the end of this time they were virtually murdered as were all sacred kings, when they were said to be asleep, not dead.

So we are told that King Arthur and his knights are sleeping in a cave below the Eildon Hills, or Snowdon or Cadbury in Somerset or in the Vale of Neath, waiting to be awakened from their magical charmed sleep to come forth at the end of time to do wondrous deeds again and save the land of Britain.

According to the *Book of Revelations* there are seven Holy Angels of the seven Churches. They are:

Raphael or Suriel

Michael

Uriel

Gabriel

Jophiel

Jephephiah

The Metatron

The number seven pervades our life:

A baby becomes a boy at 7 years of age.

A boy becomes a youth at 2 x 7 years of age, or 14 years.

A youth becomes a man at 3 x 7 years of age, or 21 years.

A man seeks a new wife after being married 7 years. This is the 7 year itch.

A man's days are numbered to three score years and ten, which is 10 x 7 or 70 years.

Seven years was sometimes considered the proper period for courting.

Every seven days a man should rest.

Four times 7 days is the time between new moons.

7 x 7 x 7 days with 7 + 7 + 7 days = 364 days - the period between one new years day and the next.

Hecate with a horse, torch and dog. She was said to appear attended by howling dogs and ghosts and was worshipped where three ways met. Hecate also presided over births, could increase flocks and herds and care for the living with Diana and Juno Lucina. She also presided over purifications.

The Moon (Luna)

Monday
Silver or White
Soft Shades
Fortune
Phoebe and Atlas
The moon when referred to as a person is Luna or Selene

the new moon, the first quarter, the full moon, the last quarter

It is associated with:

The Angel Jephephiah
SIN
or Damkina (Ishtar) the mother of Tammuz

Saint Anne

Circe, Hecate, Selene, Artemis, Dia-Anna or Diana, Astarte, Anna Perenina, Demeter, Io, Aphrodite, Acca Laurentia, Persephone, Minerva, Athene, Arianrhod, The Cailleach, Boan (the swift heifer), Don

The Willow tree, The Hawk S. 16

The moon is associated with silver, reflections and the stones crystal, pearl, opal, moonstone and milkstones but also the blood red carbuncle. It symbolises fruitfulness, changeability, fortune, envy and enchantment. It controls the head. It is complementary to the sun.

A Roman copy of a Greek statue c335 B.C. of Artemis, the Lady Huntress of Windsor Forest as described in Arthurian legend

The moon goddess Arianrhod, whose name means silver wheel, is also associated with the constellation Corona Borealis, which to the Celt was Caer Arianrhod, the Castle or Court of Arianrhod. Her sons by Gwydion were twins:

Dylan & Lleu - their titles were:

Son of the Wave & Llew Llaw Gyffes

Llew Llaw Gyffes means "the lion with a steady hand", because of his prowess as an archer.

Llew was also called Llew Lamh Farda "Light, the long handed". He was also known as Lugh the sun god, and his soul was an eagle.

However, the name for the constellation Corona Borealis may have been Carreg Arianrhod, the stone of Silverwheel because the crescent or circular shape is reminiscent of the stone, and later iron throwing axe, the shepherds rod of the Chiltern shepherds, the thunderbolt of the gods and the francisca of the Franks. When thrown, the honed axe blade caught the sun and appeared as the Silver Wheel - of Arianrhod.

It is quite possible that among the Mesolithic hunters of western Europe, before agriculture became the main source of food for mankind, the polar constellations of Draco and Ursa Major and Minor were still thought of as the representations of the gods of food, especially food in winter, when the male deer wore antlers. The great goddess instead of being the mistress of agriculture, the holder of the sickle, would have been seen as Mistress of the wild beasts, the Lady Huntress. The constellation Draco, the Dragon who was ridden by the goddess Berecynthia, became in Celtic eyes the DRAEN-ION, the Lord of the Thorns, the horned god Cernunnos. On the Gundestrup bowl he is shown holding a lunar torque (see the illustration).

The three classical constellations of Draco and Ursa Major and Minor fit well into a picture of the classical Actaeon and Artemis or Herne the Hunter and the Lady Huntress of Windsor Forest or Cernunnos and Diana.

In Britain the name of the goddess Arianrhod, meaning Silverwheel, tells us that she was the moon goddess, just as Selena, Diana and Artemis were. They, and the British Cailleach, and their priestesses the witches, could all turn themselves into hares. The hare was also the messenger and servant of the moon goddess. That is why the markings on the moon are interpreted by some not as the face of the man in the moon but as a running hare. There is a medieval floor tile in the

The shape of the hare in the moon on a medieval floor tile from Holy Trinity, Cookham, Berks

church at Cookham, Berkshire, which shows a circular design which is that of the markings on the moon interpreted as a hare (see the illustration)). Annual games were held at Cookham on Great Whitten Hare Warren on the Assumption of the Blessed Virgin Mary on 15th August.

Hares belong to the moon as they are largely nocturnal. The connection with the Cailleach, the waning crescent moon, is carried into the cornfield, where the last stand of corn is called either the hare or the hag.

The crescent of the waxing moon is the phase connected with the Lady Huntress Artemis or Diana, and the full moon with Our Lady, or the Mother Goddess Diana, whose feast day was on 13th August, the day of the death of the Blessed Virgin Mary, who rose again and ascended to heaven three days later on 15th August.

Julius Caesar records that the Britons held the hare and the goose to be sacred animals and never usually ate them. This reluctance survived in Wales, the south west of England and in Brittany into the 19th century, except for two occasions. Jugged Hare or Hare Pie was the traditional dish at Easter or Ladyday, the same feast in the Dark Ages. Similarly geese, the domesticated version of the grey lag goose (see the constellation Cygnus), were traditionally eaten only at Michaelmass.

Mars, from Bisley, Gloucestershire

Mars

Tuesday
Iron
Red
Passion or Anger

a helmet or plume and a phallic symbol

Dione and Cruis
Tiur or Ziris

Mars is associated with

The Archangel Michael (who is like god)
Nergal or Ninlil, the storm god husband of Ishtar
Saint Alban
Aries, Hercules, Mars (the red god)
The Morrigu, Zio, Tuisco, Tina, Tiur, Amathon, Bran, Camulos, Teutates
The Holly tree, the Starling, T. 11

Mars is associated with energy, iron and steel, courage and aggression. Its stones are bloodstone, flint, malachite, the yellow cairngorm and red haematite. It symbolises passion, and controls growth. It is complementary to Venus. Hence Mars was the red faced god whose month March covered the end of the old year and start of the new year on Ladyday. The equivalent British god was the giant Bran, also red faced. The alder tree was the tree of Bran, and his month in the old 13 month calendar ran from 19th February to 18th March. Just before the month of the god Bran started, on the Christian feast day of Shrove Tuesday, 13th of February when Easter is on Ladyday, the cook at Eton College in South Bucks, used to hang up a live crow over a pancake on the kitchen door, for the boys to stone to death. Since the original boys at Eton were the sons of local poor farmers and the like, they kept alive a lot of old pagan British customs such as the Eton Montem, held on the equivalent of the Welsh Twimpath Chwarae or "mound of the games". The crow stoning was probably a similar ceremony just before the start of the month of the god Bran, since his bird was bran, a crow, the bird stoned to death - elsewhere in Britain it was a tethered cock that was stoned to death as retribution against the cock that crowed as Saint Peter denied Jesus three times, before the crucifixion.

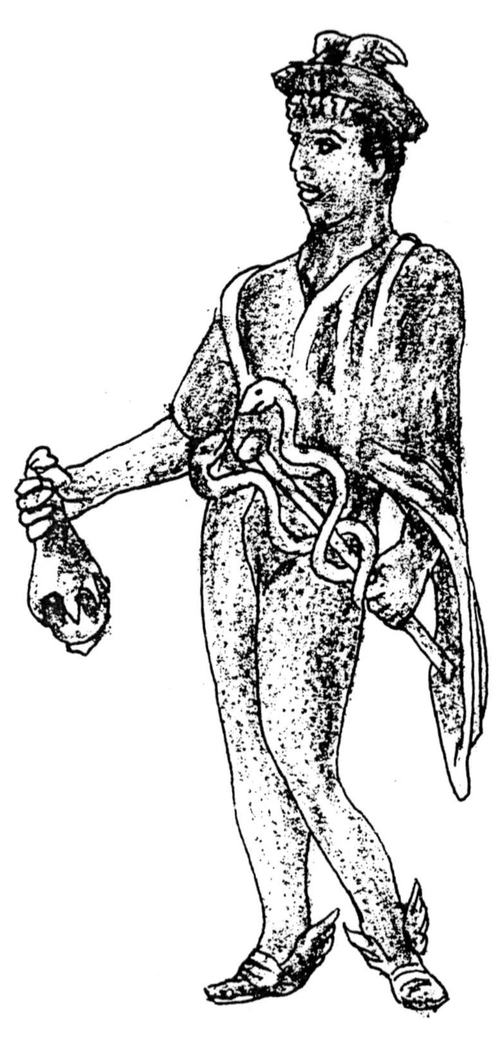

A Roman bronze of Mercury/Hermes from St. Donats, Glamorgan, restored to show his winged sandals and hat with a caduceus in his left hand

Mercury

Wednesday
Mercury (quicksilver) and tin
Grey or Navy Blue
Commerce and Avarice

a buck, the horned god,
the cog almanac sign of
St Nicholas

Metis and Coeus
Woden or Wotan
Odin

Mercury is associated with:

The Archangel Raphael (god heals) otherwise called Suriel
Nabu

Hermes, Apollo, Mercury
Ogma, Manawyddadan
The Ash tree or Hazel, the Crane

Mercury is associated with intellectuals, commerce and orators, its stones are opal, aquamarine, and banded red agate. It associates well with other moving stars, but complements none. It controls wisdom, eloquence and the lungs, hence the connection with the god Ogma or Ogimus who is shown in sculpture leading men in chains running from ears to tongue. Needless to say Ogma was honoured in Ireland, the country where Blarney castle still stands, and where kissing the Blarney Stone confers the art of oratory.

Jupiter with his thunderbolt. A 2nd century statue from Smyrna

Jupiter

Thursday
Tin and Electrum
Purple and Orange
Increase Ambition

Themis and Eurymedion
Thor

an eagle

Jupiter is associated with:

The Angel The Metatron
Marduk (possibly Tamuz)
or Ea (another husband of Ishtar) or Bel

Saint John, Saint Amphibalus
Dianus, Janus, Zeus, Juppiter, Jove

Bel or Beli, The Dagda (the good or cattle god), and Ludd
Succllus (of southern Gaul)
The Oak tree, the goldcrest wren D 12

Jupiter is associated with good fortune, the faithful and honourable and increase, but also with the conceited and fanatics. Its stones are amethyst and turquoise. It is complementary to Saturn and controls Law. In Celtic lands folk moots and parliaments were held under oak trees, and courts of Justice too. Oak was the solid wood of honesty, it would not bend like ash or fall without warning like elm.

A second century Roman bronze of Venus from Verulanium

Venus

Friday
Copper (and brass)
Blue and Pink and Green
Love

Tethys and Oceanus
Frig
Fria or Freia

the looking glass and/
or the hornless doe

Venus is associated with:

The Angel Jophiel
Ishtar, the lover of Tammuz, or Ashtoreth or Astarte or Beltis

Saint Mary Magdalene, Saint Mary Gypsy (both penitent and prostitutes), Saint Margaret and Saint Bride or Bridget (who hung up her veil on a sunbeam)

Aphrodite, Hera, Persephone, Juno, Athene, Minerva, Astarte, Ceres, Demeter

The Lady in Red, Creudyladd, Briget or Bridge, Brigantia, St Frideswide, the Gruagrach

The Apple tree, the hen, Q in the Ogham alphabet

Venus controls both love and lust.

The planet Venus is known as The Evening Star when appearing at close of day or in the night sky and is the personification of the goddess Venus or Aphrodite of the classical world, or Creudyladd or Bride to the Celts, or even of Branwen.

The same star, or rather planet, when seen at break of day is called The Morning Star or Day Star, and was the personification of the classical god Lucifer, the bringer of light. The bringer of light was also a title of Helios or Apollo to the Romans.

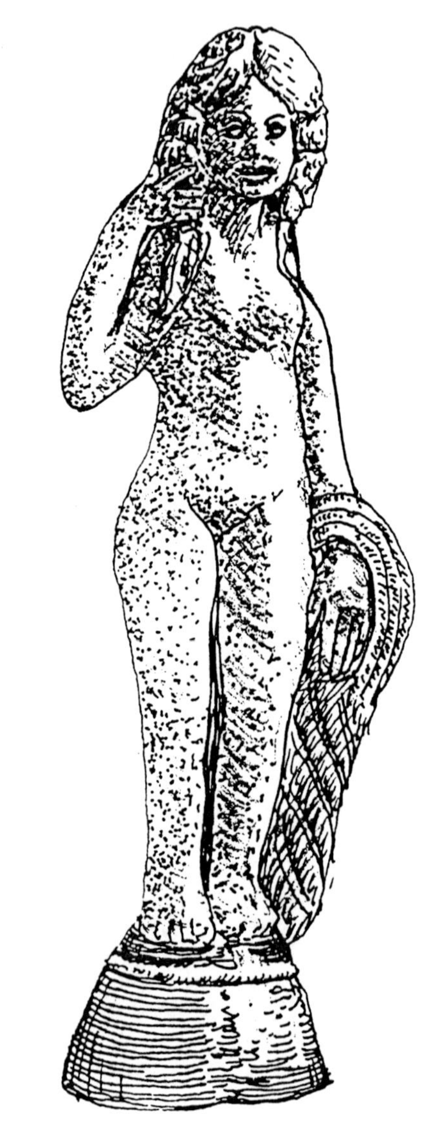

A Roman figure of Venus from London

Lucifer from a tomb in the Vatican cemetery

In Revelations 22:16 in a reference to his second coming, Jesus Christ is called The Bright, The Morning Star, and was therefore identified with the planet Venus by the early semi Christians. He was even worshipped as Christos Helios in Rome. It is through the iconography of Lucifer as shown from the illustration taken from a tomb in the Vatican cemetery that the planet Venus is linked with the sun and the sun gods who rode on white horses, like Saints George, Michael, and James, and the Celtic gods Lugh or Llew Llamfada.

The Cornish name for the planet Venus (which is therefore probably the British Celtic name) is Berlewen, a feminine noun made up from the elements: BER = short or brief, LEU or LLEW = light (an ancient form) and WEN = holy, fair, white, blessed. So Berlewen means the Holy white Light. There may be a link in part of the name with the Celtic God of Light, Llew Llaw Gyffes or Lugh.

Before the birth of the Prophet Mohamet, the planet Venus, the Morning Star, was worshipped as the personification of the goddess Uzza, the youngest of the three incarnations of the goddess, signified by the new moon. The other two incarnations were the full moon Allat and the old moon Manat. They were worshipped at Mecca until the 7th century, when Allah, the male consort of the mother goddess of the full moon Allat or AL-LAT, became the supreme and only god recognised by Mohamet. To this day the black stone set in the eastern or morning side of the cubic Kaaba in Mecca and set in a silver mount, was the personification of the goddess and was probably a meteorite, like that which represented the goddess Cybele, that was taken to Rome, or the one near St David's in Pembrokeshire associated with his birth from St Non in the centre of a stone circle. (See Meteorites under Moving Stars). Venus the planet must therefore also be associated with Aphrodite Artemis, Uzza and St Non, while Allat is equated with Rhea, Hera, Demeter or Don and Manat with the Hesperades and Fates and the Morrigu. Therefore Venus is associated with the moon.

Venus is associated with love, affection, harmony, beauty and sensuousness. Its stones are emerald and sapphire and it is complementary to Mars.

The Morning Star is called Berlewen in Cornish, which means the short white or holy light. Venus when seen before dawn is the light bringer, and according to classical astronomy is here the daughter of Jupiter and Aurora or Eos the goddess of dawn, and she drives through the sky in a chariot drawn by white horses. Her mother Aurora's dress is yellow and she carries a torch and was a daughter of Hyperion.

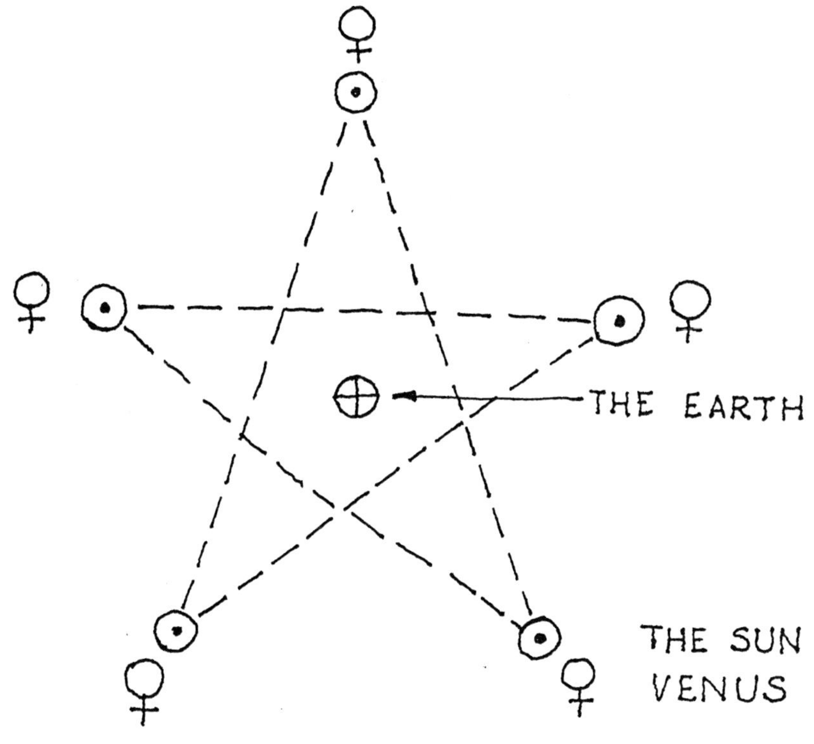

The courses of the Sun and Venus over an eight year period trace out a pentagram. The five points being the places where the Sun eclipses the planet Venus.

The Morning Star is also called Lucifer or Phosphoros. In the witches gospel it was Lucifer who married Tana (Diana) and begot their goddess Aradia at Dawn.

Vesper or Hesperos is the name of Venus as the Evening Star, hence the Hesperedes -the islands where the sun sets.

St Mary Magdalen is the Christian equivalent of the goddess Aphrodite or Venus.

To the Astronomer or Astrologer who maps the stars every 8 years, the sun and Venus appear to trace out a pentacle or five pointed star in the heavens, its points being the five places where the sun eclipses Venus during this time. This Seal of Solomon was the sign of the French organised Priory of Zion a parallel order to that of the Knights Templar.

The pentacle is also known as The Druid's footprint, and as the Seal of the Virgin.

The planet Venus was also the star of Astarte, who was known as Ashtoreth in the Bible, and Ishtar in Babylon.

The late classical authors Lucian and Herodian recorded that in their time representations of Astarte had horns, though they did not say what sort of horns. However, in ancient writings there are references to Astartes of the flocks, so she may have had rams or sheeps horns.

It may have some significance that in the 1939-1946 war against the dictatorial powers, the allies fought under the sign of a single white five point star, like that on the shield of the Arthurian hero Sir Gawain, The Seal of the Virgin, and were victorious.

Saturn

Saturday
Lead
Black and dark colours
Fatality

a scythe or sickle

Rhea and Cronos. Just as Rhea was the wife of Cronos so Ops was the wife of Saturn and her name means wealth as she gathered in the crop resulting from the seed that Saturn sowed. So Saturns Greek equivalent was Triptolemos.

Saturn is associated with:

The Archangel Gabriel (man of god)
Ninib
or Ninurta, the god of war

Saint Andrew, Saint Nicholas, Jehovah or Yhweh

Pan, Orion, Actaeon, Cronus (old father time)

Cernunnos and perhaps Manayddan and Bran

The Alder tree, the gull, F 8

Saturn is associated with teachers, and careful and laborious work and restriction. Its stones are garnet, jet and all black stones. It is complementary to Jupiter and controls fatalities and sloth and peace.

The sickle originally belonged to the hag aspect of the Great Goddess, The Terrible Reaper, Uthr Medelwr, represented by the constellation we call Ursa Major today.

A bronze relief of Pan from Pompeii

Actaeon attacked by his own dogs as he turned into a stag - from a Roman tomb in Chester

Christus-Helios from a tomb in the Vatican cemetery. The term Chrestos is "thou good and excellent man", alternatively Christos is "the anointed one". The picture is plainly Helios driving his quadriga (four horse chariot) of the Sun.

The Sun (Sol)

Sunday
Gold
Yellow or Scarlet

the sun

Theia and Hyperion

The sun is associated with:

The Archangel Uriel
Shamash or Samas
or Tammuz or Adonis
Jesus Christ
Cupid, Eros, Apollo, Helius, Sol, Phoebus, Adonis and Tammuz

Aengus Mac Oc, Lugh, Llew Llaw, Bel, Belinus, Helith

The Birch tree, the Pheasant B 5
the bull of seven fights and the stag of seven tines

The sun is associated with creativeness, ability, pride, life giving and even an overbearing nature. Its stones are the diamond, ruby, carbuncle and red sard. It is complementary to the moon.

The Sun as a person is referred to as Helios or Sol and as such is the Golden King Sol or Zul reputed to have been buried astride his golden horse under Silbury Hill, which lays near the Kennet river and Long Barrow. It is the largest Tumulus in Europe. Helios drove a chariot usually drawn by four horses. In art Helios is sometimes represented, like the Christian God, by a single open eye. Hyperion son of Coelum and Terra was the father of Sol or Helios, and Helios is paired with Selene.

Silbury Hill and its surroundings are worthy of some study in relation to the worship of a sun god in Britain by the Celts or their predecessors.

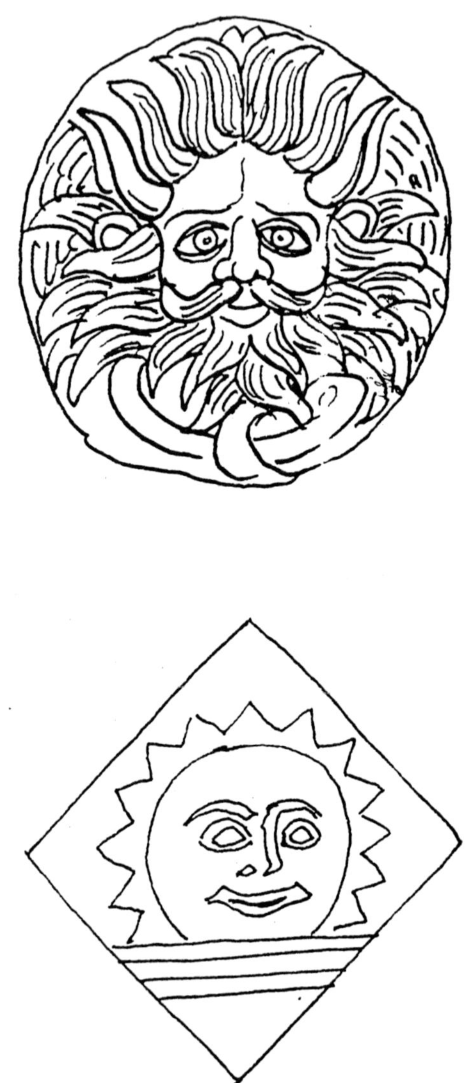

Top: Carving from the Temple of Sul Minerva at Aqua Sulis at Bath
Bottom: 12th century tile from Aylesbury

A bronze plaque of Minerva from Charlton Down, Wiltshire

Surviving tradition tells us that King Zel was buried there on horseback, and in the 18th century this had grown to be a life size figure of the king astride his horse in solid gold. Furthermore it was said that the hill had been raised in the time it took a posit of milk to seethe.

Archaeological excavation has found no chamber and no burial, though it is the largest tumulus in Europe, being 130 feet high and covering some 5.25 acres. It is recorded to have been built some 4000 years ago. The sides are steep, at a slope of 1 in 2 or about 30 degrees and it contains some 9.5 million cubic feet of material, which is more than the volume of the Great Pyramid at Gizeh. It is surrounded by a moat some 125 feet wide and 16 feet deep. It has a flat top surrounded by a slightly lower rim, with signs of some lower terraces. This suggests its use more in manner of the Welsh Twmpath Chwarae or Mound of the Games, as a raised stage for ceremonials and plays, perhaps in the manner of Dragon Hill by the Berkshire White Horse, where it is said that the Mummers Play showing Saint George's combat with the Dragon was performed. This celebration may have survived into the 18th and 19th centuries when local people still met on the summit on Palm Sunday to eat cakes and figs with sweetened water from a spring by the nearby river Kennet.

Nearby the large West Kennet Long Barrow may also be connected with solar worship as from its orientation between 85 and 90 degrees from due north, and the sun will probably shine down the length of the barrow at about the Spring and Winter Equinoxes.

The Earth

Saint Bride's Cross

Until the 19th or 20th Century, the earth was not considered in the same way as the other planets, so it is curious to find its sign astrologically in the Cross of the Virgin, the Celtic Cross.

Bibliography

Collins Concise Encyclopaedia of Green and Roman Mythology by Sabine G Oswalt, Collins of Glasgow

Taliesin Shamanism and the Bardic Mysteries in Britian and Ireland by John Matthews, The Aquarian Press of Harper Collins Publishers

A Smaller Latin English Dictionary by Sir William Smith D.C.L., L.L.D. and Theophilus D Hall M.A. and John K Ingram L.L.D., John Murray London

An Arthurian Reader by John Matthews, The Aquarian Press of Harper Collins

The White Goddess by Robert Graves, Faber and Faber Ltd

Celtic Myth and Legend by Charles Squire, The Gresham Publishing Co Ltd

Old England by Charles Knight, James Sangster & Co

The Crowning Privilege by Robert Graves, Pelican

Hutchinsons Splendour of the Heavens by the Rev T.E.R. Phillips M.A., F.R.A.S. and Dr W H Steavenson F.R.A.S., Hutchinson & Co

The Golden Bough by J G Frazer, Macmillan & Co Ltd

The Greek Myths by Robert Graves, Penguin Books

The Stars Above Us by Ernst Zimmer, George Allen and Unwin

The Golden Dolly by M Lambeth, The Cornucopia Press, 33 Stonebridge Lane, Fulbourne, Cambridgeshire

Popular Antiquities, Brand

Kecks, Keddles and Kesh by Michael Bayley, Capall Bann, Chieveley.

Celtic Heritage by Alwyn Rees and Brindley Rees, Thames and Hudson, London

The British Celts and Their Gods Under Rome by Graham Webster, B T Batsford Ltd, London

Collins Concise Encyclopaedia of Greek and Roman Mythology by Sabine G Oswalt, Collins, Glasgow

Legendary and Mythological Art by Clara Erskine Clement, Bracken Books, London

White Horses and Other Hill Figures by Morris Marples, Alan Sutton Publishing, Phoenix Mill, Strand, Gloucs

Stones, Bones and Gods by R T Pearce, Ward Lock Educational

Index

Addanc, 106, 159, 170
Alder, 192, 217, 229
Algol, 103
Allah, 226
Amathon, 113, 217
Andromeda, 23, 26, 47, 55, 92, 103-104, 128, 189-190
Aphrodite, 29, 47, 85, 128, 157, 211, 223, 226, 228
Apollo, 3, 5, 81, 85, 87, 133, 153, 157, 163, 169, 192, 219, 223, 233
Apple, 29, 33, 85, 139, 223
Aquila, 10, 23, 27, 33, 62, 75
Arctophylax, 33
Arianrhod, 9, 33, 47, 52, 57, 59, 75, 79, 178, 211, 213
Ariel, 173
Artemis, 3, 5, 7, 26, 81, 84-85, 100, 115, 125, 155, 157, 165, 167, 169, 211, 213, 215, 226
Artemis Brauronia, 115
Arthur's Chair, 41
Arthur's Harp, 9, 89
Arthur's Ship, 10, 185
Arthur's Yard, 10, 199
Ash, 141, 219, 221
Astarte, 47, 111, 123, 125, 128, 211, 223, 228
Atlas, 81, 152, 163, 211
Attis Adonis, 8, 26, 29, 43, 123, 126, 133
Augerona, 69
Auriga, 23, 31, 35, 137, 179, 203
Aurora, 199, 226
Avanc, 35

Bald Ship, 10, 185, 193
Berecynthia, 5, 7-9, 30, 39, 41, 47, 53, 67, 75, 100, 104, 111, 115, 123, 125, 128-129, 133, 137, 159, 183, 195, 213
Birch, 233
Birds Wedding day, 31
Blarney Stone, 219
Boan, 211
Bona Dea, 7
Bootes, 5, 23, 31, 33, 35, 39, 82, 106-107, 129, 170, 173, 178-179, 191
Boreas, 57, 109
Bran, 49, 77, 143, 153, 155, 187, 191-192, 199, 201, 207, 217, 229

Caer Arianrhod, 9, 57, 59, 213
Caer Gwydion, 9, 205
Caer Sidhe, 205
Cailleach, 9, 67, 82, 125, 129, 133, 139, 155, 165, 211, 213, 215
Callisto, 5, 115, 125
Campion, 197
Camulos, 217
Cardea, 30, 115
Casseopea, 10, 23, 26, 43, 45, 49, 77, 103
Celi, 39
Cephus, 26, 41, 55, 103
Cerealia, 51
Cerebus, 187
Cerne Abbas, 26

Cerridwen, 8-10, 30, 39, 41, 43, 53, 57, 67, 125-126, 129, 133
Charlemagne, 113, 135
Chiron, 169, 189
Cock Robin, 49, 51, 77, 82, 143, 155
Cog Almanac, 2, 7-8, 43, 45, 49, 51, 59, 69, 77, 133, 152, 159, 165, 219
Corn Baby, 182
Corona Borealis, 9, 23, 33, 57, 113, 178, 213
Corybantes, 126
Court of Don, 10, 29, 41, 52, 62
Crane, 219
Creudyladd, 75, 94, 149, 223
Crying the Mare, 100
Cuckoo, 82, 167
Cybele, 5, 7-9, 26, 30-31, 41, 47, 67, 111, 115, 123, 125-126, 129, 133, 226
Cygnus, 10, 23, 27, 62, 105, 215
Cyphus, 23

Damkina, 211
Delos, 1, 5, 163
Delphinus, 23, 65
Demeter, 7, 70, 100, 123, 179, 211, 223, 226
Dene Holes, 1
Dewi Sant, 109
Dia-Anna, 211
Diana, 5, 7, 26, 67, 69-70, 84, 100, 125-126, 148, 155, 167, 199, 203, 211, 213, 215, 228
Dionysus, 39-40, 43, 70, 100-101, 106-107, 126, 152, 201
Dolphin, 23, 65
Don, 3, 9-10, 29, 41, 52, 59, 62, 155, 206, 211, 226
Draco, 10, 23, 41, 67, 69-70, 104, 111, 123, 190, 203, 213
Dragon Hill, 55, 92, 103, 190, 236
Dragon, 7, 11, 23, 26, 41, 43, 47, 55, 67, 69-70, 75, 85, 92, 103-104, 106, 109, 111, 123, 128-129, 137, 159, 190, 213, 236
Druid's footprint, 228
Dylan, 213

Epona, 73, 90, 94, 98, 100
Equuelus, 23, 73, 90

Faunus, 83
Festival of Birds, 77

Gabriel, 62, 153, 187, 189, 195, 199, 201, 208, 229
Gaia, 70, 109
Galli, 126
Ganymede, 27
Godgifa, 94
Goose, 10, 62, 64, 105, 126, 167, 215
Gorgon, 55, 103
Great Nativity Day, 8, 133, 195
Gruagrach, 223
Gull, 229
Gwalchmei, 27
Gweynevere, 49
Gwydion, 9-10, 27, 62, 75, 141, 205-206, 213

Hag of Beara, 5
Hallowe'en, 62, 137, 155, 163, 165, 167
Harlequin, 115
Harvest Lord, 182
Hawk, 10, 27, 62, 105, 109, 211
Hazel, 141, 219
Helis, 75
Helith, 75, 77, 92, 233
Hellwain, 115
Hera, 5, 70, 81, 83-85, 87, 115, 144, 163, 223, 226

Hercules, 23, 39, 51, 62, 70, 75, 77, 83-85, 87, 89, 92, 104, 144, 149, 157, 169, 187, 192, 199, 217
Herelingas, 149
Herlingas, 115
Herne, 59, 69, 187, 199, 203, 213
Hippasus, 100
Hirco-cervus, 145
Hodening Horse, 100
Holly, 217
Hu Gadarn, 5, 31, 35, 39, 69-70, 106, 113, 126, 133, 149, 170, 173, 179
Hydra, 84, 144, 184, 187, 193

Iduna, 135, 201
Ishtar, 31, 211, 217, 221, 223, 228

Janus, 115, 221
Jephephiah, 208, 211
Jesus Christ, 29, 33, 126, 134, 226, 233
Jethro Tull, 179
Jolly Pinder, 135
Jophiel, 208, 223

Kern Babby, 182
King Canute, 94
King Zel, 236

Ladon, 70, 85
Lady Day, 8, 26, 30-31, 39, 43, 49, 57, 59, 62, 64, 69, 75, 115, 123, 125-126, 139, 132-133, 195, 199, 215, 217
Lady Godifu, 94
Lady Godiva, 94
Ladyday,
Lamia, 98
Latinus, 83-84
Leofric, 94, 98
Little Nativity Day, 8-9
Llew Llaw, 27, 29-30, 47, 75, 79, 83, 92, 103-104, 190, 201, 205, 213, 226, 233
Llys Don, 10, 41, 52, 59, 62, 206
Loki, 135, 201
Long Man of Wilmington, 51, 75, 77
Lucifer, 70, 223, 226, 228
Lucippe, 100
Lugh, 49, 62, 75, 77, 92, 103-104, 128, 190, 192, 206, 213, 226, 233
Lugh's Chain, 206
Lyra, 9, 23, 70, 89

Mabon, 143, 153, 157, 199, 201
Magpie, 26, 79, 128
Manawyddadan, 219
Maponus, 199, 201
Marduk, 199, 221
Mari Llwyd, 100
Marian, 128, 135
Mazes, 113
Merlin, 1-2, 9, 133
Metatron, 208, 221
Michaelmas, 49, 62, 64, 159
Milky Way, 9-10, 27, 55, 62, 184, 189, 205-206
Mordred, 49
Morning Star, 223, 226, 228
Morrigu, 217, 226
Mount Cynthus, 5
Mummers plays, 26, 47, 55, 69, 75, 92, 103, 187, 206
Myrrha, 128

Navis, 10, 185
Nemean Lion, 84, 157, 187
Nimue, 2, 133
Ninurta, 229
Non, 10, 106, 109, 111, 125, 141, 226
Nu, 109
Nun, 109

Oak, 59, 75, 221
Odin, 98, 135, 201, 219
Ogma, 75, 87, 219
Olwen, 10, 59, 67, 153, 206
On Niona, 141
Opelia, 8
Ops, 9, 41, 70, 126, 229
Orwaendel, 151, 201

Pan, 75, 148, 229
Passover, 8, 31
Path of the Fairies, 205
Pegasus, 10, 23, 49, 55, 73, 90, 94, 100, 144, 201
Perseus, 23, 26, 47, 51, 55, 83, 92, 103-104, 128, 189-190, 206
Pheasant, 233
Phoebe, 211
Poseidon, 87, 100
Priory of Zion, 228
Prydwen, 10, 185
Pythagoras, 1

Raphael, 141, 208, 219
Red Champion, 197
Regulus, 153, 155
Remus, 31
Rhea, 39, 126, 205, 226, 229
Rhiannon, 94, 98, 100, 111, 141
Robin Hood, 30, 135
Romulus, 31, 134-135, 205
Round dances, 195
Rural Mars, 170, 201

Sabazius, 39, 43, 70, 126
Sabrina, 26, 55, 103-104
Sagitta, 23, 64, 105, 169
Saint Alban, 217
Saint Andrew, 143, 229
Saint Anne, 90, 211
Saint Asaph, 35
Saint Bartholomew, 159
Saint David, 106, 109, 111, 125, 141, 226
Saint Darvell Gadarn, 35
Saint Elias, 45
Saint Frideswide, 45, 47, 126, 223
Saint George, 47, 55, 67, 92, 98, 103-104, 128, 187, 190, 206, 236
Saint James, 92, 103, 149, 169-170, 173
Saint John, 153, 221
Saint Jude, 173
Saint Katherine, 47
Saint Lawrence, 8, 51, 62
Saint Madron, 201
Saint Margaret, 43, 45, 47, 67, 104, 128
Saint Martin, 35, 165, 167
Saint Mary Magdalene, 45, 47, 51
Saint Michael, 49, 92, 103-104, 159, 170
Saint Nicholas, 165, 199, 219
Saint Simon Zelotes, 173
Saint Swithin, 43, 45
Saint Swithin's Chair, 41
Saint Thomas, 69, 149
Salii, 134-135
Salutaris, 84
Saturualia, 8
Sea goat, 131, 145, 204
Seal of Solomon, 228
Seal of the Virgin, 29, 33, 126, 178, 228
Seal, 29, 33, 65, 126, 178, 193, 228
Serpentarius, 25, 106, 109, 111, 141
Serpeus, 23
Seven Sleepers, 207-208
Shepherds rhod, 57, 155
Silbury Hill, 233
Sir Gawain, 149, 228
Sir Lancelot, 199
Sir Lavine, 199
Sol, 233

Spica, 9, 177
Stab Monkey, 39-40, 70, 107
Starling, 217
Stonehenge, 3, 133, 163
Succllus, 221
Suriel, 141, 208, 219
Swan Upping, 43, 62

Tailltiu, 49
Taliesin, 9-10, 238
Telyn Idris, 9, 89
Tempe, 3
Teutates, 217
The Great Plain, 10, 206
Thomas the Rhymer, 208
Thomasing, 69
Thor, 57, 69, 135, 201, 221
Tina, 217
Tiur, 217
Triangulum, 10, 25, 112
Tuisco, 217
Tundermans Eve, 69
Twelve Labours of Hercules, 84

Uffington Castle, 55, 90
Uffington White Horse, 90, 98
Uriel, 208, 233
Ursa Major, 10, 25, 35, 39, 41, 70, 111, 113, 115, 125, 129, 173, 190, 203, 213, 229
Ursa Minor, 10-11, 25, 39, 41, 69, 129

Venus, 8, 47, 51, 81, 125, 128, 159, 163, 173, 217, 223, 226-228

Waendel, 151, 199
Walrus, 145, 204
Wassailing, 100
Weyland, 56
White Serpent, 133
Willow, 115, 211
Wish Hounds, 187, 195

Yell Hounds, 187, 189

Zeus, 5, 39, 75, 83, 104, 106, 115, 125, 152, 165, 169, 201, 221
Zio, 217